Global Air Transport Management and Reshaping Business Models for the New Era

Kannapat Kankaew
Suan Sunandha Rajabhat University, Thailand

A volume in the Advances in Logistics,
Operations, and Management Science (ALOMS)
Book Series

Published in the United States of America by
IGI Global
Business Science Reference (an imprint of IGI Global)
701 E. Chocolate Avenue
Hershey PA, USA 17033
Tel: 717-533-8845
Fax: 717-533-8661
E-mail: cust@igi-global.com
Web site: http://www.igi-global.com

Copyright © 2022 by IGI Global. All rights reserved. No part of this publication may be reproduced, stored or distributed in any form or by any means, electronic or mechanical, including photocopying, without written permission from the publisher. Product or company names used in this set are for identification purposes only. Inclusion of the names of the products or companies does not indicate a claim of ownership by IGI Global of the trademark or registered trademark.
  Library of Congress Cataloging-in-Publication Data

Names: Kannapat Kankaew, 1973- editor.
Title: Global air transport management and reshaping business models for
   the new era / Kannapat Kankaew, editor.
Description: Hershey, PA : Business Science Reference, [2022] | Includes
   bibliographical references and index. | Summary: "This book studies the
   new era of business management on air transport aiming to reshape air
   transport business models such as, management practices, organizational
   culture, marketing strategy, technology and green transport and more"--
   Provided by publisher.
Identifiers: LCCN 2022008757 (print) | LCCN 2022008758 (ebook) | ISBN
   9781668446157 (hardcover) | ISBN 9781668446164 (paperback) | ISBN
   9781668446171 (ebook)
Subjects: LCSH: Airlines--Management. | Aeronautics,
   Commercial--Management.
Classification: LCC HE9780 .G56 2022 (print) | LCC HE9780 (ebook) | DDC
   387.7068--dc23/eng/20220223
LC record available at https://lccn.loc.gov/2022008757
LC ebook record available at https://lccn.loc.gov/2022008758

This book is published in the IGI Global book series Advances in Logistics, Operations, and Management Science (ALOMS) (ISSN: 2327-350X; eISSN: 2327-3518)

British Cataloguing in Publication Data
A Cataloguing in Publication record for this book is available from the British Library.

All work contributed to this book is new, previously-unpublished material. The views expressed in this book are those of the authors, but not necessarily of the publisher.

For electronic access to this publication, please contact: eresources@igi-global.com.

Advances in Logistics, Operations, and Management Science (ALOMS) Book Series

John Wang
Montclair State University, USA

ISSN:2327-350X
EISSN:2327-3518

Mission

Operations research and management science continue to influence business processes, administration, and management information systems, particularly in covering the application methods for decision-making processes. New case studies and applications on management science, operations management, social sciences, and other behavioral sciences have been incorporated into business and organizations real-world objectives.

The **Advances in Logistics, Operations, and Management Science** (ALOMS) Book Series provides a collection of reference publications on the current trends, applications, theories, and practices in the management science field. Providing relevant and current research, this series and its individual publications would be useful for academics, researchers, scholars, and practitioners interested in improving decision making models and business functions.

Coverage

- Risk Management
- Finance
- Production Management
- Political Science
- Networks
- Computing and information technologies
- Services management
- Decision analysis and decision support
- Operations Management
- Information Management

IGI Global is currently accepting manuscripts for publication within this series. To submit a proposal for a volume in this series, please contact our Acquisition Editors at Acquisitions@igi-global.com or visit: http://www.igi-global.com/publish/.

The Advances in Logistics, Operations, and Management Science (ALOMS) Book Series (ISSN 2327-350X) is published by IGI Global, 701 E. Chocolate Avenue, Hershey, PA 17033-1240, USA, www.igi-global.com. This series is composed of titles available for purchase individually; each title is edited to be contextually exclusive from any other title within the series. For pricing and ordering information please visit http://www.igi-global.com/book-series/advances-logistics-operations-management-science/37170. Postmaster: Send all address changes to above address. Copyright © 2022 IGI Global. All rights, including translation in other languages reserved by the publisher. No part of this series may be reproduced or used in any form or by any means – graphics, electronic, or mechanical, including photocopying, recording, taping, or information and retrieval systems – without written permission from the publisher, except for non commercial, educational use, including classroom teaching purposes. The views expressed in this series are those of the authors, but not necessarily of IGI Global.

Titles in this Series

For a list of additional titles in this series, please visit: http://www.igi-global.com/book-series/advances-logistics-operations-management-science/37170

Handbook of Research on Global Networking Post-COVID-19
Ana Pego (Nova University of Lisbon, Portugal)
Business Science Reference • © 2022 • 400pp • H/C (ISBN: 9781799888567) • US $295.00

Increasing Supply Chain Performance in Digital Society
Ramona Diana Leon (Universitat Politecnica de Valencia, Spain) Raul Rodriguez (Universitat Politecnica de Valencia, Spain) and Juan Jose Alfaro Saiz (Universitat Politecnica de Valencia, Spain)
Business Science Reference • © 2022 • 315pp • H/C (ISBN: 9781799897156) • US $250.00

Sales Management for Improved Organizational Competitiveness and Performance
José Duarte Santos (Instituto Superior Politécnico Gaya, Portugal)
Business Science Reference • © 2022 • 325pp • H/C (ISBN: 9781668434307) • US $240.00

Handbook of Research on Post-Pandemic Talent Management Models in Knowledge Organizations
Mohammad Rafiqul Islam Talukdar (American International University-Bangladesh, Bangladesh) Carmen z. Lamagna (American International University-Bangladesh, Bangladesh) Charles Carillo Villanueva (American International University-Bangladesh, Bangladesh) Rezbin Nahar (American International University-Bangladesh, Bangladesh) and Farheen Hassan (American International University-Bangladesh, Bangladesh)
Business Science Reference • © 2022 • 415pp • H/C (ISBN: 9781668438947) • US $295.00

International Perspectives on Value Creation and Sustainability Through Social Entrepreneurship
Hesham Magd (Modern College of Business and Science, Oman) Dharmendra Singh (Modern College of Business and Science, Oman) Raihan Taqui Syed (Modern College of Business and Science, Oman) and David Spicer (Bradford University, UK)
Business Science Reference • © 2022 • 300pp • H/C (ISBN: 9781668446669) • US $250.00

Examining the Vital Financial Role of SMEs in Achieving the Sustainable Development Goals
Dalila Taleb (A. Belkaid University, Algeria) Mohammed El Amine Abdelli (University Of Brest, France) Afef Khalil (University Of Tunis Carthage, Tunisia) and Asma Sghaier (University Of Sousse, Tunisia)
Business Science Reference • © 2022 • 325pp • H/C (ISBN: 9781668448342) • US $250.00

Creativity Models for Innovation in Management and Engineering
Carolina Machado (University of Minho, Portugal) and J. Paulo Davim (University of Aveiro, Portugal)
Business Science Reference • © 2022 • 300pp • H/C (ISBN: 9781668423394) • US $240.00

701 East Chocolate Avenue, Hershey, PA 17033, USA
Tel: 717-533-8845 x100 • Fax: 717-533-8661
E-Mail: cust@igi-global.com • www.igi-global.com

Table of Contents

Preface xiv

Acknowledgment xx

Chapter 1
Planning for a Trip: Selecting the Mode of Air Transport 1
    Jaime Santos-Reyes, SEPI-ESIME, ZAC, Instituto Politecnico Nacional, Mexico
    Abel Badillo-Portillo, Instituto Politecnico Nacional, Mexico

Chapter 2
COVID-19 Pandemic and Air Transport Business in Nigeria: An Analysis 20
    Oluchukwu Ignatus Onianwa, University of Ibadan, Nigeria

Chapter 3
Corporate Strategies in the Airline Industry 39
    Ferhan K. Sengur, Eskisehir Technical University, Turkey
    Doğan Kılıç, Zonguldak Bülent Ecevit University, Turkey
    Burak Erdoğan, Eskisehir Technical University, Turkey

Chapter 4
Air Transport Safety and Security 64
    Ravi Lakshmanan, GMR Infrastructure (Singapore) Pte Ltd., India

Chapter 5
Crew Resource Management Development: Characteristics, Perspectives, and Experiences 98
    Fahad ibne Masood, Modern College of Business and Science, Oman
    Bikal Jha, Modern College of Business and Science, Oman
    Hesham Magd, Modern College of Business and Science, Oman

Chapter 6
Do Ultra Long Haul Flights Attract More Premium Class Passengers? 118
    Colin C. H. Law, Singapore Institute of Technology, Singapore
    Eliver Lin, Beijing Normal University-Hong Kong Baptist University United International
        College, China

Chapter 7
Competitive Strategies in the Airline Industry 148
    Ferhan K. Sengur, Eskisehir Technical University, Turkey
    Huseyin Onder Aldemir, Özyeğin University, Turkey
    Mert Akınet, University of Turkish Aeronautical Association, Turkey

Chapter 8
Customer Experiences of Omni-Partner Services: An Insight From the Airline Alliance
Perspective 164
    Vikrant Janawade, University of Cote d'Azur, France

Chapter 9
The Image Value of Southeast Asia Airlines: A Study of Attribute That Led to Image Value of
Choosing Southeast Asia Airlines by Mean-End Theory Approach 192
    Benjapol Worasuwannarak, Cranfield University, UK
    *Kannapat Kankaew, College of Hospitality Industry Management, Suan Sunandha Rajabhat
        University, Thailand*

Chapter 10
The Impact of Customer Dissatisfaction Regarding Revenue Management on Perceptions of
Airline Experience and Loyalty 207
    Tanyeri Uslu, Altinbas University, Turkey
    İbrahim Sarper Karakadilar, Kahramanmaras Sutcu Imam University, Turkey

Chapter 11
Expect the Unexpected: Lessons From the COVID-19 Pandemic for the Future of Airport Leaders
and Managers 229
    Andreea-Iulia Iordache, Faculty of Economics, University of Porto, Portugal
    *Helena Martins, CEOS, ISCAP, Polytechnic of Porto, Portugal & University Lusófona,
        Lisbon, Portugal & NOVA SBE, Lisbon, Portugal*
    Teresa Proença, Center for Economics and Finance, University of Porto, Portugal
    Lúcia Piedade, Centre for Management Studies, Instituto Superior Técnico, Lisbon, Portugal

Chapter 12
Analysis of the Possible Relationship Model Between Knowledge Management and Job
Satisfaction: Aligning and Developing a Model as a Guideline for Service Staff Management in
the Aviation Industry 251
    Sarun Widtayakornbundit, Kasetsart University, Thailand
    Tanapoom Ativetin, Srinakharinwirot University, Thailand

Chapter 13
Model of Air Cargo Supply Chain Resilience: Way to Build by Knowing What Can Tear Your
Supply Chain Apart.. 272
    Chonnikarn Luangpituksa, School of Integrated Science, Kasetsart University, Thailand

Chapter 14
Robotic Process Automation (RPA) in the Aviation Sector 289
    R K Tailor, Manipal University Jaipur, India
    Sofia Khan, Manipal University Jaipur, India

Compilation of References 301

About the Contributors 342

Index 347

Detailed Table of Contents

Preface xiv

Acknowledgment xx

Chapter 1
Planning for a Trip: Selecting the Mode of Air Transport 1
    Jaime Santos-Reyes, SEPI-ESIME, ZAC, Instituto Politecnico Nacional, Mexico
    Abel Badillo-Portillo, Instituto Politecnico Nacional, Mexico

The chapter presents the results of selecting the mode air travel by considering other modes of transportation to highlight public's preferences of mode transport. The approach was a cross-sectional study by employing a questionnaire to a sample size of N=500; the data were collected from January to June 2019. The main conclusion of the analysis was that the preferred mode of transport was by bus (59.6%) followed by air travel (23.6%). Some of the cons and pros of air travel are the following: 1) air travel is considered too expensive (90%); it is believed that 70% of Mexicans do not participate in air travel; 2) it may be perceived as unreliable due to the unexpected such as extreme weather, earthquakes (e.g., the 19 September earthquake in 2017) and volcanic activity ("Popocatepetl" volcano eruptions); 3) it is perceived as the fastest and most comfortable compared to bus and car transportation; 4) the benefits of the air transport industry in Mexico pre-COVID-19 pandemic were that it contributed to 3.05% of the country's GDP.

Chapter 2
COVID-19 Pandemic and Air Transport Business in Nigeria: An Analysis 20
    Oluchukwu Ignatus Onianwa, University of Ibadan, Nigeria

It will be difficult for the airline transportation business to return to the pre-COVID-19 era as many changes have taken place within the COVID-19 period itself. These changes will be the catalyst for launching the industry into post COVID-19 with the emergence of different innovative ideas and digital models that will drive the growth of the sector. However, it is necessary to take stock of the effects and impact of the pandemic in the airline sector with the view to easily finding ways of adapting to the new normal created by the pandemic. Also, to achieve optimum changes in the airline transport business, unequivocal global collaboration and idea-sharing are very important in surviving the ripple effect of the pandemic. Because this is one important lesson that the pandemic has taught the global community, every country has to be with each other to make progress in airline transport. Without this in mind, there is the tendency that new business models in the airline's models might crash and ever create a series of problems equivalent to that created by COVID-19.

Chapter 3
Corporate Strategies in the Airline Industry 39
    Ferhan K. Sengur, Eskisehir Technical University, Turkey
    Doğan Kılıç, Zonguldak Bülent Ecevit University, Turkey
    Burak Erdoğan, Eskisehir Technical University, Turkey

The air transport industry is a highly regulated, dynamic industry dominated by international rules and highly competitive. In this environment, airline companies need to determine both the type and scale of their activities. In this chapter, corporate strategies, which are an essential element for airline businesses, will be explained, and their applications will be discussed, particularly for airline companies. Corporate strategies mainly consist of growth and retrenchment strategies. The first part will explain growth strategies and related and unrelated diversification strategies. Next, the second part will explain savings and liquidation strategies as retrenchment strategies and sub-strategies. The third part will explain the applications of diversification and retrenchment strategies in airline companies. In the last section, airline alliances will be explained.

Chapter 4
Air Transport Safety and Security 64
    Ravi Lakshmanan, GMR Infrastructure (Singapore) Pte Ltd., India

Over the last 20 years, the reduction in aircraft accident rates has been due to proactive and predictive safety measures implemented through state safety program and safety management system. Likewise, gradual enhancement of security measures is achieved using advanced screening technology, threat assessment, and behaviour detection through analytics and the security management system. The pandemic had a significant impact on the aviation industry, with decreased operations, revenue loss, and idle aircraft, among other things, which brought many challenges to the industry. The reactivation of the human resources and assets, especially inoperative aircraft, will be a huge task when the traffic accelerates. This chapter is a simplified form of safety and security management with processes/models to assess and mitigate the risks to ensure safety and security performance. In addition, this chapter highlights broader issues foreseen due to pandemics and describes models to evaluate additional risks comprehensively and mitigate them.

Chapter 5
Crew Resource Management Development: Characteristics, Perspectives, and Experiences.............. 98
    Fahad ibne Masood, Modern College of Business and Science, Oman
    Bikal Jha, Modern College of Business and Science, Oman
    Hesham Magd, Modern College of Business and Science, Oman

Crew resource management (CRM) is the product of a paradigm shift in safety thinking from 'finding the problem' to 'finding the solution'. Until the 'crash of the century' took place in Tenerife in 1977, the first officer was only to be seen and not heard. He was 'a good for nothing' sandbag sitting in the right seat. But all changed in 1977-1978 with the introduction of CRM, initially cockpit resource management and now crew resource management. It was so elaborate a system created out of necessity by aviation that no matter which high-reliability organization (HRO) was and is present, they took it up as the most efficient and effective method to reduce human fallibility. Starting from the civil nuclear technology sector to medical science to firefighting, all have adhered to CRM principles. The latest innovation which comes across from the experts is threat and error management (TEM), which is coincidentally the revision or version six of CRM. The aim of the present effort is to relate how CRM has come of age, the purpose behind it, and a deeper view of its successful cross-functioning into various vocations and industries.

Chapter 6
Do Ultra Long Haul Flights Attract More Premium Class Passengers?... 118
    Colin C. H. Law, Singapore Institute of Technology, Singapore
    Eliver Lin, Beijing Normal University-Hong Kong Baptist University United International College, China

Improved aircraft technologies have allowed aircraft to fly faster and farther, which offered more flexibility to the airlines to operate ultra long haul flights. This chapter reviews the development of and examines the changes in traveler demand after the introduction of ultra long haul flights. Five ultra long haul routes including Singapore/New York, Perth/London, Singapore/Los Angeles, Manila/New York, and Sydney/Houston were examined. The result has demonstrated that airlines offering ultra long haul flights are obtaining a larger market share between city pairs as passengers were attracted away from direct flights and connecting flights. There was evidence that passengers were willing to purchase premium services for more comfort on most ultra long haul markets where the origin and destination cities are large business centers.

Chapter 7
Competitive Strategies in the Airline Industry 148
    Ferhan K. Sengur, Eskisehir Technical University, Turkey
    Huseyin Onder Aldemir, Özyeğin University, Turkey
    Mert Akınet, University of Turkish Aeronautical Association, Turkey

The airline industry is a dynamic industry with intense competition. Deregulation, the international competition structure, and economic and COVID-19-like crises make the sector even more fierce. In this chapter, airline industry competitive strategies are discussed. For this purpose, following the introduction part, the concepts of strategy, business strategy, and competitive structure of the airline industry are discussed, and the place of competitive strategies in business strategies is explained. The airline industry structure is analyzed using Porter's five forces model. Two fundamental competitive strategy approaches, Porter's generic strategies and Miles and Snow's competitive strategies, are examined in detail for the airline industry. Following the presentation of the two well-known strategy frameworks, the chapter will end with a conclusion part.

Chapter 8
Customer Experiences of Omni-Partner Services: An Insight From the Airline Alliance
Perspective 164
    Vikrant Janawade, University of Cote d'Azur, France

The concept of facilitating sound service experiences has been widely discussed in the marketing landscape in recent years. Whilst the concept is highly acknowledged in service industries, it introduces some challenges when services are dovetailed and delivered to customers by multiple service providers. These aspects offer new realms to understand how customers form their experiences whilst interacting and encountering dovetailed services of networked service providers. To explore these spheres, a qualitative study employing thematic analysis was conducted to understand how networked and dovetailed services of an airline alliance influence the experiences of international airline travellers. The results of the study suggest that the alliance carriers' ability to offer extensive, synchronised, harmonised, interactive, and reciprocated services can be instrumental and pivotal for delivering sound experiences to their customers. In addition, these attributes offer new avenues to suggest that alliance carriers' services could be considered an omni-partner engagement activity.

Chapter 9
The Image Value of Southeast Asia Airlines: A Study of Attribute That Led to Image Value of Choosing Southeast Asia Airlines by Mean-End Theory Approach 192
    Benjapol Worasuwannarak, Cranfield University, UK
    Kannapat Kankaew, College of Hospitality Industry Management, Suan Sunandha Rajabhat
       University, Thailand

The Southeast Asia airline is one of the most well-known in the aviation industry where airlines represent unique culture for the value-added service standard to customers. Through the means-end theory method, the purpose of this study is to explore the value that passengers create in the decision making on Southeast Asia airlines that would result in understanding the attribute and structure of choosing Southeast Asia airlines. This study aimed to (1) investigate customer attributes in choosing Southeast Asia airlines, (2) understand the crucial value-added characteristic of Southeast Asia airlines, and (3) contribute a value-added framework for Southeast Asia airline passengers. The qualitative method is administered in this study. The interview is conducted in an interview from the mean-end-chain of the passenger. The analysis results in the expression of passenger attributes, consequences, and value of the Southeast Asia airlines and the contributions of the new framework of passenger added value.

Chapter 10
The Impact of Customer Dissatisfaction Regarding Revenue Management on Perceptions of Airline Experience and Loyalty 207
    Tanyeri Uslu, Altinbas University, Turkey
    İbrahim Sarper Karakadilar, Kahramanmaras Sutcu Imam University, Turkey

This chapter examines the effects of the complaints about the practices of revenue management (RM) on the travel experience perception and loyalty of the customers. The analysis shows that the complaints about the RM practices have positive effects on the travel experience perception, and the travel experience perception has a positive effect on the loyalty of the customer who travel short distances. The results of the detailed sub-hypothesis test performed in relation to the travel purposes of the customers and the business model adopted by an airline company show that the companies which adopt low-cost business model are obliged to manage their RM practices on a much more customer-centric basis. The companies in the sector should develop special customer programs for their customer segments which remain outside the business purpose. Thus, the operational efficiency will increase, and revenues will be maximized.

Chapter 11
Expect the Unexpected: Lessons From the COVID-19 Pandemic for the Future of Airport Leaders and Managers 229
    Andreea-Iulia Iordache, Faculty of Economics, University of Porto, Portugal
    Helena Martins, CEOS, ISCAP, Polytechnic of Porto, Portugal & University Lusófona,
        Lisbon, Portugal & NOVA SBE, Lisbon, Portugal
    Teresa Proença, Center for Economics and Finance, University of Porto, Portugal
    Lúcia Piedade, Centre for Management Studies, Instituto Superior Técnico, Lisbon, Portugal

Airports are arguably the most well-prepared structures for crises and contingencies, and their staff undergo abundant training for these types of events; however, the COVID-19 pandemic events were largely unpredictable, thus creating a somewhat rare happening in the industry: a novel type of crisis. This study aims to realize the types of strategies and elements that made a difference in positive and negative critical incidents using semi-structured interviews and the critical incident technique to managers from Portuguese and Romanian airports focusing on the type of skills that the management required and developed in a crisis. In accordance with the competency-based education framework, leadership, communication, subject matter excellence, teamwork, ethics and integrity, and resilience and innovation were crucial soft skills in critical situations. The present study contributes with new insights on airport managers and leaders facing crisis situations, key issues, and strategies during the first wave of COVID-19.

Chapter 12
Analysis of the Possible Relationship Model Between Knowledge Management and Job Satisfaction: Aligning and Developing a Model as a Guideline for Service Staff Management in the Aviation Industry 251
    Sarun Widtayakornbundit, Kasetsart University, Thailand
    Tanapoom Ativetin, Srinakharinwirot University, Thailand

This study examines the relationship between knowledge management in the aviation industry and job satisfaction among service staff through a literature review. This authors surveyed the relationship model while reversing to job satisfaction, which allowed them to develop a guideline for organizational knowledge management and the process of achieving satisfaction from practice guidelines, as well as other factors that contributed to developing the model apart from the two aforementioned variables, especially the changes from the situation that promote the continuous development of the knowledge management model because good management practices would lead to good organizational behavior and performance. Therefore, the context in which the study is conducted is the aviation industry because it has been severely affected by the crisis. The relationship management model must integrate management approaches into employee requirements by means of lessons learned from sample case studies.

Chapter 13
Model of Air Cargo Supply Chain Resilience: Way to Build by Knowing What Can Tear Your Supply Chain Apart.. 272
    Chonnikarn Luangpituksa, School of Integrated Science, Kasetsart University, Thailand

The air transport sector provides global connectivity via trade flows and tourism. The outbreak of the COVID-19 pandemic caused this sector to alternate between long periods of continued growth and long periods of negative growth. The air cargo airlines have permanently endeavored to maintain operations sufficiently robust to be resilient to the impacts of different internal and external disruptive events to maintain the guaranteed quality of services to their users and consignees. One approach to deal with disruptions in the development of air cargo supply chain systems is resilience. The resilient air cargo supply chain requires two critical capacities: the capacity for reliability and the capacity for restoration under disruptive condition.

Chapter 14
Robotic Process Automation (RPA) in the Aviation Sector... 289
    R K Tailor, Manipal University Jaipur, India
    Sofia Khan, Manipal University Jaipur, India

Robotic process automation (RPA) is an automation technology that airline sectors can benefit from because the airline business is the most global of all, and externalities are likely to have a significant influence and transform it. A generally robust global economic background, particularly earlier in the year, encouraged air passenger demand, which in turn supported employment, earnings, and company activity, as well as strong industry competition, which helped keep airfares low for passengers. Relevant to the increase in passenger numbers, operational costs were rising (i.e., the companies with huge volumes but poor margins are continuously looking for new methods to cut costs and boost efficiency). Robotic process automation (RPA) is a vital technology to meet both of these requirements. Robotic process automation (RPA) is known for its high operational accuracy, reliability, and for enabling organizations to conform rapidly and effectively. As a result, including RPA software bots into the flying experience can eliminate all the user concerns about flying.

Compilation of References 301

About the Contributors 342

Index 347

Preface

For decades, the air transport has efficiently brought people from different cities, countries, and continents around the world to connect and interact face to face. That is enhancing business, tourism, social, as well as remote area connectivity and development. The air transport activities cherish the economic, health, and living standard. It is also creating the job opportunities both direct and indirect related to air transport system. Ultimately, it furnishes fast and efficient global transportation network for passengers and goods, making it necessitate for global trade and commerce (IATA, 2012). Whereas, the mandatory infrastructure, as such an airport which accommodates passengers, cargo, and visitors also impactful to the economic. In such a way, the immense impact includes direct, indirect, and induced impact are identified. The operation of airlines and airports, commercial activities within airport parameter are good illustration example of direct impact. Whilst the employment and income from supply chain of goods and services to direct activities like utilities and fuel suppliers, cleaning services are indirect impact. And the employment and expenses of income from wages by direct and indirect are induced impact (Graham, 2014). Due to its fast and efficient transportation of people and goods, along with the advancement of modern technology have strengthening the growth of air transport dramatically. Thence, travelling by air becomes more popular and affordable price because of multiple carriers entering to the air transport market. Simultaneously, the price mechanism was used for competition and attracting customer. Today, the air transport is seen as a common service which everyone can use and there are not many differences in products and services among carriers provided. These result to the strong competition in air transport industry. Furthermore, the deregulation policy of aviation in various countries that removing government control over routes, prices and the market attracting new airlines enter to the aviation industry. This results to higher supply and higher competition in air transport business, specifically the emergence of low-cost carriers (IATA, 2013). The rise of low-cost airlines has reshaped not only the price structure but also the services of air transport. That is called no frill with simply low fare and rather no inflight services provided. Consequently, the existing legacy airlines are forced to reducing the ticket price to be competitive. The differentiate strategy of its products and services were employed in some airlines such as Singapore airlines offering four classes including suites, first class, business class, and economy class. And Emirates furnishes premium passenger seat that modifies into flat bed in a full suite with doors (IATA, 2013). Some air carriers choose to either add up frequency of flights, reschedule, finding uncapped routes or omit nonprofit routes, partnering with other airlines for code sharing flight, joining alliance, and merging or joining competition in low-cost sector. We, all, have obviously seen that many airlines breeding and collapse from the intense competition. There were some airlines pleas for the government protection. As an illustration, Thai Airways submitted the rehabilitation plan to the government avoiding bankruptcy (BBC, 2021).

Preface

Evidently, operating and managing the air transport company in modern economy is challenging since the operation of airlines itself is complex (IATA, 2012). That has to deal with various departments i.e. catering, ground service, cargo, airport, and air traffic control etc. Additionally, these stakeholders return a burden cost to air carriers. Whereas the competition is piercing and the nature of air transport industry is vulnerable to environment in terms of political, social, technology, and economic. For instance, unstable of political issues or new regulations, customer behavior changes overtime and the spread of pandemic, economic downturn, and modern technology and innovation in aviation sector. Literally, the air transport firm shall anticipate to these changing environments. For instance, the modern aircraft, seats were introduced airlines shall procure to add in its fleet in order to provide customer experience and gain preferences. However, this procurement cost a fortune to organization. Correspondingly, there has also been an analysis of Porter Five Forces revealed that air transport firms were among the least profitable industries. Due to the extreme competition, the common of products and services, low barrier to entry, suppliers and buyers have high power over the air transport company (Kankaew, 2016). Among other things, recently, the unprecedented disease COVID-19 has ruined socio-economic that the prohibition and restriction of regulations were implemented toward travelling across the frontier in multiple countries (Scarlett, 2021). On the grounds of the pandemic, there is an urgent need to address the health safety problems caused by the outbreak in all kinds of transport. In the first phase, the strict screening, vaccination, and quarantine were executed. Admittedly to the fact, the business and tourism activities were immobilized (United Nations, 2020) that surely affecting the air transport business and economic. The pandemic suppresses the air transport even worst (Sun et al., 2021). It seized the operation, and forced the airlines to readjust strategy both corporate strategy and competitive strategy to survive, rethinking on developing people's skills, employing technology, and associating to the safety (Afaq et al., 2021), and security according to public health regulations. Relatively in recovering, Thailand as an example, by the cooperation of the Ministry of Tourism and Sports, the Tourism Authority of Thailand, the Ministry of Public Health, the Department of Disease Control, the Department of Health and the Department of Health Service Support, the government and private sectors have set up the project namely "SHA". It stands for The Amazing Thailand Safety and Health Administration (SHA). This project aims to prevent and ensure the sanitation standard of Thailand's tourism products and services (Thailandsha, 2022). This would assure travelling to the country and consume the products and services are safe and sound.

Social phenomenon, the pandemic, has gained attention scholars in air transport research coping with the situation competently. The justification review in air transport amid the outbreak from (Sun et al., 2021) concluded the post pandemic air transport would develop new business air travel model i.e., super long-haul flights, the immunity passport enforcement for passenger safety, airlines, and destination trust. They further suggested future sustainable air transport, for instance green transportation. While the passengers seem more tolerant to the service performance for their safety. In the meantime, air cargo sounds elastic to the COVID-19. Apparently, the air cargo is trendy opportunity in air transport that airlines using their aircrafts carry more cargo instead of passenger. It is remarkably that online ordering and delivering become well-liked. Noticeably, as Nalisa (2021) reported that Vietjet Air revealed its profit during the attacked of COVID-19 on air transport. The Q4/2020 revenue of Vietjet Air rose 75 percent from cargo shipment. On the other perspective, Afaq et al (2021) found the passengers' attitude towards airline service after the occurrence of COVID-19, such as concerning health safety. The passenger worried the disinfection of aircraft before operation. The overcrowded at the airport and carelessness of airport staff checking the passenger's temperature. The researchers advised airlines communicate promptly to the passenger's queries by using technology like artificial intelligence (AI). On the other hand, Scheiwiller and Zizka (2021) recommended airline to manipulate crisis communication strategy during the unprecedented spreading of disease. The effective communication could deliver positive impact to organization and helping airline to focus on specific issues. Meanwhile, Lamb et al (2020) suggested airlines communicate the actions against the infectious disease, suchlike mask wearing policies, aircraft disinfectant to ensure passenger safe flying.

This book of research on global air transport sought, selected from scholars and practitioners in aviation industry around the globe. There are experts from 12 countries sharing their profound studies on current air transport as well as managerial outlook. The book aims to provide the insight idea, strategies, and theory implication to reshape the air transport model in new era. As prior stated, the air transport is sensitive to external environment which is rather unpredictably. In addition, the competition is relatively intense, especially in the emergence of low-cost airlines and technology advancement that change customer behavior. Thence, 14 chapters were selected from 25 proposals submitted. This book deals with various aspects of the air transport industry that flourish the management and practices. Precisely, it incorporates with empirical and theoretical studies, comparative case between countries, general review, and specific context in some parts of the world. Aforementioned studies could crystalize the complex chain of air transport operations. It entails the skills set of leadership, knowledge management, image value, safety and security, and strategies in air transport etc.,

The intention of this book aspires to deliver easy reading for everyone including; students, researchers, academicians, practitioners (managers and all individual who works in air transport), lecturers, or those who are interested in air transport business. The book is organized into fourteen chapters. A brief description of each chapter is given as follows:

Chapter 1 highlights reasoning the customer choose to fly, the pros and cons of air travel were discussed. The authors of this chapter dig the motivation of customers intention to fly or omit it. They compare to other modes of transportation, so that the management in air transport firms able to deploy marketing strategies in accordance to customer preferences.

Chapter 2 investigates and analyze the impact of COVID-19 on air transport and restrictive measures imposed on air transport during the pandemic. The innovative idea and digital models were proposed to absorb the impact. The author suggests lessen-learned the effects to resilience adaptive to the new normal. As well as, the adoption of technology in daily operations and institutional collaborations among stakeholders are essential.

Chapter 3 outline the significant element of corporate strategies for air transport business and the application in airline companies. The growth and retrenchment strategies were presented. The authors also stressed the important of airline alliance that create efficiency for airlines cooperation. More importantly, airline carriers shall focus on determining, planning, implementing, and controlling corporate strategy striving to the success.

Chapter 4 the author addresses the importance of safety and security in air transport both at national level and international level standards. The author draw attention to safety changes, challenges, and concern based on the analysis of aviation system during COVID-19 and the implication of the processes and models. The processes and models help to assess and mitigate the risk for the growth and continuous as normal in air transport.

Chapter 5 the crew resource management has been pinned point as man and machine interaction for safety air transport. The CRM was explored necessitate against errors and violations. Whilst the current situation artificial intelligence still does not reach full potential independence. Thence, human is needed

Preface

to ensure flight operation safety. The various stages of CRM were represented and play an important role in air transport.

Chapter 6 examines whether the ultra long haul could captivate premium passengers flying direct instead of transit flight. Enthrallingly, the international business destinations and major international hubs attract premium class passengers. The authors underlined the customer behavior change flying direct rather than connecting flight to avoid the exposure risk of the infectious disease.

Chapter 7 the competitive strategies have been raised in this chapter. The authors provide the notion to gain competitive edge in air transport business. The competitive concept and model were examined in air transport during certain uncertainty situations. Several types of competitive typologies are reviewed and presented. The authors emphasize the dynamic of air transport industry fit with cost leadership and differentiation.

Chapter 8 focuses on customer experiences create a positive perception. The network-oriented service in air transport like alliances has been assessed. The chapter accentuates to understand the customer perceived experiences of network-based services in air transport. The airline alliance concept, the customer experiences are tackled. The inductive method was applied for the insightful source of data. The author spotlights on the tendency of passenger preference flying with alliance airlines due to its capacity and synergies, as well as the information sharing among the carriers.

Chapter 9 lay stress on the new era of airlines competitiveness by image value attracting customers. The mean-end chain theory is used to understand the relationship of purchasing decision-making and behavior. The authors expand to comprehend the air transport attributes leading to image value which result to selection to fly. The significant questions regarding the customer choices and values in air transport companies were responded. Finally, the value-added framework for air transport was proffered.

Chapter 10 analyzes the effects of the complaints about the practices of revenue management (RM) on travel experiences. Whereas the RM was implied to the optimum profitability with limited seats capacity. Hence, a well-organized of RM is necessary that resulting to loyalty and re-purchase intention. The authors pronounce the airline companies revising their business models in accordance with the type of customers and customer service policies. This chapter is given a novel knowledge of customer behavior toward RM practices perspectives. It includes the effects on customer experience, perception, attitude, and complaint regarding the RM of air transport practices.

Chapter 11 explores the impact lessons from COVID-19 and canvass the outlook for airport management skills set in dealing with unprecedented crises. The authors outline the significance of human capital and soft skills in crisis. Specifically, the management of the airport was stressed on the comparative study between two countries in Europe. The in-depth analysis was performed to sort out the formulation and conclusion. The study proposes organizational interventions such as the creation of a crisis taskforce constituted of all managers and a higher leadership involvement in low level tasks and processes.

Chapter 12 synthesizes the knowledge management practices in air transport organization relate to job satisfaction on employees. Since the unprecedented attack of the pandemic has crashed the air transport business for two years. The authors present knowledge management restate and provide the employees knowledge and attitude to solve current situations, and preparedness for a dynamic future endeavor. Knowledge management is not only affected to job satisfaction, but also ameliorating the organizational capability for competitiveness.

Chapter 13 scrutinizes the resilience of air cargo transportation amid the COVID 19 disruption. The efficient and robust strategy of air cargo is dealing with the interruptions by mitigating the effects of disruption, and the ability to recover. Additionally, the author highlights supply chain agility, planning for future with recovery strategy. It is about to build a culture of continuous learning, risk management, managing and planning dynamic and unforeseen situation, and the adoption of digitalization in air cargo supply chain system.

Chapter 14 outlooks the usage of robotic process automation (RPA) in air transport system. The RPA will reduce human activity, yet it minimizes the human repetitive work. The system helps to improve the airline manufacturing supply chain by automating labor-intensive and time-consuming procedures like procuring, managing the inventory, and processing of payment. Therefore, the air transport workforce can focus on high-value tasks such as improving customer service, allowing front-line employees to recover more data at a faster pace, and making improvement every aspect of the booking experience to customer service support. The authors stressed the importance of using automation technology to increase the efficiency of flight management.

Throughout 14 chapters of this book, it reflects multi aspects of air transport revealing a profound knowledge, managerial issues, risk and crises handling, and technology adoption for a better customer experience. All contributors are the experts in the field of air transport presenting the vital details of current and outlook topics enclosed.

Kannapat Kankaew
Suan Sunandha Rajabhat University, Thailand

REFERENCES

Afaq, A., Gaur, L., Singh, G., & Dhir, A. (2021). COVID-19: Transforming Air Passengers' Behaviour and Reshaping Their Expectations Towards the Airline Industry. *Tourism Recreation Research*, 1–9. Advance online publication. doi:10.1080/02508281.2021.2008211

BBC NEWS. (2021, Jun 15). *Kān bin Thai: sān lomlalāi klāng hen chop phǣn fuñfū kitčhakān phǣm thun 'īk hā muñlā nabāt* [Thai Airways International: Central Bankruptcy Court approves business rehabilitation plan, increase capital by 50 billion baht]. Retrieved from: www. bbc.com/thai

Graham, A. (2014). *Managing Airports: An International Perspective*. Routledge.

IATA. (2012). *Introduction to the Airline Industry* (2nd ed.). IATA.

IATA. (2013). *Airline Customer Service* (3rd ed.). IATA.

Kankaew, K. (2016). Thai Airways International: The World Economy Crisis Resolutions. *Actual Problems of Economics*, 2(176), 261–265.

Lamb, L. T., Winter, R. S., Rice, S., Rustin, J. K., & Vaughn, A. (2020). Factors that Predict Passengers Willingness to Fly during and After the COVID-19 Pandemic. *Journal of Air Transport Management*, 89, 101897. doi:10.1016/j.jairtraman.2020.101897 PMID:32837029

Nalisa. (2021, Feb 2). *Wīat čhet bin fā khōwit - sipkāo čhon mī kamrai* [Vietjet flies through COVID-19 until it's profitable]. Retrieved from: www. marketeeronline.co.th

Scarlett, G. H. (2021). Tourism Recovery and the Economic Impact: A Panel Assessment. *Research in Globalization*, 3, 100044. doi:10.1016/j.resglo.2021.100044

Preface

Scheiwiller, S., & Zizka, L. (2021). Strategic Responses by European Airlines to the COVID-19 Pandemic: A Soft landing or a Turbulent Ride? *Journal of Air Transport Management, 95*, 102103. doi:10.1016/j.jairtraman.2021.102103

Sun, X., Wandelt, S., Zheng, C., & Zhang, A. (2021). COVID-19 Pandemic and Air Transportation: Successfully navigating the paper hurricane. *Journal of Air Transport Management, 94*, 102062. doi:10.1016/j.jairtraman.2021.102062 PMID:33875908

Thailandsha. (2022). *Amazing Thailand Safety and Health Administration.* Retrieved from: https://web.thailandsha.com/about/details

United Nations. (2020). *Socio-Economic Impact Assessment of COVID-19 in Thailand.* United Nations in Thailand.

Acknowledgment

The editor would like to appreciate the help and support from everyone involved in this project, specifically, all contributors and reviewers that took part along the processes. Without their support and contributions, this book would have not been launched. I am also highly grateful to all people from IGI Global who assist in preparing and aiding the publication. Once, again the editor would like to express gratitude to all reviewers who contribute their extra time and effort that shape the ideas, notion, and expand the insightful novel.

Kannapat Kankaew
Suan Sunandha Rajabhat University, Thailand

Chapter 1
Planning for a Trip:
Selecting the Mode of Air Transport

Jaime Santos-Reyes
https://orcid.org/0000-0002-3758-9862
SEPI-ESIME, ZAC, Instituto Politecnico Nacional, Mexico

Abel Badillo-Portillo
https://orcid.org/0000-0002-3209-5740
Instituto Politecnico Nacional, Mexico

ABSTRACT

The chapter presents the results of selecting the mode air travel by considering other modes of transportation to highlight public's preferences of mode transport. The approach was a cross-sectional study by employing a questionnaire to a sample size of N=500; the data were collected from January to June 2019. The main conclusion of the analysis was that the preferred mode of transport was by bus (59.6%) followed by air travel (23.6%). Some of the cons and pros of air travel are the following: 1) air travel is considered too expensive (90%); it is believed that 70% of Mexicans do not participate in air travel; 2) it may be perceived as unreliable due to the unexpected such as extreme weather, earthquakes (e.g., the 19 September earthquake in 2017) and volcanic activity ("Popocatepetl" volcano eruptions); 3) it is perceived as the fastest and most comfortable compared to bus and car transportation; 4) the benefits of the air transport industry in Mexico pre-COVID-19 pandemic were that it contributed to 3.05% of the country's GDP.

INTRODUCTION

Modern society is characterized by human mobility. In a way, all modes of transportation systems (road, air, sea) facilitate this process within and across countries worldwide. Air transport systems have contributed human mobility to such a scale since the late 1970s (Lin & Zhang, 2021). According to the IATA (International Air Travel Association, 2019a) report, in 2018, the world's airlines transported 4 billion passengers to a global network of 22,000 routes. As with any country worldwide, similar trends were

DOI: 10.4018/978-1-6684-4615-7.ch001

observed pre-pandemic in Mexico. It is believed that from 2009 to 2018, the number of air passengers was doubled over the decade; recent data have also shown that international tourism increased 9.0% (3.7 million) in 2019 when compared to 2018 (Datatur, 2019).

The growth of travel and tourism, on the other hand, is correlated to the levels of CO2 emissions (Bucks, et al., 2014, Xu, et al., 2021). Moreover, according to the World Tourism Organization and International Transport Forum (2019), 1600 million tons of CO2 resulted from tourism in 2016. Furthermore, it is argued that transport systems account for 75% of tourism related emissions, e.g., air travel (40%), car (32%). The different modes of transportation also generate higher emissions per passenger per kilometer: car (0.1135 Kg), air travel (0.1042 Kg), bus (0.03 Kg), train (0.0205 Kg).

But the fundamental questions being asked in the present work are, how modes of transport are chosen within countries? How often people travel by air in developed and developing countries? It has been argued that to be able to understand human attitudes, behavior of transport mode use, it becomes necessary for planning and management of transportation systems (Yang, et al., 2021). The subject has attracted the attention to researchers and a vast amount of literature covers it, for example, in relation to road and railways (Umbelino de Souza, et al., 2021; Mayo & Taboada, 2020; Abdullah, et al., 2021; Romao & Bi, 2021), and air travel (Nevins, et al., 2022; Wang & Gao, 2021; Xu, et al., 2021; Czepkiewicz, et al., 2018; Dempsey, et al., 2021; Dolnicar, et al., 2012).

For example, in a study on transport mode choice was found that people's attitude towards life was significant when selecting modal choice (Choo & Mokhtarian, 2004); similar findings have been reported by Chen & Petrick (2013), Czepkiewicz, et al., (2018), Dempsey et al., (2021), Dolnicar et al., (2012). Steg, et al., (2001) reported that car use is significantly associated with symbolic and affective motives. In another study by Ghani, et al., 2007, the authors found that 'latent factors' (i.e., safety, comfort, convenience, and flexibility) were significantly associated with the mode of transportation selection. Similarly, Backer-Grondahl, et, al., (2007) conducted research on risk perception and mode choice and it was found that the perceived safety did not influence for the selection of transportation mode between the cities of Oslo and Kristansand, Norway; however, attributes such as comfort, efficiency and time were important.

Research has also been published on the inequality of air travel (Mattioli, et al., 2021; Czepkiewicsz et al., 2018; Buchs & Mattioali, 2021; Hopkings & Cairns, 2021; Gosslin & Cohen, 2014). For example, Hopkins & Cairns (2021) reported that in the UK only 15% of the population accounting for 70% of all flights. According to Munguia (2019) Mexicans are the ones who travel the least by air in Latin American countries (more on this in the Discussion section).

Research on issues related to public's perceptions of travel mode selection is lacking in the context of Mexico. The chapter addresses this issue to shed some light on it to a sample population of N=500 residents of Mexico City; the questionnaire-based survey was administered from 1 January to 30 June 2019. In particular, the following hypothetical scenario as considered: "Imagine that you on your own are planning a trip to spend a weekend in Oaxaca city. *What of the following modes of transport would you choose?*" Respondents rated their answers according to the following transport modes, by air, bus, or car. The aims of the chapter are:

1. to investigate the preferred mode of transport to Oaxaca City according to the above scenario.
2. to investigate, why did respondents choose air travel?
3. to investigate, why respondents did not choose air travel?
4. to discuss the pros and cons of air travel in the context of the case study.

Planning for a Trip

The chapter is organized as follows: first, a context of air travel in Mexico followed by a brief description of the touristic city of Oaxaca is given. Second, a description of the employed materials and methods is briefly described; third, the most relevant results are presented. Fourth, the cons and pros of air travel in the context of the study is given in the discussion section; also, some limitations and future directions are given within the section. Finally, some relevant conclusions are reported.

AIR TRAVEL AND TOURISTIC HOT SPOTS IN MEXICO

Air Travel in Mexico

As in 2018, it is believed that air travel passengers (domestic and international) marked an all-time high for the seventh consecutive year, reaching a total of 97.3 million passengers (SCT, 2019); an increase of 7.6% when compared to 2017 where 90.5 million passengers were transported.

In the same year, data show that international flights exceeded 46 million, which is slightly lower than domestic flights (49 million, in the last five years domestic flights grew more than 62.5%) (SCT, 2019). Moreover, in the last twenty years the infrastructure of air transport has changed in an important way, e.g.:

a). In 1998, 81.9% of international flights had origin or destination in the United States and 7.0% in Europe.
b). In 2018 there has been an important diversification towards other regions; for example, Canada has gone from being the fifth in importance in 1998 to the second in 2018. Central America, the Caribbean and South America have seen an increase in flights to/from these countries. Moreover, in the last five years there has been an accelerated growth to destinations in Asia.

Figure 1. Airports in Mexico (SCT, 2019)

Planning for a Trip

In the country, it is believed that there are 77 airports, 64 of them accommodate international flights (Figure 1). (AICM, ASUR, GAP, OMA & ASA, are the organizations running airport infrastructure).

As with the case of international flights, in the last five years domestic flights grew more than 62.5%, with an Average Annual Growth Rate (AAGR) of 10.2%. Moreover, the 10 busiest regular domestic routes mobilize 42.7% of the total number of passengers.

In short, if an individual or family willing to travel to/from any touristic destination across the country by air, they could do it. For example, the case of a touristic city of Oaxaca, which is the subject of the next subsection.

Oaxaca City

In general, Mexico is being regarded as a touristic destination given its great diversity of natural resources, world-renowned gastronomy, and a privilege geographical location, among others (STO, 2021). An example is the city of Oaxaca, which is located 468km from Mexico City, the capital of the country (Figure 2).

Few places in Mexico have the cultural richness of the city of Oaxaca. The city that preserves the ancient traditions recreated by the indigenous peoples, its gastronomic and artisan wealth that has been recognized by thousands of tourists. For example, in 1987, the UNESCO declared the Historic Center and the "Monte Alban" archaeological zone as a cultural heritage of humanity.

Oaxaca city and its surroundings offer countless activities to do, from pedestrian tours in the historic center, tours to the museums, markets, baroque temples, convents, parks, and gardens, among others. The archaeological zones of "Monte Alban" and "Mitla" are the most important in the state.

Figure 2. Oaxaca city connected by air and road transportation

Oaxaca City International Airport provides air connections with Mexico City and other national and international destinations. The city also offers flights to beaches located in the Pacific Ocean, such as Huatulco and Puerto Escondido (not shown in Figure 2).

Oaxaca City is also well connected by road to other nearby cities, such as Mexico City, Puebla, etc. Again, the city offers touristic attractions and can be reached by road and air to spend a weekend doing leisure activities.

MATERIALS AND METHODS

A cross-sectional study was conducted by employing a questionnaire-based survey to a sample population of n=500 and the range of age was from 16 to 72 years old (Mean=28). (Respondents <18 years were mostly undergraduate students doing their degree on the subject related to Transport; it was very important for us to have their perceptions on the issues addressed herein). The sample was for convenience. It should be highlighted that what is presented here is part of a much wider research project on the public's perceptions of the transport system in a megacity such as Mexico City. Hence, the subsection dealing with the travel mode preference associated with air travel, and road transportation (bus and car) are considered. As already stated in the introduction section, the aim of the study was to investigate the respondents' perceptions on air travel.

Overall, the questionnaire was structured as follows: first, a brief description of the research project was provided; respondents were informed of their right to withdraw at any time. Further, they were informed that the questionnaire was anonymous and confidential. This section of the questionnaire was a hypothetical one and with the following scenario: "imagine that you on your own are planning a trip to spend a weekend in Oaxaca city (see the previous section). *What of the following modes of transport would you choose?"* Respondents rated their answers according to the following transport modes, by air, bus, car, or a taxi (Figure 2).

Another question was related to the following, "w*hy did you choose the mode of transport to the previous question?"* The following options were considered as possible responses: "Faster", "Cheaper", "More reliable", "More comfortable", "Safer", "I have no choice", and "Other, please specify".

Finally, the following question: "w*hy did not you choose one of the other means of transportation?"* The possible responses were the following: "Unreliable", "Uncomfortable", "Bad service", "It takes too long", "Too expensive", and "Other, please specify".

The questionnaire also contained a section of the demographics of the participants of the study (Table 1). Data from the questionnaire was collected between 1 January 2019 and 30 June 2019.

To analyze the descriptive information, frequency analysis has been conducted. The relationship between the dependent and independent variables have been assessed by employing Pearson Chi-square or Fisher's exact probability tests. The latter was employed in cases were one or more of the cells having an expected frequency less than five (Agresti & Finlay, 1986). The Statistical Package SPSS, ver. 25, has been employed to the analysis of the collected data. All the conducted tests were two-tailed, and the statistically significant results acceptance criteria were yield at $p<.05$.

RESULTS

Sample Characteristics

The sample size considered in the study was N=500 respondents (Table 1). The sample characteristics show that 59.8% of participants were male and 40.2% female. Most of the participants were low educated (86.2%), with only 13.8% reporting that they have a university degree or higher qualification (Postgraduate). Old people appeared to be underrepresented in the study, that is, only 9.6% aged 50 years and above. Participants aged between 16-30 accounted for 71% of the total sample. (See the limitations of the study in the Discussion section.)

Table 1. Demographic characteristics of the participants of the study, n=500

Variables	Measures	N	%	Total
Gender	Women	201	40.2%	500 (100%)
	Men	299	59.8%	
Age	16 – 20	148	29.6%	500 (100%)
	21 – 30	210	42.0%	
	>31	142	28.4%	
Educational level	Low	431	86.2%	500(100%)
	High	69	13.8%	

Air Transport and Oaxaca City

Regarding the preferred mode of transport to visit the city of Oaxaca, the results show that the first choice by the participants was by bus (59.6%), followed by air travel (23.6%) and by car (16.8%) came as the third option (Figure 3).

Table 2. Relationship between the demographic variables and modes of transport

		Variables [†]					
		Gender [a]		Age [b]		Level of Education [c]	
		Women N (%)	Men N (%)	16-24 N (%)	25-75 N (%)	Low N (%)	High N (%)
Modes of transport [d]	Bus	133 (66.2)	165 (55.2)	158 (57.0)	140 (62.8)	258 (59.9)	40 (58.0)
	Plane	42 (20.9)	76 (25.4)	66 (23.8)	52 (23.3)	99 (23.0)	19 (27.5)
	Car	26 (12.9)	58 (19.4)	53 (19.1)	31 (13.9)	74 (17.2)	10 (14.5)

[†]Percentages (%) are given within variables, gender, age, and educational level.
[ad]Gender: χ^2= 6.464, df=2, p= .039; Cramer's V= .114; [bd] Age: χ^2= 2.710, df=2, p= .258, Cramer's V= .074
[cd]Level of education: χ^2= .815, df=2, p= .665, Cramer's V= .040

Planning for a Trip

Figure 3. The preferred mode of transport to Oaxaca City

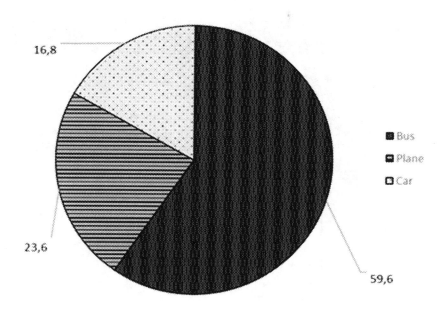

Table 2 shows that there is a significant relationship between gender and the modes of transportation ($X^2 = 6.464$, df = 2, $p < 0.039$) to the extent that women had better preferences for bus transport than men. However, there was not association between age ($X^2 = 2.710$, df = 2, $p = 0.258$), the level of education of the participants ($X^2 = .815$, df = 2, $p = 0.665$) and the modes of transportation considered in the study.

Why Air Travel?

When asked why they chose their preferred modes of transport, in general, the participants of the study considered the variables related to cost, speed, and comfort in their preferences; that is, "cheaper" (44.8%), "more comfortable" (41.2%), and "faster" (36.2%), as shown in Figure 4 (but not shown in Tale 2). The results also highlighted a statistically significant relationship between the modes of transportation and speed ($X^2 = 307.716$, df = 2, $p < 0.001$), cost ($X^2 = 178.514$, df = 2, $p < 0.001$), reliability ($X^2 = 58.251$, df = 2, $p < 0.001$), comfort ($X^2 = 70.657$, df = 2, $p < 0.001$), and safety ($X^2 = 38.485$, df = 2, $p < 0.001$).

Figure 4. Variables related to the preference of air travel

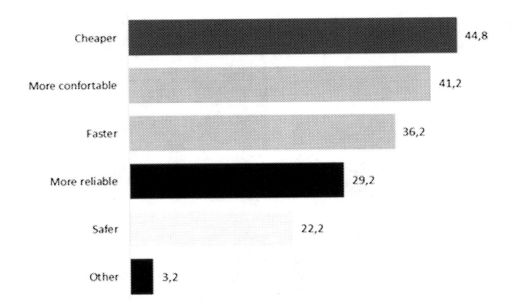

Overall, over 60% of the respondents recognized air travel as the fastest, but not cheap (42%) and 34% as more comfortable than travelling, for example, by bus. Moreover, 33% of participants >25 years old considered travelling by plane is safer than by bus. In the same way, participants with higher education perceived air travel as comfortable (47%).

Why Not Air Travel?

Figure 5 shows the results of some of the reasons why air travel is not the preferred mode of transport to Oaxaca city. That is, frequency data shows that 90% of the participants considered air travel as too expensive. As already mentioned in the previous section, travelling to Oaxaca by bus (59.6%) was the preferred choice and this is clearly seen in Figure 6. Moreover, it seems that the variable related to costs is what have an influence when selecting a mode of transportation in the context of the study and this may be the reason why air travel is not the preferred option.

Planning for a Trip

Figure 5. Why not air travel?

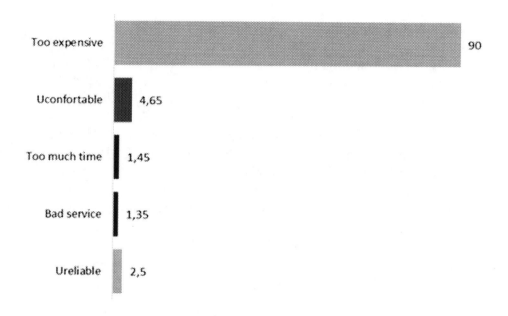

Figure 6. Air travel and other types of transportation

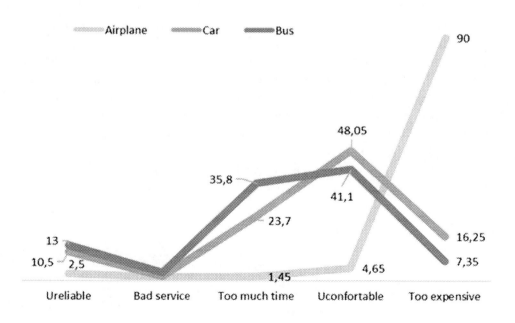

DISCUSSION

It may be argued that modern society is characterised by human mobility within and across countries worldwide. Air transport systems have made possible human mobility to such a scale. In general, the air travel industry has grown exponentially since the late 1970s (Lin & Zhang, 2021). The rate of growth varies across countries, for example, in Mexico, from 2009 to 2018, the number of air passengers has doubled over the decade; recent data have shown that international tourism increased 9.0% (3.7 million) in 2019 when compared to 2018 (Datatur, 2019).

As mentioned in the introduction section, there have been a vast amount of research on air travel and other modes of transportation (Graham et al., 2020; Delgado-Jalon, et al., 2019; Hanson, et al., 2019; Lamb, et al., 2020; Mattioli & Scheiner, 2022); however, research on public's perceptions, for example, on the modes of transport is scarce in the context of Mexico. Hence, the chapter addressed the issue related to the publics' perceptions on air travel when compared to road travel (bus & car). In the study participants were asked which mode of transport they would choose to visit Oaxaca City for a weekend. In what follows the cons and pros of air travel is discussed in the context of the study.

It is worth mentioning that since the data were collected pre Covid-19 pandemic, references to it will be given to enhance the discussion in the context of the study.

Cons

Overall, the results show that bus transport (59.6%) was selected as the preferred choice followed by air travel (23.6%) (Figure 3). Further, it has been found that air travel was considered too expensive (90%) by the respondents of the study. Hence, the results have highlighted that the variable related to costs was the contributor to the choice of bus transport to Oaxaca City. Table 3 shows the ticket fares for the types of transport considered in the analysis. The bus transport system is cheaper than air travel, even though it takes over six hours of travelling time.

In a study conducted in 2017 in the country, it has been found that 70% of Mexicans do not participate in air travel (Animal Politico, 2017). More recently, it has been reported that the number of flights per habitant in Mexico is the lowest in Latin American countries, i.e., 0.7 per year (Figure 7) (Munguia, 2019).

The above findings are consistent with what has been reported in the literature in relation to the inequality of air travel (Mattioli, et al., 2021; Buchs et al., 2018; Czepkiewicsz et al., 2018; Buchs & Mattioali, 2021; Hopkings & Cairns, 2021; Buchs et al., 2014; Gosslin & Cohen, 2014). For example, Hopkins & Cairns (2021) reported that in the UK only 15% of the population accounting for 70% of all flights, while 50% does not participate in air travel.

Table 3. Costs of travelling from/to Mexico-Oaxaca cities

Mode	Type	One-way ticket	Round ticket	Time
Air	Carrier: Aeromexico Viva Aerobús Volaris	-	US $108.20 US $105.25 US $112.91	1 h 10 min.
Road	Bus	-	US $73.70	6 h 30 min.
Road	Car	-	US $98.30	4 h 45 min.
Road	Taxi	US $343.95	-	5 h 54 min.

Figure 7. Mexicans and flights per year (Adapted from Munguia, 2019)

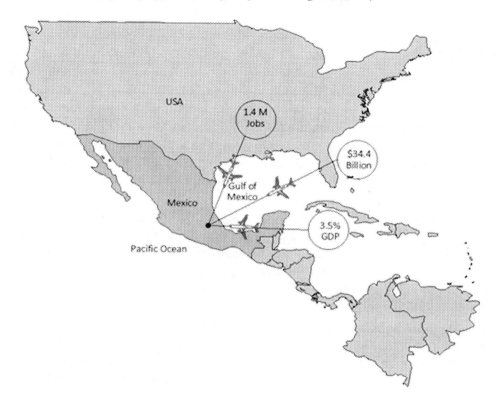

A study on the income of the employed population in Mexico reported that in the third quarter of 2019, the average income of the employed population nationwide was 203.72 USD per month (Coneval, 2019). When considering the gender of the population, men reported a monthly income of 223.16 USD and women of 173.6 USD. However, it is worth mentioning that there are high indices of unemployment. Hence, air travel may be regarded as an expensive and not all people can afford to it in Mexico. (See the limitations and future research section for more on this.)

Another issue that has been highlighted by the study is that related with the unreliability of air travel; although the percentage of respondents was 2.5% (Figures 5&6), however, it is worth discussing this feature of air travel. Given the geographical location of the country, it is affected by natural hazards such as extreme weather conditions, hurricanes, etc., that disrupt the operations of airports and therefore the cancellation of flights. For example, during 2018, 46.15% of disruptions affecting delays of flights cancellations were due to the presence of fog and then by winter and tropical storms (Herrera Gonzalez, et al., 2019). These adverse events occurred during the months of January, June, and December. Similar findings have been reported in the literature on the adverse effects on air travel due to severe weather conditions (Glass et al., 2022; Chen, et al., 2021).

Mexico and Oaxaca cities are in a highly seismic region where earthquakes occur all the time, for example, the 07 & 19 September earthquakes (Santos-Reyes, 2021). During the 19 September earthquake, about 180 flights were affected at the capital city (Yeo, 2017). Moreover, volcanic activity such as the "Popocatepetl" which is located 121 km from the capital city prompts to affect air travel. Every time it erupts, flights are cancelled (Fernandez-Roman, 2013; Milenio, 2021; Debate, 2019). Similar findings have been reported in other countries on the adverse effects on air traffic due to seismic, volcanic hazards (Minato & Morimoto, 2021; Takebayashi, et al., 2021; Reichardt, et al., 2019).

As with any technological system, accidents always occur causing disruptions in air travel (Figure 4). Unfortunately, on July 31, 2018, at approximately 3:30 p.m., an accident occurred in the state of Durango (Herrera Gonzalez, et al., 2019). The aircraft with 99 passengers and four crew members leaving the Durango airport for Mexico City had a mishap during the take-off; it was projected off the runway, moving on the ground and remaining approximately 300 meters from the runway. It is believed that during take-off, a hailstorm accompanied by strong winds broke out. Fortunately, there were no human losses, but shortly after the accident the aircraft caught fire resulting in a total loss. Usually, these adverse events are highly publicized by the mass media and have a negative influence on the public's perception on this mode of transportation system.

However, air travel may be regarded as the safest of all modes of transportation. According to a recent safety report by IATA (2021), 'all accident rate' (AAR) (accidents per one million flights) was 1.11 (or 1 accident every 0.9 million flights) in 2019 (the 5-year average (2016-2020) for the AAR was 1.38 or 1 accident every 0.75 million flights). Moreover, the reported 'Fatality risk' (FR) was 0.09 for that same year (the FR for a 5-year average was 0.13).

More recently, the Covid-19 (and the subsequent variants) have severely hit the air travel worldwide (Truong, 2021; Gao, 2022; Dube et al., 2021; Gallego & Font, 2021; Yang, et al., 2021). According to Herrera-Garcia (2020), the pandemic had a significant impact on aviation in Mexico during 2020; it generated a reduction of 52.8% in passengers served and 11.7% in cargo, compared to 2019. Further, in the report it has been argued that the effect of the pandemic in aviation in Mexico had the shape of an asymmetric "V", where the fall was accelerated and significant, while the recovery was sustained but slow.

Although the topic related to CO_2 emissions was not the subject of the study, however it has to do with what has been highlighted in the present work, i.e., the fact that 59.6% of the participants preferred a bus transport system to Oaxaca than by air. Moreover, 70% of Mexicans do not participate in air travel. This raises the question as to, whether environmental decision-makers should promote the use of road transport systems instead? As mentioned in the introduction section, air travel generates higher emissions than bus transport systems (0.1042 Kg vs. 0.03 Kg, respectively).

Given that Mexico is regarded as a developing country, it may be the case that the benefits of air travel outweigh the problems associated with CO_2 emissions. The economics of air transport systems in Mexico is discussed in the next section.

Pros

The presented results highlighted that air travel was perceived as the fastest (36.2%) and comfortable (41.2%) of the types of transport considered in the analysis. It may be argued that these features, among others, for example, quality of life, are well known and recognized worldwide (Uysal, et al., 2016; Dempsey, et al., 2021; McCabe & Diekmann, 2015; Chen & Petrick, 2013; Dolnicar, et al., 2021).

Planning for a Trip

Figure 8. The economic benefits of air transport system in Mexico (Adapted from IATA, 2019b)

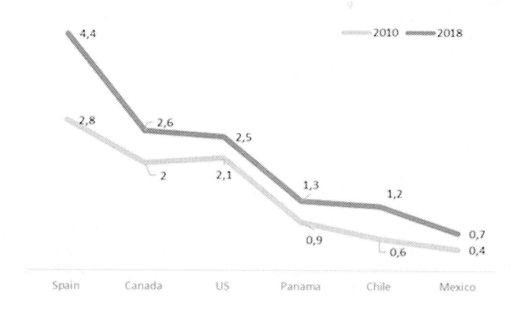

Although the variable related to the economic benefits of air travel was not considered explicitly in the study, it is worth mentioned its impact on Mexico. According to a report by IATA (2019b), 278,000 people were employed by air navigation service providers, airport operators, airport on-site organizations (retail and restaurants, among others). Moreover, 345,000 more jobs were added by the sector, by services and goods from local suppliers. Furthermore, 122,000 and 667,000 more jobs through employees' wages and those related to money spend by foreign tourists to the local economy, respectively. Overall, the air transport industry in Mexico contributed to 1.4 million jobs (Figure 8).

It is also believed that in general, the air transport system, including the supply chain and the airlines are estimated to support US $ 24.1 million of GDP and foreign tourists' spending another US $13.3 billion of GDP; by considering both totaling US $37.4 billion and therefore supporting 3.5% of the country's GDP (IATA, 2019b).

Given the economic benefits of air travel, a new international airport was inaugurated on March 21, 2022 (Felipe Angeles International Airport (AIFA), 2022). The international airport is bigger than the current international airport located in Mexico City. Moreover, it has three landing runways, it is believed that two of which can carry out air operations simultaneously. Furthermore, the airport will have the capacity to handle more than 20 million passengers a year. It is estimated that during 2022 a total of 2.4 million passengers will be transported, and by 2023 it is intended to reach 5 million travellers.

Limitations of the Study and Future Work

As with any study, the present study has several limitations; first, the sample was for convenience and therefore the results should not be generalized to the whole population of the Mexico City. In fact, as already mentioned in previous sections, the presented results are part of an ongoing research project and a study considering a representative sample of the country may be pursued to replicate the presented results herein; second, the over 50s are underrepresented and more data should be collected. Unfortunately, the pandemic contributed to the collection of more data; third, further research is needed to better understand, why Mexicans do not travel? Has it to do with the cost of air travel? Are there other factors such as the cultural issues?

Further research is also needed, for example, to increase the sample size and increasing the unrepresented population of the over 50s. Moreover, the present study has highlighted the need to further investigate why Mexicans do not participate in air travel.

CONCLUSION

Public's perceptions of different modes of transportation are crucial in understanding the phenomena of human mobility. The chapter has presented the results of an analysis of a sample population of N=500 of Mexico City. In particular, the following hypothetical scenario was considered in the analysis, what modes of transportation would you choose to travel to Oaxaca City for a weekend? The approach was a cross-sectional study by employing a questionnaire to collect the data, and it was collected from January to June 2019. The main conclusions of the analysis were that the preferred mode of transport was by road, i.e., bus (59.6%); air travel came as a second option (23.6%).
Some of the cons and pros of air travel in the context of the study are the following:

1. Air travel is being considered too expensive for the participants of the study (90%). It is believed that 70% of Mexicans do not participate in air travel.
2. Air travel may be regarded as unreliable due to the unexpected such as extreme weather, earthquakes (e.g., the 19 September earthquake in 2017) and volcanic activity ("Popocatepetl" volcano eruptions, which is located 121 km from Mexico City).
3. Air travel was perceived as the fastest and comfortable compared to the other types of transportation considered in the study.
4. The benefits of the air transport industry in Mexico pre Covid-19 pandemic were that it created 1.4 million jobs, 37.4 billion in gross value, i.e., the industry contributed to 3.05% of the country's GDP.

The results have highlighted the economic benefits of air travel, it is suggested that airline carrier operators, those running airports, touristic destination organizations, federal and local governments, should work in a collaborative way to promote air travel within the country. Moreover, marketing strategies should consider low-income consumers by promoting, for example, specially designed flying deals.

ACKNOWLEDGMENT

This project was funded under the following grant: SIP-IPN: No-20220766.

REFERENCES

Abdullah, M., Ali, N., Javid, M. A., Dias, C., & Campisi, T. (2021). Public transport versus solo travel mode choices during the COVID-19 pandemic: Self-reported evidence from a developing country. *Transportation Engineering, 5*, 100078. doi:10.1016/j.treng.2021.100078

Agresti, A., & Finlay, B. (1986). Statistical method for the social sciences (2nd ed.). San Francisco, CA: Dellen.

AIFA. (2022). *Aeropuerto Internacional Felipe Angeles* [Felipe Angeles International Airport]. Available at: aeropuertoaifa.mx

Backer-Grondahl, A., Amundse, A., Fyhri, A., & Ulleberg, P. (2007). Safe or scary? Risk perception on different means of transport. TO1 Report 913/2007, Oslo, Norway.

Büchs, M., Bahaj, A., Blunden, L., Bourikas, L., Falkingham, J., James, P., Kamanda, M., & Wu, Y. (2018). Sick and stuck at home – how poor health increases electricity consumption and reduces opportunities for environmentally-friendly travel in the United Kingdom. *Energy Research & Social Science, 44*, 250–259. doi:10.1016/j.erss.2018.04.041

Büchs, M., Bardsley, N., & Schnepf, S. (2014). Unequal emissions – unequal policy impacts: how do different areas of CO2 emissions compare? In T. Fitzpatrick (Ed.), *International Handbook on Social Policy and the Environment* (pp. 62–92). Edward Elgar. doi:10.4337/9780857936134.00008

Buchs, M., & Mattioali, G. (2021). Trends in air travel inequality in the UK: From the few to the many? *Travel Behaviour & Society, 25*, 92–101. doi:10.1016/j.tbs.2021.05.008

Chen, C.-C., & Petrick, J. F. (2013). Health and wellness benefits of travel experiences. *Journal of Travel Research, 52*(6), 709–719. doi:10.1177/0047287513496477

Chen, Z., Wang, Y., & Zhou, L. (2021). Predicting weather-induced delays of high-speed rail and aviation in China. *Transport Policy, 101*, 1–13. doi:10.1016/j.tranpol.2020.11.008

Choo, S., & Mokhtarian, P. (2004) Modeling the individual consideration of travel-related strategy bundles. Paper UCD-ITS-RR-04-7, Institute of Transportation Studies.

Coneval. (2019). *Coneval presenta informacion referente al índice de tendencia laboral de la pobreza at tercer trimestre de 2019* [Conveal presents information regarding the labor tren index of poverty in the third quarter of 2019]. Direccion de Información y Comunicación Social, Consejo Nacional de Evaluación de la Política de Desarrollo Social (CONEVAL), México.

Czepkiewicz, M., Heinonen, J., & Ottelin, J. (2018). Why do urbanites travel more than do others? A review of associations between urban form and long-distance leisure travel. *Environmental Research Letters, 13*(7), 073001. doi:10.1088/1748-9326/aac9d2

Datatur. (2019). *Results of tourism activity 2019* [Results of tourism activity in 2019]. Secretaria de Turismo, Mexico.

Debate. (2019). *Suspenden vuelos por caída de ceniza del Popocatépetl en Puebla* [Flights suspenden due to ash fall from Popocateptl in Puebla]. https://www.debate.com.mx/estados/Suspenden-vuelos-por-caida-de-ceniza-del-Popocatepetl-en-Puebla-20190615-0029.html

Delgado-Jalon, M. L., Gomez-Ortega, A., & Curiel, J. E. (2019). The social perception of urban transport in the city of Madrid: The application of the Servicescape model to the bus and undeground services. *European Transport Research Review*, *11*(37), 37. Advance online publication. doi:10.118612544-019-0373-5

Dempsey, R., Healy, O., Lundy, E., Banks, J., & Lawler, M. (2021). Air travel experiences of autistic children/young people. *Annals of Tourism Research Empirical Insights*, *2*(2), 100026. doi:10.1016/j.annale.2021.100026

Dolnicar, S., Yanamandram, V., & Cliff, K. (2021). The contribution of vacations to quality of life. *Annals of Tourism Research*, *39*(1), 59–83. doi:10.1016/j.annals.2011.04.015

Dube, K., Nhamo, G., & Chikodzi, D. (2021). COVID-19 pandemic and prospects for recovery of the global aviation industry. *Journal of Air Transport Management*, *92*, 102022. doi:10.1016/j.jairtraman.2021.102022

Fernandez-Roman, E. (2013). *Sorprende lluvia de ceniza* [Ash rain surprise]. https://archivo.eluniversal.com.mx/primera/42452.html

Gallego, I., & Font, X. (2021). Changes in air passenger demand as a result of the COVID-19 crisis: Using Big Data to inform tourism policy. *Journal of Sustainable Tourism*, *29*(9), 1470–1489. doi:10.1080/09669582.2020.1773476

Gao, Y. (2022). Benchmarking the recovery of air travel demands for US airports during the COVID-19 pandemic. *Transport Research Interdisciplinary Perspectives*, *13*, 100570. doi:10.1016/j.trip.2022.100570 PMID:35224475

Ghani, N., Ahmad, M. Z., & Tang, S. H. (2007). Transportation mode choice: Are latent factors important? *Journal of the Eastern Asia Society for Transportation Studies*, *7*, 894–904.

Glass, C., Davis, L., & Watkins-Lewis, K. (2022). A visualization and optimization of the impact of severe weather disruption to an air transport network. *Computers & Industrial Engineering*, *168*, 107978. doi:10.1016/j.cie.2022.107978

Gossling, S., & Cohen, S. (2014). Why sustainable transport policies will fail: EU climate policy in the light of transport taboos. *Journal of Transport Geography*, *39*, 197–207. doi:10.1016/j.jtrangeo.2014.07.010

Graham, A., Kremarik, F., & Kruse, W. (2020). Attitudes of aging passengers to air travel since the coronavirus pandemic. *Journal of Air Transport Management*, *87*, 101865. doi:10.1016/j.jairtraman.2020.101865 PMID:32834691

Hansson, J., Pettersson, F., Svensson, H., & Wretstrand, A. (2019). Preferences in regional public transport: A literature review. *European Transport Research Review*, *11*(1), 38. doi:10.118612544-019-0374-4

Herrera Garcia, A. (2021). Impacto de la COVID-19 en el transporte aéreo de pasajeros y carga en México durante 2020 [Impacto f COVID-19 on Passenger and cargo air transport in Mexico during 2020]. Publicacion Tecnica No. 629. IMT, Mexico.

Herrera Gonzalez, A., Zamra Domínguez, A. R., & Rivas Gutierrez, A. R. (2019). Informe anual 2018 del monitor del estado de la actividad aérea (MONITOREAA) [Annual 2018 report of the air activity status monitor (MONITOREAA)]. Publicacion Tecnica No. 572. IMT, Mexico.

Hopkinson, L., & Cairns, S. (2021). Elite Status. Global inequalities in flying. Report for Possible, London.

IATA. (2019b). *The value of air transport in Mexico-Challenges and opportunities for the future.* Available at: https://www.iata.org/contentassets/cb691a38573642d0bbfd2ba380eaf04e/americas-focus-february-2019.pdf

IATA. (2021). *2020 safety report, details airline safety performance.* Press Release No. 15.

IATA (International Air Transport Association). (2019a). *IATA Annual Review 2019.* Available at: https://www.iata.org/en/publications/annual-review/

Lamb, T. L., Winter, S. R., Rice, S., Ruskin, K. J., & Vaughn, A. (2020). Factors that predict passengers willingness to fly during and after the COVID-19 pandemic. *Journal of Air Transport Management*, 89, 101897. doi:10.1016/j.jairtraman.2020.101897 PMID:32837029

Lin, Y. H., & Zhang, C. (2021). Investigating air travellers' travel motivation during a pandemic crisis. *Journal of Air Transport Management*, 97, 102138. doi:10.1016/j.jairtraman.2021.102138

Mattioli, G., & Adeel, M. (2021). Long-distance travel. In R. Vickerman, R. B. Noland, & D. Ettema (Eds.), *International Encyclopaedia of Transportation*. Elsevier. doi:10.1016/B978-0-08-102671-7.10695-5

Mattioli, G., & Scheiner, J. (2022). The impact of migration background, ethnicity and social network dispersion on air and car travel in the UK. *Travel Behaviour & Society*, 27, 65–78. doi:10.1016/j.tbs.2021.12.001

Mayo, F. L., & Taboada, E. B. (2020). Ranking factos affecting public transport mode choice of commuters in an urban city of a developing country using analytical hierarchy process: The case of metro Cebu, Phillipines. *Transportation Research Interdisciplinary Perspectives*, 4, 100078. doi:10.1016/j.trip.2019.100078

McCabe, S., & Diekmann, A. (2015). The rights to tourism: Reflections on social tourism and human rights. *Tourism Recreation Research*, 40(2), 194–204. doi:10.1080/02508281.2015.1049022

Milenio. (2021). *Cancelación de vuelos ante ceniza del Popocatépetl afecta a más de 800 pasajeros* [Cancellation of flights due to ash from Popocatepetl affects more tan 800 passengers]. https://www.milenio.com/negocios/cancelacion-vuelos-ceniza-popocatepetl-afecta-800-pasajeros

Minato, N., & Morimoto, R. (2021). Collaborative management of regional air transport during natural disasters: Case of the 2011 East Japan earthquake and tsunami. *Research in Transportation Business & Management*, 4, 13–21. doi:10.1016/j.rtbm.2012.06.008

Munguia, A. (2019). *Los mexicanos, entre los que menos viajan en America Latina* [Mexicans, among those who travel the least in Latin America]. El Financiero. https://www.elfinanciero.com.mx/empresas/los-mexicanos-son-los-turistas-que-menos-viajan-en-america-latina/

Nevins, J., Allen, S., & Watson, M. (2022). A path to decolonization? Reducing air travel and resource consumption in higher education? *Travel Behaviour & Society, 26,* 231–239. doi:10.1016/j.tbs.2021.09.012

Político, A. (2017). *70% de mexicanos no han viajado en avión, pero la mayoría apoya las compensaciones por retrasos* [70% of Mexicans have not travelled by plane, but the majority support compensation for delays]. http://www.parametria.com.mx/estudios/70-de-mexicanos-no-han-viajado-en-avion-pero-la-mayoria-apoya-las-compensaciones-por-retrasos/

Reichardt, U., Ulfarsson, G. F., & Pétursdóttir, G. (2019). Developing scenarios to explore impacts and weaknesses in aviation response exercises for volcanic ash eruptions in Europe. *Journal of Air Transport Management, 79,* 101684. doi:10.1016/j.jairtraman.2019.101684

Romao, J., & Bi, Y. (2021). Determinants of collective transport mode choice and its impacts on trip satisfaction in urban tourism. *Journal of Transport Geography, 94,* 103094. doi:10.1016/j.jtrangeo.2021.103094

Santos-Reyes, J. (2021). Influencing factors on the usefulness of an earthquake early warning system during the 2017 Mexico City earthquakes. *Sustainability, 13*(20), 11499. doi:10.3390u132011499

SCT (Secretaria de Comunicaciones y Transportes). (2019). *Dirección General de Aeronautica Civil Aviacion Mexicana en cifras 2018* [Mexican General Directorate of Civil Aeronautics in figures 2018]. Secretaria de Comunicaciones y Transportes.

Steg, E. M., Vlek, C., & Slotegraaf, G. (2001). Instrumental-reasoned and symbolic-affective motives for using a motor car. *Transportation Research Part F: Traffic Psychology and Behaviour, 4*(3), 151–169. doi:10.1016/S1369-8478(01)00020-1

STO (Scretaria de Turismo de Oaxaca). (2021). *Estado de Oaxaca* [Oaxaca state]. STO. https://www.oaxaca.gob.mx/sectur/wp-content/uploads/sites/65/2019/10/Ciudad_de_Oaxaca.pdf

Takebayashi, M., Onishi, M., & Iguchi, M. (2021). Large volcanic eruptions and their influence on air transport: The case of Japan. *Journal of Air Transport Management, 97,* 102136. doi:10.1016/j.jairtraman.2021.102136

Truong, D. (2021). Estimating the impact of COVID-19 on air travel in the medium and long term using neural network and Monte Carlo simulation. *Journal of Air Transport Management, 96,* 102126. doi:10.1016/j.jairtraman.2021.102126

Umbelino de Souza, F. L., Larranaga, A. M., Palma, D., & Pitombo, C. S. (2021). Modelling travel mode choice and characterizing freight transport in a Brazilian context. *Transportation Letters,* 1–14. Advance online publication. doi:10.1080/19427867.2021.1976011

Uysal, M., Sirgy, M. J., Woo, E., & Kim, H. (2016). Quality of life (QOL) and well-being research in tourism. *Tourism Management, 53,* 244–261. doi:.tourman.2015.07.013 doi:10.1016/j

Wang, S., & Gao, Y. (2021). A literature review and citation analysis of air travel demand studies published between 2010 and 2020. *Journal of Air Transport Management, 97*, 102135. doi:10.1016/j.jairtraman.2021.102135

WTO (World Tourism Organization and International Transport Forum). (2019). *Transport-Related CO2 Emissions of the Tourism Sector – Modelling Results*. UNWTO.

Xu, Y., Liu, Y., Chang, X., & Huang, W. (2021). How does air pollution affect travel behaviour? A big data field study. *Environment, 99*, 103007. doi:10.1016/j.trd.2021.103007

Yang, T. T., Ruan, W. Q., Zhang, S. N., & Li, Y. Q. (2021). The influence of the COVID-19 Pandemic on tourism demand for destinations: An analysis of spatial heterogeneity from a multi-scale perspective. *Asia Pacific Journal of Tourism Research, 26*(7), 793–810. doi:10.1080/10941665.2021.1919160

Yeo, G.-L. (2017). *Mexico City airport resumes flights after earthquake*. https://www.flightglobal.com/mexico-city-airport-resumes-flights-after-earthquake/125453.article

Chapter 2
COVID-19 Pandemic and Air Transport Business in Nigeria:
An Analysis

Oluchukwu Ignatus Onianwa
University of Ibadan, Nigeria

ABSTRACT

It will be difficult for the airline transportation business to return to the pre-COVID-19 era as many changes have taken place within the COVID-19 period itself. These changes will be the catalyst for launching the industry into post COVID-19 with the emergence of different innovative ideas and digital models that will drive the growth of the sector. However, it is necessary to take stock of the effects and impact of the pandemic in the airline sector with the view to easily finding ways of adapting to the new normal created by the pandemic. Also, to achieve optimum changes in the airline transport business, unequivocal global collaboration and idea-sharing are very important in surviving the ripple effect of the pandemic. Because this is one important lesson that the pandemic has taught the global community, every country has to be with each other to make progress in airline transport. Without this in mind, there is the tendency that new business models in the airline's models might crash and ever create a series of problems equivalent to that created by COVID-19.

INTRODUCTION

The air transport is an important sector of global economy. Strong inter-industry linkages with both upstream and downstream sectors make it a strategic component of the international market. The air transport business is a major booster of international knowledge transfer and tourism. Beyond inter-industry linkages air transport is characterized by both complementarily and substitutability with other modes of transport espcaily high-speed rail on short and medium scale routes (OECD, 2020, p.1).

Between 2019 and 2022, the world was hit by one of the catastrophic pandemics ever seen in years. The outbreak of the COVID-19 pandemic took virtually all nations of the earth unawares. Different sectors of human endeavour were thrown into utter confusion as the disease began to spread across dif-

DOI: 10.4018/978-1-6684-4615-7.ch002

ferent countries (Grace, 2020, p.3). COVID-19 disrupted global activities across all economic sectors and industries (Price Water House Coopers, 2020, p.1).

The essence of this chapter is to investigate the impact of COVID-19 on the air transport business in Nigeria. It examines various restrictive measures imposed on air transport industry in the country during the pandemic. However, it implements specific focus on how COVID-19 affected both the domestic and international air transport businesses in the country. Despite the efforts to prevent the spread of the pandemic at various airports, COVID-19 kept spreading with vigour making airliners consciously cancel and consistently reschedule air travels. I argued that it will be difficult for the airline transportation business to return to the pre-COVID-19 era as many changes have taken place within the COVID-19 period itself. These changes will be the catalyst for launching the industry into post-COVID-19 with the emergence of different innovative ideas and digital models that will drive the growth of the sector. However, it is necessary to take stock of the effects and impact of the pandemic in the airline sector with the view to easily finding ways of adapting to the new normal created by the pandemic.

CONCEPTUAL CLARIFICATIONS

Air Transportation

Transportation is very essential in every aspect of human endeavour. This is because it enhances speedy movement of goods and services from one place to another. Transportation service is the port of physical distribution activity which is concerned with the actual movement of goods to their various consumers (Good and Jebbin, 2015, p.2). Transport modes are combinations of infrastructures, vehicles, operations and terminals and the modes include walking, the automobile or highway system, railroads, maritime transport like ships, water-ways, pipelines and harbors and modern aviation such as airplanes, airports and air traffic control (Adeniran and Yusuf, pp.93-94). Each transportation system operates within a larger economic, social, and physical environment (David, 2019, p.2).

Air transportation is the transportation of passengers and cargo by aircraft and helicopters. An efficient air transport contributes to economic growth and development (Ladan, 2021, p.1). Air transport allows rapid and convenient travel, including journeys to remote areas not served by other modes of transport, and facilitates economic growth, trade and investment. The connectivity that air transport provides brings individuals and businesses together, makes global supply chains possible and connects families and communities. Air connectivity is also a measure of economic potential and opportunity (FAL Bulletin, 2017, p.2).

Air transportation can be viewed as a very complex system. Not only does this systems perspective focus on the many physical and operations components that must work together for the system to be effective, but it also emphasizes the important influence air transportation has in such areas as economic development, national security, and environmental quality (Thomas, 2014, p.2). Air transportation provides employment and enables certain economic activities which are dependent on the availability of air transportation services (Mariya, 2009, p.3).

COVID-19 PANDEMIC

Coronavirus disease 2019 (COVID-19) is an infectious disease caused by new Coronavirus type 2 severe acute respiratory syndrome (SARS-CoV-2), identified for the first time in December 2019 within an atypical pneumonia outbreak in the city of Wuhan China (Jose, 2020, p.1). COVID-19 was initially reported to the World Health Organisation on December 31 2019. On January 30 2020 the WHO declared the COVID-19 outbreak a global health emergency. On March 11 2020 the WHO declared COVID-19 a global pandemic, its first such designation since declaring NINI influenza a pandemic in 2009. Illness caused by SARS-CoV-2 was termed COVID-19 by the WHO, the acronym derived from Coronavirus disease of 2019. The name was chosen to avoid stigmatizing the virus' origins in terms of population, geography or animal associations. On February 11 2020, the Coronavirus Study Group of the International Committee on Taxonomy of Viruses issued a statement announcing an official designation for the novel virus; (SARS-CoV-2) Severe Acute Respiratory Syndrome Coronavirus 2 (David 2020, p.1).

NIGERIAN AVIATION INDUSTRY: AN ANALYSIS

Since the advent of human civilization air transportation has become an important means of transportation. With the advancement of technology air transportation has become highly sophisticated and more diversified operating both at the local and international levels (Global Aviation Industry High-Level Group, 2019, p.1). Air transportation has a rich history that is part of evolution of human ideas and ingenuity which spanned over decades. According to Obadiah Mailafia (2021):

For the millennia, the dream of flying like birds in the sky dominated the imagination of visionaries, inventors, shamans, madmen and cranks. Leonard da Vinci, the greatest genius of all time, used to tie the wings of dead birds on his hands in the vain attempt to fly. As far back as the 16th century, he left behind several designs that look uncannily like the aircraft and spaceships...The inventors of the airplane, the Wright brothers, made their first successful flight on 17 December 1903. But it was not until June 1939 that the first trans-Atlantic commercial flight took place. Aviation is now highly critical for global logistics chain, trade and tourism.

1925 is widely known as the dawn of aviation in Nigeria for it was the year that the aircraft of the Royal Air Force of Britain landed in Kano on 1 November 1925. The RAF aircraft landing in Kano and Maiduguri in 1925 provided the British imperial government a view of the possibility of citing airfields in Nigeria. When the government finally decided to develop the landing grounds an official delegation of officers of the Air Ministry in London came to Nigeria in 1930 to assess the chances and feasibility of the landing grounds which were later to be developed into airports in Nigeria. Before then the Royal Air Force had consistently landed on the grounds in Kano and Maiduguri for upwards of five years annually carrying mails from England to the northern protectorate for onward transmission to the colony of Lagos (Tunde, 2008, p.22).

From 1930 there was a marked increase in the efforts at developing the landing grounds for better use not only by the Royal Air Force but also by Imperial Airways which was to begin flight operations to Nigeria from 1935. Some records indicate that the airline had begun to fly regular airmail and passenger flights to the four British West Africa colonies before 1935. These flights in addition to those of the RAF were dangerous but pioneering efforts that established certain airfields as future airports. These the Pan American Airways of the United States later made use of to execute the war plans of the US in 1944. More of this later, the challenge posed by the African interior was extremely demanding for the British air crews sent to identify potential landing grounds (Tunde, 2008. 45).

The team sent out by the British air ministry identified landing grounds which included Azare; Bauchi; Bida; Benin Kebbi; Biu; Brass Bussa; Gboko; Gusau and Katsina. The landing ground in Lagos at the time was at Apapa. The task to build these potential airports was given to the Public Works Department (PWD). All the airstrips were meant to be serviced by commuter roads. Some were the size of a football field; while the paths leading to some were so tiny that one could only get there on horseback. Over a hundred small airfields were remotely operational and were used by the Royal Air Force, Imperial Airways and the Sudan United, also called 'Interior' Mission (Tunde, 2008, p.46).

In 1937, the PWD was instructed by the colonial authorities to develop the landing strips that had been identified and in use. In addition to this was the construction of aerodromes in places that were further identified. These included Minna, Oshogbo, and Lagos. The Department began with the construction of twenty-four aerodromes. It was a challenging task and only a small number were actually completed before 1939. The general plan was to build aerodromes that could take fairly lightweight aircraft. Those constructed were each built with major runways of about 3000 feet and secondary runway of about 2400 feet (Tunde, 2008, p.47).

The colonial authorities decided to give him some authority and his position was attached to the then Ministry of Transport where he headed the Department of Civil Aviation. This department actively pursued further construction of aerodromes throughout the period of the Second World War. Additional landing fields were constructed and existing runways were further and considerably lengthened because the military aircrafts required greater length for landing and take office (Tunde, 2008, 48).

By 1945 the aerodromes that were left over from the war were left in good condition by the PWD whose responsibility it was to do so. However, development continued, and control towers and terminals were constructed in line with the plans of the Civil Aviation Department. Also, more modern radio equipment and navigational aids were progressively introduced. In 1951, a well-organized aerodrome fire service was formed with a training school at the Ikeja Airport in Lagos to provide the two main airports at Kano and Lagos with trained personnel. A school for Air Traffic Control was also set up at Ikeja and from then on started to produce air traffic control assistants (Tunde, 2008, pp.53-54).

By 1960, there was already a plan to establish a flying training school for pilots which was nearing its opening stage. Construction of a special landing field was begun, ten miles from the airport at Lagos so that the training could proceed uninterrupted and without hazard to airline operations. Distant possibilities for the use of seaplanes or amphibious aircraft to serve the creeks, the delta area and some of the towns on the Niger and the Benue were also conceived (Tunde, 2008, 54).

The Nigerian government gave more attention to air transport development in the 1970s mainly for political and social consideration rather than economy. During this period, Sixteen (16) Airports were developed and expanded. Four(4) of them simultaneously in Lagos, Ibadan, Benin, Enugu, Kaduna, Jos, Calabar, Port Harcourt, Abuja, Ilorin, Makurdi, Sokoto, Maiduguri and Kano. Lagos, Kano, and Port Harcourt have been developed to international standard. The runways aprons and terminal buildings have been completed. Lagos airport alone handles about 80% of the domestic and international passengers, which makes it to be recognized as the most viable and functional airport in the country (Afolayan, 2012, p.118).

The air transport industry in Nigeria experienced a landmark event in 1985 when entry into the domestic airline sector and air fares was formally deregulated. The narratives around the industry gradually changed from a national carrier focus to one focused on private carriers. By 2003, the industry was composed entirely of private carriers (Adebukola and Tunde, 2019, p.1).

As at 2011, there were eight international airports and twenty (20) domestic airports in Nigeria in addition to other landing stations for private organization and the Nigeria military. (Afolayan, 2012, p.1). As a result of the series of economic activity in Nigeria, in particular, oil industry business, the aviation industry has been witnessing increase patronage which in turn generates high tax revenue and boom in tourism (Abraham, 2017, p.1). There are also numerous air strips because there is high number of flight operations in Nigeria, from scheduled flights to charter services, oil and gas services and so many others (Chinedu, 2017, p.1). In 2010 there were 48 routes connecting Nigeria to urban agglomerations around the world. On average there were 3 outbound flights per day along these routes. A total of 11 of these routes were connecting Nigeria to cities of more than 10 million inhabitants, with 4.8 outbound flights per day available to passengers. Frequencies are higher to the most economically important destinations (Oxford Economics, 2012, p.5).

According to National Bureau of Statistics report in the third and fourth quarters of 2015, the Nigerian aviation saw a decline in activity between the second halves of 2014 and 2015, both in terms of the number of travelers and aircrafts, and the weight of cargo and mail moved. However, there was nevertheless a slight recovery in activity relative to the first half of 2015. Murtala Muhammed Airport in Lagos was the airport to record the most activity, accounted for 36.5% of domestic passengers, 69.2% of international passengers, 89.5% of cargo movement and 44.9% of mail movement (National Bureau of Statistics, 2016, p.1).

COVID-19 SITUATION IN NIGERIA

On December 27, 2019, Hubei Provincial Hospital of Integrated Chinese and Western Medicine reported cases of pneumonia of unknown cause to the Wuhan Jianghan Center for Disease Prevention and Control. On December 31, China informed WHO about a cluster of pneumonia cases in Wuhan, Hubei province. And, since that day, China began to release updates on the disease in accordance with the law. On January 7, 2020, a new type of Coronavirus was identified as cause by Chinese authorities. As of January 19, 2020, China was in the first stage of fighting against the epidemic, where it of was swift response to the public health emergency (Zhun, 2021, p.2). China announced its first death from the virus on 11th of January, 2020. It was the case of a 61 years old man who had bought consumables from the seafood market. Following this development, Beijing cancelled events for the Lunar New Year, slated to commence on 25th of January, 2020 (Nikkei Asia News, 2020). Wuhan was placed under quarantine with effect from 23rd January, 2020 as rail and air departures were suspended, but it was too late (Enitan et al, 2020, p.697).

The second stage, between January 20 and February 20, was the initial progress in containing the virus. During this period, newly confirmed cases in China rapidly increased. China began an all-out battle to protect Wuhan and Hubei from the COVID-19 epidemic. China mobilized nationwide resources to assist Hubei province and Wuhan city. On January 20, the National Health Commission (NHC) confirmed that the novel Coronavirus could transmit from human to human and brings the pneumonia under quarantinable infectious disease management. On January 23, the Wuhan city's outbound routes at its airports and railway stations were closed temporarily at 10 a.m. and passenger traffic into Wuhan from other parts of China by road or waterway was suspended. On February 11, the WHO announced COVID-19 as the name of the disease and the virus causing COVID-19 was officially named "SARS-CoV-2." As the most comprehensive, stringent, and thorough epidemic prevention and control campaign was launched in China, the spread of the virus was curbed preliminarily. On February 19, newly cured and discharged cases outnumbered newly confirmed ones in Wuhan for the first time (Zhun, 2021, pp.2-3).

In Africa, there was fear that the disease would spread massively and kill a huge population on the continent. According to the Director of the African Centre for Disease Control and Prevention ACDC John Nkengasong, Africa is thought to be at high risk for the spread of the Coronavirus because of the number of flights between the epicenter of them outbreak and the continent. Air traffic between the regions had risen by more than 600% in the past decade. The first confirmed case of COVID-19 in Africa was recorded in Egypt on February 14, 2020. It was a case of a foreign national who flew into the country. Within three months, the virus had spread throughout the African continent, as Lesotho, the last African sovereign state to have remained free of the virus, reported a case on 13th May, 2020 (Shaban 2020; Reuters, 2020 cited in Enitan et al, 2020, pp.700-701).

Nigeria like any other African nations had about 50 days or more to prepare for the pandemic since the outbreak started in China. The country announced its first COVID-19 case on 27th February, 2020. It was a case of a 44years Old Italian who came into the country on February 24, 2020 and displayed symptoms of the disease, while visiting Lafarge Cement Company in Ewekoro, Ogun State. Many public health experts had criticized the Nigeria Centre for Disease Control (NCDC) for not being vigilant enough to detect the Italian man at the Lagos International Airport (Enitan, 2020, p.701). The government has used different measures to control the spread of the virus. The closure by the Federal Government of Nigeria started on 30 March 2020 with Federal Capital Territory, Lagos, and Ogun States having the first share being the first states with the COVID-19 cases in the country (Abioye, et al., 2020, p.1).

As of March 27 2020, one month after the first case, ten states in Nigeria had 81 clinically confirmed cases. At this time, Lagos State had the highest number of cases (52; 64.2%). By April 5, the number of positive cases had increased exponentially to 232. The death toll had risen to five, and 33 persons had recovered while states with positive cases in Nigeria totaled 14. Within the first 30 days, the 70.0% of the individuals tested positive for COVID-19 were male, and 30.0% were female. Their ages ranged between 30 and 60 years. People aged 31-50 years were the most affected (39.0%). About 44.0% (101) of the cases were imported, some 41.0% (96) had incomplete epidemiological information; the sources of their infections were unknown. Thirty-five (15.0%) patients were known contacts of positive cases (NCDC, 2020) suggesting community transmission or cross-infection. Lagos State accounted for over 50% of the cases in Nigeria, followed by Abuja (20.3%) and Osun State 8.6% (Jimoh and Maryam, 2020, pp.3-4).

The incidence of COVID-19 grew steadily in Nigeria moving from an imported case and elitist pattern to community transmission. The case fatality stood at 2.8%. The country recorded an upsurge in transmission of COVID-19 during the short period the lockdown was relaxed (Jimoh and Maryam, 2022, pp.1-2). On 28 April 2020, the amount of positive Coronavirus cases increased by 31 percent in Nigeria, reaching, 255, 716 cases in total. As of the same date, there were about 3.114 thousand causalities and 249 thousand recoveries in the country. Nigeria is the eight highest African countries in terms of registered cases. December 21 2021 recorded the highest daily increase in cases in Nigeria since the beginning of the pandemic (Doris, 2022, p.1). As of 18 March 2022 the total number of COVID-19 cases in Nigeria amounted to 255,092. Lagos was the most impacted state, counting over 99 thousand cases. Federal Capital Territory (FCT) and Rivers had the second and third highest number of cumulative cases, respectively (Statista Research Department, 2022, p.1).

Air Transportation and COVID-19 Situation in Nigeria

The Aviation sector plays a vital role in facilitating economic growth and development, and provides numerous economic and social benefits (Oniji, 2020, p.1). Human-to-human transmission of SARS-CoV-2 is mainly through respiratory droplets from infected individuals, contact with contaminated objects and surfaces and social activities like handshaking and hugging. The aircraft and airport environment, as well as its human occupants constitute an ecological unit that permits exposure to the novel Coronavirus. In the absence of adherence to the COVID-19 safety guidelines, accidental exposure to SARS-CoV-2 can occur at any point: pre-boarding, boarding or post-boarding (Enitan, 2020, pp.701-702).

As the Coronavirus spread across the globe, the air transport industry came to a virtual standstill by the end of March 2020. The pandemic lockdown was an unusual development that modern aviation did not foresee. According to Samanth (2020):

Among all the industries hit by COVID-19, aviation suffered in two distinct ways. Most obviously, there was the fear of contagion. No other business depends on putting you into knee-by-thigh proximity with strangers for hours, while whisking potentially diseased humans from one continent to another. Less directly, there was the tumbling economy.

Following widespread national lockdowns, report from the International Civil Aviation Organization confirmed a dramatic fall in international air travel due to COVID-19 over the course of 2020 to levels last seen in 2003. The pandemic plunged in air travel demand began in January 2020, but was limited to only few countries. According to the report, with the wide-scale lockdown measures, border closures and travel restrictions being set out around the world, by April the overall number of passengers had fallen 92 percent from 2019 levels, an average of the 98 percent drop-off seen in international traffic and 87 percent fall in domestic air travel (International Civil Aviation Organization, 15 January 2021, p.1).

Air travel is predominantly elitist in Nigeria because of high rate of poverty. The political elite also bore the early brunt of COVID-19 with three state governors and some political appointees testing positive for COVID-19. Due to the initial trend, the initial perception was that COVID-19 was a disease of the elite who returned from international travels or had contact with the political bourgeoisie. Such perception, which has not dissipated, undermined control efforts (Jimoh et al., 2020).

In June 2020 the Nigerian government muted the idea of reopening the airspace to local flight operations to begin on 12 June 2020. This was a welcome development after weeks of lockdown. The reason was that the conditions attached to the partial reopening, especially physical distancing reduced maximum capacity, continued restriction of their foreign counterparts and denial of government's bailout were not in the best interest of the local aviation businesses. Government was eager to reopen the air transport because of its huge capacity to totally downgrade the operational capacity of different components of the air transport industry for COVID-19 exposed the weaknesses of the commercial aviation sector globally and Nigeria in particular (Wole, 2020, p.1).

Nigeria officially resumed international flights on September 18 2020. One month after international flights resumed in Nigeria, allegations of fraud and test certificates racketeering trail international air travels. Shortly before the band on travel was lifted, the Federal Government declared COVID-19 PCR test certificate and negative results mandatory requirements for exit or entry into the country. Government and laboratory officials collaborated with airport staff to manipulate test results and charge innocent passengers exorbitant fees and issue them fake COVID-19 testing and vaccines certificates (Chukwuma and Wole, 2020, p.1).

The National Coordinator, Presidential Task Force for COVID-19 Sani Aliyu, stated that, "international travelers from some countries had been presenting fake Polymerase Claim Reaction (PCR) results on their COVID-19 status to enter Nigeria. Some passengers presented negative COVID-19 PCR results but later tested positive for the disease and test results presented by the passengers could not be trusted" (Chukwuma and Wole, 2020, p.2). This was a serious situation that posed a serious challenge to the airlines industry. It created confusion and chaotic situations that affected airline businesses. According to the FAAN General Manager, Corporate Affairs, Henrietta Yakubu, "suspects of these illegal acts were arrested in both Lagos and Abuja for touting, illegal facilitation, forgery, loitering, theft, public nuisance and arguments amongst others" (Channels TV, 2020, p.1). Arriving passengers complained about the non-functionality of the dedicated online travel portal for pre-arrival payment for PCR test in Nigeria. They were therefore at the mercy of extortionists, multiple payments for test and officials negotiating negative status for a fee (Wole, 2020, p.1).

RESTRICTIVE MEASURES ON AIR TRANSPORTATION

Facing the COVID-19 pandemic, international organizations diligently issued recommendations and directives for countries, regarding health measures to try to contain the health, social and economic impact of the pandemic (Rivera, 2020, p.21). Before Nigeria recorded the first index case of COVID-19 in February 2020 experts argued that Nigeria had two-month window period to learn valuable lessons and get prepared for the pandemic. The need for protective preventive measures like either a shutdown of the airspace or restriction of air movements to only two airports for proper monitoring of all inbound travelers was suggested.

The Nigeria's Senate Committee on Health during an oversight function to Lagos airport was shocked that the foremost ports of entry were not secured. Lagos airport for instance had only a doctor on-duty amid inadequate support staff screening equipment, just as operating airlines were not complying with basic control directives of the Nigerian Civil Aviation Authority (NCAA). On March 23 2020, the NCAA shut down Lagos and Abuja airports and by month-end the entire airspace had closed down (Oyebade, 2021, p.1).

One important measure introduced was restriction of local and international travels at the airports across the country. These restrictive measures changed the whole spectrum of air transportation and created avenue for innovative ideas for transformation and reorganization of transport management and business activities. On 14 September, 2020 the Presidential Task Force on COVID-19 issued a provisional quarantine protocol for travelers arriving in Nigeria. It states that all travelers arriving in Nigeria must have tested negative for COVID-19 by PCR in country of departure pre-boarding. The PCR test must be within 96 hours before departure and preferably within 72 hours pre-boarding (Presidential Task Force on COVID-19, 2021, pp.1-2).

On 27 April 2021 the Federal Government of Nigeria release another provision quarantine protocol for travelers arriving in Nigeria which mandated passengers to perform a COVID-19 PCR test not more than 3 days (72 hours) before boarding. PCR test done more than 72 hours before departure is not valid and person will not be allowed to board. Rapid antigen or antibody test are not acceptable; only PCR test can be used for this purpose. Test validity commences from the time of sample collection. For passengers with multiple connections before arrival in Nigeria, the PCR test must be valid within 72 hours of boarding from the first point of departure (Presidential Task Force on COVID-19, 2021, pp.1-2).

On 22 October, 2021 another revised COVID-19 protocol for air travelers was released. It mandated travelers, who are non-Nigerians, will be refused entry and returned to the point of embarkation at cost to the airline; travelers who are Nigerians or holders of permanent resident permit will be allowed entry, but subjected to the procedure If holding foreign passport and non-resident in Nigeria, the traveler will be denied entry into the country and returned to the point of embarkation at cost to the airline. Following the removal of Brazil, Turkey, and South Africa from the red list countries, airlines were now allowed to board all intending passengers to Nigeria from these countries. This second and revised protocol came into effect on 25 October 2021(NCAA/DG/AIR/11/16/320, 2021, p.1).

On 2nd December 2021 another travel protocol rules for international flights was released. Travelers must perform a COVID-19 PCR test not more than 2 days 48 hours before boarding/departure. PCR tests done more than 48 hours before departure are not valid and persons will not be allowed to board. Rapid antigen or antibody test are not acceptable; only PCR tests can be used for this purpose. This particular protocol came into effect on 5th December, 2021 (NCAA/DG/AIR/16/327, 2021, p.1). Following the resumption of international flights into Nigeria post-COVID-19 on September 5 2020 the PTF on COVID-19 later renamed Presidential Steering Committee on COVID-19 pegged a maximum number of two hundred passengers per each international flight operating into Nigeria (NCAA/DG/AIR/11/16/319, 2021, p.1).

Rules never seen before were set for the airliners making it difficult for them to adjust to the new normal. For instance, PTF National Coordinator, Sani Aliyu, asked the aviation sector to begin to develop protocols that would lead to the resumption of domestic flight anytime from June 21, 2021 onwards. Airlines must ensure physical distancing by reducing passenger capacity and ensure the provision of sanitizers and personal protective equipment as well as carrying out temperature checks at the point of entry and departure and ensuring that airports are not congested by either travellers or airports staff (Kayode, 2020, p.1). Flight suspension was highly prevalent during the COVID-19 pandemic. Only the travelling public was allowed access into the terminal area of the airports. The departure lounge of the Murtala Muhammad International Airport, Lagos was streamlined to about 500 to avoid crowding in absence of VIP escorts, welcome parties of friends and family, trolley boys, harassing cab operators and even fake travel agencies (Wole, 2020, p.1).

Airliners were meant to restrict schedules which sounded utopian when operators were not normal. Such a development affected the airliners preparation, check-in preparation, together with how agencies interacted with customers and airlines. According to Captain Rabiu Yadudu FAAN managing Director said that: "We are moving to the digital space where physical interaction would be reduced drastically… (Wole, 2020, p.2).

The closure of all international airports in the country impacted heavily on the economy. Many of the airlines would return at full capacity, rather it would take some time for them to recover. A lot of people who relied on airline services find it difficult to survive. The President, Association of Foreign Airlines and Representatives in Nigeria, Kingsley Nwokoma, described the situation as tragic. The closure of airports to international flights is a preventive measure but cargo, which brings in supplies affected. Cargo planes bring in spare parts, medicals and other essentials (Punch, 2020, p.1).

Travel restrictions increased frustrations among air travelers. IATA's Director-General Willie Walsh said that "People were increasingly frustrated with the COVID-19 travel restrictions and even more, had seen their quality of life suffer as a result. They don't see the increasingly of travel restrictions to control the virus. And they have missed too many family moments, personal development opportunities and business priorities. In short, they miss the freedom of flying and want it restored (Wole, 2021, p.1). An airline's cancellation policy, combined with poor customer service communications and transparency negatively influence passenger's repurchase intentions (Amal et al., 2022, p,1).

Impact of COVID-19 on Nigeria's Air Transport Businesses

Generally, the Covid-19 pandemic has social, religious, political and economic effects on the Nigeria's economy. Specifically, the effects of the Covid-19 pandemic in Nigeria include jobs losses, a sharp drop in income of the informal workers and the poor, food insecurity, business and school closures, a steep decline in oil revenues and economic uncertainties (Otache, 2020, p.176). The COVID-19 pandemic has caused a major macro and micro-economic shock to countries of the world. The pandemic has a wide-reaching effect on businesses and has already taken the millions of lives globally (Abdulaziz & 2Ofili, 2021, p.1). Okeleke & Aponjolosun (2020) alluded that COVID-19 outbreak is an economic woe to the global market and economy. Its effect spread like a wild fire and has left businesses around the world counting their costs (Bukar and Umar, 2021, p.81).

Aviation is seen by most governments as a strategic sector closely linked with economic development (Zhang and Graham, 2020), and as a result is directly or indirectly supported across several parts of its value chain (Abate et l., 2020, 89). Air transport industry has attracted considerable amount of investment from both private and government (Abraham et al., 2017, p.1).

The drastic drop in demand caused by the COVID- 19 crisis pushed airlines financial resilience to the limit, with the majority of them requiring very substantial support from governments to keep them afloat (Pol, 2022, p.1). Almost all the countries probably reacted too late in their decision to reduce flights in the early stage of the pandemic. As the pandemic evolved, most countries have significantly cut the number of flight connections, especially international flights (Aming, 2021, p.1).

Ticket prices went up astronomically making it difficult for passengers to book their flights in the country (Xiaoqian, 2021, p.1). The increase in price of tickets was attributed to the exchange rate which did not favour the airliners. By a combination of demand and supply shocks, the COVID-19 pandemic policy responses caused the most significant decrease in global air transport passenger traffic in history, thereby affecting airfares (Florian, 2022, p.1). Given the fact that they wanted to meet up with the global economy that is in the recovery process the air operators increased the price of tickets with the view to generate more funds (Haleem, 2020, p.1).

Many airport and air navigation services providers in the United Kingdom, South Africa, European Union, Ethiopia and United States broached the idea of increasing their charges by $2.3 billion. As a result, The International Air Transport Association warned that increase in charges by airports and air navigation service providers would stall post-COVID-19 recovery in air transport and damage international connectivity (Oyetunji, 2021, p.1).

Closure policies adopted by the highly affected regions including European Union, United States and China, entailed low productivity and disruptions to key value chains. Ultimately, these lockdowns resulted in reduced demand for African exports with the greatest impact on countries with substantial participation in global value chains (Grace, 2020, p.1).The massive spike in price of aviation fuel made airfares unsustainable without either government's intervention or upward review in ticket prices (Okonkwo cited in Wole, 2022, p.3).

The emergence of Delta variant of COVID-19 deepened the massive loss being experience in the air transport sector. The Delta variant was detected in over ninety countries and still has potential to spread further during the period. As a result, many airliners began to put on hold their respective travel schedules across the airports in the country. For instance, Air Peace announced the suspension of its Lagos-Johannesburg flights due to the surge of COVID-19 in South Africa. The suspension was in line with the restrictions imposed by the Federal Government of Nigeria through the Presidential Task Force on COVID-19 (Juliana, 2021, p.1).

NCAA had issued detailed guidelines for officers of the agency who had recently travelled abroad to self-isolate for 14 days among other measures upon their return to Nigeria. This is just as a directive for the compilation of details of all NCAA Staff already on official assignments or training to a country where there is community transmission of COVID-19 (Maureen, 2020, p.1).

The outbreak of Omicron variant further hit the air transport sector across the globe including Nigeria with the cancellation of many domestic and internal flights (Punch, 2021, p.1). While the air transportation sector was beginning to get a sign of relieve from the effects of Delta variant of COVID-19 Omicron variant broke out again from South Africa. On December 1 2021 Nigeria announced the presence of Omicron variant in the country. The NCDC conducted case and genomic surveillance for inbound international travelers arriving in the country at it National Reference Laboratory (NRL) Abuja and network of other testing laboratories (Punch, 2020, p.1).

The Omicron variant thump the air transport heard. Many countries issued travel ban allowing their respective airlines from travel to Nigeria. Many countries began to ban flights from South Africa and other African nations including Nigeria. With that announcement countries banned flight operations to Nigeria were banned from entry North American and European countries (Chinedu, 2021, p.1). Countries such as Argentina, Britain, Canada and Saudi Arabia, Australia, Brazil, Fiji, France, Germany, Greece, India and Indonesia among others place travel ban on Nigeria (Felix, 2021, pp.1-3). The United Arab Emirates (UAE) placed a travel ban on Nigeria and other African countries while it's National Emergency Crisis and Disasters Emergency Management Authority and the General Civil Aviation Authority suspended entry for passengers from Nigeria and other African countries (Emorinken and Okunbor, 2021, p.1).

According to IATA "the outbreak of Omicron variant, attendant border closures and other protocols stalled the industry recovery. The total demand for air transportation in November 2021 was down 47.0 percent compared to November 2019. This marked an uptick compared to October's 48.9 percent contraction from October 2019. International passenger demand in November was 60.5 percent below November 2019, bettering the 64.8 percent decline recorded in October (Wole, 2022, p.1).

Amid the surge in travels and international traffic existed mandatory tests and vaccine certificates at departure and arrival terminals which cost passengers between three to eight hours of delay with serious discouragement for customers and slow industrial recovery from the pandemic (Wole, 2021, p.1). The COVID-19 pandemic saw the intense rush of airline passengers at different airports. It was expected that the airline operators would take advantage of this peak in number of passengers besieging the airport to board flights. That did not happen as the industry was heavily confronted with numerous challenges rising from the COVID-19 pandemic. The Chairman of Air Peace Airlines, Allen Onyema, revealed that, "about 20 Air Peace aircraft are in maintenance facilities overseas and some of them are expected to start coming back very soon. What has delayed the delivery of the aircraft is the COVID-19 lockdown which forced maintenance facilities to stay off work (Mikariu, 2021, p.1).

The COVID-19 severed shortage of air cargo capacity, with freighter utilization high, and wide body passenger aircraft slow to return. It pandemic led to the downsizing of air plane by airline operators

(UNICEF Supply Division, 2020, p.2). The negative impacts of the scourge on the Nigerian aviation industry include closure of airports and banning of flights, increasing industry debt profile, negative impact on tourism, increased competitive pricing and severe loss of jobs (Siyan, 2020, p.1). Many workers were laid off due to incapacity for the airliners to operate amid the pandemic (Lawani, 2020, p.1).

Travel agencies were affected by the rising COVID-19 pandemic. Many of them went out of business having incurred huge financial loss and liquidity in the airline businesses (Wole, 2021, p1.). The vary travel protocols that were put in place by some countries including Nigeria thrown international travellers into confusion (Wole, 2021, p.1). Hakeem (2021) said that the COVID-19 pandemic has changed so many travel protocols, such that many international travelers, especially those transiting, have been stranded because they were not fully aware of the rules or they just took things for granted.

FINANCIAL EFFECT OF COVID-19 ON AIR TRANSPORT SECTOR

Prior to the crisis, aviation contributed $1.7 billion to Nigeria Gross Domestic Product. The COVID-19 crisis put the Nigeria's GDP at $900 million (IATA, 2020, p.2). According to the African Airlines Association (Afraa) the COVID-19 pandemic hammered Africa's aviation industry in 2021, resulting in an estimated $8.6 billion revenue loss. While the figure is less than the $10.21 billion revenue loss recorded by the sector in 2020, it did mark a 49.8 percent decline when compared to the revenue recorded by the sector prior to the pandemic in 2019. In short, the traffic volume from January through to December was 42.3 percent less than what was recorded in 2019. According to Afraa report, Across Africa in general passenger traffic volumes remain depressed due to the unilateral and uncoordinated travel health restrictions imposed by some governments, following the outbreak of the Omicron variant of COVID-19 (Wole, 2021, p.1).

IATA noted that the disruption to air travel due to the continued spread of Coronavirus would cost Nigeria's aviation industry over $4343 million in revenue. In March IATA, projected loss of 853, 000 passenger volumes and $170 million lose in base revenues in Nigeria are the COVID-19 continued to spread. Between April and June 2020, Nigerian airlines lost $2.09 billion with passenger numbers decline by 5.32 million when compared to the corresponding periods in 2019. Similarly, former President, National Associations of Nigerian Travel Agencies, Bankole Bernard, stated that, "in the first two months of the global lockdown in 2020, the Nigerian travel industry lost more than 180 billion naira (Joseph, 2020, p1.). The Nigeria's Minister of Aviation, Hadi Sirika revealed that airlines lost nearly 17 billion naira monthly since their operations were grounded. There were safety issues and concerns (Fikayo, 2020, p.1). Also the figures from the IATA Economics gave economic impact in Africa's largest aviation market and that for Nigeria; airline revenue loss is $994 million. In terms of employment at risk in Nigeria, it is 125,370 and loss of contribution to the GDP is $885 million. These are IATA figures and because the sector has to do service delivery and it has not been able to render services, then the revenue is lost boost the service has not been rendered and that means I have lost it (Nike, 2020, p.1).

Similarly, Musa Nuhu exposed that "the pandemic has cost the airline industry almost $1 billion while the loss to Nigeria's economy is $800 billion" (British Broadcasting Corporation, 2020, p.1). As the Managing Director of the Federal Airports Authority of Nigeria, Captain Rabiu Yadudu argued, "it would take a long time before the aviation industry would recover from the devastating effect of Coronavirus pandemic" (Chinedu, 2021, p.1). It would be difficult for the airline transportation business to return to the pre-COVID-19 era as many changes have taken place within the COVID-19 period itself.

These changes will be the catalyst for launching the industry into post-COVID-19 with the emergence of different innovative ideas and digital models that will drive the growth of the sector.

CONCLUSION

The contributions of air transport industry to global as well as Nigeria's economy are inestimable. Without the air transport international travel would be impossible. The industry was booming when the COVID-19 struck. The emergence of the pandemic gave no sign as the industry was functioning normally without any prior. Just like every other sector the air transport sector was unprepared for the pandemic. It did not take seriously the health security systems with regards to prevention of any eventualities that might befall the industry. When the COVID-19 broke out the sector was thrown into confusion and utter disarray not knowing what to do mitigate the imminent disaster. With impending restrictions jobs were lost. Important travels were cancelled. Airliners could not keep their businesses running due to the pandemic. Airlines were grounded and incomes were not forthcoming. Airport staff was forced to stay home. The advent of COVID-19 variants further leveled air transportation in the country. Banning of travel by state actors at different points of the pandemic crippled the air transport businesses. To survive, airlines have to dramatically cut costs and adapted their business to whatever opportunities were available. No business model device by the airline operators that withstand the escalating pandemic rather as new models is designed to cushion the pandemic its consistent widespread changes the earlier designs. It took the effort of the scientific and health institutions and the nation's leadership to map out series of health strategies to curtail the pandemic. Series of precautionary advices given to the air transport authorities both at the official and unofficial levels helped the air transport workers to initiate new ways of working and dealing with the pandemic. As the initiatives became highly effective in contending against the spread of the disease the nations' airports were reopened for business. Indeed, the COVID-19 pandemic has called for a deeper adoption of technologies in their everyday operations and to ensure adequate health security and protection in the sector. Institutional collaborations have become more necessary in fighting against pandemic of such nature. The use of technology to ensure safety at the airports is something that the airliners should not jettison. Thus, sharing of information on latest technologies on health security and safety measures have become a priority for the global air transport industry.

REFERENCES

Abate, M., Christidis, P., & Purwanto, A. J. (2020). Government Support to Airlines in the Aftermath of the COVID-19 Pandemic. *Journal of Air Transport Management, 89*, 101931. doi:10.1016/j.jairtraman.2020.101931 PMID:32952317

Abdulaziz, M. A. & Ofili, P. N. (2021). Assessment of the Impact of Covid-19 Pandemic on the Manufacturing Sector of the Nigerian Economy. *Gusau International Journal of Management and Social Sciences, Federal University, 4*(3), 126.

Abioye, O., Ogunniyi, A., & Olagunju, K. (2020). *Estimating the Impact of COVID-19 on Small and Medium Enterprise: Evidence from Nigeria.* African Development Bank. https://aec.acfdb.org/en/papers/estimating-impact-covid-19-small-and-medium-scale-enterprises-evidence-nigerian-397

Abraham, A., Anfofum, S., & Illuno, S. Z. C. (2015). Air Transportation Development and Economic Growth in Nigeria. *Journal of Economic and Sustainable Development, 6*(2), 1. www.iiste.org

Abraham, P., Obioma, R. N., Ogunnumesi, O., & Imad, G. (2017). An Investigation into the Effect of Airport Touting from the Passengers' Perspective: A Case of Nnamdi Azikiwe Airport Abuja. International Conference on Air Transport: INAIR 2017. *Transportation Research Procedia, 28*, 69–78.

Adebowale, N. (2020, May 6). Nigeria's aviation industry loses N21 billion monthly to COVID-19-Minister. *Premium Times*. https://www.premiumtimesng.com/news/headlines/391697-nigeria-aviation-industry-losses-n21-billion-monthly-to-covid-19-minister

Adebukola, D.T.F. (2019). *Air Travel and Airline Operations in Nigeria: Market Potentials and Challenges*. IntechOpen. . doi:10.5772/intechopen.80646

Adeniran, A. O., & Yusuf, T. B. (2016). Transportation and National Development: Emphasis to Nigeria. *Developing Country Studies, 6*(9), 93-94. www.iiste.org

Adioye. (2021). Nigerians face airfare hikes, foreign airports impose 950 billion charges. *Punch*.

Afolayan, O. S. (2012). Comparative Analysis of Aircraft-Passenger Movement in Nigeria Airports. *International Journal of Business. Human Technology, 2*(6), 118.

Agency Report. (2021 December 24). Over 2,000 flights cancelled worldwide as Omicron hits holiday travel. *Punch*. https://www.punchng.com/over-2000-flights-cancelled-worldwide-as-omicron-hits-holiday-travel-/%3famp

Air transport as a driver of sustainable development in Latin America and the Caribbean: challenges and policy proposals. (2021). *FAL Bulletin, 359*(7).

Airport Staff Others Arrested for Fake COVID-19 Results Other Crimes. (2022). *Channel Television News*. https://www.channelstv.com/2022/01/10/90-airport-staff-others-arrested-for-fake-covid-19-results-other-crimes/amp/

Amal, H. A. M., William, M. G., & Ioanna, Y. (2022). The Impact of airlines' policies during COVID-19 on traveler's repurchase intentions: The case of Aegean Airlines. *International Journal of Tourism Policy, 12*(2).

Amming, Z., Xiaoqian, S., Sebastian, W., Yahua, Z., Shiteng, X., & Ronghua, S. (2021). *COVID-19, Air Transportation and International Trade in the ASEAN+5 Region*. ERIA Discussion Paper Series No. 401. ERIA-DP-2021-34.

British Broadcasting Corporation. (2020, August 9). *Coronavirus: The impact on Nigeria's airlines*. https://www.bbc.com/news/av/business-53715571

Bukar, A. B. U., & Garba, A. (2021). Effect of COVID-19 Pandemic on SME Performance in Nigeria. *Advanced International Journal of Business Entrepreneurship and SMES, 3*(7), 75–92. doi:10.35631/AIJBES.37007

Chinedu, E. (2017). 57 Years of Air Transport in Nigeria. *Thisdaylive*. https://www.thisdaylive.com/index.php/2017/10/06/57-years-of-air-transport-in-nigeria/

Chinedu, E. (2021 December 3). As Omicron Raises Another Dilemma for Africa. *Thisdaylive*. https://www.thisdaylive.com/index.php/2021/12/03/as-omicron-raises-another-dilemma-for-africa/

Chinedu, E. (2021 July 30). Nigeria: Aviation Industry's Slow Recovery From Covid-19 Devastation. *Thisdaylive*. https://www.thisdaylive.com

Chukwuma, M., & Wole, O. (2020 September 17). Fake COVID-19 Certificates bog air travel. *The Guardian*. https://guardian.ng/news/fake-covid-19-certifcates-bog-air-travel/

David, B. (2019). Transportation Systems. Transportation Engineering and Planning. Encyclopedia of Life Support System, 1.

David, J. C. (2020). *Coronavirus Disease 2019 (COVID-19)*. Medscape. https://emedicine.medscape.com/article/2500114-overview

Economics, O. (2012). *Nigeria Country Report: Economic Benefits from Air Transport in Nigeria*. Oxford Economics.

Felix, O. (2021, December 14). *Nigeria eyes diplomacy to resolve Omicron travel restrictions*. CNBCAFRICA. https://www.cnbcafrica.com/2021/nigeria-eyes-diplomatic-to-resovle-omicron-travel-restrictions/amp

Felix, R. (2021, February 12), Pandemic Results in Historic Decline in Air Passenger Traffic. *The Wire*. https://m.thewire.in/article/business/aviation-industry-covid-19/amp

Fikayo, O. (2020, May 6). Nigerian govt. reveals worst hit sector from COVID-19. *Daily Post*. https://www.google.com/amp/s/dailypost.ng/2020/05/06/nigerian-govt-revealed-worst-hit-sector-from-covid-19/%3famp

Fontanet-Pérez, P., Vázquez, X. H., & Carou, D. (2022). The impact of the COVID-19 crisis on the US airline market: Are current business models equipped for upcoming changes in the air transport sector? *Case Studies on Transport Policy*, 10(1), 647–656. doi:10.1016/j.cstp.2022.01.025

Global Aviation Industry High-Level Group. (2019). *Aviation Benefits Report 8*. Author.

Good, W., & Jebbin, M. F. (2015). Transportation and National Development. *Journal of Economics and Sustainable Development*, 6(9).

Grace, G. (2020). *Assessing the Impact of COVID-19 on Africa's Economic Development*. United Nations Conference on Trade and Development. UNCTAD/ALDC/MISC/2020/3.

Hakeem, J. (2021 September 22). *Challenging COVID-19 Protocols air travellers must know about*. https://www.premiumtimesng.com/opinion/486310-challenging-covid-19-protocols-airtravellers-must-know-about-by-hakeem-jamiu.html

Haleem, O. (2020 December 10). NCAA: Increase in air fares caused by COVID-19 pandemic. *The Cable*. https://www.thecable.ng/ncaa-increase-in-fares-caused-by-covid-19-pandemic/amp

IATA. (2020 May 6). *Calls on Nigerian Government to Support Aviation in the Face of COVID-19 Crisis*. https://www.iata.org/en.pressroom/pr/2020-05-07-01/

International Civil Aviation Organization. (2021, January 15). *2020 Passenger totals drop 60 percent as COVID-19 assault on international mobility continues*. https://www.icao.int/Newsroom/Pages/2020-passenger-totals-drop-60-percent-as-covid-19assault-on-internationalmobility-continues.aspx

Jimoh, A., Kafayat, A., & Maryam, C. D. (2020). Coronavirus outbreak in Nigeria: Burden and socio-medical response during the first 100 days. *International Journal of Infectious Diseases, 98*, 218–224. doi:10.1016/j.ijid.2020.06.067 PMID:32585282

Jose, A. Y., Cecilla, P., Samuel, R., & Marco, A. R. D. (2020). Effectiveness of COVID-19 case definition in identifying SARS-CoV-2 infection in northern Mexico. *Population Medicine, 2*(October), 1–8. Advance online publication. doi:10.18332/popmed/127470

Joseph, O. (2020, February 1). Aviation operators fear travel ban as FG mulls lockdown. *Punch*. https://www.punchng.com/aviation-operators-fear-travel-ban-as-fg-mulls-lockdown/%3famp

Juliana, A. (2021, July 3). COVID-19: Concerns as Nigerian airlines, others face fresh setback. *Punch*. https://www.punchng.com/covid-19-concerns-as-nigerian-airlines-others-face-fresh-setback/%3famp

Kayode, O. (2020, June 4). Why flights after COVID-19 will be expensive-PTF. *Punch*. https://www.punchng.com/why-flights-after-covid-19-will-be-expensive-ptf/%3famp

Ladan, S. I. (2012). An Analysis of Air Transportation in Nigeria. *Journal of Research in National Development, 10*(2). https://www.ajol.info/index.php/jorind/article/view/92699

Lawalni, M. (2021, March 25). Why flight delays, cancellations still persist after COVID-19 lockdown. *Vanguard*. https://www.vanguardngr.com/2021/03/why-flight-delay-cancellations-still-persist-after-covid-19-lockdown/amp

Lawani, M. (2020, June 28). Airfares may start from 100,000 as tough flying rules set to take effect. *Vanguard*. https://www.vanguardngr.com/2020/06/airfare-may-start-from-n10000-as-tough-flying-rules-set-effect/amp/

Mariya, A. I. (2009). *Analysis of the Interaction between Air Transportation and Economic Activity: A Worldwide Perspective* [Doctoral Dissertation]. Department of Aeronautics & Astronautics, Massachusetts Institute of Technology, Cambridge, MA.

Maureen, I. (2020, March 20). Coronavirus: Nigeria's aviation industry to lose N160 billion, 22,200 jobs. *Punch*. https://www.punchng.com/covid-19-aviation-industry-to-lose-n160bn-2220-jobs/%3famp

Moses, E., & Kelvin, O. O. (2021 December 25). Omicron now spreading at Community level, says NCDC. *The Nation*. https://www.thenationonlineng.net/omicron-now-spread-at-community-levels-says-ncdc/amp

National Bureau of Statistics. (2016). *2015 Summary Report Q3/Q4 in the Nigerian Aviation Sector*. http://nigerianstat.gov.ng

Obadiah, M. (2021). Aviation and national destiny. *Punch*, p. 1. https://www.google.come/amp/s/punch.com/aviation-and-national-destiny?%3famp

Office of the Director-General Nigerian Civil Aviation Authority, All Operators Letter DG22/21 to All Airlines Operating International Flights into and out of Nigeria from Nigerian Civil Aviation Authority/NCAA/DG/AIR/11/16/320, Revised Quarantine Protocol for Travellers Arriving Nigeria, 22nd October 2021.

Office of the Director-General Nigerian Civil Aviation Authority, All Operators Letter DG22/21 to All Airlines Operating International Flights into and out of Nigeria from Nigerian Civil Aviation Authority/NCAA/DG/AIR/11/16/319, Removal of Limitation of 200 Passengers Per Each International Flight Operating into Nigeria, 30 September 2021.

Okeleke, U. J., & Aponjolosun, M. O. (2020). A study on the effects of COVID–19 pandemic on Nigerian seafarers. *Journal of Sustainable Development of Transport and Logistics*, *5*(2), 135–142. doi:10.14254/jsdtl.2020.5-2.12

Oniji, O. (2020). *Business Outlook: Impact of COVID-19 on the Aviation Sector in Nigeria*. Academic Press.

Organisation for Economic Cooperation and Development. (2020). *OECD Policy Response to Coronavirus (COVID-19), COVID-19 and the Aviation industry: Impact and Policy Response*. https://www.oecd.org/coronavirus/policy-response-/covid-19-and-the-aviation-industry-impact-and-policy-responses-26d521c1./

Otache, I. (2020). The Effects of the COVID-19 Pandemic on the Nigeria's Economy and Possible Coping Strategies. *Asian Journal of Social Sciences and Management Studies*, *7*(3), 173–179. doi:10.20448/journal.500.2020.73.173.179

Oyebade, W. (2020, July 3). How new safety protocol changed air travel dynamics. *The Guardian*. https://guardian.ng/business-services/aviation-business/how-new-safety-protocol-changed-air-travel-dynamic/amp/

Oyebade, W. (2020, October 5). Test certificate rocks COVID-19 air travel protocol. *The Guardian*. https://theguardian.ng/news/test-certifcates-fraud-rocks-covid-19-air-travel-protocol-/

Oyebade, W. (2021 January 1). Local air travel in the year of pandemic. *The Guardian*. https://guardian.ng/business-services/aviation-business/local-air-travel-in-the-year-of-pandemic/

Oyebade, W. (2021 June 1). Travellers to face longer processing time over protocols, traffic. *The Guardian*, 1. https://guardian.ng/business-services/travellers-to-face-longer-processing-time-over-protocols-traffic/

Oyebade, W. (2021, September 17). Confusion in air travel over varying COVID-19 protocols. *The Guardian*. https://guardian.ng/business-services/confusion-in-air-travel-over-varying-covid-19-protocol/

Oyebade, W. (2021, January 22). Travel agencies to explore dynamics of new normal. *The Guardian*. https://guardian.ng/business-services/travel-agencies-to-explore-dynamics-of-new-normal/

Oyebade, W. (2021, October 8). Air Travellers express frustration over restrictions. *The Guardian*. https://guardian.ng/business-services-/aviation-business/air-travellers-express-frustration-over-resrrictions

Oyebade, W. (2022 February 10). Industry risks collapse as aviation fuel hits N400/litre. *The Guardian*. https://guardian.ng/news/industry-risks-collapse-as-aviation-fuel-hits-n400-litre/

Oyebade, W. (2022, January 14). Omicron restrictions, travel protocols stall air travel recovery. *The Guardian.* https://https:guardian.ng/business-services/omicron-restrictions-travel-protocols-stall-air-travel-recovery

Presidential Task Force on COVID-19. (2020, September 4). *COVID-19 Response: Provisional Quarantine Protocol for Travellers Arriving in Nigeria from any Country.* Academic Press.

Presidential Task Force on COVID-19. (2021, June 30). *COVID-19 Response: Provisional Quarantine Protocol for Travellers Arriving in Nigeria from any Country.* Academic Press.

Price Water House Coopers Limited COVID-19 Resources. (2020). *Impact of COVID-19 on the Supply chain industry.* https://www.pwc.com/ng/covid-19

Reporters, O. (2020). Coronavirus: Delta, Emirates, Air France, Lufthansa, KLM, others suspend flights to Nigeria. *Punch.* https://www.punchng.com/coronavirus-delta-emirates-air-france-lufthansa-klm-others-suspend-flights-to-nigeria/%3famp

Rivera, A. (2021). The impact of COVID-19 on transport and logistics connectivity in the landlocked countries of South America. Project Documents (LC/TS.2020/155), Santiago, Economic Commission for Latin America and the Caribbean (ECLAC).

Samanth, S. (2020 September 29). Inside airline industry's meltdown. *The Guardian.* https://www.theguardian.com/world/2020/sep/29/inside-the-airline-industry-meltdown-coronavirus-pandemic-/

Sasu, D. D. (2022). *Coronavirus Cumulative cases in Nigeria 2020-2022.* Statista. https://www.statista.com/statistics/1110879/coronarius-cumulative-cases-in-nigeria/

Seyi Samson, E., Surajudeen, A. J., Godwin, O. A., Kester, A. D., Adeolu, S. O., & Richard, Y. A. (2020, December 30). The Role of International Flights in Covid-19 Pandemic: Global, Africa and Nigeria's Narratives. *Iranian Journal of Health, Safety and Environment, 6*(9), 696–710. www.academiascholarlyjournal.org/ijhse/index_ijhse.htm

Siyan, P. A., & Adewale, E. A. O. (2020). Impact of COVID-19 on the Aviation Industry in Nigeria. *International Journal of Trend in Scientific Research and Development, 4*(5), 234-239. www.ijtsrd.com/papers/ijtsrd31787.pdf

Statista Research Department. (2022). *Coronavirus Cases in Nigeria March 2022 by state.* Statista. https://www.statista.com/statistics/1122620/coronavirus-cases-in-nigeria-by-state/

Thomas, E. N. (2014). The Air Transportation System in the 21st Century. Sustainable Built Environment & Encyclopedia of Life Support Systems, 2.

Tunde, D. (2008). *A History of Aviation in Nigeria, 1925-2005.* Dele-Davis Publishers.

UNICEF Supply Division. (2020). *COVID-19 Impact Assessment and Outlook on Global Logistics.* https://www.unicef.org/

Wole, O. (2020). Fresh concerns for operators as five airports reopen June 21. *The Guardian.* https://guardian.ng/business-services-fresh-concerns-for-operators-as-five-airports-reopen-june-21/

Wozny, F. (2022). The Impact of COVID-19 on Airfares: A Machine Learning Counterfactual Analysis. *Econometrics, 10*(1), 8. doi:10.3390/econometrics10010008

Xiaoqian, S., Sebastian, W., Changhong, Z., & Anming, Z. (2021), COVID-19 pandemic and air transportation: Successfully navigating the paper hurricane. *Journal of Air Transport Management, 94*, 1-13. http://www.elsevier.com/locate/jairtraman

Zhun, L. (2021). Air Emergency Transport under COVID-19: Impact, Measures and the Future. *Hindawi Journal of Advanced Transportation.*

Chapter 3
Corporate Strategies in the Airline Industry

Ferhan K. Sengur
Eskisehir Technical University, Turkey

Doğan Kılıç
https://orcid.org/0000-0003-2696-8231
Zonguldak Bülent Ecevit University, Turkey

Burak Erdoğan
https://orcid.org/0000-0001-7215-3354
Eskisehir Technical University, Turkey

ABSTRACT

The air transport industry is a highly regulated, dynamic industry dominated by international rules and highly competitive. In this environment, airline companies need to determine both the type and scale of their activities. In this chapter, corporate strategies, which are an essential element for airline businesses, will be explained, and their applications will be discussed, particularly for airline companies. Corporate strategies mainly consist of growth and retrenchment strategies. The first part will explain growth strategies and related and unrelated diversification strategies. Next, the second part will explain savings and liquidation strategies as retrenchment strategies and sub-strategies. The third part will explain the applications of diversification and retrenchment strategies in airline companies. In the last section, airline alliances will be explained.

INTRODUCTION

The airline industry is a specific service industry having high competitive tensions. According to Hitt, a strategy is "an integrated and coordinated set of commitments and actions designed to exploit core competencies and gain a competitive advantage" (Hitt et al., 2020: 4). David (2011) classified fundamental strategies into four categories in large firms and three categories in small enterprises:

DOI: 10.4018/978-1-6684-4615-7.ch003

- Corporate Strategies (Corporate Level) - CEO level
- Business Management (Competition) Strategies (Business Level)
- Functional Strategies (Functional Level)
- Operational Strategies (Operational Level)

Organizations gain strategic competitiveness by designing and executing a value creation strategy (Hitt et al., 2020: 4). Corporate strategies are the highest level strategies of a business and answer what the business wants to do and in which sector it wants to operate. According to Michael Porter, corporate strategy is concerned with two specific questions: what companies the corporation should be involved in and how the corporate management should oversee the many business divisions (Porter, 1987). Corporate strategy is the leading strategic tool as it helps a company focus its various resources on one goal. When corporate strategy is absent or unclear, companies cannot focus on their core objectives. At the same time, corporate strategy is an element that provides support to companies in measuring their success. But measuring the success of the company will not be easy if the strategy is uncertain. If the corporate strategy is well planned, it is a tool that is likely to provide growth opportunities for the company in good and bad economic conditions. In this respect, the identification and implementation of successful airline corporate strategies are essential for an airline to survive. The main objective of this chapter is to develop a new perspective by examining corporate strategies in the dimension of airline companies. For this reason, we will first explain the corporate strategies and After examining basic corporate-level strategies in general, the chapter will focus on to sample and analyze them specifically for airline companies.

CORPORATE LEVEL STRATEGIES IN THE AIRLINE INDUSTRY

Corporate strategy is mainly concerned with the field in which the business will operate and how the subunits of the business will be formed. Corporate strategy creates synergy by bringing business sub-units together. It ensures that all sub-units and employees of the business unite in a common goal (Porter, 1987:1). It enables the business to reach its goals by considering the business as a whole, by explaining its structure, core values and goals, by determining the products and services to be offered within the framework of the goals and core values of the business (Flouris & Oswald, 2016: 99). The corporate strategy of a company with more than one business (multi-business) within its structure primarily seeks to answer the fields in which it wants to work. From this, it can be concluded that corporate strategy entails entering some business areas, withdrawing from some businesses and maintaining some existing business (Spulber, 2007: 141).

The corporate strategy should address the business's problems if it decides to enter or exit an industry (Carpenter & Sanders, 2014: 220). Corporate strategies are the strategies put forward by senior managers in businesses and determine the area where activities will be carried out to gain superiority over competitors in the long run (Ülgen & Mirze, 2020: 211). Senior managers make decisions to increase the long-term performance of the business and can change their decisions according to environmental factors (Özer, 2015: 77). The success of corporate strategies determined by the top management depends on the adoption and implementation of these strategies by managers at all levels.

Decisions made at the corporate level are about how the business can best develop in the long run. It includes decisions about the number of resources to be allocated, the activities to be carried out, the areas of activity to be entered into and where operations will be reduced or stopped regarding the

Corporate Strategies in the Airline Industry

sub-brand or departments of the business. Sub-brands or departments should organize their activities by determining their strategies in line with the corporate strategies of the enterprise, making plans to achieve their strategic goals. There are basic issues that need to be determined by the top management in the business. These are as follows (Porter, 1987: 9; Macmillan & Tampoe, 2001: 176; Wilson & Gilligan, 2005: 364-365; Carpenter & Sanders, 2014: 220);

- Determination of current fields of activity
- Determining the relationship between existing business units
- Identifying the businesses that will form the basis of the corporate strategy.
- Determining the business mission and vision
- Determining the value that the business will create for the stakeholders
- Establishing the structure of the business
- Identification of new fields of activity to be entered
- How does entering a new field of activity affect competition in other fields?
- Determination of the fields of activity to be left

Corporate strategies focus on businesses that create value and decide to divest or cease operations of those that do not. Institutional strategies consist of two basic strategies: diversification and withdrawal strategies. A corporate-level strategy aims to be instrumental in outlining a company's goal for the future. Businesses choose alternative strategies to determine how they will seek strategic competitiveness while developing a strategy. In this sense, the selected strategy communicates both what the company will do and what it will not do (Hitt et al., 2020: 4). Although there are different classifications of corporate strategies, basic types of corporate strategy can be expressed as growth strategies and retrenchment strategies. Some authors add stability as a starting point of corporate strategies (Glueck & Jauch, 1984), and some have different sub-types of strategies. Moreover, it should be noted that there are also Mixed strategies that corporations may use. This chapter will examine the most prevalent corporate strategies under the growth and retrenchment strategies in detail.

GROWTH STRATEGIES

Under the growth strategies, diversification, mergers and acquisitions and alliances are the most prominent strategies for the airline industry.

Diversification Strategies

The diversification strategy is a growth strategy at the heart of the corporate strategy. Companies implement the strategy to create more value and earn above-average income by expanding their operations, entering new markets and taking advantage of the opportunities in these markets (Ülgen and Mirze, 2020: 212). Suppose the products do not attract attention in the market or reach saturation point. In that case, the company diversifies its activities by applying a diversification strategy, offering new products in its current market, or entering different markets (David, 2011: 143). The ability of the enterprise to benefit from its corporate resources and capabilities affects its competitive advantage in another sector

(Grant, 2016: 49). The main objectives of the diversification strategy are to increase the value obtained and reduce the risk.

The existence of a company in a market with a good or service brings with it some risks. One of these risks is the inability to respond to differentiated customer expectations and demands. Customers do not prefer products, seasonal and economic factors, and substitute products enter the market with low demand. Too much diversification can cause the company to turn into a more complex structure. It is easier to manage a company with simple structures than with complex structures. The increase in the number of departments of the enterprises causes both the formation of a more bureaucratic structure and the increase in office costs, thus reducing the benefits of diversification. Complexity, bureaucratic structure and spreading over too many areas negatively affect the synergy created (Carpenter & Sanders, 2014: 229).

The diversification strategy should not focus solely on allocating company risks among different sectors because company partners can buy stocks from different sectors and distribute the risk to different sectors. By providing synergy, the diversification strategy should provide more value than would be realized when operating separately and should be able to increase shareholder value more than individual investments. The product, market or sector to be diversified should be attractive enough to provide high returns and continuity (David & David, 2017: 140).

In order to create more synergies, the company should evaluate to what extent the resources they have and the activities they diversify can meet their needs. One of the issues to be considered in the evaluation is the relationship level of the enterprises. Because when associated diversification is made, the resources required by the original activity and the new activities will be similar, and the probability of creating value will increase. When unrelated diversification is overdone, the primary and new activities may not complement each other. However, the main issue in diversification is not that companies have the same resources. The main issue is the effect of complementary resources and their compatibility on competition (Carpenter & Sanders, 2014: 231). A company can also acquire poorly managed companies to reorganize their asset structure.

Various factors push a company to implement a diversification strategy. These; core capabilities are risk reduction, tax advantages, joint activities, increasing competitiveness and market share (Barney & Hesterly, 2019: 252; Hitt et al., 2020: 193). In order to increase the value of diversification strategies, costs must be reduced, or revenues must be increased to a level that competitors cannot realize.

When a company want to implement their diversification strategy, it can enter many industries and acquire a different company. However, companies want to enter areas suitable for their core company areas or areas with high profitability rates. However, entering industries with high profitability can be difficult. A company can follow three ways to overcome the difficulty of entering the market. By purchasing an existing company in the sector, entry can be made with low quantities compared to existing competitors and by providing a price advantage at low cost compared to existing competitors (Carpenter and Sanders, 2014: 239).

The reasons for a company to implement a diversification strategy can be listed as follows (Dess et al., 2019: 176; Hitt et al., 2020: 183):

- Creating more value
- Creating an economy of scope
- Increasing core abilities
- Increasing market share

- Reducing competition
- Vertical integration
- Efficient use of capital
- Company restructuring
- Poor company performance
- Legal regulations

If the company receives support from any company while applying the diversification strategy, this strategy is called the dependent diversification strategy. When an unrelated diversification strategy is adopted, a company must support it to operate in the foreign market. While the company implements the diversification strategy, the strategy it implements on its own without any support from any company is called the independent diversification strategy. A company that adopts a related diversification strategy can identify strategies more efficiently on their own.

The airline industry is an industry that is rapidly affected by economic, political and social events has low profitability rates and high risk. The responses of an airline company in the face of possible crises and the strategies they implement are significant for their survival. The diversification strategy will prevent airline companies from being dependent on a product and enable them to generate more revenue (Redpath et al., 2017: 124; Kılıç et al., 2021: 353).

The airline industry is an industry that must obtain input from catering, travel agencies, information technology and inflight entertainment services, fuel, ground handling and maintenance organizations to maintain its operations. Airline companies supply these services from different companies and carry out these activities within their structure by applying a diversification strategy. The main objectives of the airline company in implementing the diversification strategy are to reduce the bargaining power of the suppliers, control the strategic points, reduce the competition, and grow. The bargaining power of suppliers increases due to high supplier switching costs and differentiated service delivery (Aldemir et al., 2021).

Turkish Airlines, Lufthansa, Emirates and Virgin Atlantic are critical airline companies that implement the diversification strategy. It is possible to extend this list further. Turkish Airlines operates in passenger transportation, cargo transportation, maintenance and repair, production of in-flight products, fuel, catering, ground handling, flight training academy and information technologies. Lufthansa Group offers passenger transportation, cargo transportation, maintenance and catering services. Emirates offers passenger transportation, cargo transportation, maintenance and repair, ground handling, catering, in-flight cleaning, aviation university, flight training academy, security and vacation services. In addition to air transportation, Virgin Atlantic offers beverage, hotel, radio and broadcast services (THY, 2022; Lufthansa, 2022; Emirates, 2022; Virgin Atlantic, 2022). As seen in the examples airline companies apply diversification strategies in several ways and purposes. The implementation of the diversification strategy reduces the outsourcing of companies and ensures the distribution of risk to different areas. In addition, it increases the operational controls of companies and reduces their dependence on other companies. Companies such as Turkish Airlines, Lufthansa, Emirates and Virgin Atlantic continue to grow by implementing the diversification strategy.

There are different definitions and classifications in the literature regarding diversification strategies. These; related diversification strategy, unrelated diversification strategy, horizontal growth strategy and vertical growth strategy. In this study, diversification strategies will be examined under four sub-titles.

Figure 1. Diversification strategies

Related Diversification Strategy

The related diversification strategy is when a company start to do different jobs within the fields of activity in which they continue their existence or in similar fields of activity. In line with their growth objectives, the company add similar markets to their fields of activity with their previous knowledge and experience. Similar markets will ensure that the resources available to the company are used, thus reducing the costs (Ülgen & Mirze, 2020: 214).

There may be some advantages and disadvantages for a company to acquire a similar company by applying a diversification strategy. By increasing its power and reach in the market, the company can increase its bargaining power towards customers and suppliers. Therefore, it can achieve a stronger competitive position against its competitors. It will also be more robust against substitute products and new competitors to enter the market. While implementing the diversification strategy, it should also be evaluated how it will affect competitors, customers and suppliers. An enterprise may lose a customer if it enters the field of activity of the enterprise, which operates in the same field as itself and of which it is a supplier because no company wants to strengthen it's rival operating in the same field as itself (Dess et al., 2019: 179).

The related diversification strategy enables the company to share core competencies and activities with its subsidiaries and create more value. Sharing activities also requires sharing resources. The purpose of diversification is that the company wants to take advantage of the economy of scope. If companies find synergies, they can earn more than they earn by operating separately. However, the execution and coordination of operations after the sharing of activities may increase the costs. It can also cause different levels of value to be created between units (Dess et al., 2019: 175; Hitt et al., 2020: 200).

Airlines apply the relevant diversification strategy to use their core capabilities, create more value, benefit from economies of scope and generate more revenue. Qatar Airways is one of the airlines implementing a related diversification strategy. In addition to carrying out transportation activities, the airline company also carry out activities in other areas related to aviation. In addition to passenger transportation, it offers air cargo transportation with Qatar Airways Cargo, ground handling services with Qatar Aviation Services, Hamad International airport operations, private jet charter with Qatar Executive, catering services with Qatar Aircraft Catering Company (Qatar, 2022). The airline has entered the business of its suppliers by implementing an associated diversification strategy. By operating in the catering services, airport management and ground handling sectors, which are similar to its core business, it both reduces the use of outsourcing and becomes the supplier of its competitors. It increases its control over processes by reducing the use of outsourcing. Qatar Airways continues to maintain its presence in the areas where it started operations by implementing an associated diversification strategy.

Unrelated Diversification Strategy

An unrelated diversification strategy is a diversification strategy in which there is no similarity between the current company line of the company and the new company line. It is the entry of a company into a new market that they did not have previous knowledge and experience. This strategy, which seems to start a company from scratch, is riskier than the related diversification strategy (Ülgen & Mirze, 2020: 215). It is risky because it does not match its core capabilities in its original industry. It is challenging to create synergies, and the company enters new markets that it does not know beforehand and has no experience.

Although the unrelated diversification strategy is risky, there are many reasons why it is preferred. One of the main reasons for applying this risky strategy is that the current market in which the company exists is weakened due to saturation. The profitability decreases and does not grow. In this case, the company invest in markets with growth opportunities to take advantage of new opportunities. At the same time, this strategy ensures that the risk is not concentrated in a single market but distributed to different markets. While one of the operating markets is growing, the other may shrink by experiencing crises. In this case, the revenues from the growing market can provide resources for the shrinking market (Thompson & Martin, 2005: 596).

Unrelated diversification strategy is a strategy in which companies do not prefer to grow by taking advantage of the similarities in their fields of activity. They prefer to buy or become a partner in a financially distressed and low-value company with insufficient capital but high growth prospects and return on investment. The company prefer to take advantage of the opportunities provided by another company that can be successful and have high financial performance in different sectors. In order to implement the unrelated diversification strategy and be successful, the company should constantly follow the companies operating in different sectors (David & David, 2017: 131).

When a company implements an unrelated diversification strategy, it cannot use its core competencies or share activities between departments as they enter different sectors. Instead, benefits are provided by creating synergy due to the interdepartmental interaction within the hierarchical structure. The factors that reveal this synergy are that the acquired company contributes to restructuring the leading company and shares resources to achieve the goals (Dess et al., 2019: 182).

One of the companies implementing the unrelated diversification strategy is the Virgin Atlantic group in the airline industry. Besides the airline industry, Virgin Atlantic operates in many different industries. Virgin Active; It operates fitness centers in Australia, Italy, Singapore, South Africa, Thailand and the U.K. VirginBet; sports betting, Virgin Casino and Virgin Games; operates a casino. Virgin Books; publishing, Virgin Connect, Virgin Media and Virgin Telco; contact, Virgin Hotels, Virgin Voyage, Virgin Holidays; operates a travel agency and hotel (Virgin, 2022). With its successfully implement unrelated diversification strategy, Virgin aims to be affected by the contraction that may occur in a sector at the lowest level by allocating risks to different sectors. It should also be kept in mind that too much unrelated diversification may result in the underutilization of core competencies. The aviation sector is a sector that can be affected quickly by economic, political and natural events. For this reason, companies can apply the unrelated diversification strategy like Virgin Atlantic to overcome the risks and crises that may arise with the least loss.

Horizontal Integration Strategy

A horizontal integration strategy is when a company buys or merges a rival company to grow in their sectors and reduce their competitors. The main objectives of the horizontal integration strategy, which companies frequently use, are to benefit from economies of scale and to transfer assets (David and David, 2017: 137). The horizontal integration strategy is similar to the related diversification strategy but different. The main difference between the two strategies is that growth occurs in similar fields of activity and markets in the related strategy. In contrast, growth occurs in the current field of activity and the market (Ülgen & Mirze, 2020: 200).

When a company pursues growth through acquisition strategy, it should be aware that the acquisition is more likely to be successful if the company it wishes to acquire and its line of company are similar. Therefore, a company's acquisition of operating in its sector may gain more strategic power than purchasing a company operating in different sectors (Hitt et al., 2020: 219).

With the liberalization process of the airline industry, which started in the United States in 1978 and spread all over the World, most of the restrictions were lifted. Despite liberalization, states impose restrictions on the ownership of airline companies. States impose limitations on foreign nationals' ownership and management of airline shares because they want the ownership and control rights to belong to their citizens. These constraints by the states in the airline industry make it challenging to implement the horizontal growth strategy. Due to competitive conditions and growth aspirations, airline companies implement the horizontal integration strategy through acquisitions, mergers, and joint ventures despite the constraints.

One of the most important merger examples in the airline industry is the Air France-KLM partnership. Due to increased competition, the two airlines decided to merge in 2003 to combine their strengths. The Air France-KLM partnership continues as of 2022 (Air France-KLM Group, 2022). Turkish Airlines and Lufthansa are the airline companies that implement the horizontal growth strategy. Lufthansa Group includes SWISS, Austrian Airlines, Brussels Airlines, and Eurowings (THY, 2022; Lufthansa, 2022). In the partnership of these two airlines, SunExpress was established. Turkish Airlines is also a partner of Air Albania.

Horizontal growth strategy is used by airline companies to survive. By applying the horizontal growth strategy, airline companies reduce their competitors in the sector or make partnerships. One of the most important and successful examples of horizontal growth in the world is the Air France-KLM partnership. By applying its horizontal growth strategy, Lufthansa continues to be one of the most important airline companies in the European market.

Vertical Integration Strategy

The vertical integration strategy is the entry of a company's suppliers or distribution channels into the value chain into the field of activity. The growth of the company suppliers towards the field of activity is called backward integration, and the growth of the distribution channels towards the field of activity is called forward integration (David & David, 2017: 134).

Companies apply the vertical integration strategy to take advantage of opportunities and grow. However, companies apply a vertical integration strategy out of necessity in some cases. Situations compel a company to grow; control of critical raw materials, the number and status of suppliers, and the difficulty of meeting supplier and customer demands. Vertical integration is seen as a logical move as the company will enter new activities in areas they know. A company should not forget that they are entering a new industry, even though they have grown in the fields they know. For this reason, the sector and competitors where the growth will be realized should be analyzed well (Carpenter & Sanders, 2014: 232-233).

When a company consider following their vertical integration strategy, it should analyze whether this growth will provide a competitive advantage. In addition, in the case of vertical integration, it is necessary to determine how the company will provide value to its customers. Growth should give the company a competitive advantage by offering differentiated or low-cost products to customers.
The benefits and risks of vertical integration can be listed as follows (Dess et al., 2019: 180):

Benefits

- Raw material sources and distribution channels are safer.
- Control and protection of assets.
- Access to new processes and technologies developed by departments
- Simplifying procedures and purchasing

Risks

- Increase in general administrative expenses and capital costs.
- Decreased flexibility due to company growth
- Capacity problems that may occur in the value chain.
- Increase in administrative costs due to the complexity of the company structure.

Forward Vertical Integration Strategy: The entry of a company into the fields of activity of their distributors or retailers is called a forward vertical integration strategy. It is the company's growth from its processes to customer-oriented processes. Manufacturers or suppliers follow a forward vertical growth strategy by establishing websites to sell their products directly to consumers (David & David, 2017: 135).

Within the scope of the vertical integration strategy in the airline industry, airline companies try to reach their passengers through online sales channels they have established instead of reaching their passengers through travel agencies. Airline companies sell tickets both through their websites and mobile applications. The airlines' use of their distribution channels instead of travel agencies increases passenger satisfaction and reduces the fees paid to agencies.

Backward Vertical Integration Strategy: A backward vertical integration strategy is called a vertical integration strategy for a company to enter the fields of activity of their suppliers. In addition to their desire to grow, the company implement this strategy when their suppliers' costs increase, their reliability loses, and they cannot meet their needs (David & David, 2017: 136).

Airline companies have to provide a large number of inputs in order to carry out their operations. Therefore, airline companies have many suppliers. Airline companies enter the field of activity of suppliers to reduce the bargaining power of suppliers, increase their control over inputs and grow.

Airline companies get the services they need from their suppliers from a company they have established or partnered with. Turkish Airlines started to produce the service it received from suppliers in many subjects by applying its vertical growth strategy backwards. With this strategy, Turkish Airlines, in cooperation with Opet, established the Turkish Airlines Opet company in 2009 with a 50% partnership, started to supply the fuel it needed and became the supplier of its competitors. Similarly, he founded the Turkish DO&CO company in 2007 and started to supply catering products himself. In the field of ground handling services, he established Turkish Ground Services in partnership with Turkish Airlines and Havaş in 2010 and outsourced his ground handling services to his partner company. Turkish Airlines is also the supplier of these companies, of which it is a partner, and of its competitors. While increasing the number of markets in which it operates with the backward vertical growth strategy it has implemented, Turkish Airlines carries out activities that are in direct communication with passengers, such as catering and ground handling services. Carrying out these activities within its own structure enables it to control service quality more easily and increase customer satisfaction.

RETRENCHMENT STRATEGIES

A retrenchment strategy can be mentioned when a business restructures by reducing its assets and costs. During retrenchment, the management of the business is faced with operating in an environment where resources are even more limited (David & David, 2017: 131). Retrenchment can also occur in changes in the rules and procedures related to the organization (Elmelund-Præstekær & Klitgaard, 2012). When all lines of a product are in a weak competitive position and producing poor results, a company might use retrenchment (Coulter, 2012). Previous studies show that the retrenchment strategy brings success in some companies while it fails in others (Brahmana et al., 2021). Effective use of retrenchment strategies helps the business reduce financial problems and improve performance (Smith & Graves, 2005). Retrenchment is a strategy that the company must decide very well at the point of use. The importance of its planning is very high and a possible wrong step can cause the company to be in a difficult situation.

It means that companies stop a part or all of their activities for a certain period or completely. It is a strategy that is often undesirable to be implemented by managers and shareholders, as it causes companies to downsize. Companies implement this strategy because their sales or revenues are reduced due to the economic crisis, decreased market shares, technological changes and decreased demand. In addition, companies may downsize in their current markets to seize opportunities in new markets.

We can analyze the withdrawal strategy under two sub-headings as savings and liquidation strategy. In their liquidation and savings strategies, businesses can choose one of the options to increase their income and reduce their costs, reduce their assets, or apply both options together (Thompson, 2001: 539).

According to the literature, divestiture decisions should be based on corporate strategy (Montgomery, Thomas, & Kamath, 1984). Companies may lose their competitive advantage and assets in the market in which they operate due to adverse conditions. Companies have to reduce their costs in order to regain their previously lost competitive advantage and increase their assets and productivity. The strategy that companies implement to reduce expenses and increase efficiency by reviewing the processes in their activities is called savings strategy. While applying the saving strategy, it is necessary to pay attention not to lose basic skills (Dinçer, 1998: 294; Kitching et al., 2009: 20).

The liquidation strategy means that companies dispose of some or all of their unsuccessful activities (Ülgen and Mirze, 2013:201). In cases where saving strategies are not successful, this strategy is applied. If the failure cannot be avoided by the savings strategy or the disposal of a part of the company, the entire company is sold and all its activities are terminated. Although cessation of operations is an indication of failure, it is a strategy that should be implemented in order to reduce the losses of the partners investing in the company.

Like any other important choice a company makes, voluntary divestitures should take place only when the estimated income stream associated with or following a divestiture is larger than the expected income stream of continuous operation. Only in this case is it in the best interests of the shareholders to sell the unit (Montgomery et al., 1984).

MERGERS AND ACQUISITIONS

A business aiming to grow can realize that growth by using its internal resources. Another way to grow for businesses is to expand the business externally. Mergers and acquisitions are among the typical and most preferred methods of external growth of the business. Mergers and acquisitions (M&A are significant corporate strategic actions that help a company's external expansion and provide it with a competitive advantage. Although acquisitions and collaborations are strategic moves that have been implemented for a long time, it has been seen that there have been acquisitions and mergers globally and between industries, especially with the increase of individual, entrepreneurship, start-ups and technology companies in the recent decades. Globalization increases the transfer of raw materials, labor, and know-how between borders and enables and accelerates the flow of capital between borders. In the globalizing World, new business networks and business models brought about by information technologies are also transforming global marketplaces.

Industry structure may also play an essential role in defining corporate strategies. The airline industry's deregulation is an important factor leading to the increase in bankruptcies, mergers and acquisitions due to freedom of entry to the lines, increased demand for profitable lines, price reductions, and an increase in the number of carriers. The experience demonstrates this situation, especially in the United States (Kim & Singal, 1993).

A merger is often defined as two firms combining as peers (usually through the exchange of shares) to become one (Sherman & Hart, 2010). Hitt (2020) defines a merger as "a strategy through which two firms agree to integrate their operations on a relatively co-equal basis. On the other hand, an acquisition is a "strategy through which one firm buys a controlling, or 100 per cent, interest in another firm with the intent of making the acquired firm a subsidiary business within its portfolio" (Hitt, 2020). In a typical acquisition, one company—the buyer—purchases the seller's assets or shares in exchange for cash, the buyer's equities, or other valuable assets to the seller (Sherman & Hart, 2010). Although most mergers are voluntary processes that occur at the request of both parties, acquisitions can be voluntary or involuntary. A takeover is a form of purchase in which the target firm does not seek the acquiring business's proposal; as a result, takeovers are unfriendly acquisitions (Hitt, 2020).

Mergers and acquisitions can be horizontal or vertical. A horizontal acquisition is the merger or purchase of a company that competes in the same industry as the merging and acquiring firm. Horizontal acquisitions strengthen a company's market position by leveraging cost and revenue synergies. A vertical acquisition occurs when a company purchases a supplier or distributor of one or more of its goods. Vertical acquisitions result in enhanced market power since the newly formed business gains control of more value chain areas (Hitt, 2020).

In today's globalized economy, mergers and acquisitions) are increasingly being used around the World to improve company competitiveness by gaining more outstanding market share, broadening the portfolio to reduce business risk, entering new markets and geographies, and capitalizing on economies of scale, among other things. There are substantial incentives for airline mergers and partnerships. Although the reasons for the merger or acquisition decisions of companies may be based on specific reasons on a business basis, in general, businesses may choose to merge and acquire for the following reasons:

Increasing Market Power: An industry structure determines the intensity of competitive competition and, in turn, affects a firm's profitability. In order to reduce the adverse effects of intense competition and market dependencies, companies can use mergers and acquisitions. Seizing market power and strengthening its position in the market is the main reason for many collaborations and acquisitions. Market power is generally obtained from the firm's size, the quality of the resources it utilizes to compete, and its market dominance in the market(s) in which it competes. As a result, most acquisitions made to attain more market power include purchasing a rival, a supplier, a distributor, or a business in a strongly connected industry to gain a competitive position in the acquiring firm's primary market (Hitt, 2020). Through acquisitions and mergers, businesses make their closest competitors work with them. This advantage paves the way for companies to earn above-average returns. Thus, businesses naturally reduce or even eliminate competition in the industry. The airline industry is a sector where mergers and acquisitions are experienced intensively, especially with deregulation. Airline mergers and acquisitions were experienced in the U.S., and a consolidation trend was observed in the sector even in the regulated periods. With the deregulation, this trend increased and started to take place globally. As a result of these mergers and acquisitions, undesirable increases in prices or decreases in service may occur for customers. Significant increases in airfare may occur on routes impacted by airline mergers, and such increases are strongly connected with changes in concentration (Kim & Singal, 1993).

Overcoming Entry Barriers: Mergers and acquisitions may be used by corporations to enter new markets and geographies. Cross-border mergers and acquisitions have grown dramatically over time, owing mainly to a desire to avoid tariffs and nontariff obstacles imposed by international trade and taxation; to get new financing alternatives; to gain access to technology; and to spread Research & Development expenditures across a more extensive base (Vasconcellos & Kish, 2013). One of the most prevailing reasons for cross border acquisitions is to overcome barriers to entry in another country. Recent decades have witnessed that mergers and acquisitions have become one of the most prominent techniques used by commercial enterprises to enter and expand into new markets and sustain their current market position. The airline business has also seen a surge in mergers and acquisitions. Domestic and cross-border mergers and acquisitions have risen significantly in recent years (Chow & Tsui, 2017).

Acquiring Cost Advantages: In some cases, instead of buying the assets it needs from the market at a high cost, the company may merge with a company and reduce the replacement cost and choose to merge and buy. Especially in the airline industry, the airport slots owned by the airline can be a typical example of this situation. Airport slots have landing-departure rights defined at certain hours, especially at busy airports, but can change hands in return for bankruptcies or very high prices. Therefore, sometimes it is impossible to have slots even by purchasing them. As the airlines use the slots they hold in the following years due to grandparent rights practices, it becomes impossible for the airlines to enter the market to use a specific airport at a specific time. In these cases, mergers and acquisitions provide access to the resources of the airlines purchased, which is a preferred practice both to enter new markets and to arrange a flight from the airport at the desired time.

Acquiring New Sources: Internally developing new products and effectively putting them into the market frequently necessitates a significant expenditure of a firm's resources, particularly time, making it difficult to achieve a financial return rapidly (Hitt, 2020). Another critical reason for mergers and acquisitions is access to new resources and the development of existing resources. This can have the effect of saving new product development costs, or it can be in the form of expanding resources or assets by combining them with the other business's assets.

One of the main benefits of merging and acquiring with another airline is to create a network advantage in the airline industry. Suppose the network structures of the two airlines complement each other, as in airline strategic alliances. In that case, this integration will expand the network structure of the new corporation with a synergetic effect. Network expansion expands the customer base and brings significant cost advantages. Large networks outperform smaller networks in terms of both cost and demand. Travellers prefer connecting flights on the same airline to connecting flights on different carriers because "seamless" connections are often more convenient and provide more security in the case of delays on the arriving or leaving aircraft or missing luggage. Travellers also choose airlines that provide more frequent service because they provide greater travel flexibility in the case of a last-minute change of plans. Depending on the nature of the competition between the networks prior to the merger, a merger or alliance can allow the merged airline to lower costs and increase demand for its services by rationalizing the hub-and-spoke structure(s), achieving greater cost efficiencies, and offering a more comprehensive range of seamless connections. On the other hand, a merger or alliance will lessen competition and may increase market power on routes where the networks previously overlapped, particularly on spoke and hub-hub routes. (OECD, 1999).

Employing New Business Models and Increasing Diversification: Mergers and acquisitions can also be utilized to employ new business models and to diversify a company's operations. Firms often find it simpler to create and introduce new goods in markets they now serve based on their expertise and the insights gained. Each airline has a unique business model and different value propositions. (Sengur & Sengur, 2017). One of the strategies of full-service airlines to compete with low cost carriers is starting a low cost subsidiary and competing with different business models. An acquisition may serve such an aim.

On the other hand, companies find it challenging to design items that differ from their present lines for markets in which they lack experience. As a result, it is far easier for a company to diversify its product lines than to develop new items domestically. Acquisition tactics can be used to supplement both related and unrelated diversification strategies (Hitt, 2020).

Airline consolidation trends with mergers and acquisitions created today's most prominent airlines in the World. Some examples of the major mergers and acquisitions that take place in the airline industry can be seen below:

- 2001 - American Airlines merged with Trans World Airlines
- 2004 - Air France- KLM Merger

- 2010 - Southwest acquired AirTran Airways
- 2010 - Delta merged with Northwest Airlines
- 2012 - LAN and TAM merged to form LATAM
- 2012 - United Airlines acquired Continental Airlines
- 2013 - American Airlines acquired U.S. Airways

Each airline merger and acquisition should be examined independently. Although generally in mergers, companies choose one name, one brand, corporate identity, there are some exceptions. For example, in 2004, Air France acquired KLM Royal Dutch Airlines, and this acquisition changed the company name to Air France KLM. The horizontal merger of Air France and KLM attempted to retain each company's trademarks, emblems, and corporate identity, and the two airlines still operate as separate airlines. A stable and fair hub development of Amsterdam Airport Schiphol and the Dutch brand and identity might be ensured by simply forming one listed holding company like Air France-KLM Group with two operational carriers' national traffic rights. As a result, the Dutch state and two Dutch foundations retain 50,1% of KLM's voting rights, allowing it to avoid the nationality limitations placed on airline ownership under so-called bilateral rights (Friesen, 2005).

Mergers and acquisitions may also have some potential problems. Primarily cultural and organizational problems may occur.

STRATEGIC ALLIANCES

Strategic alliances, which attracted significant attention from the academic and industry after the 1990s, have entered a rapid rise around the World as a new perspective on integrating resources and cooperation (Albers et al., 2016). Today, the rate of change in the environment of businesses is high. The rapid realization of technological developments, the saturation of existing markets, the desire to reach new markets, the emergence of new business models, the increase in the importance of innovation can be cited among the reasons for this high rate of change (Foroohar, 2018). However, the universal economic and political structure situation is also changing, and it creates an obstacle for businesses to reach their strategic goals (He et al., 2020).

A strategic alliance is defined as an agreement between two or more companies to achieve common goals, usually involving a long-term partnership and interaction (Rivera-Santos & Inkpen, 2009).

Strategic alliances are cooperation between two or more companies to increase their competitive performance by sharing their resources (Ireland et al., 2002) and they create significant opportunities for businesses to develop their capabilities and optimize the value created (O'Dwyer & Gilmore, 2018). There are three types of strategic alliances:

Joint Venture: It means that two separate companies come together to form a joint third company. If the partnership is equal, it is known as a 50-50 joint venture, if one partner has more shares than the other, it is known as a majority owned venture.

Equity Strategic Alliance: An alliance formed by one company buying another at a certain rate. For instance; Pegasus Airlines has a 36.2% stake in Hitit Computer, which produces software in the field of aviation.

Non-equity Strategic Alliance: It is the sharing of knowledge of two or more companies in line with common interests. They make up the vast majority of business alliances.

Corporate Strategies in the Airline Industry

The activities of the alliances can be in the following titles: Supplier and buyer agreements, technical cooperation, joint product development, joint research projects, joint distribution agreements. The main activity of alliance may vary depending on the structure of the businesses and their current needs (Wang et al., 2018).

Along with these, we can say that strategic alliances are partnerships realized by businesses to provide mutual benefits. Even without an alliance, the business can achieve its goals. The critical point here is that with creating an alliance, the efficiency in that field increases and the cost in that field decreases. At this point, we can talk about the difference between effectiveness and efficiency. The difference between effectiveness and efficiency is this: effectiveness means achieving the goal; Efficiency means achieving the goal with minimum cost and effort.

AIRLINE ALLIANCES

Airline alliances can be defined as agreements made to coordinate, promote and jointly market the services of carriers that are members of the alliance or airline companies party to the agreement (Dresner & Windle, 1996). Airline alliances are formed to create a seamless global network to gain competitive advantage through codeshare or various joint operations. Unlike conventional airline operations, airlines in alliances are coordinated to maximize the profits of all members (Yang et al., 2021). An airline alliance is a cooperative agreement between two or more airlines that regulates joint operations to gain a competitive advantage and thereby improve the airline's overall performance (Morrish & Hamilton, 2002).

A strategic airline alliance is an alliance in which airlines pool their resources to pursue and develop shared goals. Combined resources can be terminal facilities, maintenance bases, aircraft, personnel, traffic rights or capital. If two or more airlines offer a familiar brand and a uniform service standard, it means they have consolidated their assets and entered into a strategic alliance (Doganis, 2005).

Airline alliances mean partnerships that aim to grow and develop their companies and airline industry by combining the energy that airline companies spend on competing with each other on common interests. Airline alliances are essential agreements that help achieve common predetermined strategic goals. It helps airlines strengthen their existing markets, expand their flight network by accessing new markets, and thus increase their market share by reducing costs.

The formation of alliances has arisen mainly because of the legal and regulatory structure for the international airline industry. International law assigns ownership of the airspace and a specific area around it to the countries below that area. A country's airline cannot fly into another country's airspace without the permission of that country's government. It can fly from one country to another by agreement between the two countries. The agreement is usually an air transport "bilateral agreement" that sets the flight route of each country's airlines. For example, the bilateral agreement between Germany and the USA specifies the route of German and American airlines between the two countries (Erdoğan, 2019).

In the globalizing World, airlines have sought to outdo their competitors. At this point, bilateral agreements first emerged before global airline alliances. KLM/Northwest was the first alliance (bilateral agreement) to be granted antitrust immunity by USDOT (U.S. Department of Transportation) in November 1992, shortly after the Netherlands and the United States signed an open skies agreement in September 1992 (Oum et al., 2001). Examples of other bilateral agreements are:

- U.S. Air / British Airways

- United Airlines / Lufthansa
- United Airlines / Ansett Australia
- United Airlines / British Midland

Antitrust immunity means that the airline participants in the alliance determine the fares together at the joint network (Bilotkach, 2019). The most prominent alliance types in the airline industry in recent years are codeshare agreements and global airline alliances (Cobena et al., 2019). Codeshare agreements are an integral part of global airline alliances. In addition, studies have determined that it is a factor affecting the preferences of passengers (Weber, 2005).

Gudmunsson and Rhoades (2001) list the critical partnership of airline alliances as follows:

Codeshare: Two or more airlines agree on a flight and perform this flight jointly. In Codeshare flights, each airline has its flight code for the flight. The airline that owns the aircraft and shares the flight with other airlines is an operating carrier. An example of code sharing is Scandinavian Airlines selling tickets on Turkish Airlines Istanbul - Izmir flight with its code.

Block Space: An airline purchases a certain number of seats for a flight from an operating carrier to sell it. Block space examples are abundantly available in the U.S., where regional airlines are standard. Because the USA is a vast country in terms of surface area, spread over a continent. Major US airlines have many regional companies called feeder carriers. An example of this is Piedmont Airlines, a subsidiary of American Airlines.

Revenue sharing means that two or more airlines share the revenue from a joint activity.

A wet lease is an aircraft lease with its crew and the other for a certain period.

Franchising: Airline franchising means that an airline acquires the right to assume another airline's public brand, image and related services for a fee (Denton & Dennis, 2000).

Computer Reservation System (CRS): Systems usually set up and used for the sale and reservation of tickets over the internet.

Insurance/parts pooling: Two or more airlines agree to joint purchases.

Joint Service: Two airlines offer a combined flight service.

Management Contract: An airline contracting with another airline to manage an aspect of its operation.

Baggage Handling/Maintenance/Facilities Sharing: An airline sharing different resources with another airline.

Joint Marketing: At least two airlines carry out joint marketing activities.

Equity swap/governance: Two or more airlines exchange shares and/or create joint governance structures.In addition to airlines, airports have also created alliances in recent years. While there are many dimensions to be shared in airline alliances, there is a general sharing of administrative processes in airport alliances. Airport alliances, which emerge later and are much less common than airline alliances, provide a more limited resource sharing than airline alliances.

For example, Schiphol International Airport and Fraport (Frankfurt Airport) formed and reformed the Pantares Alliance in 2001 and 2008. The purposes for doing this are; to reduce operational costs, increase the market shares of the two hub airports and provide a strong logistics network with value-added products (Jiang et al., 2019).

The reasons for the formation of airport integration in research are as follows; They argued that the goal was to generate economic gain through the transfer of know-how, including expertise in the operation, investment and marketing of airports, and to increase the technical efficiency of partner airports (Forsyth et al., 2011).

WHY AIRLINE ALLIANCES EXIST?

The regulation of the rules on entry restrictions, especially after the deregulation of the U.S. domestic market in 1978, encouraged the formation of new airlines and the airline industry's growth. Airline alliance agreements and established airline alliances, which have been widely made since the 1990s, have benefited airlines in various fields.

Oum and Park (1997) state that the reasons for airline alliances are:

- **Expansion of seamless service network:** The airline alliance aims to fly with one member in the alliance for each leg for multi-leg flights. The more destinations there are, the higher the probability that the passenger will make all of his flights within the alliance. For example, a passenger cannot find a non-stop flight between Istanbul and Sydney. On connecting flights, Turkish Airlines, a member of the Star Alliance alliance, takes them from Istanbul to Singapore. In contrast, Singapore Airlines, another member of the alliance, takes passengers to their desired destination with a flight from Singapore to Sydney. In this example, the Star Alliance alliance has provided a **seamless service network** to its passengers with codesharing it has made within itself.
- **Traffic feed between partners:** By connecting the networks of members, airline alliances can feed traffic mutually and contribute to the increase in load factor. Thus, member airlines increase their frequencies without operating their aircraft (Oum et al., 2000). As an example, we can give LOT Polish Airlines the sale of tickets for the Turkish Airlines flight between Istanbul and Ankara. When it does not organize a flight, it can sell tickets to its passengers through its alliance partner.
- **Cost efficiency:** In economies of density, the increase in traffic from joint pricing of inter-line journeys results in lower marginal costs for alliance partners (Brueckner & Whalen, 2000).
- **Improvement of service quality:** By increasing their frequencies and expanding their destinations, airlines can increase the quality of the service they offer. It is one of the contributions of the alliances to the airlines to offer the passengers flights at the desired destinations at the frequencies they want.
- **Frequent Flyer Program (FFP) and CRS display:** The fact that the frequent flyer programs of the alliances are integrated and that the passengers who fly in a member airline can use the points earned by the other airline brings a significant advantage at this point.

GLOBAL AIRLINE ALLIANCES

Global airline alliances form a partnership based on codeshare agreements between members. Leaving a member from the alliance may reduce the alliances' flight network (Klophaus & Lordan, 2018).

Nowadays, airline alliances have evolved from bilateral agreements to global strategic partnerships. There are three global airline alliances in the World:

- Star Alliance
- SkyTeam
- Oneworld

Star Alliance: It was founded on May 14 1997, by five airlines (United Airlines, Lufthansa, Air Canada, Scandinavian Airlines, Thai Airways International). As of February 2022, it has 26 members. The alliance's strategy is explained as follows: to be the World's most digital airline alliance by providing a seamless travel experience that everyone is talking about (Star Alliance, 2021). Star Alliance flies to 98% of the World's destinations. It has more than 1300 destinations worldwide.

The Star Alliance alliance established Star Alliance Circle Pacific Fare as a sub-program. The purpose of the program; Reaching passengers travelling in North America, Southwest Pacific and Asia regions, is to facilitate their travel. It covers regions where 35% of the World's population is located. Twelve airlines are involved in this program (Star Alliance, 2021).

Figure 2. Logo of Star Alliance Source: Star Alliance (2022)

The five individual pieces in the Star Alliance logo in Figure 2 represent the founding airlines.

Figure 3. Members of Star Alliance Source: Star Alliance (2022)

Oneworld: It was founded on February 1, 1999. American Airlines, British Airways, Cathay Pacific and Qantas are founder members. As of February 2022, it has 14 members. Oneworld has almost 1000 destinations worldwide.

Corporate Strategies in the Airline Industry

Figure 4. Logo and members of Oneworld Source: Oneworld (2022)

SkyTeam: It was founded on June 22, 2000. Aeromexico, Air France, Delta Air Lines and Korean Air are founder members. As of February 2022, it has 19 members. SkyTeam has more than 1036 destinations worldwide.

Figure 5. Logo and Members of SkyTeam Source: SkyTeam (2022)

57

Comparison of Global Airline Alliances

The market shares of the three major alliances according to the available seat kilometer (ASK) in 2018 were as follows:

Table 1. Comparison of global airline alliances in different dimensions

	Star Alliance	SkyTeam	Oneworld
Members	26	19	14
Destination	1300	1036	1020
Destination Countries	195	170	170
Revenue	$171 billion	$152,9 billion	$142 billion
Market Share by ASK	21,7%	16,1%	15,6%
Annual Passenger	762 million	676 million	535 million
Fleet Size	5033	3763	4196
Daily Flights	19000	15445	13000
Lounges	1000	790	600
Number of employees	423210	459781	397682

Source: Compiled from Star Alliance, SkyTeam, Oneworld

As seen in Table 1, Star Alliance is superior to other alliances in every dimension except the number of employees. At this point, Star Alliance made a difference by being the first alliance established, having more members, and having more large companies among its members than other alliances.

CONCLUSION

Corporate strategies answer the basic questions for any organization. The importance of corporate strategies for airlines has increased even more in the post-covid-19 period. Airline alliances emerged in the 1990s, and they continue to influence under the leadership of three major global airline alliances. According to ASK, the three major airline alliances have a 53.4% market share in the World (Salas, 2019). The dimensions of alliances in airlines have diversified from past to present. Initially, it was based only on bilateral codesharing agreements, but today it has evolved far beyond that into advanced global partnerships. The alliances made now enable the joint flight of a flight and provide cooperation of airlines in many fields. The use of energy to be spent on the competition for common interests will bring lower costs and increase efficiency for airlines. Vertical, horizontal diversifications and mergers and acquisitions have increased in recent decades.

In corporate strategies, companies make moves in various dimensions. However, it is of great importance to determine, plan, implement and control the corporate strategy. The result of a poorly implemented corporate strategy can even lead to the bankruptcy of the company. A properly implemented corporate strategy brings the company to a point that makes a difference in its field.

In this chapter, different corporate strategies were analyzed with examples from different companies. As a result of the analyzes made, it was determined that corporate strategies are of great and different level of importance for airlines and that they provide benefits at various points and these are expressed. The industry is under a cyclical reconstruction under its internal dynamics and external factors such as COVID-19 pandemic like crisis. Corporate strategies examined in this chapter will be more important under the new normal.

REFERENCES

Air France-KLM Group. (2022). *History*. https://www.airfranceklm.com/en/group/history

Albers, S., Wohlgezogen, F., & Zajac, E. (2016). Strategic alliance structures: An organization design perspective. *Journal of Management*, *42*(3), 582–614. doi:10.1177/0149206313488209

Aldemir, H., Kuyucak Şengür, F., & Ulukan, İ. (2021). Exploring Strategic Choices of Airlines: A Study in Turkish Air Transport Industry. *Asian Academy of Management Journal*, 1-26. doi:10.21315/aamj2021.26.2.1

Barney, J. B., & Hesterly, W. S. (2019). *Strategic management and competitive advantage: Concepts and cases*. Pearson.

Bilotkach, V. (2019). Airline Partnerships, Antitrust Immunity, and Joint Ventures: What We Know and What I Think We Would Like to Know. *Review of Industrial Organization*, *54*(1), 37–60. doi:10.100711151-018-9636-x

Brahmana, R., You, H., & Kontesa, M. (2021). Does CEO power matter for the performance of retrenchment strategy? *Journal of Strategy and Management*, *14*(1), 1–18. doi:10.1108/JSMA-10-2019-0186

Brealey, A. R., Myers, C. S., & Marcus, J. A. (2007). *Fundamentals of Corporate Finance*. McGraw-Hill.

Brueckner, J., & Whalen, W. (2000). The Price Effects of International Airline Alliances. *The Journal of Law & Economics*, *43*(2), 503–546. doi:10.1086/467464

Carpenter, M. A., & Sanders, W. G. (2014). *Strategic Management Concepts and Cases*. Pearson.

Chow, C. K. W., & Tsui, W. H. K. (2017). Organizational learning, operating costs and airline consolidation policy in the Chinese airline industry. *Journal of Air Transport Management*, *63*, 108–118. doi:10.1016/j.jairtraman.2017.06.018

Cobena, M., Gallego, A., & Casanueva, C. (2019). Diversity in airline alliance portfolio configuartion. *Journal of Air Transport Management*, *75*, 16–26. doi:10.1016/j.jairtraman.2018.11.004

Coulter, M. (2012). *Strategic Management in Action*. Pearson Education.

David, F., & David, F. (2017). *Strategic Management: A Competitive Advantage Approach, Concepts and Cases*. Pearson Education Limited.

David, F. R. (2011). *Strategic Management Concepts And Cases*. Phi Learning.

Denton, N., & Dennis, N. (2000). Airline franchising in Europe: Benefits and disbenefits to airlines and consumers. *Journal of Air Transport Management*, 6(4), 179–190. doi:10.1016/S0969-6997(00)00010-7

Dess, G. G., McNamara, G., Eisner, A. B., & Lee, S. (2019). *Strategic management: Text and cases*. McGraw-Hill Education.

Dinçer, Ö. (1998). *Stratejik Yönetim ve İşletme Politikası*. Beta Publishing.

Doganis, R. (2005). *The Airline Business*. Routledge. doi:10.4324/9780203596807

Dresner, M., & Windle, R. (1996). Alliances and Code-Sharing in the International Airline Industry. *Built Environment*, 22(3), 201–211.

Elmelund-Præstekær, C., & Klitgaard, M. (2012). Policy or institution? The political choice of retrenchment strategy. *Journal of European Public Policy*, 19(7), 1089–1107. doi:10.1080/13501763.2012.672112

Emirates. (2022). *About Us*. https://www.emirates.com/english/about-us/group-company/

Erdoğan, B. (2019). Airline Alliances and Its Effects On Airlines: Turkish Airlines Case. *The Journal of Social Science*, 33, 375–395.

Flouris, T. G., & Oswald, S. L. (2016). *Designing and executing strategy in aviation management*. Routledge. doi:10.4324/9781315576718

Foroohar, R. (2018). *Corporate elites are overlooking deglobalization*. https://www.ft.com/content/df3ded82-ce32-11e8-b276-b9069bde0956

Forsyth, P., Niemeier, H.-M., & Wolf, H. (2011). Airport alliances and mergers – Structural change in the airport industry? *Journal of Air Transport Management*, 17(1), 49–56. doi:10.1016/j.jairtraman.2010.10.011

Friesen, M. (2005, March). *Capital Market's Assessment of European Airline Mergers and Acquisitions–The Case of Air France and KLM* [Paper presentation]. In *5th Swiss Transport Research Conference*, Monte Verità/Ascona.

Glueck, W. F., & Jauch, L. R. (1984). *Business Policy and Strategic Management*. McGraw-Hill.

Grant, R. M. (2016). *Contemporary strategy analysis: Text and cases edition*. John Wiley & Sons.

Gudmundsson, S., & Rhoades, D. (2001). Airline alliance survival analysis: Typology, strategy and duration. *Transport Policy*, 8(3), 209–218. doi:10.1016/S0967-070X(01)00016-6

He, Q., Meadows, M., Angwin, D., Gomes, E., & Child, J. (2020). Strategic Alliance Research in the Era of Digital Transformation: Perspectives on Future Research. *British Journal of Management*, 31(3), 589–617. doi:10.1111/1467-8551.12406

Hitt, M. A., Ireland, R. D., & Hoskisson, R. E. (2020). *Strategic management: Concepts and Cases: Competitiveness and globalization*. Cengage Learning.

Ireland, R., Hitt, M., & Vaidyanath, D. (2002). Alliance Management as a Source of Competitive Advantage. *Journal of Management, 28*(3), 413–446. doi:10.1177/014920630202800308

Jiang, Y., Liao, F., Xu, Q., & Yang, Z. (2019). Identification of technology spillover among airport alliance from the perspective of efficiency evaluation: The case of China. *Transport Policy, 80*(C), 49–58. doi:10.1016/j.tranpol.2019.05.004

Kılıç, D., Polat, G., & Şengür, F. (2021). Havayolu İşletmelerinin Covid-19 Pandemi *Sürecindeki Yönetsel Tepkileri Üzerine Bir Araştirma*. *Uluslararası Yönetim İktisat Ve İşletme Dergisi, 17*(2), 353–377.

Kim, E. H., & Singal, V. (1993). Mergers and market power: Evidence from the airline industry. *The American Economic Review, 83*(3), 549–569.

Kitching, J., Blackburn, R., Smallbone, D., & Dixon, S. (2009). *Business Strategies and Performance during Difficult Economic Conditions*. Kingston University.

Klophaus, R., & Lordan, O. (2018). Codesharing network vulnerability of global airline alliances. *Transportation Research Part A, Policy and Practice, 111*, 1–10. doi:10.1016/j.tra.2018.02.010

Lufthansa. (2022). *Company*. https://www.lufthansagroup.com/en/company.html

Macmillan, H., & Tampoe, M. (2001). Strategic management. Academic Press.

Montgomery, C. A., Thomas, A. R., & Kamath, R. (1984). Divestiture, market valuation, and strategy. *Academy of Management Journal, 27*(4), 830–840.

Morrish, S., & Hamilton, R. (2002). Airline alliances—Who benefits? *Journal of Air Transport Management, 8*(6), 401–407. doi:10.1016/S0969-6997(02)00041-8

O'Dwyer, M., & Gilmore, A. (2018). Value and alliance capability and the formation of strategic alliances in SMEs: The impact of customer orientation and resource optimization. *Journal of Business Research, 87*, 58–68. doi:10.1016/j.jbusres.2018.02.020

OECD. (1999). *Policy Roundtables Airline Mergers and Alliances*. https://www.oecd.org/daf/competition/mergers/2379233.pdf

Oneworld. (2022). *14 Global Airlines. One Bright Alliance*. https://www.oneworld.com/members

Oum, T., & Park, J.-H. (1997). Airline alliances: Current status, policy issues, and future directions. *Journal of Air Transport Management, 3*(3), 133–144. doi:10.1016/S0969-6997(97)00021-5

Oum, T., Park, J.-H., & Zhang, A. (2000). *Globalization and Strategic Alliances: The Case of Airline Industry*. Elsevier Science Ltd.

Oum, T., Yu, C., & Zhang, A. (2001). Global airline alliances: International regulatory issues. *Journal of Air Transport Management, 7*(1), 57–62. doi:10.1016/S0969-6997(00)00034-X

Özdaşlı, K. (2012). Kurumsal (Şirket Düzeyi) Stratejiler. In F. Okumuş, M. Koyuncu, & E. Günlü (Eds.), *İşletmelerde Stratejik Yönetim*. Seçkin Publishing.

Özer, M. A. (2015). İşletmelerde Stratejinin Önemi Üzerine Değerlendirmeler. *International Journal of Economic and Administrative Studies*, 7(14), 69–84.

Porter, M. E. (1987). From competitive advantage to corporate strategy. *Harvard Business Review*, (59), 1–11. PMID:17183795

Qatar. (2022). https://www.qatarairways.com/tr-tr/about-qatar-airways/group-company.html

Redpath, N., O'Connell, J. F., & Warnock-Smith, D. (2017). The strategic impact of airline group diversification: The cases of Emirates and Lufthansa. *Journal of Air Transport Management*, 64, 121–138. doi:10.1016/j.jairtraman.2016.08.009

Rivera-Santos, M., & Inkpen, A. (2009). Joint Ventures and Alliances. In M. Kotabe & K. Helsen (Eds.), *The SAGE Handbook of International Marketing* (pp. 198–217). SAGE Publications. doi:10.4135/9780857021007.n10

Salas, E. B. (2019). *Airlines Alliances Dossier*. Statista.

Sengur, Y., & Sengur, F. K. (2017). Airlines define their business models: A content analysis. *World Review of Intermodal Transportation Research*, 6(2), 141–154. doi:10.1504/WRITR.2017.082732

Sherman, A., & Hart, M. A. (2010). *Mergers and Acquisitions from A to Z* (2nd ed.). Amazon.

SkyTeam. (2022). *SkyTeam Airline Alliance*. https://www.skyteam.com/en/about

Smith, M., & Graves, C. (2005). Corporate turnaround and financial distress. *Managerial Auditing Journal*, 20(3), 304–320. doi:10.1108/02686900510585627

Spulber, D. F. (2007). *Global Competitive Strategy*. Cambridge University Press. doi:10.1017/CBO9780511841651

Star Alliance. (2022). *About Star Alliance*. https://www.staralliance.com/en/about

Star Alliance. (2022). *Circle Pacific*. https://roundtheworld.staralliance.com/staralliance/EN/circle-pacific

Thompson, J., & Martin, F. (2005). *Strategic Management: Awareness and Change*. South Western a Division of Cengage Learning.

Thompson, J. L. (2001). *Strategic Management*. Thomson Learning.

THY. (2022). *Ortaklıklar*. https://www.turkishairlines.com/tr-tr/basin-odasi/hakkimizda/ortakliklar/

Ülgen, H., & Mirze, S. K. (2020). *İşletmelerde Stratejik Yönetim*. Beta Publishing.

Vasconcellos, G. M., & Kish, R. J. (2013). Cross-border mergers and acquisitions. In C. F. Lee & A. C. Lee (Eds.), *Encyclopedia of Finance* (pp. 515–523). Springer. doi:10.1007/978-1-4614-5360-4_43

Virgin Atlantic. (2022). https://www.virgin.com/virgin-company

Wang, C.-N., Nguyen, X.-T., Le, T.-D., & Hsueh, M. (2018). A partner selection approach for strategic alliance in the global aerospace and defence industry. *Journal of Air Transport Management, 69*, 190–204. doi:10.1016/j.jairtraman.2018.03.003

Weber, K. (2005). Travellers' Perceptions of Airline Alliance Benefits and Performance. *Journal of Travel Research, 43*(3), 257–265. doi:10.1177/0047287504272029

Wilson, R. M., & Gilligan, C. (2005). *Strategic marketing management.* Routledge.

Yang, W., Shao, J., Jiang, Y., Xu, Z., & Tsurdos, A. (2021). International Airline Alliance Network Design with Uncertainty. *Applied Sciences (Basel, Switzerland), 11*(7), 3065. doi:10.3390/app11073065

Chapter 4
Air Transport Safety and Security

Ravi Lakshmanan
https://orcid.org/0000-0002-0283-6675
GMR Infrastructure (Singapore) Pte Ltd., India

ABSTRACT

Over the last 20 years, the reduction in aircraft accident rates has been due to proactive and predictive safety measures implemented through state safety program and safety management system. Likewise, gradual enhancement of security measures is achieved using advanced screening technology, threat assessment, and behaviour detection through analytics and the security management system. The pandemic had a significant impact on the aviation industry, with decreased operations, revenue loss, and idle aircraft, among other things, which brought many challenges to the industry. The reactivation of the human resources and assets, especially inoperative aircraft, will be a huge task when the traffic accelerates. This chapter is a simplified form of safety and security management with processes/models to assess and mitigate the risks to ensure safety and security performance. In addition, this chapter highlights broader issues foreseen due to pandemics and describes models to evaluate additional risks comprehensively and mitigate them.

INTRODUCTION

Maintaining aviation safety and security is the primary goal of all parties involved in the aviation industry. Safety and security are two separate tasks but frequently overlap each other. To understand the requirements of the twin aspects, International Civil Aviation Organization (ICAO) 's Annex 19 for safety and Annex 17 for security provide the Standards and Recommended Practices (SARPs). ICAO SARPs help harmonizes aviation worldwide. Therefore, the safety and security performance and measures must adhere to ICAO SARPs. ICAO also has publications such as Documents for implementation guidelines. Documents relevant to this subject are Doc 9859- Safety Management Manual and Document 8973 - Aviation Security Manual.

DOI: 10.4018/978-1-6684-4615-7.ch004

Air Transport Safety and Security

International Air Transport Association (IATA), which represents 290 airlines in 120 countries, carrying 83% of the world's air traffic, has published manuals on many subjects, including safety and security. It also publishes safety reports, holds training programs and conducts safety and security audits. Similarly, Airports Council International (ACI), representing 1950 airports with 717 members in 185 countries, has publications on safety and security subjects. It also conducts training programs for aviation professionals and conducts webinars. In addition, its Airport Service Quality (ASQ) and Airport Carbon Accreditation programs are popular. State Regulators like FAA, EASA, and CAA (UK) provide additional guidance.

Proactive and predictive measures are the most effective ways to improve safety performance. While the States define their State Safety Program (SSP) through Acceptable Level of Safety, Service Providers apply Safety Management System (SMS). Therefore, one of the most critical service providers' tasks is developing and executing effective SMS.

Because of its vulnerabilities and the human, psychological, and economic consequences, aircraft is a target for assaults. Planes are clear targets easily connected with a specific country, and a successful assault results in many casualties. The State is solely responsible for aviation security. Nonetheless, risk-mitigation strategies enhance passengers' safety, minimize disturbance, ensure passenger convenience, and facilitate coordination with all aviation sector stakeholders. The security measures required by airlines and airports are prescribed as SARPs by ICAO, which establishes an outcome-based requirement without identifying the technology used. ICAO Doc 8973 (restricted) provides implementation guidelines. When the threat perception changes or security breaches/incidents happen, already established preventive measure processes require modifications. Also, the preventive measure processes differ from airport to airport and between the States. Even within a particular State, there is no one-size-fits-all strategy.

ACI reports that 20% of airports handled more than 1 million passengers per annum, whereas 80% handled less than 1 million passengers per annum. Out of 68% of airports that do not make a profit, most airports are small airports. On the other hand, these small airports contribute to society by connecting distant cities, feeding traffic to larger airports, and providing socio-economic benefits by bringing communities together. Hence, technology adopted for safety or security need not be the same at all airports. Some innovative ideas are required, especially on implementing security measures fulfilling ICAO SARPs.

The consequences of an accident or security breach are severe, like business loss and loss of company image, investigation cost, legal fees, compensation, increased insurance premium, loss of productivity, etc. The cost of removing the fuel spills to major ones like aircraft removal due to runway excursion and many more impacts.

The objectives of this chapter are i) to briefly describe processes /models of aviation safety and security management and ii) to highlight a few safety changes/challenges/concerns foreseen based on analysis of aviation systems during the COVID 19 period and apply the processes/models to these. Then, when the traffic accelerates to growth and gets back to the normal situation, the principles of the safety and security management systems should be applied, evaluated using the models and based on which corrective actions are required to maintain performance level.

BACKGROUND

The COVID-19 pandemic has posed unprecedented challenges to international air transport. ICAO reports that passenger traffic plunged by 60 per cent, with just 1.8 billion passengers during 2020, the first year of the pandemic, compared to 4.5 billion in 2019. Flight departures for scheduled commercial operations dropped by 42 per cent, with around 22.5 million departures in 2020, compared to more than 38 million in 2019 (ICAO, 2021b). For 2021, global RPKs are 41.6% of 2019 levels compared with 34.2% in 2020, and in absolute terms, it is nearly 50% of the pax traffic in Y 2019. The Aviation Industry has suffered substantial financial losses. According to Bloomberg calculations, about 400,000 airline workers have been fired, furloughed, or told they might lose their jobs. (Anurag Kotoky et al., 2020). According to the IATA, job losses in related industries, including aircraft manufacturers, engine makers, airports, and travel agencies, could reach 25 million.

Many of the planes were grounded and parked at the outbreak's peak. Operators hope to get them back in the air as quickly as possible when travel restrictions go away. This situation in aviation safety necessitates that all stakeholders concentrate on aircraft safety, pilots' training, and passengers' safety when they return to the skies. The air transportation system must continually adopt a holistic and integrated plan to continuously enhance safety across the industry. (AIRBUS, 2021)

A survey conducted by IATA shows that the majority of the respondents expect increased hiring this year due to anticipated passenger traffic recovery. Also, most of the respondents expect that input costs will increase in the future (IATA, 2022). When the traffic starts growing, the industry will primarily focus on increasing revenue and economical operations by reducing the operational cost by various measures, including optimizing the labour cost and improving the maintenance management systems, renegotiating the operations and maintenance contracts to mention a few of the initiatives. They would also postpone the capital expenditure planned before the pandemic for the capacity enhancement and replacement of equipment/system unless it enhances operational efficiency and reduces operating costs. To defer the capital expenditure requires maximization of asset utilization or stretching the life of the equipment. For example, Airlines would maximize their fleet utilization, less time on the ground within the limit set by the regulators. Furthermore, for the quick turnaround of aircraft, the airports, airlines, and other service providers should complete all passenger/baggage processing and the apron services faster for the flight to signal ready for push back from the aircraft stand. Similarly, Airports would try to increase the passenger throughput with the available infrastructure by introducing technology, reorganizing the processes/procedures, increasing the utilization of the assets most efficiently and improving the service quality by minimizing the processing time at each passenger service point.

Protection vs. Production

In any organization engaged in delivering services, production/profitability and safety risks (protection) are interlinked. An organization/service provider must maintain profitability to stay in business by balancing output with acceptable safety risks (and the costs involved in implementing safety risk controls). Typical safety risk controls include identifying risks, using technology, training staff, and improving processes and procedures. For the State, the safety risk controls include effective oversight, the internal processes and procedures supporting the oversight. Implementing safety risk controls comes at a price – money, time, resources – and safety risk controls usually aim to improve safety performance, not production performance. However, investments in "protection" can also enhance "production" by reducing accidents and incidents and their associated costs. Therefore, safety and Security measures should not affect production. The production here means the service level delivery and operational efficiency. Post pandemic, this aspect becomes very relevant as the service providers will try to increase production.

Air Transport Safety and Security

The issues foreseen due to the pandemic on the system could be worked out and apply relevant processes to mitigate these issues to balance production and protection. Therefore, it is essential to focus on safety and security management and performance. Otherwise, any incident or security/safety breach will hurt the traffic growth.

MAIN FOCUS OF THE CHAPTER

Changes/Challenges/Concerns due to Pandemic

After shutting down even partially for nearly two years and getting back to total production, any industry will face issues. The aviation industry is affected globally, where the highest safety and security performance is of paramount importance and firmly regulated. Therefore, any safety/security occurrence will be a setback for the sector raising. Also, most operating personnel require certification/licence, which involves training and assessment and thus, it is a time-consuming process. Because it is a service industry, the output is not tangible, and the customers' expectations are very high, and the service providers would like to meet this. Thus, bringing the infrastructures, equipment, aircraft etc., to full-fledged operational status requires considerable effort. It is just like commissioning a new asset. Due to minimum operation for a long time, some changes/concerns/challenges (broadly called issues) are foreseen in the aviation industry when the traffic accelerates to growth. These are listed in Table 1 and remarks to show why these are relevant and significant issues.

Table 1. Changes-challenges-concerns (issues)

Changes/Challenges/Concerns (Issues)	Brief Remarks
As employee hiring is expected to grow from Y 2022 in tandem with traffic growth, new joiners.	Employee rehiring will have to be in tandem with traffic. Rehiring aviation staff is time-consuming, and on rehiring, they are to be trained, certified/licensed for specific functions, security clearance completed before they are engaged in operations. The chaos on April 22 in Manchester airport is an example where the passengers waited in the queue at check-in and security check for a considerable time (more than 3 hours, many missed flights) due to a shortage of staff and unexpected traffic surge airport did not anticipate. Recruitment will be challenging, requiring people with the right technical and soft skills, especially at the leadership level.
Airport terminals being recommissioned in some major airports having multiple terminals or all systems in a terminal is being put into operation. Equipment or system not in operation for a long time is to be put into operation. Condition assessment / maintenance record of the equipment / system.	Any system, equipment, and asset not in use for a considerable time requires a lot of effort to reactivate. The equipment/system must be checked thoroughly to ensure its performance is as per design parameters or regulatory requirements. This process requires adequate staff and sufficient time to complete the task.
Introduction of new technologies- Use of AI/ML for screening machine algorithms, Air Traffic Management, Autonomous vehicles, Real-time behaviour assessment of passengers for security etc	It is anticipated that new technologies like AI/ML, autonomous vehicles, real time behaviour assessment of passengers etc will be introduced. Most of the technology up-gradation will be aimed at touch-free systems and reduce manual intervention. Require trained staff and system tested sufficiently before inducting into operation.
Changes in process/procedures	Changes in processes and procedures with revised SOPs may be introduced to improve operational efficiency or reduce cost. This requires training/retraining of staff
Focus on reduction in operational expenses. Postponing capital expenses	Focus on reduction in operational expenses and capital expenses may pose a safety issue or capacity deficiencies if not formally evaluated.
Merger/acquisitions of airlines or other service providers	Mergers/acquisitions of airlines or other service providers may bring anxiety and uncertainty among the employees.
Training to newly employed staff, retraining/refresher course for existing employees or employees whose role/duties/ responsibilities redefined. Familiarization training to new employees. Enhancement of teamwork among the employees. The team composition would have changed compared with pre-covid 19, and it is just like a transition to a new system and work environment. Require integration of team. Appropriate training through simulators may be required for pilots and cabin crew to retain currency. Also, it may be due to a change of aircraft type. Verification / revalidation of licence / certification / airport entry pass of employees/ airside operational permits as per regulatory requirement.	
Aircraft on the ground for a long time being put into operation	As aircraft induction to operation after a prolonged storage time, the safety performance depends on the maintenance during the storage and before being inducted into service. Many maintenance teams are required with so many aircraft parked at various locations. Also, Regulators should have adequate staff strength to validate or certify the checks.
It is known that passengers hate waiting at the processing points. However, due to the pandemic, the processes themselves take more time, particularly at the security check and boarding gates. Therefore, when the traffic reaches a certain level, and if the COVID 19 protocol continues, there will be a delay in processing and congestion in the terminals.	

These issues require careful consideration by the service providers to analyse the impact and scale of impact, prepare an action plan, and prioritise the activities so that the operation is not affected, safety and security are maintained, and achieve traffic growth. The scale of getting back to normal may vary between service providers, depending on the level of operation during the pandemic; however, all would face most of the items listed in Table 1. As seen from the literature review, there are already incidents reported and advised by the regulators.

Literature Review

A literature review of the current pandemic's safety, security, and operational challenges highlights certain incidents and some learnings. The literatures evaluated are included in Table 2.

Air Transport Safety and Security

Table 2. Literatures reviewed

Title	Reference
Long-time Storage of aircraft	
Federal Aviation Administration National Part 139 Cert Alert	(FAA, 2020)
Safety Information Bulletin Subject: Contamination of Air Data Systems During Aircraft Parking and / or Storage due to the COVID-19 Pandemic.	(EASA, 2021b)
Three airspeed incidents at Heathrow trigger alert over insect blockage	(Kaminski-Morrow, 2021)
COVID-19 Pandemic as a Mechanism of the Motion of an Aircraft in MIRCE Mechanics	(Knezevic, 2021)
Grounded aircraft: An airfield operations perspective of the challenges of resuming flights post COVID	(Adrienne et al., 2020)
Corrosion From Inactivity Flagged on Pratt-powered 777 Engine Parts	(Broderick, 2022)
Human Resources, Training	
Psychological distress in Spanish airline pilots during the aviation crisis caused by the COVID-19	(Ana Alaminos-Torre et al., 2021)
Are You surgically current? Lessons from aviation for returning to non-urgent surgery following COVID-19	(Hardie J.A & Brennan P.A, 2020)
Impact of COVID -19 on Pilot Proficiency – A Risk Analysis	(Rajee Olaganathan & Roli Angelo H Amihan, 2021)
Aviation trends post Covid-19	(Allianz Global Corporate & Specialty, 2021)
The effect of a safety crisis on safety culture and safety climate: The resilience of a flight training organization during COVID-19	(Byrnes et al., 2022)
Post COVID-19 fatigue management for ATCOs	(Drogoul & Cabon, 2020)
COVID-19 and airline employment: Insights from historical uncertainty shocks to the industry	(Sobieralski, 2020)
Health safety	
Air travel and COVID-19 prevention in the pandemic and peri-pandemic period: A narrative review	(Bielecki et al., 2020)
Airport pandemic response: An assessment of impacts and strategies after one year with COVID-19	(Arora et al., 2021)
Operations related	
Flight safety during Covid-19: A study of Charles de Gaulle airport atypical energy approaches	(Jarry et al., 2021)
Bird Strike at Indian Airports	(Economic Times, 2022)
US Flight Passenger Who Was Duct-Taped To Her Seat Faces Record Fine	(NDTV, 2022)
Learnings	
Aviation trends post Covid-19	(Allianz Global Corporate & Specialty, 2021)
Grounded aircraft: An airfield operations perspective of the challenges of resuming flights post COVID	(Adrienne et al., 2020)

Continued on following page

Table 2. Continued

Title	Reference
Long-time Storage of aircraft	
COVID-19 Pandemic as a Mechanism of the Motion of an Aircraft in MIRCE Mechanics	(Knezevic, 2021)
Risk of COVID-19 Transmission Aboard Aircraft: An Epidemiological Analysis Based on the National Health Information Platform	(Guo et al., 2022)
COVID-19 pandemic and innovation activities in the global airline industry: A review.	(Amankwah-Amoah, 2021)
Federal Aviation Administration National Part 139 Cert Alert	(FAA, 2020)

Table 3a and 3b lists a brief content of the literatures reviewed and these substantiates the issues described in Table 1.

Table 3a. Brief contents of literatures reviewed

Brief contents of Literatures Reviewed	Reference
FAA's guidelines on identifying suitable location at the airport to avoid safety issues. Example infringement on obstacle limitation surfaces	FAA 2020
Aircrafts on storage shall have to undergo periodic maintenance as per manufacturers recommendations. The airport where the aircrafts will be stored shall be based on a cost benefit analysis, among other things, considering storage cost and the maintenance cost.	Knezevic, 2021
Alarming trend in the number of reports of unreliable speed and altitude indications during the first flight(s) following the aircraft leaving storage, caused by contaminated air data systems. Most of the reported occurrences concerned the accumulation of foreign objects, such as insect nests, in the pitot static system. Several Rejected Take-Off (RTO) and Air Turn Back (ATB) events.	EASA 2021 b
In June 2021 UK safety regulators urged pilots to pay close attention to speed checks during the take-off roll, after three incidents in three days at London Heathrow involving suspected pitot blockage by insects	Kaminski-Morrow, 2021)
Contaminated fuel due to heat and humidity, will corrode fuel tanks and may cause wing structure damage. Thus, it requires testing of fuel frequently in those cases. EasyJet has increased testing form once a year to every 14days and testing in 21 locations instead of only one.	Knezevic, 2021
Corrosion of air/oil heat exchangers on some series of engines, prompting the FAA to mandate inspections before affected aircrafts to return to service	Broderick, 2022
Challenges of resuming flights post Covid from airfield operations perspective like aircraft to undergo maintenance before being returned to service, aircraft to undergo additional cleaning and disinfection between flights at least initially immediately after reopening.	Adrienne et al., 2020
Long layoffs have impact on individuals' skills especially in safety critical sectors such as medical surgery and aviation and need to undergo training to retain (or regain) professional 'currency' before resuming normal duties.	(Hardie J.A & Brennan P.A, 2020)
Psychological distress in Spanish airline pilots during the aviation crisis caused by the COVID-19 pandemic	Ana Alaminos-Torre et al., 2021
Extension for pilots' currency certification, who are unable to comply due to the pandemic and temporarily waiving some requirements	Rajee Olaganathan & Roll
Normally pilots operating to airfields in difficult terrain acquires required skill by repeated use of the airfield whereas if flying for the first time there is an element of risk involved. But due to shortage of pilots this risk exists.	Allianz Global Corporate & Specialty, 2021
Various safety culture and safety climate variables of an flight training organization were impacted due to the pandemic. Based on the results of the study, the organization took steps to improve the safety culture and climate.	Bymes et al., 2022
There are many human factor effects of this crisis. Among all fatigue has been identified by EASA as a major hazard for flight safety during the shutdown and during the return to service or normal operations. Managing ATCO fatigue will therefore be a key aspect during and after the pandemic, to ensure both safe and healthy working conditions. CANSO, ICAO and IFATCA have recently issued recommendations for the implementation of fatigue risk management systems (FRMS) for air traffic service providers.	Drogoul & Cabon 2020
The impact on employment is mostly on major airlines, lesser impact on low cost and regional airlines. Among the staff, passenger handling and flight operations staff were most affected. These are the people who directly contribute the safety and security in operations	Sobieralski, 2020
Response mechanism that would lead to better coordination and more control after a disease outbreak. The mechanism would distribute SARPs from the policy-level to the airports and companies involved in airport operations, similarly to what happens with security regulations. The resulting response would therefore aid in curbing disease spread, while keeping air travel safe and providing regulations that are easier to navigate for travellers. The threat level would also be categorized as green (constant vigilance to report), yellow (disease outbreak is suspected in a particular region), orange (epidemic is confirmed in a certain country/ region) and red (like COVID 19 pandemic affecting globally). Each of these traffic lights will be described with a SARPs.	Arora et al., 2021
Aircraft manufacturers have published procedures on how to clean aircraft and what products to use for years which are updated based on learnings from recent events. A pilot of an unnamed airline filed a ASRS report in spring 2020 detailing an onboard smoke event in an aircraft and found to be due to alcohol wipes that may have shorted the wires. This issue was reportedly observed on many aircrafts	Knezevic, 2021

Table 3b. Brief contents of literatures reviewed

Brief contents of Literatures Reviewed	Reference
Impact on the pilot/controller system, especially during the critical approach and landing phases evaluated. This is due to deviations from normal operations were frequent at Charlles de Gaulle Airport. These results emphasized that crises that lead to a drop in traffic should be subject to increased vigilance during the approach and landing phases. Similarly, trajectory shortenings should be monitored more closely un-stabilized approaches	Jarry et al., 2021
Incidents of air rage and unruly pax behaviour on the rise. FAA has reported a steep rise in unruly passengers since the beginning of COVID-19 pandemic. It initiated 1,099 inquiries in 2021, up from 183 in 2020 and 146 in 2019. Such unruly behaviour is a safety as well as security issue.	NDTV 2022
Even though there were very less operations at the Indian airports the number of bird and animal strike incidents in Y 2021 were more than the year Y 2020 by 19 % and 123% respectively presumably due to quieter airports during this period, thus increased the presence of wildlife habitation at aerodromes.	Economic Times 2022
Organizations are likely to adopt new measures that rectify current defects in the processes and techniques during crises. As demonstrated by Schilling (2020), such process innovations are often typified by minimizing errors and defects and discarding obsolete routines. In tandem with the process innovations are often new product innovations geared towards enhancing the marketing competitiveness of the business (Schilling, 2020). Firm innovation is often rooted in forging collaboration with customers, suppliers, and competitors to stay attentive to their concern	Amankwah-Amoah, 2021
Based on an analysis of data on all international flights to Lanzhou, China, from June 1, 2020, to August 1, 2020, it was concluded that COVID-19 may be transmitted during a passenger flight, although there is still no direct evidence	Guo et al., 2022
To avoid the problems arising due to parking of aircrafts for a long time some airlines operated the aircrafts so that they are in service. This means pilots' proficiency and licensing requirements are met and might help them to maintain their slots	Allianz Global Corporate & Specialty, 2021
During this period some airlines performed deep cleaning and heavy maintenance like C &D checks, which otherwise would be required later and that requires to withdraw the aircraft from operations when needed most	Adrienne et al., 2020

SOLUTIONS AND RECOMMENDATIONS

How the Industry Will Overcome These Issues

System or equipment is said to be operating in baseline performance when it is operating to the designed technology and human performance level and policy/procedures aiding the system and human behaviour. However, the system does not always run-on baseline performance. Instead, it drifts due to the following critical elements:

1. Technology is not operating as designed.
2. Unable to execute procedures under certain operating conditions, changes to the system, and interface with other systems.
3. Lower Human performance level due to motivational issues, safety culture, and adequacy of resources. And so on.

Activities like workarounds or shortcuts manage some deficiencies in normal operations, thus drifting from baseline performance. Such drift beyond a certain level will lead to an incident/accident or security breach. (Scott A. Snook's theory)

Safety audits, observations and monitoring expose the activities that make the performance drift through the critical elements. Therefore, the service providers need to examine these vital elements when getting back to normal operations.

The issues listed in Table 1 look normal, but the scale of these for most of the service providers and all at the same time globally is a unique situation. Also, the list is not exhaustive and complete, as there could be more issues in future. Overcoming these requires established management systems with defined and tested processes. However, we can broadly classify the problems into some categories viz. a) Due to long term storage of aircraft b) Human Resources, training, certification, c) Reactivation of infrastructures, equipment, systems, condition assessment d) Technology up-gradation e) Cost optimization.

Assessing the risks and taking corrective action necessitates understanding the principles of SMS and SeMS. It is required to carry out a safety/security risk assessment of the operations afresh, identifying the hazards that might have arisen during this pandemic. The threats may not be only hardware/technical; they could be organizational changes, staff morale, team relationship, trust, and confidence with the management. It is also required to understand the principles of accident/incident avoidance, the importance of enhanced safety and security culture and mismatches among the system components, including humans. This section describes all of these and includes health safety in brief and policy level security management, and current trends in security management. With these, the issues mentioned could be analysed and mitigated. Also included is an example of hazard identification of airport operations.

Safety Performance and Safety Management

In their annual review report, IATA mentions, "Every accident, of course, is a tragedy. And that makes the aviation industry all the more determined to improve on its safety record each successive year". While achieving a zero accident/incident scenario is impossible, a certain level of safety risk must be allowed. The State usually is responsible for determining the appropriate degree of safety.

Adhering to the safety performance and improving these continually is always challenging. Safety performance means maintaining the risks to a predetermined level called an acceptable level. ICAO defines aviation safety as "the state in which risks associated with aviation activities, related to, or in direct support of the operation of aircraft, are reduced and controlled to an acceptable level".

Safety risks are constantly present, and proactiveness is required to mitigate them before they result in accidents and incidents. Safety can be implemented in a more disciplined, integrated, and focused manner with safety management. Safety management enables the States to prioritize actions to resolve safety concerns/risks and effectively manage their resources to achieve the highest level of feasible aviation safety. The effectiveness of a state's safety management actions is enhanced when implemented in a formal and institutionalized manner and achieved through State Safety Programme (SSP) by the State and Safety Management Systems (SMS) by the Service Providers.

Safety Statistics

Yearly accident statistics indicate a decrease in both the total number of accidents and the accident rate in 2020. From 2019 to 2020, there was a 58 per cent decrease in the total number of accidents. The global accident rate of 2.14 accidents per million departures in 2020 also decreased by 27 per cent from the 2019 rate of 2.94 accidents per million departures. The number of flights on commercial jet aircraft was continuously growing before the COVID 19 pandemic. Despite this growth, the number of accidents was decreasing each decade. There were three fatal accidents and six hull losses recorded in Y 2020, and with an equivalent number of flights, it contrasts with ten fatal accidents and twenty-four hull losses recorded in 1998. These figures illustrate the continuous safety enhancement within the commercial aviation industry over recent decades. (ICAO, 2021b)

Aviation Safety processes are very well recognized. For example, surgical outcomes are often compared to safety data from commercial aviation. In addition, the aviation industry's performance is frequently referenced as an example of high reliability that should be reproduced in clinical practice (Gogalniceanu et al., 2021). Another example is that aviation and affiliated training concepts have gained a pioneering role in establishing interpersonal competence training for physicians, particularly for surgical disciplines. Strengthening interpersonal competence in conjunction with standardized processes and tools aims at implementing a safety and error culture in the clinical surroundings while improving patient safety (Hirche & Kneser, 2021)

Progress in aviation safety can be described by four approaches: technical, human factors, organizational, and total system. In the total system approach, which is adopted now, the aviation system as a whole is considered, particularly in terms of interface and coordination with other organizations and service providers functioning in the system. By implementing a State Safety Program (SSP) or a Safety Management System (SMS), several States and Service Providers have achieved a greater degree of safety maturity and thereby achieved safety benefits. States and service providers have been drawn to the interactions and interfaces between people, processes, and technology, which constitute the system's components due to the evolution of safety. Benefits are realized when coordination between service providers and between service providers and States improves.

SSP and SMS in Brief

ICAO mandates States to establish and maintain a State Safety Program (SSP) that is commensurate with the size and complexity of the State's civil aviation system. SSP is designed to be tailored to meet the specific needs of each State.

The State safety performance is indicated through acceptable level of safety performance (ALoSP).

Safety Management System (SMS)

SSP is for the State, whereas SMS is applicable for Service Providers. ICAO mandates service providers to establish and implement SMS. With SMS, safety is managed through a systematic approach with organizational structure and a set of processes and procedures.

"Service provider" refers to any organization providing aviation services. The term includes approved training organizations that are exposed to operational safety risks during the provision of their services, aircraft operators, approved maintenance organizations, organizations responsible for type design and or manufacture of aircraft, air traffic service providers and certified aerodromes as applicable.

SMS is designed to continuously improve safety performance through identification of hazards, collection and analysis of safety data and safety information and continuous assessment of safety risks. Components and elements of SSP and SMS are shown in Table 4.

Air Transport Safety and Security

Table 4. Components and elements of SSP and SMS (ICAO)

Components and Elements of SSP Framework - ICAO	
Component	**Elements**
State Safety Policy, Objectives and Resources	Primary aviation legislation
	Specific operating regulations
	State system and functions
	Qualified technical personnel
	Technical guidance, tools and provision of safety-critical information
State Safety Risk Management	Licensing, certification, authorization and approval obligations
	Safety management system obligations
	Accident investigation
	Hazard identification and safety risk assessment
	Management of safety risks
State Safety Assurance	Surveillance obligations
	Monitoring a service provider's safety performance
	State safety performance
	Management of change: State perspective
State Safety Promotion	Internal communication and dissemination of information
	External communication and dissemination of safety information

Components and Elements of SMS Framework - ICAO	
Component	**Element**
Safety Policy and Objectives	Management Commitment
	Safety Accountability and responsibilities
	Appointment of key safety personnel
	Coordination of emergency response planning
	SMS Documentation
Safety Risk Management	Hazard Identification
	Safety Risk assessment and mitigation
Safety Assurance	Safety Performance monitoring and measurement
	The management of change
	Continuous improvement of the SMS
Safety promotion	Training and Education
	Safety Communication

Safety risk management and management of change under safety assurance and safety culture are described in this chapter.

Safety Risk Management (SRM)

SRM is one of the core pillars of SMS, and this is more applicable in the post-pandemic situation, as can be seen from the description that follows. Service providers ensure they are managing their safety risks by a process is known as safety risk management (SRM), which includes identifying hazards, assessing the safety risk due to the hazards, and mitigation/acceptance of the safety risk based on the assessment. It is required to take a proactive and predictive approach to hazards to eliminate them before they cause accidents. When an incident or accident is broken down into a series of events, valuable information can be uncovered. Even though this is a reactive action an occurrence still such information provides some help to identify hazards and safety risks.

Figure 1. Safety risk management decision aid flow chart (ICAO)

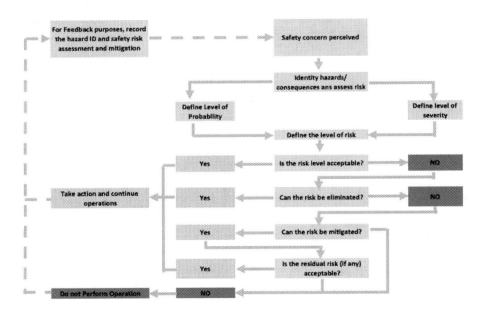

ICAO defines Hazard as "A condition or an object with the potential to cause or contribute to an aircraft incident or accident". Identification of the hazards is the first step in the SRM process to mitigate the impact of Hazard on safe operations.
ICAO lists the examples of common hazard sources in aviation as

- Design factors
- Procedures and operating practices
- Communications
- Personnel factors
- Organizational factors
- Work environment factors
- Regulatory oversight factors and

- Defences

To identify hazards, ACI suggests forming a group including, at minimum, a facilitator (who knows the risk-assessment process thoroughly) and subject-matter experts (who typically are technical or operations personnel) who are knowledgeable about the scope of the operations under scrutiny for the potential hazards. This group will look for hazards from people, machinery and equipment, organizational components and environment and the interactions among these aspects:

Methods to Identify the Hazards

The voluntary safety reporting system is an essential mechanism for proactively identifying hazards. Information collected through such reporting systems may be supplemented by observations or findings recorded during routine & periodical site inspections or audits.

Methods for identifying hazards are defined depending on the hazard identification sources and the approach to hazard identification, below

- **Reactive hazard identification methods** –After an occurrence or event hazards are recognized based on the investigation report of an accident or incident which shows the causes and preventive measures recommended. For example, Investigation of near-miss incidents and the hazard identified is an example of the reactive method.
- **Proactive hazard identification methods** - The proactive activities such as safety surveys, safety audits and safety monitoring & safety assessments may identify the hazards that exist in the system.
- **Predictive approach** is aimed at discovering future hazards that could result because of changes that is anticipated in the aviation system

Practically, both reactive and proactive methods provide an effective means of hazard identification. However, an incident investigation is still one of the most significant contributors to identifying hazards. Whereas with SMS implemented effectively, the aim is to maximize proactive approach for hazard identification.

Hazards connected to interfaces are also to be identified. Wherever possible, this should be done in collaboration with the interacting entities. One example of the interfaces is the apron services. When an aircraft is parked on the apron, various tasks such as refueling, cleaning, baggage loading/unloading, aircraft maintenance, passenger boarding / de-boarding, and so on are carried out to prepare the aircraft for departure within a given time frame. More than one service provider may be carrying out these activities simultaneously, and some hazards arise due to the interactions between different agencies. These are identified as safety concerns.

Risk Assessment

After identifying the hazard, risk assessment is the next step to determine whether the risk is acceptable by estimating the risk's probability, severity, and tolerability.

- **Safety risk probability**

Safety risk probability is the likelihood that a safety consequence or outcome will occur. It includes five categories to denote the probability related to an unsafe event or condition, the description of each category, and an assignment of a value to each category. This example uses qualitative terms, but quantitative terms could be defined depending on the availability of appropriate safety data and the organization's sophistication and operation.

- **Safety risk severity**

Safety risk severity is defined as the extent of harm depending on a hazard's potential consequences that might reasonably be expected to occur due to identified hazard. Therefore, it is essential to envisage various scenarios to consider all potential consequences. It includes five categories to denote the level of severity, the description of each category, and the assignment of a value to each category. A typical safety risk probability classification and safety risk severity classification as an example are shown in Table 5.

Table 5. Safety risk probability classification and severity classification (ICAO)

Components and elements of SSP (ICAO)

Likelihood	Meaning	Value
Frequent	Likely to occur many times (has occurred frequently)	5
Occasional	Likely to occur sometimes (has occurred infrequently)	4
Remote	Unlikely to occur, but possible (has occurred rarely)	3
Improbable	Very unlikely to occur (not known to have occurred)	2
Extremely improbable	Almost inconceivable that the event will occur	1

Components and elements of SMS (ICAO)

Severity	Meaning	Value
Catastrophic	Aircraft equipment destroyed	A
	Multiple deaths	
Hazardous	A large reduction in safety margins, physical distress, or workload such that operational personnel cannot be relied upon to perform their tasks accurately or completely	B
	Serious injury	
	Major equipment damage	
Major	A significant reduction in safety margin, a reduction in the ability of operational personnel to cope with adverse conditions as a result of an increase in workload or as a result of conditions impairing the efficiency	C
	Serious incident	
	Injury to persons	
Minor	Nuisance	D
	Operating limitations	
	Use of emergency procedures	
	Minor incident	
Negligible	Few consequences	E

Air Transport Safety and Security

- **Safety Risk Index**

The safety risk is an index that consists of an alphanumeric designator by combining the results of the probability and severity assessments. For example, a hazard will have a safety index of 5 A when the probability is assessed as frequent, and the severity assessed as catastrophic. A hazard assessed to be of remote probability and negligible severity will have an index of 3 E.

- **Safety Risk Tolerability**

The index obtained from the safety risk assessment matrix is then tabulated as a safety risk tolerability matrix to describe the tolerability criteria of the risk- tolerable, intolerable and acceptable

Figure 2. Safety risk index matrix and safety risk tolerability matrix

Safety Risk		Severity				
Probability		Catastrophic A	Hazardous B	Major C	Minor D	Negligible E
Frequent	5	5A	5B	5C	5D	5E
Occasional	4	4A	4B	4C	4D	4E
Remote	3	3A	3B	3C	3D	3E
Improbable	2	2A	2B	2C	2D	2E
Extremely improbable	1	1A	1B	1C	1D	1E

Tolerability Description	Assessed Safety Risk Index	Criteria
Intolerable	5A, 5B, 4A, 4B, 3A	Unacceptable under exixting circumstances
Tolerable	5D, 5E, 4C, 4D, 4E, 3B, 3C, 3D, 2A, 2B, 2C, 1A	Acceptable based on the safety risk mitigation. It may require management decision
Acceptable	3E, 2D, 2E, 1B, 1C, 1D, 1E	Acceptable

Safety risks in the tolerable region are acceptable if the organization implements appropriate mitigation strategies. A safety risk initially assessed as intolerable may be mitigated and moved into the tolerable region provided that such risks remain controlled by appropriate mitigation strategies. Safety risks assessed as initially falling in the acceptable region are acceptable as they are presently assessed and require no action to bring down the probability or severity.

Safety risk mitigations (ICAO) are actions that often result in changes to operating procedures, equipment, or infrastructure. Generally, safety risk mitigation strategies fall into three categories:

- **Avoidance**: The operation or activity is cancelled or avoided because the safety risk exceeds the benefits of continuing the activity, thereby eliminating the safety risk entirely
- **Reduction**: The frequency of the operation or activity is reduced, or action is taken to reduce the magnitude of the consequences of the safety risk.
- **Segregation**: Action is taken to isolate the effects of the consequences of the safety risk or build in redundancy to protect against them.

Cost-Benefit Analysis

It is essential to evaluate the cost-benefit or effectiveness of each risk mitigation measure, as these may have a significant financial impact in so0me cases.

Air Transport Safety and Security

Management of Change

One of the elements of SMS is Management of Change as any change can introduce new hazards and impact the appropriateness and or effectiveness of existing risk-mitigation measures and strategies. Therefore, whenever changes are contemplated, that would imply affecting the level of safety. Therefore, before implementing the contemplated changes, should start the change management.

Change may be external to the organization or internal. For example, for an airport, changes to the physical characteristics of the infrastructure, new technology and organizational characteristics are internal. In contrast, the introduction of new aircraft types and modifications to the regulations & standards are external. The process is to identify hazards due to the changes and carry out a risk assessment for the hazards posed by these changes by calculating the magnitude of the risk as per SRM, and action is initiated based on the region where the risk lies- tolerable, intolerable, or acceptable. These are to be monitored to ensure that the risks always lie in the acceptable region. The process flow for the management of change is shown in Figure 3.

Figure 3. Management of Change Process flow (ACI)

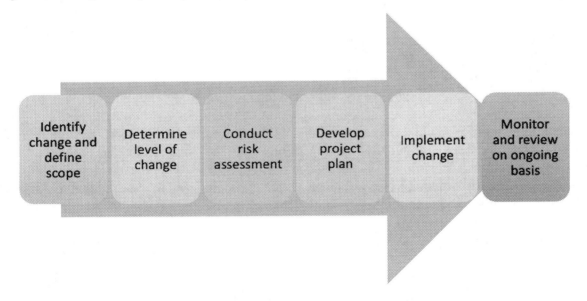

As per ACI there needs to be a formal process for the management of change. This process should address the stability of systems and operational environments, regulations and past performance, and industry and technological change. In addition, such a process should ensure that the management of change procedures addresses the impact on existing safety performance and risk-mitigation records before implementing new change. Also, it establishes procedures to ensure that safety-risk assessments of new aviation operations, processes, and equipment are completed before these are commissioned.

Human Factor

With the involvement of senior management and employees on the ground, safety performance could be improved. Understanding people's strengths, limitations, and how they interact with others in the system is all about the human factor. As a result, understanding, identifying, and mitigating hazards and optimizing human contributions to organizational safety is an essential aspect of safety management. Leadership level support is required to address how the organization influences human performance. Such support includes a commitment from management to develop the optimal working environment and safety culture to address human factors, which will impact everyone's attitudes and behaviours in the organization.

SHELL Model for the Assessment of Human Factors

Federal Aviation Administration (FAA) defines Human Factors as a "multidisciplinary effort to generate and compile information about human capabilities and limitations and apply that information to equipment, systems, facilities, procedures, jobs, environments, training, staffing, and personnel management for safe, comfortable, and effective human performance"

SHELL Model is well known and useful to illustrate the impact and interaction of the different system components, viz. software, hardware, environment on the human and between the humans (liveware). With this model, we can very well understand why the human factor is an integral part of SRM.

The model's critical focus is on the humans since they are on the front lines of operations and are portrayed in the model's centre and because humans are the least predictable and most susceptible to the effects of internal (hunger, exhaustion, motivation, etc.) and exterior (temperature, light, noise, etc.) influences of all the components in the model. As a result, despite their remarkable adaptability, humans are vulnerable to significant variations in performance. As a result, the model's remaining components must be adapted and matched to this central component, the human.

To eliminate tensions that could jeopardize human performance, it is required to understand the consequences of abnormalities at the interface between the various SHELL blocks and the core 'Liveware' block. The jagged edges of the modules represent the imperfect coupling of each module. SHELL blocks and examples of the four components of SHELL model (ICAO) is in Figure 4.

Figure 4. SHELL blocks and examples of the four components of SHELL model

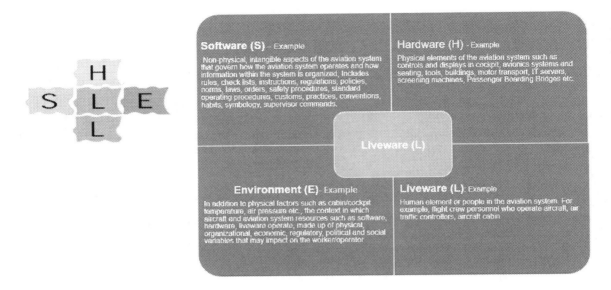

The SHELL model connects people to other system components, providing a framework for optimizing the relationship between people and their activities inside the aviation system, a major human factors issue. Human factors, according to ICAO, is a concept that encompasses people in their living and working environments, as well as their interactions with machines (hardware), procedures (software), and the environment around them, as well as their interpersonal relationships.

Most aviation disasters are attributable to mismatches at interfaces between system components, rather than catastrophic failures of individual components. Examples of the Interface mismatches are in Figure 5.

Figure 5. Interface mismatches between the components of SHELL model

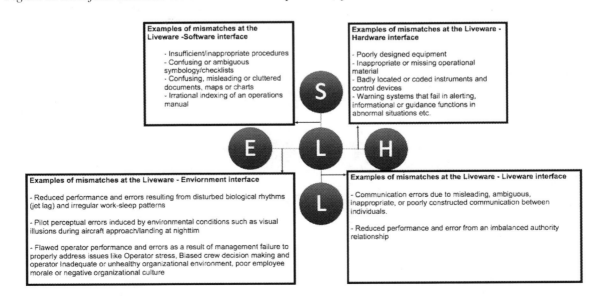

According to Boeing, human error has been shown as a primary contributor to more than 70% of commercial aviation hull-loss incidents. As a result, human error is a significant concern. Boeing's human factors professionals collaborate with engineers, pilots, and mechanics to use the most up-to-date knowledge of the interaction between human performance and commercial aeroplanes to help operators improve the safety and efficiency of their everyday operations.

Accident Causes and Ways to Minimize

The "Swiss-Cheese" Model, developed by Professor James Reason, well known to the aviation industry, illustrates that accidents involve successive breaches of multiple defences. These breaches can be triggered by several enabling factors such as equipment failures or operational errors. The model contends that complex systems such as aviation are extremely well defended by layers of defences (otherwise known as "barriers") and a single-point failure is rarely consequential. Thus, all accidents include a combination of both active failures and latent conditions. Figure 6 explains the concept of active failures and latent conditions and why latent conditions contribute to the safety occurrences.

Figure 6. Active failures and latent conditions (NTSB)

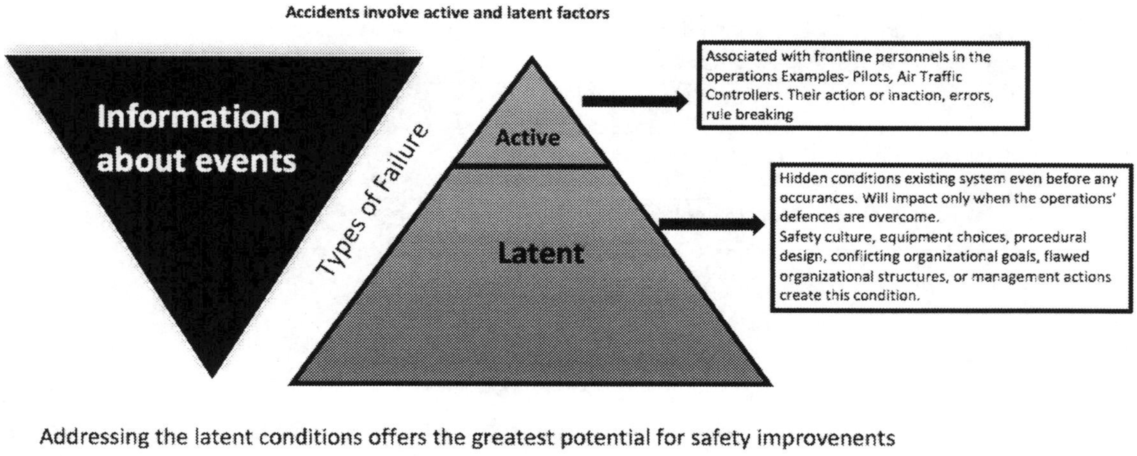

Accidents involve active and latent factors

Information about events — Types of Failure

Active → Associated with frontline personnels in the operations Examples- Pilots, Air Traffic Controllers. Their action or inaction, errors, rule breaking

Latent → Hidden conditions existing system even before any occurances. Will impact only when the operations' defences are overcome.
Safety culture, equipment choices, procedural design, conflicting organizational goals, flawed organizational structures, or management actions create this condition.

Addressing the latent conditions offers the greatest potential for safety improvenents

"Swiss–Cheese" Application

"Swiss-Cheese" Model can be used as an analysis tool. It can help safety risk management, safety surveillance, internal auditing, change management, and safety investigations. In each situation, the model can be used to determine which of the organization's defences are effective, which can or have been breached, and where new defences might be beneficial. Any weaknesses in the defences can then be filled to prevent future mishaps and incidents. It is critical to recognize that an interfacing organization can influence some defences or breaches. As a result, service providers must assess and manage these interfaces.

Figure 7. Swiss-cheese model to explain accident causation (ACI)

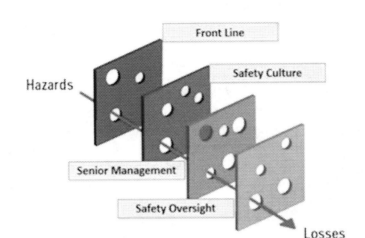

Front Line -Field level- Deficiency- Inadequate time spent on inspection, Lack of knowledge on critical aspects of the system
Safety Culture- Lack of Communication on Safety Management benefits, Safety Program did not highlight in inspection results
Senior Management- Did not follow up action on previous investigation report, little time spent on Safety Management practices by staff, Lack of budget for remedying deficiencies observed in routine inspections
Safety Oversight Mechanism- Ineffective oversight of safety implementation

Safety Culture

Dictionary meaning of culture is the beliefs and attitudes about something that people in a particular group or organization share. Indicators of poor safety culture are insufficient appreciation of risks, lack of proper intervention to recognized risks, or lack of attention to safety contribute to safety incidents/accidents. Based on the work done by (Cooper, 2000), the term safety culture can be used to refer to the behavioural aspects (i.e., 'what people do'), and the situational aspects of the company (i.e., 'what the organization has'). For example, a safety culture is an observable degree of effort by which all organization members direct their attention and actions to improve safety daily. However good the safety management system of an organization is, the way it exists on paper does not necessarily reflect the way it is carried out in practice. The organization's safety culture and safety climate will "influence the deployment and effectiveness of the safety management resources, policies, practices and procedures" (Kennedy & Kirwan, 1998). It is also worth noting that Regulators have started focusing on safety culture as a process improvement.

Air Transport Safety and Security

The achievement of an effective safety culture is recognized to be a vital element of achieving and maintaining satisfactory levels of safety performance. A Systematic Safety Culture Enhancement Process is a managerial tool allowing organizations to identify areas where safety culture may be enhanced. The enhancement process moves onto measuring and evaluating the safety culture. There are many available tools for measuring and evaluating safety culture. The selection of the appropriate measurement tools begins with the model and takes many factors into effect, including but not limited to cost, time, confidentiality requirements, ease of data analysis and usefulness of output for the planning of enhancement actions.

CANSO Safety Culture Working Group (CSCWG) (Piers Michel et al., 2009) proposed that safety culture may be defined by eight key elements/characteristics: Informed Culture, Reporting Culture, Just Culture, Learning Culture, Flexible Culture, Risk Perception, Attitudes to Safety and Safety-Related Behaviour. The Characteristics are still at a high level. They need to be expressed in more measurable terms, identified with indicators. Safety Culture maturity levels are explained as 5 levels which provides some indication about at which level the organization is presently.

Figure 8. Safety culture maturity levels (CSCWG)

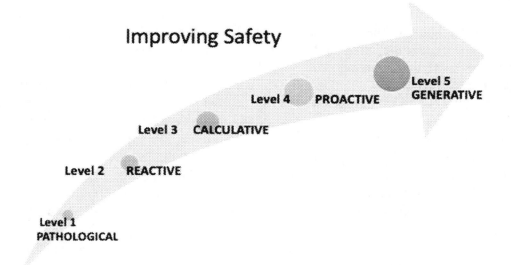

Level 1 (Pathological): Who cares as long as we're not caught
Level 2 (Reactive): Safety is important; we do a lot every time we have an accident
Level 3 (Calculative): We have systems in place to manage all hazards
Level 4 (Proactive): We work on the problems that we still find
Level 5 (Generative): Safety is how we do business around here

Assessing safety culture maturity can provide valuable insight, leading to actions by management that will encourage the desired safety behaviours. A Safety Culture assessment results are expressed in a score indicating the level of maturity of the Safety Culture present in the organization.

Self-assessment is also required to establish a process for monitoring the safety culture. There are several tools which are used to assess safety culture maturity, usually in a combination of questionnaires, interviews and focus groups, observations, and document reviews.

The primary goal of an assessment is to enhance traditional regulatory oversight by addressing organisational characteristics (latent circumstances) that would otherwise go unnoticed by regulators. Depending on the maturity of the company's safety culture, there are several ways for an organisation to measure the effectiveness of its safety culture and drivers for the assessment.

When analysing Safety Culture (through surveys, interviews, or workshops), question sets should be used that are unique to a specific domain (aircraft maintenance, flight operations, or ATC) or to a specific group of employees within an organisation. This is required since the questions pertinent to an airport maintenance team and a ground handling team will be different.

Health Safety

Article 14 of ICAO Chicago Convention (1944) describes the prevention of the spread of disease by the contracting States. ICAO Annex 9- Facilitation- specifies SARPs for passenger/cargo facilitation, including health safety. The ICAO Council has adopted amendment 29 to Annex 9 addressing national civil aviation responses to public health emergencies and the security and inspection of travel and related health documents, and some more provisions.

ICAO Council's Aviation Recovery Task Force (CART) aims to provide practical, aligned guidance to governments and industry operators to restart the international air transport sector and recover from the impacts of COVID-19 on a coordinated global basis. The CART's work on its recovery report and the accompanying 'Take-Off' guidance for international aviation have kept the health, safety, and security of the travelling public of paramount concern throughout. A Public Heath Corridors (PHCs) under CART is formed when two or more States agree to mutually recognize the implemented public health mitigation measures on one or more routes between their States.

ICAO's Collaborative Arrangement for the Prevention and Management of Public Health Events in Civil Aviation (CAPSCA) brings together international, regional, national, and local organizations to combine efforts to improve preparedness planning and response to public health events that affect the aviation sector.

In-flight infection probability is approximately 1 per 27 million passengers due to in-flight protocols such as highly efficient filtering, rapid testing, and regular disinfection (Bielecki et al., 2021). Aeroplane manufacturers specify that the planes have systems to help maintain a healthy cabin environment. The air inside the aircraft is filtered using HEPA filters that capture 99% of viruses and bacteria and thus minimizing the spread of airborne contaminants. 20-30 air changes per hour also ensure fresh air. Cabin air flows primarily from ceiling to floor in a circular pattern and leaves through the floor grilles near the same seat row where it enters. Aeroplane manufacturers also specify a clear program and methodology for disinfection of the cabin.

The proactive measures by Airports, ACI and IATA are described in the Table 6

Air Transport Safety and Security

Table 6. Proactive measures by airports, ACI and IATA

Airports Contactless / touchless were introduced by many airports in passenger terminal buildings, with self-check-in kiosks, self-bag drops, web check-in, passenger-printed boarding pass and luggage tags, biometric use, and e-boarding etc. The use of personal protective equipment (PPE) was made mandatory for employees. The streamlined boarding / deboarding process ensured social distancing. Temperature checking of passengers and personnel (which, according to some research, is ineffective and should be supplemented with testing) and wearing masks by everyone were mandated. Sanitizer dispensers were strategically placed throughout the terminals, and disinfection was performed on a regular basis for counters, seating, checked bags, baggage trolleys, trays, floors, and any other touchpoints. MERV 13 filters, more air changes, UV lights in the return air etc., improved the air conditioning system. Some airports utilize robots to detect people without masks and conduct temperature scans. Some airports have replaced their cabin baggage screening scanners with CT technology, allowing passengers to keep their laptops and other electronic goods in their bags. American Society of Heating Refrigerating and Airconditioning Engineers (ASRAE) published core recommendations for reducing airborne infectious aerosol exposure in closed spaces in buildings. These are applicable for passenger terminal buildings as well. The problem areas were maintaining social distance, contactless at all processes, health document verification means more time and space required in the processes, RT/PCR testing facility at the airports, waiting area requirement for arriving or departing pax awaiting RT/PCR test results, non-uniform covid health document requirement, quarantine requirement and testing requirements etc.
ACI ACI has developed a program to assess how airports' health and safety measures align with ACI's Aviation Business Restart and Recovery guidelines through Airport Health Accreditation (AHA). As of date, there are 400 airports accredited. ACI's Airport Health Measures Audit program, launched in partnership with Bureau Veritas, offers ACI members worldwide a comprehensive onsite audit of all airport processes, the airport-specific audit is based on internationally recognized SafeGuard™ standards. Also, ACI has developed Airport Health Measures Portal where airports can directly provide information about the measures in place at individual airports to passengers and industry stakeholders.
IATA IATA's initiative of a mobile app named 'Travel Pass' with which: • Governments can verify the authenticity of tests or vaccines, as well as the identities of persons presenting their credentials • Airlines have the capacity to deliver correct test requirements information to their passengers and verify that a passenger meets the travel requirements. • Laboratories can issue certificates to passengers that will be recognized by governments. • Travelers get accurate information on test requirements, where they can get tested or vaccinated, and the ability to securely communicate the results/certificates to airlines and border authorities. IATA's Medical Advisory Group brings together airline medical experts from around the globe. IATA has produced an Emergency Response Plan and Action Checklist for use by air carriers in the event of a public health emergency. Guidelines for aircraft cleaning and disinfection are specified in.(IATA, 2021)

Aviation Security

Worldwide Terror Incidents during the 1970s to 2000s show that hijack is a significant terror attack, and the number of hijack attacks reduced from 80 to 10 in 2000 (Gillen & Morrison, 2015). Unlike IATA and ICAO's statistics and specifics on safety matters, no equivalent information on security is publicly available. However, when significant security incidents or breaches occur, they are widely reported in the media. Similarly, there are no publicly available investigation reports on security events or violations.

Changes in a State's security threats, on the other hand, are shared with other States as a warning to take preventive measures. Security information is treated as highly secret, and only necessary authorities and agencies with strict confidentiality agreements are given access(Gillen & Morrison, 2015)

Aviation security management includes regulations, practices and procedures involving multiple stakeholders such as airlines, airport operators, air navigation service providers, police authorities, security service providers and intelligence organizations. The primary objective of States regarding aviation security is to ensure the protection and safety of passengers, crew, the public, aircraft, and facilities at an airport. While civil aviation security is a top priority, it is also an obligation to maintain an efficient air transport system by the airport operator and airline operator and facilitation of passengers as per ICAO SARPs.

Security Regulators in the States are responsible for laying down Aviation Security Standards in their National Civil Aviation Security Program (NCASP) according to Annex 17 and monitor and implement security rules and regulations, ensuring personnel implementing security controls are appropriately trained and possess all competencies required to perform their duties and planning and coordination of aviation security matters. Service providers are responsible for adhering to ICAO Annex 17, implementation as per ICAO Doc 8973, State's NCASP and applicable national and regional laws.

Effective implementation of security measures requires the security authority's involvement from the conceptual stage to the design and implementation of airport facilities. Therefore, the planners should consult with the authority, address security concerns, and facilitate the design of security systems and operational processes to aid passenger facilitation, operational efficiency, and compliance with all security requirements.

With the traffic growth projected to double in 20 years, there will be pressure to enhance and maintain a secure environment at airports and on flights. The criticality of and dependence on technologies that enable safety, security, and resilience for this growth cannot be underestimated.

Security and facilitation go together. Therefore, ICAO requires that the State should, whenever possible, arrange for the security controls and procedures to cause a minimum of interference with or delay to civil aviation activities, provided the effectiveness of these controls and procedures is not compromised. This is to ensure that for example, the turn-round time of the aircraft is not affected, and passengers/crew are not inconvenienced due to the security measures subject to the condition that there is no compromise on the specified procedures.

Entity Security Programme

ICAO mandates

1. Airports to
    - Establish, implement, and maintain a written airport security programme appropriate to meet the National Civil Aviation Security Program (NCASP) requirements
    - Ensure that an officer at each airport serving civil aviation is responsible for coordinating the implementation of security controls
    - Form an airport security committee at each airport serving civil aviation
    - Ensure that airport design requirements shall include the architectural and infrastructure-related requirements necessary for implementing the security measures in the national civil

Air Transport Safety and Security

aviation security programme. Such provision is for the construction of new facilities and alterations to existing facilities at airports.

2. Aircraft operators to
    - Ensure that they have established, implemented, and maintained a written 'operator security programme' that meets the requirements of the NCASP of that State from which they are operating.

Implementation of Security through programs at the State level to service providers level is depicted in Figure 9. Hence, any change in security implementation procedures must align with NCASP.

Figure 9. Implementation of aviation security through programs (ICAO)

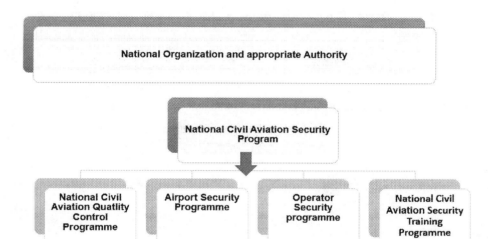

Preventive Measures

The objective of the preventive measures as per ICAO is to establish measures to prevent weapons, explosives or any other dangerous devices, articles, or substances, which may be used to commit an act of unlawful interference, the carriage or bearing of which is not authorized, from being introduced, by any means whatsoever, on board an aircraft engaged in civil aviation. States are mandated to fulfil this objective. ICAO recommends promoting the use of random and unpredictable security measures. Unpredictability could contribute to the deterrent effect of security measures. It also recommends integrating behaviour detection into its aviation security practices and procedures.

Under preventive measures ICAO provides SARPs for measures relating to access control, aircraft, passengers & cabin baggage, hold baggage, Cargo/mail/ other goods, special categories of passengers, landside, and cyber threats. All these preventive measures are to comply with, as required by ICAO, using appropriate technology depending on the threat perception and past events. The technology is regulated by the respective State's security regulator like CAA (UK), TSA or BCAS in India.

ICAO Global Aviation Security Plan (GASeP) provides guidance for priority-setting at the international, regional, and State levels. It creates a framework within which ICAO, States and stakeholders can work together to meet shared objectives. Additionally, the GASeP supports ICAO's 'No Country Left Behind' initiative to address common challenges, and it guides efforts to enhance aviation security jointly further. One of the five priority actions of the GASeP is to develop security culture and human capability. The promotion of effective security culture is critical to achieving good security outcomes. A strong security culture must be developed from the top management across and within every organization. A well-trained, motivated, and professional workforce is a critical prerequisite for effective aviation security.

Security Management System (SeMS)

SeMS is like SMS to be a proactive and formalized way of managing security. It improves the effectiveness of security implementation, focusing on a risk-based approach and outcome-based. SeMS should enable an organization to identify and address security risks, identify gaps considering the available barriers and strengthen the defences. Like safety risk assessment, with threat assessment, available defences against such threats and their weaknesses and severity of the security breach could formalize a security risk assessment. Elements of SeMS defined by CAA (UK) and IATA are shown in Figure 10.

Figure 10. Elements of SeMS defined by CAA(UK) and IATA

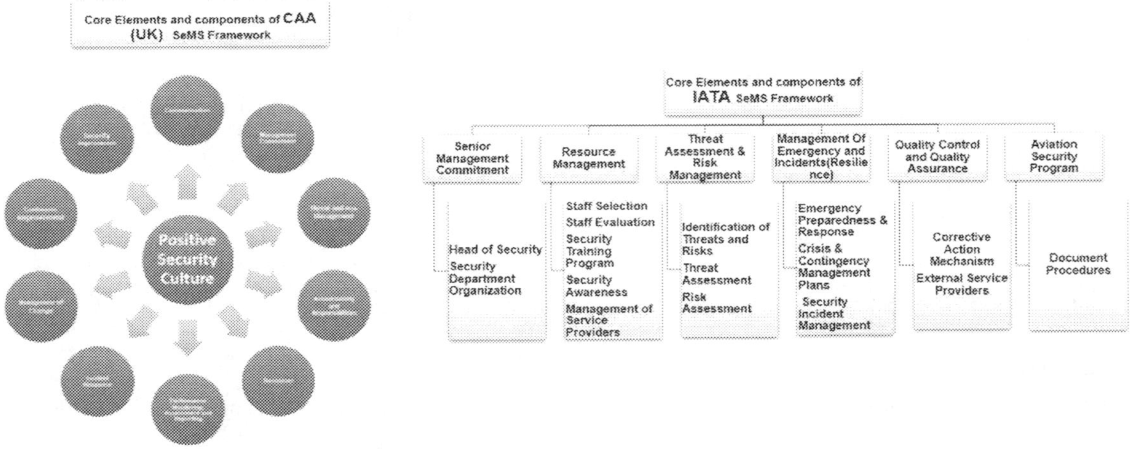

Among all the above components of SeMS, the most relevant elements for this chapter considering the post pandemic situation are management of change and security culture.

Security Culture

It is a set of norms, beliefs, values, attitudes, and assumptions that are inherent in the daily operation of an organization and are reflected by the actions and behaviours of all entities and personnel within the organization (ICAO). Security should be everyone's responsibility - from the ground up. Security culture

Air Transport Safety and Security

is effective when it is recognized that it is critical for business success; when employees appreciate the positive security practices, there is an alignment with business goals. Most importantly, security culture is seen as core value, not an obligation or burdensome expense.

The benefits of an effective security culture could be seen in employee engagement and taking responsibility for security issues. As a result, there is an increase in compliance; employees act in security-conscious ways resulting in a reduction in risk of incidents and breaches, voluntary reporting of concerns on security issues, and reduced expenditure with improved security.

Management of Change

As a part of SeMS the organization would have detailed the process to identify internal and external changes that would have an adverse impact on security. These are to be viewed and action taken for mitigation. For example, new technology or process introduced in the security system. The impact due to the changes should consider the criticality of systems and activities, the stability of systems and operational environments and past performance. The organization should also implement a security governance process to take care of planned business model changes.

The SeMS document includes a description to effectively plan, communicate, implement, and measure the effect of changes to security policy and procedures and monitor and measure the effects of change on security and facilitate action as appropriate. These are required to be implemented due to the changes that have happened. Another component very relevant to the chapter is security education, wherein there is a need to evaluate the employee's level of security awareness.

Current Trends in Security Management

ACI has published Smart Security Vision 2040, which describes the program for security and the process that should be assessed for the future based on what is available presently. The publication details the aviation trend, including COVID 19, changing passenger expectations and evolving security threats. The program also mentions the need for change in regulations (ACI, 2020).

A point of entry into the air transportation system is an airport. A wide range of security measures have been adopted to counter possible risks in response to a wide range of attacks on the air transportation system over the last few decades. A proactive strategy is essential to deliver a trouble-free passenger experience while operating more efficiently. This necessitates a future needs assessment to adapt the security system. It is critical to have as much knowledge as possible about a system's general structure when coping with the uncertainty that future-oriented decisions frequently imply (Cole, 2014)

(Qingbin & Dangen, 2021) in their paper has brought out the advantages of blockchain technology. Using blockchain facilitates data sharing of data information interaction across regions, levels, subjects, and processes. For example, air transport security management is increasingly dependent on data and the application of data information.

Public dilemmas about security measures in the field of civil aviation were studied by (Juvan et al., 2020) The study recommends that if the legitimacy of the civil aviation industry is to be preserved while implementing new security measures, the societal concerns such as privacy, human rights, and health care to be considered and taken into account.

Segregating Passengers Based on Risk Profile

The Transportation Security Administration's PreCheck program allows airline passengers assessed as low risk to be directed to faster screening lanes. For the PreCheck program, the passenger should enrol in person, including fingerprinting for background checks. More than 200 airports and 81 airlines provide PreCheck (as of Feb 22). With PreCheck, passengers wait for less time in the screening process (less than 5 min for 97% pax in Jan 22) as there's no need to remove shoes, belts, liquids, laptops, or light jackets when going through airport security.

Risk Based and Randomised Security Measures

Perceived costs and benefits that drive the acceptability of risk-based security screenings at airports has been studied and this show that although this strategy has advantages for low-risk travellers (reduced wait times), it is contentious because it requires identifying and classifying individuals' risk levels. This online study suggest that risk-based security checks are not considered a sufficient replacement for the conventional common security check approach since they are frequently connected with a perceived loss of both security and fairness (Stotz et al., 2020). A randomized check is where only a specific number of passengers are chosen for security screening. The effects of such a change in security procedures on travelers' security perceptions and the deterrence of criminal activities were investigated in this paper. The study finds that people perceive traditional security checks to be safer than randomized security checks, and randomized security leads to a lower perception of security.

Behaviour Detection through Analytics

In addition to use of conventional security checks using equipment and monitoring through CCTV of the security area, now a days, behaviour detection through analytics is being employed. Humans can detect abnormal or suspicious behaviour of other human and this can be an added methodology to take preventive action, which otherwise could result in a security incident. Intelligence input is also a feature of security reinforcement measures. Airport program of Gatwick airport, wherein the passenger hold bags are collected at home and processed till loading into the plane so that the pax can avoid checking in or dropping the bag at the airport and go through other processes. This reduces passenger processing time in check-in/bag drop and the screening process.

Summary of Solution and Recommendations for the Issues due to Pandemic

Table 7 specifies the relevant process/model viz. SRM, management of change, SHELL model and Swiss Cheese model for each of the issues foreseen and listed.

Air Transport Safety and Security

Table 7. Process/model that could be adopted for the issues listed out.

Issues	Process / Model
As employee hiring is expected to grow from Y 2022 in tandem with traffic growth.	**Management of Change** – Identify the changes and hazards, carryout risk management process and mitigate. Action plan required for staggered hiring.
Airport terminals being recommissioned in some major airports having multiple terminals or all systems in a terminal is being put into operation. Equipment or system not in operation for a long time is to be put into operation. Condition assessment / maintenance record of the equipment / system	**SRM**- Identify Hazards through maintenance record, actual performance parameters compare it with design parameters. Based on this Risk management process to be adopted.
Introduction of new technologies- Use of AI/ML for screening machine algorithms, Air Traffic Management, Autonomous vehicles, Real-time behaviour assessment of passengers for security etc	**Management of Change** – Identify changes and hazards, carryout risk management process and mitigate. Apply the principles of **SHELL to identify** and mitigate mismatches between the operating personnel (L) and other components.
Changes in process/procedures	**Management of Change** – Identify changes and hazards, carryout risk management process and mitigate. Apply the principles of **SHELL to identify** and mitigate mismatches between the operating personnel (L) and other components.
Focus on reduction in operational expenses. Postponing capital expenses	**Management of Change**- Required to carry out a risk benefit analysis of the changes. Identify hazards and mitigation. Capacity analysis included.
Merger/acquisitions of airlines or other service providers	**Management of Change** – Identify hazards, carryout risk management process and mitigate.
Training, retraining, license/certification, team integration etc	**Management of Change** – Identify changes and hazards, carryout risk management process and mitigate. Required to carryout assessment of safety and security, organization culture. Identify mismatches using **SHELL** model and mitigate
Aircraft on the ground for a long time being put into operation	**SRM**. Aircraft manufacturers input would be required. Already few cautions issued based on the incidents noted. Proactive/predictive method of hazard identification required.
It is known that passengers hate waiting at the processing points. However, due to the pandemic, the processes themselves take more time, particularly at the security check and boarding gates. Therefore, when the traffic reaches a certain level, and if the COVID 19 protocol continues, there will be a delay in processing and congestion in the terminals.	**Management of Change** – Identify changes and hazards, carryout risk management process and mitigate. Reassess the capacity of the terminals for various scenarios.
Above are applicable for both Safety and Security.	

Just to recap the reference models. Figure 1 is for the risk assessment and management process. Whether the risk is acceptable or not is decided as per Figure 2. Figure 3 illustrates a method for change management, from identifying the scope of the change to implementing the change, which may require a risk assessment. The change includes organizational change. The third process/model is to identify and rectify mismatches between human performance and other three components, viz. software, environment, and hardware and is done based on the concept of the SHELL model explained in Figure 5. The fourth one is to ensure that all the defences/barriers are in place and review the latent conditions as illustrated in Figures 6 and 7. Service providers proactive approach should be to restart operations as if a new asset has been commissioned and identify the risks in the operation. Safety / security audits, emergency mock drills, encouraging voluntary reporting of safety/security risks during operations (with no punitive actions) are the few initiatives that will identify the risks.

Human factor improvements are another initiative necessary through training and retraining on the job as well as soft skills, improving staff morale, communicate to the personnel with the organization plans for growth to remove uncertainty from their minds, team meetings, exercises on improvement to the organization, safety, and security culture among the staff. Figure 11 contains a checklist of elements that must be reviewed for airport operations, mainly infrastructure, as an example of checks and audits. Such review necessitates the technical ability to assess the performance of systems and equipment and the ability to do so in a formal manner utilising processes of safety and security management discussed here. Service providers should also apply change management principles. Operating personnel should understand how to avoid an incident/accident and the need for coordination and matching between human resources, the environment, and software and between personnel, especially for new technology and modifying procedures or processes.

Figure 11. Hazard identification- examples- airport operations

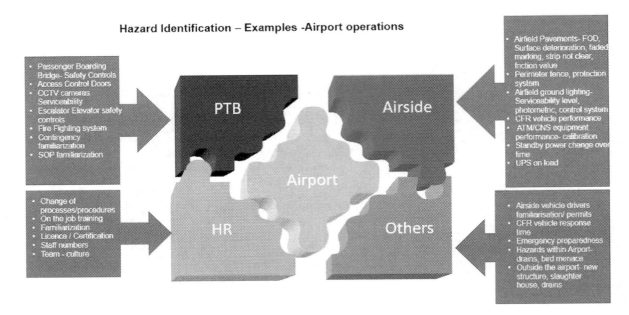

FUTURE RESEARCH

Concerns about aviation safety and security during the pandemic and guidelines, alerts, and lessons learned would be an excellent resource for the industry. A comprehensive collection of such data from State Regulators, IATA, ICAO and ACI and analysis of these could be the next step. The subsequent study could include the impact of cyber security and increased drone and eVTOL aircraft operations on this subject. Finally, the transportation of dangerous goods is another topic to explore.

CONCLUSION

The COVID 19 pandemic has affected the air transport industry globally. One of the lessons learnt is how the businesses should cater for the sudden and steep fall in traffic if it happens in the future and still make the business sustainable. Such business strategies will invite some challenges in managing aviation safety and security. This chapter emphasizes significant and relevant safety and security management processes/models that help to evaluate the risk and mitigate as the business accelerates growth and returns to normal. The issues highlighted and suggested process /models are examples of overcoming these challenges. As a first step, it is essential to identify the hazards and mitigate them through safety/

security risk assessment. As change is inevitable, adopting a change management process is continuous. Assessing and improving organizational, safety, and security culture, particularly during this transition period from low to high operation levels, as well as applying SHELL and Swiss Cheese models, for the operations, to eliminate system mismatches of components and failures of barriers, as well as identifying and minimizing latent conditions, are all critical. Airport operators can determine capacity at each process with various scenarios and prepare to facilitate and ensure safety and security performance.

REFERENCES

ACI. (2020). *Smart Security Vision 2040 Achieving a Seamless Airport Security Screening Experience for Passengers*. Retrieved from: www.aci.aero/publications

Adrienne, N., Budd, L., & Ison, S. (2020). Grounded aircraft: An airfield operations perspective of the challenges of resuming flights post COVID. *Journal of Air Transport Management*, *89*, 101921. Advance online publication. doi:10.1016/j.jairtraman.2020.101921 PMID:32901184

AIRBUS. (2021). *A Statistical Analysis of Commercial Aviation Accidents A Statistical Analysis of Commercial Aviation Accidents* (Issue 5). https://safetyfirst.airbus.com/news-a-statistical-analysis-of-commercial-aviation-accidents-1958-2020/

Alaminos-Torre, Martinez-Locra, De Sola, Lopez-Ejeda, & Marrodan. (2021). Psychological distress in Spanish airline pilots during the aviation crisis caused by the COVID-19. *Ergonomics*.

Allianz Global Corporate & Specialty. (2021). *Aviation trends post Covid-19*. www.agcs.allianz.com

Amankwah-Amoah, J. (2021). COVID-19 pandemic and innovation activities in the global airline industry: A review. In Environment International (Vol. 156). Elsevier Ltd. doi:10.1016/j.envint.2021.106719

Arora, M., Tuchen, S., Nazemi, M., & Blessing, L. (2021). Airport pandemic response: An assessment of impacts and strategies after one year with COVID-19. *Transportation Research Interdisciplinary Perspectives*, *11*, 100449. Advance online publication. doi:10.1016/j.trip.2021.100449 PMID:34458721

Bielecki, M., Patel, D., Hinkelbein, J., Komorowski, M., Kester, J., Ebrahim, S., Rodriguez-Morales, A. J., Memish, Z. A., & Schlagenhauf, P. (2020). Reprint of: Air travel and COVID-19 prevention in the pandemic and peri-pandemic period: A narrative review. *Travel Medicine and Infectious Disease*, *38*, 101939. Advance online publication. doi:10.1016/j.tmaid.2020.101939 PMID:33291000

Bielecki, M., Patel, D., Hinkelbein, J., Komorowski, M., Kester, J., Ebrahim, S., Rodriguez-Morales, A. J., Memish, Z. A., & Schlagenhauf, P. (2021). Air travel and COVID-19 prevention in the pandemic and peri-pandemic period: A narrative review. In *Travel Medicine and Infectious Disease* (Vol. 39). Elsevier Inc. doi:10.1016/j.tmaid.2020.101915

Broderick, S. (2022). *Corrosion From Inactivity Flagged On Pratt-powered 777 Engine Parts*. Academic Press.

Byrnes, K. P., Rhoades, D. L., Williams, M. J., Arnaud, A. U., & Schneider, A. H. (2022). The effect of a safety crisis on safety culture and safety climate: The resilience of a flight training organization during COVID-19. *Transport Policy*, *117*, 181–191. doi:10.1016/j.tranpol.2021.11.009 PMID:34803245

Cole, M. (2014). Towards proactive airport security management: Supporting decision making through systematic threat scenario assessment. *Journal of Air Transport Management*, *35*, 12–18. doi:10.1016/j.jairtraman.2013.11.002

Cooper, M. D. (2000). Towards a model of safety culture. *Safety Science*, *36*(2), 111–136. doi:10.1016/S0925-7535(00)00035-7

Drogoul, F., & Cabon, P. (2020). *Post COVID-19 fatigue management for ATCOs*. ResearchGate.

EASA. (2021a). *Review of Aviation Safety Issues Arising from the COVID-19 Pandemic-V2, April 2021 Review of Aviation Safety Issues Arising from the COVID-19 Pandemic Version 2-April, 2021*. https://www.easa.europa.eu/contact-us

EASA. (2021b). *Safety Information Bulletin Subject: Contamination of Air Data Systems During Aircraft Parking and / or Storage due to the COVID-19 Pandemic*. https://www.easa.europa.eu/sites/default/files/dfu/easa_sib_2020-14r1_1.pdf?msclkid=e2891536bbd511ec8be890d3d3d928f2

Economic Times. (2022). Bird Strike at Indian Airports. *Economic Times*. https://economictimes.indiatimes.com/industry/transportation/airlines-/-aviation/limited-flights-but-bird-animal-strike-incidents-rose-significantly-at-indian-airports-in-2021/articleshow/90470596.cms?utm_source=contentofinterest&utm_medium=text&utm_campaign=cppst

FAA. (2020). *Federal Aviation Administration National Part 139 Cert Alert*. FAA.

Gillen, D., & Morrison, W. G. (2015). Aviation security: Costing, pricing, finance and performance. *Journal of Air Transport Management*, *48*, 1–12. doi:10.1016/j.jairtraman.2014.12.005

Gogalniceanu, P., Calder, F., Callaghan, C., Sevdalis, N., & Mamode, N. (2021). Surgeons Are Not Pilots: Is the Aviation Safety Paradigm Relevant to Modern Surgical Practice? *Journal of Surgical Education*, *78*(5), 1393–1399. doi:10.1016/j.jsurg.2021.01.016 PMID:33579654

Guo, Q., Wang, J., Estill, J., Lan, H., Zhang, J., Wu, S., Yao, J., Yan, X., & Chen, Y. (2022). Risk of COVID-19 Transmission Aboard Aircraft: An Epidemiological Analysis Based on the National Health Information Platform. *International Journal of Infectious Diseases*, *118*, 270–276. doi:10.1016/j.ijid.2022.03.024 PMID:35331931

Hardie, J. A., & Brennan, P. A. (2020). Are You surgically current? Lessons from aviation for returning to non-urgent surgery following COVID-19. *Journal of Oral and Maxillofacial Surgery*.

Hirche, C., & Kneser, U. (2021). What We Really can Learn From Aviation: Checklist-based Team Time-Out in Conjunction With Interpersonal Competence Training for the Daily Management of a Surgical Department. *Surgical Innovation*, *28*(5), 642–646. doi:10.1177/15533506211018439 PMID:34319815

IATA. (2022). *Airline Business Confidence Index Weighted Score (50 = No Change)*. www.iata.org/economics

ICAO. (2020). *Doc 10144 ICAO Handbook for CAAs on the Management of Aviation Safety Risks related to COVID-19*. ICAO.

ICAO. (2021a). *COVID Restart Risk Assessment Post-COVID Risk Assessment Checklist-V1.0.* https://www.icao.int/Security/COVID-19/Documents/COVID_Restart_Risk_Assessment_v1_1Nov2021.pdf?msclkid=7e03b659be1b11ecb2bce1954cd3c3f1

ICAO. (2021b). *Safety Report 2021 Edition.* https://www.icao.int/safety/Documents/ICAO%20Safety%20Report%202021%20Edition.pdf

Jarry, G., Delahaye, D., & Feron, E. (2021). Flight safety during Covid-19: A study of Charles de Gaulle airport atypical energy approaches. *Transportation Research Interdisciplinary Perspectives, 9,* 100327. Advance online publication. doi:10.1016/j.trip.2021.100327 PMID:33623897

Juvan, J., Prezelj, I., & Kopač, E. (2020). Public dilemmas about security measures in the field of civil aviation. *Security Journal, 34*(3), 410–428. doi:10.1057/s41284-020-00240-8

Kaminski-Morrow, D. (2021). Three airspeed incidents at Heathrow trigger alert over insect blockage. *Flight Global.* https://www.flightglobal.com/safety/three-airspeed-incidents-at-heathrow-trigger-alert-over-insect-blockage/144142.article?msclkid=17de37f4bbd911ecb32ecedbde9c1615

Kennedy, R., & Kirwan, B. (1998). *Development of a Hazard and Operability-based method for identifying safety management vulnerabilities in high risk systems.* Academic Press.

Knezevic, J. (2021). COVID-19 Pandemic as a Mechanism of the Motion of an Aircraft in MIRCE Mechanics. *American Journal of Engineering and Technology Management, 6*(1), 1. doi:10.11648/j.ajetm.20210601.11

NDTV. (2022). *US Flight Passenger Who Was Duct-Taped To Her Seat Faces Record Fine.* https://www.ndtv.com/world-news/woman-on-us-flight-who-spit-at-headbutted-crew-faces-record-81-950-fine-2887078

Olaganathan & Amihan. (2021). Impact of COVID -19 on Pilot Proficiency – A Risk Analysis. *Global Journal of Engineering and Technology Advances, 6*(3), 1–13. doi:10.30574/gjeta.2021.6.3.0023

Piers, Montijn, & Balk. (2009). *Safety Management System and Safety Culture Working Group Safety Management System and Safety Culture Working Group (SMS WG) Safety Culture Framework For The ECAST SMS-WG.* Academic Press.

Qingbin, C., & Dangen, X. (2021). Research on Application of Blockchain Technology in Airport Aviation Security. *Proceedings of 2021 IEEE 3rd International Conference on Civil Aviation Safety and Information Technology, ICCASIT 2021,* 454–459. 10.1109/ICCASIT53235.2021.9633615

Sobieralski, J. B. (2020). COVID-19 and airline employment: Insights from historical uncertainty shocks to the industry. *Transportation Research Interdisciplinary Perspectives, 5,* 100123. Advance online publication. doi:10.1016/j.trip.2020.100123 PMID:34173453

Stotz, T., Bearth, A., Ghelfi, S. M., & Siegrist, M. (2020). Evaluating the Perceived Efficacy of Randomized Security Measures at Airports. *Risk Analysis, 40*(7), 1469–1480. doi:10.1111/risa.13474 PMID:32356923

Chapter 5
Crew Resource Management Development:
Characteristics, Perspectives, and Experiences

Fahad ibne Masood
Modern College of Business and Science, Oman

Bikal Jha
Modern College of Business and Science, Oman

Hesham Magd
Modern College of Business and Science, Oman

ABSTRACT

Crew resource management (CRM) is the product of a paradigm shift in safety thinking from 'finding the problem' to 'finding the solution'. Until the 'crash of the century' took place in Tenerife in 1977, the first officer was only to be seen and not heard. He was 'a good for nothing' sandbag sitting in the right seat. But all changed in 1977-1978 with the introduction of CRM, initially cockpit resource management and now crew resource management. It was so elaborate a system created out of necessity by aviation that no matter which high-reliability organization (HRO) was and is present, they took it up as the most efficient and effective method to reduce human fallibility. Starting from the civil nuclear technology sector to medical science to firefighting, all have adhered to CRM principles. The latest innovation which comes across from the experts is threat and error management (TEM), which is coincidentally the revision or version six of CRM. The aim of the present effort is to relate how CRM has come of age, the purpose behind it, and a deeper view of its successful cross-functioning into various vocations and industries.

DOI: 10.4018/978-1-6684-4615-7.ch005

INTRODUCTION

If it is looked in detail, the work on CRM officially started with the 'decision' in the 1977 with the infamous Tenerife disaster. Decision to take off without being sure the runway was clear of traffic in heavy fog at Tenerife, the Canary Islands (Accidentes, 1978). Although there had been bar-talks on requirement of such a system since a long time amongst pilots as well as researchers since start of heavier than air flights in 1903. Hence, lifespan of the CRM is rather short-lived looking at its past. There have been unquestionable improvements like those of latest addition of the TEM (Threat & Error Management) domain, bringing the greater number of grey areas into light. More specifically, pilot CRM skills provide countermeasures against risk and error in the form of threat and error avoidance, detection, and management (Robert L. Helmreich, 2001). Both academia and industry, even with all their differences, have agreed on the requirement of CRM. Although, there have been a lot of successes due to 'teamwork' but has never made the headlines. On the other hand, the losses did 'stop the press' because they emoted sensation and in turn sales. Though fear mongering and sensationalism are by no means new to journalism, the enhanced pressure of deadlines and competition in the 24/7 news era lends itself to irresponsibility in the newsroom (Friedman, 2009). At the end of the millennium, CRM training was defined as an instructional strategy "designed to improve teamwork in the cockpit by applying well-tested training tools (e.g., performance measures, exercises, feedback mechanisms) and appropriate training methods (e.g., simulators, lectures, videos) targeted at specific content (i.e., teamwork knowledge, skills, and attitudes)" (Blickensderfer, 1998). There were five versions of CRM (Helmreich, 1999) till year 2005-2006 and subsequently evolved into the sixth in form of TEM. The objective of penning down research on the various aspect of CRM relates to diversity of the concept, its acceptance in various industries and touch upon the future of idea.

BACKGROUND

We, as humans, have been aspired by the birds staying aloft since times unknown. Drew about it, wrote about it but never really understood the true essence of the phrase 'birds of a feather flock together'. Research is needed to tie cultural models to aviation human factors and CRM so that the variability among cultures can lead to synergy in the cockpit (Redding, 1984). Aviation has come of age in all technological aspects of it but the human element has not evolved to stay parallel to what the redundancies have been applied on the machine side. Further uses involving safety-critical systems have utilized redundancy as a method of achieving high-availability and/or fault-tolerant operation. (Hecht, 2004) (Isermann, 2006). Hence, there is an inevitable requirement observed in finding increased methods to ensure that there is improvement in this all-important domain of human factors, Crew Resource Management.

CRM was so elaborate a system created out of necessity by aviation that no matter which High-Reliability Organization (HRO) was and is present, took it up as the most effective method to reduce human fallibility. Starting from the Civil Nuclear Technology sector to medical science, all have adhered to the principles of CRM. It was elaborated as the utility of diverse 'resources' available to the aviation industry which should be brought into play in order to enable learning & developing the art and the skill required for safe & efficient operations in all airborne facets while ensuring landings equal the all takeoffs of whole flight deck managers while using excellent ergonomics. This was the outcome of research of NTSB's well-cited mind doctor John K. Lauber in 1984.

Human factor studies are overawing the big picture of CRM. The latest innovation that comes across from the experts is "Threat & Error Management (TEM)" which is coincidentally the revision or version six of CRM. Barbara G. Kanki et al in their 2019 academic writing on Crew Resource Management mention that negative connotations attached to realization of hazards into risks are referred to as 'threats' & actions/inactions by aviators at large which result in extrapolation of the threats can be called 'errors. They also elucidate importance of having all crew members on the same frequency and wavelength remains mission critical to success in all commercial operations. (Krieger, 2005); (Brian K. Sperling, 2011). There is an absolute connection between human performance enhancement and a shared mental model. USHRI (Ultra Safety High Risk Industries) teams require to share mental models. Amy L Fraher in 'Thinking through crisis: Improving teamwork and leadership in high-risk fields' book from 2011 reinforces the idea of 'Mindfulness' (shared situational awareness/coherent mental modeling) which leads to pre-emptive safety risk management as well as continuous compliance to rules & regulations. (Fraher, 2011) (Krieger, 2005).

Shared mental models improve squad efficacy by providing the support for keeping an eye on joint routine acts as well as act as redundancy to decision-making & mannerisms. It is via shared mental models, group affiliates opt if, when, and what type of compliance and support is suitable and essential. The synergistic effect of a team operating in mind coherence, may it be follies, errors, or successes, will relate to greater gains in aviation operations through mutual support which has been aptly discussed in the ground-breaking book 'Errors in the Heat of Battle: Taking a Closer Look at Shared Cognition Breakdowns Through Teamwork' by Wilson; Salas; et al in 2007.

DEVELOPMENT OF CRM

Before 'The Start'

Human Factor studies were initiated mainly during the inter-war period (Dempsey, 1985) for the purpose of mere biological and therapeutic reasons. Like, effects of g-onset were considered on human beings and animals alike. "Angular accelerations were produced by a 20 ft -diameter centrifuge, while a swing was used to produce linear acceleration" (Moroney, 1995). Study of 'physical measures of a person's size' resulted in the G-suit in late 30's. Edwin Link coined the concept of flight simulator although some decent change (coins) was made in the process via sharing the technology for sake of amusement. Air-Crew Classification Test Battery was devised in WW-II (Taylor, 1993) for the purpose of gauging combat training success. "Probably, the best-known researcher during World War II was Paul Fitts, who worked with his collaborators on aircraft controls and displays" (Fitts, 1947). One of the subsequent pioneers in human factors domain Arthur David Beaty (28 March 1919 – 4 December 1999) successfully sowed seeds of how does the pilot or its team enables or disables safe aviation operations through his landmark book 'The Human Factor in Aircraft Accidents' in 1969 as well as other works to set the ball rolling in the correct direction. Mr. Beaty initiated by outlining all improvements in aircraft design and performance but although 'professional error' accidents decreased, 'human error' mishaps increased (Beaty, 1969).

Crew Resource Management Development

The Start

Time, a few minutes past five in the evening, date 27 March 1977, on a foggy weather condition at Tenerife islands runway 12/30, then CFI of KLM, Captain Jacob Veldhuyzen van Zanten initiated takeoff roll of his majestic KLM Boeing 747 Flight 4805 ended up colliding with Pan Am 747 Flight 1736, killing 583 souls on board. CRM was born (Krause, 2003). One of the findings in the accident investigation related to the 'poor decision-making' of the captain. (Jenny A. Walker, 2016). Communications is and always have been at the heart of safe aviation operations and it could not have been truer for the aforementioned accident, nicknamed 'the crash of the century'. (Investigation, 2006). Prima facie purpose of Crew Resource Management was to ensure all possible valuable additions – equipment, information, people – are synergized (David Meister, 2010) to ensure a singular and greater whole.

1st Generation CRM: In start of 1980's, one of the first airlines to officially imbibe this paradigm was the KLM, maybe because of organizational guilt of the Tenerife Disaster, and the United Airlines (David Meister, 2010). "First-generation CRM training was based largely on existing management training approaches and was psychological in nature (i.e., focusing on psychological testing and general interpersonal behaviors, such as leadership)" (Kantowitz, 2010). Something amiss in this system was Team-related behaviors which directly impacted the safe aviation operations. Rudimentary flight simulators were introduced to gain interest of the common man and later build on domains of teamwork in the multi-crew cockpit. Majority of the preliminary efforts were focused on altering the individual – the pilot (Eduardo Salas, 2010). Captains were over-bossy and first officers were meant to be seen not heard, hence lacked the all-important 'assertiveness' to speak in times of adversity in order to save their own and the passengers lives in the bargain. "The roots of crew resource management training in the United States are usually traced back to a workshop, Resource Management on the Flight deck (Cooper, 1980) sponsored by the National Aeronautics and Space Administration (NASA) in 1979" (Robert L. Helmreich A. C., 1999). More than a few aircraft accidents were researched to generate this output by NASA.

2nd Generation CRM: For the idea to get grounded, it took about half a decade. Aviation industry, especially with all the conservative culture, was not willing to learn something new that rattled the rather vertical cockpit authority gradient. The word 'cockpit' came into perspective to bring along with itself some amount of teamwork on the flight deck. "Second-generation CRM training evolved 5 years later in 1986, and a shift was made from psychological testing to cockpit group dynamics" (David Meister, 2010). Focus started shifting from a one man show to group of professionals in the cockpit to achieve a singular aim. As per Kantowitz (2010), the inertia was so big within the American airline industry that it took ten years for FAA (Federal Aviation Administration) to provide detailed guidance through Advisory Circular 120-51D for all to follow suit in making CRM a part of day-to-day operations of the airlines. "Th e resistance to initial CRM training by segments of the pilot community (Helmreich R. L., 1992) led to a revision of the original approach, thus, giving birth to the second generation of CRM training" (Kantowitz, Human Factors in Transportation, 2010). A gradual influx of new information resulted into mix of varying modules like that of decision-making, stress management, error chain, SA (situational awareness), communications, leadership, attitudes etc. Active aim was still to enable flight deck performers to become better at their job. Whereas the latent intent related to improve safety performance with upgraded teamwork.

3rd Generation CRM: Revisiting aircraft occurrences, extensive role playing & non-aviation related activities were at core of first as well as second generation CRM training syllabi. Mark difference between the technical and soft skill training was maintained with direct intent to maintain clear delineation (Kantowitz, Human Factors in Transportation, 2010). The next jump took place with the advent of glass-cockpits which ushered the era of the 3rd generation CRM. The sphere of trainings expanded with addition of continuously changing scenarios within cognitive domains vis a vis minor teams while maintaining similar frequency and wavelength to achieve objective (Orasanu, 1993). Computer technology was becoming a major player in the aviation in general and flight deck management, in specific. A greater requirement was felt to achieve a successful man-machine interface which was focus of tertiary level CRM innovation. The concept of basic flight operational units – aircraft/crew system & flight/cabin crew system – was introduced in order to improved system performance (Kantowitz, Human Factors in Transportation, 2010). A few modules were added to the previously used ones from 1st & 2nd generation CRM, namely human reliability, vigilance, automation management, stress/fatigue management and mental models etc. Safety was also given an upgrade while considering it to be a more proactive rather than a reactive process. Which had a direct influence of weaning away from role-playing & non-aviation games to a more subtle approach towards flying-related activities. Enhanced amalgamation of human-factor beyond operations and into training regimes resulted into reducing red lines between 'NOTECHS' (Non-Technical Skills) & 'TECHS' (Technical Skills) (Kantowitz, Handbook of Aviation Human Factors, 2010).

Fourth Generation CRM: In the 1990's, the world 'Globalization' was related to, with both positive and negative connotations attached to it. Aviation related to it in the positive where it was connected to the "consequence of the global health of the system" (Daniel E. Maurino, 2010). Aeronautical sciences is truly a global phenomenon. For example, one has to only mentally absorb the ICAO Annex documents once and then stay abreast with amendments, he or she will be considered a specialist in the field. Revision four of CRM was all about whole-part-whole improvement of aviation. Meaning the complete aviation 'system' will improve only if its components improve the and generate a better system. Amongst the many topics, 'synergy' was one word used by the innovators for the very first time officially. Other than this inclusion of 'role & status', 'shared mental models', 'team interactions' came to the table and have stayed there till date. The buzz sentence was "safety is one positive outcome of the system's health" (Daniel E. Maurino, 2010). Syllabi was also diversified to bring into its fold topics related to flight operations or dispatch duties officers (Chidester, 1993), ATM/ATC (Air Traffic Management/Control) (Baker, 1995) as well as maintenance (Robertson, 1995). Decisions taken to act or not to act, in addition to, succumbing to indecision circumstances were also investigated (Maurino, 1992). Terms such as Organizational Resource Management (ORM) reverberated with industry and academia alike for it was the whole 'system' that needed to evolve.

Fifth and Sixth Generations of CRM: Interestingly, where it was seen in previous versions, expansion of CRM to achieve an organization-wide effect, TEM (Threat & Error Management) came up in version five where it related to achieving the core mission of CRM i.e., 'Safe Flights'. "Threat and Error Management, as a concept, was born in the late 1990s, based on the studies at the University of Texas and their close liaison with Continental Airlines in the development of the line operations safety audit (LOSA)" (Daniel E. Maurino, 2010). Line Operation Safety Audits (LOSA) program was introduced to gain insight on anonymous & de-identified data to process into information and generate insight on points to improve within the flights or flight legs. It was identified that 'Human Error' is inevitable but a few teams as well as individuals are able to put CRM practices to good use and mitigate these errors. Error Management was a three-prong effect, first avoid or mitigate it, secondly if error committed catch it early and last but not the least reduce its aftershocks (Kantowitz, Human Factors in Transportation, 2010). Flight deck managers knew that one aspect of their job profile was to 'manage threats' from out-

Crew Resource Management Development

side, but it was never articulated well enough before the concept of Threat Management in TEM. Hence, the concept is growing as core of wholesome & safe aviation operations till date.

CRM in USHRI's

Ultra-Safe High-Risk Industries (USHRI's) or HRO's (High Reliability Organizations) are rare groups where a minor mistake on someone anyone in the chain of command leads to a catastrophic failure with immense loss of human lives or finance. The three tiers of any HRO are intertwined to a degree of enormous connect where one incorrect decision at strategic, operational or tactical level will have a near irreversible effect on the system leading to mayhem (Dekker, 2009). Various examples include sectors like Nuclear (May it be military or civil), health care, mining, electric power generation, large-scale telecommunication & computers network, maintenance organizations and last but not the least aviation. "High-reliability organizations (HROs) have emerged across a number of highly technical, and increasingly automated industries (e.g., aviation, medicine, nuclear power, and oil field services)." (Mark P. Alavosius, 2017). CRM was introduced and still continues to be a focus of attention in especially large complex organizations which are looking to synergize its many components including the workforce through teamwork, singular purpose i.e., mission & vision statement. A calamity at sea made headlines of international news as well as with USHRI's strategic bosses now known as Deep water Horizon oil rig disaster on 20 April 2010, which was the tipping point for CRM in HRO's (Mark P. Alavosius, 2017). Root cause analysis (RCA) of the event related to a history of risk-prone actions by the team at the rig resulted into the disaster as per study done by Deepwater Horizon Study Group of Center for Catastrophic Risk Management in 2011 (Group, 2011). Automation has crept up slowly but surely to ensure ease of operations in all HRO's but it has brought along with itself challenges as well. Ergonomics or man-machine interaction plays a pivotal role in securing assets worth millions and lives worth gazillions of dollars as displayed by Captain Sullenberger in the successful 'water-landing' in Hudson River (Sullenberger, 2009). Replicating the high-fidelity simulators of aviation sector, the medicine industry has started using the same in surgery and patient care (Simon, 2000) to ensure that there is greater teamwork at achieve singular mission: save lives. Till date the influence has spawned many conceptual frameworks in USHRI's while taking lead from aviation CRM designs to ensure synergistic effect and evolving system to improve efficiency, safety and security.

CHARACTERISTICS OF CRM

The main purpose of developing Crew Resource Management as a tool for airlines to conduct smooth flight operations, was so that their flight crew members could inhabit these 6 major characteristics of CRM and display them during the flight hours. When it comes to the general concept of CRM, this tool addresses certain human behavior or characteristics that are required to be considered while performing in a complex situation which brings uncertainty and ambiguity. The 6 characteristics of CRM come under the concept of "soft skills". Soft skills are an individual's interpersonal ability to deal with other people when found in a complex situation. The term soft skills is further reflected in Non-technical skills (NOTECH). These 6 characteristics come under NO-TECH and they are classified as follows: (Alavosius et al., 2017).

Communication: Adequate communication occurs when the recipient of the conversation receives and understands the information that they have gained. It is a management's responsibility to make sure that there is effective communication at all levels of the organization. There should be clearly written and understood objective manuals that the staff, as well as the flight crew, can understand and follow. Adequate communication between the flight crew is also crucial as it helps in creating situational awareness. The main importance for pilots to have communication between themselves is so that they can address risks and increase the level of safety among them during flight operations. Poor communications have been one of the major causes of flight accidents in the initial stages of air travel. There are many issues that can arise out of miscommunications like Information overload, Pronunciation issues, Misunderstanding.

Operational crew members like pilots, co-pilots, cabin crew, and air traffic controllers are required to learn English, which is their core language of communication, and this has been adopted by ICAO. During the communications between the ATC and the flight crew, their main priority is to establish the "operational context", which can specify the reason for the transmission, information of their location, the flight direction, and the expected timeline. The effectiveness and efficiency of representing one of the most important pillars of flight safety, and every airline and flight operator must make sure that no miscommunication takes place so that an aircraft accident or incident will not take place (Gilstrap, 2019).

Situational Awareness: It is mandated and required of every flight crew member to be aware of their surroundings and of the situation around them. Being situationally aware makes it possible for them to identify situational hazards and risks that come along with them. This is a major factor in reducing the effects of the risk. There are five levels of situational awareness which can influence the flight crew's actions. Informational influences (Information derived from other flight crew and the ATC), Environmental influences (Information derived from radars and surveillance about the surroundings of the aircraft), Personal influences (Information derived from the individual's perceptions and assumptions), and Organizational influences.

Gaining or deriving and maintaining situational awareness consists of a process that includes three steps:

1. The perception of what is happening
2. The understanding of what has been perceived
3. The use of what is understood to think ahead

During the whole process of deriving situational awareness, there are again three levels involved in the process:

1. Perception (Scanning and gathering information): In order to create a mental image or situation of the environment, it is important that pilots gather enough information by using their senses of vision, hearing and touch. During the first level, it is important for pilots to associate and compare the most important aspects of their surroundings with their knowledge and experience of flying.
2. Representation (Understanding and creating the mental modal): Every understanding of the pilots is often built upon their observations from the surroundings and their knowledge and experience. The flight crew can effectively develop a mental modal of their environment by successfully matching their observations with their knowledge.
3. Projection (Thinking ahead and updating the modal): The understanding of the pilot's allows them to think further ahead and project the future condition of their environment. This step is very im-

portant as it contributes to the pilot's decision-making process and can have a major effect on their final decision. (Situational awareness, 2022).

Decision-Making: Good decision-making comes along with sound judgment. Before a flight crew member can make a decision, they must be able to judge the situation correctly. Good judgement and decision-making come with training and experience. Crew members must also be able to differentiate between their perception and the reality of the situation. The perception of an individual plays a major role in decision making and if done wrong, can risk safe flight operations.

Aeronautical decision-making is strongly dependent upon situational awareness and all the possible alternatives that are available for the flight crew members (Hoc and Amalberti, 1995). The choice of response and the final decision made by the pilot depends on the level of the pilot's situational awareness. This shows that decision-making and situational awareness are interdependent factors. Certain studies that have been done have only been focused on an individual's decision-making. However, the cockpit in the aircraft has a group of pilots who must work together to make sound decisions. This is not only for the pilots but also for the cabin crew as well as the ground handlers and all their efforts are coordinated. There are certain steps taken when it comes to making a collective decision:

- Assess the same information either directly or by sharing and communicating the information received to the team members.
- Build collective situational awareness of all the pilots and build one common understanding of the overall picture of the environment.
- Complete the achievement of flight goals and mutually agree on the goals that have been set.
- Choose and accept the course of action that needs to be taken
- Execute the course of action after the process of execution is being planned by all and the duties and tasks allocated to each member of the flight crew.
- Providing valuable feedback
- Expressing concerns and doubts that need to be addressed.

Every decision that is made by the pilot involves a certain amount of risk. The choice made on the alternative chosen depends on what the pilot expects to happen, and the amount of risk failure involved in each alternative (Decision making, 2022).

Leadership: Leadership is a quality that individuals possess or develop, and it is often easy to recognize. When an individual shows forth or exercises good leadership skills, it is known that the team will have a better chance at being successful. Every pilot must understand that in order to achieve good leadership skills, they must be able to understand the elements of an effective leadership style, as well as the negatives of poor leadership. When goals are being established among the members of the team, it lays out a clear vision which aligns with the set goals and mission of the whole organization. During the time of when members of a team work together towards a common goal, they create interlocking contingencies. This behaviour of being interlocked with one another, makes every crew member to be in contact with the other. When it comes to CRM, the leader is the one who is responsible for making sure that all the crew members have the required competencies so that they do their tasks effectively and efficiently. Captains of the flight crew must be able to show their leadership quality during the command. They must be able to provide and maintain standards, moreover, they must be able to provide a plan to reach those standards and coordinate with the co-pilots.

Teamwork: CRM inculcates teamwork among the flight crew members which indirectly increases the levels of co-operation among them. It helps in understanding their pre-determined rules and this leads to an enhanced safety environment. As it is well known, the aviation industry is a very high-risk industry, and this is why effective teamwork is a very critical and important factor in CRM. An effective teamwork can only be achieved when every member of the team, whether on the ground or in the air, performs and contributes their best in achieving the common goals of their team (Writers, 2019). It can have a major impact on risk and safety and the need to get people together and to work as a team is crucial in-flight operations. The ATC is one major area in aviation that exemplifies teamwork. They are the essential link in the chain of keeping aviation safe on the ground and also in the air. Co-ordination is also an important factor when it comes to controlling the air traffic, whether it is between the individuals themselves in the ATC or between the aircraft and the ATC tower, or the tower and ground staff. The flight cabin crew members also are being trained to improve their teamwork capabilities through CRM. The crew members learn how emergency situations can be caused through a series of events, and that if they lack in communication and teamwork, it can lead to many further risks and an aircraft accident (Green, 2021).

Van Avermaete (1998) had created a different approach to CRM and had further summarized the 6 characteristics into 4 general categories, which are:

- Co-operation: CRM increases the co-operation among the flight crew members. An increase in the co-operation can lead to fast decision-making skills, which become very beneficial during complex situations that require fast decisions to be made. Co-operation among flight crew members also decreases confusion and dilemma among them, which can reduce arguments and conflicts among the flight crew members.
- Leadership: Leadership is a quality that individuals possess or develop, and it is often easy to recognize. When an individual shows forth or exercises good leadership skills, it is known that the team will have a better chance at being successful. Every pilot must understand that in order to achieve good leadership skills, they must be able to understand the elements of an effective leadership style, as well as the negatives of poor leadership.
- Situational awareness: It is mandated as required of every flight crew member to be aware of their surroundings and of the situation around them. Being situationally aware makes it possible for them to identify situational hazards and risks that come along with it. This is a major factor in reducing the effects of the risk.
- Decision-making: Good decision-making comes along with sound judgment. Before a flight crew member can make a decision, they must be able to judge the situation correctly. Good judgment and decision-making come with training and experience. Crew members must also be able to differentiate between their perception and the reality of the situation. The perception of an individual plays a major role in decision making and if done wrong, can risk safe flight operations.

In this approach towards CRM, communication does not come as a separate category but falls under the four categories.

Crew Resource Management Development

CREW RESOURCE MANAGEMENT BEHIND THE COCKPIT

The Management: According to statistics regarding aircraft accidents and incidents, it has shown that the industry has reached a very high level of safety and is now one of the safest industries in the world. This was possible due to the improvements made in technology, but better crew performance also contributed in a major way to the safety in flight operations. This is because CRM has significantly contributed to crew performance and teamwork performance. CRM was started initially by management as an intervention for team development within airlines. In the year 1979, NASA had sponsored and implemented a workshop called CRM ad the main purpose of this workshop was to address human errors and factors in accidents and accident prevention. (Helmreich and Wilhelm, 1991). During the initial stages of the development of CRM by NASA, it was only implemented in management interventions for the private sectors. CRM was then implemented by many airlines only at the management level. But since the scope of CRM has increased along with its benefits towards the industry, it was further extended into the operational level of other industries as well. Industries that function in very high-risk areas like air traffic control, oil and gas, nuclear power, healthcare, and so on, have also initiated the implementation of CRM in their work domains. There are many reasons as to why CRM has to be implemented by the management. Given below are a few reasons:

- Most researched team interventions: Many companies spend a lot of their money of trying to develop workshops and programs as a way to develop team performance in their workplaces and among their management teams. It has been 40 years since CRM has been developed and there are many scientists and practitioners who are further studying them, as the implementation of CRM has become extremely beneficial for any management.
- Great man theory: Some management companies still focus on the great man theory, in which the CEO of the company is the "great man" who dominates the team. The management teams of the aviation industry have proved to be ahead of this method, as they have effectively implemented CRM and have improved their team performance.
- Dynamic environment: The environment in the cockpit has proved to be very dynamic and complex in nature. This creates a lot of room for errors, and it tests the interpersonal skills of the pilot. CRM allows the flight crew to enhance their skills in order to face any given situation in the cockpit, which can only be done if the management implements CRM training.

Present your perspective on the issues, controversies, problems, etc., as they relate to theme and arguments supporting your position. Compare and contrast with what has been, or is currently being done as it relates to the chapter's specific topic and the main theme of the book.

Flight Crew: CRM is a teamwork tool that is used by the flight crew to enhance the safety and efficiency of flight operations. Non-technical skills are very essential, and CRM promotes those skills as mentioned above. It promotes skills like decision making and teamwork which allows the pilots to be aware of their situation and surroundings and promote threat and error management. CRM is used at every phase of flight operation's; from the moment the flight crew enters the aircraft till the time they checkout from the aircraft. It is used during the pre-flight decisions phase, all the way till they taxi to the ramp after landing. The flight crew members can identify, avoid and mitigate threats only through the process of CRM. It allows them to communicate the hazards and threats to another and thus form plans to avoid the risks.

Ground Handlers: CRM has extended its use to RRM (Ramp Resource Management) which also describes the use of resources efficiently but in ground handling. This training aims at improving communication, teamwork, safety, and efficiency in ground handling operations. The purposes of Ramp Resource Management are the following:

- Increasing the efficiency of ground handling operations
- Increasing the awareness of how human factor influences aircraft turnaround
- Reducing the number of operational disruptions
- Decreasing the equipment or aircraft damage and individual injuries
- Improving safety in ground handling operations

RRM was created with the goal is to prevent and reduce the number of accidents and incidents during the time of the aircraft turnaround process. The target group involved for the RRM training is the ramp personnel. After the training has been given to the ramp personnel, the training will be further extended to the ramp planners and managers, so that it can have an influence in their decisions related to aircraft handling and turnaround. (Ramp Resource Management, 2021).

Overall Importance of Crew Resource Management in the Flight Operations Management

In order to understand the overall importance of CRM in flight operations management, we should first look at the causes of poor resource management. The following are the some of the causes:

- Lack of proper training: When there is a lack of good training for crew members in CRM, they can start to exhibit the nature of poor resource management and will not understand the importance of CRM in flight operations.
- Poor technical knowledge: If a pilot lacks the ability to perform technically well, it can have an adverse effect on his performance. This can further lead to confusion and lack of self-confidence in making decisions.
- Disruptive organizational culture: Due to very high integration in the hierarchy system, some organizational structures prevent people from speaking out or providing valuable input to seniors.
- Not considering the seriousness of a situation: The lack of technical knowledge and interpersonal skills can affect one's understanding of how serious a cockpit situation can be and can lead them to misconstrue or misjudge a situation.
- Prejudice: If a flight crew member has a negative behaviour towards his co-pilot because of his background, gender or culture, their interactions will not be done in a positive manner.

Mentioned above are a few causes of poor resource management and all these causes can be eradicated by the implementation of CRM in flight operations.

In Nutshell, CRM is a strategic aviation tool and an intervention that focuses more on reducing human errors to conduct safe flight operations, ground handling operations and managerial operations. CRM is done through training and tries to culminate the skills of communication, situational awareness, decision-making, teamwork, and leadership among the crew members. All the characteristics of CRM are interlinked with the other and cannot be mastered with any of them excluded. When there is maintenance

Crew Resource Management Development

and effective training of CRM, there are more chances to increase the safety during any operation, and it keeps the employees from making mistakes that can create a catastrophe.

CRM: EXPERIENCES

Since the 1970's, and for some, even before that time CRM has played a pivotal role in success and failure of human performance in relation to various activities related to aviation in general and flight deck actions in specific. As mentioned in the 'CRM Development' component of this chapter, crew resource management has been imbibed by the world of USHRI's & HRO's, the focus of this segment will be on the various experiences, good or bad, which different professionals have experienced till date.

CRM in Aviation Sector: Since the crash of the century took place in 1977 at Tenerife with the two Jumbo jets colliding (Eduardo Salas, 2010) there have still been many irrationalities, where countless lives and aircrafts alike, have been lost due to human errors (Dan Maurino, 2010) and violations. A steady growth in research & development has been witnessed since then through the various versions of CRM as mentioned in the development section and its importance cannot be undermined with successes like Sully's Miracle on the Hudson like events. Captain Sullenberger relates CRM to the event while stating "We had a crew briefing at the beginning of the trip, on Monday, January 12, where we aligned our goals, we talked about a few specifics, set the tone, and opened our channels of communication. So, we functioned very well the entire time" (Langewiesche, 2010).

There have been many studies performed on pros and cons of the paradigm but one aspect that has come afront over and over again is the all players refer to it as 'useful' but not as stand-alone training programs but amalgamation of its principles into the complete spectrum of aviation operations, may it be ground-based or air-related (Beaubien & Baker, 2001). Experiential research on aspects of efficacy & effectiveness has been few and far between and those who have ventured this path have been left wanting in domains of evaluation design, smaller population samples etc. (Salas, et al., 2001). Another example of 'assertive' CRM experience was the Airbus A320 with 144 passengers on board Northwest Airlines Flight 188 which was supposed to land at Minneapolis, overshot destination by about 100 miles but was only brought back to earth safely due to an intercom call of a flight stewardess. This communication done by the non-flying cabin crew to the flight deck managers was the 'causal factor' for survival of both men and machine (Press, 2009). Another experiential trend witnessed in the past and even is displayed in airlines, especially in the developing part of the world, is the 'macho' attitude of the 'autocratic' captain, who tends to manage the flight deck as a single-seat fighter aircraft. This brashness was first truly identified in the periodical Aviation, Space, and Environmental Medicine (Foushee, 1982) and rekindled in the disclosures of human factors in aviation (Foushee & Helmreich, 1988) where "a co-pilot's attempts to communicate an air traffic control speed restriction were met with an order to 'just look out the damn window' " (Helmreich & Foushee, 2010).

On the flipside, to operate at extremes like the one from an over-control to an under-control fatal occurrence of Boeing 727 Fort Worth, Dallas was and is not the best way of going about doing business in the field of aviation. This incident was an intra-cockpit communication failure related to confusion due distraction and as a result failed to select correct flap settings for takeoff profile (NTSB, 1988). Continuous evolution of the paradigm has resulted in both successful and unsuccessful stories of examples as well as application of CRM process in the complete sphere of the concept in aviation.

CRM in Healthcare Sector: "CRM was adopted by the medical community in the 1990s, specifically in the surgical and nursing areas, to prevent untoward outcomes and infections" (Griffith, et al., 2015). Due to the robustness of CRM, there have been more than a few emulations in more than a few HRO's and healthcare is no exception (Gross, et al., 2018). As it comes from aviation there is a famous unwritten rule: Mission First! Safety ALWAYS! This is a big reason for CRM to be chosen for all HRO's where not adhering to safety or better known as today by phrase of 'Risk Management' can result into immense human, fiscal (in form of insurance claims) and reputation loss.

"The goal of the CRM is to organize a group of individuals to think and act as a team with the common goal of safety." (McConaughey, 2008). Use of similar technology like that of interactive sessions, case studies, vide clips etc. are used to enhance the capability of the 'team' with special focus on both within the professionals and outside the sphere. Two specific types of knowledge i.e., "Declarative knowledge" & "Procedural knowledge" were put into exercise while using the literature and practical exercises. "Humans are bound to err" and this statement held valid for healthcare as well. Current & incorrect behavior was displayed by teams and later corrected with apt debriefs focusing on learning and 'take-home' points to ensure improvement in subsequent efforts in training and real-time operations (Salas, et al., 2006). As said, two minds are better than one. Same is the case in healthcare, the synergistic effect of two plus two is not four but twenty-two. The two components of personality relate to 'Attitude' & 'Behavior' and the latter if performed coherently relates to enhanced teamwork (Beaubien & Baker, 2004). Considering the organizational efforts put into the accept and utilize the efficacy of the CRM, some sections of Medicare have been left wanting e.g., nurses as well as physicians could have been better facilitated (Oriol, 2006).

The output of any healthcare sub-division is to improve patients' health as early as possible and as best as possible. Knowledge of CRM has moved from the books to becoming common information. Now known to majority of the masses as 'teamwork'. Patients who are about to go under the scalpel, feel more comfortable, assured, hopeful and relatively full of belief when they have prior knowledge of successful CRM practices taking place at a hospital (Pratt, et al., 2007). There has been relatively a lot of research on applying aspects of aviation CRM training principles to healthcare and safe to say decent successes have been achieved till date. United Nations is one of the biggest, if not the biggest Human Development well-wisher at a global scale. UN-HDI (United Nations Human Development Index) has also looked at research with same if not greater concern and satisfaction (UNDP, 2015). "The interconnection between culture and CRM programs has previously been described at the national, organizational and professional levels." (Gross, et al., 2018).

CRM in Nuclear Technology: The world has seen a few major scares of this type of technology going haywire. One was the 'Three Mile Island' event where Unit 2 reactor showed a partial meltdown in Pennsylvania, USA in 1979 and the Second was the infamous Chernobyl disaster in mid-eighties close to Pripyat, north of the Ukrainian SSR, Soviet Union (KIM & BYUN, 2011). Not to mention the Fukushima nuclear disaster which was in the aftermath of the 2011 Tohoku earthquake with subsequent tsunami. In the recent past with the advent of improved DigiTech, things have gotten even more complicated in the civil nuclear technology business. This is in direct relationship to what the aviation world is facing contemporarily. Pilots are now Flight Deck Managers having more to do with managing the affairs of making the destination good instead of 'flying' the plane. Greater the digitization involved in any sector, greater amount of cognitive comprehension required to ensure safe and efficient operations by reducing human errors & violations (Byun & Lee, 2001). CRM gained worldwide recognition due to its successful use in commercial aviation where it was determined through CVRs (Cockpit Voice Recorders) &

FDCVRS (Flight Data Cockpit Voice Recorders) that human factors and related errors/violations were at the core of loss of life and machine both resulting into major degradation of capability (CAA, 2006).

Various researches conducted have resulted into understandings of how best to mitigate risks of nuclear technology. Methodical method of risk management & human factors (CRM) along with integration of engineering &human error statistics (Hamilton, et al., 2013). Application of CRM in nuclear industry has paid dividends beyond the conventional, hence there is trainings being conducted in all developed countries ranging from UK, USA, France etc. With the intent of imbibing human performance improvements from CRM domain, INPO "Institute of Nuclear Power Operations" centered in Atlanta, GA, USA has evolved simulator-based training of 28-hour syllabi with the purpose of improving aspects related to critical actions, conflict resolution, leadership-followership and communications (U.S-NRC, (n.d.)). Situational Awareness (SA) is considered one of the highest forms of cognitive processes in all HRO's. Once lost, SA is challenging to regain, especially if the risks are dynamically changing and gravity of scenario gradually increasing as well, which is one of the most important factors in nuclear power processes. There have been various tools introduced and tested in USHRI's for quantification and measurement purposes known as "SAGAT" (Situational Awareness Global Assessment Technique). "SPAM" (Situation Present Assessment Method) as well as qualitative instrument, namely the "SART" (Situational Awareness Rating Scale etc. (Endsley, 1995b).

CRM in Fire Services: Firefighting is as hazardous as aviation, if not more because it the fire-fighter is in direct line of fire and one incorrect step can be difference between life and death. Keeping in view of the above, emergency & fire services for the first time around 1995 started to absorb the concepts of human factors training in general and crew resource management in specific along with Incident Command Systems workshops with the purpose to mitigate human errors in n firefighting & first aid during ambulance service (Lubnau II & Okray, 2001). In context of leadership-followership domain Lubnau II & Okray (2001) mentioned that the concept of "lead dog" is not valid because it's not the front-runner but the synergy within the team that matters. There have been incidents like the Storm King Mountain fire of 1994 where more than half a dozen fire fighters lost their lives which is taken as flash point for change in training systems while learning from aviation & healthcare versions of CRM but about twenty-odd years later same dilemma revised in Yarnell fire while killing nineteen firemen (Griffith, et al., 2015) (Leschak, 2013). NIOSH (National Institute of Occupational Safety and Health) has gone to the extent of mentioning failures in CRM domains, namely leadership, task allocation, SA & communications etc. as causal & contributing factors to "Firefighter Line-of-Duty Death Reports" (IAFC, 2005). Since the last twenty years, no matter how hard the firefighters train but their performance over a period has levelled-off at a specific number (Okray & & Lubnau II, 2004). Lubnau & Okray (2001) had gone to extent of stating.

The fire service now finds these proven concepts knocking at its door. Equipment is becoming more and more reliable. Firefighting techniques and strategies are becoming scientifically honed, and new technologies for firefighter safety are being brought to the market daily. At the same time, firefighter fatalities and injuries on the emergency scene have plateaued.... The time has come for these aviation principles to be adopted by the fire service. However, for that to happen, a whole new mind set and organizational culture will need to be instilled from the top down. Modifying an organization's leadership style from military and authoritarian to team leadership takes extensive training and a courageous release of control by those in command.... The fire service needs to take on a new and tried approach that takes advantage of the entire team's skills and senses, not just those of the leader. Leaders must buy into the concepts of CRM completely if these principles are to be successfully adopted (p. 8).

Fire Services have evolved the term 'Crew Resource Management' to 'Team Resource Management' but still holding on to the previous CRM training modules only to bring in their own subjective contextualizing related to aspects fire-fighting case studies (Hagemann, et al., 2012). CRM in fire services, as in all HRO's, aims to provide training with the intent to make decision-making efficient with share mental model within the team.

CONCLUSION AND FUTURE DIRECTION

CRM has become a necessity from being a 'fashion symbol' in USHRI's. It has shown its dividends in more ways than one as mentioned above. And with the advent of improved technology and associated redundancies, the human element has to stand up and be counted. Otherwise, the parity in the man-machine interface will be on an ever-decreasing trend for the 'man' in the equation. CRM is an excellent method to ensure the team maintains it defense mechanisms against errors & violations. For all future purposes, till artificial intelligence does not reach complete 'independence', the man is *chargé d'affaires* and needs to ensure safe and efficient operations in all HRO's starting from aviation to healthcare to nuclear to firefighting and more. In this world of change, change is the only constant. One needs to remain in sync with evolution to stay relevant otherwise, it will perish. CRM has gone through it stages and it needs to keep improving with connect of academia and industry working uniformity in direction and magnitude towards enhanced systems. Possible improvement in the CRM version seven can be related to the access of data and predictive modelling capability involved with all domains of operations in USHRI's, CRM can also benefit to a degree beyond normal. This means to process data into information for use on finding short-comings in the 'Team' method of performing day-to-day functions as well as to enhance synergistic results in avoiding errors from inside the cockpit and evading threats from outside the flight deck. Better judgment through improved SA via the enhanced knowledge of systems in place as well as operating discipline, skill and proficiency is where CRM can play an even greater role.

ACKNOWLEDGMENT

We, the researchers, have worked as a CRM team to achieve this academic research document. Thank you all for your relevant efforts. This research received no specific grant from any funding agency in the public, commercial, or not-for-profit sectors.

REFERENCES

Accidentes, C. d. (1978). Colision aeronaves. In *C. d. Accidentes, Colision aeronaves*. Ministerio de Transportes y Comunicaciones, Subsecretaria de Aviacion Civil.

Alavosius, M. P., Houmanfar, R. A., Anbro, S. J., Burleigh, K., & Hebein, C. (2017). Leadership and Crew Resource Management in High-Reliability Organizations. A Competency Framework for Measuring Behaviors. *Journal of Organizational Behavior Management, 37*(2), 142–170. doi:10.1080/01608 061.2017.1325825

Baker, S. B. (1995). *Team resource management in ATC—interim report*. EUROCONTROL.

Beaty, D. (1969). *The Human Factor in Aircraft Accidents*. Stein & Day.

Beaubien, J. M., & Baker, D. P. (2001). *Airline Pilots Perceptions of and Experiences in Crew Resource Management (CRM) Training*. Society of Automotive Engineers, Inc.

Beaubien & Baker. (2004). The use of simulation for training teamwork skills in health care: how low can you go? In *Qual Saf Health Care* (pp. i51–i56). Academic Press.

Blickensderfer, E. C.-B. (1998). Assessing team shared knowledge: A field test and implications for team training. In *Proceedings of the 42nd Annual Meeting of the Human Factors* (p. 1630). Santa Monica, CA: HFES. 10.1177/154193129804202379

Brian K. Sperling, A. R. (2011). *Complementary information distribution to improve team performance in military helicopter operations: An experimental study*. Academic Press.

Byun, S. N., & Lee, D. H. (2001). *Preliminary Safety Review on the Design of Korea Next Generation Reactor: A Human Factors Evaluation of Advanced Control Facilities in Korea Next Generation Reactor* (404th ed.). Korea Institute of Nuclear Safety.

CAA. (2006). *Crew Resource Management Training: Guidance for Flight Crew, CRM Instructors and CRM Instructor-Examiners*. Safety Regulation Group.

Chidester, T. (1993). Role of dispatchers in CRM training. In *Proceedings of the Seventh International Symposium on Aviation Psychology* (pp. 182–185). Columbus, OH: The Ohio State University.

Cooper, G. E. (1980). Resource management the flightdeck. In *Proceedings of a NASN Industry Workshop* (Rep. No. NASA CP-2120). Moffett Field, CA: NASA-Ames Research Center.

Crew Resource Management (CRM). (2021, December 8). *SKYbrary Aviation Safety*. Retrieved January 28, 2022, from https://skybrary.aero/articles/crew-resource-management-crm

Dan Maurino, M. C. (2010). Human Factors in Aviation: An Overview. In E. Salas (Ed.), *Human Factors in Aviation* (p. 5). Elsevier.

Daniel, E., & Maurino, P. S. (2010). Crew Resource. In Human Factors in Transportation (pp. 10-4 to 10-5). Boca Raton, FL: CRC Press.

David Meister, V. G. (2010). Measurement in Aviation Systems. In *V. D. John A. Wise, Handbook of Aviation Human Factors* (pp. 9–11). CRC Press, Taylor & Francis Group.

Decision-Making (OGHFA BN). (2022, February 13). *SKYbrary Aviation Safety*. Retrieved February 14, 2022, from https://skybrary.aero/articles/decision-making-oghfa-bn#:%7E:text=The%20 decision%2Dmaking%20process%20produces,the%20conduct%20of%20a%20flight

Dekker, S. W. (2009). The high reliability organization perspective. In *Human factors in aviation* (2nd ed., pp. 123–146). New York, NY: Wiley.

Dempsey, C. A. (1985). *50 years of research on man in flight*. Wright-Patterson AFB.

Eduardo Salas, D. M. (2010). *Human Factors in Aviation*. Academic Press, Elsevier.

Eduardo Salas, M. L. (2010). Team Dynamics at 35,000 Feet. In D. M. Eduardo Salas (Ed.), Human Factors in Aviation (pp. 250-291). Elsevier.

Endsley, M. R. (1995b). Measurement of situation awareness in dynamic systems. *Human Factors*, *37*(1), 65–84. doi:10.1518/001872095779049499

Fitts, P. M. (1947). *Psychological aspects of instrument display. I. Analysis of 270 "pilot-error" experiences in reading and interpreting aircraft instruments* (Rep. No. TSEAA-694-12A). Dayton, OH: Aeromedical Laboratory, Air Materiel Command.

Foushee, H. (1982). The role of communications, socio-psychological, and personality factors in the maintenance of crew coordination. *Aviation, Space, and Environmental Medicine*, *53*, 1062–1066. PMID:7150164

Foushee, H., & Helmreich, R. (1988). Group interaction and flight crew performance. In E. Wiener & D. Nagel (Eds.), *Human factors in aviation* (pp. 189–227). Academic Press.

Fraher, A. L. (2011). *Thinking through crisis: Improving teamwork and leadership in high-risk fields*. Academic Press.

Friedman, T. (2009, October 10). *Pigs in a Barrel*. Retrieved from https://taylorfriedman.wordpress.com/2009/10/10/fear-mongering-in-the-21st-century-newsroom/

Gilstrap, J. (2019, November 1). *Importance of Communication in Aviation. E2b Calibration Aerospace*. Retrieved February 14, 2022, from https://calibration.aero/importance-of-communication-in-aviation/

Green, P. (2021, March 8). *The Importance of Teamwork from a Cabin Crew Perspective*. CareerAddict. Retrieved February 14, 2022, from https://www.careeraddict.com/the-importance-of-teamwork-from-a-cabin-crew-perspective

Griffith, J. C., Roberts, D. L., & Ph.D., R. T. (2015). A Meta-Analysis of Crew Resource Management/Incident. *Journal of Aviation/Aerospace Education & Research (JAAER)*, *25*(1), 1-25.

Gross, B., Rusin, L., Kiesewetter, J., Zottmann, J. M., Fischer, M. R., Prückner, S., & Zech, A. (2018). *Crew resource management training in healthcare: A systematic review of intervention design, training conditions and evaluation*. BMJ Open.

Group, D. H. (2011). *Investigation of the macondo well blowout disaster*. Retrieved from https://ccrm.berkeley.edu/pdfs_papers/bea_pdfs/dhsgfinalreportmarch2011-tag.pdf

Hagemann, V., Kluge, A., & Greve, J. (2012). Measuring the effects of team resource management training for the fire service. *Human Factors and Ergonomics Society Annual Meeting*. 10.1037/e572172013-504

Hamilton, I. W., Kazem, N. M. L., He, X., & Dumolo, D. (2013). Practical human factors integration in the nuclear industry. In *Cognition* (pp. 5–12). Technology & Work.

Hecht, H. (2004). Systems reliability and failure prevention. In H. Hecht (Ed.), *Systems reliability and failure prevention*. Artech House.

Helmreich, R. L. (1992). Fifteen years of CRM wars: A report from the trenches. In *Towards 2000—future directions and new solutions* (pp. 73–88). The Australian Aviation Psychology Association.

Helmreich, R. L. (1999). *The Line/LOS Checklist, Version 6.0: A checklist for human factors skills assessment, a log for external threats, and a worksheet for flightcrew error management*. Austin, TX: The University of Texas Team Research Project Technical Report 99-01.

Helmreich, R. L., & Foushee, H. C. (2010). Training, Why CRM? Empirical and Theoretical Bases of Human Factors. In B. G. Kanki, R. L. Helmreich, & J. Anca (Eds.), *Crew Resource Management*. Academic Press, Elsevier. doi:10.1016/B978-0-12-374946-8.10001-9

Helmreich, R. L., & Wilhelm, J. A. (1991). Outcomes of Crew Resource Management Training. *The International Journal of Aviation Psychology*, *1*(4), 287–300. doi:10.120715327108ijap0104_3 PMID:11537899

IAFC. (2005). Crew resource management manual. Fairfax, VA: IAFC.

Investigation, A. C. (Director). (2006). *Crash of the Century* [Motion Picture].

Isermann, R. (2006). Fault-diagnosis systems: an introduction from fault detection to fault tolerance. In R. Isermann (Ed.), *Fault-diagnosis systems: an introduction from fault detection to fault tolerance*. Springer.

Jenny, A., & Walker, G. M. (2016). *Human Factors of Leadership: What the Tenerife Plane Crash Taught the World About Cockpit Communication Dynamics. Human Factors and Applied Psychology*. Embry Riddle Aeronautical University.

Kantowitz, B. H. (2010). *Handbook of Aviation Human Factors*. Taylor & Francis Group.

Kantowitz, B. H. (2010). *Human Factors in Transportation*. Taylor & Francis Group.

Kim, S. K., & Byun, S. N. (2011). Effects of Crew Resource Management Training on the Team Performance of Operators in an Advanced Nuclear Power Plant. *Journal of Nuclear Science and Technology*, *48*(9), 1256–1264. doi:10.1080/18811248.2011.9711814

Krause, S. S. (2003). *Aircraft Safety: Accident Investigations, Analyses, & Applications* (2nd ed.). McGraw-Hill.

Krieger, N. (2005). *Embodiment: A conceptual glossary for epidemiology*. Academic Press.

Langewiesche, W. (2010). *Fly by Wire: The Geese, the Glide, the Miracle on the Hudson* (2nd ed.). Picador.

Leschak, P. (2013, July 13). *Star Tribune*. Retrieved February 17, 2022, from https://www.startribune.com/opinion/commentaries/215309681.html

Lubnau, I. I. T., & Okray, R. (2001, August 1). *Crew resource management for the fire service.* Retrieved February 17, 2022, from https://www.fireengineering.com/articles/print/volume154/issue-8/features/crew-resource-management-for-the-fire-service.html

Mark P. Alavosius, R. A. (2017). Leadership and Crew Resource Management in High-Reliability Organizations: A Competency Framework for Measuring Behaviors. *Journal of Organizational Behavior Management*, 142–170.

Maurino, D. E. (1992). Shall we add one more defense? In R. Heron (Ed.), *Third Seminar in Transportation*. Montreal, Canada: Transport Canada Development Centre.

McConaughey, E. (2008, April). Crew Resource Management in Healthcare: The Evolution of Teamwork Training and MedTeams. *The Journal of Perinatal & Neonatal Nursing, 22*(2), 96–104. doi:10.1097/01.JPN.0000319095.59673.6c PMID:18496068

Midura, D. (2021, February 3). *CRM Risk Analysis & Management.* Technology Advisors. Retrieved January 28, 2022, from https://www.techadv.com/blog/crm-risk-analysis-management

Moroney, W. R. (1995). Evolution of human engineering: A selected review. In Research techniques in human factors. Englewood Cliffs, NJ: Prentice-Hall.

NTSB. (1988). Aircraft Accident Report, Delta Airlines, Inc. National Transportation Safety Board, Bureau of Accident Investigation.

Okray, R., & Lubnau, I. I. T. (2004). *Crew resource management for the fire service.* Penn Well Publishers.

Orasanu, J. M. (1993). Shared problem models and flight crew performance. In N. M. A. N. Johnston (Ed.), *Aviation psychology in practice* (pp. 255–285). Averbury Technical.

Oriol, M. (2006). Crew resource management: Applications in healthcare organizations. *JONA, 36*(9), 402–406. doi:10.1097/00005110-200609000-00006 PMID:16969251

Pratt, S., Mann, S., Salisbury, M., Greenberg, P., Marcus, R., Stabile, B., McNamee, P., Nielsen, P., & Sachs, B. P. (2007). Impact of CRM based team training on obstetric outcomes and clinicians' patient safety attitudes. *Joint Commission Journal on Quality and Patient Safety, 33*(12), 720–725. doi:10.1016/S1553-7250(07)33086-9 PMID:18200896

Press, T. A. (2009, December 16). *CBS News.* Retrieved February 16, 2022, from https://www.nbcnews.com/id/wbna34447873

Ramp Resource Management. (2021, September 14). *SKYbrary Aviation Safety.* Retrieved January 29, 2022, from https://skybrary.aero/articles/ramp-resource-management

Ramyar Gilani, J. L. (2022). *Vascular Complications of Surgery and Intervention.* Springer. doi:10.1007/978-3-030-86713-3

Redding, S. (1984). Cultural effects on cockpit communications in civilian aircraft. In *Flight Safety Foundation Conference.* Washington, DC: Flight Safety Foundation.

Robert L. Helmreich, A. C. (1999). The Evolution of Crew Resource Management Training in Commercial Aviation. *The International*, 19-32.

Robert, L., & Helmreich, J. A. (2001). Culture, Error, and Crew Resource Management. In Improving Teamwork in Organizations (p. 28). CRC Press.

Robertson, M. M. (1995). Maintenance CRM training: Assertiveness attitudes eff ect on maintenance performance in a matched sample. In N. J. R. Fuller (Ed.), *Human factors in aviation operations* (pp. 215–222). Averbury Technical.

Salas, E., Burke, C. S., Bowers, C. A., & Wilson, K. A. (2001). Team training in the skies: Does resource management training really work? *Human Factors, 43*(4), 641–674. doi:10.1518/001872001775870386 PMID:12002012

Salas, W., KA, B. C., & DC, W. (2006). Does crew resource management training work? An update, an extension, and some critical needs. *Human Factors*, 392–412.

Simon, R. L. (2000). A successful transfer of lessons learned in aviation psychology and flight safety to health care. In Patient Safety Initiative (pp. 45–49). The MedTeams System.

Situational Awareness (OGHFA BN). (2022, February 12). *SKYbrary Aviation Safety*. Retrieved February 14, 2022, from https://skybrary.aero/articles/situational-awareness-oghfa-bn#:%7E:text=In%20other%20words%2C%20situational%20awareness,future%2C%20to%20feed%2Dforward

Sullenberger, C. (2009). *Highest duty: My search for what really matters*. William Morrow & Company.

Taylor, H. L. (1993). Military psychology. In Encyclopedia of Human Behavior (pp. 503–542). San Diego, CA: Academic Press.

UNDP. (2015). Work for human development. New York, NY: United Nations Development Programme.

U.S-NRC. (n.d.). *Human-System Interface and Plant Modernization Process: Technical Basis and Human Factors Review Guidance. NUREG/CR-6637, BNL-NUREG-52567*. US Nuclear Regulatory Commission.

Van Avermaete, J.A.G. (1998). *NOTECHS: Non-technical skill evaluation in JAR-FCL*. Academic Press.

Chapter 6
Do Ultra Long Haul Flights Attract More Premium Class Passengers?

Colin C. H. Law
https://orcid.org/0000-0001-8964-4707
Singapore Institute of Technology, Singapore

Eliver Lin
Beijing Normal University-Hong Kong Baptist University United International College, China

ABSTRACT

Improved aircraft technologies have allowed aircraft to fly faster and farther, which offered more flexibility to the airlines to operate ultra long haul flights. This chapter reviews the development of and examines the changes in traveler demand after the introduction of ultra long haul flights. Five ultra long haul routes including Singapore/New York, Perth/London, Singapore/Los Angeles, Manila/New York, and Sydney/Houston were examined. The result has demonstrated that airlines offering ultra long haul flights are obtaining a larger market share between city pairs as passengers were attracted away from direct flights and connecting flights. There was evidence that passengers were willing to purchase premium services for more comfort on most ultra long haul markets where the origin and destination cities are large business centers.

INTRODUCTION

Air transport has been playing an important role in generating benefits for air travelers by offering speedy connectivity between destinations. The improved technology allowed aircraft to fly faster and further, which gave convenience to air travelers by reducing travel time with less technical stops. In the early years of aviation, flying over long distances required multiple stopovers for refueling purposes. The travel time between New York and Los Angeles (3,935 km) in the 1930s was 19 hours with 3 fuel stops (Burke, 2013). The era of mass travel began with the introduction the jetliners in the 1950s which greatly

DOI: 10.4018/978-1-6684-4615-7.ch006

reduced travel time and introduced long haul travel. The first long haul commercial service, London and Johannesburg, was launched by British Overseas Airways Corporation (BOAC) in 1952 (Hollingham, 2017). The flight was served by the De Havilland Comet with 36 passengers onboard, and took 23 hours and 40 minutes with five stops, Rome, Beirut, Khartoum, Entebbe and Livingstone (Villamizar, 2021). The De Havilland Comet had reduced the travel time by 15.2% compared to the piston-engine Hermes airliners which took 27 hours and 55 minutes (BBC, 2007). The aircraft model also allowed BOAC to operate flights to the far east, Tokyo in Japan with 9 stops in 36 hours compared with more than 86 hours using the piston aircraft (Egmond & Westra, 2019). The introduction of widebody aircraft in the 1970s had further changed the air transport industry. The jumbo jet allowed airlines to carry more passengers, fly to greater distances and lower operating costs by almost 50% (Slutsken, 2020). The first B747 flight took off with 324 passengers onboard from New York on 22 January 1970 and arrived in London 7 hours and 20 minutes later. Flying time was greatly reduced by more than 32% compared with the B707 which required a stopover in Newfoundland for refueling purposes (London Air Travel, 2018).

The new aircraft technology has significantly increased the aircraft's flying distance and minimized the need for technical stops. In addition, the relaxation of the regulation of allowing aircraft to fly long distances over water with Extended-range Twin-engine Operational Performance Standards (ETOPS) has given the opportunities and flexibility to the airlines to expand their international network by offering long haul and ultra long haul (ULH) flights (Pandey & Smith, 2014). A previous study by Qantas (2019) claimed that non-stop long haul flight is more popular among passengers. However, non-stop flights are normally 15 – 20% more expensive than direct or connecting flights due to their convenience and the higher operating cost (Hoeller, 2015).

According to the Air Operator Certificate Requirements from the Civil Aviation Authority of Singapore, airlines operating ULH flights are required to deploy an additional 25% of flight crew members (CAAS, 2017), therefore a higher operating cost. On the other hand, other research has argued that ULH travel may pose a serious health risk to some air travelers (Feldscher, 2019), which maintained the attractiveness of connecting flights to many travelers. This study attempts to fill the research gaps of whether (1) air travelers would shift from direct and connecting flights to the ULH non-stop flights; and (2) whether there will be a higher occupancy rate of premium classes with the launch of ULH flights. The finding of this chapter provides evidence to the market performance of the aviation industry so that better decisions can be made by regulators and industry practitioners in further developing the ULH market.

FLIGHT CLASSIFICATIONS AND THE HISTORY OF ULTRA LONG HAUL TRAVEL

Airline flights can be classified based on the routing and flight length.

Routing

Airlines flights are generally divided into three categories based on the routing. Nonstop flights are flights that operate between two cities without any intermediate stop. Direct flights are flights that operate between two cities and make stop(s) in one or more cities before arriving at the destination airport. Generally, these flights carry the same flight number for the entire journey. Connecting flights are flights that operate between two cities and make a change of flights (different plane and flight number) of the same airlines or on other airlines in one or more cities before arriving at the destination airport (Law & Doerflein, 2014). With most airlines are operating hub and spoke networks, the majority of customers are traveling on connecting flight routing.

Flight Length

There was no standardized definition of the types of flights according to their length. As shown in Table 1, there are different versions of definitions of the types of flights based on flying time or flight distance. IATA, ICAO and IFALPA defined short haul flights as the flights that fly less than 6 hours, long haul flights as the flight time ranges between 6 – 16 hours, and ULH flights as those fly more than 16 hours (IATA, ICAO, & IFALPA, 2015; CAPA, 2021). However, a different viewpoint was identified in the U.S. market, short-haul flights are those up to 3 hours flight time, while medium-haul flights take between 3-6 hours. A long-haul flight flies for 6-12 hours, whilst a ULH flight operates for 12 hours or more (Wilkerson, et al., 2010). Eurocontrol measures the length of flights based on the flying distance. Route shorter than 1,500 km is considered short haul, the distance between 1,500 km to 4,000 km is considered medium haul and long haul flights are those flies more than 4,000 km. There is no classification of ULH flights in Europe (Eurocontrol, 2021).

Table 1. Definitions of the types of flights.

	Short Haul	Medium Haul	Long Haul	Ultra Long Haul
IATA, ICAO, IFALPA	<6 hr	-	6 hr – 16 hr	>16 hr
USA	<3 hr	3 hr – 6 hr	6 hr – 12 hr	>12 hr
Eurocontrol	< 1,500km	1,500 km – 4,000 km	> 4,000 km	NA

Aircraft Technology and Ultra Long-Haul Operations

The inauguration of the state of the art aircraft, the Boeing B747 model, was an advancement in the air transport industry. The aircraft allowed airlines to carry more passengers and cargo over a longer distance. The aircraft has greatly enhanced the reliability of operating long haul flights of more than 8,000 km with a capacity exceeding 300 passengers (Billet, 1969). The increased capacity allowed airlines to earn higher profits from long haul services. Flying long distances, especially over large bodies of water had been challenging to airline operations. Twin engine aircraft flying over the Pacific Ocean in the early years were bounded by many restrictions due to the operational constraints of aircraft. The introduction of the quart engine B747 in the 1970s allowed airlines to operate extensive over-water flights (Byington & Miltiadous, 1990). The jumbo jets were capable to fly longer ranges at faster speeds and the increased capacity allowed airlines to offer profitable long haul nonstop transcontinental and transoceanic flights. The Boeing B747-400 was one of the most famous aircraft for long haul operation (Grimme, Bingemer, & Maerten, 2020). Table 2 and figure 1 shows the development of the transpacific route between San Francisco and Hong Kong by Pan American Airways from 1930s to 1970s using different aircraft types. In the 1930s the airline operated a 5 sectors flight from San Francisco to Hong Kong with a B317 clipper

Do Ultra Long Haul Flights Attract More Premium Class Passengers?

and the trip lasted for a total of 7 days. In the 1970s, the introduction of the B747 aircraft allowed the airlines to operate nonstop flights and the trip time has greatly reduced to 14 hours.

Table 2. *The development of Pan American Airways Pacific route between San Francisco and Hong Kong from 1930s to 1970s.*

Year	Route	Aircraft type	Trip time
1930s	San Francisco – Honolulu – Midway Island – Wake Island- Gum – Manila – Hong Kong	B317 Clipper	7 days
1950s	San Francisco – Honolulu – Tokyo - Hong Kong	Stratocruiser	40 hours
1960s	San Francisco – Honolulu - Hong Kong	DC 8	24 hours
1970s	San Francisco - Hong Kong	B747	14 hours

Figure 1. *The route map of Pan American Airways, Pacific route between San Francisco and Hong Kong from 1930s to 1970s. (Source: Delta Flight Museum)*

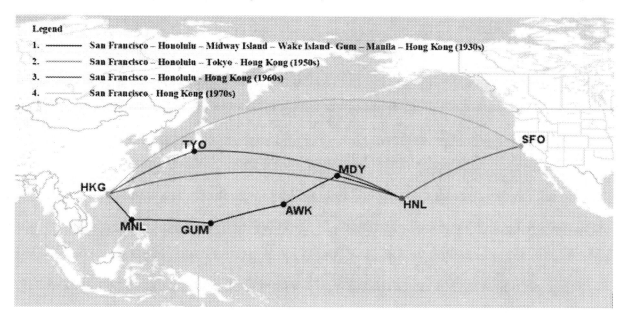

The first ULH flight on a B747-400 was flown by South Africa Airways in 1991 between Johannesburg and New York. The flight flew over a distance of 12,824 km in 17.5 hours (Beveridge, 1991). The record was later broken by United Airlines in 2001 when the U.S. carrier launched a B747-400 nonstop flight between Hong Kong and New York. The flight was made available thanks to the opening up of the China and Russian air space which had shortened the flying distance and time (approximately 2 hours) between Asia and North America continent by allowing airlines to operate transpolar routes (Drescher, 2017). The United Airlines flight covered more than 13,500 km in approximately 15 hours and 40 minutes (Jaffe, 2015). However, due to the operational constraints of restricted payload and the flight was not profitable. The Hong Kong to New York B747-400 service was stretched close to its maximum range, the flight was greatly affected by weight restrictions and unable to carry a full load on some days due to weather and other restrictions. United Airline had operated the route for a few months and decided to withdraw it from the network after the 9-11 incident in the fall of 2001.

Aircraft technology further improved in the 1990s which offered more flexibility to the airlines in their operations. Airbus has introduced the 4 engines A340 series aircraft targeting long haul operations. The aircraft is capable to operate up to 14,450 km with more than 300 passengers onboard. However, the aircraft is not economically efficient for airlines due to its high operating cost leading to a few operators (Airways Magazine, 2020). Singapore Airlines launched the first ULH flight with the A340-500 from Singapore to Los Angeles (16 hours) and later Singapore to New York (18 hrs.) in 2004. Thai Airways has also launched a flight service between Bangkok and New York (17hrs 55 mins) in 2005 using the same aircraft model. However, these services were withdrawn in 2013 and 2008 respectively due to the increasing fuel prices which led to massive losses to the airlines from the operation of the four-engine aircraft (Pande, 2020). Many airlines turned to the twin engine aircraft. The introduction of the newer aircraft design and improved engine reliability permitted airlines to operate long distance over water flights with twin engine aircraft by the Extended-range Twin-engine Operational Performance Standards (ETOPS) rating certification (DeSantis, 2013). The twin engine aircrafts B777 was able to operate on long haul over water flights under special conditions which were favorable to those airlines operating nonstop flights over the Pacific Ocean at lower operating costs. Both the B777-200LR and B777-300ER were the ideal model for airlines to service long-haul intercontinental routes. Compared with the 4 engine aircraft, the operating cost of the extended range version B777-300ER is 15% lower than the B747-400 and 23-25% lower than the A340-500 due to significantly lower fuel burn (Aircraft Commerce, 2018; Boeing, 2013). Continental Airlines launched its Hong Kong to New York services weeks before the United Airlines nonstop service in 2001 covering approximately 12,970 km with the twin engine B777-200ER aircraft. In 2005, Airbus introduced the A380 aircraft to challenge the Boeing 747's dominance of the high capacity long haul market. The four engine A380 aircraft can accommodate 555 passengers and fly up to 15,000 km in range (Olejniczak & Nowacki, 2019). Emirates replaced the nonstop flight between Dubai to Los Angeles from the B777-200LR aircraft with A380 which has been the world's longest Airbus A380 commercial route since 2013 (Loh, 2021). However, this aircraft model was not popular among airlines. Airlines perceived that the aircraft is inefficient to the airlines due to its high operating cost and airlines were facing difficulties in filling the seats of this high capacity aircraft (Thomas, 2019).

The introduction of the new generation aircraft, B787 and A350 has further allowed airlines to operate long haul flights with higher economic feasibility. The first B787 long haul commercial service was launched by All Nippon Airways between Tokyo and Frankfurt in 2012 and the A350 long haul flights were introduced in 2014 by Qatar Airways between Doha and Frankfurt (Hofmann, 2012; Mutzbaugh, 2014). The new aircraft models have improved airline revenue due to higher capacity, better range performance and a significantly lower operating cost, hence a higher profit margin (Kumar, 2015). The Boeing B787-9 Dreamliner was capable to operate up to 14,010 km with a capacity of about 290 passengers (Boeing, 2021) and the Airbus A350-900 can carry up to 315 passengers and fly the range of 15,000 km, the ultra long range version of the A350-900ULR is capable to fly up to 17,960 km with a modified fuel tank design (Airbus, 2021). These new aircraft technologies allowed airlines to further expand their network by operating ULH flights and enabling greater connectivity across the globe.

Do Ultra Long Haul Flights Attract More Premium Class Passengers?

Table 3 shows the specification of aircraft used by airlines to operate long haul and ULH services. The table shows the typical three cabin classes (First, Business and Economy) and two cabin class (Business and Economy) capacity of each aircraft type and the maximum range. Figure 2 shows the comparison of the range and capacity of the ultra long range capable aircraft.

Table 3. Specification of aircraft operating long haul and ULH services. (Source: Airbus 2021, Boeing 2021)

Aircraft Model	Number of Engines	Typical Seat Capacity[1] F: First, C: Business, Y Economy	Max Range
B747-400	4	416 (23F/78C/315Y)	14,045 km
A340-500	4	313 (12F/42C/259Y)	16,670 km
B777-200ER	2	305 (24F/54C/227Y)	13,900 km
B777-200LR	2	301(16F/58C/227Y)	15,843 km
B777-300ER	2	365 (22F/70C/273Y)	13,649 km
A380	4	525 (10F/76C/ 439Y)	15,000 km
B787-9	2	290 (28C/262Y)	14,140 km
A350- 900	2	315 (48C/267Y)	15,000 km
A350-900ULR	2	315 (48C/267Y)	17,960 km

Remark: [1] Manufacturer recommended cabin configuration

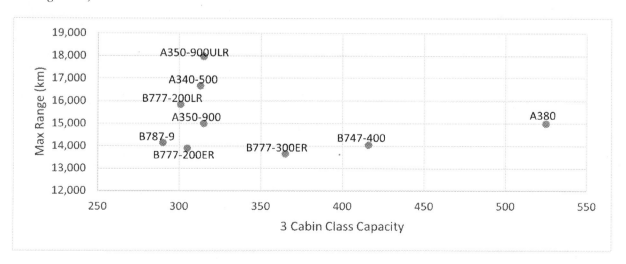

Figure 2. Comparison of the range and capacity of the ultra long haul aircraft. (Source: Airbus 2021, Boeing 2021)

Ultra Long-Haul Routes

The introduction of the new generation aircraft has returned the feasibility of ULH operations due to their cost efficiency (Lee, Li, & Wong, 2019). The majority of the ULH services operated the Trans-Pacific eastbound routes from Asia and Oceania to North America. Based on Statista (2021) data, the world's longest nonstop flight is between Singapore to New York which covered over 15,000 km with a flying time of 18 hours and 40 minutes.

Cabin Classes

The introduction of the wide body aircraft allowed airlines to offer a variety of onboard services to customers. Qantas was the first airline that introduced a separate cabin, business class, from the traditional first class and economy class in 1979. Qantas's business class was available on its long haul B747 operation between Australia and the United States and charged 15% more than the economy fare (Chamberlin, 2021). The concept was adopted by many other airlines and 3 class services on long haul flights have become a norm within the industry ever since. In 1992, EVA Air introduced the premium economy class on its B747 aircraft, which is positioned as the middle ground between economy class and business class. A four cabin classes service was offered on the Taipei to Los Angeles operations (Lazare, 2017). Since then, many airlines have offered four classes services making it an accessible alternative cabin class for all kinds of travelers. However, with the lack of demand and the changes in airline business strategy, some airlines have shed the first class cabin from their service list (Lyon, 2018).

Table 4 and figure 3 shows the detail of the 10 longest nonstop flights as of February 2021. Airlines operating ULH flights have reduced their capacity on the aircraft which aimed to give more room and comfort to the customers. For example, Singapore Airlines' flight between Singapore and New York offered two cabin classes services including business class and premium economy class. Some airlines are employing a different strategy in keeping the traditional 3 cabin classes services such as Emirates and Air India while others are putting their focus on the business class by eliminating the first class such as Qatar Airway, United Airlines, Philippines Airlines and Singapore Airlines.

Table 4. Detail of the 10 longest nonstop flights as of February 2021.

Route	Operating Airlines	F*	C*	P*	Y*	Operating Aircraft	Distance (KM)	Published flying time
Singapore « New York	Singapore Airlines	-	67	94	-	A350-900ULR#	15,347	18hr 40m
Auckland « Doha	Qatar Airways	-	42	-	230	B777-200ER	14,525	18hr 05m
Perth « London	Qantas	-	42	28	166	B787-9#	14,499	17hr 45m
Auckland « Dubai	Emirates	14	76	-	399	A380	14,419	17hr 10m
Singapore « Los Angeles	Singapore Airlines	-	67	94	-	A350-900ULR#	14,096	17hr 50m
Bangalore « San Francisco	Air India	8	35	-	195	B777-200LR	14,001	17hr 45m
Sydney « Houston	United Airlines	-	48	63	141	B787-9#	13,829	17hr 35m
Sydney « Dallas Fort Worth	Qantas	14	64	35	371	A380	13,801	17hr 20m
Manila « New York	Philippine Airlines	-	30	24	214	A350-900 #	13.690	16h 35m
Singapore « San Francisco	Singapore Airlines / United Airlines	-	42 / 48	24 / 63	187 / 141	A350-900#/ B787-9#	13,575	17h 35m

Remark: *F: First Class; C: Business Class; P: Premium Economy Class; Y: Economy Class, # New generation aircraft.

Figure 3. Route map of the 10 longest non-stop flights as of February 2021. (Source: Compiled by authors)

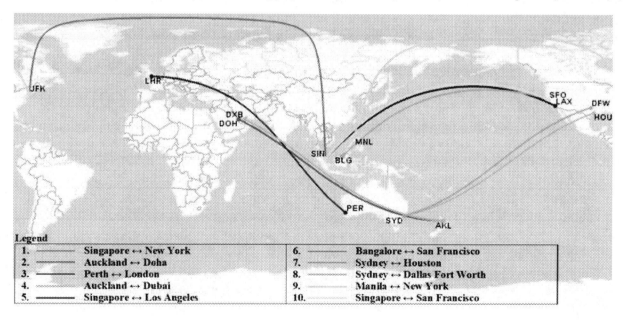

LITERATURE BACKGROUND

Despite the increasing number of ULH flights operating, there were a few studies that covered the ULH flight market. Some previous studies on ULH operation were focused on the economic and operational aspects of the airlines while limited studies focused on the passenger demand perspective. The majority of the previous studies on passenger demand perspective were carried out prior to the introduction of the ULH operations mainly focusing on long haul nonstop operations.

Multiple researchers have studied the fatigue risk management of the flight crew members on ULH flights and the necessity of deploying additional crew onboard to allow adequate inflight rest breaks (Singh, 2003; Werfelman, 2015; Berg, Signal, & Gander, 2019). Some other previous studies have reviewed the commercial viability of ULH flights. Bauer (2019) study has claimed that airlines used ULH services as premium products thus being able to sell at a higher price. The introduction of nonstop flights also stimulated travel demand. According to the study by Grimme, et al. (2020), after Singapore Airlines relaunched the nonstop flight between Singapore and New York in 2018, the number of air travelers between the city pair has increased by 40%. In addition to the passenger load, previous studies have also focused on the airline cargo operation on ULH operation. The study of Baxter, Srisaeng & Wild (2018) has examined and compared the cargo payload of the A350-900XWB and B787-9 operating the route between Singapore and San Francisco. The result of the study has indicated that both aircraft types allowed airlines to carry sufficient air freight even with a full load of passengers achieving operating profits. The profitability of the airline was also contributed by the reduction of the operating cost. The newer aircraft technology has reduced the airlines' operating costs by about 15% which increased the feasibility of airlines operating ULH flights (Bauer, Bloch, & Merkert, 2020).

ULH flight is enabled by advanced technology which allows airlines to offer new nonstop services to passengers. Nonstop flights serving distant cities are appealing to passengers due to the reduced travel time and elimination of hassle at connecting airports. A number of previous studies have researched the passenger satisfaction level of an airline and claimed that airlines offering non-stop flights are favorable compared to those airlines that offer connecting flights. The study of Gilbert and Wong (2003) indicated that nonstop service offered by airlines is an important attribute to the key purchase criteria of air travelers in Hong Kong. Similar findings were also identified in the U.S. market where the airlines operating nonstop flights were more attractive to the passengers (Coldren, et al., 2003; Adler, Falzarano, & Spitz, 2005; Cho, Windle, & Dresner, 2017). Hunt and Truong (2019) have studied the transatlantic market and concluded that comfort, service, convenience and amenities are important to long haul passengers. Milioti, Karlaftis and Akkogiounoglou (2015) have further identified that air travelers are concerned about the flight schedule when making their airline choice, especially business travelers, who were less price sensitive. These passengers have a higher tendency to choose airlines that provide nonstop flights as it saves their time by removing the inconvenience of changing planes. A similar finding was also found in Thailand where the majority of air travelers are favoring nonstop flights and avoid connecting flights (Law, 2017). To compensate, some researchers argued that passengers are more willing to pay for additional services when they are traveling on long haul flights. These included Wi-Fi connectivity and seat selections (Chiambaretto, 2021). Some passengers were also willing to pay extra to upgrade for a better seat on long haul flights. A study by Airbus in 2013 claimed that new generation economy class passengers were ready to pay more on long haul flights. They are willing to pay more for better seat selection such as those on the bulkhead and exit rows and opt for an upgrade in search of more comfort (Kositchotethana, 2013). Kuo and Jou (2017) have identified that some passengers departing from Taipei on long haul flights were willing to pay an average of US$ 454 for a roundtrip upgrade from economy class to premium economy class for more comfort. In addition, there was also a large group of passengers who exchange their mileage points from the airline loyalty program for upgrade awards for longer haul flights.

Flying long haul or ULH flights might not be always favorable to all air travelers. Russon and Vakil (1995) argued that as distance or travel time increases, passenger demand will decrease after reaching a peak. The major concern of taking long haul flights are health and physical discomfort. Zhang and Jiang (2019) claimed that ULH flights flying across multiple time zones would create post health problems to air travelers due to failure to sleep, dehydration, starvation and lack of movement. Yao and Vink (2019) also found that some air travelers have negative perceptions of long haul air travel due to the physical discomfort and feeling of boredom. The corporate air travel survey conducted by IATA (1997) found that jetlag and boredom emerged among business travelers on long haul flights which affect their choice of flights. According to previous health studies, the occurrence of deep venous thrombosis (DVT) and superficial vein thrombosis (SVT) on long haul flights (flights more than 12 hours) is posing a high risk (Scurr, 2002; Aubrey, 2007). As a result, some air travelers preferred taking direct or connecting flights which allowed them to move around while waiting at the connecting airport. In addition, non-stop flights are often more expensive than connecting flights on long haul routes and ULH routes. This is mainly because long haul flights bear a higher business risk compared to other airlines operating a hub and spoke system. The hub and spoke operations allowed airlines to operate with a lower operating cost and higher load factor (Lin, 2010) which allowed the airline to offer lower airfares compared to the nonstop flight in attracting passengers to compensate for the extra travel time required (Lijesen, Rietveld, & Nijkamp, 2002). According to the McKinsey report, direct and connecting flights is still favorable to many air travelers on intercontinental routes who are looking for lower airfares (Bouwer, Krishnan, & Saxon, 2020).

METHODOLOGY AND DATA

To measure the changes in air passenger travel class choices on ULH flights, passenger load data of 5 city pairs were collected including Singapore/New York, Perth/London, Singapore/Los Angeles, Manila/New York and Sydney/Houston. The passenger load data included the total number of passengers per airlines per route as well as the distribution of the passenger load among different cabin classes per route. These five routes were chosen as they are all operated with the newer generation aircraft models and these routes were introduced in a similar period between 2018 to 2019. The Singapore to San Francisco route is not included in the study as the flight was introduced in 2016 which falls outside the study period. Table 5 shows the city's gross domestic product (GDP) and the number of airlines operating at the major airports. The city GDP shows the monetary value of goods and services in the city which also reflects its economic condition while the number of airlines operating at the airport indicates the degree that which the airport is served as a hub with feeding traffic.

Table 5. City GDP and the number of serving airlines. (Source: Compiled by author from various government websites and CAPA, 2021.)

City	Airport	City GDP (billion US$) 2019	Number of serving airlines
London	Heathrow Airport	642	76
New York	John F. Kennedy International Airport, Newark Liberty International Airport, New York LaGuardia airport.	884	74, 28, 9
Houston	George Bush Intercontinental Airport	512	27
Perth	Perth Airport	105	12
Manila	Manila Ninoy Aquino International Airport	192	39
Los Angeles	Los Angeles International Airport	1,088	62
Sydney	Sydney Airport	348	39
Singapore	Changi Airport	339	70

Two sets of monthly data were collected (1) the number of air passengers traveling in both directions between the origin and destinations of the airlines serving the five identified routes. This included those passengers traveling on direct and connecting flights. (2) The number of air passengers traveling on each cabin class in both directions between the origin and destinations on direct, connecting and nonstop flights.

The monthly data between January 2017 to March 2020 (39 months) collected were derived from the OAG traffic analyser. This period was chosen due to the availability of data. The study focuses on the comparative time series analysis to identify the changes in the travel pattern of air travelers. The comparative time series analysis is widely used in air transport demand studies (Weatherford, Gentry, & Wilamowski, 2003; Pitfield, 2007; Faraway & Chatfield, 2008), as it is useful in studying trend changes (Srihari, Mousumi, & Srivatsa, 2020). The data collected for this study were analyzed through the use of the number of air travelers between the two cities and the number of passengers in each cabin class. The moving average of the premium services for each route was calculated to examine the trend of the raw observations in the time series data. Following this, an analysis was completed to compare the studied periods to determine any trends of air travelers shifting between direct flights, connecting flights and the ULH nonstop flights. Additionally, to determine whether there is a cabin class demand changes before and after the launch of ULH flights.

RESULT

This section compares the passenger statistic of the ULH flights, direct flights and connecting flights of the studied route, the market share of the operating airlines and the market share distribution between the premium class and the economy class over the studied period.

Singapore / New York

The flight route between Singapore to New York was served by multiple carriers including those from North America, Asia Pacific, the Middle East and Europe. The larger players for the route included

Do Ultra Long Haul Flights Attract More Premium Class Passengers?

Singapore Airlines, United Airlines, Cathay Pacific, Japan Airlines, EVA Air and Emirates. Other than Singapore Airlines, all other airlines offer connecting flights through their hub or connecting city. Passengers taking United Airlines and Japan Airlines are required to make an aircraft change in Tokyo, those traveling with Cathay Pacific in Hong Kong, EVA Air in Taipei and Emirates in Dubai. Singapore Airlines was the only airline that offered ULH flights between the two cities since 2004. The airline started the nonstop flight service between Singapore and New York in 2004 using the A340-500 aircraft. However, the service was dropped in 2013 due to being unprofitable. The airlines returned the aircraft to the manufacturer for a better deal for the new generation aircraft, the A380 (Rusi, 2013). The shorter range of the A380 required the flight to add a stopover at Frankfurt. In 2018, Singapore Airlines relaunched the ULH flight between Singapore and New York with the new A350-900ULR aircraft offering business class and premium economy class while the services through Frankfurt were also maintained. The ULH flight offered by Singapore Airlines using the new generation aircraft allowed the airlines to offer more comfortable and convenient services to the travelers which helps the airlines gain a higher market share.

Figure 4 shows the air passenger demand of flight types between connecting flights (connect), direct flights (direct) and non-stop ultra long haul flights (ULH). Soon after the introduction of the ULH flight in September 2018, a significant number of passengers were shifted from the connecting flight and the number of passengers taking direct flights also shows a decline.

Figure 4. Passenger demand by flight types. (Source: OAG traffic analyser).

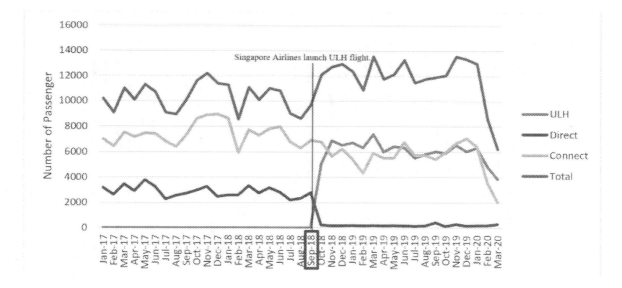

Figure 5 shows that after Singapore Airlines (SQ) introduced the ULH flight, its market share has increased from about 25% in September 2018 to over 48% in October 2019. The market share of the other airlines operating connecting flights between the two cities was diminishing. Cathay Pacific (CX) experienced the greatest reduction followed by United Airlines (UA) and other airlines were also experienced similar conditions.

Figure 5. Market share distribution between operating airlines (Source: OAG traffic analyser).
Remark: EK: Emirates, BR: EVA Air, JL: Japan Airlines, CX: Cathay Pacific, UA: United Airlines, SQ: Singapore Airlines.

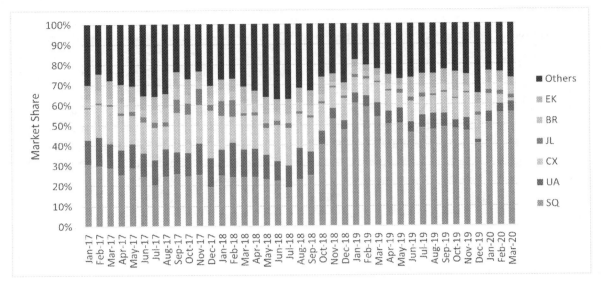

Figure 6. Market share distribution between premium class and economy class. (Source: OAG traffic analyser).

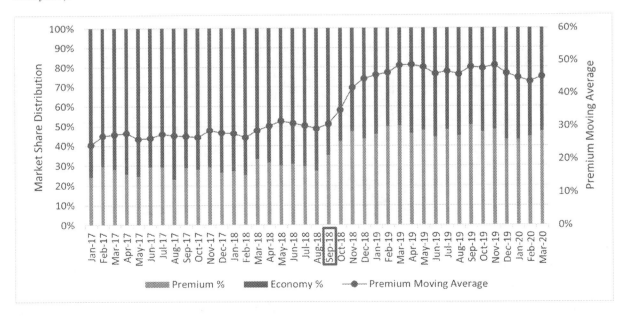

Figure 6 shows the market share of the premium classes and economy class on the Singapore and New York route between 2017 to 2020. The premium cabins consists of the first class, business class and premium economy class. The result shows that after Singapore Airlines introduced the premium ULH flight between Singapore and New York, there was a significant increase in the number of passengers purchasing premium services with an average market share of 64.19% between September 2018 to March 2020. Prior to the introduction of the nonstop service, the market share in the premium service was accounted for an average of 28% between January 2017 to September 2018. Singapore Airlines' market share increased to an average of 46% between October 2018 to March 2020. The results indicated that a significant number of passengers were shifting away from economy class to premium classes. The moving average of the premium classes has also shown a significant increase from September 2018, after the introduction of the ULH service.

Perth / London

The air connectivity between the United Kingdom and Australia (known as the kangaroo route) has a long history dating back to the 1930s connecting the former British colony with its motherland. Traditionally, the passengers are taking Qantas from Brisbane to Singapore and change to Imperial Airways from Singapore to London on a 12.5 day trip. By 1947, Qantas began flying the entire route all by itself by using a newly purchases Lockheed Constellations aircraft. The flight took 58 hours trip from Sydney to London via Darwin, Singapore, Calcutta, Karachi, Cairo, Castel Benito, and Rome (Curran, 2020). The kangaroo route has been one of the most competitive routes in the world today. In 2018, more than 20 airlines were participating in the sector mainly from the Asia Pacific including Cathay Pacific through Hong Kong, Singapore Airlines through Singapore, Garuda Indonesia through Jakarta, Thai Airways through Bangkok and Malaysia Airlines through Kuala Lumpur (Smith, 2018). Over the last decade, airlines from China and the Gulf also joined the battle. With a distance of over 15 thousand kilometers apart, operating direct flight was impossible in the early years. The introduction of the Boeing 747 in the 1970s has offered higher operational efficiency allowing the airlines to minimize the multiple connecting stops to one stop only. In March 2018, Qantas further extended the kangaroo route to a nonstop operation. The extended range of B787-9 aircraft allowed Qantas to offer 17 hours ULH flights between

Figure 7. Passenger demand by flight types. (Source: OAG traffic analyser).

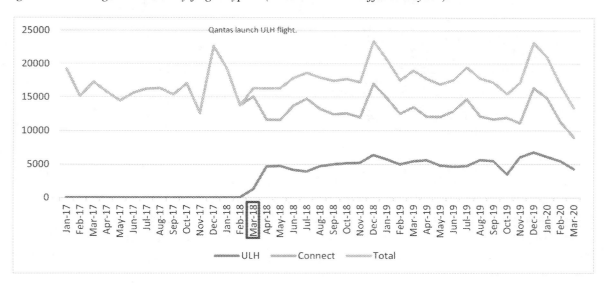

Figure 8. Market share distribution between operating airlines. (Source: OAG traffic analyser).
Remark: SQ: Singapore Airlines, QR: Qatar Airways, MH: Malaysia Airlines, EY: Etihad Airways, EK: Emirates, QF: Qantas Airways.

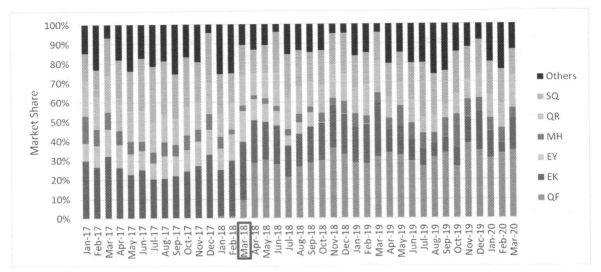

Figure 9. Market share distribution between premium class and economy class. (Source: OAG traffic analyser).

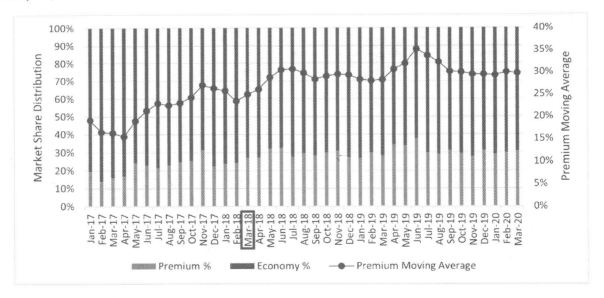

UK and Australia. Qantas flight QF10 operates from Melbourne to Perth then continues to London replacing the 25 hours flight from Melbourne to London via Dubai.

The nonstop kangaroo flight offered by Qantas allowed the airlines to offer more convenience to travelers. Figure 7 shows the air passenger choice of flights between connecting flights and ULH flights. The ULH service by Qantas in March 2018 has attracted a total of 1,274 passengers in the starting month.

Do Ultra Long Haul Flights Attract More Premium Class Passengers?

The total passenger demand between the two cities has shown some increment. The passenger load maintained steady from April 2018 to Mar 2020 with an average of over 5,000 passengers per month. The demand of the airline operating connecting flights was affected in the first few months.

Figure 8 has shown the market share of airlines offering services between Perth and London. Prior to the ULH flight, Qantas' market share was positioned at around 1.1% with passengers traveling from Perth to Singapore and connecting to the London bound flight from Sydney. The airlines' market share significantly increased to an average of 30% soon after the launch of the ULH flight between Perth and London and became the biggest player on this route. Meanwhile, the market share of other competitor airlines has decreased notably, especially the airlines offering premium services such as Emirates and Etihad. Prior to Qantas entering the market, Emirates and Etihad have gained about 30% and 12% of the market share respectively. Emirates' market share had diminished to an average of 16% between April 2018 and March 2020 while Etihad had exited the fiercely competing market in October 2018.

Figure 9 compares the premium classes and economy class market share of the Perth and London service between 2017 and 2020. The result shows that after Qantas initiated the nonstop flight between Perth and London, there was some increment of passengers purchasing premium services. The result is showing that some passengers have shifted away from the economy class to premium services. Prior to the introduction of the nonstop service, the average market share of the premium service was 22% from January 2017 to February 2018 and increased to an average of 30% between March 2018 and March 2020. The moving average of the premium class market share has demonstrated growth since March 2018.

Singapore / Los Angeles

The Singapore and Los Angeles is a highly competitive route with many airlines offering connecting services. The major players included United Airlines which connects passengers through Hong Kong and Tokyo; and Singapore Airlines via Taipei and Seoul. Many other airlines in the Asia Pacific also offers connecting through their hub including Cathay Pacific via Hong Kong, China Airlines via Taipei, Japan Airlines via Tokyo and Korean Air via Seoul to name a few. Singapore Airlines launched Singapore to Los Angeles ULH flights in 2004 with its A340-500 and B777-200LR aircraft. However, the ULH services were terminated in 2013 due to unprofitable and the connecting flight via Seoul resumed afterward (CAPA, 2013). The ULH flights between Singapore and Los Angeles were relaunched by United Airlines in 2017 with 3 cabin classes (Business, Premium Economy and Economy) B787-9 aircraft. The services lasted for about a year when United Airlines terminated the ULH flight in 2018 and started the second daily nonstop flight to San Francisco. The ULH services between Singapore and Los Angeles were picked up by Singapore Airlines in the same year using 2 cabin classes (Business and Premium Economy) A350-900ULR aircraft.

Figure 10 shows the air passenger choice of flights between connecting flights, direct flights and ULH flights for the route between Singapore and Los Angeles. The passenger demand has significantly increased by 177% between September and November 2017 after United Airlines launched the ULH flight between Singapore and Los Angeles in October 2017. The passenger demand on direct and connecting flight have encountered a decrease of 11% and 2% respectively. As United Airlines ended the ULH service in October 2018, the number of passengers traveling on the connecting flights was observed an increase. However, soon after Singapore Airlines started the ULH route in November 2018, the passenger demand for the ULH returned. After the launch of the ULH flights, there were still a significant number of passengers taking connecting flights offered by the respective airlines.

Figure 10. Passenger demand by flight types. (Source: OAG traffic analyser).

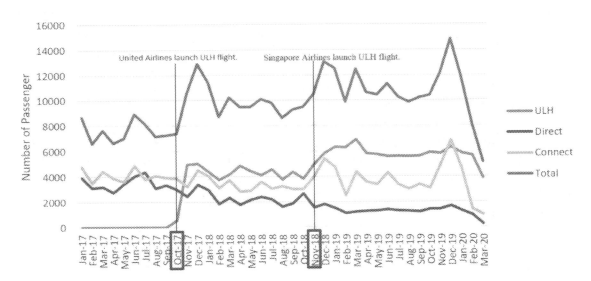

Figure 11. Market share distribution between operating airlines (Source: OAG traffic analyser).
Remark: CZ: China Southern Airlines, CI: China Airlines, CX: Cathay Pacific, BR: EVA Air, UA: United Airlines, SQ: Singapore Airlines.

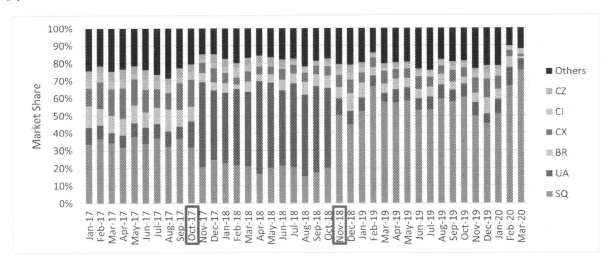

Figure 11 shows the market share among the airlines offering services between Singapore and Los Angeles. United Airlines' market share has gained significant growth after launching the ULH service. The market share of United Airlines has increased from an average of 8% prior to the launch of the ULH service (January 2017 to September 2017) to an average of 43% after the launch of the ULH service (October 2017 to October 2018). As the airline dropped the market, its market share has declined to

Do Ultra Long Haul Flights Attract More Premium Class Passengers?

Figure 12. Market share distribution between premium class and economy class. (Source: OAG traffic analyser).

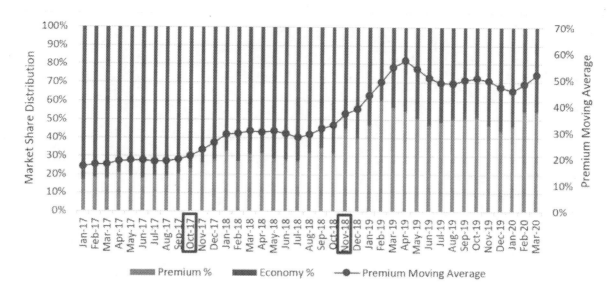

an average of 7% between November 2018 to March 2020. On the other hand, Singapore Airlines have taken over the ULH service in November 2018, its market share has increased from an average of 27% between January 2017 and October 2018 to an average of 57% between November 2018 and March 2020.

Figure 12 shows the share of the premium classes and economy class of the Singapore and Los Angeles route between 2017 and 2020. The result indicates that after United Airlines introduced the nonstop flight, there was some shift of passengers from economy service to premium services. Prior to the introduction of the nonstop service, the market share of the premium services was accounted for an average of 19% between January 2017 and September 2018. The premium service's market share expanded to an average of more than 29% between October 2018 and October 2019. As Singapore airlines picked up the service in November 2019, the premium service market share has further increased to an average of 50% in the period between November 2019 and March 2020. The results indicate a significant increment of the moving average of premium classes from October 2017 after the ULH flight was first launched.

Manila / New York

The long history of connectivity between the Philippines and America has made the route one of the oldest transpacific routes. The Philippines was the first U.S. colony since the 18th century and air transport has played an important role to connect the Philippines to its motherland. In the 1940s, Pan American Airways operated transpacific flights between New York and Manila via Honolulu, Wake Island and Guam. Today, there were many airlines in North Asia and the Middle East offering connecting services between Manila to New York through their hub airports. These airlines included Cathay Pacific via Hong Kong, Japan Airlines and All Nippon Airways via Tokyo, Korean Air and Asiana through Seoul, Qatar through Doha and Emirates via Dubai. The introduction of modern airliners allowed Philippines Airlines to begin direct flights between Manila to New York with a transit stop in Vancouver in 2015

Figure 13. Passenger demand by flight types. (Source: OAG traffic analyser).

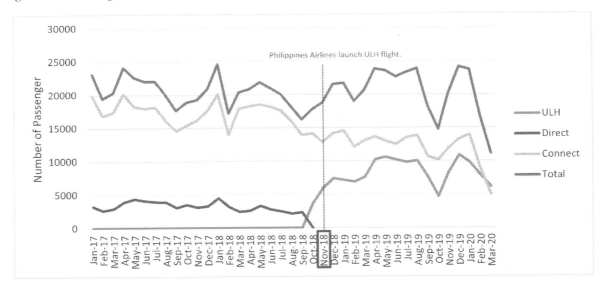

Figure 14. Market share distribution between operating airlines. (Source: OAG traffic analyser).
Remark: OZ: Asiana Airlines, KE: Korean Air, CX: Cathay Pacific, CI: China Airlines, BR: EVA Air, PR: Philippines Airlines.

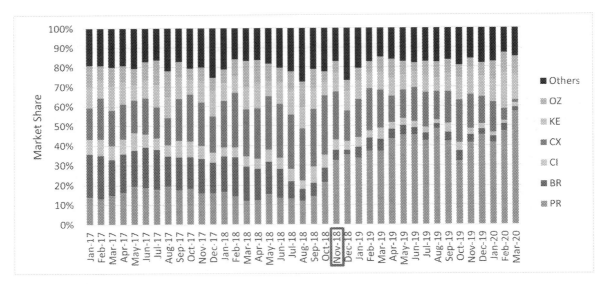

(Vancouver Airport Authority, 2015). In 2018, Philippines Airlines have further strengthened the service by offering ULH service between the two metropolitans using the newly purchased A350 aircraft and dropped the connecting flight service. Philippines Airlines offer 3 class cabins (Business, Premium Economy and Economy) on this 16 plus hour flight which is categorized as one of the longest routes in the world in 2018 (Ellis, 2018).

Figure 15. Market share distribution between premium class and economy class. (Source: OAG traffic analyser).

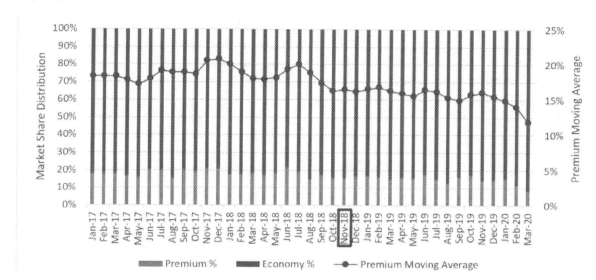

Figure 13 shows the air passenger demand of connecting flights, direct flights and the ULH flight. The introduction of the ULH flight by Philippines Airlines between Manila and New York in October 2018 has attracted some air traveler demand from the direct and connecting flights. The total passenger demand between the two cities maintained steady with an average of over 19,000 passengers a month and the demand for connecting flights has been observed to decline.

Figure 14 shows the market share among the airlines offering services between Manila and New York. Philippines Airlines' market share has gained sufficient growth after the introduction of the ULH service. The airlines' market share has increased from an average of 15% prior to the launch of the ULH (January 2017 to September 2018) to an average of 41% in the period between October 2018 to March 2020. EVA Air and Cathay Pacific Airways were heavily affected. Prior to the launch of the ULH flight, EVA Air and Cathay Pacific Airways' market share were 16% and 21% and their market share has decreased to 4% and 10% respectively.

Figure 15 shows the share of the premium classes and economy class on the Manila and New York route between 2017 to 2020. The result indicates that the premium market share was steadily sustained at an average of 19% prior to October 2018. The premium classes market share shows a trend of a decrease to an average of 15% between October 2018 to March 2020.

Sydney/ Houston

The nonstop flight between Sydney and Houston was launched in January 2018 by United Airlines which makes it one of the longest routes in the world using the B787-9 aircraft. As a major hub and gateway to Latin America and the Caribbean, Houston was a strategic location that allowed travelers to make connections to more than 170 destinations. Prior to the introduction of the ULH flights, travelers traveling between Sydney and Houston are required to make a connection at Auckland, San Francisco, Los

Figure 16. Passenger demand by flight types. (Source: OAG traffic analyser).

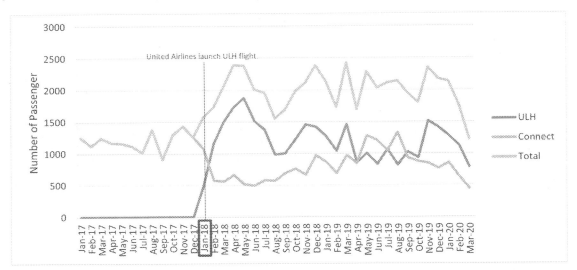

Figure 17. Market share distribution between operating airlines
Remark: QF: Qantas Airways, NZ: Air New Zealand, UA: United Airlines.

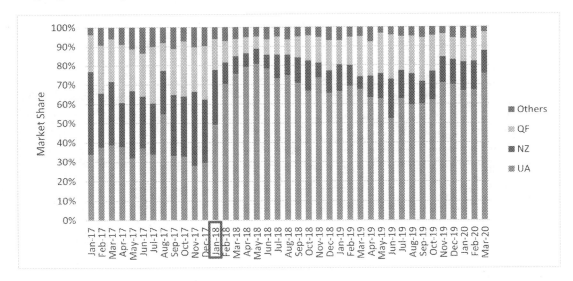

Angeles or Vancouver. The ULH flight service has given air travelers convenience by reducing waiting time at the connecting airports.

Figure 16 shows the air passenger demand between connecting flights, direct flights and ULH flights for the route between Sydney and Houston. A significant increase in total passenger demand was observed from January 2018. The passenger demand has increased about 90% in January 2018 compared to the previous month. The growth was observed after United Airlines introduced the ULH flight and

Figure 18. Market share distribution between premium class and economy class.

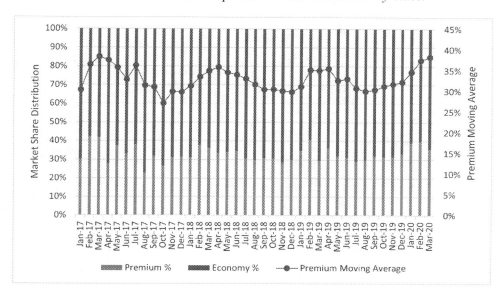

the passengers traveling on connecting flights were observed a significant drop in January and February 2018 and became steady for around a year.

Figure 17 shows the market share of airlines offering services between Sydney and Houston. United Airlines' market share has gained a significant increment after the introduction of the ULH service. The airlines' market share has increased from 30% in December 2017 to about 70% in February 2018. United Airlines have obtained an average market share of about 70% for the air transport market between Sydney and Houston from January 2018 to March 2020. Air New Zealand and Qantas market shares were heavily affected. Air New Zealand's market share has decreased from an average of 31% prior to the launch of the ULH service (January 2017 to January 2018) to an average of about 13% in the period between February 2018 and March 2020 while Qantas' market share has declined from an average of 24% to 14%.

Figure 18 shows the share of the premium classes and economy class of the Sydney and Houston air transport service between 2017 to 2020. A little increment of passengers traveling in premium classes was observed, which indicated that limited passengers have shifted from economy class to premium services after the introduction of the ULH service. Prior to the introduction of the nonstop service, the market share of the premium service was accounted for an average of 33% between January 2017 and December 2017. The premium service market stayed steadily at an average of 33% between January 2018 and March 2022.

Table 6 shows the summary of the average market share to the percentage changes of the airlines operating ULH flights and Table 7 shows the average percentage of premium services on the chosen routes. The airlines that offered ULH flights were observed to have significant positive percentage changes to the market share for all routes. The premium services of Singapore – New York, Singapore – Los Angeles and Perth – London were observed to have increased after the launch of the ULH flights. A decline was observed in the Manila – New York route while Sydney – Houston was observed unchanged.

Table 6. Summary of the average market share to the percentage changes of the airlines operating ULH flight

Route	ULH airlines	Average Market Share Prior to ULH	Average Market Share After ULH	Percentage Change
Singapore – New York	Singapore Airlines	Jan 2017 - Aug 2018	Sep 2018 - Mar 2020	+100%
		25%	50%	
Singapore – Los Angeles	United Airlines	Jan 2017 – Sep 2017	Oct 2017 - Mar 2020	+438%
		8%	43%	
	Singapore Airlines	Jan 2017 - Oct 2018	Nov 2018 - Mar 2020	+111%
		27%	57%	
Manila – New York	Philippines Airlines	Jan 2017 - Oct 2018	Nov 2018 - Mar 2020	+163%
		16%	42%	
Perth - London	Qantas	Jan 2017 - Feb 2018	Mar 2018 - Mar 2020	+13,536%
		0.22%	30%	
Sydney - Houston	United Airlines	Jan 2017 - Dec 2017	Jan 2018 - Mar 2020	+86%
		37%	69%	

Table 7. shows the average percentage of premium service before and after the launch of the ULH.

Route	Average Premium Service % Prior to ULH	Average Premium Service % After ULH	Percentage Change
Singapore – New York	Jan 2017 - Aug 2018	Sep 2018 - Mar 2020	+64%
	28%	46%	
Singapore – Los Angeles	Jan 2017 – Sep 2017	Oct 2017 - Mar 2020	+72%
	29%	50%	
Manila – New York	Jan 2017 - Oct 2018	Nov 2018 - Mar 2020	-21%
	19%	15%	
Perth - London	Jan 2017 - Feb 2018	Mar 2018 - Mar 2020	+36%
	22%	30%	
Sydney - Houston	Jan 2017 - Dec 2017	Jan 2018 - Mar 2020	0%
	33%	33%	

DISCUSSION

The introduction of ULH flights has created some changes to the industry. The results from the study have indicated that airlines offering ULH flights are obtaining a larger market share between cities pairs. The ULH flights are attracting passengers away from those airlines offering connecting flights. The result is in line with the study of Gilbert & Wong (2003); Adler, Falzarano, & Spitz (2005); Coldren, Koppelman, Kasturirangan, & Mukherjee (2003); Cho, Windle, & Dresner (2017) which their studies indicated that airlines operating nonstop flights were more attractive compared to those offering connecting flights.

The result of this study also shows evidence of passengers are willing to purchase premium services for more comfort in some ULH markets. The result is also in line with the study of Kositchotethana (2013); Kuo & Jou (2017); Law (2017). However, the study has also concluded that certain ULH markets might not generate additional passengers taking premium classes such as Manila/New York and Sydney/Houston. Many potential factors could influence the passengers' choice including the affordability of the passengers, hub airports with feeding airlines, airline alliances and airline quality.

a.   Affordability of the passengers

The purchasing power of the passengers from the catchment areas of the origin and destination airport would have a direct impact on the number of passengers purchasing premium services. Business destinations generally have a higher number of business travelers who are less price sensitive and will pay more for comfort. However, as shown in Table 5, the city GDP of Manila in 2019 was accounted for 192 billion US dollars which is relatively lower compared with other cities in the Asia Pacific region. With a lower GDP, the number of business travelers who could afford the airlines' premium services might be less compared to other routes in this study. The lower GDP also indicated that the economic activity in Manila is limited, which might not generate a sizeable market of business travelers for ULH flight services. The GDP of Perth is the lowest amongst all the cities as shown in Table 5. The following section will explain the possible reason that the performance of the route Perth/London is much better than Manila/New York.

b.   Hub airports with feeding airlines

The number of airlines serving an airport influences the passenger load of the premium cabin classes. Table 5 showed that airports in London, New York, Los Angeles and Singapore have a significantly higher number of serving airlines while Sydney, Houston, Perth and Manila have a limited number of serving airlines. The findings suggest that the route connecting two major hub airports with a large number of serving airlines at both ends can provide feeding traffic of business travelers to the ULH premium services. The route of Singapore/New York and Singapore/Los Angeles support this argument. When one end of the route is not serving at a major hub airport, then it depends on if there is a specific route that carries strong feeding traffic of business travelers to ULH flights. The Qantas' Perth to London service showed strong evidence that the ULH flight was supported by the feeding passengers from Melbourne, which is a strong origin of the feeding traffic of business travelers. Since the distance between Melbourne and London exceeds the flying range of all types of aircraft, Qantas operated Perth/London ULH service to serve travelers from Melbourne. In the case of Manila/New York, Manila is not a major hub airport while there is lacking specific routes that can bring strong business traffic to feed the ULH premium classes. The route of Sydney/Houston is a case where both ends of the route are not major hub airports, there was no increment to the premium services after the launch of the ULH service.

c.   Airline Alliances

Airlines belonging to an alliance network could also help to feed passengers. Philippines Airlines does not involve in any airline alliance and therefore they are unable to enjoy the passenger traffic generated by other airlines.

d. Airline Quality

Air travelers choose an airline based on the quality of facilities and services offered. This is extremely important to business travelers as they have higher expectations compared with other traveler types. These travelers normally select an airline based on the quality. Comparing the airlines in this study, Singapore Airlines scored 5 stars in the Skytrax certified rating, Qantas and Philippines airlines graded with 4 stars and United Airlines with 3 stars (Skytrax, 2022). The result has shown some evidence that airlines with lower quality are attracting fewer premium customers.

CONCLUSION AND REMAINING ISSUES FOR FUTURE RESEARCH

This chapter has reviewed the history and development of ULH flights in international air transport. The development of aircraft technologies gave airlines the flexibility to operate long haul operations with profitability. The 5 ULH routes were examined which shows that air travelers were shifted from the direct and connecting flights to the ULH flights. Interestingly, not all ULH flights attract premium travelers. Those flights operate between international business destinations and major international hubs tend to attract more passengers traveling in the premium class. As a result, the airlines should only operate ULH flights with city pairs where there are sufficient business travelers and feeding customers at the hub airports. The study has concluded that the novel phenomenon of ULH flights is generating a competitive advantage for the operating airlines. In addition, the COVID-19 pandemic might have changed the air travelers' behavior as it is likely that air travelers will try to avoid connecting flights to minimize the exposure risk at the stopover airports. This gives the airlines plenty of opportunities to launch and/or expand their ULH flights serving more destinations.

However, there were many other potential factors influencing the ULH operations. These include the zero emission air transport rules beyond 2030 and the air travelers' behavior toward premium cabins on ULH flights in the new normal era. These factors should be raised and addressed in future air transport research works to further evaluate the ULH business model.

REFERENCES

Adler, T. J., Falzarano, S., & Spitz, G. (2005). Modeling Service Trade-Offs in Air Itinerary Choices. Transportation Research Record: Journal of the Transportation Research Board, (1), 20–26.

Airbus. (2021). *A350-900 Sharping the Future of Air Travel.* Airbus. https://aircraft.airbus.com/en/aircraft/a350/a350-900

Aircraft Commerce. (2018). *A350-900/-1000 fuel burn & operating performance.* Aircraft Commerce. https://www.aircraft-commerce.com/sample_article_folder/121_FLTOPS_A.pdf

Airways Magazine. (2020). A340-600's Progressive Withdrawal. *Airways Magazine.* https://airwaysmag.com/airlines/a340-600-withdrawn/

Aubrey, A. (2007). *Move Around on Long Flights to Prevent Blood Clots.* National Public Radio. https://www.npr.org/templates/story/story.php?storyId=12593776

Bauer, L. (2019). *The Commercial Viability of Ultra Long-Haul Operations. Evidence from Qantas' Perth-London Service.* GRIN Verlag.

Bauer, L., Bloch, D., & Merkert, R. (2020). Ultra Long-Haul: An emerging business model accelerated by COVID-19. *Journal of Air Transport Management, 89*, 101901. doi:10.1016/j.jairtraman.2020.101901 PMID:32839647

Baxter, G., Srisaeng, P., & Wild, G. (2018). The Air Cargo Carrying Potential of the Airbus 350-900XWB and Boeing 787-9 Aircraft on their Long Haul Flight: Case Study for flights from San Francisco to Singapore. *Transport and Telecommunication, 19*(4), 301–314. doi:10.2478/ttj-2018-0025

Berg, M. J., Signal, T., & Gander, P. (2019). Perceived Workload Is Associated with Cabin Crew Fatigue on Ultra-Long Range Flights. *The International Journal of Aerospace Psychology, 3-4*(3-4), 74–85. doi:10.1080/24721840.2019.1621177

Beveridge, D. (1991). *South African resumes flights to N.Y. Pittsburgh Post Gazette.*

Billet, A. B. (1969). *Hydraulic System State-of-the-Art Advances on the 747 Airplane.* AE Technical Paper 690670, 1969, 1-11.

Boeing. (2013). *Made with Japan: A Partnership on the Frontiers of Aerospace.* Boeing.

Boeing. (2021). *Boeing 787 Dreamliner.* Boeing. https://www.boeing.com/commercial/787/#/family

Bouwer, J., Krishnan, V., & Saxon, S. (2020). *Will airline hubs recover from COVID-19?* McKinsey.

British Broadcasting Corporation (BBC). (2007). *1952: Comet inaugurates the jet age.* British Broadcasting Corporation (BBC). http://news.bbc.co.uk/onthisday/hi/dates/stories/may/2/newsid_2480000/2480339.stm

Burke, K. (2013). How the DC-3 Revolutionized Air Travel. *Smithsonian.* https://www.smithsonianmag.com/history/how-the-dc-3-revolutionized-air-travel-5444300/

Byington, M. R., & Miltiadous, M. (1990). Optimized Engine-Out Procedures to Extend the Range of Jet. *Journal of Aviation/Aerospace Education Research, 1*(1), 17–37. doi:10.15394/JAAER.1999.1007

Center for Asia Pacific Aviation (CAPA). (2013). *Singapore Airlines upcoming termination of non-stops to US spells end to ultra long-range travel.* CAPA. https://centreforaviation.com/analysis/reports/singapore-airlines-upcoming-termination-of-non-

Center for Asia Pacific Aviation (CAPA). (2021). *Aviation Industry Glossary.* CAPA. https://centreforaviation.com/about/glossary

Chamberlin, C. (2021). Did Qantas really 'invent' business class? *Executive Travelers.* https://www.executivetraveller.com/did-qantas-invent-business-class

Chiambaretto, P. (2021). Air passengers' willingness to pay for ancillary services on long-haul flights. *Transportation Research Part E, Logistics and Transportation Review, 147*, 102234.

Cho, W., Windle, R., & Dresner, M. (2017). The impact of operational exposure and value-of-time on customer choice: Evidence from the airline industry. *Transportation Research Part A, Policy and Practice*, *103*, 455–471.

Civil Aviation Authority Singapore (CAAS). (2017). *Air Operator Certificate Requirements*. Civil Aviation Authority Singapore. Retrieved from: https://www.caas.gov.sg

Coldren, G., Koppelman, F. S., Kasturirangan, K., & Mukherjee, A. (2003). Modeling aggregate air-travel itinerary shares: Logit model development at a major US airline. *Journal of Air Transport Management*, 6, 361–369.

Curran, A. (2020). *The History of the Kangaroo Route*. Simple Flying. https://simpleflying.com/kangaroo-route-history/

Delta Flight Museum. (2022). *Family Tree*. Delta Flight Museum. https://www.deltamuseum.org/exhibits/delta-history/family-tree/pan-am

DeSantis, J. A. (2013). Engines Turn or Passengers Swim: A Case Study of How ETOPS Improved Safety and Economics in Aviation. *Journal of Air Law and Commerce*, 77(4), 1–68.

Drescher, C. (2017). Why Airplanes Sometimes Fly Over the North Pole. *Condé Nast Traveler*. https://www.cntraveler.com/story/why-airplanes-sometimes-fly-over-the-north-pole

Egmond, R. v., & Westra, A. (2019). *Shell and aviation. The story of more than a century of collaboration*. Shell International B.V. HR.

Ellis, C. (2018). *PAL's non-stop Manila – New York JFK flight among world's longest*. Aerotime Hub. https://www.aerotime.aero/21979-pal-s-non-stop-manila-new-york-jfk-flight-among-world-s-longest

Eurocontrol. (2021). *EUROCONTROL Data Snapshot #4 on CO_2 emissions by flight distance*. Eurocontrol. https://www.eurocontrol.int/publication/eurocontrol-data-snapshot-co2-emissions-flight-distance

Faraway, J., & Chatfield, C. (2008). Time series forecasting with neural networks: A comparative study using the airline data. *Journal of the Royal Statistical Society Applied Statistic Series C*, *47*(2), 231–250.

Feldscher, K. (2019). *The potentially unfriendly skies*. Harvard T.H Chan. https://www.hsph.harvard.edu/news/features/the-potentially-unfriendly-skies/

Gilbert, D., & Wong, R. K. (2003). Passenger expectations and airline services: A Hong Kong based study. *Tourism Management*, *24*(5), 519–532.

Grimme, W., Bingemer, S., & Maerten, S. (2020). An analysis of the prospects of ultra-long-haul airline operations using passenger demand data. *Transportation Research Procedia*, *51*, 208–216.

Hoeller, S.-C. (2015). Here's the difference between a nonstop and direct flight. *Business Insider*. https://www.businessinsider.com/the-difference-between-a-nonstop-and-direct-flight-2015-9

Hofmann, K. (2012). ANA begins first 787 long-haul service. *Aviation Week*. Retreived from: https://aviationweek.com/air-transport/airports-routes/ana-begins-first-787-long-haul-service

Hollingham, R. (2017). *The British airliner that changed the world*. South African History Online. https://www.bbc.com/future/article/20170404-the-british-airliner-that-changed-the-world

Hunt, J., & Truong, D. (2019). Low-fare flights across the Atlantic: Impact of low-cost, long- haul trans-Atlantic flights on passenger choice of Carrier. *Journal of Air Transport Management, 75*, 170–184.

IATA, ICAO, & IFALPA. (2015). Fatigue Risk Management Systems (FRMS) implementation Guide for Operators. IATA, ICAO, IFALPA.

International Air Transport Association (IATA). (1997). *Corporate Air Travel Survey*. IATA Aviation Information and Research.

Jaffe, S. D. (2015). *Airspace Closure and Civil Aviation: A Strategic Resource for Airline Managers*. Routledge.

Kositchotethana, B. (2013). Economy passengers willing to pay more for comfort. *Bangkok Post*. https://www.bangkokpost.com/business/381103/economy-passengers-willing-to-pay-more-for-comfort

Kumar, D. (2015). *Building Sustainable Competitive Advantage: Through Executive Enterprise Leadership*. Routledge.

Kuo, C.-W., & Jou, R.-C. (2017). Willingness to pay for airlines' premium economy class: The perspective of passengers. *Journal of Air Transport Management, 59*, 134–142.

Law, C. (2017). The Study of Customer Relationship Management in Thai Airline Industry: A Case of Thai Travelers in Thailand. *Journal of Airline and Airport Management, 7*(1), 13–42.

Law, C., & Doerflein, M. (2014). *Introduction to Airline Ground Service*. Cengage.

Lazare, L. (2017). EVA Air's long love affair with the iconic Boeing 747 is officially over. *Chicago Business Journal*. https://www.bizjournals.com/chicago/news/2017/08/22/eva-airs-longlove-affair-with-the-iconic-boeing.html

Lee, M., Li, L. K., & Wong, W. (2019). Analysis of direct operating cost of wide-body passenger aircraft: A parametric study based on Hong Kong. *Chinese Journal of Aeronautics, 32*(5), 1222–1243.

Lijesen, M. G., Rietveld, P., & Nijkamp, P. (2002). How do carriers price connecting flights? Evidence from intercontinental flights from Europe. *Transportation Research Part E, Logistics and Transportation Review, 28*(3-4), 239–252.

Lin, C. (2010). The integrated secondary route network design model in the hierarchical hub- and-spoke network for dual express services. *International Journal of Production Economics, 123*(1), 20–30.

Loh, C. (2021). *Record Smashing: What Is The Longest Airbus A380 Flight?* Simple Flying. https://simpleflying.com/longest-airbus-a380-flight/

London Air Travel. (2018). *60 Years of the Transatlantic Jet Age*. London Air Travel. https://londonairtravel.com/2018/10/04/the-transatlantic-jet-age/

Lyon, J. (2018). First class is shrinking on airlines and it may disappear altogether. *Business Insider*. https://www.businessinsider.com/first-class-shrinking-airlines-may-disappear-altogether-2018-11

Milioti, C., Karlaftis, M. G., & Akkogiounoglou, E. (2015). Traveler perceptions and airline choice: A multivariate probit approach. *Journal of Air Transport Management, 49*, 46–52.

Mutzabaugh, B. (2014). World's first Airbus A350 route will be Doha-Frankfurt. *USA Today*. https://www.usatoday.com/story/todayinthesky/2014/10/20/worlds-first-airbus-a350-route-will-be-doha-frankfurt/17644483/

Olejniczak, D., & Nowacki, M. (2019). Assessment of the selected parameters of aerodynamics for Airbus A380 aircraft on the basis of CFD tests. *Transportation Research Procedia, 40*, 839–846.

Pande, P. (2020). *How The Airbus A340-500 Opened The Door To The Longest Flight*. Simple Flying. https://simpleflying.com/airbus-a340-500-longest-flight/

Pandey, M., & Smith, B. (2014). *ETOPS: Expansion in the North Pacific Market*. Boeing. https://www.boeing.com/commercial/aeromagazine/aero_04/fo/fo01/index.html

Pitfield, D. E. (2007). Ryanair's Impact on Airline Market Share from the London Area Airports: A Time Series Analysis. *Journal of Transport Economics and Policy, 41*(1), 75–92.

Porter, S. (2018). *The world's longest non-stop flight takes off from Singapore*. British Broadcasting Corporation. https://www.bbc.com/news/business-45795573

Qantas. (2019). *New Qantas Research Reveals What Customers Really Want on Ultra long Flights*. Qantas Airways. https://www.qantasnewsroom.com.au/media-releases/new-qantas-research-reveals-what-customers-really-want-on-ultra-long-haul-flights/

Rusi, S. (2013). *Singapore Airlines gives up the longest non-stop operating route (Newark – Singapore)*. Airlines Travel. https://en.airlinestravel.ro/singapore-airlines-has-discontinued-the-longest-non-stop-newark-singapore-route.html

Russon, M., & Vakil, F. (1995). Population, convenience and distance decay in a short-haul model of United States air transportation. *Journal of Transport Geography, 3*(3), 179–195.

Scurr, J. (2002). Travellers' thrombosis. *Perspectives in Public Health, 122*(1), 11–13.

Singh, J. (2003). Study on Pilot Alertness Highlights Feasibility for Ultra Long Range Flight Operations. *ICAO Journal, 58*(1), 14–15.

Skytrax. (2022). *World Airline Star Rating*. Skytrax. https://skytraxratings.com/about-airline-rating

Slutsken, H. (2020). *Five ways Boeing's 747 jumbo jet changed travel*. Cable News Network (CNN). https://edition.cnn.com/travel/article/boeing-747-jumbo-jet-travel/index.html

Smith, P. S. (2018). *'Kangaroo Route' Dynamics See New Market Entrants*. Aviation International News (AIN). https://www.ainonline.com/aviation-news/air-transport/2018-02-04/kangaroo-route-dynamics-see-new-market-entrants

Srihari, A., Mousumi, P., & Srivatsa, K. (2020). A Comparative Study and Analysis of Time Series Forecasting Techniques. *SN Computer Science, 1*, 175.

Statista. (2021). *The World's Longest Non-Stop Flights*. Statista. https://www.statista.com/chart/3761/the-worlds-longest-non-stop-flights/

Thomas, D. (2019). *Why did the Airbus A380 fail?* British Broadcast Corporation (BBC). https://www.bbc.com/news/business-47225789

Vancouver Airport Authority. (2015). *Philippine Airlines Flies Between Manila, Vancouver and New York*. Vancouver Airport Authority. https://www.yvr.ca/en/media/news-releases/2015/philippine-airlines-flies-between-manila-vancouver-and-new-york

Villamizar, H. (2021). Today in Aviation: First Commercial Jet Flies to South Africa. *Airways Magazine*. https://airwaysmag.com/today-in-aviation/first-commercial-jet-south-africa/

Weatherford, L. R., Gentry, T. W., & Wilamowski, B. (2003). Neural network forecasting for airlines: A comparative analysis. *Journal of Revenue and Pricing Management*, *1*, 319–331.

Werfelman, L. (2015). *In It For the Ultra-Long-Haul*. Flight Safety Foundation. https://flightsafety.org/asw-article/in-it-for-the-ultra-long-haul/

Wilkerson, J., Jacobson, M., Malwitz, A., Balasubramanian, S., Wayson, R., Fleming, G., Naiman, D., & Lele, S. (2010). Analysis of emission data from global commercial aviation: 2004 and 2006. *Atmospheric Chemistry and Physics*, *2010*(10), 2945–2983.

Yao, X., & Vink, P. (2019). A Survey and a Co-creation Session to Evaluate Passenger Contentment on Long-haul Flight, with Suggestions for Possible Design Improvements to Future Aircraft Interiors. In *2nd International Comfort Congress August 29th and 30th, 2019* (pp. 1-9). Università degli Studi di Salerno.

Zhang, C., & Jiang, X. (2019). Ultra Longhaul Flight and Its Impact on Air Travellers. *Journal of Transport & Health*, *14*, 100756.

KEY TERMS AND DEFINITIONS

Connecting Flights: Flights that operate between two cities and make a change of flights of the same airlines or on other airlines in one or more cities before arriving at the destination airport.

Direct Flights: Flights that operate between two cities that make stop(s) in one or more cities before arriving at the destination airport.

Extended-Range Twin-Engine Operational Performance Standards (ETOPS): A certification allowing twin engine aircraft flying at least 60 minutes away from the nearest airport.

Nonstop Flights: Flights that operate between two cities without any intermediate stop.

Premium Cabins: Airline cabins offers a higher level of comfort and space compared with economy class. It consists of first class, business class and premium economy class.

Ultra Long Haul Flights: Flights operate over a very long distance that could last over 16 hours.

Chapter 7
Competitive Strategies in the Airline Industry

Ferhan K. Sengur
Eskisehir Technical University, Turkey

Huseyin Onder Aldemir
https://orcid.org/0000-0002-8083-0447
Özyeğin University, Turkey

Mert Akınet
https://orcid.org/0000-0002-0805-9731
University of Turkish Aeronautical Association, Turkey

ABSTRACT

The airline industry is a dynamic industry with intense competition. Deregulation, the international competition structure, and economic and COVID-19-like crises make the sector even more fierce. In this chapter, airline industry competitive strategies are discussed. For this purpose, following the introduction part, the concepts of strategy, business strategy, and competitive structure of the airline industry are discussed, and the place of competitive strategies in business strategies is explained. The airline industry structure is analyzed using Porter's five forces model. Two fundamental competitive strategy approaches, Porter's generic strategies and Miles and Snow's competitive strategies, are examined in detail for the airline industry. Following the presentation of the two well-known strategy frameworks, the chapter will end with a conclusion part.

INTRODUCTION

In today's globally competitive world, businesses operating in a turbulent environment constantly interact and thus ensure their sustainability. Businesses must be flexible to maintain their competitive structure to ensure sustainability in the ever-changing competitive environment. They must constantly compare with their competitors to realize the best practices in the sector and perform their activities efficiently

DOI: 10.4018/978-1-6684-4615-7.ch007

Competitive Strategies in the Airline Industry

and effectively by focusing on their core competencies (Porter, 1996). Competition is defined as the tactical struggles between businesses in an industry to gain a competitive advantage (Grant, 2005). Porter stated that a consistent competitive strategy must be successfully implemented to achieve a long-term competitive advantage (Kling & Smith, 1995). Today, while businesses are looking for the most suitable strategy for themselves, they plan counteractions by monitoring the competitiveness and strategies of their competitors.

The competitive strategy aims to gain a competitive advantage against its competitors in the market (Porter, 1980) and defines how the business should take a position against its competitors while continuing its activities. In other words, a competitive strategy can be defined as a long-term action plan by which a company aims to gain a competitive advantage after examining and comparing its strengths and weaknesses against its competitors (Okumus, Altinay, & Chathoth, 2010).

The airline industry is one of the sectors where intense competition is experienced in the global sense today. The airline industry is competitive in origin, and as a service-oriented industry, competition and interaction within the industry are very high. Several unpredictable exogenous forces have plagued the airline industry in recent decades, including major worldwide events. The September 11 attacks, SARS crisis, economic crisis, and lastly, the COVID-19 pandemic has significantly impacted the industry. Due to the COVID-19 pandemic, air transport almost stopped in initial reactions. While most passenger flights have been cancelled due to the epidemic, cargo flights have been cancelled, and only relief flights, referred to as "rescue flights" by countries, continued (Kiliç & Sengur, 2021). In recent years, innovative business models have also resulted in industrial transformation. While industries have witnessed the low-cost revolution against the full-service carriers for the last decades, today, hybridization became an industry reality (Sengur & Sengur, 2017). In this turbulent environment, airline companies must accurately analyze themselves, their competitors and the structure and competitive environment of the market to ensure their permanent sustainability in the market in which they operate, maintain their market share and reach their predetermined targets (Brueckner, Lee, & Singer, 2013).

Internal and external environmental factors and the industry's structure are among the main determinants of competition conditions for businesses. Airlines formulate and implement competitive strategies to survive and prosper in the competitive environment. The main aim of this study is to reveal the competition (business management) strategies, which is one of the basic strategies at the application level implemented by the airlines. The well-known strategic management approaches to creating competitive advantage are Porter's generic strategies, Miles and Snow's typology, resource-based view, outpacing approach, and blue ocean strategies (Aldemir et al., 2021). The chapter will first examine the competitive structure of the airline industry with Porter's Five Forces Framework and then will focus on the two well-known strategy frameworks, the "Generic Strategies" determined by Porter and "four typologies" determined by Miles &Snow for the airline industry. There are three general strategic approaches to outperforming other businesses operating in an industry: cost leadership, differentiation, and focus strategy (Porter, 1980). For businesses to be successful, they need to achieve cost leadership in their production or processes or differentiate their products. Businesses can also achieve success by focusing on the market they operate (Helms, Dibrell, & Wright, 1997). In addition to Porter's classification of competition strategies, the classification made by Miles and Snow in 1978 has also been widely studied in the literature, specific to competition strategies. (Miles & Snow, 1978). Following the presentation of the two models, the chapter will end with a conclusion part.

COMPETITIVE STRUCTURE OF THE AIRLINE INDUSTRY

The first to examine the concept of competition is the discipline of Industrial Economics, which is under the science of Economics. The concept of competition in the industrial economy has been handled as perfect competition and aimed to explain the functioning of economic units in industries (Devine et al., 1993). As an encyclopedic definition, competition is a market behavior that manifests itself in the form of a competition between economic units that want to obtain goods or services with limited supply or, conversely, to avoid an abundance of supply (Great Larousse, 1986). Competition is the tactical struggles of businesses in an industry with each other to gain a competitive advantage (Grant, 2005). Every business must create competitive differentiation to compete successfully. This differentiation can be achieved with different abilities and approaches that make the business different from other businesses. Competition rules might regulate the economic life of the countries.

Every industry creates a competitive environment. Companies within the industry have to keep up with changes both within the industry they operate and in the industry's environment. This structure requires companies to adapt quickly to every change in their competitive environment. The airline industry has an oligopoly market structure. Imperfect competition in which a small number of enterprises dominate the sector. Since oligopoly businesses are interconnected and create comparable outputs and compete with their industry rivals, each move taken by a firm is noticed by its competitors. As a result, competitors may respond with price cuts or other initiatives to increase market share (Rubin & Joy, 2005). The market strength of a particular firm is subject to erosion by its competitors or new market entrants (Rubin & Joy, 2005).

Even the best-formulated and best-practised strategies can become obsolete as a business's internal and external environment changes. Therefore, it is essential that strategists systematically review, evaluate and control the implementation of strategies and their industry environment. Porter's Five Forces Model present an excellent framework for examining the industry structure. The following part will analyze the airline industry through Porter's Five Forces Model.

Porter's Five Forces Model

Businesses use various analytical methods to analyze and evaluate their competitive environment as operating in a constantly changing and turbulent environment. One of the most widely applied methods is the "Five Competitive Power Model" developed by M. Porter. In his article titled "How Competitive Forces Shape Strategy", published in 1979, Porter first identified the five elements of the competitive environment that shape the strategies of businesses. These five forces are "The Threat of New Entrants", "The Bargaining Power of Suppliers", "The Bargaining Power of Customers", "The Threat of Substitute Products", and "The Competition among Existing Competitors". Porter stated that competitive pressure for a business comes from five different sources and that businesses must struggle with them to maintain their sustainability and profitability in the long run. The five competitive forces determine the intensity of competition in an industry and the sector's profitability. The most vital forces come to the fore for business strategy formation. Managers should evaluate how the five forces affect the industry's competitive environment and make inferences about how they may affect it in the future. Thus, managers will determine the most suitable position in the sector for their businesses. The five power models that affect the competitive environment of businesses are shown in Figure 1 and will be explained in detail.

Competitive Strategies in the Airline Industry

Figure 1. Five competitive power model (Porter M., 1979)

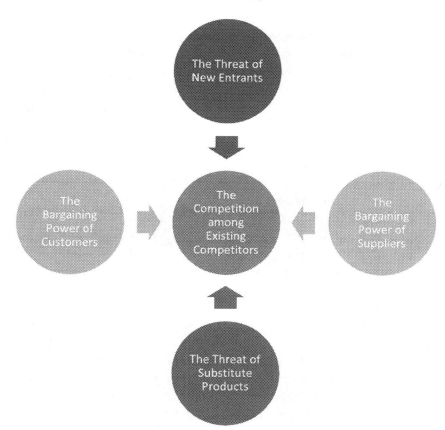

The Threat of New Entrants: New enterprises that will enter the sector create a production capacity and the danger of reducing the profit share of the enterprises that already exist in that sector. In other words, the new companies entering the sector increase the competition in the sector and this causes a decrease in the general prices of the products. For example, the continuous increase in the number of low-cost carriers in the aviation sector in the same market increases competition. Each new airline company poses a potential threat to the sector. On the other hand, there are various potential entry barriers for new entrants to the sector, explained below.

1. Economies of Scale: Thanks to the economies of scale, which can be defined as the cost advantage of production in large volumes (Johnston & Ozment, 2011), the new enterprises that will enter the sector are deterred by difficulty. The increasingly competitive environment in the aviation industry of the US after 1978 and today's competitive market structure led aviation companies to make strategic alliances (Budd & Ison, 2020). This situation created a potential barrier to entry for new businesses entering the sector. Thus, businesses could benefit from economies of scale by accessing broader markets with their established alliances.
2. Product Differentiation: With product differentiation, known as highlighting the different and attractive features of a good or service in the eyes of the consumer, existing businesses in the sector

ensure customer loyalty and create barriers for potential entries. Businesses in the airline industry differentiate their products with privileges such as in-flight services, catering and additional services, creating an obstacle for new businesses (Hazledine, 2011).

3. Capital Requirements: The total investment and risk, including the infrastructure and working capital required to enter an industry, is a significant threat to new entrants. Since the airline industry is in an important position, especially for countries, there is usually a limitation on the initial capital and the minimum number of aircraft. These figures can pose a threat to new entries.

4. Cost Disadvantages Independent of Size: Cost disadvantages of existing enterprises such as product knowledge and technology, appropriate access to raw materials, advantageous establishment location, trained and experienced workforce and managers, which are independent of scale, constitute an essential barrier to entry for new enterprises. For example, grandparent rights in the aviation industry can create a cost disadvantage independent of scale for new entrants. Grandfather rights can be defined as an air carrier that has used a slot in the last summer or winter period can use their rights in the current summer or winter period (Sieg, 2010). Airlines prevent other businesses from getting their qualifications thanks to grandparent rights by reusing their previously used slots.

5. Access to Distribution Channels: Existing businesses reach the consumer easily with controlled and robust distribution channels, thus posing a threat to potential entries. The airline industry has direct and indirect distribution channels. Direct distribution channels are airline companies' ticket and sales offices, reservation and sales applications via call centers and airline companies' websites. In contrast, travel agencies and other sales offices are usually indirect distribution channels. Today, with the widespread use of the internet, airline companies' influence and control on distribution channels continue to increase, and customers can be easily reached at a point of need. This situation poses a potential risk for businesses that will enter the market.

6. Government Policy: Laws and government practices regulating industries can limit and complicate entry into the industry. Thus, costs increase for businesses entering the sector, creating a difficult obstacle. Today, with the protectionist government policies, the aviation industry has become a market with its unique structure and limitations. Giving an example from airline companies, governments have imposed restrictions on their own airline companies' foreign capital property rights. In addition, governments have developed practices to encourage airline businesses to develop regions in their countries in various aspects. (Uzgör & Şengür, 2021). In addition, governments have taken measures to support their airline businesses, especially flag carrier airlines, economically and to protect them from the adverse effects of the Covid-19 pandemic (Abate, Christidis, & Purwanto, 2020).

In the article published in 1979, Michael E. Porter listed six potential entry barriers for businesses that will enter a sector, and then the following barriers were added in his study titled "The Five Competitive Forces that Shape Strategy" (Porter M., 2008) and other academic studies in the literature (Grundy T., 2006).

7. Switching Cost: Switching costs, known as the sum of monetary and non-monetary costs that a customer incurs to leave the business they have already purchased and move to a new business, create risks for new entrants to the industry (Yang & Peterson, 2004). Airlines offer their customers privileged services through loyalty programs such as the Frequent Flyer Program (FFP) to increase switching costs. Customers can easily use their savings after each flight on their future flights. In

this case, customers will prefer other businesses less, and there will be a potential obstacle, especially for a business that will enter the sector.
8. Learning and Experience Curve Effect: With the knowledge and experience of the existing companies in the aviation sector, their certification, qualified personnel, and a certain level of knowledge, the new companies that will enter the sector may perceive the market as uncertain and a potential entry barrier is created. With the power of experience, an element whose presence is felt more especially in times of crisis, aviation enterprises could protect themselves from the negative situations they experience (Grundy & Moxon, 2013).

Factors that make a new entry into the sector difficult may vary depending on the sector-specific characteristics. Factors such as the fact that new entries in the aviation sector require long-term investments, the legal requirement to maintain a specific budget, and that existing enterprises can quickly put additional flights on the necessary lines create potential barriers to entry. Each new airline operating in the aviation sector poses a potential risk to other airlines already in the sector, and there is a risk of reducing their market share.

The Bargaining Power of Suppliers: By raising the prices of the products they offer or reducing the quality, suppliers can gain significant bargaining power over the existing businesses in the sector. This situation may be possible, especially if there are limited suppliers in the sector. In addition, the bargaining power of suppliers increases due to high supplier switching costs and differentiated service delivery (Aldemir, Kuyucak Şengür, & Ulukan, 2021). In the airline industry, the bargaining power of the suppliers is relatively high, as specialized services such as ground handling, catering and air traffic control services are in the hands of one or more companies. Air traffic control service in various countries has a monopoly structure. All airline operators must purchase the minimum services offered to carry out their activities, regardless of the price difference.

The Bargaining Power of Customers: Customers who buy the goods or services produced by the business can use their bargaining power by forcing the prices to decrease or demanding to buy the best product with the minimum payment. Large purchases, undifferentiated product demands, low replacement costs and flexibility increase buyers' bargaining power. In the airline sector, the low switching costs increase the bargaining power of buyers. Especially with the widespread use of the internet, customers can see and compare the prices of the airline companies they want. On the other hand, airline companies are trying to reduce the bargaining power of buyers by trying to increase the switching costs with the loyalty programs such as Frequent Flyer Programs (FFP).

The Threat of Substitute Products: A substitute product is another good or service that performs the same function as a good or service. Businesses in one sector may compete directly or indirectly with substitute products in another sector. The presence of substitute products may impose an upper limit on the products of a sector and reduce the sector's profitability by meeting similar needs. The most important substitute for the airline industry is other modes of transport. Another substitute product that reduces profitability in the aviation industry is the global development of video conferencing communication, which has emerged due to technological developments. Parallel to this development, most businesspeople attend domestic or international meetings via video conference today. On the other hand, the high-speed train, widely used today, is considered a substitute product for airline companies, concise and medium distances (Socorro & Viecens, 2013).

The Competition among Existing Competitors: The competitive situation, which has the most intense effect among the five competitive forces, constitutes the competitive elements such as price, quality, marketing and customer service among the existing competitors in the sector. Competition increases when the number of competitors increases or when competitors converge in market share. In today's globally competitive environment, managers should define the level of competition in the sector and implement the most suitable strategies. On the other hand, in the airline sector, businesses are mutually dependent, and the competitive move of one business creates a direct or indirect effect on the other business. Today, competitive races such as price, improved customer service and technology prevail, especially among existing competitors in the aviation industry. Reducing the barriers to entry in the airlines, especially after liberalization, has increased the number of competitors and competition in the sector. In addition, the cheap service offered by low-cost airline companies to the industry has brought prices down and increased competition.

On the other hand, especially during the Covid-19 period, states' support of flag carrier airlines with various practices can create unfair competition for other airlines. During the crisis, other airline companies operating in the same region had to continue their activities under unfair and difficult conditions due to the state support given to flag carriers such as Air France, Lufthansa, and SAS operating in the European region. Governments should primarily protect competition in the sector which has critical importance, such as the airline industry (Abate, Christidis, & Purwanto, 2020).

Managers struggling with competitive forces will try to protect their businesses from the pressure of the five powers. They will try to position their businesses in a strong position in the competitive environment. Thanks to the Five Forces Model developed by Porter, which shows a systematic way to understand the competition in an industry better, businesses analyze and evaluate the competitive environment. The Five Forces Model, which analyzes environmental forces with an analytical approach in a macro framework, presents a broad picture for businesses.

AIRLINE COMPETITION STRATEGIES

Competitive strategies are all decisions and behaviors that create value for customers in a particular market and provide a competitive advantage by using existing core capabilities (Hitt et al., 2003). Although there are different classification schemes for strategies, according to the application levels, the basic strategies are grouped into four groups in large businesses and three groups in small businesses (David, 2011):

- Corporate Strategies (Corporate Level) - CEO level: Strategies determined and implemented at the Senior Management level
- Business Management (Competition) Strategies (Business Level): Strategies determined and implemented at the level of central business units.
- Functional Strategies (Functional Level): At the finance, production, marketing, information systems, R&D, and human resources manager.
- Operational Strategies (Operational Level): Departmental strategies determined and implemented at the lower management level.

Porter's Generic Strategies

Porter (1985) emphasizes that businesses should earn above-average income to gain a competitive advantage. To achieve this, it shows businesses two different ways:

- It is the business's competitive advantage by producing goods and services at low cost and selling them at market prices, making more profit than their existing competitors in the market.
- As a result of the business's differentiation in its goods and services, it establishes a competitive advantage by selling it to the customer at a higher price than other goods and services in the market, providing profit and higher returns.

These two main ways that Porter (1985) created competitive strategies are "Cost Leadership Strategy" and "Differentiation Strategy" in competitive strategies. These two main competitive strategies are called "Focus Strategies" when used in narrower and different market platforms instead of a broad market platform. When both Cost Leadership and Differentiation Strategies are used together by a business, "Combined Competitive Strategies" are in question (Porter, 1985).

Cost leadership requires aggressively building effective-scale facilities, tracking cost reductions from experience, tight cost and overhead control, avoiding marginal customer accounts, and minimizing costs in services such as R&D, service, salesforce, and advertising. A great deal of managerial attention to cost control is required to achieve these goals. Low-cost relative to competitors becomes the running theme throughout the entire strategy, although quality, service, and other areas cannot be overlooked (Porter, 1980). The cost leadership strategy is based on reducing costs in all activities rather than reducing the prices of goods and services. Cost leadership as a competitive strategy should ensure cost reduction without affecting or compromising quality. It should not be expected that every activity in a business will necessarily be less costly than competitors. What matters is the importance of that activity in creating value and the magnitude of the value created. Cost leadership strategy is preferred by businesses that do not change rapidly and produce common goods and services.

Cost leadership strategy achieves by utilizing a fuel-efficient fleet, short or mid-haul flights, point to point model, single service class -generally economy class- direct sales and extra charges for extra pre-flight or in-flight services (Shaw, 2007). For this reason, cost leadership is a strategy mainly geared toward internal efficiency (Ülgen & Mirze, 2013). Global airlines that implement a cost leadership strategy are generally called Low-Cost Airlines (LCC), such as Southwest Airlines, Ryanair Airlines, and Pegasus Airlines.

A low-cost position provides the business with above-average returns in the industry, despite strong competitive forces. The cost position provides the business with a defence against competition from competitors. A low-cost position creates a defensive shield against strong suppliers while defending the business against strong buyers, providing more flexibility to deal with input cost increases. Factors leading to a low-cost position often also provide significant barriers to entry in terms of economies of scale or cost advantages (Porter, 1980).

Differentiation strategy differentiates the firm's product or service offering, creating something perceived as unique across the industry. Differential approaches can take many forms: design or brand image, technology, features, customer service, dealer network or other dimensions. It should be emphasized that the differentiation strategy does not allow the firm to ignore costs, but rather that costs are not the primary strategic objective (Porter, 1980). The basis of the differentiation strategy is to direct the customer's preference towards their goods and services by behaving differently from the practices of other businesses. Differentiation strategy creates a competitive advantage by differentiating in all value-creating business activities and providing above-average returns. In this strategy, the business tries to achieve a return above the industry average by fulfilling customer expectations differently from its competitors and supplying its goods and services at a higher price than the customer is willing to pay. Differentiation strategies can create loyal customers (Ülgen & Mirze, 2013). Businesses that implement a differentiation strategy are generally called full-service carriers, such as Lufthansa, Singapore Airlines, and Turkish Airlines. Airlines have always been necessary to be innovative to be successful in the differentiation strategy. Emirates added Airbus A380 large aircraft in their fleet with accessible in new developments in-flight services.

Focus strategy focuses on a particular buyer group, product line segment or geographic market; as with differentiation, focus can take many forms. While low cost and differentiation strategies aim to achieve their goals across the entire industry, the focus strategy serves a particular goal very well. Each functional policy is developed with this in mind. The strategy assumes that the firm can serve its narrow strategic objective more effectively or efficiently than competitors that compete more broadly. As a result, the business succeeds either by differentiation, serving at lower costs, or both. While the focus strategy may not provide low cost or differentiation from the market's perspective, it achieves one or both of these positions to a narrow market target (Porter, 1980).

Focus strategies involve a narrower sub-market and goods and services whose characteristics are tailored to the market to which they are addressed. Narrowing the market platform to particular customer groups reduces the number of competing businesses and makes the market more specific. The market platform can be narrowed down in three ways (Ülgen & Mirze, 2013):

- Geographical/regional segmentation,
- Narrowing the market according to different customer requests, needs and expectations,
- Creating a different and new market for producing goods and services with different characteristics.

Porter's Generic Strategies are alternative and viable approaches to dealing with competitive forces. The fact that the business cannot develop its strategy in at least one of the three directions and is in a fragile strategic situation indicates it is stuck in the middle. Such businesses lack market share and capital investment. They must decide to differentiate, create a low-cost position, or focus on industry-wide or limited space. The low profitability of a stuck-in-the-middle business is guaranteed. They either lose out on high-volume customers who demand low prices or sacrifice their profits to divert the business from low-cost firms. A stuck-in-the-middle business likely also suffers from an uncertain corporate culture and conflicting organizational arrangements and motivation systems (Porter, 1980). FedEx and UPS are directly dealing with the air cargo operations in the aviation sector, and they are an excellent example of focusing strategy on the airline industry. They strongly emphasized critical, urgent packages and valuable goods that need to be sent with airlines.

Miles and Snow's Competitive Typology

Miles & Snow (1978) developed a theoretical framework consisting of the adaptation cycle and strategic typology and linked this theoretical framework with existing management theories. Miles & Snow (1978) proposed a typology indicating four strategic types of organizations: defenders, prospectors, analyzers, and reactors. Miles et al. (1978) created this system by interpreting existing literature and studies in printing textbooks, electronics, food processing, and health industries. This study developed an adaptation process called the "adaptation cycle". Accordingly, only a part of the organization's behavior is predetermined by environmental conditions. The choices made by top management are fundamentally critical to the structure and process of the organization. According to Miles & Snow (1978), the success of the organization is based on external (environment) and internal (strategy, structure, process and ideology) harmony (Martins & Kato, 2010). This process begins with the organization adapting to the market to meet customers' current and future needs. This harmony creates the strategy of the business. In other words, this type of analysis tries to evaluate the organization's adaptation to the changing environment by studying the relationship between strategy, structure and process (Miles & Snow, 1978). Snow & Hrebiniak (1980) also demonstrated the applicability of this typology in the automotive, plastics, air transport and semiconductor industries. The stages of this strategy, which is called the adaptation cycle and includes adaptation to the competitive environment, consist of the solutions given to the following questions (Miles et al., 1978):

- Entrepreneurial Problem: Monitoring product-market space, success status, environment and growth policies.
- Engineering Problem: Technological objectives, scope and orientation.
- Administrative Problem: Main administrative function, organizational structure, planning behavior, and control.

Zahra & Pearce (1990) based the typology of Miles and Snow on three main pillars. First, successful organizations have developed a systematic and definable approach to environmental compliance over time. Miles and Snow's typology clarified the general physiology of the adaptation cycle and organizational behavior by conceptualizing the main elements of adaptation and considering their relationship. The second pillar is the four strategies they have developed in the industry. The main difference between these strategies is the rate of change in the organization's sphere of influence. The third is that if defender, prospector and analyzer strategies are applied appropriately, it will lead to a compelling performance. They are based on internal consistency between the three elements of the adjustment cycle. Each type emphasizes different functions to produce sustainable, different competencies. The reactor type lacks a coherent strategy. As a result, the typology suggests that the defenders, the prospectors, and the analyzers will be superior to the reactors.

Defenders: Defenders are organizations with narrow product markets. In such organizations, senior managers are highly specialized in the limited areas of their organization but are not inclined to seek new opportunities outside of their field. Consequently, these organizations rarely make significant changes to their technology, structure, or way of working due to this restrained focus. Instead, they prioritize improving the efficiency of current operations (Miles & Snow, 1978).

Defenders are pretty much the opposite of prospectors. A defender's strategy is to offer a relatively stable set of services (narrow segment) to defined markets. The defender's strategy focuses on doing the best possible work in the field of expertise. This strategy tries to increase business production and efficiency to reduce costs continuously. It also emphasizes strict control, particularly on cost and efficiency matters. Defenders aggressively strive to prevent competitors from entering their limited niches or areas. They perform standard economic actions such as competitive pricing or producing high-quality products. Defenders tend to disregard developments outside of product line areas. They do little environmental monitoring and limited product development. Financial and production experts manage decision-making (Gibcus & Kemp, 2003).

According to Snow & Hrebiniak (1980), defenders perceive differential competence in general management, manufacturing, applied engineering, and financial management. According to Desarbo et al. (2005), organizations that follow defensive strategies need strategic capabilities in marketing and marketing contexts for optimum performance.

Prospectors: Prospectors are organizations that constantly seek market opportunities and regularly experiment with potential responses to emerging environmental trends. Those organizations are commonly the creators of the changes and uncertainties that their competitors have responded to their actions. However, due to their vital concern for product and market innovation, these organizations are often not entirely efficient (Miles & Snow, 1978).

Prospector organizations are often the cause of changes in the industry. A business that follows a prospector strategy tailors its products and services and constantly attempts to be first in the market. Such a business emphasizes innovation and flexibility to respond quickly to changing market conditions. Marketing and research and development are the dominant functions. Decision making is more decentralized, and coordination and communication structure is simple. 3M (Minnesota Mining and Manufacturing) company is a well-known enterprise that follows the prospector strategy (Gibcus & Kemp, 2003).

According to Snow & Hrebiniak (1980), prospectors demonstrate different abilities in general management, manufacturing, market research, product research and development, and basic engineering. According to Desarbo et al. (2005), prospectors have balanced marketing, technology, information technology and management skills.

Analyzers: Analyzers operate in two types of product-market areas, one relatively consistent and the other volatile. These organizations operate orderly and efficiently through formalized structures and processes in their stable regions. In their more turbulent regions, their executives closely monitor their competitors for new ideas and quickly adopt the most promising ones (Miles & Snow, 1978).

Analyzers are between the two extremes of stable and effective defenders and dynamic and more effective prospectors. They combined the characteristics of both types. An analyst's strategy is to enter selected new areas as committed while maintaining a relatively stable base of products and services. They position themselves as defenders in a more stable market environment and focus on production efficiency and low-cost factors. However, they oversee new developments in more turbulent markets to jump in as soon as they see a booming trend. An analyzer emphasizes formal planning processes and seeks to balance cost control and efficiency with risk-taking and innovation. The analyzer prefers to be the second, not the first, observer in the market. They move to innovations and new markets only after the market's viability has been proven by organizations implementing prospector strategies. They live by imitation. Organizations that implement analyzer strategies must have the capability to respond to leading organizations, but operational efficiency must also be ensured. They tend to have fewer profit margins than researchers. The structure of the analyzer strategy is quite complicated due to its hybrid character. IBM is a business that pursues analyzer strategies (Gibcus & Kemp, 2003).

According to Snow & Hrebiniak (1980), analyzers demonstrate differential competence in general management, production, applied engineering, and marketing. According to Desarbo et al. (2005), organizations implementing analyzer strategies have balanced marketing, technology, information technology and management capabilities.

Reactors: Reactors are organizations in which senior managers cannot respond effectively, although they generally perceive the change and ambiguity in their organizational environment. Since this type of organization does not have a coherent strategy-structure relationship, they rarely make any adjustments until they are challenged by environmental pressures (Miles & Snow, 1978).

Reactors are organizations that do not have a coherent strategy. Reactor strategies are challenging to classify unambiguously, as they can show attributes of each of the other strategy types at different times.

Organizations that implement reactor strategies respond inappropriately, work poorly, and are reluctant to implement a particular strategy (Gibcus & Kemp, 2003).

According to Snow & Hrebiniak (1980), reactors do not have consistent perceptions of discriminative efficacy. According to Desarbo et al. (2005), organizations that implement reactor strategies need strategic marketing capabilities for optimum performance.

Application of the Competition Strategies to Airlines

Bahaee (1992) researched the competitive strategic orientations of the regional airlines operating in the US since regional airlines fit the definitions of small and homogeneous firms. The author sent questionnaires to all 204 regional airlines; however, he gathered 82 usable returns. As a result of questionnaires applied to 82 regional airlines, 9 prospectors, 19 defenders, 24 analyzers, and 30 reactors were revealed. Bahaee (1992) explained that he expected few airlines to implement prospector strategies since limited resources were allocated to regional airlines in this industry. Having such a high number of reactor airlines has demonstrated the deregulation in 1978. These airlines did not articulate their long-term strategies and aims. They missed the opportunities that deregulation offered.

Kling & Smith (1995) determined and grouped the competitive strategies of nine major US passenger airlines according to Porter's Generic Strategies. It was determined that American, Delta and United Airlines implemented the differentiation strategy, while America West implemented the cost leadership and Southwest focused strategies. USAir, Northwest, Continental, and TWA were clustered as stuck in the middle.

Aldemir et al. (2021) studied the competition strategies of eight passenger airlines (5 scheduled and 3 charter). Their research demonstrated that an airline company might implement hybrid strategies of Miles and Snow typology like analyzer-defender. One most striking result of their research is that the airlines, applying pure cost leadership and "integrated cost and differentiation strategy," matched with analyzer-defender strategies. In conclusion, while the scheduled airline companies of Turkey were mostly revealed to adopt hybrid analyzer-defender competition strategies, charter airlines were closer to following Miles and Snow's pure strategies. Furthermore, some airline firms in Turkey state that they implement all of Porter's generic strategies simultaneously, supporting Dostaler & Flouris (2006) and Heracleous & Wirtz, 2009) results which indicate an "integrated cost and differentiation strategy". Aldemir et al. (2021) also concluded that implementing hybrid strategies might offer more strategic options and provide flexibility in the turbulent environment of the airline industry.

NEW ERA AND FUTURE OF AIR TRANSPORTATION

For a few years, the airline industry has struggled with the coronavirus pandemic and its effects. As of March 11th, 2020, the World Health Organization (WHO) declared COVID-19 a pandemic. First, airline companies tried to ensure their sustainability in the market due to this pandemic, which negatively affected global service sectors such as the aviation sector and brought airline transportation back to the 2008 global financial crisis levels. Countries have set international flight restrictions to prevent the spread of the virus. Due to the applied restrictions and global concern, airline companies ceased their operations on a large scale by grounding the fleets and maintaining sustainability with the least possible employees. The runways at some airports had to be turned into aircraft parking areas.

Furthermore, aircraft manufacturers had to stop or delay their orders. Precautions are taken at the airports, such as vaccination passports, temperature measurement during the flight, clean air in the cabin, masks, and distance. Therefore, the operations continue increasingly due to the decrease in the spread of the virus in immunity.

The Five Forces Model developed by Porter to determine the competitive dynamics in the industry has been reshaped for the aviation industry with the coronavirus pandemic. Firstly, the threat of new entrants has considerably decreased, but many airlines have gone bankrupt. The threat of substitute products has become the most critical threat to the sector, natural competitors such as highways and high-speed trains have come to the forefront, and online communication channels have become increasingly widespread. The competitive dynamics of the airline industry are being reshaped according to the Five Forces Model under such new threats.

Specific to Porter's generic strategies, focusing strategies have been developed for the air cargo sector, the least affected by the coronavirus epidemic. Airline companies tried to increase their revenues by converting their current aircraft to cargo aircraft and focusing on the air cargo market.

CONCLUSION

The airline industry is one of the service industries where global competition exists. The deregulations of domestic markets and liberalization and open skies trends have already contributed to competition's intensity. In addition, crises such as 9/11, SARS, global economic crisis, wars, and the COVID-19 pandemic make the competitive structure difficult for competing airlines to survive.

This chapter examined the airline industry structure and two distinct competitive typologies based on industry dynamics. The cost leadership strategy is defined as the firm's strengthening of its position and competitive advantage through low costs compared to rivals. According to Porter, the enterprise's privileged access to natural resources, technology, and economies of scale is vital to deliver low cost and form the foundation of this approach. A low-cost position gives the business a higher-than-industry return, despite intense competition. On the other hand, businesses that follow a cost leadership strategy should consider that other businesses can imitate their savings tactics in the market reduction.

Differentiation competitive advantage strategy can be defined that products having different and unique characteristics from their competitors, and customers value the company's products more than competing products. Businesses should create customer loyalty with the goods or services they offer to the market and use this as a competitive tool. Differentiation as a business management strategy aims to achieve above-average returns in all value-creating business activities. Approaches to leading differentiation can take different forms, such as different designs or images of goods or services, the technology used, and customer service provided. Businesses that follow the differentiation strategy today differentiate themselves at several different points according to the wishes and needs of the customers instead of a single point. Businesses offer their goods or services at higher prices and generally achieve higher profit rates with the differentiation strategy. On the other hand, businesses that follow a differentiation strategy should avoid making differentiations that may cause prices to increase too much compared to competitors.

Miles and Snow developed four strategic typologies in competitive strategies named after them. These are classified as defensive, leading, analytical and reactive strategies. In organizations that follow a defensive strategy, senior managers are experts in their fields and are not inclined to seek new opportunities outside of their field. Organizations that follow defensive strategies often try to increase their productivity and have narrow product markets. Organizations that follow a pioneering strategy constantly seek market opportunities and pursue creative strategies against environmental factors. Formal structures and processes continue regularly and efficiently in businesses that implement analytical strategies, and these businesses monitor and analyze new ideas in turbulent market regions. Organizations that follow a reactive strategy react to change or fail to respond effectively.

REFERENCES

Abate, M., Christidis, P., & Purwanto, A. J. (2020). Government Support to Airlines in the Aftermath of the COVID-19 Pandemic. *Journal of Air Transport Management*, *89*, 101931. doi:10.1016/j.jairtraman.2020.101931 PMID:32952317

Aldemir, H. O., Sengür, F. K., & Ulukan, I. C. (2021). Exploring Strategic Choices of Airlines: A Study in Turkish Air Transport Industry. *Asian Academy of Management Journal*, *26*(2), 1–26. doi:10.21315/aamj2021.26.2.1

Bahaee, M. S. (1992). Strategy-Comprehensiveness Fit and Performance. *Australian Journal of Management*, *17*(2), 195–215. doi:10.1177/031289629301700202

Brueckner, J., Lee, D., & Singer, E. (2013). Airline Competition and Domestic US Airfares: A Comprehensive Reappraisal. *Economics of Transportation*, *2*(1), 1–17. doi:10.1016/j.ecotra.2012.06.001

Budd, L., & Ison, S. (2020). *Air Transport Management: An International Perspective*. Routledge. doi:10.4324/9780429299445

David, F. R. (2011). *Strategic Management Concepts and Cases* (13th ed.). Pearson Education Inc.

DeSarbo, W. S., Di Benedetto, C. A., Song, M., & Sinha, I. (2005). Revisiting the Miles and Snow Strategic Framework: Uncovering Interrelationships Between Strategic Types, Capabilities, Environmental Uncertainty, and Firm Performance. *Strategic Management Journal*, *26*(1), 47–74. doi:10.1002mj.431

Devine, P. J., Lee, N., Jones, R. M., & Tyson, W. J. (1993). *An Introduction to Industrial Economics* (4th ed.). Routledge.

Dostaler, I., & Flouris, T. (2006). Stuck In the Middle Revisited: The Case of the Airline Industry. *Journal of Aviation/Aerospace Education Research*, *15*(2), 33–45. doi:10.15394/jaaer.2006.1502

Gibcus, P., & Kemp, R. G. M. (2003). *Strategy and Small Firm Performance*. Research Report H200208, SCALES Scientific Analysis of Entrepreneurship and SMEs, Netherlands: Zoetermeer (EIM, Business & Policy Research).

Grant, R. (2005). *Contemporary Strategy Analysis*. Backwell Publishing.

Great Larousse. (1986). *Dictionary and Encyclopedia* (Vol. 16). Gelisim Publishing.

Grundy, M., & Moxon, R. (2013). The Effectiveness of Airline Crisis Management on Brand Protection: A Case Study of British Airways. *Journal of Air Transport Management*, *28*, 55–61. doi:10.1016/j.jairtraman.2012.12.011

Grundy, T. (2006). Rethinking and Reinventing Michael Porter's Five Forces Model. *Strategic Change*, *15*(5), 213–229. doi:10.1002/jsc.764

Hazledine, T. (2011). Legacy Carriers Fight Back: Pricing and Product Differentiation in Modern Airline Marketing. *Journal of Air Transport Management*, *17*(2), 130–135. doi:10.1016/j.jairtraman.2010.10.008

Helms, M. M., Dibrell, C., & Wright, P. (1997). Competitive Strategies and Business Performance: Evidence from the Adhesives and Sealants Industry. *Management Decision*, *35*(9), 689–703. doi:10.1108/00251749710186531

Heracleous, L., & Wirtz, J. (2009). Strategy and Organization at Singapore Airlines: Achieving Sustainable Advantage Through Dual Strategy. *Journal of Air Transport Management*, *15*(6), 274–279. doi:10.1016/j.jairtraman.2008.11.011

Hitt, M. A., Ireland, R. D., & Hoskisson, R. E. (2003). *Strategic Management: Competitiveness and Globalization* (5th ed.). Thomson South-Western.

Johnston, A., & Ozment, J. (2011). Concentration in the Airline Industry: Evidence of Economies of Scale? *Journal of Transportation Management*, *22*(2), 59–74. doi:10.22237/jotm/1317427500

Kiliç, D., Polat, G., & Sengur, F. (2021). Havayolu İşletmelerinin Covid-19 Pandemi Sürecindeki Yönetsel Tepkileri Üzerine Bir Araştırma. *Uluslararası Yönetim İktisat ve İşletme Dergisi*, *17*(2), 353–377.

Kling, J., & Smith, K. (1995). Identifying Strategic Groups in the US Airline Industry: An Application of the Porter Model. *Transportation Journal*, *35*(2), 26–34.

Martins, T. S., & Kato, H. T. (2010). *An Analytical Framework for Miles and Snow Typology and Dynamic Capabilities*. XXXIV Encontro da ANDAP.

Miles, R. E., Snow, C. C., Meyer, A. D., & Coleman, H. J. Jr. (1978). Organizational Strategy, Structure, and Process. *Academy of Management Review*, *3*(3), 546–562. doi:10.2307/257544 PMID:10238389

Okumus, F., Altinay, L., & Chathoth, P. (2010). *Strategic Management in the International Hospitality and Tourism Industry*. Routledge. doi:10.4324/9780080940465

Porter, M. (1979). *How Competitive Forces Shape Strategy*. Harvard Business Review.

Porter, M. (1980). *Competitive Strategy: Techniques for Analyzing Industries and Competitors*. The Free Press.

Porter, M. (1985). *Competitive Advantage: Creating and Sustaining Superior Performance*. The Free Press.

Porter, M. (1996). What is Strategy? *Harvard Business Review*, *76*(4), 61–78. PMID:10158474

Porter, M. (2008). The Five Competitive Forces that Shape Strategy. *Harvard Business Review*, 25–40. PMID:18271320

Rubin, R. M., & Joy, J. N. (2005). Where Are the Airlines Headed? Implications of Airline Industry Structure and Change for Consumers. *The Journal of Consumer Affairs*, *39*(1), 215–228. doi:10.1111/j.1745-6606.2005.00010.x PMID:32336778

Sengur, Y., & Sengur, F. K. (2017). Airlines Define Their Business Models: A Content Analysis. *World Review of Intermodal Transportation Research*, *6*(2), 141–154. doi:10.1504/WRITR.2017.082732

Shaw, S. (2007). *Airline Marketing and Management*. Ashgate Publishing Limited.

Sieg, G. (2010). Grandfather Rights in the Market for Airport Slots. *Transportation Research Part B: Methodological*, *44*(1), 29–37. doi:10.1016/j.trb.2009.04.005

Snow, M., & Hrebiniak, D. C. (1980). Strategy, Distinctive Competence and Organizational Performance. *Administrative Science Quarterly*, *25*(2), 317–336. doi:10.2307/2392457

Socorro, M., & Viecens, M. (2013). The Effects of Airline and High Speed Train Integration. *Transportation Research Part A, Policy and Practice*, *49*, 160–177. doi:10.1016/j.tra.2013.01.014

Ülgen, H., & Mirze, S. K. (2013). *İşletmelerde Stratejik Yönetim* (6th ed.). Beta Basım A.Ş.

Uzgör, M., & Sengur, F. (2021). Havayolu Sektöründe Devlet Destekleri: Türkiye'deki Teşvikli Uçuş Hatlarının İncelenmesi. *Anadolu Üniversitesi Sosyal Bilimler Dergisi*, 851-870.

Uzgör, M., & Sengur, F. (2022). Investigating an Underutilized Subsidized Routes Scheme: Underlying Reasons and Policy Recommendations. *Case Studies on Transport Policy*, *10*(1), 287–299. doi:10.1016/j.cstp.2021.12.010

Yang, Z., & Peterson, R. (2004). Customer Perceived Value, Satisfaction, and Loyalty: The Role of Switching Costs. *Psychology and Marketing*, *21*(10), 799–822. doi:10.1002/mar.20030

Zahra, S. A., & Pearce, J. A. II. (1990). Research Evidence on The Miles-Snow Typology. *Journal of Management*, *16*(4), 751–768. doi:10.1177/014920639001600407

Chapter 8
Customer Experiences of Omni-Partner Services:
An Insight From the Airline Alliance Perspective

Vikrant Janawade
University of Cote d'Azur, France

ABSTRACT

The concept of facilitating sound service experiences has been widely discussed in the marketing landscape in recent years. Whilst the concept is highly acknowledged in service industries, it introduces some challenges when services are dovetailed and delivered to customers by multiple service providers. These aspects offer new realms to understand how customers form their experiences whilst interacting and encountering dovetailed services of networked service providers. To explore these spheres, a qualitative study employing thematic analysis was conducted to understand how networked and dovetailed services of an airline alliance influence the experiences of international airline travellers. The results of the study suggest that the alliance carriers' ability to offer extensive, synchronised, harmonised, interactive, and reciprocated services can be instrumental and pivotal for delivering sound experiences to their customers. In addition, these attributes offer new avenues to suggest that alliance carriers' services could be considered an omni-partner engagement activity.

INTRODUCTION

Experience of consumers have become subject of discussions during the last few decades. Since 1980's, scores of articles offer a rich landscape to understand not only the roles of businesses to offer sound experiences to consumers, but they also offer an understanding on how businesses could facilitate decent experiences to consumers (Bitner, 1995; Berry et al, 2006). In addition, studies also offer several insights on how service providers could shape consumers experiences during their service encounters (Otto & Ritchie, 1996; Bitner et al, 2000; Bolton et al, 2007), their customer journeys (Lemon & Verhoef, 2016),

DOI: 10.4018/978-1-6684-4615-7.ch008

Customer Experiences of Omni-Partner Services

their value creation processes (Vargo & Lusch,2008; Lusch et al, 2010; Heinonnen et al, 2010; Jaakkola et al,2015) and their experiences in dyadic (service setting made of one service provider and their respective customers) or network-oriented (multiple actors providing services to their customers) contexts (Lusch & Webster, 2011; Story et al, 2020; Lipkin & Heinonnen, 2022).

In recent years, studies related to consumers experiences and their value creation process in dyadic and network-centric environments have emerged as highly discussed topics. The insights gained from these studies offer a spectrum of understanding on how businesses could facilitate sound experiences to their consumers in dyadic or network-centric service environments (Story et al, 2020; Trischler et al, 2021). Whilst facilitating sound experiences in a dyadic context depends entirely on the service provider (Bitner,1995; Berry et al, 2006; Heinonnen et al, 2010; Lemon & Verhoef,2016), however facilitating sound experiences in network-oriented environments can be considered highly complex (Story et al, 2020). To offer more light on this aspect, Sir Colin Marshall (former Chairman of British Airways) shared his experiences in an interview with Steven Prokesch (1995). Their discussions suggest that the objective of British Airways was to facilitate not only an unbeatable travel experience to their customers, but to create seamless services by dove-tailing their route networks, flight schedules and sharing codes for multi-legged flights often operated by their alliance partners/airlines (alliance carriers). This approach offered travellers to reserve a trip which entailed legs flown with two or more alliance carriers and making it easier and pleasant to transfer between the alliance partners (Prokesch, 1995). These discussions suggest dovetailing amongst alliance carriers (airline partners) to provide sound travel experience can be highly complex and comes with daunting challenges. But how consumers perceive these services, raises a new set of service experience discussions. To date, not much is explored to understand how consumers develop their holistic perceptions of their experiences in network-oriented service environments. Furthermore, to make matters murkier, little is known about the experiences of consumers in network- oriented service environments which are designed and driven by dove-tailed services, such as airline alliances. Therefore, the objective of this study is to understand firstly, how customers perceive their experiences whilst using network-oriented service environments such as the airline alliance services. And eventually, to understand the consumers' attributes of perceived experiences of network-based services offered by airline alliances.

THE RESEARCH CONTEXT

Over the last few decades, airline industry has gone through a chain of developments to meet the demands of the customers. Two types of approach are currently employed in the airline industry, the low-cost approach, and the full-service approach. The low-cost approach is adopted to provide no-frills and point-to-point services at competitive fares (Dennis, 2005; Papatheodorou & Lei, 2006). The full-service approach is often run by legacy carriers, which adopt a full-service approach and operate through their own fleet and hubs (Lohmann et al, 2009). Quite often full-service airlines engage in developing partnerships with other airlines by using code-share agreements. Whilst some airlines have created bilateral agreements, others have created multi-lateral agreements, such as multi-lateral strategic airline alliance to defend or expand their market presence (Park & Zhang, 1998). The carriers of an airline alliance have multi-lateral agreements and make use of each other's fleet and airports and hence provide inter-lined services through their joint-marketing approaches (Gudmundsson et al, 2002; Fan et al, 2001). Consequently, airline alliances have dominated the inter-continental routes, where providing quality services are the source of service differentiation between large, federated airline networks and their competitors (Tiernan et al, 2008).

Airline alliances are an unique example for strategic alliances. An airline alliance is a muti-lateral strategic alliance. They do not inherit a long history, nor they associate themselves to any country. They are made of a consortium of cherry-picked alliance carriers from several regions of the world. They have a federated structure, and they employ joint operational and marketing activities for dove-tailing their services and route operations. These aspects have the permitted alliance carrier'ss ability to facilitate and create values for their partners (Moller & Rajala, 2007; de Man & Luvison, 2019). What is apparent to the customers, is their ability to create a new sort of representation for providing seamless airline services. This sort of collaborative approach could offer a distinct perception towards dovetailing of airline services and create a new figure for the airline alliance. Therefore, the dove-tailed services of the airline alliance and the effects of its joint marketing activities could be seen as a new set of experiences for customers (Kleymann & Seristo, 2017). Therefore, in this section of the study, the subsequent discussions focus on the drivers for forming airline alliance, and the benefits

Airline Alliance

Since 1970's, airline industry witnessed a period of restructuring in American airline operations. The advent of these restructuring schemes facilitated several airlines to create a new business model by employing hub and spoke networks (Gillen & Morrison, 2005). This model invited airlines to forge partnerships with other airlines which led to development of large network of airlines (Pels, 2001) universally known as multi-lateral alliance (Gudmundsson et al, 2002). Whilst the dawn of airline alliances began just four decades ago, however they are growing at an exponential pace. Airline industry is a highly competitive industry (Doganis, 2019). And airlines face competition from all sides of the compass. Some airlines are joining an airline alliance not only to seek opportunities to create new routes for destinations, but they also seek means to evade any contest landing in their own back yards. For instance, some airlines like British Airways and Qantas co-ordinated their operations and created a new route called the "Kangaroo Route" which links European and Australian markets through transits from America and Far East (Fan et al, 2001). In other cases, some alliance carriers have formed partnerships with other alliance carriers to increase their capacities and destinations which would be difficult to accomplish otherwise. These partnerships are mainly observed in countries that have highly regulated aviation markets (Gudmundsson & Rhoades, 2001).

An airline alliance services are different to non-alliance carriers. There are several differences in the way an airline alliance operates as against a non-alliance carrier. An airline alliance pools all their alliance carriers' resources (fleets, airport hubs, etc) and uses joint-marketing activities to expand their service networks to destinations, where they did not previously operate. By doing so, an airline alliance strengthens its services and its market positions in other international airline markets. The co-operation between alliance carriers in joint alliance marketing involves co-ordination of schedules, ticketing services, passenger services and a complete integration of alliance carrier's operations (Lu, 2003).By synergising their activities, alliance carriers are not only co-ordinating their services with other alliance carriers (Brueckner, 2001), but they are also increasing traffic volumes in some specific routes by feeding new carriers through their partner airlines (Park & Zhang, 1998). These sorts of co-ordinated engagements and activities are not only demonstrating the highlights of what airline alliances can achieve through their consortium-based marketing activities, but it also suggests the driving forces behind the growth of airline alliances.

In an airline industry context, strategic alliance marketing is an informal description of the joining of different skills sets, complementary experience, networks, and resources (people, money, and time) to achieve a common objective. A strategic marketing alliance can possibly combine the expertise of alliance members and make use of the networks of participating groups. For example, alliance carriers can form a strategic marketing alliance with other groups to enhance organisational capacity, resources, and achieve specific marketing objectives (Kramer, 2010). Joint marketing activities offer several advantages to alliance carriers. Firstly, it facilitates alliance carriers to expand their services on a global scale by highlighting their extensive global connectivity through joint networks of the alliance carriers. In other words, code-sharing network offered by the alliance carriers offers development of capacities and markets (Goh & Uncles, 2003; Gayle, 2008; Brueckner et al, 2011). Secondly, joint marketing facilitates offers economies of scale (Morley, 2003). Thirdly, joint marketing facilitates overall developments in their customer relationship management and loyalty marketing through joint/alliance-wide loyalty programme (Frequent flyer programme/FFP) initiatives taken by all the members of the airline alliance (de Boer, 2018). Therefore, facilitating better service experiences to all the customers of their respective alliance carriers remains pivotal for the growth and development of an airline alliance.

In airline alliance context, some of the benefits of alliance marketing are clear. This is because, the alliance carriers form marketing alliances with other larger airlines that serve in other markets thereby increasing the destinations and widening consumer choice for travels. Therefore, marketing alliance will help alliance carriers to tap other markets and to achieve benefits of scope without making further investments or buying the shares of another airline company (Doganis, 2019). Whilst the benefits for the alliance carriers remain clear and discussed widely in literature. However, complete understanding of the experiences of airline alliances' services requires a holistic understanding from the customers' lenses. Therefore, this study makes an attempt to understand the what do consumers make of their respective experiences whilst using airline alliances' services. And hence the objective of this study.

THEORETICAL FRAMEWORK

The prominence of providing sound service experience and quality services is highly epitomised in several businesses and particularly in service industry. Several businesses, such as hotels, retail stores and airlines have made considerable investments in their service environment to provide an excellent service experience for their customers (Bolton et al, 2007). Consumers perceive the service environment by what they see, smell, taste, sound, and their touch, as clues, during their service consumption experience. They filter consciously and unconsciously these clues as a set of impressions in a rational or emotional way as experiential clues. These experiential clues eventually help create a service experience for a consumer. A sound consumer experience can hence be considered as a good consumer service, and the service consumed by the user is the experience (Berry et al, 2006). By understanding the significance of experience of consumers, this section tries to provide different facets of studies related to experience of the consumers. Firstly, this section provides an understanding on how experiences of consumers were addressed in marketing literature. Secondly, this chapters offers some understanding about the relationship between service experience and customer experience. Thirdly, the discussions are extended to understand how experience of customers is observed from dyadic and network-centric relationships. Fourthly, this section offers some understanding about relationship between experience of customers and their value creation process. And finally, this section offers an understanding on experience of the consumers can be influenced during the customer journey.

Customer Experience

Whilst observing the chronicles and origins of studies related to consumers experiences, one can find that literature on experiences of consumers is often intertwined. And to-date several studies have examined experience of consumers in diverse spheres, which makes it a highly assorted subject weaved through several aspects of marketing. Studies suggest that during 1960's -1970's, experiences of consumers were examined in the form of consumers buying behaviour and their process. From 1970's–2000, experiences of consumers were examined through the lenses of customer satisfaction, customer loyalty, relationship marketing and customer relationship concepts. From 2000-2010, studies have examined experience of customers from a customer-centric spirits of businesses and their customer-centric approaches. In recent years, experience of consumers is examined through customer engagement perspective, wherein consumers involvement and participation in an experience take the spotlight (Lemon & Verhoef, 2016). Whilst some studies, describe customer's role in an experience through customer engagement, other studies describe how businesses could facilitate positive experiences by identifying, designing, mapping, and delivering appropriate service provisions to their customers (Lemon & Verhoef, 2016). As a consensus, one can find that studies related consumers' interactions and encounters, have not only placed consumers and their experiences in the spotlight, but they also offer several theoretical and managerial implications as well.

Besides the previously mentioned aspects, it appears that some of the sources related to consumers' experience in a service setting can be traced from the service experience related studies. A service experience is considered not only as an amorphous construct but a distinct offering that is absolutely desired by the consumer. They are usually wrapped with a traditional service offering to make it more appealing for a consumer (Pine & Gilmore, 1998). Service experience can hence be defined as "the customer's direct experience of the service process, which concerns the way service provider deals with the customer. It includes customer's personal interaction with the organisation, its customer-facing staff, technology, and its facilities." Johnston & Clark (2008, p.8). During the service delivery process, consumer's encounter series of services during their interactions and involvements with service staff and technology-enabled services. The infusion of technology can further facilitate the service staff to provide suitable services to the consumers during service delivery phases (Bitner et al, 2000). Consumer's assessments are often shaped during these interactions and service encounters, which is why they represent the consumers service experience (Bitner, 1995; Bitner et al, 2000). Therefore, service experience appraisals focus on the consumer's psychological and affective representation of the experiential, hedonistic and symbolic benefits of a service setting during a consumer's service consumption process (Otto & Ritchie, 1996).

To broaden these discussions related to experiences of consumers, some studies have explored in detail to understand the relationships between service experience and customer experience. The concepts of service experience and customer experience have been observed to share several features and conceptualised similarly, in some ways. However, there are some key differences which makes them as two different concepts (Bueno et al, 2019). The concept of service experience addresses their stakeholders, including their customers. Service experience encompasses the service providers and social experiences of networks of people implicated in the service sphere (Heinonen & Strandvik, 2009; Bueno et al, 2019). On the flip side of the coin, customer experience is alluded to be a subjective and an internal customer's response to a service (Dagger & Sweeney, 2013; Bueno et al, 2019). It focusses on the experience of the customers as the main actor (Jaakkola et al, 2015; Bueno et al, 2019). Therefore, that the main differences amongst these two concepts depend on the subjects who are implicated in the experiences. Despite these differences, it is suggested that service experience is a marketing construct which is usually employed to measure customer experiences of a service (Bueno et al, 2019). However, in some studies, it is found that the complementary aspects amongst the two concepts have been used to describe customer service experience. This implies that customer service experience could be used as the means or a dimension of service experience which depicts customers reactions to a service encountered (Heinonen & Strandvik, 2009; Bueno et al, 2019). As a consensus, customer experience can be considered as a multi-dimensional construct which focusses on the cognitive, emotional, behavioural, sensorial, and social responses of the customers during their entire customer journey towards service offerings (Verhoef et al, 2009; Lemon & Verhoef, 2016).

In addition to the previous discussions, one can find that the literature of experience of consumers are further examined from a dyadic or network-centric approach. In other words, experience of consumers offers wide range of topics which are examined from dyadic relationship (consumers and service provider) to a network-oriented relationships (). From a dyadic perspective, experiences of the consumers are related to their response to a service providers' stimuli and services (Bitner, 1995; Bitner et al, 2000). In this approach, a service provider is in control of the interfaces related to service provision and service delivery to the consumers. In addition, the service provider can shape the experiences for the consumers during their service delivery through their service staff and technology-based services (Bitner et al, 2000; Berry et al, 2006; Bolton et al, 2007; Lipkin & Heinonen, 2022). From a network-centric perspective, consumers experiences can be considered as consumers' assessment towards experiences derived during their service encounters. The assessment the consumers experience can occur during dynamic or static facets whilst interacting with the touchpoints. These touchpoints and settings might remain not only within or beyond the service providers control but also the circumstantial factors which surround the service environment (Story et al, 2020; Trischler et al, 2021; Lipkin & Heinonen, 2022).

By gathering several aspects from the aforementioned discussions, it appears that consumers experiences can be influenced from both dyadic and network centric service environments. These aspects can play a pivotal role in the customers journey and their value creation processes. From a dyadic perspective, customers' journey can be shaped by the service provider who is offering the service by themselves (without any partners). The service provider can facilitate better experiences during the service encounters to the customers, because they design the service provision and eventually deliver the services to their consumers respectively (Bitner et al, 2000; Berry et al, 2006; Bolton et al, 2007). In addition to the businesses roles to shape of customer journey through dyadic approach, businesses also play key role in value facilitation for the consumers (Lusch et al, 2010; Lusch & Webster, 2011). Experience of the consumers can be treated as an immediate outcome of their value creation processes (Heinonnen et al, 2010; Jaakkola et al, 2015; Lipkin & Heinonnen, 2022). This is because consumers' experiences are specific to the subjective elements, the contexts of the service settings, and phenomenologically identified by the consumers as an outcome of their value creation process (Jaakkola et al, 2015; Lipkin & Heinonnen, 2022). Albeit consumers differ in their segments and in their respective customer journeys, however the role of service providers is to identify and facilitate conditions for supporting consumers for offering not only their much-desired experiences (Verhoef, 2020), but also facilitate values for them (Trischler et al, 2021; Lipkin & Heinonnen, 2022). Therefore, a proper understanding on how customer experience services across their entire customer journeys remains a quintessential element.

In a network-centric service environment, service provision is more complex as there are several partners who are involved in several phases of legs of the service process. In this approach the service design is composed to several service providers who provide their respective services when requested. To amplify the experience of the consumers, businesses offer linkages of their services through touch points and channels to their partners services during different phases of the customers' journey. Therefore, network-oriented approach can offer consumers several opportunities to interact with several channels and wide range of touch points to develop their experiences (Lemon & Verhoef, 2016).

In a network-centric approach, offering decent experiences to the consumers requires a proper service design along with proper management of touchpoints and channels from all the participants of the network. These aspects should be designed to facilitate steady, cohesive, pertinent, and proper inter-connectivity amongst all the actors of the network. By managing these operations, actors could facilitate better services amongst the partners and facilitate value for the end users (Lusch & Webster, 2011; Homburg et al, 2017; Story et al, 2020). In addition, the supporting roles of all the actors, who are visible or partially visible or invisible to the consumers should also be considered highly important during steady and interrupted service situations (atypical services). In other words, all the supporting actors should play their respective role in facilitating sound service experiences to the consumers during regular service situations and during service failure context as well (Story et al, 2020).

A good example of network-centric environments which facilitates sound experiences to the consumer is found in airline industry. In airline industry, the core service of the airlines is to transport people and cargo from a point of departure to their respective destination. However, there are several services providers which play a key role in the entire airline's operation. The services offered by other service providers can facilitate not only better flight operations for the airlines, but also contribute to the consumers experiences during check-in, security checks, baggage handling, personal announcements, real-time flight information, boarding, disembarking, food consumption and airport lounges services (Goh & Uncles, 2003; Doganis, 2019). In airline industry, the entire airline operations and services are complex because of the inter-relationships between the actors' service provision and delivery mechanisms (Goh & Uncles, 2003; Doganis, 2019: Story et al, 2020). The actors involved in the service provision and service delivery play an autonomous and balancing role for synchronising their services to offer holistic services experiences to their customers. Therefore, consumers' experiences are often influenced not only by the complexity in service provider's service provision, but also by the service delivery of the visible service providers (frontline staff) or service providers who remain partially visible or invisible to the consumers, i.e., fuelling, airline safety checks, air traffic control, baggage handling etc (Goh & Uncles, 2003; Doganis, 2019: Story et al, 2020).

In addition, airlines belonging to a particular airline alliance, develop co-operation through joint marketing activities. The co-operation amongst alliance carriers' have facilitated them to improve their co-ordinated code-share agreements and frequent flier programmes amongst alliance carriers (de Boer, 2018). By co-ordinating their service operations with the respective alliance carriers, alliance partners are developing several means to harmonise and integrate their products and services processes. These engagements facilitate alliance carriers to facilitate smooth travel operations (Holtbrugge et al, 2006) and facilitate alliance-wide (joint) loyalty programme-based services for their customers (de Boer, 2018). Therefore, the synchronisation and co-ordination of services orchestrated by the service providers plays an essential role for facilitating sound experiences for the consumers during regular and interrupted service scenarios (Story et al, 2020).

Whilst the aforementioned aspects are often discussed in literature, however, little is known, on how customers' experience services when they are served by multiple service providers i.e., airlines and airports belonging to an airline alliance. In addition, consumers perceptions of the service operations of alliance carriers which are served through dove-tailed service mechanisms, remains a bit murky. Therefore, by following disparities observed in previous discussions, this study explores the perception of the experience of the customers during the entire (upstream and downstream) journey in an airline alliance service setting.

RESEARCH METHODOLOGY

This study employs qualitative research methodology for conducting the research. Qualitative research methodology facilitates the study to analyse the data from direct observations from the fieldwork, in-depth and open-ended interviews. Qualitative study permits a representational assessment whilst studying the real-world situations inductively to create rich narrative explanations. By using these approaches, a study can yield patterns and themes, which are considered fruitful for the research (Patton, 2005). Before conducting the actual research, an appropriate method for sampling, interviews, and data analysis are considered pivotal for presenting the results of the study. Therefore, this offers an overview of the sampling method, sampling technique, interview method, and data analysis method employed in this study.

Sample

Probability and non-probability sampling methods are generally used in research (Koerber & McMichael, 2008). However, studies suggests that sampling methods employed in qualitative studies differ from quantitative studies. Usually sampling methods are employed in quantitative studies to reduce bias and increase generalisability. Whilst sampling methods are employed in qualitative research to offer window or mirror like perspective of a phenomenon or a situation under examination (Giacomini & Cook, 2000; Koerber & McMichael, 2008). Furthermore, it is suggested that researchers could employ non-probability sampling methods, when confidence levels are considered not that crucial or when probability samples are uneasy to acquire (Koerber & McMichael, 2008). In qualitative research, non-probability sampling has been employed in some studies by using snowballing or purposeful or convenience sampling techniques (MacNealy, 1999; Koerber & McMichael, 2008). Convenience sampling comprises of participants who are easy to reach and often available for discussions. Whilst purposeful sampling comprises of participants who have certain qualities and traits who are considered appropriate and suitable for the study under examination (Koerber & McMichael, 2008).

Unlike the previous two techniques, snowball technique is employed when the subjects belong to an unique or hard to reach population under examination. This method involves finding one or more subjects initially and eventually requesting them to recommend other subjects (Higginbottom,2004). This chain referral approach might facilitate the researcher to be a part of the subjects who have encountered the experiences under examination. Therefore, this sampling technique facilitates research to develop trust amongst the subjects and enter in certain spheres where conventional practices would find it daunting (Atkinson & Flint, 2001). In terms of the sample size, studies suggest the sample size for qualitative studies depends on the context of the study, and it differs from phenomenology-based studies, grounded theory-based study, or a case study-based research (Gentles et al, 2015). However, it was suggested that interviews could be conducted until nothing new is encountered (Cohen et al, 2000; Gentles et al, 2015) or no new themes could be generated from the study (Higginbottom,2004).

Interviews

Once the samples are sorted, interview methods are considered highly pivotal for qualitative studies. Interviews can be used in many different formats (Cassell, 2005). And they have been categorised as structured, semi-structured and unstructured (Whiting,2008). The benefits of using a structured interview or unstructured interview or semi-structured interview are usually assessed before commencing the interviews. A structured interview uses a set of regulated closed questions which are raised to all the participants as in initial screening process to assess and compare the participants responses (Mathis & Jackson, 2008). Whereas, unstructured interviews are informal, they usually do not have predetermined set of questions to follow. Unstructured interviews are known as non-directive interviews or as an informant interview. The information which emerges during the interviews, facilitates the researcher to direct the interviews. In other words, the respondents' discussions facilitate the researcher to guide the interviews conducted, moving forward (Saunders *et al.*, 2015; Axelson et al, 2010). Unlike structured and unstructured interviews, semi-structured interviews are often referred to as informal, conversational, and soft interviews. Semi-structured interviews permit the investigator to develop a few sets of questions which they want to cover. However, the order of the questions can differ depending on the flow of information gathered from the participant's discussions. Depending on the requirement of the research, supplementary questions can be added to explore new information or to seek adequate responses to the research questions under study Therefore, semi-structured interviews facilitate to stimulate discussions from a respondent to explore new issues, which were unexplored or unaddressed previously (Longhurst, 2003).

Considering the above-mentioned interview methods and, by understanding the requirements of this research study, a semi-structured interview was chosen as an appropriate methodology for this study. A series of semi-structured interviews were conducted in France with American, European, Asian, North African, and South American airline travellers. In total, 23 respondents participated in the interviews. Respondents who participated in the interviews were of both genders and in equal ratio. The participants were aged between 22 to 67 years old and were business professionals, scholars, entrepreneurs, and international students. Interviews were conducted in French and English, and the overall duration of the interviews was approximately 25 minutes. All the participants had frequently travelled on international flights and had a good experience flying with airline alliances' carriers. To meet the objectives of this study, participants prior knowledge and experience about inter-lined flights of an airline alliance were considered crucial. Based on the requirements of the interviews, participants who have suitable profile were contacted through social contacts and snowballing techniques.

Data Analysis

Whilst reviewing literature, it is found that there are several methodologies for analysing qualitative data. Studies suggests that content analysis and thematic analysis are the two widely used methodologies in qualitative research. Content analysis is used in analysing data to facilitate establishment of categories and eventually counts the number of occurrences. In other words, content analysis helps to determine the frequency of occurrences in certain categories (Joffe & Yardley, 2003). Whilst quantification remains the distinguishing feature of content analysis (Franzosi,2008), thematic analysis can be more helpful for not only analysing the data through codes, but it also facilitates to pool the analysis of the frequency of the codes with the analysis of their meaning in their respective contexts (Joffe & Yardley, 2004). Therefore, this method facilitates not only to get a proper sense of the interview data, but it can also assist to get a proper sense of what is being discussed by the participants as a group (Liamputtong, 2009; Minichiello et al, 2019).

There are few steps to carry out a proper thematic analysis. Firstly, it is suggested to get acquainted with the data by transcribing and reading the entire data to create some initial ideas about the data (Braun & Clarke, 2006). Secondly, after having acquainted with the data, it is considered appropriate to develop some lists of ideas about what is rooted in the data and what sort of information could emerge with it (Braun & Clarke, 2006). During this phase of data analysis, the development of initial codes from the data collected remains pivotal. Whilst the initial processes of coding are typically basic. However, it is crucial to get to the bottom of the issues under examination and pay detailed attention to the data under analysis. A coding framework can be established, and this could be done in several ways. Firstly, coding could be done based on the theoretical interests and the previous research findings which could facilitate the study to respond to the research questions. Secondly, coding could also be done based on the issues that emerge from the data collected. And lastly, it could be through both ways. Coding can be done either manually or through computer aided software programmes (Braun & Clarke, 2006; Liamputtong, 2009). In addition, depending on the research objectives, the coding framework may possibly be based on the pre-established criteria. These criteria could be based on particular words or topics, on repeated issues emerging from the data, or on a set of theoretical constructs which unfolded systematically, as the analysis were developed (Attride-Stirling, 2001). It is also suggested that the codes in the coding framework should draw frontlines that can be described to make sure they are not inter-changeable. This approach helps to focus on the object of the analysis, whilst avoiding to code, every phrase or sentence of the data under assessment. Hence this approach becomes a highly interpretive step during the data analysis (Attride-Stirling, 2001).

Once the initial codes are generated, it is recommended to organise the codes and collate them into some tentative sub- themes and eventual themes (Clarke & Braun, 2017). It is also suggested to gather all the data that can potentially related to a particular sub- theme and themes and eventually revise the themes that are initially developed. By using this sort of approach, the researchers can help to create themes required for analysis and check if the codes extracted from the data work in co-ordination with the themes generated. this process reaches a broader level, wherein several themes are identified from the different codes. Essentially, the researchers are required to analyse the codes and consider or reconsider what sorts of codes might merge to form an all-encompassing theme (Braun & Clarke, 2006; Clarke & Braun, 2017). Once the themes are generated, it is suggested to select the themes for further refinement. This process permits the study to check if the generated themes are distinct, non-repetitive, and offer strong linkages of patterns in the analysis. In addition, it facilitates the study to check if the themes are wide enough to capture a set of notions or ideas required for enriching the study. This approach facilitates the study to develop manageable set of relevant and significant themes which concisely encapsulates the data under examination (Braun & Clarke, 2006). Once these steps are accomplished, it is suggested to create a thematic map of the analysis and eventually define and name each of the themes respectively (Braun & Clarke, 2006). Following the benefits and the methods used for thematic analysis, this study has employed the thematic approach for data analysis. This sort of approach has been found to be fruitful to identify themes by extracting data from the participants discussions. In addition, thematic analysis can be conducted from the data collected from the participants' discussions through the interviews (Braun & Clarke, 2006; Fereday & Muir-Cochrane, 2008; Clarke & Braun, 2017).

RESULTS AND DISCUSSIONS

As the perceived service of an airline are usually assessed by understanding the consumer's perception of how the services were delivered and what services were offered (Liou & Tzeng, 2007). All the participants of the interview were briefed about the purpose of the interview. The objective aspect of the discussion was about airline alliance service offering, their service delivery during service encounters and the service environments where services were delivered. However, the subjective aspect of the interviews were focussed to understand participants' perceptions of the service offerings, service deliveries of the airline alliance as an entity and the overall experiences of their perceptions of the alliance carriers' service. In addition, as the discussions were semi-structured, this methodology allowed the further clarification of certain issues concerning the airline alliance's online services and other peripheral services (call centre and self-help kiosks). Overall, the semi-structured methodology gave a better idea to understand what sort of airline alliance services were served by alliance carriers and how were the participants' experiences whilst encountering the services delivered to them. All the participant discussions were recorded on a laptop with the permission of the participants and consequently their discussions were translated and transcribed. Based on participant's request, all the participant's names, their occupation, their experiences with airline alliances, alliance carriers', airports, aircrafts, cities, and transits are held anonymous in this study. The transcripts were analysed to develop codes, clusters of sub-themes and themes. The themes that emerged from the interviews explain the participant attributes of service experience of an airline alliance. Therefore, the participants' discussion brought certain clues to understand how consumers form perceptions of an airline alliance's service experience.

Discussions which emerged from the respondents suggest that participants have a good idea of the services offered by the alliance as against the non-alliance carriers' services. Participants' discussions also facilitated to develop attributes related to customers experiences of airline alliance services. The results from the interviews conducted could be considered in a stage of exploration. The results however can be useful for providing some clues for service experience attributes of an airline alliance. The results also offer some key information related to collaborative service provision and service delivery of airline alliances. Several aspects addressed during the participant's discussion has facilitated the study to offer some attributes of the perceived service experiences of an airline alliance. In this study, several sub-themes were developed. Eventually these sub-themes facilitated the study to create two themes. The first theme is termed as Network capacity and Synergies and the second theme is termed as Enhanced and shared Information services. Both the themes and sub-themes are mentioned in the following discussions and together they offer the study to understand the customers' attributes of airline alliance's service experience.

Theme 1: Network Capacity and Synergies

Participants' discussions suggest that airline alliances' extended networks and their inter-lined co-ordinated arrangements were considered as two key factors offered by alliance carriers to travel with ease. Participants expressed their thoughts and opinions about all the extensive services offered by joint activities of the alliance carriers. Several participants believe that their decision to fly with an airline alliance was largely based on the choices they get by using an airline alliance services. A choice for the participants is based on the number of options they can get. An option for the participants referred to the services which included increased number of flights, transit options, flight schedules, increased destinations, extended loyalty programmes, increased use of airport lounges, and extended online services offered by the alliance carriers. In addition, the participants' choice to fly with an airline alliance were based not only on the number of options offered by the airline alliance network, but also the synchronisation and harmonisation of services offered by the alliance carriers. So, the joint-marketing services offered by the airline alliance are appealing to the participants in several ways and they reckon it would be clumsy to have these sorts of services otherwise from a non-alliance airline company that operates on their own limited fleet, routes, and hubs. Based on participants' discussions, this study developed three sub-themes to facilitate the understanding of customers experiences of alliance carriers' services. These three sub-themes facilitate the study to understand the customers' perception of airline alliance's service experiences, in terms of the alliance carriers' extensive service networks, their synchronised services and the harmonisation of services developed amongst the alliance carriers.

Extensive Service Network

In an airline alliance context, sometimes one alliance carrier markets and issues tickets to consumers who are travelling to different destinations. But the flights, on which the airline passengers have booked their flight, could be operated by other carriers which belong to their respective airline alliance. Therefore, the airline passengers could be travelling on an alliance carrier that is just operating on behalf of the alliance carrier that sold the flight ticket. So, these sorts of networks of inter-lined arrangements have created a wide range of travel itineraries, which seems to be appealing to airline passengers.

Participant discussions suggest that the choice to fly with an airline alliance is based on the options made available by the airline alliance for the passengers. However, the options made available by an airline alliance are largely based on the services offered by the alliance carrier network. And the services that participants discussed were (a) wide range of destinations; (b) a greater number of flights to select for flying to certain destinations; (c) high frequency of flights to destination; (d) option to select a combination of alliance carriers to fly to a destination; (e) option of flying on a direct and a non-direct flight; (f) option of choosing an airport transit as against another transit airport; (g) option of flying at any given time of the day. Participant discussions suggest that the wide range of options made available for the passengers would help them to cherry pick the options and build their own itinerary. This sort of cherry-picking scheme and creating one's own itinerary is considered as an attribute of the perceived service quality of an airline alliance. Some of the participant thoughts and perceptions are discussed as mentioned below

Informant 19, Male, North African "The benefits, it is already the question of, what I mean is already, for sure the air fare. And then, we have the choice, like we have lot of choice of choosing an airline (alliance carrier) to fly, any date to fly. And then there is the question of quality, for example, you have choice of choosing any flight to travel on any date. Therefore, you have choice to fly on any date. Then you have choice of choosing a transit which permits you to reduce the time of the journey".

Informant 20, Male, European, "We have a lot of possibilities, we have a lot of destinations, we have a lot of flights for each destination, which gives flexibility for travel and more choices. We can choose a flight that corresponds to our travel requirements, where we can arrive at a convenient time. So, there is flexibility. Flexibility, I mean the group (airline alliance) has several airlines (alliance carriers), we can choose which airline company to fly, to which destination and we can choose a transit in a particular country, as against other transit countries etc. And this helps the passenger to plan their travel itinerary".

Informant 21, Male, North African "If I am flying by an airline company which operates on its own fleet of airlines and does not have partnerships with other airlines. I might take 24 hours to reach to a destination. But for example, If I take a flight (through an airline alliance) where there are two or more flights from other companies (alliance carriers) with transits for taking the next connecting flight. And, if I can save 6 hours or 8 hours to arrive at final my destination by taking these airlines (airline alliance members). I can arrive to my destination early. So, I see that this system is more practical especially for frequent flyers, for business travellers who travel frequently. So, customers can find flexibility through these flights".

Informant 23, Female, European "I think, I first choose the destination and then the most interesting will be the time. How will I take, how long will it take to get to the place to the destination. And plus, the service they are offering what type of service on board, also service before the departure and after I will get to the airport that I don't know. Some services like they will also provide somebody for helping me to find a taxi or something how to get out of the airport".

Informant 25, Male, European "Yes, it's true that rather by flying with one airline company (operating with its own fleet). I can travel around the world (with an airline alliance network): I mean by proper travelling around the world, by visiting several countries around the world with a choice of 900 or so destinations. And so, I imagine it is a 100 percent benefit. So, this is exceptional. Rather than travelling with one company, I can travel anywhere, without searching another airline company for travelling, where you must pay for other supplementary fares. And once you are in a country, it is hard to buy another airline ticket to travel further".

Informant 26, Female, Asian "Airport K and Airport M there is more choice. And later the transit time at the transit airport is also very important to me. Because if I take an airline with a transit in Airport X. For example, Airport A–B- C. At B, I must wait for 8 hours or 9 hours to take the connecting flight. But, if I choose to use another route and transit in X or Y, then I will spend just two hours for taking the next connecting flight from this transit airports. And that is all you need (less stop over time)".

Participant discussions suggest that the results match some of the previous scholarly works on marketing strategies of an airline alliance. Previous studies have illustrated the importance of extensive network arrangements offered by the airline alliance. It is noted from other scholarly works that an extended network is beneficial to airline alliance. The alliance carrier's network connects to a larger network of flight routes and destinations of other alliance carrier's flight networks. The most common type of alliance marketing tools are code-sharing agreements between alliance carriers. However, the concept is extended amongst all the members of the multi-lateral alliance, making it a multi-lateral code-sharing agreement (Dennis,2000; Goh & Uncles, 2003; Weber & Sparks, 2004, Weber,2005, Iatrou & Alamdari,2005; de Man et al,2010; Redondi et al,2011).

So, due to the massive expansion of airlines alliances in many parts of the world, alliance carriers are marketing and promoting large number of interlined itineraries. All the interlined itineraries are made of by combination of two or more alliance carrier's fleet and route networks. So, these forms of interlined itineraries are becoming increasingly popular as they offer large number of destinations, choice of flights to pick, choice of schedules to fly during any part of the day, choice of transits and finally choice of selecting a combination of flight to travel to a particular destination. This ease of forming a travel itinerary has been well marketed by the airline alliance carriers. And this form of inter-lined arrangements and are now extended to all the alliance carriers' network (Wright et al, 2010) which has helped airline alliances to reduce fares on city pairs (Bamberger et al, 2001). Therefore, these sorts of inter-lined arrangements made among the alliance carriers, which are also called code-share arrangement, have an advantage of gaining access to seats availability and inventory on some flights operated by other alliance carriers. Through these inter-lined arrangements all the alliance carriers can serve several destinations on a global scale. And this would be realised by the large extension of other alliance carrier's route networks, their supporting fleets, and their facilitating hubs. Besides all the massive increase in the choice of destinations through code-share arrangements, the code-share arrangements can also pool a massive demand from alliance carrier's fleet, which would result in economies of scale, a benefit that is purely enticing for any alliance carrier (Topaloglu, 2012).

Synchronisation of Services

Consecutive interviews with participants suggest that the synchronising of flight schedules among the airlines, ground services offered at transit airport, and synchronising the baggage services between two airlines are important features that determine the quality of the airline alliance network. Passengers' discussions suggest that all the inter-linked airlines operating under the airline alliance network dovetail their services at all the transit airports. Alliance carriers' dovetail their services by synchronising their flight schedules to reduce layover time and distribute baggage services for connecting flights. Participants' discussions also suggest that some alliance carriers are using a dedicated terminal at airports that are specifically designed to cater to the alliance carriers of a particular airline alliance. This system of using dedicated terminals assigned to a particular airline alliance helps passengers to save time for taking their connecting flights and this also helps alliance carriers to operate in one terminal to facilitate smooth operations at major hubs of the alliance carriers. Therefore, participants consider all these above-mentioned services to determine the attributes of service quality of the airline alliance. Participant's discussions suggests that the synchronisation of the flight schedules between the alliance carriers and the ground services offered by the alliance carriers at the transit airport during flight connections can explain the overall efficiency of the dove-tail services of the alliance network.

Informant 21, Male, North African "I think co-ordination among the flights is important especially between two airline companies because it is important for the customers who fly by two airlines which includes a connecting flight. It is important for the flights to co-ordinate their operations between themselves for satisfying the airline passengers. It is important for the airlines to co-ordinate and synchronise their operations for saving their time, respecting the customers for their food requirements, and satisfying the airline passengers. It is important for the airlines to co-ordinate their services and it is clear from the

18 airlines of the alliance which have chosen to be the members of the airline alliance, there is certain level of co-ordination among the airlines of the alliance. Therefore, the choice of a destination and the choice of an airline company is more practical, and it is more favourable for the airline passengers to travel with an airline alliance than travelling with an airline operating through its own fleet".

Informant 13, Male, European "Hmmm yes. Absolutely there is, I mean those airlines which are co-operating with each other they have a good co-operation (co-ordination of flights) and it all helps you for a smooth, smooth sailing. But what I think is, that you know a certain culture in exists in these hubs. It is less actually; this is the airline. But you have the same culture (airline service culture) when you are in Airport A, or you are in Airport B or you are in Airport C".

Informant 25, Male, European "Yes, it depends on what sort of services are proposed. Because, for example, if I drop my bags at the airport, and I am travelling for two days with the transits. If for example, if I am picking my bags at Hong Kong during transit with my suitcases and backpack and have 1 hour of transit time to take my connecting flight then it bothers me. And if there is a service that follows the co-ordination (baggage and flight connection). I think if you are travelling to a far of destination on the other side of the world, this co-ordination can be of an advantage. And it is important that the whole travel should not be long and tiring. So, the travel should less tiring and not for long time. Yes, fluidity is important, and it should not be a long wait".

Informant 26, Female, Asian "Yes, if the all the 18 alliance carriers work in the same terminal, its more practical not only for the passengers of the airline alliance but also for the alliance carriers, as it is easier for communicating. And for us(passengers), we don't wait, we don't wait for 12 hours or 8 hours for taking the next connecting flight. And we don't have to move and don't take any shuttle services to move to another terminal. And this is practical. We don't want to be lost in the airport, because as you know the airport in City X is massive".

Participant discussions provide important clues about the co-ordinating functions of an airline alliance which explains the seamless travel experience offered by alliance carriers. It is interesting to note that, participants' discussions about co-ordination among the alliance carriers which determines the smoothness of the dove-tail services can be related to some scholarly works on seamless travel. Previous studies explain seamless travel experiences offered by an airline alliance is a marketing arrangement between alliance carriers of an airline alliance that facilitates passengers to have quick, efficient, and smooth travel from check-in counter of the departing airport to baggage collection at the destination airport. (Belobaba et al,2009; Steven & Merklein,2012). During the whole process, passengers of the alliance carriers (the airline that sold the air ticket and the alliance carriers that partly or fully provide the transportation service) are provided to make use of the respective alliance carrier's check-in counters, baggage dropping, baggage collections, airport lounges, transit halls, boarding gates, ground personnel assistance and in-flight services. This arrangement also includes passengers to go through efficient flight connections between two connecting flights of an airline alliance. Moreover, in an event of missing a connecting flight or cancellations of flight, airline alliances provide alternative flights for passengers to reach their respective destinations quickly and hence improving the efficiency of the airline alliance services to passengers. Therefore, it is to be noted that, the co-operation among the alliance carriers exceeds simple agreements to more integration and firm co-ordination (Kleymann & Seristo, 2017).

Customer Experiences of Omni-Partner Services

Harmonisation of Services

Consecutive interviews with participants suggest that most participants often find that the on ground and on-board services offered by alliance carriers are almost similar or "Quasi-similar". Most participants also believe that the services offered by airline staff at the airport and the cabin crew are almost similar among all the alliance carriers. Participants reckon that, unlike low-cost airlines, the alliance carriers are full-service providers and provide proper services to their passengers. Furthermore, as the alliance carriers are made of full-service providers and not low-cost airlines that have no-frills service policies. The participants discussions suggest that there is some sort of resemblance of services among the alliance carriers in terms of the process of serving passengers, starting from check-in to baggage handling services at the destination airports.

Informant 13, Male, European "When I look at the alliance, which are (European carriers) Airline A, Airline B and Airline C .For example, which I am using very often. I have the feeling that all these airlines, in terms of their culture they continue their own culture which is (Country's cultural background of the) Airlines A or an Airline B's culture or Airline C. I mean these three airlines are similar because they are from the same sort of geographic region. And so I think there was from the, from the beginning there was probably a homogeneity in this, in this three.".

Informant 21, Male, North African "And more important is there is certain homogeneity among the airlines of the alliance, because there is no Airline X (A low-cost company) in the airline alliance. I mean these airlines (alliance carriers) are full-service providers and are quite similar in terms of characteristics, and services etc. I mean for someone who is flying on a flight from country in Africa and is flying on several flights, but it will good find food that suits the passenger's food choice and requirements. For example, if you are taking two or three flights for your entire flight journey and it is good if the airlines are providing two different types of food on the flights. The customers will be better satisfied when you offer two types of services".

Informant 19, Male, North African "For now, I have been using Airline 1 and Airline 2, and for transits, I have not noticed any difference in quality. And for the in-flight services, the qualities were good. And for transits, I had one hour or one hour and half, I guess. The time spent for taking the connecting flight was alright. I did not notice any major difference in the quality of service on board (Airline 1 and Airline 2) and even with the quality of service of the cabin crew. And food service was almost the same. And yes, voila, especially, I have not noticed any major differences in service quality (among the airlines). Like I told you, the only time I have used transits is in Airport A, Airport B, Airport C. It worked well for me during my return flights with transits and quality services on board".

Informant 20, Male, European "What I find interesting for me are the quality of services that are offered by the airlines, they are quite similar. Sometimes on a flight journey, the airline companies which serve the flight journey, I mean there is homogeneity in quality, the airlines adapt to the requirements of the customers, like food requirements of the customers coming from different cultural backgrounds. The quality of the service is quite similar from one company to the others, which helps to have a level of homogeneity in services on an entire flight journey".

Informant, 25, Female, European "Yes, I guess, and if I compare the service quality of) Airline 1 and Airline 2, (European alliance carriers) they have same level of quality. I have never flown with Airline C (European Alliance carrier) and so I am afraid I don't know much about its quality. The other airline I flew was Airline X (European alliance carrier) and it's very good. And, it has the same level of quality like Airline 1 and Airline 2. When I talk about the quality I talk about the seat comfort, the service, the food, the service attendance of the cabin crew and things like this"

Informant, 22, Female, South American "Hmmm, Well the the airlines that I have taken. Well, they are homogeneous concerning the... the food, they have snacks, then dinner and then breakfast before we arrive (land). Yes, the only thing that are usually quite different is the television. And the entertainment (In-flight Entertainment-IFE), I think because some of them (aircrafts) have their own individual televisions (IFE), some of them no.".

Informant, 29, Male, European "With respect to, the levels of quality of services offered by the airlines. And talking about the quality of service of an airline. In my opinion, it is all about the seating comfort, the cabin crew, the aircraft itself, a new aircraft etc. So, there are a lot of things I consider like, food, the seats where you can sleep. There are economic class of some flights that are different from other. Overall, I judge the airline service levels based on these things. Then its fine for me".

Participants' discussions suggest that the alliance carriers also have similar approaches for serving their respective customers. These services can be related to reservation, cancellation, air miles registration, customer assistance through their respective call centres or through online service platforms. In addition, discussions suggest that the alliance carriers have similar approaches concerning customer services (ground, on-board and online services) for international customers. And hence try to deliver harmonised sort of services in any possible way they can. Besides these opinions, participants also suggested that they find few minor differences in services among the alliance carriers, and they suppose these differences are due to the food and beverage services. Participants believe that the difference in food and beverage services among the alliance carriers are based on the alliance carrier's ability to meet the regional taste of the markets they service. These aspects consequently influence the hospitality and service culture of an airline's cabin services, food and beverage services. For instance, an Asian alliance carrier could serve passengers based on its cultural background and offer passengers a cultural flavour on food and beverages. However, with the advent of airline alliance network most intentional alliance carrier offer a choice to select food that suits American, European, Asian travellers. Participant discussion suggest that alliance carriers therefore offer a wide range of options for selecting food and drinks to maintain international and regional influences on their food and drink section.

Previous studies suggest that airline alliances are making improvements to organise their network to harmonise the services among all the alliance carriers with other alliance carriers (Holtbrugge et al, 2006). It is found that the service quality performance levels (flight arriving on-time, reports on baggage, and cancellations of flight) of alliance carriers have improved (Tiernan et al, 2008) and there is also convergence of quality (delays in flight, mishandling of baggage, denial of boarding and complaints registered by passengers) within the alliance carriers (Tsantoulis and Palmer, 2008).

Theme 2: Enhanced and Shared Information Services

Participant discussions therefore suggest the services offered online are key drivers which facilitate customers to experience useful and beneficial service from an airline alliance extended online networks. Therefore, the presence of online service of an airline alliance network is of a great benefit to the participants. Participants' discussion suggest that the information services developed by airline alliance offer an efficient system to communicate with their customers travel related activities. These services include, reservation, updating their loyalty programmes and seeking updated flight schedules and flight status information. The participants' discussions also appear to be in-line with the recent studies related to investments made by alliance carriers for enhancing their online services and infrastructure to facilitate seamless online services to their customers and their respective alliance partners. In addition, studies suggests that airline alliances have been involved in joint information technology activities, and this helps in general harmonisation and integration of all the information technology systems among the alliance carriers (Oum & Park, 1997; Li, 2000; Morrish & Hamilton, 2002).

Participants' discussions also suggest that the reciprocal and mutual alliance-wide loyalty programme (Frequent Flier Programme or FFP) offered by alliance carriers' online services are an additional benefit and convenience. Participant discussions suggest that the alliance-wide loyalty programme services facilitate their customers to accrue and redeem miles from all the members of the airline alliance. The alliance-wide loyalty programme facilitates the customers to have one alliance carrier's FFP membership, rather than registering to several individual alliance carriers' FFP membership. This sort of loyalty programmes permits alliance wide customers to avail FFP benefits of all the members of the airlines. Based on the participants' discussions, the shared and reciprocated services offered by alliance-wide loyalty programme services are considered as pivotal features which offers sound service experiences to the customers. These discussions appear to be in-line with the few studies, which explain the benefits and advantages of alliance-wide loyalty programme services. These studies suggest that under one FFP airline alliance programme, all alliance members recognise and register the individual alliance carrier's FFP schemes (Goh & Uncles, 2003; Weber,2005; de Boer,2018). Based on participants' discussions, this study developed two sub-themes to facilitate the understanding of customers experiences of alliance carriers' online information services. The first sub-theme is termed as Interactive services and the second sub-theme is termed as Shared and reciprocated services. Both these two sub-themes facilitate the study to understand the customers' perception of airline alliance's online services.

Interactive Services

Successive discussions with participants suggest that most interviewees reckon that the airline alliance offer a wide range of services on the internet that is off a huge benefit for the passengers. Participants said that the online services offered by the alliance carriers helps them to access flight information like; flights serving to a particular destination, departure and arrival times, frequency of flights in a day or week, duration of the entire flight journey, transits to be used, etc for reserving their airline tickets. The website also helps to select their dietary and other travel requirements whilst booking their flight tickets. And finally, the participants said that the online presence has helped them for accessing their frequent flier programs for registering their air miles and updating priority status.

Informant 26, Female, Asian "Reservation online is practical to use because I can connect to my loyalty program account and the air miles get accumulated automatically. And if I reserve an airline ticket, there is clarity about the list of flight details (name of the alliance carrier/s operating, name of the alliance selling the flight ticket, flight schedule, airfare, duration of the flight, transit, lay over time). So, If I do not have a lot of flight information or if I have the better information on flights and then if we have a list of flight details. So, you can compare (and decide to buy the flight ticket). Well Airline A* and Airline B* provide information that is clearer and this is another benefit. If I must reserve a flight ticket with 17 routes to travel for one week and there is one price so I would choose this as it is more practical. And it is better to reserve this than going to a travel agency for reserving the flight. And what else can think of the website service is the question of online security of the use of bank (credit/debit) cards. And this is assured, because Airline A and Airline B have verification of 3D (an online security tool) for their online transactions. So, there is security for my bank (credit/debit) card transactions online".

Informant 24, Female, European "I think the service of the website is well done and it's attractive and I think they have system of organising the website, which is in an American way "Information on your fingertips". And information available on the website for reservation are like Airline A and Airline C. We can say that it's clear and easy to use".

Informant, 22, Female, South American "Yes, I think that is useful and very good. Because I am used to buy things online. But I usually feel comfortable if I have the impression that the site, the homepage is serious or if they do not omit any information and give all the things that you want to know. It's for me a sign that they are a very serious and they are not going to do anything and misguiding".

Informant 28, Male, European "There is a difference between the information available on the website and through a travel agency. Perhaps a person working in a travel agency might make mistakes (to provide information about the flights). But the information available on the website is proper. It is efficient. And yes, and there will fewer errors on the website. The website is made to provide all the information required (to the passengers) if you search it well".

Informant 29, Male, European "I think the website is a good thing because we use internet all the time, every day. And it is much better to access information from the website than a travel agency. Because you can access information through the website at any time, as it allows flexible timing. Whereas the timings of the travel agency are fixed. The other thing is the price and sale of airline tickets between the airline company's website and with the travel agency. Sometimes, perhaps in one travel agency, they might sell airline tickets of one company as against the others. So, it (website) allows the customer to be free and to choose any airline ticket in easy way and not getting stressed by the travel agency as well."

Shared and Reciprocated Services

Participant discussions suggest that alliance carriers have mutual understanding with their partners. And due to their mutually exclusive services and high-level reciprocal service agreements. Alliance carriers offer a whole bunch of services for the airline alliance passengers. Participants suggest that alliance carriers offer passengers mutual recognition and registration of loyalty programs that belong to their alliance. In case of flight cancellation alliance carriers also offer alliance passengers to fly with other

Customer Experiences of Omni-Partner Services

alliance carriers belonging to their airline alliance. Therefore, the mutual and reciprocal services offered by an airline alliance are considered as determinants that illustrate the quality of services offered by an airline alliance.

Informant 13, Male, European "But it comes to other things organisational issues like hmmm mileage points that you can switch and… and use them all together that is of course a, I think it's a great advantage. Hmmm, also that the networks are bigger, that you can switch within them (airline alliance). If you come late by Airline A, it puts you on Airline B's plane and so on and so. These are things which make your life much easier for the traveller"

Informant 19, Male, North African "There is also something that I wish, and I imagine this may not be the case (with all the alliances). In case of flight delay, I mean if I miss my connecting flight due to flight delays. I wish the alliances (all the alliances) propose another flight to take, without paying any extra air fare to board another connecting flight, and this system exists in an airline alliance. In this case, this is very important. If you miss your connecting flight due to flight delay from one of your flights, you can take another connecting flight (connecting through an alliance partner airline company) without waiting from one hour or two hours or sometimes one day. You can take next connecting flight immediately".

Informant 17, Male, European "An airline alliance is like the menu (a la carte with choice of entre, main course and desert) of simplicity, efficiency, and rapidity. And yes, an airline company can bring its usual network, I mean it can bring its usual customers, who use the company regularly, and benefit the loyalty services of the company in fact … the loyalty card (frequent flyer programme). And so, this form of loyalty, we can say, it doesn't limit to just Airline 1, it will extend its limit of Airline 1 and open the loyal customers of Airline 1. It will open the possibility of using the other airline companies that comes under the alliance, the alliance which Airline1 is from. And, so, we can say that the customers know they have choice. In fact, I mean, if they don't choose Airline1. But take another flight of the alliance and they know, they will benefit, all the travels they make, and the air miles will be also registered in their loyalty program. And this will encourage I mean Airline1 and other companies of the alliance".

Informant 20, Male, European "We can earn air miles from each airline company (alliance carrier) of the group (airline alliance). So this helps for the loyalty programmes (of the alliance carrier): wherein we can accumulate the air miles of the airlines and this scheme helps customers to climb up the priority status of the loyalty programs in less time and faster".

From the following discussion it is evident that alliance carriers extend their services to cater the requirements of other alliance carrier's customers. of an Alliance carriers' customers can earn and redeem air miles from flights operated and marketed by any alliance carrier belonging to the airline alliance. These discussions appear to offer similar perceptions found in other studies related the airline alliance loyalty programmes. Previous studies suggest that alliance carriers facilitate the customers to accrue their air miles from any alliance carrier quicker and thereby improve their priority status swiftly and finally redeem their air miles with any member of the alliance (Goh & Uncles, 2003; Weber, 2005).

CONCLUSION

An airline alliance is made of several alliance carriers that provide different types of services (on ground, onboard, web and call centres) to passengers travelling to several destinations on economy class, business class and first class. Interviews from the discussants suggest that, unlike non-alliance carriers, the services offered by an airline alliance network are on a massive scale and often comes with complexities. These complexities arise due to the introduction of the new entrant's (alliance carriers' membership) services and their respective airline operations. As the enlargement continues, the airline alliances are constantly offering new destinations and upgrading their services through their joint-marketing activities. Therefore, whilst airline alliances' services could be offered on a colossal scale, however, the quality of the services provided to global consumers could be met with several challenges.

This exploratory study is in an infant stage to identify the attributes of the consumer perceived experiences of an airline alliance. However, this exploratory study, in its present form offers new insights about the attributes of consumer's perception of airline alliance's services. Discussions with the interviewees, suggest that the participants tended to make decisions to fly with an airline alliance based on the overall experiences pooled from the alliance carriers. Furthermore, participants chose to fly with an airline alliance due to two reasons firstly, due to the number of increased network capacity and synergies offered by the airline alliance, and secondly, due to the enhanced and sharing of information amongst the alliance carriers.

The increased network capacity and synergies refers to the co-operative and synergetic services offered by the alliance carriers to provide increased number of flights, destinations, schedules, frequencies. Additionally, the increased network capacity refers to the participants' ability to choose not only the alliance carriers when flights are inter-linked, but also the right transit airport in case of layover, etc. Interviews suggest that participants prefer to have the upper hand in decision making process. This is because participants wish to seek sound experiences and benefits for the price, they paid to receive the services from an alliance carrier. Participants' discussions suggests that they preferred to create their benefits by designing their own journeys, creating their own itineraries, and maintaining their frequent flyer programme accounts. Therefore, participants consider number of options offered by the airline alliance, can assist them to design their respective, trajectories, choose the service providers (alliance carriers), develop their loyalty programme relationships. Participants discussions also reveal that participants considered the synchronisation and harmonisation amongst the alliance carriers as another important factor to judge the seamless service delivery of the alliance carriers. The dove-tailed, and harmonised service provisions amongst the alliance carriers can facilitate consumers to seek seamless services during their journeys.

Participants discussions also reveal that participants considered the enhanced and sharing of information amongst the alliance carriers as another important factor to determine not only the seamless service delivery of the alliance carriers, but also to assess the customers experiences. The alliance carrier's ability to develop not only mutual and reciprocal arrangements amongst the alliance carriers, but also to offer interactive services for their respective customers can considered an important attribute for the participants. The mutual and reciprocal arrangements amongst the alliance carriers are made possible because of the alliance carriers' ability to create, share, integrate, pool, and synergise alliance carriers' service operations amongst other alliance carriers belonging to their alliance. Furthermore, another additional dimension which offers decent experience to the consumers are the interactive services offered by the alliance carriers. Participants discussions suggest that interactive services offered by alliance carriers largely depend on the entire alliance carriers' framework to share and pool the flight and customers information amongst the alliance carriers. The interactive services delivered online (web-based) to their respective customers could be related to flight reservations, modifications, flight information updates, baggage handling, airport services, customers' accounts, customer relationships, and their loyalty programmes. Therefore, this study suggests that consumers could determine their experiences based on not only the increased network capacity and synergies of the alliance carriers, but also on the enhanced and sharing of information amongst alliance carriers' services and operations. Both these dimensions could facilitate customers to synthesise their holistic experiences. Additionally, the experiences of customers towards alliance's carriers' services may also assist them in their value creation process moving forward.

Overall, this study suggests that participants consider the services offered by the alliance carriers as an omni-partner engagement. This transcends our existing understanding of omni-channel engagements found within a sole service provider. In this study, the participant discussions indicate that the alliance carriers' service appear to offer omni-partner based services. This suggests that alliance carriers not only offer omni-channel services to their customers, but they also tend to offer omni-partner services by weaving, synchronising, and harmonising their services with other members of their respective alliance. These sort of approaches and engagements, permitted the participants to have access to alliance carriers' services and experience seamless services during their entire customer journeys.

REFERENCES

Atkinson, R., & Flint, J. (2001). Accessing hidden and hard-to-reach populations: Snowball research strategies. *Social Research Update*, *33*(1), 1–4.

Axelson, R., Kreiter, C., Ferguson, K., Solow, C., & Huebner, K. (2010). Medical school preadmission interviews: Are structured interviews more reliable than unstructured interviews? *Teaching and Learning in Medicine*, *22*(4), 241–245. doi:10.1080/10401334.2010.511978 PMID:20936568

Bamberger, G. E., Carlton, D. W., & Neumann, L. R. (2004). An empirical investigation of the competitive effects of domestic airline alliances. *The Journal of Law & Economics*, *47*(1), 195–222. doi:10.1086/386274

Belobaba, P. (2009). The Airline Planning Process. In P. Belobaba, A. Odoni, & C. Barnhart (Eds.), *The Global Airline Industry* (1st ed., pp. 153–181). John Wiley & Sons, Ltd. doi:10.1002/9780470744734.ch6

Berry, L., Wall, E., & Carbone, L. (2006). Service Clues and Customer Assessment of the Service Experience: Lessons from Marketing. *The Academy of Management Perspectives*, *20*(2), 43–57. doi:10.5465/amp.2006.20591004

Bissessur, A., & Alamdari, F. (1998). Factors affecting the operational success of strategic airline alliances. *Transportation*, *25*(4), 331–355. doi:10.1023/A:1005081621754

Bitner, M. J. (1995). Building service relationships: It's all about promises. *Journal of the Academy of Marketing Science*, *23*(4), 246–251. doi:10.1177/009207039502300403

Bitner, M. J., Brown, S. W., & Meuter, M. L. (2000). Technology infusion in service encounters. *Journal of the Academy of Marketing Science*, *28*(1), 138–149. doi:10.1177/0092070300281013

Bolton, R. N., Grewal, D., & Levy, M. (2007). Six strategies for competing through service: An agenda for future research. *Journal of Retailing*, *83*(1), 1–4. doi:10.1016/j.jretai.2006.11.001

Braun, V., & Clarke, V. (2006). Using thematic analysis in psychology. *Qualitative Research in Psychology*, *3*(2), 77–101. doi:10.1191/1478088706qp063oa

Braun, V., & Clarke, V. (2012). Thematic analysis. In H. Cooper, P. M. Camic, D. L. Long, A. T. Panter, D. Rindskopf, & K. J. Sher (Eds.), APA handbook of research methods in psychology, Vol. 2. Research designs: Quantitative, qualitative, neuropsychological, and biological (pp. 57–71). American Psychological Association. doi:10.1037/13620-004

Brueckner, J. K. (2001). The economics of international codesharing: an analysis of airline alliances. *International Journal of Industrial Organization*, *19*(10), 1475-1498.

Brueckner, J. K., Lee, D. N., & Singer, E. S. (2011). Alliances, codesharing, antitrust immunity, and international airfares: Do previous patterns persist? *Journal of Competition Law & Economics*, *7*(3), 573–602. doi:10.1093/joclec/nhr005

Bueno, E. V., Weber, T. B. B., Bomfim, E. L., & Kato, H. T. (2019). Measuring customer experience in service: A systematic review. *Service Industries Journal*, *39*(11-12), 779–798. doi:10.1080/02642069.2018.1561873

Cassell, C. (2005). Creating the interviewer: Identity work in the management research process. *Qualitative Research*, *5*(2), 167–179. doi:10.1177/1468794105050833

Clarke, V., & Braun, V. (2016). Thematic analysis. *The Journal of Positive Psychology*, *12*(3), 297–298. doi:10.1080/17439760.2016.1262613

Cohen, M. Z., Kahn, D. L., & Steeves, R. H. (2000). *Hermeneutic phenomenological research: A practical guide for nurse researchers*. Sage Publications. doi:10.4135/9781452232768

Dagger, T. S., Danaher, P. J., Sweeney, J. C., & McColl-Kennedy, J. R. (2013). Selective halo effects arising from improving the interpersonal skills of frontline employees. *Journal of Service Research*, *16*(4), 488–502. doi:10.1177/1094670513481406

De Boer, E. (2018). The Different Types of Frequent Flyer Programs. In Strategy in Airline Loyalty. Frequent Flyer Programs. (pp. 29-57). Palgrave Macmillan. doi:10.1007/978-3-319-62600-0_2

De Man, A. P., & Luvison, D. (2019). Collaborative business models: Aligning and operationalizing alliances. *Business Horizons*, *62*(4), 473–482. doi:10.1016/j.bushor.2019.02.004

De Man, A. P., Roijakkers, N., & De Graauw, H. (2010). Managing dynamics through robust alliance governance structures: The case of KLM and Northwest Airlines. *European Management Journal*, *28*(3), 171–181. doi:10.1016/j.emj.2009.11.001

Dennis, N. (2000). Scheduling issues and network strategies for international airline alliances. *Journal of Air Transport*, *11*(3), 175–183. doi:10.1016/j.jairtraman.2004.07.004

Dennis, N. (2005). Industry consolidation and future airline network structures in Europe. *Journal of Air Transport Management*, *6*(2), 75–85. doi:10.1016/S0969-6997(99)00027-7

Doganis, R. (2019). *Flying Off Course: airline economics and marketing* (5th ed.). Routledge. doi:10.4324/9781315402987

Fan, T., Vigeant-Langlois, L., Geissler, C., Bosler, B., & Wilmking, J. (2001). Evolution of global airline strategic alliance and consolidation in the twenty-first century. *Journal of Air Transport Management*, *7*(6), 349–360. doi:10.1016/S0969-6997(01)00027-8

Fereday, J., & Muir-Cochrane, E. (2006). Demonstrating rigor using thematic analysis: A hybrid approach of inductive and deductive coding and theme development. *International Journal of Qualitative Methods*, *5*(1), 80–92. doi:10.1177/160940690600500107

Franzosi, R. (2008). Content analysis: Objective, systematic, and quantitative description of content. *Content Analysis, 1*(1), 21-49.

Gayle, P. G. (2008). An Empirical Analysis of the Competitive Effects of the Delta/Continental/Northwest Code-Share Alliance. *The Journal of Law & Economics*, *51*(4), 743–766. doi:10.1086/595865

Gentles, S. J., Charles, C., Ploeg, J., & McKibbon, K. A. (2015). Sampling in qualitative research: Insights from an overview of the methods literature. *Qualitative Report*, *20*(11), 1772–1789. doi:10.46743/2160-3715/2015.2373

Giacomini, M. K., & Cook, D. J.Evidence-Based Medicine Working Group. (2000). Users' guides to the medical literature: XXIII. Qualitative research in health Care B. What are the results and how do they help me care for my patients? *Journal of the American Medical Association*, *284*(4), 478–482. doi:10.1001/jama.284.4.478 PMID:10904512

Gillen, D., & Morrison, W. G. (2005). Regulation, competition and network evolution in aviation. *Journal of Air Transport Management*, *11*(3), 161–174. doi:10.1016/j.jairtraman.2005.03.002 PMID:32572312

Goh, K., & Uncles, M. (2003). The benefits of airline global alliances: An empirical assessment of the perceptions of business travelers. *Transportation Research Part A, Policy and Practice*, *37*(6), 479–497. doi:10.1016/S0965-8564(02)00054-X

Gronroos, C. (2008). Service logic revisited: Who creates value? And who co-creates? *European Business Review*, *20*(4), 298–314. doi:10.1108/09555340810886585

Gudmundsson, S. V., de Boer, E. R., & Lechner, C. (2002). Integrating frequent flyer programs in multilateral airline alliances. *Journal of Air Transport Management*, *8*(6), 409–417. doi:10.1016/S0969-6997(02)00043-1

Gudmundsson, S. V., & Rhoades, D. L. (2001). Airline alliance survival analysis: Typology, strategy and duration. *Transport Policy*, *8*(3), 209–218. doi:10.1016/S0967-070X(01)00016-6

Heinonen, K., & Strandvik, T. (2009). Monitoring value-in-use of e-service. *Journal of Service Management*, *20*(1), 33–51. doi:10.1108/09564230910936841

Heinonen, K., Strandvik, T., Mickelsson, K. J., Edvardsson, B., Sundström, E., & Andersson, P. (2010). A customer-dominant logic of service. *Journal of Service Management*, *21*(4), 531–548. doi:10.1108/09564231011066088

Higginbottom, G. (2004). Sampling issues in qualitative research. *Nurse Researcher*, *12*(1), 7–19. doi:10.7748/nr2004.07.12.1.7.c5927 PMID:15493211

Holtbrugge, D., Wilson, S., & Berg, N. (2006). Human resource management at Star Alliance: Pressures for standardization and differentiation. *Journal of Air Transport Management*, *12*(6), 306–312. doi:10.1016/j.jairtraman.2006.07.006

Homburg, C., Jozić, D., & Kuehnl, C. (2017). Customer experience management: Toward implementing an evolving marketing concept. *Journal of the Academy of Marketing Science*, *45*(3), 377–401. doi:10.100711747-015-0460-7

Iatrou, K., & Alamdari, F. (2005). The empirical analysis of the impact of alliances on airline operations. *Journal of Air Transport Management*, *11*(3), 127–134. doi:10.1016/j.jairtraman.2004.07.005

Ito, H., & Lee, D. (2005). Domestic codesharing practices in the US airline industry. *Journal of Air Transport Management*, *11*(2), 89–97. doi:10.1016/j.jairtraman.2004.09.003

Ito, H., & Lee, D. (2007). Domestic code sharing, alliances, and airfares in the US airline industry. *The Journal of Law & Economics*, *50*(2), 355–380. doi:10.1086/511318

Jaakkola, E., Helkkula, A., & Aarikka-Stenroos, L. (2015). Service experience co-creation: Conceptualization, implications, and future research directions. *Journal of Service Management*, *26*(2), 182–205. doi:10.1108/JOSM-12-2014-0323

Joffe, H., & Yardley, L. (2003). Content and thematic analysis. In D. Marks & L. Yardley (Eds.), Research Methods for Clinical and Health Psychology (pp. 56-68). SAGE Publications, Ltd.

Johnston, R., & Clark, G. (2008). *Service operations management: improving service delivery* (3rd ed.). Prentice Hall.

Kankaew, K., & Vadhanasindhu, C. (2020). Airline's human capital development: A case study of ground service officer in Thailand. *Journal of Critical Reviews*, *7*(11), 1780–1787.

Kleymann, B., & Seristö, H. (2017). *Managing strategic airline alliances*. Routledge. doi:10.4324/9781315249858

Koerber, A., & McMichael, L. (2008). Qualitative sampling methods: A primer for technical communicators. *Journal of Business and Technical Communication*, *22*(4), 454–473. doi:10.1177/1050651908320362

Kramer, L., Fowler, P., Hazel, R., Ureksoy, M., & Harig, G. (2010). *Marketing guidebook for small airports*. Transportation Research Board.

Lemon, K. N., & Verhoef, P. C. (2016). Understanding customer experience throughout the customer journey. *Journal of Marketing*, *80*(6), 69–96. doi:10.1509/jm.15.0420

Li, M. Z. (2000). Distinct features of lasting and non-lasting airline alliances. *Journal of Air Transport Management*, *6*(2), 65–73. doi:10.1016/S0969-6997(99)00024-1

Liamputtong, P. (2009). Qualitative data analysis: Conceptual and practical considerations. *Health Promotion Journal of Australia*, *20*(2), 133–139. doi:10.1071/HE09133 PMID:19642962

Liou, J. J., & Tzeng, G. H. (2007). A non-additive model for evaluating airline service quality. *Journal of Air Transport Management*, *13*(3), 131–138. doi:10.1016/j.jairtraman.2006.12.002

Lipkin, M., & Heinonen, K. (2022). Customer ecosystems: Exploring how ecosystem actors shape customer experience. *Journal of Services Marketing*, *36*(9), 1–17. doi:10.1108/JSM-03-2021-0080

Lohmann, G., Albers, S., Koch, B., & Pavlovich, K. (2009). From hub to tourist destination–An explorative study of Singapore and Dubai's aviation-based transformation. *Journal of Air Transport Management*, *15*(5), 205–211. doi:10.1016/j.jairtraman.2008.07.004

Longhurst, R. (2016). Semi-structured interviews and focus groups. In N. Clifford, M. Cope, T. Gillespie, & S. French (Eds.), *Key methods in geography* (3rd ed., pp. 143–156). SAGE Publication.

Lu, A. (2003). *International airline alliances: EC Competition Law, US Antitrust Law and International Air Transport*. Kluwer Law International.

Lusch, R. F., Vargo, S. L., & Tanniru, M. (2010). Service, value networks and learning. *Journal of the Academy of Marketing Science*, *38*(1), 19–31. doi:10.100711747-008-0131-z

Lusch, R. F., & Webster, F. E. Jr. (2011). A stakeholder-unifying, cocreation philosophy for marketing. *Journal of Macromarketing*, *31*(2), 129–134. doi:10.1177/0276146710397369

MacNealy, M. (1999). *Strategies for empirical research in writing*. Longman. doi:10.2307/358974

Mathis, R., & Jackson, J. (2008). *Human resource management* (12th ed.). Thomson/South-western.

Minichiello, A., Hood, J., & Harkness, D. (2018). Bringing User Experience Design to Bear on STEM Education: A Narrative Literature Review. *Journal For STEM Education Research*, *1*(1-2), 7–33. doi:10.100741979-018-0005-3

Moller, K., & Rajala, A. (2007). Rise of strategic nets—New modes of value creation. *Industrial Marketing Management*, *36*(7), 895–908. doi:10.1016/j.indmarman.2007.05.016

Morley, C. L. (2003). Impacts of international airline alliances on tourism. *Tourism Economics*, *9*(1), 31–51. doi:10.5367/000000003101298259

Morrish, S. C., & Hamilton, R. T. (2002). Airline alliances—Who benefits? *Journal of Air Transport Management*, *8*(6), 401–407. doi:10.1016/S0969-6997(02)00041-8

Otto, J. E., & Ritchie, J. B. (1996). The service experience in tourism. *Tourism Management*, *17*(3), 165–174. doi:10.1016/0261-5177(96)00003-9

Oum, T. H., & Park, J. H. (1997). Airline alliances: Current status, policy issues, and future directions. *Journal of Air Transport Management*, *3*(3), 133–144. doi:10.1016/S0969-6997(97)00021-5

Papatheodorou, A., & Lei, Z. (2006). Leisure travel in Europe and airline business models: A study of regional airports in Great Britain. *Journal of Air Transport Management*, *12*(1), 47–52. doi:10.1016/j.jairtraman.2005.09.005

Park, J. H., & Zhang, A. (1998). Airline alliances and partner firms' outputs. *Transportation Research Part E, Logistics and Transportation Review*, *34*(4), 245–255. doi:10.1016/S1366-5545(98)00018-0

Patton, M. (2014). *Qualitative Evaluation and Research Methods: Integrating Theory and Practice* (4th ed.). Sage Publications.

Pels, E. (2001). A note on airline alliances. *Journal of Air Transport Management, 7*(1), 3–7. doi:10.1016/S0969-6997(00)00027-2

Pine, B. J., & Gilmore, J. H. (1998). Welcome to the experience economy. *Harvard Business Review, 76*(4), 97–105. PMID:10181589

Prokesch, S. E. (1995). Competing on customer service: An interview with British Airways' Sir Colin Marshall. *Harvard Business Review, 73*(6), 100–112.

Rabionet, S. E. (2011). How I learned to design and conduct semi-structured interviews: An ongoing and continuous journey. *Qualitative Report, 16*(2), 563–566.

Redondi, R., Malighettu, P., & Paleari, S. (2011). Hub competition and travel times in the world-wide airport network. *Journal of Transport Geography, 16*(6), 1260–1271. doi:10.1016/j.jtrangeo.2010.11.010

Saunders, B., Kitzinger, J., & Kitzinger, C. (2015). Anonymising interview data: Challenges and compromise in practice. *Qualitative Research, 15*(5), 616–632. doi:10.1177/1468794114550439 PMID:26457066

Steven, M., & Merklein, T. (2013). The influence of strategic airline alliances in passenger transportation on carbon intensity. *Journal of Cleaner Production, 56*, 112–120. doi:10.1016/j.jclepro.2012.03.011

Story, V., Zolkiewski, J., Verleye, K., Nazifi, A., Hannibal, C., Grimes, A., & Abboud, L. (2020). Stepping out of the shadows: Supporting actors' strategies for managing end-user experiences in service ecosystems. *Journal of Business Research, 116*, 401–411. doi:10.1016/j.jbusres.2020.04.029

Tiernan, S., Rhoades, D., & Waguespack, B. (2008). Airline alliance service quality performance—An analysis of US and EU member airlines. *Journal of Air Transport Management, 14*(2), 99–102. doi:10.1016/j.jairtraman.2008.02.003

Topaloglu, H. (2012). A duality-based approach for network revenue management in airline alliances. *Journal of Revenue and Pricing Management, 11*(5), 500–517. doi:10.1057/rpm.2012.8

Trischler, J., & Westman Trischler, J. (2021). Design for experience–a public service design approach in the age of digitalization. *Public Management Review*, 1–20. doi:10.1080/14719037.2021.1899272

Tsantoulis, M., & Palmer, A. (2008). Quality convergence in airline co-brand alliances. *Managing Service Quality, 18*(1), 34–64. doi:10.1108/09604520810842830

Vargo, S. L., & Lusch, R. F. (2008). From goods to service (s): Divergences and convergences of logics. *Industrial Marketing Management, 37*(3), 254–259. doi:10.1016/j.indmarman.2007.07.004

Verhoef, P. (2020). Customer experience creation in today's digital world. In B. Schlegelmilch & R. Wilner (Eds.), *The Routledge companion to strategic marketing* (pp. 107–122). Routledge. doi:10.4324/9781351038669-9

Verhoef, P. C., Lemon, K. N., Parasuraman, A., Roggeveen, A., Tsiros, M., & Schlesinger, L. A. (2009). Customer experience creation: Determinants, dynamics and management strategies. *Journal of Retailing, 85*(1), 31–41. doi:10.1016/j.jretai.2008.11.001

Weber, K. (2005). Travelers' perceptions of airline alliance benefits and performance. *Journal of Travel Research, 43*(3), 257–265. doi:10.1177/0047287504272029

Weber, K., & Sparks, B. (2004). Consumer attributions and behavioral responses to service failures in strategic airline alliance settings. *Journal of Air Transport Management, 10*(5), 361–367. doi:10.1016/j.jairtraman.2004.06.004

Whiting, L. S. (2008). Semi-structured interviews: guidance for novice researchers. *Nursing Standard, 22*(23), 35-40.

Wright, C. P., Groenevelt, H., & Shumsky, R. A. (2010). Dynamic revenue management in airline alliances. *Transportation Science, 44*(1), 15–37. doi:10.1287/trsc.1090.0300

Chapter 9
The Image Value of Southeast Asia Airlines:
A Study of Attribute That Led to Image Value of Choosing Southeast Asia Airlines by Mean–End Theory Approach

Benjapol Worasuwannarak
Cranfield University, UK

Kannapat Kankaew
https://orcid.org/0000-0003-1127-5627
College of Hospitality Industry Management, Suan Sunandha Rajabhat University, Thailand

ABSTRACT

The Southeast Asia airline is one of the most well-known in the aviation industry where airlines represent unique culture for the value-added service standard to customers. Through the means-end theory method, the purpose of this study is to explore the value that passengers create in the decision making on Southeast Asia airlines that would result in understanding the attribute and structure of choosing Southeast Asia airlines. This study aimed to (1) investigate customer attributes in choosing Southeast Asia airlines, (2) understand the crucial value-added characteristic of Southeast Asia airlines, and (3) contribute a value-added framework for Southeast Asia airline passengers. The qualitative method is administered in this study. The interview is conducted in an interview from the mean-end-chain of the passenger. The analysis results in the expression of passenger attributes, consequences, and value of the Southeast Asia airlines and the contributions of the new framework of passenger added value.

INTRODUCTION

In recent years, the airline business has grown at a breakneck pace. The industry's supply and demand sides have increased significantly during the last decade. Recent changes have been fuelled by legal,

DOI: 10.4018/978-1-6684-4615-7.ch009

political, and cultural trends rather than technological considerations. Legal and structural factors have shaped the market structure, while cultural factors have influenced geographical mobility and features. Profitability is a recurring theme in the carrier sector on a worldwide scale. Its cycles are inexorably tied to global financial markets (Doganis 2006).

Additionally, airlines have three business models: full-service, low-cost, and charter (Gillen, 2006). Low-cost airlines operate point-to-point for various routes, whereas full-service and charter airlines use hub and speak for greater operational ease and flight frequency (Pels, 2008; Bachman 2017). The term "full-service" refers to food served as a service and in-flight entertainment. Full-service prefers to fill cheap tickets for unoccupied seats (Pels, 2008). According to Trethewey (2011), low-cost providers are eroding the market share of full-service providers and profiting from it.

Customer customisation is the job of an airline's customer service or customer experience department, primarily responsible for arranging individualised treatment in response to demand variations. Numerous clients fly with reputable carriers. As a result, customer satisfaction can assist in retaining consumers from other airlines. The airline industry's worth is in its passengers. Airlines that fail to satisfy and keep passengers are at risk of losing them (Wang and Shu, 2016). As a result, satisfaction in value-added procedures becomes ingrained in the airline sector as a means of assessing and sustaining passenger pleasure and loyalty. Airlines employ various customer satisfaction techniques to maintain client demand; they highlight the value-added service and product features that contribute to long-term commitment. In addition, airlines may use their experience, previous journeys, and ancillary purchases to push new items and services on customers.

Southeast Asia's airline sector has entered a new era of competitiveness. Southeast Asia's economic development demonstrates an increase in travel demand despite the external environment's influence on the business (Hogan, 2017). The ASEAN aviation industry's compound annual growth rate (CAGR) is constantly increasing, and it has the potential to become the world's largest aviation market by 2036. (IATA, 2017). Therefore, the development viewpoint for company competitiveness in retaining and acquiring customers is critical for survival (Calisir et al., 2016). ASEAN airlines' marketing strategy must focus on long-term pleasure (Akamavi et al., 2011). Airlines' customers in this region are multi-national and culturally diverse, which affects their wants and demand.

Additionally, in a rapidly increasing industry, the airline must provide a plan to close the gap between customer happiness and loyalty for the survivor (Tsafarakis et al., 2018). Additionally, developing a positive image for the airline is critical for its attractiveness (Hussain et al., 2015). Therefore, the research study focuses on deciphering the characteristic of selecting a Southeast Asia airline using the mean-end theory technique and developing a value-added framework for the Southeast Asia airline image.

ASEAN COMMUNITY

The Association of Southeast Asian Nations or ASEAN was established in 1967 with ten nations members including Brunei Darussalam, Cambodia, Indonesia, Laos, Malaysia, Myanmar, Philippines, Singapore, Thailand, and Vietnam. Some nations have diverse economic, cultural, environmental, legal, financial, and political structures. ASEAN wants to integrate the economy among nations and bring the significant challenge of import, export, investment, capital, and knowledge in the association for the internal and external region benefit.

"The ASEAN Economic Community (AEC) is the realisation of the end-goal of economic integration as outlined in the ASEAN Vision 2020, to create a stable, prosperous and highly competitive ASEAN economic region" (ASEAN-Secretariat, 2003 the Declaration of ASEAN Concord II, Section B paragraph 1). It intends to free flow in the region in skills workers, goods, capital, and service. According to Nandan (2006) conclude the mandatory economic of AEC:

1. AEC is building the community of Southeast Asia nations, integrating the ASEAN cultural community, and increasing the contribution among members.
2. AEC is the respondent of economic strategy for the growth rate in GDP and export. It is also the strategic involvement in foreign investment.
3. AEC is the respondent of globalisation emerging into other regions.
4. AEC is the primary factor of regional economic integration among ten nation's members.

Furthermore, ASEAN faces a significant challenge among all nations as a single market outcome of economic growth. Therefore, it also focuses on building the competitive financial perspective that can drive market, infrastructure, innovation, knowledge, and sustainable development.

ASEAN AIRLINE BUSINESS ENVIRONMENT

There is different characteristic of ASEAN airlines (Forsyth et al., 2004). Aviation policy in each nation comprises nation and customer characteristics that can strengthen the industry (Forsyth et al., 2004; Zhang et al., 2018). For example, Singapore has a liberal Air Service Agreement (ASAs) with other countries outside the region in which Singapore only serves the international market from the size of the country. As a result, Singapore airlines have a high purchase power from customers compared to countries like Cambodia. On the other hand, Cambodia has low buying power despite its large country area compared to Singapore.

In contrast, Cambodia has a small domestic airline market. Therefore, ASEAN airlines are an aggressive international market as the challenged player. Therefore, developing lower fair and new routes is a bold point that airlines contribute. ASEAN Single Aviation Market (ASEAN-SAM) is the policy of aviation in ASEAN established in 2015 that wants to expand the aviation industry in the region into a single aviation market like the European Union. The full liberalisation and deregulation have been discussed in this agreement with two main characteristics. 1) Access all countries in Southeast Asia with unlimited flight. 2) The ownership of the airlines.

Those are the main point of ASEAN-SAM as the road map of success. This road map plan can increase the market challenge of all airlines in the region and gain more revenue when under deregulation in the ASEAN. But unfortunately, since 2015, only the 5th freedom of rights has been provided in the ASEAN aviation industry with no answer about extending into another freedom of rights has been talked. Hence, it can be said that ASEAN-SAM is not the success story of the ASEAN yet as one single aviation market need to develop and provide more potential for deregulation for success.

The further development of ASEAN-SAM can bring the growth rate of airlines in the region where the positive impact of deregulation brings the value of all airlines for the challenge of routes and number of passengers. Hence, the challenge among the government in each country, culture, market stability, and customer demand characteristic. It is hard to understand and adapt to all diversity, but it will significantly change the aviation industry after understanding overall concepts.

ASEAN AIRLINE CUSTOMER BEHAVIOUR

The customer of airlines focuses on their behaviour attitude in purchasing the airline's ticket (Byun and Jang, 2018). There are varieties of intentions to travel with the airline, including the travel season and duration of the journey (Gilbert, 1996; Sanyal et al., 2014). with types of travelling are business traveller and leisure travellers. Typically, business passengers look for a product that answers their needs and demands rather than price sensitivity. Flight schedule and flight time are more relevant to travelling than the ticket price. While leisure passengers are concerned about ticket prices as the trip can adapt more flexibly than the business traveller (Hwang and Hyun, 2018). Customer behaviour is the individual purchasing character as the emotion, expectation, and perception. The behaviour can come from self-life style, experiences, family, friends, or social groups that can impact behaviour intention (. Therefore, it is crucial to understand airlines' customer behaviour as it is overcome to understand customer preference of need. Also, it brings value to increase the profit and airline image.

Airlines' customer behaviour comes from experiences and satisfaction (Byun and Jang, 2018). Customer attitude from the behaviour perception in airlines brings into airlines both product and service development perspectives to answer the needs and demands of customers for satisfaction (Bolton and Drew, 1991). As ASEAN nations are consist of culture and behaviour diversity. It is indeed to understand the image value of airlines in the region within the decision-making and value attribute. The decision-making approach comes from behaviour intention. In airlines, decision-making comes from the airline's service to customers (Parasuraman et al., 1994; Hwang and Hyun, 2017). Customers are measuring airlines from the service approach. The service is the effective attribute of decision-making in customers, especially in Southeast Asia, where passengers like good service even though lower price.

However, ASEAN airlines' customer behaviour varies depending on self-characteristic and experience in airlines. They show the behaviour in decision-making from service that airlines offer to them. Furthermore, service quality can be the crucial factor of ASEAN airlines as the image value and extending the understanding.

MEANS END CHAIN THEORY OF THIS STUDY

The means-end chain theory is the theory that links the characteristic of a product and the cause of the product (Gutman, 1982). It is the theory to study the understanding of purchasing decision-making in which review the primary process and condition factor that affect purchasing behaviour. The Means-end process is also a conceptual framework that refers to consumer interview procedures—concerning decision-making and describing the purchaser by linking to the resulting outcome. Li et al. (2016) explain that the buyer or consumer will have multiple decision-making processes. Decisions are related to choosing or acting on an item or both. The means-end chain theory can describe the product and service that engage into customer behaviour and even environment according to the study of Ramirez et al. (2015) that study this theory into a consumer product that shows significant value-added. It can help the researcher understand the structure of the study's product and service, especially in cognitive (Lin and Fu, 2017a). It also directly represents the elements of product or service characteristics (Patrick and Xu, 2018). This means that the consumer's purchasing decision must be evaluated by the purchaser's discrimination or conduct, understanding the purchaser's behaviour (Xiao et al., 2017; Borgardt, 2018)). There are two processes of the Means end chain theory.

1. Marketing must be clearly stated, and the student must understand four fundamental factors: consumers, decision-making processes, decision-making context, and decision-making options. In addition, the following points must be addressed:
   1.1 Who are the key customers, or which customer decisions do we need to understand?
   1.2 What behaviours or purchasing decision-making processes are most relevant to the customer group?
   1.3 What social traits or physical contexts drive buying behaviour?
   1.4 What choices consumers are aware of, which are crucial to decision making
2. Researchers need to understand what is valuable to a buyer's purchasing decision; the criteria used to assess those options, and why those factors are essential to the buyer. The endpoint is the buyer's desire to buy those things or services to which brands have to find answers.

The purpose of this research is to fill in the gaps in information regarding passenger attributes that influence airline selection in Southeast Asia, significant value-added characteristics of Southeast Asia airlines, and a methodology for evaluating Southeast Asia airline business competitiveness. This study contains critical research findings.

1. There are varieties of the characteristic of Southeast Asia passengers that choose Southeast Asia airlines.
2. Most passenger relies on Southeast Asia brand image before choosing the airline.
3. Passengers contribute to the value-added to the airline before making a purchase decision.

To overcome critical study findings, it is essential to understand the factors influencing a passenger's choice of airline in Southeast Asia. As Oliver (1999) criticised, passengers often choose an airline based on their behaviour and happiness. Additionally, a strong customer relationship management programme focuses on the satisfaction and loyalty of consumers as a complete circle of attention (Farooq et al., 2018). This study aims to extend the mean-end framework of passenger attributes to include satisfaction and image of Southeast Asian airlines. Also, it will strengthen the strategic framework to learn ASEAN customer attributes via the laddering technique.

Figure 1. Conceptual framework of mean-end approach (Reynold and Olson, 2001)

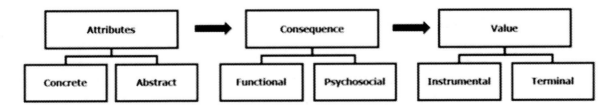

A study of laddering interviews found that academic thinkers were described as follows: Reynolds and Olson (2001) stated that hierarchical interviews were interviews for acquiring characteristics outcomes. The product or service's value is subject to the buyer's decision. There are two essential processes of hierarchical interviewing. Process 1, the interviewer must specify the criteria. Or necessary conditions that the purchaser uses as a criterion when considering choosing a product or service. Process 2, the interviewer must know why the requirements or needs are essential. Distinguished or has a relationship with buyers. Functions in the second process are accomplished by asking questions using "why". Wansink (2000) explained that hierarchical interviews using formal means-end theory are preferable in qualitative research. It is an in-depth interview. The interviewees can answer independently. The questions will be open-ended. The hierarchical interview is structured by sequencing questions and using questions to achieve what the interviewees want, with the same schedule and question format as the other interviewees. Using a face-to-face interview method to understand how important product features are to them, the hierarchical interview must be ongoing to find out the critical value behind the consumer's abstract purchasing decision and why. It must be asked continually until the value of the purchase is revealed before it can begin to be asked again.

According to Cesare and Gianluigi (2011), Mattila (1999) represents the attribute, consequences, and values related to this study of image value of Southeast Asia airlines as shown in Table 1.

Table 1. Attribute, consequences, and value that related to this study of image value of Southeast Asia airlines

Attribute	Consequences	Value
Quality	Well-treated	Security
Comfort	Communication	Happiness
Image	High quality	Enjoyable
Brand	Brand value	Self-fulfilment
Price	Comfortably	Accomplishment
Service	Safe	Image
Speed of service	Convenience	Social group acceptance
Secure	Efficiency	Self-presentation
Reliability	Relaxation	Gratification
Fulfil task	Status symbol	Self-confident

All attributes, consequences, and value come from the study and previous study of customer relationship management of Southeast Asia airline that the researcher has been studying as the literature review related to this topic of this study. It found that Southeast Asia passengers are looking to all those attributes, consequences, and values of the Southeast Asia airlines that have a relationship among the variables (Rahimi et al., 2017; Nyadzayo et al., 2016). Hence, all those variables have become the primary variable of this study.

RESEARCH METHODOLOGY

This study will be conducted qualitatively with a laddering interview based on Mean-end-chain theory. There will be 30 purposive sampling from passengers travelling with Southeast Asia airlines two times a year which are a sufficient sample size to determine the relationship according to other studies of the means-end theory that 20-30 samples represent the best benefit for the interview (Hudders et al., 2014). The age group of participants is between 20-40 years old because of the narrow age group with the ability to travel with airlines. The laddering interview will take place as by one in-depth discussion (Li et al., 2016) for the best result of the study in attribute, consequence, and value of Southeast Asia airlines with Mean-end-chain model (Ha and Jang, 2013).

Laddering interviews will be conducted in a comfortable atmosphere to make the interviewee feel comfortable and willing to give the best answer to the questions (Reynold and Olson, 2001). The interviewee will provide the channel and place for the interview. The process of discussion is including.

1. General information about the interview, including age, education, occupation.
2. General information about the passenger in Southeast Asia airlines, including which Southeast Asia airline are you travelling to, how often do you travelling with Southeast Asia airline, how do you purchase the ticket
3. Laddering interview, this part of the interview will ask about the decision making of Southeast Asia airlines with the step of the attribute, consequence, and value (Wansink, 2000).

Data analysis will be conducted with hierarchical value map (HVM) from Ladder maps program (Reynold and Olson, 2011) with the stage of study including;

1. Declare and group data from the interview is the process to declare and group attribute, consequence, and value of factor from the interview.
2. Find the relationship component in each group; it is the process of finding the relationship between attribute, consequence, and value.
3. Analyse data from the relationship, and it is the process to analyse all data from attribute, consequence, and value.
4. Input group of the word in Ladder map program and check all components. It is the process of analysing the relationship of the attribute, consequence, and value in the Ladder map program into Hierarchical Value Map (HVM).
5. Present the relationship in Hierarchical Value Map (HVM); it is the process to represent and show the result of the study.

Those are the research methodology in this study of The Image Value of Southeast Asia Airline:
A Study of Attribute that led to Image Value of Choosing Southeast Asia Airlines by Mean-End Theory Approach.

SOLUTION AND RECOMMENDATION

The laddering interview from 30 sampling sizes in of The Image Value of Southeast Asia Airline:

The Image Value of Southeast Asia Airlines

A Study of Attribute that led to Image Value of Choosing Southeast Asia Airlines by Mean-End Theory Approach. After that, analyse the relationship of the attribute of Southeast Asia airlines towards the consequence of purchasing.

There is a 30-sampling size consisting of 15 males and 15 females with seven persons at the age of 26-30 years, and another seven persons are 31-35 years of age, while the majority group is the age between 36-40 with 16 persons. In education, there is 70 to 30 per cent of undergraduate and postgraduate. In terms of occupation, all of them work in private sector organisations. Also, Table 2 illustrates the airlines that the interviewee is likely to travel with, the number of travels year 2019 (before the pandemic), and the channel of purchasing a ticket.

Table 2. Detail on general information about the passenger in Southeast Asia airlines

Person	The airline that is likely travelling with	Number of times	channel of purchasing a ticket
1.	Thai AirAsia	6	Airline's website
2.	Thai AirAsia	4	Airline's website
3.	Thai AirAsia	4	Airline's website
4.	Singapore Airlines	5	Airline's website
5.	VietJet	4	Airline's website
6.	VietJet	5	Airline's website
7.	Lion Air	8	Airline's website
8.	Lion Air	6	Airline's website
9.	AirAsia	10	Airline's website
10.	AirAsia	6	Airline's website
11.	Bangkok Airways	5	Airline's website
12.	Thai VietJet	5	Travel Agency
13.	Lion Air	8	Airline's website
14.	Thai AirAsia	8	Airline's website
15.	Thai AirAsia	10	Airline's website
16.	Singapore Airlines	8	Airline's website
17.	Malaysia Airlines	5	Travel Agency
18.	AirAsia	4	Airline's website
19.	AirAsia	5	Airline's website
20.	Singapore Airlines	4	Airline's website
21.	VietJet	6	Airline's website
22.	Garuda Indonesia	9	Travel Agency
23.	Lion Air	5	Airline's website
24.	Lion Air	10	Airline's website
25.	Thai Airways	4	Airline's website
26.	Bangkok Airways	3	Travel Agency
27.	Nok Air	6	Airline's website
28.	Nok Air	7	Airline's website
29.	Nok Air	8	Airline's website
30.	Garuda Indonesia	6	Airline's website

Table 2 shows that Thai AirAsia is the most dominant airline from this interview with 16.67 per cent, while the second one is AirAsia in Malaysia with 13.33%. In contrast, the least travelling airline in this interview is Singapore airlines, Nok Air, and Thai VietJet at 10%. The average number of travel is at six times with airline's website is the most channel of ticket purchasing.

In terms of the interview on the attribute, consequences, and value of Southeast Asia airlines, the researcher has analysed with Laddermap program with the result in the number that interviewee has been mentioned when talking about airlines they likely travelling.

Table 3. Attribute terms from the interview

Attribute	Number of mentioned
Quality	14
Comfort of seat	60
Image	58
Brand	79
Price	65
Service	17
Speed of service	15
Secure	0
Reliability	19
Fulfil task	0

Table 4. Consequences term from the interview

Consequences	Number of mentioned
Well-treated	59
Communication	40
High quality	68
Value	104
Comfortably	76
Safe	66
Convenience	166
Efficiency	16
Relaxation	78
Status symbol	0

Table 5. Value term from the interview

Value	Number of mentioned
Security	105
Happiness	188
Self-confident	92
Self-fulfilment	133
Accomplishment	87
Image	133
Social group acceptance	66
Self-presentation	2
Enjoyment	68
Self-confident	89

The brand is the most concerned attribute factor were mostly sampling size likely to travel with their trust airline. The second factor is the price, where the price of the airline is still the attribute that needs to focus on and considerable concern. Finally, the image is reliable with the brand where they comprise each other.

In terms of consequences, convenience is the most mentioned term that interviewees were cited as the critical consequence. In contrast, value and high quality are among the second terms mentioned where they are about the brand value-added of airlines and the quality in both product and service that airline show to passengers. Finally, status symbol is something that no one was mentioned in this topic of airlines image.

Happiness is the term mentioned the most in which all customers feel happy when talking about the airline. Also, self-fulfilment is the second dominant term that is quite similar to happiness in terms of feeling fulfilled when talking about the following airline. Finally, image is roughly the same as self-fulfilment term in value while none of any period has been discussed.

The characteristics of Southeast Asia Airlines in attribute, consequences, and value are collected. The researcher then used the terminology that linked the relationship between components according to Mean-end chain theory by compiling the Ladder Map program. Next, the researcher must select a cutoff value to simplify the correlation diagram to process the data. The cutoff degree allows significant data to be displayed on a correlation diagram with no theory or statistical criteria. Finally, to select a configuration level Cutoff, These configurations are generally based on the use of data that is critical to affinity plan management (Grunert and Grunert, 1995).

Figure 2. Hierarchical Value Map of the image of Southeast Asia airlines

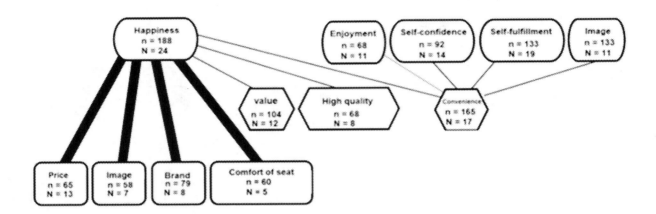

From figure 2, the hierarchical Value Map illustrates the relationship between attributes, consequences, and value of the image of Southeast Asia airlines from the interview. N means the number of the person who takes vital of the term while n means the total number that this term has been mentioned. For example, the word "Happiness" has 24 people said, and there are 188 times discussed in this term.

The attribute's characteristic includes price, image, brand, and seat comfort. The example of the interview from this attribute characteristic that brought it to the happiness of passengers when choosing to fly with this airline;

"The comfort of the seat makes me always choose to fly this airline where it is suitable for the price that I spend for this trip."

"This airline provides the right image with cost-efficiency that I am willing to pay and flying with this price."

"The priority to choose the airline to come from the brand, it must be the trusty brand with reasonable price."

"I always feel happy when spending with this price of the ticket from the trust brand and image of this airline."

"This airline has a very comfy seat for the long haul flight."

On the other hand, value and quality have a relationship with happiness. From this perspective, passengers feel happiness from the airline's value and quality from the interview example.

"I like the quality of all amenities that airline offer to the passenger."

"Airline always shows the value of service and product to me, and it is always beyond my expectation."

"I feel that when I fly with this airline, I never doubt with quality of everything that makes me so happy when flying with the airline."

"The reason I always fly with this airline because of the quality of the food, seat, and in-flight entertainment that I feel that the airline has high value-added of those service than other airlines"

"Value is important to me, and I am expecting something with high value or something with beyond expectation value. I believe that my chosen airline has all of that value for my happiness."

However, passengers who fly with Southeast Asia airlines have a high value of price, image, brand, and seat comfort that show significant happiness when flying with the mentioned airline from the interview. In contrast, value and high quality of product and service are among the role of the consequence of happiness. Moreover, the consequences of convenience brought the value of enjoyment, self-confidence, self-fulfilment, and passenger image.

CONCLUSION

From the described knowledge gaps, this research aims to expand passengers' understanding of Southeast Asia airlines in terms of attributes that lead to the image value of choosing Southeast Asia Airlines by the Mean-End theory approach. Passengers can feel happiness and value-added to the measurement of the product and service that they received. The mean-End theory will measure the purchasing decision-making process of passengers to Southeast Asia airlines by investigating the factor that creates the purchase situation. It is like a conceptual framework to interview passengers about final decision-making that links to the related result of the attribute (Li et al., 2016) as airline passenger has a process of decision making where relevant to behaviour. Therefore, this study significantly understands the passenger perspective of choosing the brand value-added of Southeast Asia airlines. The result of this study gives competitive advantages to Southeast Asia airlines in;

1. Understand the passenger's value-added image, price, quality, brand, and comfort in choosing the Southeast Asia airlines.
2. The attribute, consequences, and value of passengers in the marketing framework of the Southeast Asia airline is essential to understanding customer behaviour.

However, Southeast Asia airlines must show the attribute in price where passengers find it is the sign of happiness while image and brand are among the representative value of the airline that faces the challenge of making passengers happy to selecting the airline. The seat's comfort is another attribute that directly relates to happiness. The Mean-End approach attribute may or may not be essential to study passenger decision-making. It shows that self-fulfilment, enjoyment, self-confidence, and image of the passenger have a vital component of value to the convenience of passengers. Still, the result of this study shows the impact outcome factor to the Southeast Asia airline to provide the competitive advantages to the current passenger and the new passenger in the future.

DISCUSSION

From the objective of this study aimed to: (1) investigate customer attributes in choosing Southeast Asia airlines, (2) understand the crucial value-added characteristic of Southeast Asia airlines and (3) contribute a value-added framework for Southeast Asia airline's passengers, Southeast Asia airline passenger happiness is the primary value-added from the attribute of price, image, brand, and comfort of the seat. Most Southeast Asia airline passengers focus on airline brands as the reputation of attribution towards happiness to choose the airline. As well seat comfortable is another primary concern. In terms of consequence, the quality of the airline and the value of the airline represent the happiness of passengers. The follow-up attributes, including enjoyment, self-confidence, self-fulfilment, and image, are attributes from the consequence of convenience. Passengers expect convenience from the airline that brings about the significant challenge of attribute mostly in airline brand image and self-fulfilment. It means that Southeast Asia airline passengers are focusing on airline image and something that fulfils their achievement as the purpose of choosing the airline in this region.

Therefore, the future study of the means-end chain theory can expand the investigation into another region of airline passengers that might illustrate the passenger's different attributes, consequences, and values. For example, Southeast Asia passengers might be the same or different from other region passenger. Therefore, it is significant for further study as Southeast Asia airlines might understand more from other region passengers despite form only Southeast Asia passengers.

REFERENCES

Akamavi, R. K., Mohamed, E., Pellmann, K., & Xu, Y. (2015). Key determinants of passenger loyalty in the low-cost airline business. *Tourism Management, 46*, 528–545. doi:10.1016/j.tourman.2014.07.010

Bachman, J. (2017). *Airlines Make More Money Selling Miles than Seats*. Retrieved March 16, 2022, from https://www.bloomberg.com/news/articles/2017-03-31/airlines-make-more-money-selling-miles than-seats

Borgardt, E. (2018). Conventional and extended versions of Means-End Chain theory. *Zeszyty Naukowe Uniwersytetu Ekonomicznego w Krakowie, 3*(975), 191–204. doi:10.15678/ZNUEK.2018.0975.0312

Borgardt, E. (2019). Extending Means-End Chain theory by integrating a self-concept approach and behavioural perspective model. *Zeszyty Naukowe Uniwersytetu Ekonomicznego w Krakowie, 979*(1), 47–61. doi:10.15678/ZNUEK.2019.0979.0103

Byun, J., & Jang, S. (2018). Open kitchen vs. closed kitchen: Does kitchen design affect customers' causal attributions of the blame for service failures? *International Journal of Contemporary Hospitality Management, 30*(5), 2214–2229. doi:10.1108/IJCHM-03-2016-0167

Calisir, N., Basak, E., & Calisir, F. (2016). Key drivers of passenger loyalty: A case of Frankfurt–Istanbul flights. *Journal of Air Transport Management, 53*, 211–217. doi:10.1016/j.jairtraman.2016.03.002

Cesare, A., & Gianluigi, G. (2011). Determinants of purchasing intention for fashion luxury goods in the Italian market: A laddering approach. *Journal of Fashion Marketing and Management, 15*(1), 123–136. doi:10.1108/13612021111112386

Doganis, R. (2002). *Flying Off Course: the Economics of International Airlines*. Routledge.

Farooq, M. S., Salam, M., Fayolle, A., Jaafar, N., & Ayupp, K. (2018). Impact of service quality on customer satisfaction in Malaysia airlines: A PLS-SEM approach. *Journal of Air Transport Management, 67*, 169–180. doi:10.1016/j.jairtraman.2017.12.008

Forsyth, P., King, J., Rodoifo, C. L., & Trace, K. (2004). *Preparing ASEAN for open sky. AADCP Regional Economic Policy Support Facility Research Project 02/008*. Monash International Pty Ltd.

Gilbert, D. (1996). *Airlines*. Paul Chapman Publishing.

Gillen, D. (2006). Airline business models and networks: Regulation, competition and evolution in aviation markets. *Review of Network Economics*, *5*(4), 366–385. doi:10.2202/1446-9022.1103

Grunert, K. G., & Grunert, S. C. (1995). Measuring Subjective Meaning Structures by the Laddering Method: Theoretical Considerations and Methodological Problems. *International Journal of Research in Marketing*, *12*(3), 209–225. doi:10.1016/0167-8116(95)00022-T

Gutman, J. (1982). A Means-End Chain Model Based on Consumer Categorization Processes. *Journal of Marketing*, *46*(2), 60–72. doi:10.1177/002224298204600207

Ha, J., & Jang, S. (2013). Attributes, consequences, and consumer values: A means-end chain approach across restaurant segments. *International Journal of Contemporary Hospitality Management*, *25*(3), 383–409. doi:10.1108/09596111311311035

Hussain, R., Al Nasser, A., & Hussain, Y. K. (2015). Service quality and customer satisfaction of a UAE-based airline: An empirical investigation. *Journal of Air Transport Management*, *42*, 167–175. doi:10.1016/j.jairtraman.2014.10.001

Hwang, J., & Hyun, S. S. (2017). First-class airline travellers' perception of luxury goods and its effect on loyalty formation. *Current Issues in Tourism*, *20*(5), 497–520. doi:10.1080/13683500.2014.918941

Hwang, J., & Lyu, S. O. (2018). Understanding first-class passengers' luxury value perceptions in the US airline industry. *Tourism Management Perspectives*, *28*, 29–40. doi:10.1016/j.tmp.2018.07.001

Hwang, J., & Ok, C. (2013). The antecedents and consequence of consumer attitudes toward restaurant brands: A comparative study between casual and fine dining restaurants. *International Journal of Hospitality Management*, *33*(1), 121–131. doi:10.1016/j.ijhm.2012.05.002

Li, E. Y., Chang, L. S., & Chang, L. F. (2016, June). Exploring Consumer Value of CrossBorder Online Shopping: an Application of means-End Chain Theory and Maslow's Hierarchy of Needs. In PACIS (p. 359). Academic Press.

Lin, C. F., & Fu, C. S. (2017a). Advancing the laddering and critical incident techniques by incorporating dramaturgical theory to reveal restaurant niches. *Service Industries Journal*, *37*(13–14), 801. doi:10.1080/02642069.2017.1351551

Mattila, A. S. (1999). The role of culture in the service evaluation process. *Journal of Service Research*, *1*(3), 250–261. doi:10.1177/109467059913006

Nyadzayo, M. W., & Khajehzadeh, S. (2016). The antecedents of customer loyalty: A moderated mediation model of customer relationship management quality and brand image. *Journal of Business & Economic Research, 5*(2), 55-64.

Oliver, R. L. (1999). Whence consumer loyalty. *Journal of Marketing*, *63*(4), 33–44. doi:10.1177/00222429990634s105

Parasuraman, A., Zeithaml, V. A., & Berry, L. L. (1994). Alternative scales for measuring service quality: A comparative assessment based on psychometric and diagnostic criteria. *Journal of Retailing*, *70*(3), 201–230. doi:10.1016/0022-4359(94)90033-7

Patrick, K., & Xu, Y. (2018). Exploring generation y consumers' fitness clothing consumption: A means-end approach. *Journal of Textile & Apparel. Technology & Management, 10*(3), 1–15.

Pels, E. (2008). Airline network competition: Full-service airlines, low-cost airlines and long-haul markets. *Research in Transportation Economics, 24*(1), 68–74. doi:10.1016/j.retrec.2009.01.009

Rahimi, R., Köseoglu, M. A., Ersoy, A. B., & Okumus, F. (2017). Customer relationship management research in tourism and hospitality: A state-of-the-art. *Tourism Review, 72*(2), 209–220. doi:10.1108/TR-01-2017-0011

Ramirez, E., Jimenez, F. R., & Gau, R. (2015). Concrete and abstract goals associated with the consumption of environmentally sustainable products. *European Journal of Marketing, 49*(9/10), 1645–1665. doi:10.1108/EJM-08-2012-0483

Reynolds, T. J., & Olson, J. C. (Eds.). (2001). *Understanding consumer decision making: The means-end approach to marketing and advertising strategy*. Psychology Press. doi:10.4324/9781410600844

Sanyal, S. N., Datta, S. K., & Banerjee, A. K. (2014). Attitude of Indian consumers towards luxury brand purchase: An application of 'attitude scale to luxury items'. *International Journal of Indian Culture and Business Management, 9*(3), 316–339. doi:10.1504/IJICBM.2014.064696

Tretheway, M. (2011). Comment on "legacy carriers fight back". *Journal of Air Transport Management, 17*(1), 40–43. doi:10.1016/j.jairtraman.2010.10.009

Tsafarakis, S., Kokotas, T., & Pantouvakis, A. (2018). A multiple criteria approach for airline passenger satisfaction measurement and service quality improvement. *Journal of Air Transport Management, 68*, 61–75. doi:10.1016/j.jairtraman.2017.09.010

Wang, S. W., & Hsu, M. K. (2016). Airline co-branded credit cards—An application of the theory of planned behavior. *Journal of Air Transport Management, 55*, 245–254. doi:10.1016/j.jairtraman.2016.06.007

Wansink, B. (2000). New techniques to generate key marketing insights. *Marketing Research*, (Summer), 28-36.

Xiao, L., Guo, Z., & D'Ambra, J. (2017). Analysing consumer goal structure in online group buying: A means–end chain approach. *Information & Management, 54*(8), 1097–1119. doi:10.1016/j.im.2017.03.001

Zhang, Y., Zheng, X., & Lu, W. (2018). Measuring the openness of Chinese International Air Transport Policy. *Transport Policy, 72*, 208–217. doi:10.1016/j.tranpol.2018.03.014

Chapter 10
The Impact of Customer Dissatisfaction Regarding Revenue Management on Perceptions of Airline Experience and Loyalty

Tanyeri Uslu
https://orcid.org/0000-0001-6006-6579
Altinbas University, Turkey

İbrahim Sarper Karakadilar
Kahramanmaras Sutcu Imam University, Turkey

ABSTRACT

This chapter examines the effects of the complaints about the practices of revenue management (RM) on the travel experience perception and loyalty of the customers. The analysis shows that the complaints about the RM practices have positive effects on the travel experience perception, and the travel experience perception has a positive effect on the loyalty of the customer who travel short distances. The results of the detailed sub-hypothesis test performed in relation to the travel purposes of the customers and the business model adopted by an airline company show that the companies which adopt low-cost business model are obliged to manage their RM practices on a much more customer-centric basis. The companies in the sector should develop special customer programs for their customer segments which remain outside the business purpose. Thus, the operational efficiency will increase, and revenues will be maximized.

DOI: 10.4018/978-1-6684-4615-7.ch010

INTRODUCTION

The number of airline companies operating in the civil aviation sector has conspicuously increased especially after the 2000s (Lindenmeier & Tscheulin 2008; Mason & Alamdari 2007; Teichert et al.,2008). The services that airline companies are provided for their customers are evaluated, it is seen that each company has unique and different business models. Therefore, the level of service perceived by their customers is different. The diversification of the profile of an airline's customers requires that heterogeneous customer segments which are made up of different demographic features should be given simultaneous service, especially during short-distance flights. Airlines categorize different short-distance /short-haul flight routes from airport to airport (point-to-point) as (i) flights lasting less than 120 minutes and (ii) flights lasting between 120 and 180 minutes (An &Noh, 2009). Under these circumstances, the expectations of the airline company's customers relating to the quality of the service given to them during a flight are different from each other. Service perceptions that customers have experienced during the flight are different from each other due to different expectations of business versus leisure travellers Xu and Li (2016) which is a challenge for airline companies.

The intense competition in the market makes it crucial for airline companies to maximize their operational profits for the necessity of the continuation of their existence in the market. This pressure that the airline companies feel on their shoulders makes it a sectorial necessity for them to benefit from the revenue management (RM) tactics without any exceptions (Lindenmeier & Tscheulin 2008; Mathies et al., 2013). The approach which is called "dual entitlement" means the obtainment of the revenues by the companies that they need for the continuation of their existence in the marketplace. However, when the companies are obtaining these revenues, it is also necessary that they should render services to their customers at fair prices under suitable conditions (McMahon-Beattie et al., 2016; Wirtz et al., 2003). For all that, the RM practices of the airline companies are not always perceived as fair by their customers and cause displeasure and complaints.

As emphasized above, revenue management practices and how the economic burden on the customers is perceived by them should be evaluated within the scope of the "dual entitlement theory". The dual entitlement theory suggests that price increases made without adding value to the service given to the customer are not found just by the customers. Within this context, the equity theory should be utilized for the purposes of measuring the justice perception, because the equity theory contains the perception of how just is the situation of a person in comparison to others (Campbell, 1999). In the prospect theory which is developed by Kahneman and Tversky (1979), how people make choices among alternatives when they are under uncertain circumstances is explained. Therefore, by making use of the prospect theory at the same time, it is necessary to deal with how the customer's buying behavior is by time and price. It is also aimed at examining to what extent a passenger finds it just when he/she detects that he/she has paid more in comparison to some other passenger or that some other airline gives many more service possibilities for the same price. For this reason, it is necessary to examine the customer reactions from a general perspective by attributing the conditions relating to the RM practices to theoretical supports and converting them to standardized cases.

On the other hand, the company's concerns for profit maximization create a conflict with the customers' concern for buying the service for the optimal price. Coping with this is only possible by the simultaneous realization of airline companies' customer-centric marketing applications and their RM (Mathies et al., 2013; McMahon-Beattie et al., 2016). Within this context, the critical element is that the perception of injustice should be eliminated on a customer basis by dealing effectively with the customer complaints relating to the RM practice (Lapre, 2011; Xu & Li, 2016). Thus, as a result of the elimination of the displeasure of a complaining customer, positive thinking is created in the customer concerning the re-purchase intention of the airline company the customer in the future (Kim & Lee, 2009).

Within this scope, the main target of the study is to examine the effects of the complaining reaction of the customers about the RM practices (i.e. price discrimination and ancillary revenue practices) on the flight experiences perceived (i.e. service quality, perceived value and trust) by the customers and on their loyalty. Kimes (2010) states that RM can be applied to any business that has a relatively fixed perishable inventory capacity, which is demanded by inventories, has high fixed costs and low variable costs, and has varying customer price sensitivity (Kimes, 2010). One of the examples of these businesses is airlines. Such businesses use price-related RM practices for revenue growth, such as airline tickets purchased at different prices and at different times.

Accordingly, each sub-dimension examined concerning the perceived flight experience for RM practices and at what level the interaction is realized with the loyalty constitutes the fundamental research question of this study:

Research Question 1: On which one of the following are the complaints of airline customers about the RM practices most effective: whether the factors relating to the loyalty of the customer or the factors relating to the flight experience (i.e. service quality; perceived value; trust)?

As we previously mentioned customers have diverse evaluation criteria based on purpose of travel. According to the three different travel reasons which are dealt with within the scope of this study, the effects of the interactions of the customers to the RM practices on the variables which constitute the airline experience perception are examined.

Research Question 2: On which one of the factors relating to the customer's loyalty and flight experience is the complaints about the RM practices of the airline customers travelling for the business is the most effective?

Research Question 3: On which one of the factors relating to the customer's loyalty and flight experience is the complaints about the RM practices of the airline customers travelling for touristic/leisure purposes is the most effective?

Research Question 4: On which one of the factors relating to the customer's loyalty and flight experience is the complaints about the RM practices of the airline customers travelling for visiting their families and friends and for other purposes is the most effective?

Similarly, it is also explored about how the companies' business models affect the customer's perception during the flight. In this sense, how the RM practices affect the customer's complaints about customers perceived flight experience and their loyalty is investigated.

Research Question 5: Which one of the factors relating to the customer's loyalty and flight experience is the most affected by the complaints of the customers about the RM practices when travelling with a Full-Service Carrier?

Research Question 6: Which one of the factors relating to the customer's loyalty and flight experience is the most affected by the complaints of the customers about the RM practices when travelling with the Low-Cost Carrier?

Through these questions it is aimed to find out about what the airline companies should be careful about their RM practices in the short-distance air travel market where the customer's loyalty is low. Thus, airline companies can obtain hints about revising their business models according to the customer type and their customer service policies. By this means, the companies can have advantages of competition by producing fully customer-focused services; and with the betterment of the customers' flight experiences, they will be preferred by the customers (Kim & Lee, 2009; Lapre, 2011).

BACKGROUND

Today, the revenue management (RM) practices, it is aimed at using the limited seat capacity under control to provide for operational profitability by creating different flight classes at different price levels. This method is called the seat inventory control application (Lindenmeier & Tscheulin, 2008). Thus, the aim here is to maximize the airline's total customer revenue for each flight operation by setting a balance between the number of seats sold at discounted rates giving the customer limited rights and the number of seats sold at high prices by providing flexible options. Therefore, in order to provide for the optimum use of the limited capacity held, the plane tickets are put up for sale before the date when the flight will be made (Wirtz et al., 2003). In this case, the customers pay for ticket prices at different price levels for ticket alternatives which constitute the same conditions depending upon the density of the demand for the services at different periods when they are buying their tickets. This is called price discrimination in RM practices (Mathies et al., 2013).

The ancillary revenue was defined as revenue gains beyond the sale of tickets that is generated by direct or indirect sales to customers (O'Connell & Warnock-Smith, 2013). At the scope of this study, the ancillary revenue practices are selected such as extra payment for food and beverage services, and extra payment for seat selection. The empirical studies made recently have drawn attention to the fact that RM practices causing some negative results in the eye of the customer. Among these issues are such critical factors as a presentation of inconsistent customer services, perceived injustice, declining customer trust and loyalty levels (Mathies et al., 2013; McMahon-Beattie et al., 2016). Cui et al. (2018) consider ancillary revenue has become a valuable source of revenue generation. They have found a correlation between consumers' main service and ancillary service valuations. They have concluded that unbundling the ancillary service and using main service price discrimination are strategic complements. Ancillary revenue in the airline industry has an impact on revenue management practices (Bockelie, & Belobaba, 2017; Duenyas, 2015).

The fact that the customer does not obtain service under the conditions that he/she desires and/or the service quality does not meet the expectations of the customer firstly disturbs the customer and this leads to their complaint (Xu & Li, 2016). For this reason, the service providing companies should consider the customer's complaints and continuously improve their service processes so that the expectations with respect to the matters of the complaint can be met (Xu et al., 2019). But, most of the customers are not happy about the companies' dealing with their complaints and finding solutions methods (Lapre, 2011). However, the companies' decreasing their service failures makes important contributions to the development of sustainable business models. For an effective practice of the RM tactics, understanding the customers' behaviors clearly has critical importance (McMahon-Beattie et al., 2016). For this purpose, the negative reactions of the customers to the RM practices in the airline sector should be linked with the flight experiences of the customers with the airline company, and then these negative reactions and flight experiences should be evaluated by considering this relation (An &Noh, 2009).

RESEARCH MODEL AND HYPOTHESES

Within the scope of this study, firstly the service quality is dealt with among the variables relating to the airline experience perceptions of the customers examined. While the service quality is being evaluated, all the factors affecting the travel experience in the process when the air transportation service is given should be taken into consideration (Kim & Lee, 2011). Besides, the other sub-dimensions examined are related to the airline experience of the customers are the perceived value and trust. It will be better to deal with these factors from the viewpoint of evaluation of all sorts of material and immaterial negative effects of the airline's RM practices on the customers. Accordingly, the customers' perception of the service they receive does not only consist of material value. It also includes such burdens as the effort and time that the customer has spent in the whole process (Hapsari et al., 2017; Zins 2001). Once the customers start having trust in a service provider due to their efforts to ameliorate the services, the perceived risks regarding the quality of the flight experience decrease, and the flight process is realized more comfortably (Akamavi et al., 2015). As a result of the positive flight experiences, together with the increasing trust of the customer, their preference for a particular company becomes a habit. And this leads to developing an intention (Dick & Basu, 1994) in the mind of the customer for using the same airline in the future; and this is the most critical performance criteria for the aviation industry.

Literature shows that the airlines' customers are quite sensitive to the price (Kim &Lee 2011; Truong et.al, 2020; Lee et.al, 2018; Hassan &Salem 2021). The meaning of this is that the customers are inclined to prefer the airlines which give low price service for short-distance flights (Tsai, 2016). Due to this characteristic nature of air transportation, in this study, we opted for the dimension of loyalty to be separated from the dimension of price, and it is only dealt with in the dimension of preferring the same company in the future flights.

Since the RM practices on customers' perception in this study have been examined, it is decided to consider the customer response of the research model to the RM practices as an independent variable. So, in order to conceptualize the RM practices, three significant RM practices have been found which are directly related to the flight experiences of passengers by making in-depth interviews with the experts in the sector and by also making a wide scoped literature review. Because the final goal of the study is to develop suggestions for increasing customer loyalty in the civil aviation sector where customer loyalty is low, the dependent variable is determined to be loyalty. Hence the service quality is included in the research model as the antecedent variable which is effective in the development of loyalty attitude in the customers, and the perceived value and trust dimensions are included as perceived airline experience. The holistic research model developed in this regard is designed as shown in Figure1.

Figure 1. Holistic research model (created by the authors)

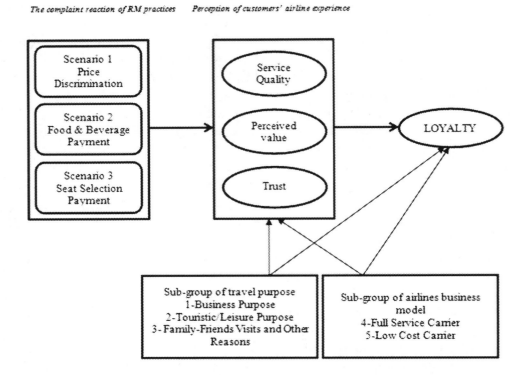

The relations partly examined before regarding the variables in the research model in the literature have been assessed, and hypothesis suggestions have been developed within the scope of this study. Firstly, when the relationship between the complaint reactions of the customers to RM practices and the flight experiences of the customers are looked at, the arguments that (Tsai, 2016) emphasized in their study are taken into consideration. If the customers do not complain to the airline about service quality, this displeasure leads to the fact that the negative attitude against the company becomes permanent and the company most probably is not preferred again. On the other hand, if the displeased customers complain about this gives the company another chance for future flights. If the improvement of the service is experienced, then a positive attitude is shown to the company (Kim & Lee, 2011). In this context, the first generic hypothesis proposed by this study is expressed as follows.

Hypothesis One-a: Airline customers' complaints about RM practices positively affect customers' perceptions of the airline experience.

The effects on customers' loyalty attitude of the variables which constitute the customers' perceptions about air transportation have been examined in the literature. Accordingly, statistically strong relations have been detected in the studies of An and Noh (2009) as well as Kim and Lee (2011) between the company policy, quality of the service given by the employees and the loyalty. Likewise, there are some literature supports between the perceived value and loyalty in the studies of Zins (2001) and Hapsari et al. (2017), besides that between trust and loyalty in the studies of Akamavi et al. (2015). Therefore, the second generic hypothesis put forth in this study comes up as follows.

The Impact of Customer Dissatisfaction

Hypothesis One-b: Airline customers' perceptions of airline experience positively affect loyalty to the airline company.

Sub-Hypotheses According to the Travel Purposes of the Customers

The fact that air transportation service provider alternatives have increased nowadays and are more economical today caused changes in the classical target mass of airlines (Teichert et al., 2008). In the past, the target customers of airlines generally consisted of travelling for business purposes with paying high prices. Since airline tickets have become cheaper during the last ten years, those who travel for touristic purposes or for visiting families/friends have also become targeted customers for airline companies (Balcombe et al., 2009; Tsai & Chen, 2019; Wen & Lai, 2010).

The fact that the customer mass who benefit from the air transportation services are divided into different customer segments within itself helps the airline companies not to be able to address all their customers equally through their customer service policies which they make by using the RM tactics. For instance, on the one hand, the work- doing- principles of the airline companies focus on meeting the expectations of their customers who fly for business purposes and are sensitive to time, on the other hand, the airline companies also need to simultaneously meet the expectations of their customers who fly for touristic/leisure purposes and are sensitive to price (Wirtz et al., 2003).

Especially the becoming widespread flights and due to the decrease in the ticket prices, a conspicuous change in the lifestyles of young people in societies is witnessed. This young generation started preferring to spend their weekends in some other city or country (Francis et al., 2007). Such changes in societies allow airlines to effectively use their capacities so that they can direct the customers in different segments by way of manipulating them through the RM practices or making estimations about their behaviors of them (Wirtz et al., 2003). And, in order to realize that, there is a need to clearly define the customer profile in each segment and for making analyses to see whether or not the new customer approaches to be developed comply with the business model and service policies of the company.

In this context, the sub-hypotheses are defined the generic hypotheses proposed above will be tested from the viewpoint of the assessment of the travel purposes of the customers which is one of the categorical variables of the research model.

Hypothesis Two-a: Airline customers' complaints about RM practices in their business travels directly and positively affect the airline experience perceived by customers.

Hypothesis Two-b: Airline customers' perceptions of airline experience in their business travels directly and positively affect the loyalty of the customers to the airline company.

Hypothesis Three-a: Airline customers' complaints about RM practices in their touristic/leisure travels directly and positively affect the airline experience perceived by customers.

Hypothesis Three-b: Airline customers' perceptions of their touristic/leisure travels directly and positively affect the loyalty of the customers to the airline company.

Hypothesis Four-a: Airline customers' complaints about RM practices in their travels for other purposes such as visiting family/friends, directly and positively affect the airline experience perceived by the customers.

Hypothesis Four-b: Airline experience perceived by the customers in their travels for other purposes such as visiting family/friends directly and positively affects their loyalty to the airline company.

Sub-Hypotheses According to Airline Business Model

In the past when the airline sector was protected by regulations and when there was not so much price competition in the market, the airline companies adopted only the full-service business model and gave luxury service to their customers. With the deregulation in the developed countries and emerging markets relating to the civil aviation sector, and as a result of market economy applications, companies adopting the low-cost carrier business model have emerged in the sector, and their number has nowadays increased dramatically (Balcombe et al., 2009; Francis et al., 2007). Low-cost carriers decrease their operating costs in the flight process by giving standard and simple services, and thus, they can serve their customers with prices lower at a rate of 10-20% (Teichert et al., 2008; Wensveen & Leick, 2009).

While traditional airlines giving full service adopt the principle of reaching all sorts of different destinations by way of connecting flights with a wide network, low-cost carriers mostly fly to short-distance destinations on a point-to-point basis (Marcus &Anderson, 2008). Due to the fact that the contest between the two business models in the airline sector intersects especially in short-distance flights, we can fairly say that the severe competition in the sector occurs on these routes. In these short-distance flights, the full-service giving airlines have to apply their RM tactics much more aggressively in order to be more competitive in respect of price (Tsai, 2016). But, low-cost carriers have to improve their service quality and the flight experience perceptions of their customers in addition to lowering their costs by way of ensuring operational effectiveness in to maintain their business models (Akamavi et al., 2015).

When both business models are evaluated from the perspective of the customers, it is understood that the customers prefer the airlines which offer a suitable quality at the most competitive price (Kim & Lee, 2011). The meaning of this is that the balance of service quality received the customers who are not fully satisfied start looking for another alternative and they do not show loyalty attitude for their future flights. Starting from this concern, the airlines' business models should be assessed by bearing in mind the market realities in a customer-focused way. After this assessment, if necessary, reform proposals about providing services to be more competitive and sustainable business model should be made. Thus, it is beneficial to test the basic hypotheses proposed within the scope of this study from the point of view of the business model which is adopted by the airline company and which is the second categorical variable of the study.

Therefore, the sub-hypotheses in relation to the airline business model may be expressed as follows.

Hypothesis Five-a: Airline customers' level of complaining about the RM practices in their travels on a Full-Service Carrier directly and positively affects the airline experience perceived by the customers.

Hypothesis Five-b: Airline customers' perceptions of airline experience in their travels on a Full-Service Carrier directly and positively affect the loyalty of the customers to the airline company.

Hypothesis Six-a: Airline customers' level of complaining about the RM practices in their travels on a Low-Cost Carrier directly and positively affects the airline experience perceptions for the airline.

Hypothesis Six-b: Airline customers' perceptions of airline experience in their travels on a Low-Cost Carrier directly and positively affect the loyalty of the customers to the airline company.

METHOD

The data used in this study is gathered via a scenario-based survey that gauged airline customers' perception of revenue management (RM) practices employed by airlines in Turkey. The survey has been applied to people who had an air trip at least once. It was targeted to reach more participants who prefer different airline business models. Thus, the research was conducted with participants who fly short-distances with different airlines for different purposes have been obtained by online survey in Turkey. As other researchers Hapsari et al. (2017); Lindenmeier and Tscheulin (2008) have conducted previously, the simple random sampling method is benefited. This method is the simplest and most common method which is used by assuming that the universe is homogeneous and each individual in the universe has an equal chance of being selected as a sample (Singh, 2003).

The overall research methodology consists of the development of a scenario-based survey and customers' flight experiments related to well-known confirmed scales (i.e. service quality, perceived value, trust and loyalty). Gathering information about participants' attitudes vis-à-vis how they will react to a certain event which is fictionalized based on an assumption by presenting scenarios to them is applied as an effective method in the examination of the issues encountered by the airline's customer market (Wen & Lai, 2010). Data collection through scenarios is highly reliable and it gives one the possibility of measuring the customer attitudes (Teichert et al., 2008).

The data relating to the RM practices of airlines (i.e. price discrimination; ancillary revenue) have been gathered through a scenario-based questionnaire. For this purpose, an independent variable which is made up of three items and which contains the measuring values included in the conditions in scenarios 1-2-3 is formed. By this means, it will be possible to examine the reactions of the customers regarding the RM practices and the effect of their complaining tendencies on the scales representing the airline customer experience and loyalty attitude.

A total of 1037 respondents have participated in the research. However, within the scope of this research, when the attitudes of the loyalty of the customers were being measured, the research was carried out of 741 survey responses, because only those who make the buying decision themselves should be included in this research (Dick & Basu, 1994; Zins, 2001). Since scenario-based data were collected in this study; in order to examine both the relationship between the constructs and construct validity; confirmatory factor analysis (CFA) and structural equation modeling (SEM) was used.

RESULTS

Demographic Results

The survey's participants proportion as shown in Table 1 occurred like this: 59% of the questionnaires used in the research were filled in by male customers, and the densest age group was 25-34 at a rate of 30.6%. While the ratio of unmarried customers was 55.1%, the rate of university graduates plus those with post-graduate education was 81%. The survey participant profile shows similarities with the studies made before in respect of airline operations and customer relations (Akamavi et al., 2015; Kim & Lee, 2009; O'Connell &Williams, 2005). Moreover, 25.5% of the survey participants travel for business, 45.4% travel for touristic/leisure and 29.1% travel for visits. In the sample, while full-service carriers were preferred at a rate of 50.2%, the rate of those choosing low-cost carries is 49.8%, so it is a balanced representation. Approximately 60% of those travelling on business and 53% or so of those travelling for touristic purposes prefer full-service carriers. Almost 62% of those other visiting purposes (such as for visiting families/friends) preferring low-cost carriers.

Table 1. Sampling profile

Categorical variables	Frequency	Percent	Categorical variables	Frequency	Percent
Age of respondents			*Education degree of respondents*		
Below 25	180	24.3	High school degree	57	7.7
25 - 34	227	30.6	Vocational school degree	69	9.3
35 - 44	141	19.0	Undergraduate (faculty) degree	417	56.3
45 - 54	86	11.6	Graduate (master/PhD) degree	183	24.7
55 and above	106	14.5	Other	15	2.0
Gender of respondents			*Marital status of respondents*		
Male	437	59.0	Unmarried	408	55.1
Female	304	41.0	Married	333	44.9
Preferred airlines business model			*Travel purpose of respondents*		
Full-service carrier	372	50.2	For business	189	25.5
Low-cost carrier	369	49.8	Leisure/touristic	336	45.4
			Visiting family/friends	216	29.1

Notes: N=741

Construct Validity Analysis

A critical prerequisite in the process of carrying out multivariate analyses is the proof of the normality of the distribution of research items. Research items has value interval between +2.0 and -2.00 considering the Skewness and Kurtosis values (George & Mallery, 2019). All the variables in the model are put into the unrotated factor analysis in the SPSS to prove the common method of bias by performing Harman's single factor test. As gathering of related variables under a triple structure (complaint reaction, perception of experience, and loyalty attitude) which means the common method bias doesn't create a problem (Kaynak & Hartley, 2008; Podsakoff et al., 2012). Cronbach's alpha (Hapsari et al., 2017; Lindenmeier & Tscheulin, 2008) calculations were made so that the validity and reliability analysis of the measurement items used in testing the hypotheses suggested and informing the research model can be made and to make an internal consistency assessment of the scales. After that, the exploratory factor analyses; An and Noh (2009); Hapsari et al. (2017); Lindenmeier and Tscheulin (2008) were carried out, and as a result, in order to test the discriminant validity according to factor loadings, average variance extract (AVE) and construct reliability (CR) analysis calculations were made (Akamavi et al., 2015; Hapsari et al., 2017; Kim & Lee, 2011). As is seen in Table 2, the results obtained conform to the threshold values it is revealed that the measurement questions used in this test measure the relevant structure and that they are not related to other structures (Fornell & Larcker, 1981; Hair et al., 2010).

The Impact of Customer Dissatisfaction

Table 2. Construct-validity analysis results

Factor components and questionnaire items	EFA*	CR**	AVE***	Cronbach's alpha
The complaint reaction of RM practices		.86	.665	α = .76
Scenario 1: price discrimination.	.712			
Scenario 2: payment for Food & Beverage.	.867			
Scenario 3: payment for seat selection.	.858			
Perception of customers' airline experience		.94	.623	α = .96
The 1st sub-dimension of airline experience:	*Service quality*			
This airline company supports the services that it offers.	.760			
Employees of this airline company are reliable in providing the service I expect.	.791			
Employees of this airline company understand what kind of needs I have.	.712			
Employees of this airline company are competent in providing the expected service.	.766			
Employees of this airline company are available to answer my service-related questions.	.745			
Service of this airline company is excellent in meeting my expectations.	.739			
The 2nd sub-dimension of airline experience:	*Perceived value*			
I believe that I got in return for what I paid.	.733			
I am proud of myself for choosing this airline company.	.764			
I believe that I got benefit in return for what I paid for this airline company.	.771			
The 3rd sub-dimension of airline experience:	*Trust*			
This airline company is generally trusted.	.858			
I trust this airline company.	.860			
I have great confidence in this airline company.	.836			
This airline company has high integrity.	.856			
I can depend on this airline company to do right things.	.835			
Loyalty		.85	.581	α = .89
I am a loyal customer of this airline company.	.802			
I have good feelings about this airline company.	.712			
I am proud of telling others that I prefer this airline company.	.758			
I would not give up this airline company easily.	.775			

Notes: N=741
Kaiser-Meyer-Olkin measure of sampling adequacy = .956; Total variance explained = 70.982
*EFA: Exploratory factor analyses (Principal component analysis with Varimax rotation) >0.50
**CR: Construct reliability > 0.70
***AVE: Average variance extract >0.50

Correlation Analysis and Confirmatory Factor Analysis

At this stage of the study, firstly the correlation between the variables which frame the research model is taken into consideration, and then the probability of whether multicollinearity problem has taken place is evaluated. For this purpose, according to the average value of the measurement items which constitute all the variables making up research model, the composite variable is transformed, and then we consider whether the correlation between the variables is r<0.7 (Hair et al., 2010). If the correlation coefficient r between the flight experience perceptions of the customers and the loyalty attitude is greater than 0.7, then this indicates a probable multicollinearity problem. Therefore, the variance inflation factor (VIF) results are considered, and it is observed that the VIF value is 1.02 which is within the ideally acceptable threshold value of 2.1, thus there is no multicollinearity problem for this research model construct (Hair et al., 2010, p. 204).

Table 3. Correlation coefficients

Research model variables	The complaint reaction of RM practices	Perception of customers' airline experience	Loyalty
The complaint reaction of RM practices	*.815*		
Perception of customers' airline experience	.121**	*.789*	
Loyalty	.199**	.722**	.762

Notes: The lower triangular matrix shows correlation coefficients and **correlation is significant at the 0.01 level (2-tailed Pearson correlation); the upper triangular matrix which is typed bold and italic representing the square root of AVE; VIF value is calculated as 1.02 ; N=741

In this context, in order to prove that the research model structure specifically meets the condition of discriminant validity, the correlation coefficients between the variables are compared to the resulting square root of the AVE value of that variable. The fact that the correlation coefficient between the variables themselves is lower than each variable's AVE value's square root score is an important indicator showing that the dissociation validity is provided (Camison &Lopez, 2010). As a result, as reported in Table 3, each variable's square root of the AVE value is higher than the correlation coefficient between the variables. Thus the dissociation validity has been provided.

And finally, the Confirmatory Factor Analysis (CFA) results of the research model provide for good-model-fit, and the evaluated criteria ($x2/df= 4.28$; GFI = .91; CFI = .96; RMSEA = .067) have given suitable results to prove the construct validity in general.

Hypothesis Tests

The relation is examined between the complaints of customers regarding the price discrimination and requesting extra charges for obtaining ancillary revenues which are the independent variable of this research and the flight experience perceptions of the customers; and also how these variables affect the loyalty is examined. Accordingly, the analysis results are as indicated in Table 4. In general, it is witnessed that the customers' complaints about revenue management (RM) practices positively affect the customers' perceptions statistically, and the H_1a hypothesis is supported. The positive perception created by the customers' travel experiences positively affects the loyalty of the customer to the airline almost twice as much ($\beta = 1.84$), and thus, the H_1b hypothesis is strongly supported as expected.

The Impact of Customer Dissatisfaction

Table 4. Hypothesis test results

Hypothesized paths		regression weight (β)	t-value and P-level sig.	Result
	Generic model			
H₁a:	The complaint of RM practices → Customers' perceptions	.134	2.97 **	Supported
H₁b:	Customers' perceptions → Loyalty attitude	1.840	4.31 ***	Supported
	Business purpose			
H₂a:	The complaint of RM practices → Customers' perceptions	.026	0.32 N.S.	*Not-supported*
H₂b:	Customers' perceptions → Loyalty attitude	8.281	0.36 N.S	*Not-supported*
	Touristic/leisure purpose			
H₃a:	The complaint of RM practices → Customers' perceptions	.179	2.31 *	Supported
H₃b:	Customers' perceptions → Loyalty attitude	1.039	3.33***	Supported
	Family/friends visits and other reasons			
H₄a:	The complaint of RM practices → Customers' perceptions	.263	3.65 ***	Supported
H₄b:	Customers' perceptions → Loyalty attitude	1.532	4.74 ***	Supported
	Full-Service Carrier Business Model			
H₅a:	The complaint of RM practices → Customers' perceptions	.024	0.51 N.S.	*Not-supported*
H₅b:	Customers' perceptions → Loyalty attitude	7.856	0.56 N.S.	*Not-supported*
	Low-Cost Carrier Business Model			
H₆a:	The complaint of RM practices → Customers' perceptions	.209	2.28 **	Supported
H₆b:	Customers' perceptions → Loyalty attitude	1.287	4.39 ***	Supported
Notes: ***P value is significant at the 0.001 level, **P value is significant at the 0.01 level, *P value is significant at the 0.05 level				

According to the sub-groups data in the study, the analysis results are also examined taking into account how the interaction in the research model is realized. In order to carry out the tests between the groups represented in the data set, the multi-group analysis is realized through the AMOS Graphics program as suggested by Byrne (2004). At the end of the analyses, in compliance with the criteria indicated by Chin and Dibbern (2010 p.188), meaningful differences between the sub-groups in both categorical variables in the research model (i.e. travel purpose and business model) are observed. That is, while the airline customer profile shows a heterogeneous structure, it is found that the groups have a homogeneous structure within themselves.

At this stage, firstly the assessments are made for the customers who travel for business, and the hypothesis test results are considered. However, because no meaningful results are obtained statistically, the suggested hypotheses H₂a and H₂b are not supported. In other words, it is found that for the customers who travel for business the RM practices have neither positive nor negative effects on their airline experience perceptions.

In touristic travels, although the suggested H₃a hypothesis is supported, a low level meaningful relationship is observed between the complaints about the RM practices and the customers' perceptions (t-value= 2.31 and p<0.05). Similarly, despite the fact that the H₃b hypothesis is supported, it is seen that in travels for touristic purposes the effect of the customers' travel experience perception on the loyalty of the customers is at a low level ($\beta = 1.039$). These relatively low hypothesis test results show that for customers travelling for touristic purposes the RM practices of airline companies and the service level perception are partially effective on the loyalty. From these results, it is understood that for those customers who fly short-distances for touristic purposes the cost of the flight is much more important.

The hypotheses H₄a and H₄b which are most strongly supported statistically were measured in travels made for visiting family/friends, and other reasons. And this result shows that in actuality among the customers who travel short-distances, those who are the most sensitive to the RM practices and have the inclination to be loyal to the airline company based on the travel experience perceptions are the people in this group. Therefore, it will be helpful for airline companies to develop their customer relation policies for short-distance lines by focusing on this customer segment.

When the criteria of the business model of the airline company are taken into consideration, the hypotheses H₅a and H₅b which are proposed for full-service airlines for their short distance flights are not found statistically meaningful and not supported. And this result should be found logical because as indicated in previous studies Xu et al. (2019) the expectations of the customers from full-service airlines are rather for long-distance travels than short-distance travels. Thus, the fact that the hypothesis is not supported should not be surprising.

On the other hand, the case is different for low-cost airlines. Because an acceptable level of service is expected from these airlines in return for a low price more remarkable results are obtained and the hypotheses H₆a and H₆b are supported. However, the effect of travel experience perceptions on the loyalty to the airline (approximately $\beta = 1.3$) is relatively low. And so, this result shows us that the low prices of the ticket fees are more prominent and important in respect of loyalty than the fact that the customers' travel perceptions affect the loyalty for low-cost airlines.

Figure 2. Summary of hypotheses testing results (created by the authors)

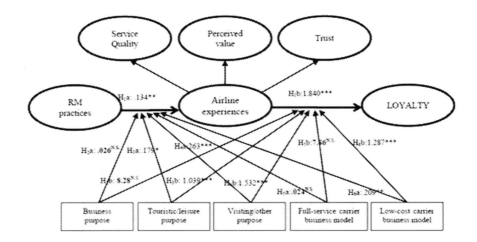

The Impact of Customer Dissatisfaction

A detailed examination of the interaction between each sub-variable which comprises the research model structure is given in Table 5. The indirect effects on each variable of the RM practices which affect the price paid (such as paying higher at last minute and paying some more for food/beverage and seat selection) for airline transport service in relation to the customers' perceptions are analyzed at this stage. For RQ-1, the indirect effect on each factor examined in this research model regarding the customers' complaints about the RM practices which change the cost of the travel is considered. In comparison to the other factors relating to the travel experience perception, the complaints about the RM practices are rather effective on the customers' loyalty (approximately $\beta = .25$).

When these effects are evaluated according to the purpose of travel, it is noted that the indirect effects of the complaints of customers about the RM who travel for business and other visiting purposes (such as visiting family/friends) are most effective on the loyalty (respectively, $\beta = .216$ and $\beta = .403$). Whereas, in travels for touristic purposes, this can show close effects on all the factors, but it affects service quality the most ($\beta = .234$). In fact, this different result in travels for touristic purposes should be considered logical, because those customers travelling for touristic purposes do not travel on the same route every time. Thus, it is not expecting that using the same airline would be a habit. On the other hand, in travels for touristic purposes, it is an acceptable result for the individual to focus on the quality of service because her/his main expectation is to relax.

When the customers' responses are assessed particularly from the viewpoint of the business model of the airline companies, it is seen that the complaints about the RM practices affect the loyalty the most for both business models (respectively $\beta = .192$ and $\beta = .269$). Therefore, the companies adopting the two business models are advised that they should handle the complaints carefully and/or should inform their customers that they are financially obliged to apply these methods in order to give the customers sustainable services. Thereby, they would have the chance to make their customers aware of this fact.

Table 5. The indirect effect of RM complaints' for each individual variable

Group categorization	Path 1	Path 2	Path 3	Path 4
	The complaint of RM practices → Service-quality perception	The complaint of RM practices → Perceived value perception	The complaint of RM practices → Trust perception	The complaint of RM practices → Loyalty attitude
RQ-1: Generic model	.171	.131	.134	**.246**
RQ-2: Business purpose	.034	.024	.026	**.216**
RQ-3: Touristic/leisure purpose	**.234**	.173	.179	.186
RQ-4: Family/friends visits-purpose	.308	.269	.263	**.403**
RQ-5: Full-Service Carrier Business Model	.029	.027	.024	**.192**
RQ-6: Low-Cost Carrier Business Model	.254	.197	.209	**.269**

SOLUTIONS AND RECOMMENDATIONS

This paper contributes to the existing literature with new empirical findings which have been obtained by virtue of the complaints of the customers about the revenue management (RM) practices (i.e. price discrimination and ancillary revenue practices) relating to their airline experiences. Within this scope, first of all, the interaction is examined between the complaints of the customers about the RM practices in relation to their flight experience perceptions and the loyalty of the customers. Secondly, the customer types who travel for different purposes are considered, and at what level the intensity of these effects occurs in respect of different airline business models are also examined. Accordingly, comparisons are made with the findings in the literature which have been obtained before, and the research results which are discussed in detail below are attained.

When the findings obtained are generally assessed (excluding the customer groups who travel on business and the planes of full-service carriers), it is noted that there is a positive interaction which is statistically meaningful although this is at a low level of effect. As will be noted in this finding, if an airline understands the complaints of the customers and tries to find solutions, it becomes possible to eliminate the complaints of the customers and to turn the dissatisfaction into a positive perception.

In the sample of the research, the hypothesis test results suggested for the customers who travel on business are not supported statistically. This may be interpreted that the customers who travel on business do not care about the RM practices, and thus, the flight experience perception is not influential on the loyalty. This conspicuous outcome supports the findings of the study made by Teicher et al. (2008) which defines the profile of those who travel on business. That is to say, the criteria affecting the preference of those travelling for a business concerning an airline company are related to such concretely observable criteria as flight schedule, flexibility, punctuality rather than perceptional factors, and the outcome of this study indirectly supports this claim (Teichert et al., 2008). However, maybe due to the fact this customer segment is not the direct respondent to the cost of the flight, they are willing to make payments for potential customer rights offered at high prices (such as free ticket cancellation).

This study related hypotheses is low level supported, it is understood that indicated in the previous studies the customer group travelling for touristic/leisure purposes give importance to the cost of the flight and prefer the airline accordingly (Tsai & Chen, 2019). One of the important findings of this study is that customers traveling for touristic purposes give more importance to the quality of service than customers traveling for other purposes.

Based on this research finding, other visiting reasons such as family/friend visits customer group are to remain loyal to the airline company depending upon the flight experience perceptions and who are the most sensitive group to the RM practices in short-distance flights. Therefore, by focusing on this customer group who use a certain route regularly and travel between two points frequently, it will be helpful to develop services devoted to their flight behaviors to provide for effective capacity management of airline companies.

In this research, the hypotheses suggested for full-service airline companies are not supported in the analyses for short-distance flights. But still, it must be kept in mind that the most important factor why the customers prefer full-service airlines for their short-distance flights is the reliability of the service offered. For this reason, full-service airlines should continue spending efforts to improve the flight experience perceived by the customers by maintaining the standard of the services offered (O'Connell &Williams, 2005).

For the companies which adopt a low-cost business model, the hypotheses put forth in the research model are strongly supported. But, when the effects of the assessment factors dealt with within the scope of this study on loyalty are considered, it is noted that they are relatively weak. In fact, this result means that loyalty takes place because of the low ticket prices as indicated in the literature rather than the effect of the travel perceptions of the customers on the loyalty to the low-cost airlines (O'Connell &Williams, 2005). However, the point that the airlines which adopt a low-cost business model should be most careful about is the price competition between many companies which adopt similar business models. Therefore, in the short-distance customer-carrying market, airline companies should not rely on customer loyalty so much. Low-cost airlines should be in a struggle, on the one hand, to offer low prices by decreasing their costs, and on the other hand, they should give their customers flight experience quality (Kim & Lee, 2011). Yet, the customers do not fully aware of low cost-carrier business model because they expect to get value from price-performance comparatively the service provided by full-service carriers. Otherwise, the activities of low-cost airlines only to sell cheap tickets and offer a simple service quality in order to be competitive will not be a sustainable business model. The research outcome shows that low-cost companies in the short-distance market should be managed in a much more customer-centric way in order to survive in the market.

FUTURE RESEARCH DIRECTIONS

Since this paper has been prepared as a context-specific study (it focuses on short distance flights), it is not possible to generalize its findings to all sorts of flights such as long-distance flights. Customers who represent different cultures have not been evaluated within this research. Future studies should focus on different customer profiles and various flight distances. There is a critical deficiency of this research model is that the frequent flyer program (FFP) membership is not included. Therefore, it will be useful to include the FFP applications in the research model suggested in this study the way dealt with by Mathies et al. (2013).

In the future, wider scoped researches based on the dyadic approaches research design may be made to develop such specific suggestions aimed at sectorial implementations. Further, researches in the airline market may be conducted concerning the ticket fees with different customer segments will be willing to pay and also about their service expectations during flights. In this way, from both the airline companies and the targeted customer segments clear findings, may be put forth to develop a customer-focused business model and a service policy.

CONCLUSION

This study makes some contributions to the existing knowledge accumulation about customer behaviors in the airline industry with a new viewpoint. It focuses on explaining the effects on the customer experience perception and loyalty attitude of the customer complaint reactions created by the RM practices related directly and indirectly to the price in line with the theories supporting the research model proposed by this study. By this means, contributions have been made to the literature by developing a new model proposal which holistically evaluates the scenarios involving RM practices and customers' flight experiences. It can be fairly said that an important contribution has been made to the literature by dealing with the variables for the first time within the scope of the research model uniquely.

The awareness put forth by the model proposed by this study may be used as a way of differentiation from the competitors in an environment of competition from the viewpoint of companies. Based on this research it will also be possible to develop a more effective service policy directed toward the targeted customer groups. In this context, it has also been put forth whether an airline company has created a differentiation from the viewpoint of the perceptions of customers groups who travel with different purposes.

Furthermore, the focus is made on efficiency and optimization studies by rather using numerical methods in the studies made in the literature regarding airline revenue management. In this context, one of the most important features that differs the study from others is that it measures the customers' reactions in general based on scenarios. In the previously made similar customer focused studies, the data evaluated were collected longitudinally. Unlike those, in this study, customer attitudes have been examined by collecting data based on the newly developed scenario in a wide scope in a cross-sectional study in such a way as to represent the customers.

As a result, this study sheds light on the matters which airline companies should be careful about for increasing customer loyalty in the realization of revenue management practices when airline companies are developing business models and service policy for customer subgroups. By this means, within the context of creating a positive customer perception, when an airline company is developing a business model and service policies, the goal here is to create awareness in respect of re-dealing with revenue management practices.

REFERENCES

Akamavi, R. K., Mohamed, E., Pellmann, K., & Xu, Y. (2015). Key determinants of passenger loyalty in the low-cost airline business. *Tourism Management*, *46*, 528–545. doi:10.1016/j.tourman.2014.07.010

An, M., & Noh, Y. (2009). Airline customer satisfaction and loyalty: Impact of in-flight service quality. *Service Business*, *3*(3), 293–307. doi:10.100711628-009-0068-4

Balcombe, K., Fraser, I., & Harris, L. (2009). Consumer willingness to pay for in-flight service and comfort levels: A choice experiment. *Journal of Air Transport Management*, *15*(5), 221–226. doi:10.1016/j.jairtraman.2008.12.005

Bockelie, A., & Belobaba, P. (2017). Incorporating ancillary services in airline passenger choice models. *Journal of Revenue and Pricing Management*, *16*(6), 553–568. doi:10.105741272-017-0100-6

Byrne, B. M. (2004). Testing for multigroup invariance using AMOS graphics: A road less traveled. *Structural Equation Modeling*, *11*(2), 272–300. doi:10.120715328007sem1102_8

Camison, C., & Lopez, A. V. (2010). An examination of the relationship between manufacturing flexibility and firm performance: The mediating role of innovation. *International Journal of Operations & Production Management*, *30*(8), 853–878. doi:10.1108/01443571011068199

Campbell, M. C. (1999). Perceptions of price unfairness: Antecedents and consequences. *JMR, Journal of Marketing Research*, *36*(2), 187–199. doi:10.1177/002224379903600204

Chin, W. W., & Dibbern, J. (2010). An introduction to a permutation based procedure for multi-group PLS analysis: Results of tests of differences on simulated data and a cross cultural analysis of the sourcing of information system services between Germany and the USA. In *Handbook of partial least squares* (pp. 171–193). Springer. doi:10.1007/978-3-540-32827-8_8

Cui, Y., Duenyas, I., & Sahin, O. (2018). Unbundling of ancillary service: How does price discrimination of main service matter? *Manufacturing & Service Operations Management, 20*(3), 455–466. doi:10.1287/msom.2017.0646

Dick, A. S., & Basu, K. (1994). Customer loyalty: Toward an integrated conceptual framework. *Journal of the Academy of Marketing Science, 22*(2), 99–113. doi:10.1177/0092070394222001

Duenyas, I. (2015). *Unbundling of Ancillary Service: How Does Price Discrimination of Main Service Matter?* Academic Press.

Fornell, C., & Larcker, D. F. (1981). Evaluating structural equation models with unobservable variables and measurement error. *JMR, Journal of Marketing Research, 18*(1), 39–50.

Francis, G., Dennis, N., Ison, S., & Humphreys, I. (2007). The transferability of the low-cost model to long-haul airline operations. *Tourism Management, 28*(2), 391–398. doi:10.1016/j.tourman.2006.04.014

George, D., & Mallery, P. (2019). *IBM SPSS statistics 26 step by step: A simple guide and reference.* Routledge. doi:10.4324/9780429056765

Hair, J. F., Black, W. C., Babin, B. J., & Anderson, R. E. (2010). *Multivariate Data Analysis: A Global Perspective* (7th ed.). Pearson Prentice Hall Publishing.

Hapsari, R., Clemes, M. D., & Dean, D. (2017). The impact of service quality, customer engagement and selected marketing constructs on airline passenger loyalty. *International Journal of Quality and Service Sciences, 9*(1), 21–40. doi:10.1108/IJQSS-07-2016-0048

Hassan, T. H., & Salem, A. E. (2021). Impact of Service Quality of Low-Cost Carriers on Airline Image and Consumers' Satisfaction and Loyalty during the COVID-19 Outbreak. *International Journal of Environmental Research and Public Health, 19*(1), 83. doi:10.3390/ijerph19010083 PMID:35010341

Kahneman, D., & Tversky, A. (1979). Prospect Theory: An Analysis of Decision Under Risk. *Econometrica, 47*(2), 263–291. doi:10.2307/1914185

Kaynak, H., & Hartley, J. L. (2008). A replication and extension of quality management into the supply chain. *Journal of Operations Management, 26*(4), 468–489. doi:10.1016/j.jom.2007.06.002

Kim, Y. K., & Lee, H. R. (2009). Passenger complaints under irregular airline conditions–cross-cultural study. *Journal of Air Transport Management, 15*(6), 350–353. doi:10.1016/j.jairtraman.2008.11.007

Kim, Y. K., & Lee, H. R. (2011). Customer satisfaction using low cost carriers. *Tourism Management, 32*(2), 235–243. doi:10.1016/j.tourman.2009.12.008

Kimes, S. E. (2010). *Strategic pricing through revenue management.* Academic Press.

Lapré, M. A. (2011). Reducing customer dissatisfaction: How important is learning to reduce service failure? *Production and Operations Management, 20*(4), 491–507. doi:10.1111/j.1937-5956.2010.01149.x

Lee, C. K., Ng, K. K. H., Chan, H. K., Choy, K. L., Tai, W. C., & Choi, L. S. (2018). A multi-group analysis of social media engagement and loyalty constructs between full-service and low-cost carriers in Hong Kong. *Journal of Air Transport Management, 73*, 46–57. doi:10.1016/j.jairtraman.2018.08.009

Lindenmeier, J., & Tscheulin, D. K. (2008). The effects of inventory control and denied boarding on customer satisfaction: The case of capacity-based airline revenue management. *Tourism Management, 29*(1), 32–43. doi:10.1016/j.tourman.2007.04.004

Marcus, B., & Anderson, C. K. (2008). Revenue management for low-cost providers. *European Journal of Operational Research, 188*(1), 258–272. doi:10.1016/j.ejor.2007.04.010

Mason, K. J., & Alamdari, F. (2007). EU network carriers, low cost carriers and consumer behaviour: A Delphi study of future trends. *Journal of Air Transport Management, 13*(5), 299–310. doi:10.1016/j.jairtraman.2007.04.011

Mathies, C., Gudergan, S. P., & Wang, P. Z. (2013). The effects of customer-centric marketing and revenue management on travelers' choices. *Journal of Travel Research, 52*(4), 479–493. doi:10.1177/0047287513478499

McMahon-Beattie, U., McEntee, M., McKenna, R., Yeoman, I., & Hollywood, L. (2016). Revenue management, pricing and the consumer. *Journal of Revenue and Pricing Management, 15*(3), 299–305. doi:10.1057/rpm.2016.17

O'Connell, J. F., & Warnock-Smith, D. (2013). An investigation into traveler preferences and acceptance levels of airline ancillary revenues. *Journal of Air Transport Management, 33*, 12–21. doi:10.1016/j.jairtraman.2013.06.006

O'Connell, J. F., & Williams, G. (2005). Passengers' perceptions of low cost airlines and full service carriers: A case study involving Ryanair, Aer Lingus, Air Asia and Malaysia Airlines. *Journal of Air Transport Management, 11*(4), 259–272. doi:10.1016/j.jairtraman.2005.01.007

Podsakoff, P. M., MacKenzie, S. B., & Podsakoff, N. P. (2012). Sources of method bias in social science research and recommendations on how to control it. *Annual Review of Psychology, 63*(1), 539–569. doi:10.1146/annurev-psych-120710-100452 PMID:21838546

Singh, S. (2003). Simple random sampling. In *Advanced sampling theory with applications* (pp. 71–136). Springer. doi:10.1007/978-94-007-0789-4_2

Teichert, T., Shehu, E., & von Wartburg, I. (2008). Customer segmentation revisited: The case of the airline industry. *Transportation Research Part A, Policy and Practice, 42*(1), 227–242. doi:10.1016/j.tra.2007.08.003

Truong, D., Pan, J. Y., & Buaphiban, T. (2020). Low cost carriers in Southeast Asia: How does ticket price change the way passengers make their airline selection? *Journal of Air Transport Management, 86*, 101836. doi:10.1016/j.jairtraman.2020.101836

Tsai, T. H. (2016). Homogeneous service with heterogeneous products: Relationships among airline ticket fares and purchase fences. *Journal of Air Transport Management, 55*, 164–175. doi:10.1016/j.jairtraman.2016.05.008

Tsai, T. H., & Chen, C. M. (2019). Mixed logit analysis of trade-off effects between international airline fares and fences: A revenue management perspective. *Current Issues in Tourism*, *22*(3), 265–275. doi:10.1080/13683500.2017.1402869

Wen, C. H., & Lai, S. C. (2010). Latent class models of international air carrier choice. *Transportation Research Part E, Logistics and Transportation Review*, *46*(2), 211–221. doi:10.1016/j.tre.2009.08.004

Wensveen, J. G., & Leick, R. (2009). The long-haul low-cost carrier: A unique business model. *Journal of Air Transport Management*, *15*(3), 127–133. doi:10.1016/j.jairtraman.2008.11.012

Wirtz, J., Kimes, S. E., Theng, J. H. P., & Patterson, P. (2003). Revenue management: Resolving potential customer conflicts. *Journal of Revenue and Pricing Management*, *2*(3), 216–226. doi:10.1057/palgrave.rpm.5170068

Xu, X., & Li, Y. (2016). Examining key drivers of traveler dissatisfaction with airline service failures: A text mining approach. *Journal of Supply Chain and Operations Management*, *14*(1), 30–50.

Xu, X., Liu, W., & Gursoy, D. (2019). The impacts of service failure and recovery efforts on airline customers' emotions and satisfaction. *Journal of Travel Research*, *58*(6), 1034–1051. doi:10.1177/0047287518789285

Zins, A. H. (2001). Relative attitudes and commitment in customer loyalty models: Some experiences in the commercial airline industry. *International Journal of Service Industry Management*, *12*(3), 269–294. doi:10.1108/EUM0000000005521

KEY TERMS AND DEFINITIONS

Customer Loyalty: The preference of the customer for an airline in respect of his/her future flights starts becoming a habit. And this leads to developing an intention in the mind of the customer for using the same airline in the future.

Deregulation: It means that the market becomes more competitive and customer oriented as legislative impediments to air transportation are removed, as are barriers to the entrance of private capital ventures in the sector.

Full-Service Carrier: Full-service provider airlines can manage connecting flights by linking aircraft traffic to routes in multiple flight networks. Airlines that provide this type of expensive service (flexibility such as cancelling a ticket or changing the ticket date to make the trip at a later time) compete in the market by shifting demand in their favor.

Low-Cost Carrier: To be able to cover the operational costs of flight schedules with low ticket prices, hereby the costs expended on each flight will be reduced by lowering the quality of service and comfort provided to the passengers. To reduce operational costs by making the most of their aircraft assets by streamlining and boosting the efficiency of their business procedures.

Perceived Value: Value perceived by the passengers in the process of benefiting from the flight service does not only include the monetary value paid by the customer. In addition to the monetary value paid, it also includes such burden as the endeavor and time that the passenger has spent in the whole process from the moment of his/her going into action for obtaining this service to the moment when he/she has received his/her luggage at the destination airport.

Service Quality: Airline service quality dimensions include the quality of the physical facility owned by the airline company; the level of capability of the airline company to give the service to its customers reliably and correctly; the intention and skills of the airline company for helping the passenger; focusing on the individual requirements and needs of the passengers; giving confidence in the company's organizational work doing model and competence of its employees to the customers.

Trust: Trust is related to the passengers start having been sure about the airline's service standards, the perceived risks regarding this quality of the flight experience decrease, and the flight process is realized more comfortably.

Chapter 11
Expect the Unexpected:
Lessons From the COVID-19 Pandemic for the Future of Airport Leaders and Managers

Andreea-Iulia Iordache
Faculty of Economics, University of Porto, Portugal

Helena Martins
CEOS, ISCAP, Polytechnic of Porto, Portugal & University Lusófona, Lisbon, Portugal & NOVA SBE, Lisbon, Portugal

Teresa Proença
https://orcid.org/0000-0001-6982-847X
Center for Economics and Finance, University of Porto, Portugal

Lúcia Piedade
Centre for Management Studies, Instituto Superior Técnico, Lisbon, Portugal

ABSTRACT

Airports are arguably the most well-prepared structures for crises and contingencies, and their staff undergo abundant training for these types of events; however, the COVID-19 pandemic events were largely unpredictable, thus creating a somewhat rare happening in the industry: a novel type of crisis. This study aims to realize the types of strategies and elements that made a difference in positive and negative critical incidents using semi-structured interviews and the critical incident technique to managers from Portuguese and Romanian airports focusing on the type of skills that the management required and developed in a crisis. In accordance with the competency-based education framework, leadership, communication, subject matter excellence, teamwork, ethics and integrity, and resilience and innovation were crucial soft skills in critical situations. The present study contributes with new insights on airport managers and leaders facing crisis situations, key issues, and strategies during the first wave of COVID-19.

DOI: 10.4018/978-1-6684-4615-7.ch011

Copyright © 2022, IGI Global. Copying or distributing in print or electronic forms without written permission of IGI Global is prohibited.

INTRODUCTION

Before the pandemic, the aviation industry had showed consistent growth in number of passengers at a global level (Mazareanu, 2020). In the first quarter of 2020, the scenery for the aviation industry was optimistic and promising with a 4.1% increase in demand, until the pandemic hit mid-March of 2020 (Mazareanu, 2020).

Airports are highly oriented towards safety and security structures, especially since the terrorist attacks of 9/11 in 2001 which resulted in increased security procedures and screening of passengers, luggage, etc. (Blalock et al., 2007). Standard procedures state that each airport should have a preparedness plan that must include information about the type of "communication with the public, screening, logistics (transport of travelers to health facilities), equipment, entry/exit controls, and coordination with the local/regional/national public health authority" (ACI, 2009). Therefore, airport authorities strive to be "one step ahead" and have a plan for any of the possible scenarios that might occur.

Airport and airline safety managers have a set of procedures for each kind of foreseeable emergency, but because crisis follow no one patter, those plans must be highly adaptable to the dynamic nature of situations (Enoma et al., 2009).

On the 11th of March 2020 the WHO declared COVID-19 a global pandemic (WHO, 2020a) due to the extent it was affecting the health and putting in risk the global population.

Consequently, countries started closing borders and nearly all international travel was halted, leaving people all over the world in a state of uncertainty, sometimes near panic trying to return to their home countries (Alper & Bloom, 2020). An unprecedented crisis in air travel all over the world ensued, with an inordinate amount of people flooding the airports to get a passage home, often ignoring safety and security indications from organisms of different natures in society.

Some of the main challenges that air travel management had to face during the COVID-19 pandemic were trying to follow as strictly as possible the safety and health rules, manage the cancelled or delayed flight passengers that were waiting to be sent back to the country of origin, storage of airplanes that were no longer flying because of the pandemic conditions, and shifting the handling division to a more cargo-oriented traffic (IATA, 2020b).

In the aftermath of COVID19 the aviation sector is reported to have taken one of the biggest hits economically speaking (IATA, 2020b). In this context, airport management had to face a lot of challenges including the effectiveness of the health safety, assuring that the passengers feel safe and trust the airport management and staff, certifying that the handling capacity is maintained and finding an optimum strategy to be financially efficient and not to limit the passenger flux (Airport Research Center, 2020).

As crisis will be less predictable and more serious, the airport community needs to be able to adapt at an even greater speed, to quicky evaluate past events and constantly improve contingency plans, to better tackle the next crisis. It is arguable that the COVID-19 pandemic was paradigm-shifting and a herald of forthcoming crisis that are bound to be ever more eminent due to risks like terrorism, extreme weather events from climate change, as well as other pandemics or epidemics (European Commission, 2019).

In the aftermath of these paradigm-shifting events, it is important to understand how these critical issues have been dealt with and what were the key elements for success and failures in dealing with this unexpected crisis situation and what are the lessons to be learned from this situation for the future crisis, which is what this chapter proposes to do.

Because of the nature of this theme and its specificities, semi-structured interviews based on the critical incidents technique were conducted with managers of the Portuguese and Romanian airports.

The goal was to study specifically the first wave of COVID19 and see how this event was coped with and how disruptive contexts can be best dealt with. The study will explore a major gap in the literature, as most of the studies are focused on airline companies and pilots, and few attentions is given to the airports and the airport management.

This study is pertinent to the aviation industry, respectively, the airport community to understand the impact of the COVID-19 pandemic, and to support airport management in dealing with future crisis.

BACKGROUND

Emergency, Crisis and Disaster

The terms emergency, crisis and disaster are often used interchangeably although they represent different levels of severity (Al-Dahash, 2016). The United Nation Office for Disaster Risk Reduction (UNDRR) (s.d.) states that an emergency refers to events like biological disasters or health issues, that do not have a serious impact and do not provoke a grave disruption at the community level; a crisis can be considered "a disruption that physically disrupts a system as a whole and threatens its basic assumptions, its subjective sense to self and its existential core" (Al-Dahash, 2016, pp. 2) and a disaster is an event of serious matter, that causes a big disruption, at a local, regional or national level and causes a big negative impact on the society. This includes negative impacts in the economy, losses of lives, material losses, etc. Out of the three, the disasters are considered to have the biggest severity (UNDRR, s.d.). In this work crisis the three types of events will be considered crisis as to simplify analysis and since they since these concepts are comparable (Al-Dahash et al., 2016), including in the disorder and urgency they create (Zhang et al., 2012).

Pan- and Epi-Demics

According to Porta (2008, pp. 79) an epidemic is "the occurrence in a community or region of cases of an illness, specific health-related behavior, or other health-related events clearly in excess of normal expectancy" whereas a pandemic is "an epidemic occurring worldwide or over a very wide area, crossing international boundaries, and usually affecting a large number of people" (Porta, 2008, pp. 179).

The risks and effects of the epidemics are not new to the civil aviation industry, which have faced several epidemics before the COVID10 pandemic (e.g. Severe Acute Respiratory Syndrome (SARS) from 2002, Middle East Respiratory Syndrome Coronavirus (MERS-CoV) in 2012 (de Groot et al., 2013) and the Ebola pandemic (Read et al., 2014)); airports tend to be considered high risk for these types of situations since they are crowded places, with many possibilities of disease of transmission.

According to Clegg (2010), ever since the first outbreaks that seriously threatened the globe, the countries tried to collaborate to stop the viruses to spread, with the first convention held in France in 1851.

Airports have been faced with different events of this nature and tried to assimilate procedures deried from these lessons. One example is the severe acute respiratory syndrome (SARS) from 2003, which was an outbreak that started in December 2002 in China in the Guangdong region and slowly spread worldwide, registering 812 deaths. This outbreak was alarming and over a two-year period, cases slowed down and disappeared, but this questioned the capacity of the authorities to understand the transmission path and to implement measures to stop the spread (Likhacheva, 2006). The limitations over the right of travel or returning home have been questioned, because while there are international laws and right that allow international movements, in the case of an emergency like an outbreak, it was consensual that this should be reconsidered (Gostin et al, 2009).

According to Nathanial and Van der Leyden (2020), in the case of COVID-19 pandemic, there are different phases for the management of the crisis: (1) look for patterns from the past crisis and try to apply the measures that were taken before in a similar situation; (2) get deeper into understanding the situation and how it should be tackled; (3) explanation of the decisions that will be made, applying the measures that were previously agreed and (4) to evaluate the strategy for improvement purposes.

Over the past 20 years and until the pandemic hit, the aviation industry had globally become one of the most promising industries, exhibiting constant growth, despite crisis like the SARS epidemic or the global economic crisis (Sehl, 2020). The economic impact of the COVID19 pandemic over the aviation industry was a drastic one, which had a negative impact of around 61.2% on the expenditure on flights and air travel (IATA, 2020a). This meant less financing for the airports and harsh times for the airlines, with a forecasted loss of 118 billion dollars in 2020 for the whole industry. Airports, a remarkably preparedness-oriented segment, faced an important challenge, which was to understand what kind of phenomena was actually being faced and what measures to put in place in a rare unpredicted event.

Impact of COVID-19 Pandemic on Airport Management

As mentioned before, the COVID-19 not only affected the airlines and travelers, but also the airports and their staff. The grounding of the flights and travel bans imposed by the E.U. and other countries like Australia (Doherty, 2020; BBC, 2020) and the decision of the former-U.S. president Donald Trump to ban all the flights coming from the European Union (Alper & Bloom, 2020) have caused a big disruption, leaving the airports to deal with unexpected and unpreceded issues, due to the passengers that were stuck in the airports, looking to get back to their home countries. The main challenges that airport management and staff had to face were, according to Airport Research Center (2020) were the effectiveness of health safety measures, passenger confidence in said safety measures, limited number of permitted travelers, guaranteeing handling capacity, and the financial strain this event represented for the air travel business. Each of the main challenges had a realistic objective that was focused on decreasing the overall negative impact of the COVID-19 pandemic in the airport community.

Importance of Human Capital and Soft Skills in a Crisis

During an event like a crisis, human capital should not be disregarded, and the organizations should keep focusing on the aspect, despite the situation of uncertainty (Sorribes et al., 2021). Management is one of the stakeholders of the airport, and it should be involved in the crisis resolution, without disregarding soft skills like communication or situational awareness during the process (Mantzana et al., 2020).

Soft skills include the ability to communicate, deal with an urgent situation and the ability to work under pressure (Dixon et al., 2010) and can be crucial for a fast response. When a disruption like the COVID-19 pandemic occurs, it is important for leaders to communicate the problem, maintain an active role in the organization and to adapt to the situation with a good and strong response to the situation (Dirani et al., 2020).

There has been a lack of in-house training for soft skills, recognized by the ICAO (2019). The organization highlighted that the aviation industry must find ways of training soft-skills and compete with

Expect the Unexpected

other specialized institutions, although it is fully aware that they cannot fulfill the existing training needs completely, suggesting internships and volunteering as a solution for the gap (ICAO, 2019); yet, hard skills (technical) keep being overwhelmingly more valued than soft skills (human) (Uchronski, 2011).

In the event of a crisis in an airport, I has been argued that small decisions or actions taken by lower-level employees that could destabilize the entire system in case of an emergency like a health-related one as is the case of the catering department and the employees that handle food, as this is considered also a danger when goods are mishandled and delivered improperly to the aircraft for the passengers (Bongiovanni & Newton, 2019).

The likelihood of an emergency-type situation is based on several factors specific to each of the airport (individual, task, tools & tech, environmental, cultural, etc.); an airport that mostly manages traffic from low-cost airlines tends to be more likely to have breaches in the safety procedures, as the staff is either scarce or the time between the flights, or other aircraft-related verifications could not allow a thorough check from the health safety point of view (Bongiovanni & Newton, 2019).

According to the ACI (2009), each airport should have a preparedness plan that should include information about the type of communication with the public, screening, logistics (transport of travelers to health facilities), equipment, entry/exit controls, and coordination with the local/regional/national public health authority. Another crucial aspect is providing the staff all the equipment and the sanitizing substances that are needed.

Robert and Lajhta (2002) emphasize that, in most of the cases, top management, which could give a good support in crisis, is not involved in the events and there is a noticeable absence of soft skills among the people which directly face the events. Soft skills training can improve the communication and collaboration between people and organizations, increase resilience and awareness of the situation, all which can contribute to a better crisis management (Lucini, 2020).

Thus, although tackling a crisis has been highly linked to hard skills, and less importance given to soft skills, the literature suggests they could be the key factor to a good approach on the management of the crisis and that they could be trained.

Competency-Based Education Framework

The Competency-Based Education Framework is a framework for aviation management programs important for the development of aviation leaders. The framework aims to bridge the gap on soft skill training in aviation management, being generally focused on members of the aviation industry, like flight attendants or pilots (Mott et al., 2019). The need of soft skills among the airport managers is crucial as their capabilities of interaction, communication and general behavior can have a strong impact on the other members of the organization (Gov & Çoten, 2021), thus influencing the process of crisis management. This framework is based on six key competencies: leadership, subject matter excellence, ethics and integrity, communication, teamwork, and individual resilience and innovation.

Summary

The aviation industry is well known for being prepared, however, due to the complexity and constant change, crises are becoming harder to be anticipated and be tackled with standard measures. Skills are crucial in a crisis, and although training for soft skills has long been established for pilots and cabin crew, there has been less focus on training soft skills for airport management workers. A framework studied in airport management programs could be the key to developing soft skills among the management of the airport and preparing for a future crisis and will be further applied on the two airport managements which have been included in this study. It is important to understand how the airport management tackled the COVID-19 pandemic and how it adapted to the situation.

MAIN FOCUS OF THE CHAPTER

Semi-structured interviews using the Critical Incidents Technique (CIT), a qualitative method commonly used in the cases of studying the skills and the factors in the case of a critical situation (Butterfield et al., 2005) was used to address the first wave of COVID19 (the most unexpected moment of the pandemic crisis) in managers at the airport of Lisbon (Portugal) (N=4) and Bucarest (Romania) (N=4).

The selection of the two countries was a convenience driven one, since originally there was only one country in the research project, but a multitude of factors (overwhelming workloads, high uncertainty regarding the future of work, organizational instability, etc) led subjects to be extremely uncooperative and interviews to be extremely hard to procure; hence, it became evident that to collect more data, the chapter would benefit from the inclusion of another airport. On the other hand, the comparison and analysis two countries can provide a better perspective on how the crisis management was done in two different environments.

Qualitative approaches are the suggested methods in the case of in-depth analysis of the events and the situation in which the subjects found themselves; qualitative research should indicate the relevant information, how the results may be used for further purposes, and what are the resources available for this kind of research (Patton, 1987).

In data treatment, summaries of each interview were created, as a way of getting an overview and an understanding of the data in the interview transcripts. This strategy allowed the researchers to focus on the key points and principal themes that emerge from the interviews (Saunders et al. 2007). The analysis procedure involved four main activities. These activities are categorization of data, unitizing data, relationship recognition and, finally, testing and drawing the conclusions. We organized the interview data according to the interview questions, and categorized the responses, then, the categorized interview data was reviewed and categories were iteratively identified. The differences between the countries were summarized in tables after each category, to aid the formulation of conclusions.

The COVID-19 Pandemic in Portugal and Romania

Portugal and Romania, the countries studied n this chapter, are both member-states of the European Union, which means both countries had to follow European directives during the COVID-19 pandemic, and ICAO regulations and recommendations. At a local level each of the national authority imposed own states of emergency and laws according to the pandemic situation in the respective countries.

In Portugal, the first registered COVID-19 case was in the beginning of March 2020, a 60-year-old male who had recently travelled to Italy and presented symptoms on 29th of February (Rico, 2020). On 19th of March 2020, the president of the Portuguese Republic declared the State of Emergency in Portugal following the declaration of a pandemic of the WHO on the 11th of March 2020. The state of emergency restricted rights given by the Constitution, such as the right of travel or commute, both inside the national territory and internationally, the transition to remote work or to a lay-off regime, highlighting that traveling should be avoided and controls and screenings are applied (Decreto do Presidente da República n.º 14-A/2020, 2020).

In Romania, the state of emergency was declared on 16th of March 2020 by the President of Romania, which restricted right of travel or commute, both inside the national territory and internationally, the right of property, economic freedom, among others, while measures such as closure of borders and limitation of movement were taken (Decret nr. 195, 2020). The measures taken were related to the decrease of the number of cases of SARS-CoV-2, as well as avoiding the spread of the disease among the citizens.

At the European Union level, the European Council has held various meetings and tried to mitigate the impact of the COVID-19 crisis, encouraging the Member States to cooperate in order to stop the spread of the virus, by creating plans and strategies to tackle the possible increase of SARS-CoV-2 (European Council, 2020a). On March 2nd the European Council activated the Integrated Political Crisis Response (IPCR) in "full mode", allowing the European Union members to "take rapid decisions when facing major cross-sectoral crises requiring a response at EU political level" (European Council, 2020b).

Regarding the aviation sector, the European Union adopted a "slot waiver" in order to ease the airlines' struggle facing the pandemic (European Council, 2020c). Before the waiver, the airlines complied with the airport slot requirements, which obliged them to use 80% of more of the take-off and landing slots, in order to maintain them in the following year. The measure was taken with the goal of helping airlines during the traffic drop caused by the COVID-19 pandemic (European Council, 2020c). As per the European Union structure, both countries studied followed the issued measures by the council.

Sample

Both countries and their aviation leadership had different strategies and different contingency plans, but both acted accordingly to the European Union directive regarding the COVID-19 pandemic and according to the main aviation regulator, International Civil Aviation Organization (ICAO).

Each of the leaders interviewed held roles in the Strategy department, Statistic, Airport handling, Human Resources, Supply or Public Relations. All the interviewees had to coordinate human or material resources during the pandemic and the processes they were responsible for were strictly related to the airport processes.

Table 1. Study participants

Interviewee code	Country	Occupation
B1	Portugal	Human Resources Manager
B2	Portugal	Operational Manager
B3	Portugal	Commercial Director
B4	Portugal	Supply Assistant
A1	Romania	Airport Manager
A2	Romania	Handling Director
A3	Romania	Airport Planning
A4	Romania	Spokesperson

A Competency-Based Education Framework Approach to Key Elements in Dealing with the First Wave of Pandemic

When analyzing the responses provided by our subjects regarding key elements that made or broke the different situations, leaders' soft skills stood out in a very clear manner, which led us to develop our analysis in strid with the Competency-Based Education Framework (CBEF) (Mott et al, 2019). The CBEF has 6 major categories that will guide our analysis: leadership, subject matter excellence, ethics and integrity, communication, teamwork and individual resilience and innovation comparing the presence of the previously mentioned in the behavior during the COVID-19 pandemic crisis.

1. Leadership

In Portugal, managers confronted the pandemic crisis having in mind both the welfare of the employees and the financial cost of the crisis. Given the nature of the crisis, the employees were reportedly worried about their health, the future, and the unpredictability of the pandemic. However, managers reported having empathized with them, understanding their fears, and tried to give as much support as possible. Another important aspect which requires leadership skills is the power to adapt and lead the organization during uncertain times. Managers also referred having to deal with budget cuts, contract termination and other financial aspects, all the while trying not to forget the human side of the situation.

"In terms of motivation at the organizational level also, because the people weren't ready, we all had a lot of fear, and this must be managed at the company level. Also, there was the financial aspect that was associated. [...] We had to handle people that started to become sick, and especially family members of colleagues that had COVID-19. We were forced to deal with death among the colleagues and their families" – B1

"Because of the breach in the aviation and the infection situation, we tried as much as possible to have the teams working from home and we adjusted quickly. [...] We tried to measure the impact that the situation had at a budget level and we saw that it was way bigger than believed. We "took the machine, unplugged most of it and only let the heart beating". We analyzed from A to Z where we could cut costs." – B2

"The most important lesson of this pandemic is that we have to be agile and show great flexibility when making fast decisions and making decisions that you might need to change the next day." – B3

Romanian managers referred mostly having to motivate their team and the employees during the transition to remote work or dealing with incidents at the airport facility. Leadership skills were demonstrated when the airport management had to make decisions regarding the future investments and had to demonstrate a quick reaction to the crisis, by adapting and making decisions fast. Subject A1, for example, stated that there was a necessity of quick adaptation to the situation, creating sort of a "taskforce" with managers, directors, and other leaders from the airport community in order to plan the way the crisis was going to be tackled.

"We didn't have a special crisis management department, we have contingency plans, but at that time, no one thought about this scenario, were all the planes would be grounded. We managed to create an "emergency group" created by all the managers and directors of the company. – A1

"What was challenging, and it was new for me was to find new methods of motivate the people, which were already in quarantine at home, partially not updated to the informational flux. […] It was difficult to organize them, it was a new element, they needed moral support, encouragement, I had to empathize with each person and their own personal problems." – A3

The management of the handling company that served the airport in Romania required leadership skills in relation to shareholders, and the financial decisions taken that affected them and the future of the organization.

"For us, the biggest challenge was given by the fact that in 2019 we made massive investments in order to open the Cargo division in 2020. We had converted all our reserves that were allocated to a crisis like COVID to invest and develop in 2020. Then things changed. The biggest challenge was to take responsibility for the fact that we couldn't deliver what we promised to our business partners, because we didn't know how long the COVID-19 pandemic would take. I could say that the decisions we made were about business sustainability." – A2

If there is a crisis tomorrow, would I have resources? If up until now we thought about contingency plans for sustaining a business for a 6-month period, now we enhanced it to 12 months" – A2

Table 2. Comparison of leadership actions taken in Portugal and Romania during the COVID-19 pandemic

Portugal	Romania
• Empathizing with staff and team members during the pandemic • Empathizing during periods of illness • Assisting other employees and the team members in the processes • Making quick decisions and adjustments • Flexibility and resilience together with the team members and other employees • Budget reduction and better management of the available cash	• Empathizing, motivating, and giving support to the team members during the pandemic • Making quick decisions and adjustments • Assisting other employees and the team members in the processes • Assuming responsibilities and risks before the shareholders • Flexibility and resilience during the crisis

As per the table above, the leadership-based decision taken in both countries were similar, both managements having related behavior regarding the management of the COVID-19 crisis, with a small accent on financial aspects from the Portuguese airport management, which emphasized the necessity of cost-cutting more than the Romanian airport management.

2. Subject Matter Excellence

According to the interviewed managers from the analyzed countries, health measures among the airport employees and the passengers were taken from the beginning of the pandemic. As safety and health measures, apart from the basic measures, the airport management from Portugal implemented remote work for the processes that didn't require presence at the airport, while the for the on-site processes and tasks, back-up teams had been established, in order to reduce the contact between the members of the organization and track easier the COVID-19 cases, if existed. Improvement of touchless and digitalized processes was also a priority, along with remote work.

"We already had everything digitalized, we don't use paper. We have never had remote work like this before, but it was very easy to install it, since we were all ready to work from home. Basically, all the administrative roles and support went home and for the roles that required presence at the airport, we ended up working with back-up employees." – B1

"In the case of the Ramp team, we didn't make changes, because we had a lot of activity in the Cargo segment and for this, we need a bigger staff at the ramp. [...] In the Passenger area, we had to place people in remote work, have the minimum number of teams working at the office and avoid the infection and the contact between the teams, it was an immediate action." – B2

In Romania, remote work was also implemented in the departments that didn't require presence at the airport, having some designated members of the organization going to the headquarters when necessary to complete basic tasks. In some departments, members were taking turns to go to the airport, respecting the social distancing and using masks in the premises.

"Amongst the first measures that were taken and had an impact in the department that I mange was remote work. We had to reduce the presence of the personnel on the airport by 80-90% and switch to remote work, which was interesting because we weren't ready for such thing" – A3

As for the passengers, the screening was made a different way, there was a screening of the passengers made in tents outside, in the parking lot of the airport, which were sent in small groups to the check-in, and then the people that were going along with them had to cross the border, go back, and pick more people up.

"We had to set everything up in the parking lot of the terminal, in Departures. We did a screening and a pre-check-in there, after that, we were doing the boarding. We were taking 10-15 people at a time through the screening, so it was a big resource consumption. As an airport, we had to give support through this process. They were taking the people from the screening tents, through the frontier to the gates, and were coming back to take more" – A1

Table 3. Comparison of subject matter excellence actions taken in Portugal and Romania during the COVID-19 pandemic

Portugal	Romania
• Health safety measures • Implementing remote work where possible • Implementing back-up teams for on-site work employees	• Health safety measures • Implementing remote work in necessary departments • Turn-taking system for on-site work employees • Restructuring/creating designated spaces for health screening

Expect the Unexpected

3. Ethics and Integrity

As studied above, during the COVID-19 pandemic, managements from Portugal and Romania exhibited leadership skills based on ethic decisions, that were health-related. The members of the organization demonstrated integrity, by following the recommendations of health regulators and respecting the health etiquette imposed.

"There is here a public health situation, and it is important to preserve the health of the people, this situation is fundamental, and, if we see the Maslow's pyramid, the health is in the bottom. We have to protect the passengers, the employees and we had to take actions that we have never taken before, we had to adapt buildings, everything related to cleaning, improve the touchless and biometric processes." – B3

There is, however, one concern that should be highlighted in the case of the Portuguese management. Due to the changes made by Handling, during uncertain times, under different circumstances – low traffic –, the switch might cause incidents that could be related to the integrity of the staff.

"Restructuring and testing with low traffic and then say that it was a positive change, that you cannot say, because we are talking about different fluxes of traffic. I think that the negative part was that this was not well thought, and the decision was rash; we are in a more dangerous situation that we think. Firstly, we still didn't measure it because of the countries opening and closing borders all the time […] my greatest fear is that the alterations might create some kind of accident or incident among the teams, or maybe even among the passengers. Usually, in aviation, when we are in the peak of the operations, everyone is on alert and no errors are made. After the peak, we feel confident that we did a good job and we let our guards down, and this is how accidents happen" – B2

Table 4. Comparison of ethics and integrity actions taken in Portugal and Romania during the COVID-19 pandemic

Portugal	Romania
• Respecting respiratory etiquette and health measures imposed • Switch to a new management model in Handling	• Respecting respiratory etiquette and health measures imposed

4. Communication

During the COVID-19 pandemic, communication was crucial, as the unpredictability of the decisions that were taken was high and people needed to communicate, whether about the organizational decisions or the personal welfare (sickness, tracing the origin of the infection, etc.)

In Portugal, the interviewees didn't draw attention to any major communication flaws, and the transition to remote work as done smoothly, without any major incidents to be mentioned. The communication was done well in the departments and the airport organizations studied, the transition to remote work was successfully done.

"The flexibility aspect, having the capability to take the work home overnight, the flexibility to do so. Those things, we used to do from time to time, remotely. This capability of resilience and change that we had, wouldn't have been possible, hadn't existed a crisis like this." – B3

In Romania, the airport management confronted three communication issues: with the passengers, the authorities and in the internal processes of the organization. During the first weeks of the pandemic, when the State of Emergency was implemented, the passengers coming from repatriation flights didn't have enough information and the airport officials could not offer exact details, as rules and conditions were rapidly changing. However, due to an extent effort, this was normalized as the time passed and there was a better coordination among the airport community members. The authorities were not giving exact information regarding the procedures, and the situation was normalized later, after some months, when the Government issued a clearer set of rules, according to one of the interviewees. The airport management from Romania was proactive and worked together with the authorities to create a set of procedures that could be followed. The internal communication was poor in the beginning of the pandemic crisis, as the employees weren't given resources to perform their tasks from work (access to the company's system, computers, telephones) and the employees had to use their own equipment. This situation was also solved as the time passed.

"We can say that until July, it was a bit of a chaos, considering the decisions that were made each and every day, the flight restrictions on some countries, while the planes were already cruising. The authorities' intervention, the decisions were a little bit chaotic. There was no coordination, no one knew what to do, each one of us was making decisions however we saw fit at that time. Somewhere in July we became more organized, we also received a Minister Order that included the measures we were supposed to take." – A1

"Even though they were receiving e-mails, working from home is different than being at the office." – A3

"There was a funny situation, the software incompatibility. Each of us was using their own version of Excel and I had to redo a lot of the reports, because the information was not harmonized. I had to merge the work of each of the five of my co-workers so that the information would be coherent." – A3

"The number of passengers was lowering, we didn't know what to communicate to them, because we didn't have enough information (from the authorities) and we were some kind of pioneers, because we had to come up with some procedures and then we would transmit them to the authorities. It was a difficult period, because the country was in a State of Emergency, and everyone was affected." – A4

Overall, in both countries, communication was done well between the members of the organization, as they could manage the crisis without any major problems. This is crucial in an environment like an airport since it could create a disruption and cause safety problems.

Expect the Unexpected

Table 5. Comparison of communication actions taken in Portugal and Romania during the COVID-19 pandemic

Portugal	Romania
• Remote work and back-up teams successfully implemented • Relatively good communication during crisis period • Overall, good communication between the members of the organization	• Lack of communication with the authorities and the passengers during the first weeks of the pandemic • Lack of material resources, which caused small issues in the coordination • Overall, good communication between the members of the organization

5. Teamwork

Portugal also showed good teamwork skills during the COVID-19 crisis, notably among the back-up teams that were created to reduce the probability of infection.

"A group of people would work in the airport and other people were preserved, to minimize the contact between different persons and allowing, in case there was an outbreak in one of the teams, to have someone in back-up, at home." – B1~

The teams working on-site were well harmonized with the remote employees, being assisted by their leaders during the whole period of the pandemic. The high resilience, which will be further explained, and flexibility, played an important part in the executed processes and the good coordination among the teams.

"The people's will to give in and the level of comprehension were much bigger. They have been more tolerant and accepted the need of change easier. In aviation, we are always prone to change and sometimes there is a resistance. I think has been more tolerance and comprehension." – B2

"The unity between the employees facing the adversity created by the COVID-19 pandemic allowed the company to keep working, even though the conditions were though" – B4

In Romania, leaders of the teams and departments became more than that, as they helped with the processes that had to be made, the changes in tasks and the other processes that weren't theirs on a normal basis. In one department, the team had to work together on new reports generated for COVID-19, help with the tasks of other departments, while at the airport facilities, different employees from completely different departments (protocol, special needs, business lounges) formed a team to help on the screening area. This change of tasks that weren't included in the job description was well dealt with and served as a lesson for future crisis.

"Of course, each of us has their own activities, but we realized that it becomes useful if we know what the other does, so that, if I cannot work, who will replace me at the office can do my tasks […] What we get from here is that we can do it, there is a bigger openness, we taught each other some particularities of our tasks" – A3

"We learned. People that used to work in business lounges started to do the management of the mass of people at the arrivals. They help people with filling the forms. We also moved people from the mobility service, and probably in a future situation, we will be more coordinated. We learned that we can do things that are not necessary in our job description" – A1

Table 6. Comparison of teamwork actions taken in Portugal and Romania during the COVID-19 pandemic

Portugal	Romania
• Remote work facilitated by the teamwork and cooperation • Back-up teams that eased the processes when on-duty teams couldn't • Involvement of the leaders in all the processes	• Completing tasks out of the job description • Reallocating employees to other areas • Team spirit when needed to complete processes • Involvement of the leaders in all the processes

6. Individual Resilience and Innovation

In both analyzed countries, resilience was the skill that was mentioned the most, as all interviewees saw it as a positive outcome after the COVID-19 pandemic. Airport leaders from both Portugal and Romania declared that the resilience of each of the employees was a crucial factor during the crisis. As per Rai et al. (2021), openness, high availability was among the characteristics noted in the behavior of the people. Along with resilience, innovation was an important skill that emerged during the COVID-19 pandemic, as airport managements had to adapt, and create new methods to function. Portugal airport management experienced resilience in all the departments studied, this making the crisis easier to be tackled. The decisions that need to be made were faster than the usual, given the fact that there was an ongoing crisis, and people complied and executed the tasks, despite the unpredictability.

"Because we had no idea about the traffic forecasts, we didn't know what it was going to happen. We had to go and speak to the regulator and explain that we didn't have the capacity for the model, at the time […] either we were doing the forecasts as usual and we would have had crazy forecasts, either we were stalling and and we would leave our confort zone. We adapted to a new timing and the taxes were applied starting 1st of April instead of 1st of January." - B3

Remote work and digitalizing the tasks and meetings could be considered an innovation that could be adopted in the future crisis and on a daily basis, as it could bring real benefits to the organization.

"An important aspect was the remote work, which managed to allow us, especially the ones that have children, to spend more time with them […] I finished work earlier, I went to pick my child up from kindergarten and we went to the park. It is a positive thing to understand that there are other ways to get organized during remote work and there is some flexibility that we hadn't had explored yet." – B1

However, a decision like restructuring during COVID-19 pandemic, could go both ways, either be considered as an innovation and success or as a failure due to the lack of data to perform such change.

Expect the Unexpected

"Restructuring made on the run might not give a good result. The fact that we have time, we start to think, and it is no longer outside the box, there is no more box and too ahead. The lesson that I take from this is that restructuring in crisis times is dangerous, we didn't have time to evaluate it because we still don't have the traffic that we had so we could see the impact" – B2

"Planning a crisis is very important. The flexibility of managing a crisis, believing in the ability of adapting and in the resilience of the people is essential. This crisis will end, but in fact, it was a big earn" – B1

"There are unpredictable factors that could have serious negative impact on the activity of the company. Nothing is guaranteed." – B4

Having to make quick and confident decisions and be fast is also an important lesson when facing a crisis.

"It is not every four months; it is making quick decisions and not being afraid of doing so." – B3

In Romania, the resilience was observable in the interaction between organization members and in the interaction with external organizations. While the communication skill was sometimes lacking, as previously mentioned, this was compensated by the resilience of the leaders and the employees. New tasks were created, new sets of rules were adopted, this giving the opportunity of acquiring new job-related skills to the people. Resilience skill triggered innovation, meaning that in a future crisis, issues will be easier to tackle and the reaction to the change will have less of a negative impact on the organization as a whole.

"We are ready to manage even worse situations that we had before in our emergency plans. We are paying more attention on the measures so that we can be responsive when something like this happens" – A1

"In terms of lessons, in my opinion, also as an economist, I believe that one of the most important lessons was to use all the tools that you have available and how to use them in a crisis. If there is a crisis tomorrow, would I have resources? If up until now we thought about contingency plans for sustaining a business for a 6-month period, now we enhanced it to 12 months" – A2

"The responsibility. No one from our team felt like they cannot continue, even thought it was human to not be able to continue. I see that the level of responsibility of each of the team member was above the expectations and above the limits, even though not all the activities were in our job description. It matters a lot to have a team for which the responsibility is important, I believe this kind of people should be appreciated and kept" – A3

"We learned a lot of lessons, one of the main ones was to act and be responsive, think in advance. Another lesson was that if today everything is fine and it seems that nothing could go wrong, well, it could." – A4

Table 7. Comparison of individual resilience and innovation actions taken in Portugal and Romania during the COVID-19 pandemic

Portugal	Romania
• Quick decision-making process • Innovating through remote work and digital processes • Openness and low resistance to change	• Quick decision-making process • Innovating through remote work and digital processes • Openness and low resistance to change • Compensate lack of communication by high resilience and cooperation

SOLUTIONS AND RECOMMENDATIONS

As previously mentioned, there seems to be a gap in soft skills training, which is more focused on the elements that are directly linked to the airport-related tasks and disregards the management. In 2014, the aviation regulator published a document that included a framework for Crisis management, where several categories of events are explained and what their impact would be on different sectors (ICAO, 2014). In the case of "Airborne spread diseases/Pandemic", the category "Persons" discusses the health and workload of personnel, passenger, and flight crew, however, the framework is not extended to management, nor soft skills are mentioned.

Based on our findings this work suggests that an adapted framework by Mott et al. (2019) can be adequate to complement the ICAO Crisis management framework as recommendations thusly:

- Leadership involvement in low level tasks and processes
- Psychological support for leaders and their teams
- Creation of a crisis taskforce constituted of all managers
- In-depth personal and professional ethics training
- Creation of a clear communication protocol
- Regular taskforce meetings for a better communication
- Switching from individual tasks to more team-oriented tasks
- Scenario-based training to test resilience

In order to maximize the learnings from the upon the events during the beginning of the COVID-19 pandemic, aviation authorities should implement the measures presented above as part of a crisis framework. It is important to understand the importance of the airport management in the decision-making process and how critical soft skills training is in such crisis.

Figure 1. Recommendation on implementing the studied framework for soft skills

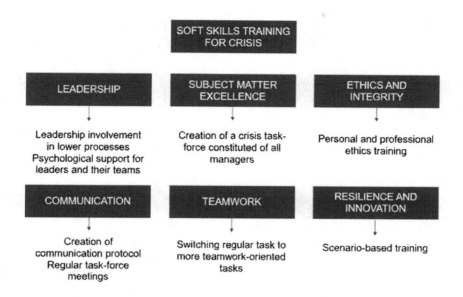

The recommendations for soft skills training in aviation authorities are highly linked to the involvement of management in low-level tasks management, since it is noticeable that during a crisis like the COVID-19, leadership, resilience, teamwork, communication, ethics, openness, and empathy are crucial. The soft skills displayed by the managers from the two countries in this study could be found in the Competency-Based Educational framework, some being more frequently mentioned than others. Upon a comparison between the skills in the framework and the ones displayed by the managers, leadership competencies were aligned, although the sub-competencies mentioned which were "achieving mission, goal and vision and utilizing situation, context, and cultural aspects of organizations effectively" (Mott et al., 2019, pp. 8) were not mentioned managers interviewed. Subject Matter Excellence competencies can be highly linked to Ethics and Integrity and Leadership, as they were noticeable in the managers' behavior during the COVID-19 pandemic. Communication skills, however, were an issue for the managers as the unpredictability of the crisis caused disruptions and difficulty in communicate problems and decisions. Teamwork is a competency which was highly valued and visible, as managers coordinated teams and involved themselves in the basic tasks. Lastly, individual resilience, which was a crucial skill during the crisis, lead to an innovation in the airport management processes. This pandemic was paradigm shifting in the sense that management had to adapt and innovate, which may have resulted in extraordinary resilience.

Although, all the six pillars of the framework should be taken into consideration, it should be stressed that not all should be treated equally, as soft skills such as leadership, communication, teamwork, and individual resilience and innovation were most required in the analyzed situation. Despite their overall importance to aviation, in crisis contexts the categories "ethics and integrity" and "subject matter excellence", do not appear to be as relevant as the afore mentioned ones. Our results indicate that leadership should be considered the foundation of the framework, as the other soft skills are highly linked to it.

CONCLUSION

Despite their high levels of preparedness for crisis situations, the COVID19 hit airports and air travel management in many unexpected ways (Center, 2020). This chapter aimed to realize the types of strategies and elements that made a difference in positive and negative critical incidents, using semi-structured interviews and the critical incident technique, to Portuguese and Romanian airport managers. Our results showed that soft skills made the biggest difference in the management of this unexpected crisis situation according to our subjects.

The Competency-Based Education Framework (Mott et al, 2019) which is already in place for training other elements of the airport community (namely pilot and cabin crew training) proved to be an adequate basis also for managers, but in their case, leadership should be the main focus of training, followed by, communication, teamwork, resilience and innovation and finally ethics and integrity and subject matter excellence.

The present study further proposes other organizational interventions such as the creation of a crisis taskforce constituted of all managers and a higher leadership involvement in low level tasks and processes.

In all, this chapter reinforces the importance soft skills for leadership behavior in a crisis, like the one caused by the recent COVID-19 pandemic. Soft skills are aptitudes which leaders should be trained in, because, despite being currently given a secondary role, are crucial in crisis management in the aviation industry. The Competency-Based Education Framework can be considered relevant starting point for a further soft skill training of airport management and can be applied and adapted for future crisis.

FUTURE RESEARCH DIRECTIONS

The findings of this study revealed that it was a relevant subject for aviation and the research could be extended to other European airports or airports from other countries which didn't have a higher authority. Also, this study can be broadened to other organizations related to the airport management, such as airlines or it can be done from the perspective of employees which had to deal directly to passengers. As qualitative research, this study was time consuming, the results cannot be generalized and there was a certain difficulty in obtaining data (Queirós et al., 2017); it would therefore be relevant to test these findings in a larger sample with the aid of quantitative methodologies.

REFERENCES

Airports Council International. (2009). *Airport preparedness guidelines for outbreaks of communicable disease.* Retrieved from: https://aci.aero/wpontent/uploads/2020/01/Airport_preparedness_guidelines_for_outbreaks_of_c ommunicable.pdf

Airport Research Center. (2020). *Airport Challenges in Reacting to Covid-19.* https://arc.de/consulting/airport-challenges-in-reacting-to-covid-19/

Al-Dahash, H. & Thayaparan, M., & Kulatunga, U. (2016). *Understanding the Terminologies: Disaster, Crisis and Emergency.* Academic Press.

Alper, A., & Bloom, D. (2020). *Trump curbs travel from Europe as coronavirus disrupts schools, sports.* Retrieved January 05, 2020. https://www.reuters.com/article/us-health-coronavirus-usa/trump-curbs-travel-from-europe-as-coronavirus-disrupts-schools-sports-idINKBN20Y1Z0

Blalock, G., Kadiyali, V., & Simon, D. (2007). The Impact of Post-9/11 Airport Security Measures on the Demand for Air Travel. *The Journal of Law & Economics*, *50*(4), 731–755. doi:10.1086/519816

Bongiovanni, I., & Newton, C. (2019). Toward an epidemiology of safety and security risks: An organizational vulnerability assessment in international airports. *Risk Analysis*, *39*(6), 1281–1297. doi:10.1111/risa.13238 PMID:30452779

Butterfield, L., Borgen, W., Amundson, N., & Maglio, A. (2005). Fifty years of the critical incident technique: 1954-2004 and beyond. *Qualitative Research*, *5*(4), 475–497. doi:10.1177/1468794105056924

Clegg, C. (2010). The Aviation Industry and the Transmission of Communicable Disease: The Case of H1N1 Swine Influenza. *J. Air L. & Com.*, *75*(437). https://scholar.smu.edu/jalc/vol75/iss2/5

Decreto do Presidente da República n.º 14-A/2020. Diário da República: Série I n.º 55 (2020) https://dre.pt/pesquisa/-/search/130399862/details/maximized

Decret nr. 195 din 16 martie 2020. Monitorul Oficial nr. 212 (2020) https://legislatie.just.ro/Public/DetaliiDocumentAfis/223831

de Groot, R. J., Baker, S. C., Baric, R. S., Brown, C. S., Drosten, C., Enjuanes, L., Fouchier, R. A., Galiano, M., Gorbalenya, A. E., Memish, Z. A., Perlman, S., Poon, L. L., Snijder, E. J., Stephens, G. M., Woo, P. C., Zaki, A. M., Zambon, M., & Ziebuhr, J. (2013). Middle East respiratory syndrome coronavirus (MERS-CoV): Announcement of the Coronavirus Study Group. *Journal of Virology*, *87*(14), 7790–7792. doi:10.1128/JVI.01244-13 PMID:23678167

Dirani, K., Abadi, M., Alizadeh, A., Barhate, B., Garza, R. C., Gunasekara, N., Ghassan, I., & Majzun, Z. (2020). Leadership competencies and the essential role of human resource development in times of crisis: A response to Covid-19 pandemic. *Human Resource Development International*, *23*(4), 380–294. doi:10.1080/13678868.2020.1780078

Dixon, J., Belnap, C., Albrecht, C., & Lee, K. (2010). The importance of soft skills. *Corporate Finance Review*, *14*(6), 35.

Doherty, B. (2020). *Thousands of Australians stranded overseas as countries close borders over Covid-19 fears.* https://www.theguardian.com/world/2020/mar/20/thousands-of-australians-

Enoma, A., Allen, S., & Enoma, A. (2009). Airport redesign for safety and security: Case studies of three Scottish airports. *International Journal of Strategic Property Management*, *13*(2), 103–116.

European Commission. (2019). *Orientations towards the first Strategic Plan implementing the research and innovation framework programme Horizon Europe.* https://ec.europa.eu/research/pdf/horizon-europe/ec_rtd_orientations-towards-the-strategic-planning.pdf

European Council. (2020a). *Council Conclusions on COVID-19.* https://data.consilium.europa.eu/doc/document/ST-6038-2020-INIT/en/pdf

European Council. (2020b). *COVID-19 outbreak: the presidency steps up EU response by triggering full activation mode of IPCR*. https://www.consilium.europa.eu/en/press/press-releases/2020/03/02/covid-19-outbreak-the-presidency-steps-up-eu-response-by-triggering-full- activation-mode-of-ipcr

European Council. (2020c). *COVID-19: EU adopts slot waiver to help airlines*. https://www.consilium.europa.eu/en/press/press-releases/2020/03/30/covid-19-eu-adopts-slot-waiver-to-help-airlines

Fearn-Banks, K. (2011). *Crisis communications. A casebook approaches*. Routledge.

Gostin, L. O., Bayer, R., & Fairchild, A. L. (2003). Ethical and Legal Challenges Posed by Severe Acute Respiratory Syndrome: Implications for the Control of Severe Infectious Disease Threats. *Journal of the American Medical Association, 290*(24), 3229–3237.

Heath, L., & Palenchar, M. (2009). Strategic issues management. *Sage (Atlanta, Ga.)*.

IATA. (2020a). *Slower but Steady Growth in 2019*. https://www.iata.org/en/pressroom/pr/2020-02-06-01/

IATA. (2020b) *Economic Performance of the Airline Industry*. https://www.iata.org/en/iata-repository/publications/economic-reports/airline-industry-economic-performance---november-2020---report/

ICAO. (2014) *ICAO Crisis Management Framework*. https://www.icao.int/eurnat/eur%20and%20nat%20documents/forms/allitems.aspx?RootFolder=%2FEURNAT%2FEUR%20and%20NAT%20Documents%2FEUR%20Documents%2FEUR%20Documents%2F031%20ICAO%20Crisis%20Management%20Framework%20Document%202014&FolderCTID=0x012000DAF95319EADD9946B510C5D7B595637D00AA5EB47B299B9A4BAD1968B24E18655C&View=%7BE414A939-5FB4-4CB9-9139-466754ED0FA9%7D

ICAO. (2019) *Education and performance in aviation: Realising and sustaining benefits*. https://www.icao.int/Meetings/a40/Documents/WP/wp_408_en.pdf

INE PORDATA. (2018). *PORDATA - Base de Dados de Portugal Contemporâneo. Obtido em 6 de dezembro de 2020, de Tráfego de passageiros nos principais aeroportos: Lisboa, Porto e Faro*. https://www.pordata.pt/Portugal/Tr%C3%A1fego+de+passageiros+nos+principais+aeroportos+Lisboa++Porto+e+Faro-3248

Likhacheva, A. (2006). SARS Revisited. *AMA Journal of Ethics, 8*(4), 219–222. doi:10.1001/virtualmentor.2006.8.4.jdsc1-0604

Lucini, B. (2020). Soft skills for governing new threats: training methods for LEAs in preventing and countering violent extremism and radicalisation. *Sicurezza, Terrorismo e Società, 45*.

Mantzana, V., Georgiou, E., Chasiotis, I., Gkotsis, I., Stelkens-Kobsch, T. H., Kazoukas, V., & Komninos, F. (2020). Airports' Crisis Management Processes and Stakeholders Involved. *Annals of Disaster Risk Sciences, 3*(1).

Martins, H., Rouco, C., Piedade, L., & Borba, F. (2020). Soft Skills for Hard Times: Developing a Framework of Preparedness for Overcoming Crises Events in Higher Education Students. *17th International Conference on Intellectual Capital, Knowledge Management & Organizational Learning*.

Mazareanu, E. (2020). *Annual growth in global air traffic passenger demand from 2006 to 2021.* https://www.statista.com/statistics/193533/growth-of-global-air-traffic-passenger-demand/

Mott, J. H., Hubbard, S. M., Lu, C. T., Sobieralski, J. B., Gao, Y., Nolan, M. S., & Kotla, B. (2019). Competency-based education: A framework for aviation management programs. *The Collegiate Aviation Review International, 37*(1).

Patton, M. Q. (1987). *How to Use Qualitative Methods in Evaluation* (4th ed.). SAGE.

Porta, M. (2008). *A Dictionary of epidemiology. American Journal of Epidemiology.*

Queirós, A., Faria, D., & Almeida, F. (2017). Strengths and limitations of qualitative and quantitative research methods. *European Journal of Education Studies.*

Read, J. M., Diggle, J. P., Chirombo, J., Solomon, T., & Baylis, M. (2014). Effectiveness of screening for Ebola at airports. *Lancet, 9962*(385), 23–24.

Rico, C. (2020). *Confirmado primeiro caso de coronavírus em Portugal. Segundo caso aguarda contra-análise.* https://www.tsf.pt/portugal/sociedade/confirmados-dois-primeiros-casos-de-contagio-pelo-novo-coronavirus-em-portugal-11876592.html

Saunders, M., Lewis, P., & Thornhill, A. (2007). *Research methods for business students.* Pearson Education.

Sehl, K. (2020). *How the Airline Industry Survived SARS, 9/11, the Global Recession and More.* https://apex.aero/articles/aftershocks-coronavirus-impact/

Sorribes, J., Celma, D., & Martínez-Garcia, E. (2021). Sustainable human resources management in crisis contexts: Interaction of socially responsible labour practices for the wellbeing of employees. *Corporate Social Responsibility and Environmental Management, 28*(2), 936–952.

UNDRR. (n.d.). *Disaster.* Retrieved December 01, 2020, from https://www.undrr.org/terminology/disaster

United Nations. (2015). *Sendai Framework for Disaster Risk Reduction 2015 – 2030.* Available at: https://www.preventionweb.net/files/43291_sendaiframeworkfordrren.pdf

World Health Organization. (2020a). *Archived: WHO Timeline - COVID-19.* Retrieved January 08, 2021 from https://www.who.int/news/item/27-04-2020-who-timeline---covid-19

World Health Organization. (2020b). *Ebola virus disease.* https://www.who.int/health-topics/ebola/#tab=tab_1

Zhang, Z., Jia, M., & Gu, L. (2012). Transformational leadership in crisis situations: Evidence from the People's Republic of China. International Journal of Human Resource Management, 23(19), 4085–4109.

ADDITIONAL READING

Bajaj, G., Khandelwal, S., & Budhwar, P. (2021). COVID-19 pandemic and the impact of cross-cultural differences on crisis management: A conceptual model of transcultural crisis management. *International Journal of Cross Cultural Management, 21*(3), 569–601. doi:10.1177/14705958211060189

Klebe, L., Felfe, J., & Klug, K. (2021). Healthy Leadership in Turbulent Times: The Effectiveness of Health-Oriented Leadership in Crisis. *British Journal of Management, 32*(4), 1203–1218. doi:10.1111/1467-8551.12498

Platje, J., Harvey, J., & Rayman-Bacchus, L. (2020). COVID-19 – reflections on the surprise of both an expected and unexpected event. *Central European Review of Economics and Management, 4*(1), 149–162. doi:10.29015/cerem.874

Wu, Y., Shao, B., Newman, A., & Schwartz, G. (2021). Crisis leadership: A review and future research agenda. *The Leadership Quarterly, 32*(6), 101518. doi:10.1016/j.leaqua.2021.101518

KEY TERMS AND DEFINITIONS

Competency-Based Education Framework: A framework for aviation management programs important for the development of aviation leaders, aiming to bridge the gap on soft skill training in aviation management; generally focused on members of the aviation industry, like flight attendants or pilots.

Crisis: An event that causes disruption of the system as a whole and threatens its basic assumptions and existence.

Critical Incidents Technique: A qualitative method where respondents identify incidents that occurred in a crisis, emergency or disaster situation and reflect upon them; it is commonly used in the cases of studying the skills and the factors in the case of a critical situation.

Disaster: An event of serious matter, that causes a big disruption, at a local, regional, or national level and causes a big negative impact on the society.

Emergency: An event that despite representing serious risk for individuals and need for immediate response, does not have a serious impact nor provoke a grave disruption at the community level.

Epidemic: The occurrence of a heath issue in a community or region that is clearly more than would be expectable.

Human Capital: The personal attributes that contribute towards the organizational goals, strategies, and values. Includes knowledge, skills, attitudes as well as personality and education, among others.

Pandemic: worldwide epidemic.

Soft Skills: Generic term referring to skills that relate with the human aspects at work, including dealing with oneself and others. Examples of soft skills include the ability to communicate, deal with an urgent situation and the ability to work under pressure.

Chapter 12
Analysis of the Possible Relationship Model Between Knowledge Management and Job Satisfaction:
Aligning and Developing a Model as a Guideline for Service Staff Management in the Aviation Industry

Sarun Widtayakornbundit
https://orcid.org/0000-0001-9521-8958
Kasetsart University, Thailand

Tanapoom Ativetin
Srinakharinwirot University, Thailand

ABSTRACT

This study examines the relationship between knowledge management in the aviation industry and job satisfaction among service staff through a literature review. This authors surveyed the relationship model while reversing to job satisfaction, which allowed them to develop a guideline for organizational knowledge management and the process of achieving satisfaction from practice guidelines, as well as other factors that contributed to developing the model apart from the two aforementioned variables, especially the changes from the situation that promote the continuous development of the knowledge management model because good management practices would lead to good organizational behavior and performance. Therefore, the context in which the study is conducted is the aviation industry because it has been severely affected by the crisis. The relationship management model must integrate management approaches into employee requirements by means of lessons learned from sample case studies.

DOI: 10.4018/978-1-6684-4615-7.ch012

INTRODUCTION

The aviation industry is one of the passenger transportation industries that is growing and expanding continuously. According to the International Civil Aviation Organization (ICAO) report, revenue passenger-kilometers (RPK) over a 20 year-period is estimated to grow at a rate of 4.5-4.6% per year. This is in line with the forecast of RPK growth over the next 20 years of Airbus Industries which has anticipated that the growth would reach 4.8% per year, especially the growth in the Asia-Pacific region which would reach up to 5.5% per year, with an estimated global aviation industry growth of 4.7% per year, and the growth of 5.7% per year in Asia (excluding China). In this regard, one of the key factors driving the growth of the aviation industry is the growth of tourism industry even though in 2019 or before the COVID-19 pandemic, the said industry grew at a moderate rate of 3-4% (CAAT, 2021). This is due to the effect of some circumstances, such as the trade war between the United States and China, global economic slowdown, and Brexit, while there have been some positive factors, such as an increase in the proportion of the middle class in emerging economies in China, India and Russia.

However, the overall situation has changed drastically after the spread of the COVID-19 that began in December 2019, continued into the first quarter of 2020, and has ongoing impact. As a result, the global tourism industry has been disrupted for a long time. This is well reflected by the number of international tourists which recorded a negative growth of 22.7%, compared to the same period in 2019, and remained stagnant until April 2020 with a decline of tourists by up to 97%, compared to the same period in 2019. This is the lowest record over the past 10 years after the 2009 global financial crisis. According to the Association of Asia Pacific Airlines (AAPA), there was a sharp decline in the number of international passengers in the first six months of 2021 globally. This is mainly due to the strict travel control measures in each country. As a result, the number of international passengers in January-June 2021 saw a sharp drop by 88.7%, compared to the same period last year (Ministry of Tourism & Sports in Thailand, 2021).

There are various measures applied to air traffic controllers, ranging from the dismissal, salary reduction, termination of apprenticeship, to voluntary resignation projects. Certainly, these measures would have a severe impact in the long run, so the aviation service must be linked with work and the environment that creates knowledge (Smith, Collins, & Clark, 2005). Crisis management knowledge is the situational management of the external environment. Internal knowledge is knowledge management in an organization that understands the requirements of employees. Therefore, the capability of the organization is to create knowledge from exchanging information (Goll, Johnson, & Rasheed, 2007). Creating a good guideline would create a good work experience for employees. As a result, service employees would be more open to organizational policies and have more trust. This focuses on human resource management strategies in the service industry with the customer-centric goals, and learning enables the organization to adjust and formulate strategies to achieve the goals (Appelbaum & Fewster, 2002, 2003). Therefore, developing employees with the airline's approach is learning as a team and improving service, making customers aware of what they receive from the organization. The overall picture is a guideline for the development of service innovations from the gathering of new ideas and employees' problem solving (Lee & Hyun, 2016). Service employees should be prepared to be qualified and adequately trained in aircraft safety. This must rely on continuous training and self-development only. Investing in human resources is therefore significant. However, the decreased subsidy budget during the COVID-19 epidemic would have a wide impact on the aviation industry worldwide, especially during the time when various businesses begin to recover and resume normal flight operations. Even before the epidemic crisis, job satisfaction is involved in issues regarding the allocation of personnel sufficient to meet the requirements

Analysis of the Possible Relationship Model

and workload because it is one of the hygiene factors that provoke dissatisfaction with organizational policies, working conditions, and job instability (Jalal Sarker, Crossman, & Chinmeteepituck, 2003; Karia & Hasmi Abu Hassan Asaari, 2006), resulting in the impact on the operation of the aviation as a whole (Beuren, dos Santos, & Theiss, 2021). Creating a guideline coupled with employee experience will form the understanding that the organization does not ignore employees, and helps enhance employees' potential at the same time. The purpose of this chapter is to present

1. Knowledge management is rehabilitating employees and providing employees with knowledge to solve problems when facing any situation, as well as preventing problems that may arise in the future by presenting the concept of knowledge management coupled with job satisfaction, focusing on the dynamics of knowledge management guidelines.
2. In general research, knowledge management tends to lead to job satisfaction, but knowledge management is possibly based on feedback from employees' work experiences in the organization because the creation of each type of guidelines often results from interacting with employees and recognizing their actual requirements.

Therefore, the content of this section presents rationale and thought-provoking issues for the service industry in order to develop the necessary guidelines for creating employees' job satisfaction and knowledge management for organizations to apply in the future.

BACKGROUND

Job Satisfaction and the Relationship that Creates Value in the Organization

Definition and Meaning

Job satisfaction refers to how the individual reacts to their job (Locke, 1976 cited by Gruneberg (1979), and Aldas-Manzano, Ruiz-Mafe, Sanz-Blas, and Lassala-Navarré (2011) referred to Locke (1976, p 1300) that it is "a pleasure or positive emotional state resulting from the appraisal of one's job." In addition, it was contextually defined by Oliver (1989) as a psychological procedure that has an emotional effect on unconfirmed expectations that come from people's emotions about the experience of interaction, with the aim to assess expectations that cannot confirm outcomes. Then, when the person gains the benefit from the outcome, that benefit will be compared with the expected benefit in order to determine the relationship of the interaction experience and lead to satisfaction.

Job satisfaction is assessed by a task, job, or project (Boer, Deinert, Horman, & Voelpel, 2016). Oliver and Swan (1989), cited by Rojas-Méndez, Vasquez-Parraga, Kara, and Cerda-Urrutia (2009) explained that job satisfaction, by definition, is related to the response assessment, attitude, and emotion. Satisfaction is beyond the scope of a product or service. It can be applied to organizations, such as physical facilitation, and employee interaction. Satisfaction is also the foundation of trust. This is consistent with the definitions given by Muterera, Hemsworth, Baregheh, and Garcia-Rivera (2016) in their research where change leaders influence satisfaction factors as work-related feelings. Emotional traits are based on job descriptions and work environments in which workers seek reward for fulfillment and satisfaction, or sometimes it can cause frustration, upset, and dissatisfaction. Therefore, job satisfaction is an expression of good emotional state as assessed by the work experience of the person or the assignment. Most of the organization's success is derived from employee satisfaction, and job satisfaction increases the productivity of individuals and organizational performance through employee responses.

Being applied in a study related to education, Dutta and Sahney (2016) explained that most teachers' satisfaction is primarily based on realizing the importance of their work, followed by behaviors which are based on the experience gained from their work. Factors that promote the quality of work provided by educational leaders are both tangible (salary, monetary compensation, etc.), and intangible (working conditions, authorization, etc.). Teachers' job satisfaction lies in having control over the classroom and support from the director in order to direct the school to achieve productivity that leads to student success. Teachers' satisfaction refers to the satisfaction behavior of personnel who utilize their experiences to carry on their work in accordance with the objectives of the organization (Nazim Cogaltay, Mikail Yalcin, & Engin Karadag, 2016).

Related Theories and Concepts for Creating Job Satisfaction

Job satisfaction consists of 3 components. Based on Noe, Hollenbeck, Gerhart, and Wright (2014), job satisfaction differs according to the perception of values or values of individual views. The organization will be able to create employees' job satisfaction only when implementing the concept of job disposition, job tasks and roles, supervisors and co-workers, and pay and benefit. Therefore, job satisfaction is related to the following components: Satisfaction relevant to personal value which is a form of desire that comes from consideration and not consideration of what is obtained; the difference in each employee which results in different employees' perceptions will affect the perceived value differently, resulting in different levels of satisfaction; and perception-based satisfaction does not always have a perfect objective or measure because it depends on the situation. Each individual compares the job based on the characteristics and the value received from the same job. Each person's perception is different. The relevant theories as cited by Campbell et al. (1970) from Gruneberg (1979: 9-26) include: Content theory - a theory that is the key factor contributing to job satisfaction; and Maslow's needs theory (1943) – a theory that describes the sequence of needs that satisfy employees and promote work achievement.

However, the weakness of this theory was mentioned by Locke (1976) that it was only a natural human need, not what a human need to do to obtain it. Some needs may arise at that moment and be predominant to other needs, and each individual circumstance, such as occupation, may cause individual motivations to be different, possibly not even have the highest needs. Furthermore, Maslow's theory was not initiated to achieve job satisfaction. Next is Herzberg's two-factor theory, a theory that describes two factors of job satisfaction, namely, the motivator that leads to job satisfaction without leading to absolute dissatisfaction, and the hygiene factor that leads to basic satisfaction, and when it is insufficient, it will lead to job dissatisfaction, but when it is sufficient, it will lead to job satisfaction. However, the weakness of the theory is that the motivator does not always lead to more advanced needs like self-actualization or personal development. Sometimes realizing the quality of the motivating factor is considered leading to satisfaction, despite not exploring the needs that must be achieved. In terms of the hygiene factor, it lacks a psychological perspective because it aims to adjust the bad things, but if the original working conditions are not good, it will lead to bad adjustments as well. In addition, the process theories are variables associated with job satisfaction, focusing on the needs, values, and expectations of individuals related to their work, and the consideration is made based on the working environment. Satisfaction considers between what the job offers and individual expectations to find out personal

Analysis of the Possible Relationship Model

needs and values. Related theories include the following: (1) Expectation and equity theory - this is the theory of job satisfaction. Employees will be satisfied with something when they put their effort into the job, such as compensation, or reward, etc. If employees do not receive what they expected or what they worked, it will affect their performance; (2) Reference group theory is a theory continued from the equity theory explaining that a person's understanding of a reference group affects their understanding of satisfaction. Group expectations are complementary to the factors of personal knowledge, individual needs, and values that individuals consider relating to job satisfaction; (3) Need/value fulfillment theory is the difference between individuals in work valuation which will affect their satisfaction. Vroom (1964) classified value fulfillment into 2 types as follows: (3.1) Subtractive model - Satisfaction is a negative relationship with the difference between individual needs and the scope of work as required. Those who have more needs would be less satisfied. Nevertheless, if there is a lot of cooperation, the satisfaction would be increased, without being able to look at very specific needs; (3.2) Multiplicative model is to use individual fulfillment needs to create a standard of job satisfaction. The disadvantage would be the difficulty in identifying how much each person needs that thing, as well as not knowing whether the person needs the provided thing.

Satisfaction is mainly derived from work experience that produces different positive and negative feelings and emotions because each employee will expect what they will get from work. Work always has its benefits, either big or small ones. Satisfaction is a concept that can be applied in many contexts. An element of satisfaction is something provided by the organization, such as compensation, benefits, or job descriptions. Therefore, the basic theories related to the job satisfaction concept are largely related to needs, such as content theory, Herzber's two factors, or process theory. Satisfaction in related theories is to fulfill any missing part or gaps in the employee's expectations from work. It is an interactive reaction. Satisfaction comes from the accumulation of past experiences that may also interact with work experience because the interaction of people with the organization is always possible even without change, while a general environment and the individuality of workers may affect general behavior.

Knowledge Management for Desirable Behavior Through Experience

Definitions and Meaning

Knowledge management is a modern concept that takes the interaction between technology and people to create the perceptions necessary to manage knowledge in the form of self-management and publication of knowledge (Tergan, Gräber, & Neumann, 2006). This became a new perspective of learning and innovation from integrating technology into knowledge transfer as an absorptive capacity (Selivanovskikh, Latukha, Mitskevich, & Pitinov, 2020) through the process of bringing information into the knowledge management system to allow learners to access learning resources as much as possible (Li & Herd, 2017). Knowledge management is a strategy that is integrated across disciplines or adapted to the context in order to provide relevant personnel with the necessary information and to build on the efficiency from lessons learned in the organization (Ammirato, Linzalone, & Felicetti, 2020). In other words, knowledge management is a guideline for managing information to encourage human capital to use the existing resources in the organization to its full potential.

To apply to the business context is necessary to take into account the resource perspective theory that deals with economic management of organizations in accessing resources to achieve competitive advantages (Helfat & Peteraf, 2003). Knowledge management in business operations is a networked learning style where knowledge acquisition is related to knowledge exploitation to create a competitive advantage in development or create something new for the business of the organization (Grandinetti, 2016). Particularly, when economic values change dynamically, knowledge is an important asset, whether it be information used in the network, sharing the results of knowledge, or the relationship between internal and external networks (Gold, Malhotra, & Segars, 2001). Knowledge management needs to distribute knowledge that exists in both people and systems to people's perceptions in a structured way, so people in the network can use their own resources to adapt to the context of the organization to the fullest potential (Irma Becerra-Fernandez, 2001). Knowledge management is like the immunity from the impact of knowledge change within organizational networks. This is consistent with supply chain management, where there is an adaptive form of management of knowledge flow and knowledge sharing between departments, leading to learning within network and accurate judgment of acquired knowledge (Kalogeraki, Apostolou, Polemi, & Papastergiou, 2018). Therefore, knowledge management is necessary for a business system in which the organization's administrators or leaders must take into account the nature of knowledge that the organization will acquire, including guidelines for managing knowledge to be thoroughly perceived by all people in the organization in order to be ready for the changes and outcomes of the organization in the future.

The Movement of Knowledge Management

Knowledge management is an idea to support members of the organization to realize how to use and share knowledge in the organization. That does not refer to only new knowledge, but it is the awareness of using the existing knowledge within the organization to improve and find error so that the knowledge is up to date and appropriate with the current situation (Cho & McLean, 2009). This is in line with the concept of Huang, Chang, and Henderson (2008) who studied strategies of knowledge management through knowledge transfer among a product development team in Taiwan, using the theory of cultural activities related to history. In addition, the study of Hasan and Gould (2001) combined knowledge management with the process of creating knowledge and ideas, aiming to observe knowledge being passed on barriers between teams through the SECI model (Takeuchi & Nonaka, 2004), combining planning strategies, development, and business processes with the reduction of the formality of the administrative system and work at all levels. The results of the strategies in the study group were transmitted by the medium like the Corporate Communications Department. This could enhance the work efficiency, especially the product development group which had excellent communication with the marketing department and the research and development department. However, it is certain that coins have two sides. During the communication process, if the message is converted to give more advantage to any specific department, it may impair knowledge communication and acquisition of knowledge along the way.

THE STUDY OF RELATIONSHIP BETWEEN VARIABLES

Relationship between Knowledge Management and Job Satisfaction

The Value of Knowledge Management to Work Experience

Knowledge would be valuable or usable through the exchange of information, especially the service industry in which knowledge can be acquired through learning and getting feedback. Likewise, the airline business has shared knowledge in order to improve service outcomes to satisfy customers who receive the service. Knowledge will arise from both external and internal parties working in harmony. Service providers will understand the needs of the administration along with perceiving consumer's needs. Thus, working in the service industry requires more than consumer satisfaction, but it is to establish guidelines for ensuring employee engagement and creating employee satisfaction, or kinds of good behavior to achieve the results that positively affect customers and gain better understanding of the job (Bose & Sugumaran, 2003; Strong, 2006). Satisfaction is another outcome of employee behavior that improves performance. The better attitude of employees towards their work, the better their performance will show in the same direction. Therefore, the organization must try to find ways to make work improvement so that employees agree to work. This is a model derived from the social exchange theory, a theory that encourages employees to perform according to the operating target, which requires exchanges and interactions between people. This is to exchange the results of work with resources from individuals, including knowledge, skills, and abilities (Bontis, Richards, & Serenko, 2011). The relationship model is a form of interdependence along with trust between the organization and its employees. Knowledge management is one of the factors for harnessing the potential and guiding good behavior in human capital. Knowledge management may rely on the needs of employees to design practices that are appropriate and consistent with current work contexts and trends.

From Knowledge to Practice Community: An Alternative to Knowledge Creation

Knowledge management is part of the development of business management concepts in various organizations because it takes into account the cooperation in refining knowledge of the members of the organization for the benefit of the company. In addition, knowledge management also provides a competitive advantage and enables sustainable business growth. The form of knowledge management can be divided into several dimensions, such as knowledge acquisition, knowledge conservation, knowledge application, and knowledge protection (Shaabani, Ahmadi, & Yazdani, 2012). The model is to use the knowledge management guideline to affect job satisfaction and then affect the organization's performance in the form of profit, employee behavior, or accomplishment of the firm objective (Figure 1).

Figure 1. Knowledge management and job satisfaction framework

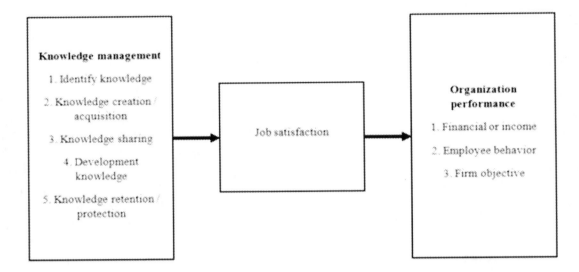

Knowledge management is a modern concept featuring the interaction of technology and people management to realize knowledge that is relevant to the situation or necessary for the profession. Therefore, knowledge management is in the form of self-management and knowledge dissemination to the outside, resulting in a new perspective of learning and innovation from integrating technology with knowledge transfer as an absorptive capacity (Selivanovskikh et al., 2020). Through the process of bringing information into the knowledge management system to enable learners to access learning resources as much as possible, knowledge management is initiated as a cross-disciplinary or adaptive strategy to provide relevant personnel with the necessary information and build on the efficiency gained from learning lessons in the community. To apply to the business context is imperative to take into account the resource perspective theory that deals with economic management of organizations which access resources for competitive advantages, especially when economic values change dynamically. Thus, knowledge is an important asset, whether it be information used in the network, sharing the results of knowledge, or the relationship between internal and external networks. Knowledge management needs to distribute knowledge that exists in both people and systems to people's perceptions in a structured way, so people in the network can use their own resources to adapt to the context of the community to the fullest potential (Caputo, Garcia-Perez, Cillo, & Giacosa, 2019). Knowledge management is necessary for a business system in which the organization's administrators or leaders must take into account the nature of knowledge that the organization will acquire, including guidelines for managing knowledge to be thoroughly perceived by all people in the organization in order to be ready for the changes and outcomes of the organization in the future.

Reverse Relationship Between Job Satisfaction and Knowledge Management

Most studies suggested that the use of knowledge management would affect job satisfaction because it is a form of tool used to manage performance and the outcomes of desirable behaviors. Satisfaction

Analysis of the Possible Relationship Model

is often used as a mechanism for the effectiveness of the individual in generating results. However, in reverse view, if setting the job satisfaction as an initiator to stimulate knowledge management in the organization, can this be done?

The Process of Adjusting the Characteristics of Satisfaction

Individual job satisfaction is often attributed to a variety of job-related feelings (Spector, 1997). Therefore, satisfaction is a journey through the perspective of work experience, learning through the performance of tasks, and the creation of value in the path of perception through the operations (Locke, 1976; Roberts & Foti, 1998). The tools to measure satisfaction are quite diverse and depend on the method used by the organization, so job satisfaction is a measure that indicates the satisfaction of employees in many ways. The study of Al-Abdullat and Dababneh (2018) mentioned about the use of employee engagement, employee empowerment, turnovers-absenteeism, work environment, and salary as indicators to present how knowledge management would be extended or integrated. In this regard, the organizational culture is an independent variable, and job satisfaction is a mediating variable to achieve knowledge management in the organization. Such a relationship is a tool-building model based on the feelings and understanding of the personnel. This reverse concept is an awareness of employee needs. Then, it is applied as a method or tool to improve or enhance the organization's performance.

Figure 2. Job satisfaction as driven of knowledge management (Al-Abdullat & Dababneh, 2018)

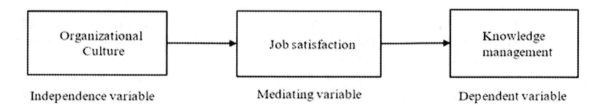

Satisfaction is a need that responds to a specific type of interaction because each need responds in a unique emotional way. La Guardia, Ryan, Couchman, and Deci (2000) provided an explanation of the individual's response to management approaches as follows: Perceiving that the relationship needs are fulfilled with emotional sincerity; responding with relationship stability where different exchanges are part of the need for independence; and the need for performance arises when there is instability in the emotional attachment of each other because it is difficult to build relationship with performance critics. To make it easier to perceive predictable emotional attachment lies in the need for relationship and independence. The understanding of these needs gains from the rational interpretation of each party in response to interpersonal experiences, contributing to the well-being in the organization. Well-being is considered a basic human need (within-person). As a result, the need for satisfaction in the self-determination theory is often the mediating variable between the stability of emotional attachment and well-being. Group relationships have different models in the relationships of individuals in different groups. In reality, one cannot perceive the need for satisfaction from the other party. The experience becomes the deciding factor that leads to the knowledge management guideline that the organization must design properly.

Creating a Process of Reversing Value from Employee Needs

Learning is a social mediator because group processes and indicators of work culture are influenced by interpretive factors. Motivation or tendency often leads to the creation of activities for learning. In Figure 2, organizational culture creation reflects on the needs from the experience of employees to raise an understanding of how to create a process used as a tool. Actually, knowledge management is found not preceding the learning process. Gherardi (2006) explained that knowledge is diverse, so competence techniques need to be developed. Learning is strongly associated with trust in social competency relationships through expertise that is transmitted and willing to learn and develop into creative competencies. Therefore, competencies and social relationships are considered to be mediators in the learning approach. The guideline mediator is also considered a component of other practices, for example, performance is a new knowledge component for creating technological innovation. Learning has the status of an experiment. The scope of competency acquisition is to apply diverse abilities and resources, while norms are used to position new knowledge. The dynamics of this section have been the interaction between the daily and institutional approaches of abstract practice. Therefore, norms are interpreted as a guideline, but revised guidelines may make it impossible to recognize the level of the organization's norms. The approach management can be identified in 4 levels, namely, individual, group, organization, and network. Situational analysis is required to be made as follows:

- **The First Step: is to prepare learners to be practitioners**. It is the transmission and receipt of information on the knowledge acquisition approach. The indicators are initially learned. This section will design a curriculum based on the learners' experiences gained from work.
- **Second Step: Managing the boundaries**. It is the relationships between groups of members in an organization which cooperate with each other. The context of each member group will focus on learning, responsibilities, and the impact from the expertise gained.
- **Third Step: Upgrading the practice guideline**. This is managing the part that makes the learning experience negatively affect learners' satisfaction behavior. Therefore, contextual and situational management depends on finding a sustainable model in the creation of new practices as a unique approach to knowledge management in order to modify and develop better guidelines from the needs of learners.
- **Final Step: Cultural practices** in inter-organizational networks link institutional diversity with organizational actors to be compiled into a knowledge structure of the institutional process. This demonstrates the creation of sustainable knowledge in society through discussion and mediation.

The author demonstrated a model in which learners receive knowledge management to become practitioners for communities in the organization. This reflects on experience sharing after assessing the acquisition of knowledge gained from work to create a new knowledge management approach. The author applied the concept of Gherardi (2006) to organizational learning, which is expressed in the conceptual framework in Figure 3.

Analysis of the Possible Relationship Model

Figure 3. Loop of learning experience

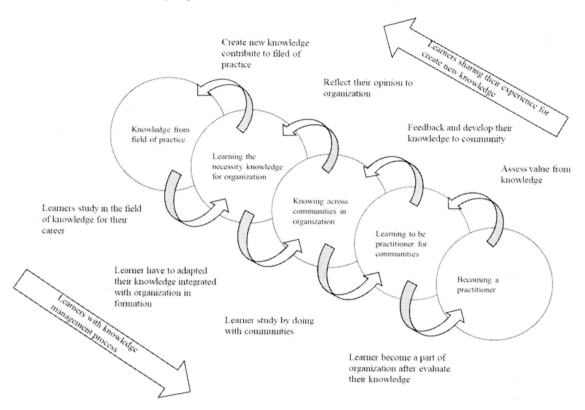

Smith and Sadler – Smith (2006) explained how to motivate learning from learners' behaviors by determining the direction, with relevant factors including attitudes, motivations, and needs, while focusing on individual analysis. According to the study, learners' attitudes were different, so learning directions had to be adjusted according to the situation based on opinions, personal beliefs, and traits. Therefore, management depends on the level of agreement with the learners. The variable that affects attitudes is skill, but attitudes that influence learning can be in the perspective of curiosity. The person who determines the direction of learning is guided by attitudes, followed by the experience gained, and this affects the learning activities, which determines the direction of development. Thus, individuals increase their satisfaction through learning experiences. This leads to the support that inspires lifelong learning and human resource development policies. Then, learners are motivated to design their learning as well. Motivation is an internal process that controls external behaviors to get stabilized and adapted, or maintain the perspective in designing learning and general human resource development procedures. However, sometimes trends of learners may be wrongly predicted. Therefore, motivation predominates over attitudes because it empirically determines behaviors and external perceptions in different situations. Motivation theory is considered a part of organizational psychology.

Personal motivation is therefore the application of skills for learning development. The theory is divided into two groups: Content theory (with work that stimulates learning) is a theory that creates understanding and explains the needs that are inherent to employees, so this theory is related to organizational behavior; Process theory is a motivation theory that attempts to explain the role of personal perception from the beginning, reversing, and ending. The three theories as mentioned above will help understand learners' motivation in the human resource development process. (a) Goal setting is the definition of the learning context, and the degree of the desire for success. (b) Self-Efficacy is to have high self-expectations that lead to success. This is a component of the direction and objectives as set out. Trying hard will lead to new knowledge and skills. There is a relationship between expectation and motivation. (c) Equity is a social comparison on perceptions of fairness affecting work. The more injustice will cause a lot of stress and lead to higher motivation to act. This is related to the beginning, maintenance, and tendency involved in the human resource development process.

The Research Methodology

The study applied the case study methodology to examine the relationship between knowledge management and job satisfaction. The context in the study were determined by surveys on aviation service in COVID-19 pandemic crisis. At the beginning, the study declared the impact of aviation business and explain overall picture during the crisis. This study has realized the applied knowledge management practices in aviation employees and evaluated the effect by consider job satisfaction as amplifier to other behavior or even organization performance. The knowledge management process is selected to present the implementation in work system.

The qualitative of study plays an important role to decode organization system and employee behavior in aviation business context. The result of case study alone might not adequately proof of the relation between knowledge management and job satisfaction but the literatures that applied in the story can partially explained the concept and reach a finite discussion. The method provides the relation of variables based on interaction among aviation communities. This can reflect to human resource management process in term of development, managing the crisis, and flexibility in employee. The aviation business is huge industry, should have the ability to adapt and integrated any practice for solve problem during the crisis. The information of the case study will be transcribed and interpreted to the conclusion. The finding will explain the necessary of variable for aviation business concept.

CASE STUDY

The Aviation Industry and the Epidemic Crisis

The Endless Cycle of Problems and Crises

The aviation business had faced a lot of difficulties with managing aviation problems during 2020-2021, the period of the COVID-19 pandemic crisis, because of the closure of international borders affecting a large number of workers, especially crews who work for the airlines. According to the data from the European Transport Worker's Federation (ETF), the samples were collected from members in various sectors of the aviation industry, including crew members, pilots, ground service personnel, and air traffic controller (ATM). At present, the operation of these people is being affected in several aspects: Reduced working hours; dismissal; or being forced to be furloughed, and many of them completely lost their career. According to the latest survey, it was found that as many as 58.5% of airport-based employees were unemployed, including those who did not get paid temporarily and those who were permanently

Analysis of the Possible Relationship Model

laid off. The number of people laid off in Europe currently exceeds 191,000. However, based on the nature of jobs in the aviation industry which are seasonal, temporary, or irregular jobs, the real number of layoffs could soar to nearly 250,000. From such information, it is evident that in Europe, the short-term solution is layoffs due to the ongoing crisis which caused each airline to deplete their capital reserves. In addition, the government sector was unable to provide supports for all of them.

The overall circumstances also have the impact on the gross economy. Some countries have to decide to delay proposals on air traffic levy on airline operators who are struggling with financial liquidity. As a result, air traffic operators continue to work amid reduced wages or may not be paid at all. In fact, the air traffic service is a job that requires continuous service. No matter how dense the air traffic conditions are, there have been fixed costs that need to be managed and cannot be reduced quickly as the situation changes. When the air traffic service is under all around pressure to implement flexible measures during this situation, it will undoubtedly affect the employees who are the direct operators. Aviation industry personnel need to adjust their operational competencies to conform to the changing service context. Originally, the heart of service was the time that customers, service recipients, or passengers spend with service personnel. The factors that affect the decision of customers are the quality of service provided. Although customers may not be able to recognize the service staff, what to remember may be conversations with the staff, the convenience provided by the service staff, baggage handling method, as well as the punctuality and safety of traveling to the destination. This impressive experience will encourage customers to show their appreciation by returning to the same airline again in the future.

The study of Vinnicombe's (1984) described the process of creating job satisfaction through exchanging within the airline. The special feature of air travel is relatively short flight time which means crews have the opportunity to create positive interactions with passengers or colleagues within a limited amount of time. Another thing is the policy of serving food and beverages to passengers regardless of route or flight duration. As a result, crew members have to work almost all the time of the flight. In addition, the number of crew members, grouping of staff, and the roles of each staff will vary depending on the aircraft model. In the case of large commercial aircraft, there will be approximately 15 staff, or only 5 staff in the case of small aircraft. In this regard, the number of crew members is fixed and does not vary according to the number of passengers, and the roles and duties of employees will be allocated differently according to the level of the employee's position. Problems that occur during the flight will be reported to the supervisor (a different person from the air purser) in the form of an official report. Then, it will be further reported to the management level. At the same time, the air purser is responsible for managing the crew members, in terms of the allocation of allowances, leave days, medical benefits, or in the case of a letter of compliment or complaint from a passenger. Most of the supervisors' work on the ground, but in some cases, they may also work on flights as a special member of staff in accordance with the labor union agreement that shows differences between ground staff and crew members. As the two groups of employees are controlled under different unions, the gap between them has been widened.

Therefore, the internal interaction is quite essential. The nature of the work requires crews to operate far from the operations center. As a result, these crews have rather low interaction with supervisors. Meanwhile, the working system has not been designed. It is very necessary for all parties to cooperate with one another. A form of communication is necessary because all service staff must know all of their duties, and have a lot of expertise in their own work, as well as the ability to convey clear, accurate information and choose the appropriate communication method with the target audience. In addition, this may include the ability to share information openly and honestly with respect to others. The skill of a good listener coupled with choosing the appropriate communication method that contributes to the communicated messages is the key success factor of the communication process. This also includes knowing how to communicate in a calm and cautious manner under certain pressures. In addition, teamwork involves treating others with fairness and respect, as well as being able to share resources and information with other members, plus seeking opportunities to provide assistance to colleagues without request. Thus, a key to operate as a team of crew members is that a task cannot be accomplished until all team members complete the task.

Finding a Balanced Solution of Management in a Relaxing Crisis Situation

In late 2021 and early 2022, the epidemic has subsided despite detecting more new strains of coronavirus. The organizations and employees in the aviation industry have made adjustments during the post-COVID-19 pandemic. According to Deloitte's report titled 'Engaging Frontline Workers in the Airline Sector: Challenges and Imperatives Post-Pandemic', the epidemic has affected not only the financial status of airlines, but also the health and wellness of all employees operating in the industry, especially the frontline workers who were reported having the lowest operational morale since the data has ever been collected, not to mention the mental health problems of the staff as a result of concerns about the situation when working with passengers who do not respect the rules, such as refusing to wear masks. This is reflected in the TSA (Transportation Security Administration) report reminding crew members to pay close attention to self-care information during work under the epidemic crisis due to the continuous increase in the number of passengers on flights.

Service staff should adjust themselves to the situation when customers feel insecure about flying. Therefore, the airline has to make employees understand the situation in order to ensure viability of business. This is in line with the case study of Bamford and Xystouri (2005) which described how to revitalize the international airline business with the business strategy focusing on maintaining relationships with existing customers along with building relationships with new customers. Dale's (2003) concept was used to find success for businesses recovering from impacts, comprising the following components: Consumer perceptions and expectations; supportive technology factors; and competitiveness. Therefore, the interactions that occur during the service process are taken into consideration for management purpose. The focus will be on the service provider's role as a person who delivers and maintains the quality of service. The details of each component are as follows: (a) Consumer perceptions and expectations - In today's society where consumers are wealthier while the additional utility of products becomes decreased, people tend to spend more on services. This growing consumer demand is the result of expectations for service quality; (b) Supportive technology factors - Computers and innovations have become important tools in shaping business practices and service models, and one of factors highly influencing the delivery of quality services. These state-of-the-art technologies help create opportunities to improve service quality, and increase competitiveness in the end; and (c) Competitiveness - Organizations are currently striving for progress. Therefore, much attention has been paid to methods that can help differentiate themselves and their competitive advantages. As the information is disseminated rapidly through the phenomenon of globalization and intense competition, any mistake is unacceptable for the business.

Flexibility and adaptability are essential for airline staff due to the dynamic nature of work in terms of the context and workplace. The working environment and communities to be interacted with are diverse. Working hours are subject to change every month, including colleagues each day. However, the service model may differ depending on the airline, so it is necessary to competently adapt to the passengers. The practitioners for airline communities also needs to adapt to one another in order to improve quality

Analysis of the Possible Relationship Model

of working relationships for performance development along with good staff relationships within the organization.

Filling the Gap between Knowledge Management and Airline Job Satisfaction

The causal relationship between human resource approaches and employee outcomes influences each other. Most knowledge management practices tend to be guided by managers, aiming to anticipate the outcomes of attitudes and behaviors. Employee perceptions on practices escalated from perceptions from colleagues to perceptions on diverse knowledge from situations or contexts. Attitudes and behaviors that affect work experience or job satisfaction may be associated with existence in the organization and being late and absent at work. Therefore, knowledge management systems are based on the employment relationship in which the organization has invested in skills, reviewed, and stimulated the value of work in relation to the investment in organizational knowledge management guidelines. The measure of behavioral performance does not have only a single factor, but also various organizational performance factors.

Figure 4. Moderation variable in relationship of knowledge management and job satisfaction

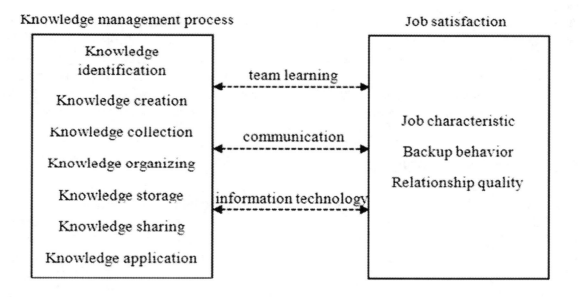

The aforementioned case study can be established as a model of the relationships between knowledge management and job satisfaction. It is concluded to be the reciprocal causal relationship. The process models of Masa'deh, Shannak, Maqableh, and Tarhini (2017) and Latif, Afzal, Saqib, Sahibzada, and Alam (2021) are applied to the case study on knowledge management of the aviation crisis that requires the necessary knowledge to adapt to the situation (knowledge identification). When airline employees are aware of the problem, they cooperatively create appropriate knowledge for the organization to deal with the situation (knowledge creation). Good knowledge must gain from a variety of perspectives. Gaining knowledge from every department will raise awareness of all the problems that need to be solved.

Creating and collecting knowledge in each community of practice will provide a guideline for the entire organization to acknowledge and understand the crisis (knowledge collection). Next step is to rearrange to make it easier to understand (knowledge organizing) and to store in a common area (knowledge storage) by using technology as a component to distribute knowledge to each section, or even the flexibility of working that enables employees to receive news and access information from the back-office management system of the organization (knowledge sharing). When everyone in the organization gains knowledge, it will be used and shared to make improvements (knowledge application), which will create job satisfaction in the future.

Job satisfaction can be attributed to a variety of reasons. Based on the case study, job satisfaction management is also dependent on the job itself due to differences in organizational tasks and different responsibilities. Job supervision and assessment must be designed to be specific to each job (Hackman & Oldham, 1976). The design of the job according to the job characteristics must be consistent with the acquisition of knowledge. Next is the backup behavior that encourages the organization's members to help each other to achieve the purpose of the action or to achieve the organization's goals (Dickinson & McIntyre, 1997). In addition, the concept that responds to working with a set of behaviors, such as relationship quality behaviors, supports or enhances the level of job satisfaction (Lee, 2016; Widtayakornbundit & Phinaitrup, 2021). These components will clarify behaviors relevant to job satisfaction to meet the organization's objectives.

The extraneous variables in the case study enable knowledge management to better create job satisfaction. Team learning is derived from assistance provided for the team to learn from success or failure at work. Nevertheless, if they cooperate with each other, they may improve the accuracy of learning outcomes or reduce learning errors, and accelerate learning. As for the use of technology and communication, it can be integrated together for the efficiency and effectiveness of knowledge that can quickly spread, as well as acquiring new knowledge in a timely manner, and creating unity for the organization.

MANAGERIAL IMPLICATIONS

The result of this study provided the assess their social exchange relationship with aviation business responsibility, employees function, organization work system, and effect to consumer. The acknowledgment in its variables implement on dyad relationship that coverage on one approach to employee behavior in organization. The aviation industries would also address at a more satisfying understanding of knowledge management and job satisfaction if the study on crisis context. The case study shown remarkable development whereas others hospitality service might have other option to improve. A knowledge management is an organization where has an enhanced ability or skill to handle the changing environment from crisis. The uncertainty occurrences force organization find the right practice for survive among competitors. For gaining capabilities and solving situation, the competitive advantage is the lasting key success in critical process. The important factor is top management in organization that must know the suitable behavior to response from employee. Job satisfaction could support their feedback from organization practices. The knowledge management is one of human resource management process that could support the infrastructure and strategy in organization. The applications of knowledge management in the case study provide more than job satisfaction on employee behavior. Although it shown the other impact from job satisfaction such as organization performance, contingency plan in future, or even positive behavior in workplace. The adaptation on aviation employee to online workplace in pandemic crisis were different from ordinary management. The new perspective is utilizing knowledge management concept to sharing the necessary knowledge or information to make it on dynamic changing environment. The holistic knowledge management in this case study shown the combination between effect on job satisfaction and organization results to complete organization practices and achieving their goal to cope the crisis and survive in the aviation market.

RECOMMENDATION AND FUTURE STUDY

This is a study from literature and textbooks to explore the relationship between job satisfaction and knowledge management in the aviation service industry amid crisis. The current guideline for knowledge management needs to change. Although some employees were removed during the crisis, existing organizations need to manage personnel in their own organizations, and even if the compensation is reduced, the operation management requires both proactive and reactive readiness. Knowledge is available in all departments of the organization as new knowledge gained from situations requires adjustments and upgrades. Creating guidelines for knowledge management for employees is necessary. Nevertheless, the stress or mental instability of employees requiring organization management should not be ignored. An organization's understanding of guideline management also needs to include work related requirements.

Therefore, the extraneous variables are important in managing the reverse picture of job satisfaction to knowledge management. There have been a few studies being conducted in this way because most of the studies are related to existing knowledge management guidelines. There has not been any survey on the use of employee requirements after measuring the satisfaction to improve and upgrade knowledge management for reassessment of job satisfaction. This is because knowledge management guidelines generate behaviors expected by organizational leaders, such as job satisfaction, and then leading to the performance as required by leaders in the organization. Whether at the departmental level or the organizational level, knowledge from the local community must be developed. Future studies are necessary to be long-term studies after the current crisis in order to create exemplary practices and standards of organizational operations to be widely recognized in the industry.

For the future study, these issues can explore the objects in differences case study that involve with a type of knowledge management in air transportation services. The study is a portrait of process to develop member in aviation organization and the result of case study presented interest with adequate empirical explanation. This could be said to provide an in-depth understand of other relation which related to knowledge management and job satisfaction. The role of aviation service in the business area has been studied extensively but not enough to survey on human capital in the industry. The longitudinal study must find out the best practice to develop in knowledge management concept for human capital outcome which, in this case, is employee behavior and organizational performance. The understand of the role of knowledge management and job satisfaction could be beneficial to the management formulation in air transport concept.

CONCLUSION

Job satisfaction is a variable widely used in research. General studies only measured levels without further development. Therefore, the content of this section specifically shows that satisfaction is not just a variable to measure the level, but it is an assessment to create a learning guideline for those who set operating guidelines for the organization, especially the fundamental of knowledge management. Thus, the applicable context is the airline industry that has been greatly affected by the epidemic. Learning is not the only guideline for employees, but employers need to understand the problems that arise from the stability of the situation and the mentality of employees. The author wishes to clarify for readers that behavioral research is not just to study cause and effect. This case study is applied to make use of the results for improvements in order to upgrade research and knowledge for development of organizational knowledge management as well. Future approaches may require to further study other variables so that they can be adapted for effective future research studies on the relationship between these two variables. In this regard, management must depend on the cooperation of all departments in the organization in order to enable guidelines and policies for employee and organizational development to achieve results in the same direction.

REFERENCES

Al-Abdullat, B. M., & Dababneh, A. (2018). The mediating effect of job satisfaction on the relationship between organizational culture and knowledge management in Jordanian banking sector. *Benchmarking*, *25*(2), 517–544. doi:10.1108/BIJ-06-2016-0081

Aldas-Manzano, J., Ruiz-Mafe, C., Sanz-Blas, S., & Lassala-Navarré, C. (2011). Internet banking loyalty: Evaluating the role of trust, satisfaction, perceived risk and frequency of use. *Service Industries Journal*, *31*(7), 1165–1190. doi:10.1080/02642060903433997

Ammirato, S., Linzalone, R., & Felicetti, A. M. (2020). Knowledge management in pandemics. A critical literature review. *Knowledge Management Research and Practice*, 1–12. doi:10.1080/14778238.2020.1801364

Appelbaum, S. H., & Fewster, B. M. (2002). Global aviation human resource management: Contemporary recruitment and selection and diversity and equal opportunity practices. *Equal Opportunities International*, *21*(7), 66–80. doi:10.1108/02610150210787226

Appelbaum, S. H., & Fewster, B. M. (2003). Global aviation human resource management: Contemporary employee and labour relations practices. *Management Research News*, *26*(10/11), 56–69. doi:10.1108/01409170310784069

Beuren, I. M., dos Santos, V., & Theiss, V. (2021). Organizational resilience, job satisfaction and business performance. *International Journal of Productivity and Performance Management*. doi:10.1108/IJPPM-03-2021-0158

Boer, D., Deinert, A., Horman, A. C., & Voelpel, S. C. (2016). Revisiting the mediating role of leader-member exchange in transformational leadership: The differential impact model. *European Journal of Work and Organizational Psychology*, *25*(6), 883–899. doi:10.1080/1359432X.2016.1170007

Bontis, N., Richards, D., & Serenko, A. (2011). Improving service delivery: Investigating the role of information sharing, job characteristics, and employee satisfaction. *The Learning Organization*, *18*(3), 239–250. doi:10.1108/09696471111123289

Bose, R., & Sugumaran, V. (2003). Application of knowledge management technology in customer relationship management. *Knowledge and Process Management, 10*(1), 3–17. doi:10.1002/kpm.163

Caputo, F., Garcia-Perez, A., Cillo, V., & Giacosa, E. (2019). A knowledge-based view of people and technology: Directions for a value co-creation-based learning organisation. *Journal of Knowledge Management, 23*(7), 1314–1334. doi:10.1108/JKM-10-2018-0645

Cho, Y., & McLean, G. (2009). Successful IT start-ups' HRD practices: Four cases in South Korea. *Journal of European Industrial Training, 33*(2), 125–141. doi:10.1108/03090590910939030

Cogaltay, N., Yalcin, M., & Karadag, E. (2016). Educational Leadership and Job Satisfaction of Teachers: A Meta-Analysis Study on the Studies Published between 2000 and 2016 in Turkey. *Eurasian Journal of Educational Research, 26*(62), 255–282. doi:10.14689/ejer.2016.62.13

Dickinson, T. L., & McIntyre, R. M. (1997). *A conceptual framework for teamwork measurement. In Team performance assessment and measurement: Theory, methods, and applications.* Lawrence Erlbaum Associates Publishers.

Gherardi, S. (2006). *Organizational Knowledge: The Texture of Workplace Learning.* Wiley-Blackwell.

Gold, A. H., Malhotra, A., & Segars, A. H. (2001). Knowledge Management: An Organizational Capabilities Perspective. *Journal of Management Information Systems, 18*(1), 185–214. doi:10.1080/07421222.2001.11045669

Goll, I., Johnson, N., & Rasheed, A. (2007). Knowledge Capability, Strategic Change, and Firm Performance: The Moderating Role of the Environment. *Management Decision, 45*, 161-179. doi:10.1108/00251740710727223

Grandinetti, R. (2016). Absorptive capacity and knowledge management in small and medium enterprises. *Knowledge Management Research and Practice, 14*(2), 159–168. doi:10.1057/kmrp.2016.2

Gruneberg, M. M. (1979). *Understand job satisfaction.* The Macmillan Press Ltd. doi:10.1007/978-1-349-03952-4

Hackman, J. R., & Oldham, G. R. (1976). Motivation through the design of work: Test of a theory. *Organizational Behavior and Human Performance, 16*(2), 250–279. doi:10.1016/0030-5073(76)90016-7

Helfat, C. E., & Peteraf, M. A. (2003). The dynamic resource-based view: Capability lifecycles. *Strategic Management Journal, 24*(10), 997–1010. doi:10.1002mj.332

Irma Becerra-Fernandez, R. S. (2001). Organizational Knowledge Management: A Contingency Perspective. *Journal of Management Information Systems, 18*(1), 23–55. doi:10.1080/07421222.2001.11045676

Jalal Sarker, S., Crossman, A., & Chinmeteepituck, P. (2003). The relationships of age and length of service with job satisfaction: An examination of hotel employees in Thailand. *Journal of Managerial Psychology, 18*(7), 745–758. doi:10.1108/02683940310502421

Kalogeraki, E.-M., Apostolou, D., Polemi, N., & Papastergiou, S. (2018). Knowledge management methodology for identifying threats in maritime/logistics supply chains. *Knowledge Management Research and Practice, 16*(4), 508–524. doi:10.1080/14778238.2018.1486789

Karia, N., & Hasmi Abu Hassan Asaari, M. (2006). The effects of total quality management practices on employees' work-related attitudes. *The TQM Magazine*, *18*(1), 30–43. doi:10.1108/09544780610637677

La Guardia, J. G., Ryan, R. M., Couchman, C. E., & Deci, E. L. (2000). Within-person variation in security of attachment: A self-determination theory perspective on attachment, need fulfillment, and well-being. *Journal of Personality and Social Psychology*, *79*(3), 367–384. doi:10.1037/0022-3514.79.3.367 PMID:10981840

Lee, K.-H., & Hyun, S. S. (2016). An extended model of employees' service innovation behavior in the airline industry. *International Journal of Contemporary Hospitality Management*, *28*(8), 1622–1648. doi:10.1108/IJCHM-03-2015-0109

Lee, Y. (2016). Relationship Quality and Its Causal Link to Service Value, Satisfaction, and Word-of-Mouth. *Services Marketing Quarterly*, *37*(3), 171–184. doi:10.1080/15332969.2016.1184541

Li, J., & Herd, A. M. (2017). Shifting Practices in Digital Workplace Learning: An Integrated Approach to Learning, Knowledge Management, and Knowledge Sharing. *Human Resource Development International*, *20*(3), 185–193. doi:10.1080/13678868.2017.1308460

Locke, E. (1976). The Nature and Causes of Job Satisfaction. The handbook of industrial and organizational psychology, 31.

Ministry of Tourism & Sports in Thailand. (2021). *Tourism Economic Review*. https://www.mots.go.th/more_news_new.php?cid=581

Roberts, H. E., & Foti, R. J. (1998). Evaluating the Interaction Between Self-Leadership and Work Structure in Predicting Job Satisfaction. *Journal of Business and Psychology*, *12*(3), 257–267. doi:10.1023/A:1025067128193

Selivanovskikh, L., Latukha, M., Mitskevich, E., & Pitinov, S. (2020). Knowledge Management Practices as a Source of a Firm's Potential and Realized Absorptive Capacity. *Journal of East-West Business*, *26*(3), 293–325. doi:10.1080/10669868.2020.1716129

Shaabani, E., Ahmadi, H., & Yazdani, H. (2012). Do interactions among elements of knowledge management lead to acquiring core competencies? *Business Strategy Series*, *13*(6), 307–322. doi:10.1108/17515631211286164

Smith, K. G., Collins, C. J., & Clark, K. D. (2005). Existing Knowledge, Knowledge Creation Capability, and the Rate of New Product Introduction in High-Technology Firms. *Academy of Management Journal*, *48*(2), 346–357. doi:10.5465/amj.2005.16928421

Smith, P. J., & Sadler-Smith, E. (2006). *Learning in Organizations: Complexities and Diversities*. New York: Routledge.

Strong, C. (2006). The influence of employee behavioural performance on customer focus strategies. *Service Industries Journal*, *26*(2), 147–163. doi:10.1080/02642060500369180

The Civil Aviation Authority of Thailand (CAAT). (2021). *Aviation Industry Review 2021*. https://www.caat.or.th

Widtayakornbundit, S., & Phinaitrup, B.-A. (2021). A study of leadership in educational institution using dual systems and the effects on personal behavior: A case study of Thailand private vocational system. *Kasetsart Journal of Social Sciences*, *42*(3), 527–534. doi:10.34044/j.kjss.2021.42.3.12

ADDITIONAL READING

Garvin, D. A. (2003). *Learning in Action: A Guide to Putting the Learning Organization to Work*. Harvard Business Review Press.

Nonaka, I., & Takeuchi, H. (1995). *The knowledge-creating company: How japanese companies create the dynamics of innovation*. Oxford University Press.

Scharmer, C. O., Kaufer, K., & Shepherd, W. (2013). *Leading from the emerging future: From ego-system to eco-system economies*. Barrett-Koehlers, Inc.

Senge, P., Scharmer, C. O., Jaworski, J., & Flowers, B. S. (2004). *Presence*. Crown Business.

Senge, P. M. (2014). *Dance of Change: The challenges to sustaining momentum in a learning organization*. Random House US.

Ungemah, J. (2015). *Misplaced talent: A guide to making better people decisions*. Wiley. doi:10.1002/9781119157496

KEY TERMS AND DEFINITIONS

Community of Practice: Defined as group created within a project, this must be individuality of the project group. The other teams do not contractually connect together.

Employee Behavior: defined as employee output as their create to positive or negative behavior or ability to applied to the new idea which effect to people in organization or organization performance. The behavior of employee may have various dimension that can relate to other behaviors.

Job Satisfaction: This behavior inferred to positive emotional state which reflect from experience involve their job.

Knowledge Management: The procedure is separate between knowledge and management which is the method to utilize all knowledge to develop organization and encourage members. the practices response to provide all state of managing knowledges.

Needs Satisfaction: Defined as possible emotional preferences for employees with a clear comprehending in each individual's needs that can motivate employees' action in organization.

Organizational Performance: It is overall productivity or pleasurable output. The organization performance is depended on how achieve organization's goals or their objectives

Value Creation: The value was created by transform knowledge between organization and employee. The goal of value creation in this context is decoding the value from generate the necessity knowledge in community of practice to resolving problem and combine new knowledge to their work for new value in organization.

Chapter 13
Model of Air Cargo Supply Chain Resilience:
Way to Build by Knowing What Can Tear Your Supply Chain Apart

Chonnikarn Luangpituksa
https://orcid.org/0000-0001-5054-2869
School of Integrated Science, Kasetsart University, Thailand

ABSTRACT

The air transport sector provides global connectivity via trade flows and tourism. The outbreak of the COVID-19 pandemic caused this sector to alternate between long periods of continued growth and long periods of negative growth. The air cargo airlines have permanently endeavored to maintain operations sufficiently robust to be resilient to the impacts of different internal and external disruptive events to maintain the guaranteed quality of services to their users and consignees. One approach to deal with disruptions in the development of air cargo supply chain systems is resilience. The resilient air cargo supply chain requires two critical capacities: the capacity for reliability and the capacity for restoration under disruptive condition.

INTRODUCTION

The most recent global risk, the occurrence of COVID-19 pandemic, has severely disrupted business operations across all industries. The air transport sector provides global connectivity. External factors such as infectious disease spread, exchange rates, and oil prices have a significant impact on it. The airline industry is notorious for its volatility. Its fluctuations have tracked those of the global economy over time, albeit with greater ferocity. Long periods of sustained growth have been followed by brief periods of negative growth in the sector, which is heavily reliant on business activity, trade flows, and tourism.

Air cargo transportation has a significant impact on global economic development by connecting a diverse range of cities and facilitating global trade movement. This occurrence had a direct impact on

DOI: 10.4018/978-1-6684-4615-7.ch013

the air cargo industry. Carriers investigated cargo overbooking prior to the COVID-19 disruption, then decided whether to accept or reject cargo orders (Lin et al., 2017). Several studies, such as contracts between airlines and single freight forwarders, have also been used to aid in cargo capacity management and allocation (Amaruchkul et al., 2011). When an airline receives cargo from multiple freight forwarders and total cargo demand exceeds route capacity, capacity allocation models are used to maximize the airline's profit by allocating capacity to multiple freight forwarders (Amaruchkul and Lorchirachoonkul, 2011).

Following the emergence of the COVID-19 pandemic, the global border lockdown has resulted in aircraft limitations and cancellations, resulting in a 42 percent decrease in cargo capacity compared to capacity in 2019. Because of the unpredictability of cargo demand and capacity, a complex demand unbalancing between existing capacity and demand has occurred, according to Maneenop and Kotcharin (2020). Normally, airlines issue bookings and sell cargo capacity twelve months before a flight's departure. Several freight forwarders book or purchase cargo space through long-term contracts or spot market transactions (Gupta, 2008). The airline determines network capacity and assigns aircraft to each route based on projected demand during the planning stage. Carriers typically face paradoxical demand-capacity mismatches on various routes following the planning stage. In some routes, freight forwarders order cargo that exceeds capacity (hot-selling), while in others, the cargo ordered is insufficient to fill even half of the capacity (underutilized).

Air cargo is an important mode of transportation for the globalized world's valuable consumer items and manufacturing components. It enables global economies and international trade through its function in the supply chain. Air cargo will undoubtedly continue to play an important role in the global economy as a business enabler, with time-definite international transactions in an increasingly globalized and complex supply chain, as well as increased production flexibility and speed that characterizes much of the new economy. However, demand for air freight is influenced by external factors and does not exist in isolation. It can be volatile at times, influenced by local and global economic cycles as well as external shocks. As a result, if air cargo carriers are to survive in the long run, they must develop a plan. Ordinary people frequently believe that only a few air cargo specialists develop and implement an air freight strategy.

One aspect of strategic management is connecting a company to its environment in order to achieve long-term goals. Strategic management also includes the development and implementation of a company's top management's primary goals and initiatives on behalf of its owners, based on resource considerations and an assessment of the company's internal and external environments (Nag, Hambrick, & Chen, 2007). Managers are constantly looking for new ways to connect the company's strengths and weaknesses with the environment's opportunities and risks. The key challenge for managers involved in business strategy is how organizations generate a lasting competitive edge in the industry in which they operate.

They are related to the efficient and successful adaptation to ever-changing and uncertain situations in the field of corporate strategy (Junni, Sarala, Tarba, & Weber, 2015). Firms that rely on their supply chain to compete in a volatile market must be more agile in identifying and creating opportunities, more responsive to disruptions, and more resilient to external threats (Battistella et al., 2017). In recent years, there has been a greater emphasis placed on supply chain interruption risk management (Parast and Shekarian, 2019). This increased emphasis is the result of a widespread recognition that all supply chains are vulnerable to a variety of disruptions that can have both immediate and long-term consequences for the supply chain (Habermann et al., 2015). The importance of supply chain risk management is demonstrated by supplier capacity constraints caused by supply process breakdowns and supply disruptions (Stank et al., 2011).

The development of flexibility, agility, and responsiveness is widely acknowledged as a critical component in reducing the risk of disruption (Parast and Shekarian, 2019). According to Nishat, F. M., et al. (2006), information sharing, supply chain agility, trust, and collaborative partnerships are enablers for supply chain disruption mitigation. According to Singh (2015), in order to have a responsive supply chain, senior management must be proactive in considering and implementing various measures to optimize resource usage and plan implementation. According to Gunessee et al. (2018), when confronted with catastrophic vulnerability, firms with limited agility and adaptability expose themselves to the terrible effects of such shifts and events. Flexibility, collaboration, agility, and redundancy are all significant factors in improving supply chain resilience, according to Parast and Shekarian (2019).

The effects of COVID-19 disruptive incidents have also had an influence on air freight movements. They have had an impact on the impacted airports, forcing airspace to be restricted and forcing airlines to cancel flights. During airspace closures, airlines routinely reroute their flights, resulting in lengthy delays and even cancellations. This has been the case despite the fact that the air freight industry has played an important role in global trade and economic development. In such circumstances, air cargo airlines have consistently worked to ensure that their operations are sufficiently robust to withstand the effects of various internal and external disruptive events, in order to maintain the guaranteed quality of services to their users-freight shippers and consignees. The interruptions highlight the fact that supply chain disruptions not only have an impact on operations, but they also frequently result in financial harm that extends far beyond the immediate operational impacts. The development of robust supply chain systems is one strategy for dealing with interruptions. However, the concept of resilience, which is at the heart of much of our current thinking about supply chain risk and management, is frequently ill-defined and fraught with ambiguity. Two critical capabilities are required for a resilient supply chain: the ability to resist and recover. The first term, resistance, refers to the supply chain's ability to delay and mitigate the effects of a disruption. The second term, recovery, refers to the ability of the supply chain to recover after a disruption.

BACKGROUND

Covid-19 has a significant impact on the air transportation business, which offers worldwide linkages between trade, tourism, and investment. Using event research technique, the overview of passenger, Maneenop and Kotcharin (2020) investigates the short-term impact of the COVID-19 epidemic on 52 listed airline firms throughout the world. According to the findings, airline stock returns fall more dramatically than market returns following the announcements of reported cases outside of China, the outbreak in Italy, and the WHO declaration. During these events, investors react in a variety of ways. In the aftermath of the event, the World Health Organization's and President Trump's official statements sparked the most outrage. In the aftermath of the event, the World Health Organization's and President Trump's official statements sparked the most outrage. Kim and Sohn (2022) looked at how passengers, airlines, and government policy responded to the COVID-19 pandemic in South Korea, and they offered policy recommendations for both the pandemic and the post pandemic eras. Passengers react to both internal and external stimuli, and the reduction in worldwide COVID cases and vaccine distribution will enhance their appetite for travel. South Korean airlines have adopted a variety of strategies to combat declining passenger numbers, including domestic route changes, freight transportation growth, and mergers and acquisitions; Korean Air's entrance into cargo transport in 2020 resulted in a profit.

Because of the technological, geographical, institutional, and, most importantly, economic complexity that those involved face, air transportation is critical in Africa's floriculture supply chains, according to Kenneth Button (2020). The critical link between short-distance, surface transportation at the African end of the chain and the intercontinental air-transportation haul to markets in Europe and, increasingly, Asia is highlighted. A substantial portion of the account is qualitative in nature. There is not only a lack of data to conduct any meaningful econometric study, but qualitative factors also tend to dominate many supply chain decisions, reducing the impact of flexibility and agility on supply chain disruptions.

The air cargo industry disruptions caused by Covid-19, for instance, Shaban et al. (2021) hypothesized that a demand imbalance in cargo routes occurs when demand exceeds capacity, and the route is underused when demand is insufficient to meet capacity. To deal with this issue, the Puppet Cournot model was created. The Puppet Cournot model is a duopoly game that pits hot-selling routes against underused routes, but the airline controls the whole game. The model generates the optimal solutions for each route, allowing airline and freight forwarder discussions to be based on these quantity restrictions. Li, T. (2020) investigated China's air freight industry in light of the country's unique condition in the wake of the epidemic. This article examines four characteristics that are positive and unfavorable for its future development, based on the belief that it would emerge from recession more quickly than China's air passenger sector: (1) strengths (economic development and the increase of freight-only airline, (2) weaknesses (insufficient cargo capacity and less business internationalization), (3) opportunities (top authority support, expanding e-commerce demand, and new technical momentum), and (4) obstacles (uncertain trade environment and increasing profitability pressure).

In the Covid-19 epidemic, the air cargo approach has achieved a responsiveness that is often characterized by flexibility, agility, and resilience. Shekarian et al. (2020) investigate a supply chain with several locations, different transportation channels, and numerous product plans throughout multiple periods, all while dealing with supply and demand risk. They evaluate the link between three objective functions relating to responsiveness, risk, and the cost of new and seasonal items using a numerical example, and then examine the influence of flexibility and agility on supply chain disruption mitigation. Janić, M. (2019) discusses how to estimate the resilience of an airline cargo transportation network that has been impacted by a large-scale disruptive event. Airports are network nodes, and the flights and air routes that connect them are network connections. The proposed methodology for assessing an affected network's resilience over time, i.e., before, during, and after the impact of a given disruptive event, was applied to a real airline cargo network (FedEx Express, United States) that was impacted by a large-scale disruptive event (extreme snowstorm - the so-called nor'easter), which was characterized by its duration, intensity, and spatial scale. According to the findings, the network's resilience was influenced differently depending on the performance measures. Another survival strategy for airlines is to implement loyalty programs. COVID-19, Pascual and Cain (2021) uses a case study technique to look at how American Airlines managed its loyalty program to withstand a pandemic and reduce the financial consequences of constrained and restricted travel. The fact that the pandemic was still a threat at the time of study constrained the case. The findings of this case study extend beyond the airline business and may provide insight into the advantages of loyalty programs in times of financial difficulty for other hospitality and tourist firms.

Management of airport post-disaster adaptation following a tragedy, Qin et al. (2021) investigate airport operations management. Because of the high volume of aircraft traffic and the need for relief freight transportation in a short period of time, the airport runway and cargo processing hangar accommodating capabilities should be effectively coordinated. Any inefficiency in runway and cargo hangar operations could result in significant losses and potentially disrupt the airport's critical post-disaster relief operating mode. During normal operations, air traffic and ground activities are frequently congested. Because each arriving mission flight is critical for relief cargo loading/unloading duty, aggregate congestions and delays should not be underestimated, especially in post-disaster aid scenarios.

COVID-19 IMPACT ON AIR CARGO INDUSTRY

From cargo chart book (IATA,2021) and world air cargo forecast 2020–2039 (Boeing, 2020), the global economy is in its deepest slump in decades, as the COVID-19 pandemic continues to exert a stranglehold on economic activity. All major economies are affected, though to varying degrees. The nature of the crisis is also very different from previous recessions. As a large external shock, the majority of the economic damage is caused by an externally imposed restriction on economic activity rather than by economic imbalances or necessary corrections. The pandemic has highlighted the value of a quick and flexible trade solution, such as air cargo. Personal protective equipment and medical devices were critical components of the early pandemic response. In the short term, increased goods consumption at the expense of reduced services consumption will aid in the recovery of merchandise trade. Some of the longer-term effects of the economic disruptions, such as a shift to more online work and shopping, are beneficial to air cargo growth. Rapid technological adoption may eventually lead to increased demand in traditional air cargo-intensive sectors such as semiconductors. There are numerous risks to this economic outlook. The unpredictability of the COVID-19 pandemic remains the most important variable. A decisive solution to the health crisis, such as an effective vaccine, on the other hand, could release pent-up demand fueled by excess savings. In any case, the recovery from one of history's deepest recessions will dominate economic and trade patterns for the foreseeable future. Additional risks to global trade, such as trade-related protectionism and populism, will remain a challenge. The ongoing COVID-19 crisis is wreaking havoc on the world's aviation services. Current travel restrictions, combined with a significant drop in demand, have resulted in the grounding of passenger flights, effectively shutting down the global air transport market and severely disrupting cross-border trade carried by passenger widebody aircraft. Today, only 20% of the widebody passenger capacity is still operational.

Supply chain congestion is a hot topic in air cargo and the wider economy right now. During the pandemic, unprecedented levels of joint fiscal and monetary support have been deployed. As a result of the shift in consumer purchasing habits, there was a significant increase in e-commerce sales. On the other hand, COVID-19-related measures, labor shortages, insufficient production of key inputs such as semiconductors, and a lack of capacity have all had an impact on supply chain operations. The average delivery time is longer, implying that the majority of businesses report longer delivery times. Because supply chain disruptions are unlikely to abate significantly in the first half of 2022, the gradual return of capacity on passenger aircraft belly may allow air cargo to benefit even more from long delivery times. Global manufacturing activity and trade have slowed due to congestion, input and labor shortages, but remain broadly supportive.

Manufacturing activity, new export orders, and confidence have all declined as a result of supply chain issues and inflation, but they remain generally supportive of air cargo. Furthermore, as businesses rush to meet demand during the critical year-end period, air cargo continues to outperform other modes of transportation due to its competitive pricing and speed. Cargo volumes on the busiest cargo trade lanes have now stabilized after recovering from the pandemic's initial stage. Due to supply chain congestion, missing inputs, and inflation, business and consumer confidence, as well as new export orders, have declined since Q2 2021. Meanwhile, high demand and a rush to get goods to consumers before the end of the year have resulted in cargo rates that have surpassed the peak reached in May 2020. As is typical during economic upturns, when businesses face a rapid increase in demand and the need to replenish inventories, resulting in a low inventory-to-sales ratio, air cargo continues to outperform container shipping and global goods trade. Furthermore, when delivery speed is considered, air cargo remains cost competitive when compared to container shipping.

Air cargo traffic has decreased by 3% as a result of global economic growth and weakened industrial production. The impact of the loss of long-haul passenger belly capacity from widebody fleets created a significant air cargo capacity shortfall as COVID-19 spread quickly. Passenger belly cargo capacity accounts for approximately 54% of total global air cargo capacity. To compensate for the lower cargo, hold shortfall, freighter operators have operated at higher-than-normal utilization levels.

Furthermore, the pressing need to meet demands for transporting medical supplies to all regions in response to COVID-19 created a one-of-a-kind and unprecedented environment. Because of declining air cargo capacity and high demand for medical supplies, yields skyrocketed to the high double digits in the second quarter of 2020. With these market conditions, freighter operators are in an exceptional position to meet market demands for high levels of speed, reliability, and security that only air cargo can provide. With high cargo yields and significantly reduced long-haul international networks, many airlines have discovered that converting some of their passenger widebody fleets to cargo-only operations can generate much-needed cash flow. By the end of September, nearly 200 airlines had flown 2,500 passenger planes solely for cargo operations. Through September, air cargo traffic was down 12%, mirroring previous recessionary declines. This would result in poor financial performance for air cargo operators in a normal year. However, by 2020, nearly a quarter of air cargo capacity will have been lost. Because of limited air cargo capacity, yields increased by more than 40%, while revenue in the air cargo industry increased by 16%.

The 2020 World Air Cargo Forecast considers the near-term disruption to air cargo markets, but it does not assume that the current dynamics of constrained widebody passenger belly capacity will continue in the long term. Long-haul widebody passenger traffic will return in the coming years, and air cargo market dynamics will resemble those seen prior to the COVID-19 disruption. Prior to the pandemic, e-commerce was already expanding at double-digit rates, and its impact on the air cargo market has grown. Express carriers fared well as a result of the market turmoil in 2020. By the end of September, they had increased their traffic by 14%. The only other growing air cargo business model is all-cargo carriers, which are up 6%. This forecast takes into account the ongoing structural growth and surge in demand caused by COVID-19.

Global industrial output and global manufacturing supply chains have a high impact on air cargo. However, some supply chain reorganization was already underway prior to the COVID-19 pandemic. For the past two decades, China had been the preferred location for many Western manufacturing firms due to its low labor costs relative to other developing countries. As a result, in recent years, some manufacturing has shifted away from China and toward other Asia-Pacific countries. However, depending on the complexity of the product, supply chain movement can take years to implement. For example, air cargo imports from China to the United States are nine times greater than those from the next Asia-Pacific country.

This emphasizes China's current dominance as a source and supplier of manufacturing. To reduce risk, early indications point to a trend toward supply chain diversification rather than onshoring. Other modes of freight transport's developments may have an impact on the growth of the air cargo industry. The maritime industry, which transports nearly 90% of global merchandise trade, has experienced significant market disruption over the last decade. Yields have collapsed as a result of several years of overcapacity and weakening trade. As trade slowed, the major shipping companies' introduction of ultra-large containerships (vessels with more than 15,000 20-foot equivalent units of capacity) contributed to overcapacity. The industry has seen player consolidation, reduced capacity growth, and firming yields over the last five years. While the maritime industry is not typically a competitor to air cargo, the changing nature of container shipping may benefit air cargo. Containership capacity constraints, as well as manufacturers seeking to de-risk their supply base and disperse manufacturing sites into lower-cost Asia-Pacific regions, may drive an increase in air cargo use.

The COVID-19 pandemic has highlighted the significance of main-deck freighters in our global air transportation system, as has the long-term trend of dedicated freighters carrying more than half of global air cargo traffic despite expanding widebody passenger fleets. While more capable passenger widebody planes have aided the growth of the air cargo industry in the last decade, dedicated freighters are expected to account for at least half of all global air cargo traffic carried.

There are several major reasons why freighters are preferred in air cargo flows:

1. The majority of passenger belly capacity is not used to serve vital cargo trade routes.
2. Twin-aisle passenger schedules frequently fall short of shipper deadlines.
3. Freight forwarders prefer palletized capacity, which single aisle aircraft lack.
4. Passenger bellies are unable to serve hazardous materials and project cargo, which is a critical component of air cargo flows.
5. On passenger planes, payload-range considerations may limit cargo carriage, lowering the likelihood of cargo arriving on time.

The freighter fleet will grow by more than 60% over the next two decades, from 2,010 to 3,260 units. There are 2,430 freighters scheduled to be delivered, roughly half of which will replace retiring planes and the rest will expand the fleet to meet projected traffic growth. Over 60% of deliveries will be freighter conversions, with the remaining 72% being standard-body passenger planes. Medium widebody freighters are expected to account for slightly more than half of the 930 new production freighters.

AIR CARGO BUSINESS STRATEGY FOR BUSINESS CONTINUITY

The COVID-19 pandemic is vastly different from previous natural disasters, posing a new set of challenges. This note calibrates lessons from previous experiences that destabilized governments and economies to reflect today's unique realities. The ability to respond through human action and interaction is and potentially will be severely hampered for an extended period of time due to the ongoing public health challenge of COVID-19 due to spatial distancing imperatives. Because the pandemic spans continents and economies, high-income countries' ability to assist developing countries will be tested. Regardless, governments around the world are expected to provide adequate resources for the health sector while also balancing and funding the costs of remote work across the public sector. Governments may have access to a variety of financial tools in times of emergency, and ministries of finance, in particular, may use a variety of financial tools. Reserve funds, contingent spending arrangements, contingent loan facilities, and risk transfer instruments are examples of these.

Supply Chain Planning

Supply chain managers' practices had to change as a result of the completely new challenges. Normally, planning priorities have centered on increasing forecasting accuracy from already high levels to extremely high levels. This was challenging due to the challenges imposed by poor data quality, changing product life cycles, and frequent promotions. However, during a pandemic, planners face entirely different and more fundamental challenges (Kumar and Mishra, 2020). Their well-established ERP planning systems, which rely on statistical forecasting models, are incapable of adapting quickly to new demand realities. Any traditional forecasting approach based on historical time series requires a longer time period to capture new levels and trends. Customers also acted completely abnormally, and frequently completely irrationally. The most well-known example is toilet paper, which was nearly out for weeks due to replenishments that did not always make it onto the shelf. Many customers bought into the psychological fallacy and began stockpiling in preparation for uncertain times. Furthermore, it was difficult to anticipate and incorporate dynamics based on government decisions in planning processes, and data on downstream inventories and lead times, which could provide some insight into demand trends, were difficult to obtain. As a result, during this crisis, demand planning priorities have shifted significantly toward enabling forecasts adequate for reasonable scenario planning. It's critical to have a realistic idea of the minimum and maximum demand, with a range that's ideally as narrow as possible, for cost-intensive decisions like plant openings, layoffs, or sourcing contracts. If demand exceeds the maximum anticipated, companies must expedite shipments, find expensive alternative suppliers, and waste time training more workers. Excess inventories accumulate when demand falls below the minimum expected, orders must be canceled, and staffing costs rise (Xiong and Helo, 2006).

Digitization Supply Chain

Humans are still largely in charge of supply chains today. But, as the current crisis has demonstrated, what happens when people are unable to leave their homes? Investing wisely in technology-based tools and products is the key to a resilient future. Digitization is the only way for businesses to be future-ready. It also necessitates an iterative approach. Such a transformation can be driven by cross-functional, collaborative teams that integrate supply chain operations, business, and technology (Ordieres-meré, 2020). Despite the fact that challenges persist, businesses are seizing opportunities to invest in technologies such as demand sensing, inventory optimization, and transportation planning, which can help them keep up with changing customer behaviors, improve business performance, and maximize resources. Accelerating e-commerce activity, labor constraints, and the need to provide an omnichannel business experience are driving businesses of all sizes to adopt digital-first strategies (Ulas, 2019). Businesses use digital technology to redesign business processes in order to increase efficiency, reduce costs, and innovate. A component of the digital transformation is the practical application of the internet as a data-driven management model in design, production, marketing, sales, and communication. The digitization of the supply chain has the potential to improve supply sustainability practices (Doyle and Cosgrove, 2019). Digitization and sustainability practices should be incorporated into long-term strategic plans for organizations of all sizes. There is a significant and positive relationship between the use of information technology (IT) and various corporate social responsibility (CSR) initiatives. Digital payments, particularly mobile money, are a critical digital transformation priority for businesses in the post-pandemic era (Shaikh et al.,2019).

To ensure business continuity, the necessary controls to support value for money, reduce fraud and corruption, and maintain citizen trust and confidence will be required. In many cases, open and innovative approaches to treasury operations, such as efficiently making cash available to pay for public services, processing and disbursing payments with minimal bureaucratic layers, and reporting in a timely and accurate manner to ensure transparency, will be required. Agile operations should ensure operational efficiency, flexibility, and responsiveness while maintaining transparency, integrity, and accountability. The lexical recipe remains the same in today's post-pandemic economy, and these three words still have the same value:

1. Supply Chain Flexibility

Williams et al. (2013) identified capabilities that reflect how supply chain managers determine whether to adjust production quantity and quality in response to changes in demand and supply. They discovered that the literature on responsiveness focuses on tactical flexibility at the business unit level, rather than flexibility associated with specific functions or lower-level operations. According to Brusset and Teller (2017), flexibility abilities increase resilience. Supply chain agility, according to Swafford et al. (2008), represents the aggregate supply chain's speed in providing a responsive supply chain, whereas supply chain flexibility represents operational capabilities within supply chain functions. According to some studies, flexibility is a driver of agility, and greater supply chain flexibility leads to greater agility (Betts and Tadisina, 2009) In their study, Zhang et al. (2003) looked at external flexibilities like mix flexibility and volume flexibility. They also proposed that flexibility is a concept that addresses adaptability in production/delivery quantities and quality as a result of changes in customer demand and supply. When internal and external integration with key suppliers and customers are considered, external flexibility is one of the three direct antecedents of a firm's supply chain agility (Williams et al., 2013; Braunscheidel and Suresh, 2009).

2. Supply Chain Agility

Firms must manage supply chain risk in today's turbulent and uncertain global environment in order to improve the agility and resilience of their supply chain systems (Tang and Tomlin, 2008). According to the literature, supply chain agility is a concept used to address competitiveness in a fast-paced and unpredictable industrial environment (Brusset, 2016; Gligor et al., 2015). Santos, B. E., and Hanna, M. D. define agility as a system's ability to reconfigure itself quickly (2009). Furthermore, agility is required to improve the supply chain's ability to respond to changes in customer demand more quickly and, as a result, to improve the supply chain's responsiveness (Gunasekaran et al., 2008; Yusuf et al., 2004). According to Gligor (2016), supply chain agility is distinct from supply chain responsiveness. In contrast, agility is a skill that enables businesses to be more efficient and responsive. According to Braunscheidel and Suresh (2009), supply chain agility is a company's internal and external ability to respond in a timely manner to market changes, as well as potential and actual disruptions. According to Chan et al. (2017), two organizational flexibility factors are critical antecedents to supply chain agility: strategic flexibility and manufacturing flexibility. They demonstrated how strategic and manufacturing flexibility can improve supply chain agility. Supply chain agility is possible through the synergy of flexibility, and it can facilitate resource efficiency, a high level of customer service, and supply chain responsiveness (Mohammed et al., 2019; Um et al., 2017; Swafford et al., 2008).

3. Supply Chain Resilience

Resilience is a reactive capability that occurs following a disruption or shock. Others see resilience as more proactive efforts to assist the company in preparing for a disruption. The resilience has been defined as follows: (i) the sum of the passive survival rate (reliability) and the proactive survival rate (restoration), reflecting their robustness while operating under disruptive conditions (Foster, 1993; Youn et al., 2011); (ii) the intrinsic ability to adjust the system's functionality in the presence of disturbances and unexpected changes (Hollnagel et al., 2006); and (iii) the ability to sustain external and internal disruptions The ability of an airline cargo network to withstand and remain operational at the required level of safety during the impact of a given disruptive event is defined as resilience. This definition explicitly considers only actions taken during the impact of the disruptive event, and implicitly only recovery actions in the aftermath. A common reaction to a disruptive event is to delay or cancel affected flights. Furthermore, the resilience of a specific airline cargo transport network can be evaluated independently or jointly at two levels: (i) the physical level, which addresses the impact of a given disruptive event on infrastructure-airports and airspace/air routes; and (ii) the service level, which addresses the impact of a given disruptive event on airline cargo transport services-flights. (2018) (Bao and Zhang) Formalized paraphrase.

Building Resilience

The duration and intensity of the COVID-19 epidemic are currently unknown. The company must also begin planning for the future and developing a recovery strategy in the aftermath of COVID 19. Supply chains all over the world have been thrown into disarray. Many businesses struggle to create a supply chain that is both durable and efficient while dealing with complicated markets. While organizations strive for cost efficiency, there is growing recognition that it frequently clashes with resiliency, which necessitates the ability to respond swiftly by adjusting production, sourcing, or distribution. (Albers and Rundshagen, 2020). Organizations have traditionally regulated their supply chains through relatively stable networks, policies, and modes of transportation. Nonetheless, in today's volatile world, this strategy is no longer viable. Old supply chain planning methods based on static assumptions simply cannot keep up. COVID19 discovered flaws in the majority of supply chains across industry verticals, revealing that the vast majority are not built for resilience (Sheffi & Rice, 2005). Business executives recognize that they must now have a thorough understanding of the disruption's effects, potential consequences, and any sacrifices that may be required to restore operations as soon as possible in order to maintain business continuity.

Continuous Supply Chain Design with Risk Management

Supply chain design is increasingly shifting away from cost and efficiency-focused techniques and toward value creation, continual evaluations, and multi-sourcing robustness. While this may be a difficult transition for many supply chain executives, it is also an opportunity. During times of change, market leadership is often forged, and company executives who manage successful supply chain transformation can outmaneuver their peers. The finest judgments necessitate a careful mix of profitability, service, risk, and long-term viability (Larson, 2011; Jabbarzadeh et al., 2017). Supply chain design, which involves reviewing and realigning the nodes, modes, flows, and policies that drive a supply chain to business objectives, can no longer be considered as an episodic, project-based exercise. The development and constant improvement of ideal supply chain structures, regulations, and flows is referred to as continuous design. This is accomplished through the use of end-to-end digital models powered by AI and sophisticated computational engines for analysis, scenario planning, and simulation (Fahimnia and Jabbarzadeh, 2016).

The risk management for the continuous supply chain design is begin with building a resilient supply chain is to create a strong supply chain risk management model. Kleindorfer and Saad (2005) distinguish two types of risks in supply chain networks: operational risks, which deal with inherent supply chain uncertainties like equipment malfunctions and unforeseen supply discontinuities, and so on, and disruption risks, which are caused by natural and man-made disasters (e.g. natural hazards, terrorism, and political instability, etc.). The various strategies to provide in managing risks have been discussed to alleviate and manage the negative impact of supply chain risks: (a) Postponement (Yang and Yang, 2010): Postpone the shipment time and the position of manufacturing the final product until customers' orders become realized. Two types of postponement were defined as time postponement: avoid that product become prepared for future but unrealized customers' orders and form postponement: avoid manufacturing products in advance based on detail specifications which is not specified by realized customers' orders. (b) Dual sourcing (Trkman and McCormack, 2009): The practice of using two suppliers for a given component, product or service. (c) Redundancy (Sheffi, 2005): A company must pay for the redundant stock, capacity, and workers.

Supplier Management

As a result of the pandemic, supplier management has been thrust into the spotlight. Businesses are feeling the effects of critical component shortages and cash flow constraints, which are slowing supply chain movement. As a result, businesses must approach supplier management methodically in order to identify and correct problem areas. Suppliers play an important role in the development of new innovations, and supply management plays an important role in the innovativeness of a company. Because supply management exists at the intersection of a company and its suppliers, it is critical for the company to participate in the early stages of innovation and product development in collaboration with suppliers, especially in terms of sustainability (Hallstedt et al., 2013). Furthermore, the ability of suppliers to provide innovative and sustainable solutions, as well as the development of integrated supply chain solutions, adds value to both sustainability and business success (Windahl and Lakemond, 2006). Transportation is classified as a service factory due to its significant investment in facilities and equipment, resulting in significant but standard service outcomes. Customers, in other words, rely more on the facility/equipment than on the service to people. As a result, when assessing the customer attractiveness of the mass service market, profitability based on customer input is a key indicator of economic value. Customer profitability refers to a customer's contribution to a supplier's profits. When calculating customer profitability, suppliers typically take both margin and sales volume into account (Reinartz and Kumar 2003). The following is a step-by-step approach to supplier management.

Step 1: To form a centralized team to facilitate the open and consistent flow of information between key supply chain stakeholders. This team can spearhead supplier assessment and risk management initiatives, as well as work to reconfigure the supplier network following the pandemic.

Step 2: To identify the most critical supply chain vulnerabilities, conduct a thorough risk identification and assessment exercise. This is accomplished by investigating the relationship between supplier risk and supplier cost. Companies now have a list of who their high risk/high impact suppliers are. Once the high risk/high impact suppliers have been identified, the central team can track down the suppliers who operate in the most vulnerable areas to disruption. Contracts with those suppliers must then be thoroughly reviewed, and appropriate provisions can be accommodated after due consideration if necessary.

Step 3: Conducting a classification assessment of suppliers and understanding the risk associated with each supplier This entails determining the level of disruption to the supplier's daily operations. The central team must then assess whether the pandemic's financial impact on suppliers is short-term or long-term, and whether this jeopardizes business continuity. It is also critical to understand how transparent your suppliers are in terms of information-sharing parameters, as well as whether they have backup action plans. If a substitute is required, the team must determine how easy it will be to switch to another supplier and how this will affect timeliness, quality, and overall cost.

CONCLUSION

The most current worldwide danger, the COVID-19 pandemic, has seriously affected company operations across many industries. One of the first industries to be touched by this incident was the aviation freight business. Because cargo demand and capacity are unpredictable, a complicated demand unbalancing between current capacity and demand has arisen. Connecting a firm to its surroundings in order to accomplish long-term goals is one aspect of strategic management. Supply chain flexibility, which reflects operational skills within supply chain activities, and supply chain agility, which represents the aggregate supply chain's quickness in delivering a responsive supply chain, will be required to ensure company continuity. Supply chain agility is required to improve the supply chain's ability to adapt to changes in customer demand more quickly and thus increase responsiveness. Under disruptive conditions, "resilience" is defined as the sum of the passive survival rate (reliability) and the proactive survival rate (restoration).

Establishing strong supply chain systems is one method for dealing with disruptions. However, the concept of resilience, which is at the heart of much of our current supply chain risk and management thinking, is frequently vague and ill-defined. A strong supply chain necessitates two key capabilities: the ability to resist and the ability to recover.

In the aftermath of COVID 19, the corporation must also begin planning for the future and establishing a recovery strategy. (i) Continuous Design is one technique to develop a robust supply chain. Organizations must place a greater emphasis on the adoption of capabilities that are aligned with their business goals, as well as the eradication of functional and data silos, which are barriers to continuous design. They may be able to build a culture of continuous learning, planning, and execution among supply chain decision-makers as a result of their efforts. (ii) Supply chain risk management, a strong supply chain risk management model is the first step in building a resilient supply chain. This paradigm splits risks into known and unknown hazards, which are then managed independently. (iii) Managing suppliers as a result of the pandemic, the function of supplier management has been thrown into the limelight. Businesses are being hampered by critical component shortages and cash flow concerns, which are impeding supply chain activity. (iv) Supply chain planning, it was impossible to foresee and incorporate dynamics based on government choices, and data on downstream stocks and lead times, which may give some insight into demand trends, was difficult to collect. As a result, demand planning goals have moved dramatically during this crisis to permitting projections strong enough for realistic scenario planning. (v) Supply Chain Digitization, Businesses can only be future-ready through digitization. It also demands a step-by-step process. Cross-functional, collaborative teams that combine supply chain operations, business, and technology can drive this change.

REFERENCES

Albers, S., & Rundshagen, V. (2020). European airlines' strategic responses to the COVID-19 pandemic. *Journal of Air Transport Management*, *87*, 87. doi:10.1016/j.jairtraman.2020.101863 PMID:32834690

Amaruchkul, K., Cooper, W. L., & Gupta, D. (2011). A Note on Air-Cargo Capacity Contracts. *Production and Operations Management*, *20*(1), 152–162. doi:10.1111/j.1937-5956.2010.01158.x

Amaruchkul, K., & Lorchirachoonkul, V. (2011). Air-cargo capacity allocation for multiple freight forwarders. *Transportation Research Part E, Logistics and Transportation Review*, *47*(1), 30–40. doi:10.1016/j.tre.2010.07.008

Baird, A., & Raghu, T. S. (2015). Associating consumer perceived value with business models for digital services. *European Journal of Information Systems*, *24*(1), 4–22. doi:10.1057/ejis.2013.12

Bao, D., & Zhang, X. (2018). Measurement methods and influencing mechanisms for the resilience of large airports under emergency events. *Transportmetrica A: Transport Science*, *14*(10), 855–880. doi:10.1080/23249935.2018.1448016

Battistella, C., De Toni, A. F., De Zan, G., & Pessot, E. (2017). Cultivating business model agility through focused capabilities: A multiple case study. *Journal of Business Research*, *73*, 65–82. doi:10.1016/j.jbusres.2016.12.007

Betts, T., & Tadisina, S. (2009). *Supply chain agility, collaboration and performance: how do they relate*. Academic Press.

Blackhurst, J., Dunn, K., & Craighead, C. (2011). An empirically derived framework of global supply resiliency. *Journal of Business Logistics*, *32*(4), 374–391. doi:10.1111/j.0000-0000.2011.01032.x

Boeing. (2020). *World air cargo forecast 2020-2039*. https://www.boeing.com/commercial/market/cargo-forecast/

Braunscheidel, M. J., & Suresh, N. C. (2009). The organizational antecedents of a firm's supply Chain agility for risk mitigation and response. *Journal of Operations Management*, *27*(2), 119–140. doi:10.1016/j.jom.2008.09.006

Brusset, X. (2016). Does supply chain visibility enhance agility? *International Journal of Production Economics*, *171*, 46–59. doi:10.1016/j.ijpe.2015.10.005

Brusset, X., & Teller, C. (2017). Supply chain capabilities, risks, and resilience. *International Journal of Production Economics*, *184*, 59–68. doi:10.1016/j.ijpe.2016.09.008

Button, K. (2020). The economics of Africa's floriculture air-cargo supply chain. *Journal of Transport Geography*, *86*, 102789. doi:10.1016/j.jtrangeo.2020.102789 PMID:32834672

Chan, A. T. L., Ngai, E. W. T., & Moon, K. K. L. (2017). The effects of strategic and manufacturing flexibilities and supply chain agility on firm performance in the fashion industry. *European Journal of Operational Research*, *259*(2), 486–499. doi:10.1016/j.ejor.2016.11.006

Doyle, F., & Cosgrove, J. (2019). Steps towards digitization of manufacturing in an SME environment. *Proc. Manuf.*, *38*, 540–547. doi:10.1016/j.promfg.2020.01.068

Fahimnia, B., & Jabbarzadeh, A. (2016). Marrying supply chain sustainability and resilience: A match made in heaven. *Transportation Research Part E, Logistics and Transportation Review*, *91*, 306–324. doi:10.1016/j.tre.2016.02.007

Foster, H. D. (1993). Resilience Theory and System Evaluation. Verification and Validation of Complex Systems: Human Factors Issues. Academic Press.

Gligor, D. M. (2016). The Role of Supply Chain Agility in Achieving Supply Chain Fit. *Decision Sciences*, *47*(3), 524–553. doi:10.1111/deci.12205

Gligor, D. M., Esmark, C. L., & Holcomb, M. C. (2015). Performance outcomes of supply chain agility: When should you be agile? *Journal of Operations Management*, *33-34*(1), 71–82. doi:10.1016/j.jom.2014.10.008

Gunasekaran, A., Lai, K., & Edwin Cheng, T. C. (2008). Responsive supply chain: A competitive strategy in a networked economy. *Omega*, *36*(4), 549–564. doi:10.1016/j.omega.2006.12.002

Gunessee, S., Subramanian, N., & Ning, K. (2018). Natural disasters, PC supply chain and corporate performance. *International Journal of Operations & Production Management*, *38*(9), 1796–1814. doi:10.1108/IJOPM-12-2016-0705

Gupta, D. (2008). Flexible carrier–forwarder contracts for air cargo business. *Journal of Revenue and Pricing Management*, *7*(4), 341–356. doi:10.1057/rpm.2008.29

Habermann, M., Blackhurst, J., & Metcalf, A. Y. (2015). Keep Your Friends Close? Supply Chain Design and Disruption Risk. *Decision Sciences*, *46*(3), 491–526. doi:10.1111/deci.12138

Hallstedt, S. I., Thompson, A. W., & Lindahl, P. (2013). Key elements for implementing a strategic sustainability perspective in the product innovation process. *Journal of Cleaner Production*, *51*, 277–288. doi:10.1016/j.jclepro.2013.01.043

Hollnagel, E., Woods, D., & Leveson, N. (2006). *Resilience Engineering: Concepts and Precepts*. Academic Press.

Holmström, J., & Partanen, J. (2014). Digital manufacturing-driven transformations of service supply chains for complex products. *Supply Chain Management*, *19*(4), 421–430. doi:10.1108/SCM-10-2013-0387

IATA. (2021). *Cargo chartbook Q4 2021*. https://www.iata.org/en/iata-repository/publications/economic-reports/cargo-chartbook---q4-2021/

Jabbarzadeh, A., Fahimnia, B., & Sabouhi, F. (2018). Resilient and sustainable supply chain design: Sustainability analysis under disruption risks. *International Journal of Production Research*, *56*(17), 5945–5968. doi:10.1080/00207543.2018.1461950

Janić, M. (2019). Modeling the resilience of an airline cargo transport network affected by a large scale disruptive event. *Transportation Research Part D, Transport and Environment*, *77*, 425–448. doi:10.1016/j.trd.2019.02.011

Junni, P., Sarala, R. M., Tarba, S. Y., & Weber, Y. (2015). The Role of Strategic Agility in Acquisitions. *British Journal of Management*, *26*(4), 596–616. doi:10.1111/1467-8551.12115

Kim, M., & Sohn, J. (2022). Passenger, airline, and policy responses to the COVID-19 crisis: The case of South Korea. *Journal of Air Transport Management*, *98*, 102144. doi:10.1016/j.jairtraman.2021.102144 PMID:34539103

Kindström, D., & Kowalkowski, C. (2014). Service innovation in product-centric firms: A multidimensional business model perspective. *Journal of Business and Industrial Marketing*, *29*(2), 96–111. doi:10.1108/JBIM-08-2013-0165

Kumar, R., & Mishra, R. S. (2020). COVID-19 global pandemic: Impact on management of supply chain. *International Journal of Emerging Technology and Advanced Engineering*, *10*(04), 132–139. doi:10.46338/IJETAE0416

Larson, P. D. (2001). Designing and Managing the Supply Chain: Concepts, Strategies, and Case Studies, David Simchi-Levi Philip Kaminsky Edith Simchi-Levi. *Journal of Business Logistics*, *22*(1), 259–261. doi:10.1002/j.2158-1592.2001.tb00165.x

Li, T. (2020). A SWOT analysis of China's air cargo sector in the context of COVID-19 pandemic. *Journal of Air Transport Management*, *88*, 101875. doi:10.1016/j.jairtraman.2020.101875 PMID:32834695

Lin, D., Lee, C. K. M., & Yang, J. (2017). Air cargo revenue management under buy-back policy. *Journal of Air Transport Management*, *61*, 53–63. doi:10.1016/j.jairtraman.2016.08.012

Maneenop, S., & Kotcharin, S. (2020). The impacts of COVID-19 on the global airline industry: An event study approach. *Journal of Air Transport Management*, *89*, 101920. doi:10.1016/j.jairtraman.2020.101920 PMID:32874021

Mohammed, A., Harris, I., Soroka, A., & Nujoom, R. (2019). A hybrid MCDM-fuzzy multi-objective programming approach for a G-resilient supply chain network design. *Computers & Industrial Engineering*, *127*, 297–312. doi:10.1016/j.cie.2018.09.052

Nag, R., Hambrick, D. C., & Chen, M.-J. (2007). What is strategic management, really? Inductive derivation of a consensus definition of the field. *Strategic Management Journal*, *28*(9), 935–955. doi:10.1002mj.615

Nishat Faisal, M., Banwet, D. K., & Shankar, R. (2006). Supply chain risk mitigation: Modeling the enablers. *Business Process Management Journal*, *12*(4), 535–552. doi:10.1108/14637150610678113

Ordieres-meré, J. (2020). *Digitalization: An Opportunity for Contributing to Sustainability From Knowledge Creation.* Academic Press.

Parast, M. M., & Shekarian, M. (2019). The Impact of Supply Chain Disruptions on Organizational Performance: A Literature Review. In G. A. Zsidisin & M. Henke (Eds.), *Revisiting Supply Chain Risk* (pp. 367–389). Springer International Publishing. doi:10.1007/978-3-030-03813-7_21

Pascual, M. E., & Cain, L. N. (2021). Loyalty programs: the vital safety feature for airlines to survive COVID-19. *International Hospitality Review*.

Pettit, T., Fiksel, J., & Croxton, K. (2010). Ensuring supply chain resilience: Development of a conceptual framework. *Journal of Business Logistics*, *31*(1), 1–21. doi:10.1002/j.2158-1592.2010.tb00125.x

Qin, Y., Ng, K. K. H., Hu, H., Chan, F. T. S., & Xiao, S. (2021). Post disaster adaptation management in airport: A coordination of runway and hangar resources for relief cargo transports. *Advanced Engineering Informatics*, *50*, 101403. doi:10.1016/j.aei.2021.101403

Reinartz, W. J., & Kumar, V. (2003). The impact of customer relationship characteristics on profitable lifetime duration. *Journal of Marketing*, *67*(1), 77–99. doi:10.1509/jmkg.67.1.77.18589

Santos Bernardes, E., & Hanna, M. D. (2009). A theoretical review of flexibility, agility and responsiveness in the operations management literature. *International Journal of Operations & Production Management*, *29*(1), 30–53. doi:10.1108/01443570910925352

Seuring, S. (2013, March). A review of modeling approaches for sustainable supply chain management. *Decision Support Systems*, *54*(4), 1513–1520. doi:10.1016/j.dss.2012.05.053

Seuring, S. (2013). *A review of modeling approaches for sustainable supply chain management.* Academic Press.

Shaban, I. A., Chan, F. T. S., & Chung, S. H. (2021). A novel model to manage air cargo disruptions caused by global catastrophes such as Covid-19. *Journal of Air Transport Management*, *95*, 102086. doi:10.1016/j.jairtraman.2021.102086 PMID:34548768

Shaikh, A. A., Glavee-Geo, R., Karjaluoto, H., & Ebo Hinson, R. (2019). *How is the use of mobile money services transforming lives in Ghana?* Marketing and Mobile Financial Services. doi:10.4324/9781351174466-12

Sheffi, Y. (2005). Building a resilient supply chain. *Harvard Business Review*, *1*(8), 1–4.

Sheffi, Y., & Rice, J. B. (2005). A supply chain view of the resilient enterprise. *MIT Sloan Management Review*, *47*(1), 41–48.

Shekarian, M., Reza Nooraie, S. V., & Parast, M. M. (2020). An examination of the impact of flexibility and agility on mitigating supply chain disruptions. *International Journal of Production Economics*, *220*, 107438. doi:10.1016/j.ijpe.2019.07.011

Singh, R. K. (2015). Modelling of critical factors for responsiveness in supply chain. *Journal of Manufacturing Technology Management*, *26*(6), 868–888. doi:10.1108/JMTM-04-2014-0042

Stank, T. P., Paul Dittmann, J., & Autry, C. W. (2011). The new supply chain agenda: A synopsis and directions for future research. *International Journal of Physical Distribution & Logistics Management*, *41*(10), 940–955. doi:10.1108/09600031111185220

Swafford, P. M., Ghosh, S., & Murthy, N. (2008). Achieving supply chain agility through IT integration and flexibility. *International Journal of Production Economics*, *116*(2), 288–297. doi:10.1016/j.ijpe.2008.09.002

Tang, C., & Tomlin, B. (2008). The power of flexibility for mitigating supply chain risks. *International Journal of Production Economics*, *116*(1), 12–27. doi:10.1016/j.ijpe.2008.07.008

Trkman, P., & McCormack, K. (2009). Supply chain risk in turbulent environments—A conceptual model for managing supply chain network risk. *International Journal of Production Economics*, *119*(2), 247–258. doi:10.1016/j.ijpe.2009.03.002

Ulas, D. (2019). Digital transformation process and SMEs. *Procedia Computer Science*, *158*, 662–671. doi:10.1016/j.procs.2019.09.101

Um, J., Lyons, A., Lam, H. K. S., Cheng, T. C. E., & Dominguez-Pery, C. (2017). Product variety management and supply chain performance: A capability perspective on their relationships and competitiveness implications. *International Journal of Production Economics*, *187*, 15–26. doi:10.1016/j.ijpe.2017.02.005

Williams, B. D., Roh, J., Tokar, T., & Swink, M. (2013). Leveraging supply chain visibility for responsiveness: The moderating role of internal integration. *Journal of Operations Management*, *31*(7), 543–554. doi:10.1016/j.jom.2013.09.003

Windahl, C., & Lakemond, N. (2006). Developing integrated solutions: The importance of relationships within the network. *Industrial Marketing Management*, *25*(7), 806–818. doi:10.1016/j.indmarman.2006.05.010

Xiong, G., & Helo, P. (2006). An application of cost-effective fuzzy inventory controller to counteract demand fluctuation caused by bullwhip effect. *International Journal of Production Research*, *44*(24), 5261–5277. doi:10.1080/00207540600600114

Yang, B., & Yang, Y. (2010). Postponement in supply chain risk management: A complexity perspective. *International Journal of Production Research*, *48*(7), 1901–1912. doi:10.1080/00207540902791850

Youn, B. D., Hu, C., & Wang, P. (2011). Resilience-Driven System Design of Complex Engineered Systems. *Journal of Mechanical Design*, *133*(10), 101011. doi:10.1115/1.4004981

Yusuf, Y. Y., Gunasekaran, A., Adeleye, E. O., & Sivayoganathan, K. (2004). Agile supply chain capabilities: Determinants of competitive objectives. *European Journal of Operational Research*, *159*(2), 379–392. doi:10.1016/j.ejor.2003.08.022

Zhang, Q., Vonderembse, M. A., & Lim, J.-S. (2003). Manufacturing flexibility: Defining and analyzing relationships among competence, capability, and customer satisfaction. *Journal of Operations Management*, *21*(2), 173–191. doi:10.1016/S0272-6963(02)00067-0

Chapter 14
Robotic Process Automation (RPA) in the Aviation Sector

R K Tailor
https://orcid.org/0000-0001-6096-458X
Manipal University Jaipur, India

Sofia Khan
Manipal University Jaipur, India

ABSTRACT

Robotic process automation (RPA) is an automation technology that airline sectors can benefit from because the airline business is the most global of all, and externalities are likely to have a significant influence and transform it. A generally robust global economic background, particularly earlier in the year, encouraged air passenger demand, which in turn supported employment, earnings, and company activity, as well as strong industry competition, which helped keep airfares low for passengers. Relevant to the increase in passenger numbers, operational costs were rising (i.e., the companies with huge volumes but poor margins are continuously looking for new methods to cut costs and boost efficiency). Robotic process automation (RPA) is a vital technology to meet both of these requirements. Robotic process automation (RPA) is known for its high operational accuracy, reliability, and for enabling organizations to conform rapidly and effectively. As a result, including RPA software bots into the flying experience can eliminate all the user concerns about flying.

INTRODUCTION

The Definition and RPA Applied in the Airline Industry

Robotic Process Automation (RPA) refers to the automation of service processes that mimic human activity. The automation is carried out with the assistance of software robots or AI employees that are capable of doing repetitive jobs properly. The developer creates the job instructions by employing screen capturing and setting variables (Ribeiro, 2021). RPA must become "smarter" in order to gain wider ac-

DOI: 10.4018/978-1-6684-4615-7.ch014

ceptance. More complicated and less specified jobs may be assisted with the use of Artificial Intelligence (AI) and Machine Learning (ML) techniques (Wil M. P. van der Aalst, 2018). Every now and again, a technology emerges that changes the way things are "normally done" in a company (Anagnoste, 2017). Robotic Automation Process (RPA) is the next step after the internet, Enterprise Resource Planning (ERP), Customer Relationship Management (CRM), cloud computing, and other technologies. Robotic Process Automation (RPA) simplifies and automates rules-based business processes and operations, resulting in improved quality, accuracy, adherence, and cost savings (uipath, n.d.). It is where complicated technologies like Machine Learning, Artificial Intelligence, Optical Character Recognition (OCR), and Text Analytics come into play. The devastating impact of the coronavirus epidemic on aviation has brought home the importance of these attributes. We are not going back to business as normal, as the industry restart has demonstrated. Airport operations will alter dramatically, airlines will go out of business, and nations will emerge from the crisis at varying paces and with varying attitudes. Artificial intelligence (AI)-enabled Robotic Process Automation (RPA) has emerged as a key sector in the digitization of the economy (Beerbaum, 2020). Robotic Process Automation Smart process automation or cognitive RPA or intelligent automation refers to the same use of analytics and artificial intelligence approaches to boost the effectiveness of RPA-driven solutions in general. Artificial Intelligence (AI) has grown in maturity and strength as a result of advances in science and technology and is now a universal phenomenon in the micro-perspective present market (Ning Zhang, 2018). Robotic process automation (RPA) is a type of software that mimics human behavior using a computer interface to automate repetitive operations.

Robotic Process Automation (RPA) is the next generation of technology. Robotic Process Automation (RPA) is cutting-edge technology in the fields of computer science, electrical and communications engineering, mechanical engineering, and information technology (Somayya, 2019). It's a mix of hardware and software, networking, and automation that allows you to accomplish simple tasks. Robotic process automation technologies are becoming a requirement for conducting business operations in enterprises around the world. Robotic process automation (RPA) is a new type of business process automation that is based on software robots or artificial intelligence workforce. This cutting-edge technology is the most powerful of the twenty-first century's technologies. New hardware, software, and smart device technologies will dramatically aid the way businesses do business, people do official employment, and the public everyday lives. Human lifestyles are evolving throughout the world as a result of worldwide partnerships, international organizations, and new IT developments like RPA. An RPA framework is provided that allows auditors to focus on jobs that demand professional judgment rather than repetitive and low-judgment audit duties (Feiqi, 2019). RPA is a technology that consists of software agents known as bots that emulate a human's manual path through a variety of computer programs while executing certain activities in a business process (Rehan, 2019). RPA is a software-based solution, despite the fact that the phrase "Robotic Process Automation" conjures up images of real robots strolling about workplaces performing human duties (Willcocks, 2015). A "robot" is the RPA equivalent of one software license. Robotic process automation uses rules-based software to carry out a wide range of back-office operations at a high rate and volume. Automating time-consuming tasks like filling out forms and copying data frees up pricey human resources for more strategic or difficult tasks (IBM, 2021).

Robotic Process Automation (RPA) in the airline sector can be beneficial as for different departments it can produce various packages of work, files can be retrieved from systems, data can be managed effectively, scheduling of crew can be done, travelers can get the update faster, lost revenue outflows can be identified. Customers may easily raise a trip request by stating several origin sources and the destination using an aviation group booking facility. When the system gets the request, it generates the best

Robotic Process Automation (RPA) in the Aviation Sector

possible quote. This is feasible because the software calculates the fee based on many pre-determined factors. Customers can negotiate group fares with the use of a negotiating tool. Payment and name list submission reminders must be sent out on time for group bookings. Automatic follow-up ensures that there are no or fewer errors. Today's digital consumer has the capacity to change the rules of the aviation industry, and airlines must adapt their business models to become far more dynamic and adaptable. Consumers' priorities have shifted in the aviation industry, forcing firms to adopt new business models and align processes to meet and respond to customer and business requirements. Consumers' travel choices, travel plans, demand digital interactions and content, online transactions, and 0 touch customer support are forcing businesses to adopt innovative business models. These new businesses have a thorough understanding of departmental responsibilities, roles, and operations of interconnected systems. Business transformation is not a new concept in any industry, but there is a need to create a clear process heat chart related to business priorities, complexity, Return on Investment (ROI), and work frequency as the foundations for interlinking and developing an Enterprise Business Model that can be used to push the value chain in implementing and accommodating such transitions. Airline process automation is a technical solution that inspires both consumers and businesses by making people truly count. Staff intervention is only required for final inspections when repetitive operations are automated. This helps to save time and intellectual resources for staff to work on front-line activities, such as offering additional higher-value services to the customer. Other benefits of automation in the aviation sector include business metrics reporting, responsiveness, expenditure control, client retention, etc. Automated real-time tracking and reporting assists firms in identifying business trends. It also creates unexpected business possibilities and aids in the overall management of operations. The amount of time spent on administrative activities may add up quickly. However, with automated procedures, activities may be completed more quickly. High-volume processes may be completed with more precision and fewer manual errors due to automation, allowing staff to focus on other essential company activities. Employees can track real-time expenditure and view information from a centralized place, which was previously impossible with traditional solutions. Automated self-booking systems have allowed for more time to be spent on other aspects of the business. Bundles of statements and invoices may now be handled quickly, even after client revisions. Customers' conversations may not need to finish once the trip is completed. Businesses might use emails and advertisements to remain in touch with clients after they've traveled in order to build loyalty. Customers who looked on the site but did not check out may be targeted with the use of automation, and AIRLINES can send campaigns with suitable offers based on their travel history. Passenger Revenue Accounting (PRA), Cargo Revenue Accounting (CRA), Ticket, Tax, Commission, as well as other services of audit, all benefit from RPA. Domain areas like the accounting of revenue, auditing, and others more face major issues and become inefficient and ineffective with a lack of automation. Semi or partial automation can save between 25% and 40% of the money. The development of the Robotic Process Automation (RPA) bots that will do the semi-automated activities is the only significant additional expense. Bots can replicate important data records by accessing other aviation apps to identify and enter missing data, as well as update or approve particular processes or stages when all relevant checks and acceptability ranges have been completed. Robotic Process Automation (RPA) may even send pre-designed email requests to an airline, interpret the answer, and update the related area inside the Passenger Revenue Accounting (PRA) system. Bots may even be programmed to find out the proper data value using smart derivation or aggregation and checks if, for example, exchange coupon numbers are not reported properly. Documents can be compared and reissued as appropriate.

In these cases, the benefits of RPA range from a decrease in labor to shorter response times, as well as fewer human mistakes and income leakages. In general, efficiency, productivity, processing quality, and declarations of income have all improved. It also implies that human labor is put to greater use. This can result in a variety of benefits, including happier employees and higher employee retention. Robotic Process Automation (RPA) is undoubtedly a clear road to increased company potential and optimization. For aviation firms, it is perhaps the finest value for money in the whole technological industry. The RPA-business alignment will help businesses increase their productivity and quality. The ideal practice of implementing RPA in an organization will result in a win for the customer, a win for the workers, and a win for the stakeholders (Ning Zhang, 2018). A robot is an electromechanically built machine that can be programmed by a computer and can perform a complicated set of activities on its own (Somayya Madakam, 2019). RPA technology allows businesses to become more competitive by lowering expenses and boosting financial performance, it increases process efficiency by introducing new, sustainable practices, such as digitalization and automation of specific operational operations and whole business processes (Siderska, 2021).

COVID-19 has prohibited individuals from traveling across countries and around the world, and citizens in many countries have been encouraged to stay at home and engage in minimum social activities. A majority of the airline has reduced their flight capacity and number of flights to historic lows, putting a strain on its bottom line. In addition, the airline has taken some bold steps, like offering unpaid leave to a few of its workers across the world.

The aviation industry can ensure continuity of operations with fewer people and greater operational efficiencies by using attended and unattended automation in finance and accounting, supply chain, HR, and IT operations. Crew management, operations control, luggage handling, booking management, billing process and settlements, and network planning are among the identified process possibilities.

RPA installation is similar to employing a digital workforce that can handle the mundane, repetitive jobs that your human employees despise (cigen, 2021). Software robots may be programmed to duplicate the activities of human employees and can be taught in the same way. They have virtual workstations where they may electronically read the screen. Deploying RPA to aid your human staff may result in cost savings, improved service delivery, and a return on investment (ROI) within the first year of adoption.

In the aviation industry, Robotic Process Automation (RPA) can facilitate the development of better, faster, and less expensive processes, or enhanced operational performance. Because it decreases mistakes and omissions caused by human error, RPA enhances the consistency and accuracy of the processes that are conducted. According to a Bain & Company survey, 84 percent of organizations across industries aim to accelerate automation investments.

Robotic Process Automation in the Aviation Industry

- Work packages creation for numerous departments

Each day, numerous employees must work together to do the business operations manually, and this makes it monotonous, boring, and time-consuming, exactly the type of activity that puts employees under a lot of stress, reduces their job satisfaction and increases chances of errors. With the use of RPA, only one employee is required to oversee the process and manage any potential exceptions when using RPA for package generation and the outcome can be that manpower is saved, better task management, shorter cycle times, and better service (IATA, 2020)

- Keeping travelers up to date

Travelers may be kept updated about flight schedules and booking status using attentive RPA robots and chatbot systems. Chatbots can also react to travelers' questions, always offering the correct response and increasing their satisfaction with the organization's services. The use of robotic process automation in aviation shows how RPA may improve customer satisfaction. The airline department teams must give information to the number of travelers on flight schedules, flight cancellations, and booking status. Because doing it manually can cause processing delays. RPA may be used to swiftly complete the actions required to keep travelers informed about the issue. Chatbots may also respond to passenger queries, always providing the correct response and keeping them happy with the services. As a result, both RPA and chatbots have the potential to lead the airline sector in delivering seamless service and increasing consumer happiness.

- Scheduling of Crew

Robotic Process Automation (RPA) can assist you in assigning responsibilities within the team and effectively managing duty demands. The use of automated notification notifications allows crew members to be notified of any changes. Also, the epidemic made it much more probable that changes will occur, so be prepared to deal with them effectively is an asset one would not want to lose. Bots may be used to plan work, allocate them, and efficiently manage team responsibility needs. The bot may also handle the automation of notification messages, ensuring that crew members are kept up to date on any changes (IATA, 2020) .

Robotic Process Automation (RPA) Helps to Improve the Aviation Sector

As the aviation business becomes more automated, airline service providers are concentrating on various onboard technology to automate the business activities (Beresnevicius, 2019). The aviation sector plays a significant part in global economic activity, and increased capabilities afforded by technological advancements must be fully utilized to ensure the safe and effective functioning of aviation firms (Tetiana, 2020). Artificial Intelligence (AI) is used in the aviation and aerospace sectors in a way that AI is an employed cutting-edge technology to increase the efficiency of developing aviation systems at every stage of their lifetime, therefore strengthening their security and their capacity to learn, improve, and forecast tough scenarios. Another sort of automation technology that airlines can benefit from is robotic process automation (RPA) (Featsystems, n.d.). It can provide a hand in carrying out or eliminating time-consuming, repetitive tasks in the procedures. For example, managing air ticket cancellations and bookings, issuing refunds, generating tickets prior to boarding, and so on. This would enable the airline service to attract more passengers by providing a pleasant experience that will encourage them to return or fly more than once. It can also be used for regulatory compliance. Because different airlines are overseen by different boards, following the laws might be challenging. RPA, on the other hand, is known for its high process accuracy and for enabling organizations to comply swiftly and efficiently. As a result, including RPA software robots in the flying experience can eliminate all of the customer's concerns about flying. Implementation of automated application in aviation can improve and create enhanced awareness of any situation as Human participation is decreasing, and automation is taking over the aviation business, therefore the odds of errors are decreasing as well (Beresnevicius, 2019). This implies that the systems will be able to provide a greater understanding of the scenarios in which the flight will take off, fly, and land. This decreases the risk of air collisions, accidents, and flying in the incorrect direction, among other things. The greatest benefit for airline service providers is a decrease in operational costs because computer systems conduct the majority of the job, the operational costs are significantly reduced.

Challenges and the Opportunities Faced by the Aviation Sector

Today's digital client has the capacity to change the rules of the aviation industry, and airlines must adapt their business models to become far more dynamic and adaptable (INFOTECH, 2020). Business transformation is not a new concept in any industry, but there is the need to create a clear process based on priorities of business, sophistication, Return on Investment (ROI), and task frequency as some of the foundations for interlinking and developing an Enterprise Business Model that is used to drive the value chain when adopting and accommodating those very transformations.

Robotics and automation are the crucial causes of change for the aviation industry from a technological standpoint, others include cybersecurity, virtual reality, augmented reality (VR or AR), the Internet of Things (IoT), new designs of aircraft, and so on. Automation is likely to open new possibilities, changing how people and gadgets are tracked and targeted in real-time. Life becomes easier, activities become faster, and efficiency improves. Quality, cost savings, faster cycle, consistency, and operational efficiency are just a few of the advantages of automation. Robots are increasingly working alongside humans, doing physical and repetitive activities, while humans offer value in areas where AI has not yet taken hold. The advancements in robotics and automation in the aviation sector aim to increase productivity, minimize mistakes, and drastically enhance asset and service reliability. With the confluence of information technology (IT) and operation technology (OT), malicious individuals have more opportunities to sabotage and disrupt operations. Because of the increasing danger, cybersecurity is quickly rising to the top of the aviation industry's priority list and cybersecurity will take center stage in the coming years to yield significant advantages.

Robotic Process Automation (RPA) in the Aviation Sector

Figure 1. Number of scheduled passengers boarded by the global airline industry from 2004 to 2021
Source: https://www.itcinfotech.com/wp-content/uploads/2020/09/ITC-Infotech-Automation-Playbook-Airlines.pdf; 10:53 PM

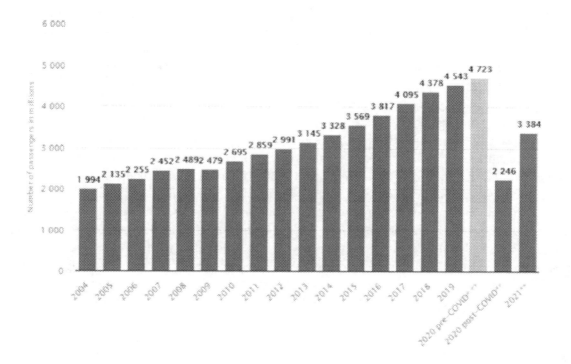

The increased number of passengers flying will have a direct influence on service costs and IT expenses. This, along with increasing competition and small margins, is a major source of concern for any airline firm. As a result, automating some of the labor-intensive procedures becomes a critical first step. Some statistics of industry suggests personnel, about 22% of procedures in the aviation sector may be streamlined or eliminated, which supports our proposals for process- and persona-driven automation (INFOTECH, 2020). Another benefit of automation may be observed in the decrease in running costs. For example, good flying performance may cut fuel consumption, lower operational costs, and increase profits. To increase profit margins by making flight performance more efficient and effective, data created in aircraft computer systems during a flight must be consumed in order to evaluate and improve performance. As the time to consume data decreases, automated procedures and systems can aid in the speedier generation of outcomes. Other benefits of automation in the aviation sector include metrics of business, reporting, reactivity, expenditure control, and client retention, among others. Automated real-time tracking and reporting assists firms in identifying business trends. It also creates unexpected business possibilities and aids in the overall management of operations. The amount of time spent on administrative activities may add up quickly. However, with automated procedures, activities may be completed more quickly. High-volume processes may be completed with more precision and fewer manual errors thanks to automation, allowing staff to focus on other essential company activities, the tedious operations of manually entering codes have become a seamless and pleasant process due to Robotic Process Automation. Automated self-booking systems have allowed for more time to be spent on other aspects of the business. Stacks of statements and invoices may now be handled quickly, even after client revisions. Customers' conversations may not need to finish once the trip is completed. Businesses might use emails and advertisements to remain in touch with clients after they've traveled in order to build loyalty. Customers may easily raise a trip request by stating several origin sources and the destination using an Airlines group booking facility. When the system gets the request, it generates the best possible quote. This is feasible because the algorithm calculates the fee based on many pre-determined factors. Customers can negotiate group fares with the use of a negotiating tool. Payment and name list submission reminders must be sent out on time for group bookings. As a result, Airways that are serious about their company objectives, plans, and priorities should automate their business operations in order to optimize profitability.

Many legacy carriers struggle to adapt swiftly to changing consumer demands and expectations, owing to their outdated, inefficient, and prone to failure in older IT systems (Aviation & defence universe, n.d.). Dealing with this not only costs the airline money, but also has an impact on the company's flexibility, growth, and customer service quality. Because complete IT system overhauls are both expensive and disruptive, several airlines are looking to RPA as a solution. RPA is a technology solution that attempts to return humans to the center of the travel business. It can automate a wide range of repetitive operations performed by employees in practically every business, including travel. The program may replace human contact and take over the tiresome tasks that were previously performed by people by utilizing computer vision. Travel agencies often manage a large number of high-volume transaction-based procedures and work with a variety of airlines, ranging from legacy carriers with out-of-date IT systems to newer low-cost carriers. As a result, workers frequently engage with a variety of management systems, invoice types, agendas, procedures, and data, raising the risk of mistakes. After implementing RPA, this data may be simply saved in the appropriate location, verified, and accessed at any time. The time and expense savings are substantial because only the last inspections are performed by employees. As a result, airline businesses may allocate their personnel to more front-line and customer-focused roles. Furthermore, RPA enables quick expansion, allowing airlines to scale at a faster and more manageable pace due to the automated workflows that have been established and deployed across the organization's many divisions. As a result, they are able to increase their trip frequency.

Changes in client behavior, unexpected weather conditions, and a complicated network of distribution systems have all caused issues for airlines. However, Covid 19 has had a greater influence on the airline industry recently, making it difficult for employees to manage many elements of corporate tasks such as a sudden surge in sales for cancellations, refund applications, and so on. Because the task involves a large amount of data and takes time. As a result, it is more difficult for the employee to manage and finish this high-volume manual effort properly and on time. Customer happiness is a major priority for airlines, as we all know. Due to the delays, customer service is being harmed, the brand's reputation is being harmed, and fines for non-compliance are being imposed. Therefore, as a result, airline firms must adopt RPA since it delivers exactly what aviation needs in today's climate.

Significance and Development of Robotics Process Automation (RPA) in the Aviation Industry

Robotics Process Automation (RPA) is a type of software that allows robots to do a variety of repetitive rules-based operations that are typically performed by humans on computers (Aviation & defence universe, n.d.). RPA can automate business processes and tasks by simulating employee actions and operations as they carry out their duties manually. Many operational functions, such as fare auditing and passenger data validation checks, are automated with RPA. It also helps to improve the airline manufacturing supply chain by automating labor-intensive and time-consuming procedures like procuring, managing the inventory, and processing of payment. Most relevantly, as personnel is released from the burden of regular, boring, and repetitive manual work, they are able to focus on high-value tasks such as improving customer service, allowing front-line employees to recover more data at a faster pace, and making improvement every aspect of the booking experience to customer service support. As a result, employee happiness is higher, and employees are more productive, resulting in improved customer service and favorable feedback from travelers. RPA is a relatively new technology that is rapidly gaining ground. RPA as an industry has developed significantly, and by 2024, it is estimated to be worth $USD5 billion. The financial industry has been fast to embrace RPA. Most airline firms, like financial institutions, confront the same difficulties of aging, legacy IT systems, and large transaction volumes. As a result, airlines are beginning to adopt RPA, especially as the advantages become clear. RPA, for example, can assist in overcoming one key challenge: the existing use of old and inefficient IT systems that limit development and innovation. UiPath is presently collaborating with major and small airlines worldwide, including Lufthansa. One of the big international airlines has begun to use the order to cash (O2C) system for Shared Services billing. To make bills for their customers, they need to access two distinct SAP-Systems (ERP) and an extra repository. The use of UiPath resulted in a quick return on investment and significantly decreased the previously manual labor. Marketing automation will be used to personalize communications and interactions even more. The program can anticipate prospective holiday locations, make restaurant suggestions, and even advise on leisure activities for users based on the data available about their interests. RPA, in conjunction with AI, may allow chatbots and support contact centers, boosting customer engagement and service even further by collecting feedback and continuing to enhance the consumers' experience. Robotic Process Automation (RPA) helps in improving health of airlines and improve the performance of the crew (Ameria, 2019). Airlines face a big issue in guaranteeing aircraft health in order to reduce the rising costs of delayed and cancelled flights. Unplanned maintenance accounts for about a third of all delay time. This is going to change in the near future.

CONCLUSION

The aviation sector has made great progress in terms of automation, and this trend is expected to continue in the future years. Automation not only improves the aircraft's security, but it also saves a lot of manual work, lowering the total airfare. Efficiency is the watchword in the aviation sector, from low-cost carriers to full-service airlines. And using automation to reduce operating expenses while improving work production is efficiency. Since a result, automation benefits both customers and airlines, as decreased operating costs translate into cheaper ticket prices. Airlines have more consumers as a result of decreased ticket pricing, which means more profit. RPA is appropriate for any organization with a high rate of data entry and switching between different applications. It is not limited to a single type of airline. RPA is used to automate specific operations, particularly those that are repetitive and monotonous. The impact on airlines will be significant due to the large number of positions in an airline company's back end that include a high percentage of operations linked to data gathering and processing. Furthermore, RPA is popular with airline carriers who want to give a greater level of customer care, particularly in terms of speed and accuracy. Because 95% of jobs in mature organizations are repetitive, airlines will be able to use UiPath's RPA technology to mimic human behavior and liberate their staff from tiresome and monotonous chores, allowing them to focus more on customer connection. RPA will enable existing legacy operators to overcome many of the obstacles that their older IT systems present. RPA will allow emerging carriers to expand at a far faster rate, perhaps outfighting their more established competitors. More complicated procedures are also being automated by RPA technologies, helping airlines to improve the quality and timeliness of their services. Customer experience is only likely to improve as Artificial Intelligence (AI) becomes more widely used and has the capacity to manage increasingly bigger volumes of unstructured data. Intelligent automation, which combines RPA and AI, will almost certainly result in a more personalized travel experience. Natural language processing, generating suggestions, and providing online customer service are examples of jobs that demand complicated decision-making and analysis. At the same time, RPA may automatically alter flight pricing according to demand, weather, seasonality, and other factors. Airline process automation is a technical solution that empowers both employees and consumers by making people truly count. Staff deployment is only required for final inspections when repetitive operations are automated. This allows more time and mental resources for staff to work on front-line activities, such as offering additional customer support, when employees and customers are happier, the airline firm has a better reputation, and personnel retention is greater. All of these factors contribute to a considerable reduction in processing time and expenses. Furthermore, the usage of dispersed RPA across many departments makes it easier for airlines to expand. Overall, robotic process automation is an opportunity that should not be left up.

In recent years, the aviation sector has undergone several transformations in order to improve the services it provides. In the aviation industry, advances in robotics and automation are aimed at increasing productivity, reducing errors, and dramatically improving asset and service reliability. Malicious persons have increased opportunity to sabotage and disrupt operations when information technology (IT) and operation technology (OT) collide. Cybersecurity should be to the top of the aviation industry's priority list as a result of the growing threat. The airline business has seen a lot of changes as a result of the implementation of numerous new technologies, from offering luxury cabins that resemble hotel rooms to giving inflight entertainment services to clients. In the coming years, the aviation sector should expand in order to deliver high-end services to clients and consumers. However, the aviation sector should keep trying to keep up with the ever-increasing demand for air travel, as airlines and airports throughout the world confront pilot and other labor shortages. Automation is the use of various control systems and technologies to eliminate the need for human intervention. Automation of different operations should be done in the aviation sector, such as traffic control systems should be undertaken a number of automation projects in order to identify meteorological conditions and minimize the likelihood of air accidents and crashes. With the advent of new technologies to the market, the use of computers has become unavoidable since they give excellent performance while doing specialized activities. While automation should improve the speed with which a work is completed, it has a significant impact on the duties of operators whose roles are switched from performer to checker. It is critical in today's world for all airlines to explore automation in order to conduct very complicated and dynamic duties with ease. Automation should be used to increase or regulate the efficiency of flight management in the aviation company. Currently, the aviation sector should concentrate on automation, particularly in air traffic control operations.

REFERENCES

Ameria, H. (2019, August 16). *Mindtree*. Retrieved from www.mindtree.com: https://www.mindtree.com/insights/blog/aviation-flying-future-wings-robotics-automation-and-cybersecurity

Anagnoste, S. (2017). *Robotic Automation Process - The next major revolution in terms of back office operations improvement*. DeGruyter. doi:10.1515/picbe-2017-0072

Aviation & Defence Universe. (n.d.). Retrieved from aviation-defence-universe.com: https://www.aviation-defence-universe.com/robotics-process-automation-rpa-a-futuristic-technology-just-right-for-the-airline-industry-now/

Beerbaum, D. (2020). *Artificial Intelligence Ethics Taxonomy - Robotic Process Automation (RPA) as Business Case*. ResearchGate.

Beresnevicius, R. (2019, May 24). *Aerotime*. Retrieved from www.aerotime.aero: https://www.aerotime.aero/23162-automation-aviation-industry

CIGEN. (2021, February 8). Retrieved from cigen.com: https://www.cigen.com.au/6-real-world-use-cases-robotic-process-automation-aviation/

Featsystems. (n.d.). Retrieved from featsystems.com: https://www.featsystems.com/rpa-airline

Feiqi Huang, M. A. (2019). Applying robotic process automation (RPA) in auditing: A framework. *International Journal of Accounting Information Systems*, 11.

IATA. (2020, June 18). *The benefits of Robotic Process Automation*. Retrieved from airlines.iata.org: https://airlines.iata.org/white-papers/the-benefits-of-robotic-process-automation

IBM. (2021). *Automation and RPA in the enterprise*. IBM.

INFOTECH. (2020). *Automation playbook airlines/aviation (AL)*. ITC Infotech.

Jorge Ribeiro, R. L. (2021). Robotic Process Automation and Artificial Intelligence in Industry 4.0 – A Literature review. Elsevier.

Professor Leslie Willcocks, P. M. (2015). The IT Function and Robotic Process Automation. *The Outsourcing Unit*, *15*(5).

Rehan Syeda, S. S. (2019). *Robotic Process Automation: Contemporary themes and challenges*. Elsevier.

Siderska, J. (2021). *The Adoption of Robotic Process Automation Technology to Ensure Business Processes during the COVID-19 Pandemic*. MDPI.

Somayya Madakam, R. M. (2019). *Journal of Information Systems and Technology Management*, 16.

Tetiana Shmelova, A. S. (2020). Artificial Intelligence in Aviation Industries: Methodologies, Education, Applications, and Opportunities. IGI Global.

UIPATH. (n.d.). Retrieved from uipath.com: https://www.uipath.com/resources/covid-automations/process-opportunities-airlines

Wil, M. P., & van der Aalst, M. B. (2018). *Robotic Process Automation.* Springer Fachmedien Wiesbaden GmbH.

Zhang, N. B. L. (2018). *ICCSE'18: Proceedings of the 3rd International Conference on Crowd Science and Engineering.* Academic Press.

Compilation of References

Airport Staff Others Arrested for Fake COVID-19 Results Other Crimes. (2022). *Channel Television News*. https://www.channelstv.com/2022/01/10/90-airport-staff-others-arrested-for-fake-covid-19-results-other-crimes/amp/

Abate, M., Christidis, P., & Purwanto, A. J. (2020). Government Support to Airlines in the Aftermath of the COVID-19 Pandemic. *Journal of Air Transport Management*, *89*, 101931. doi:10.1016/j.jairtraman.2020.101931 PMID:32952317

Abdulaziz, M. A. & Ofili, P. N. (2021). Assessment of the Impact of Covid-19 Pandemic on the Manufacturing Sector of the Nigerian Economy. *Gusau International Journal of Management and Social Sciences, Federal University*, *4*(3), 126.

Abioye, O., Ogunniyi, A., & Olagunju, K. (2020). *Estimating the Impact of COVID-19 on Small and Medium Enterprise: Evidence from Nigeria*. African Development Bank. https://aec.acfdb.org/en/papers/estimating-impact-covid-19-small-and-medium-scale-enterprises-evidence-nigerian-397

Abraham, A., Anfofum, S., & Illuno, S. Z. C. (2015). Air Transportation Development and Economic Growth in Nigeria. *Journal of Economic and Sustainable Development*, *6*(2), 1. www.iiste.org

Abraham, P., Obioma, R. N., Ogunnumesi, O., & Imad, G. (2017). An Investigation into the Effect of Airport Touting from the Passengers' Perspective: A Case of Nnamdi Azikiwe Airport Abuja. International Conference on Air Transport: INAIR 2017. *Transportation Research Procedia*, *28*, 69–78.

Accidentes, C. d. (1978). Colision aeronaves. In *C. d. Accidentes, Colision aeronaves*. Ministerio de Transportes y Comunicaciones, Subsecretaria de Aviacion Civil.

ACI. (2020). *Smart Security Vision 2040 Achieving a Seamless Airport Security Screening Experience for Passengers*. Retrieved from: www.aci.aero/publications

Adebowale, N. (2020, May 6). Nigeria's aviation industry loses N21 billion monthly to COVID-19-Minister. *Premium Times*. https://www.premiumtimesng.com/news/headlines/391697-nigeria-aviation-industry-losses-n21-billion-monthly-to-covid-19-minister

Adebukola, D.T.F. (2019). *Air Travel and Airline Operations in Nigeria: Market Potentials and Challenges*. IntechOpen. . doi:10.5772/intechopen.80646

Adeniran, A. O., & Yusuf, T. B. (2016). Transportation and National Development: Emphasis to Nigeria. *Developing Country Studies*, *6*(9), 93-94. www.iiste.org

Adioye. (2021). Nigerians face airfare hikes, foreign airports impose 950 billion charges. *Punch*.

Adler, T. J., Falzarano, S., & Spitz, G. (2005). Modeling Service Trade-Offs in Air Itinerary Choices. Transportation Research Record: Journal of the Transportation Research Board, (1), 20–26.

Adrienne, N., Budd, L., & Ison, S. (2020). Grounded aircraft: An airfield operations perspective of the challenges of resuming flights post COVID. *Journal of Air Transport Management*, *89*, 101921. Advance online publication. doi:10.1016/j.jairtraman.2020.101921 PMID:32901184

Afaq, A., Gaur, L., Singh, G., & Dhir, A. (2021). COVID-19: Transforming Air Passengers' Behaviour and Reshaping Their Expectations Towards the Airline Industry. *Tourism Recreation Research*, 1–9. Advance online publication. doi:10.1080/02508281.2021.2008211

Afolayan, O. S. (2012). Comparative Analysis of Aircraft-Passenger Movement in Nigeria Airports. *International Journal of Business. Human Technology*, *2*(6), 118.

Agency Report. (2021 December 24). Over 2,000 flights cancelled worldwide as Omicron hits holiday travel. *Punch*. https://www.punchng.com/over-2000-flights-cancelled-worldwide-as-omicron-hits-holiday-travel-/%3famp

Air France-KLM Group. (2022). *History*. https://www.airfranceklm.com/en/group/history

Air transport as a driver of sustainable development in Latin America and the Caribbean: challenges and policy proposals. (2021). *FAL Bulletin*, *359*(7).

AIRBUS. (2021). *A Statistical Analysis of Commercial Aviation Accidents A Statistical Analysis of Commercial Aviation Accidents* (Issue 5). https://safetyfirst.airbus.com/news-a-statistical-analysis-of-commercial-aviation-accidents-1958-2020/

Airbus. (2021). *A350-900 Sharping the Future of Air Travel*. Airbus. https://aircraft.airbus.com/en/aircraft/a350/a350-900

Aircraft Commerce. (2018). *A350-900/-1000 fuel burn & operating performance*. Aircraft Commerce. https://www.aircraft-commerce.com/sample_article_folder/121_FLTOPS_A.pdf

Airport Research Center. (2020). *Airport Challenges in Reacting to Covid-19*. https://arc.de/consulting/airport-challenges-in-reacting-to-covid-19/

Airports Council International. (2009). *Airport preparedness guidelines for outbreaks of communicable disease*. Retrieved from: https://aci.aero/wpontent/uploads/2020/01/Airport_preparedness_guidelines_for_outbreaks_of_communicable.pdf

Airways Magazine. (2020). A340-600's Progressive Withdrawal. *Airways Magazine*. https://airwaysmag.com/airlines/a340-600-withdrawn/

Akamavi, R. K., Mohamed, E., Pellmann, K., & Xu, Y. (2015). Key determinants of passenger loyalty in the low-cost airline business. *Tourism Management*, *46*, 528–545. doi:10.1016/j.tourman.2014.07.010

Al-Abdullat, B. M., & Dababneh, A. (2018). The mediating effect of job satisfaction on the relationship between organizational culture and knowledge management in Jordanian banking sector. *Benchmarking*, *25*(2), 517–544. doi:10.1108/BIJ-06-2016-0081

Alaminos-Torre, Martinez-Locra, De Sola, Lopez-Ejeda, & Marrodan. (2021). Psychological distress in Spanish airline pilots during the aviation crisis caused by the COVID-19. *Ergonomics*.

Alavosius, M. P., Houmanfar, R. A., Anbro, S. J., Burleigh, K., & Hebein, C. (2017). Leadership and Crew Resource Management in High-Reliability Organizations. A Competency Framework for Measuring Behaviors. *Journal of Organizational Behavior Management*, *37*(2), 142–170. doi:10.1080/01608061.2017.1325825

Albers, S., & Rundshagen, V. (2020). European airlines' strategic responses to the COVID-19 pandemic. *Journal of Air Transport Management*, *87*, 87. doi:10.1016/j.jairtraman.2020.101863 PMID:32834690

Albers, S., Wohlgezogen, F., & Zajac, E. (2016). Strategic alliance structures: An organization design perspective. *Journal of Management*, *42*(3), 582–614. doi:10.1177/0149206313488209

Compilation of References

Al-Dahash, H. & Thayaparan, M., & Kulatunga, U. (2016). *Understanding the Terminologies: Disaster, Crisis and Emergency*. Academic Press.

Aldas-Manzano, J., Ruiz-Mafe, C., Sanz-Blas, S., & Lassala-Navarré, C. (2011). Internet banking loyalty: Evaluating the role of trust, satisfaction, perceived risk and frequency of use. *Service Industries Journal*, *31*(7), 1165–1190. doi:10.1080/02642060903433997

Aldemir, H., Kuyucak Şengür, F., & Ulukan, İ. (2021). Exploring Strategic Choices of Airlines: A Study in Turkish Air Transport Industry. *Asian Academy of Management Journal*, 1-26. doi:10.21315/aamj2021.26.2.1

Allianz Global Corporate & Specialty. (2021). *Aviation trends post Covid-19*. www.agcs.allianz.com

Alper, A., & Bloom, D. (2020). *Trump curbs travel from Europe as coronavirus disrupts schools, sports*. Retrieved January 05, 2020. https://www.reuters.com/article/us-health-coronavirus-usa/trump-curbs-travel-from-europe-as-coronavirus-disrupts-schools-sports-idINKBN20Y1Z0

Amal, H. A. M., William, M. G., & Ioanna, Y. (2022). The Impact of airlines' policies during COVID-19 on traveler's repurchase intentions: The case of Aegean Airlines. *International Journal of Tourism Policy*, *12*(2).

Amankwah-Amoah, J. (2021). COVID-19 pandemic and innovation activities in the global airline industry: A review. In Environment International (Vol. 156). Elsevier Ltd. doi:10.1016/j.envint.2021.106719

Amaruchkul, K., Cooper, W. L., & Gupta, D. (2011). A Note on Air-Cargo Capacity Contracts. *Production and Operations Management*, *20*(1), 152–162. doi:10.1111/j.1937-5956.2010.01158.x

Amaruchkul, K., & Lorchirachoonkul, V. (2011). Air-cargo capacity allocation for multiple freight forwarders. *Transportation Research Part E, Logistics and Transportation Review*, *47*(1), 30–40. doi:10.1016/j.tre.2010.07.008

Ameria, H. (2019, August 16). *Mindtree*. Retrieved from www.mindtree.com: https://www.mindtree.com/insights/blog/aviation-flying-future-wings-robotics-automation-and-cybersecurity

Amming, Z., Xiaoqian, S., Sebastian, W., Yahua, Z., Shiteng, X., & Ronghua, S. (2021). *COVID-19, Air Transportation and International Trade in the ASEAN+5 Region*. ERIA Discussion Paper Series No. 401. ERIA-DP-2021-34.

Ammirato, S., Linzalone, R., & Felicetti, A. M. (2020). Knowledge management in pandemics. A critical literature review. *Knowledge Management Research and Practice*, 1–12. doi:10.1080/14778238.2020.1801364

Anagnoste, S. (2017). *Robotic Automation Process - The next major revolution in terms of back office operations improvement*. DeGruyter. doi:10.1515/picbe-2017-0072

An, M., & Noh, Y. (2009). Airline customer satisfaction and loyalty: Impact of in-flight service quality. *Service Business*, *3*(3), 293–307. doi:10.100711628-009-0068-4

Appelbaum, S. H., & Fewster, B. M. (2002). Global aviation human resource management: Contemporary recruitment and selection and diversity and equal opportunity practices. *Equal Opportunities International*, *21*(7), 66–80. doi:10.1108/02610150210787226

Appelbaum, S. H., & Fewster, B. M. (2003). Global aviation human resource management: Contemporary employee and labour relations practices. *Management Research News*, *26*(10/11), 56–69. doi:10.1108/01409170310784069

Arora, M., Tuchen, S., Nazemi, M., & Blessing, L. (2021). Airport pandemic response: An assessment of impacts and strategies after one year with COVID-19. *Transportation Research Interdisciplinary Perspectives*, *11*, 100449. Advance online publication. doi:10.1016/j.trip.2021.100449 PMID:34458721

Atkinson, R., & Flint, J. (2001). Accessing hidden and hard-to-reach populations: Snowball research strategies. *Social Research Update*, *33*(1), 1–4.

Aubrey, A. (2007). *Move Around on Long Flights to Prevent Blood Clots*. National Public Radio. https://www.npr.org/templates/story/story.php?storyId=12593776

Aviation & Defence Universe. (n.d.). Retrieved from aviation-defence-universe.com: https://www.aviation-defence-universe.com/robotics-process-automation-rpa-a-futuristic-technology-just-right-for-the-airline-industry-now/

Axelson, R., Kreiter, C., Ferguson, K., Solow, C., & Huebner, K. (2010). Medical school preadmission interviews: Are structured interviews more reliable than unstructured interviews? *Teaching and Learning in Medicine*, *22*(4), 241–245. doi:10.1080/10401334.2010.511978 PMID:20936568

Bachman, J. (2017). *Airlines Make More Money Selling Miles than Seats*. Retrieved March 16, 2022, from https://www.bloomberg.com/news/articles/2017-03-31/airlines-make-more-money-selling-miles-than-seats

Bahaee, M. S. (1992). Strategy-Comprehensiveness Fit and Performance. *Australian Journal of Management*, *17*(2), 195–215. doi:10.1177/031289629301700202

Baird, A., & Raghu, T. S. (2015). Associating consumer perceived value with business models for digital services. *European Journal of Information Systems*, *24*(1), 4–22. doi:10.1057/ejis.2013.12

Baker, S. B. (1995). *Team resource management in ATC—interim report*. EUROCONTROL.

Balcombe, K., Fraser, I., & Harris, L. (2009). Consumer willingness to pay for in-flight service and comfort levels: A choice experiment. *Journal of Air Transport Management*, *15*(5), 221–226. doi:10.1016/j.jairtraman.2008.12.005

Bamberger, G. E., Carlton, D. W., & Neumann, L. R. (2004). An empirical investigation of the competitive effects of domestic airline alliances. *The Journal of Law & Economics*, *47*(1), 195–222. doi:10.1086/386274

Bao, D., & Zhang, X. (2018). Measurement methods and influencing mechanisms for the resilience of large airports under emergency events. *Transportmetrica A: Transport Science*, *14*(10), 855–880. doi:10.1080/23249935.2018.1448016

Barney, J. B., & Hesterly, W. S. (2019). *Strategic management and competitive advantage: Concepts and cases*. Pearson.

Battistella, C., De Toni, A. F., De Zan, G., & Pessot, E. (2017). Cultivating business model agility through focused capabilities: A multiple case study. *Journal of Business Research*, *73*, 65–82. doi:10.1016/j.jbusres.2016.12.007

Bauer, L. (2019). *The Commercial Viability of Ultra Long-Haul Operations. Evidence from Qantas' Perth-London Service*. GRIN Verlag.

Bauer, L., Bloch, D., & Merkert, R. (2020). Ultra Long-Haul: An emerging business model accelerated by COVID-19. *Journal of Air Transport Management*, *89*, 101901. doi:10.1016/j.jairtraman.2020.101901 PMID:32839647

Baxter, G., Srisaeng, P., & Wild, G. (2018). The Air Cargo Carrying Potential of the Airbus 350-900XWB and Boeing 787-9 Aircraft on their Long Haul Flight: Case Study for flights from San Francisco to Singapore. *Transport and Telecommunication*, *19*(4), 301–314. doi:10.2478/ttj-2018-0025

BBC NEWS. (2021, Jun 15). *Kān bin Thai: sān lomlalāi klāng hen chop̄ phæn fun̄fū kitčhakān phæm̄ thun 'īk hā mun̄lā nabāt* [Thai Airways International: Central Bankruptcy Court approves business rehabilitation plan, increase capital by 50 billion baht]. Retrieved from: www. bbc.com/thai

Beaty, D. (1969). *The Human Factor in Aircraft Accidents*. Stein & Day.

Compilation of References

Beaubien & Baker. (2004). The use of simulation for training teamwork skills in health care: how low can you go? In *Qual Saf Health Care* (pp. i51–i56). Academic Press.

Beaubien, J. M., & Baker, D. P. (2001). *Airline Pilots Perceptions of and Experiences in Crew Resource Management (CRM) Training.* Society of Automotive Engineers, Inc.

Beerbaum, D. (2020). *Artificial Intelligence Ethics Taxonomy - Robotic Process Automation (RPA) as Business Case.* ResearchGate.

Belobaba, P. (2009). The Airline Planning Process. In P. Belobaba, A. Odoni, & C. Barnhart (Eds.), *The Global Airline Industry* (1st ed., pp. 153–181). John Wiley & Sons, Ltd. doi:10.1002/9780470744734.ch6

Beresnevicius, R. (2019, May 24). *Aerotime.* Retrieved from www.aerotime.aero: https://www.aerotime.aero/23162-automation-aviation-industry

Berg, M. J., Signal, T., & Gander, P. (2019). Perceived Workload Is Associated with Cabin Crew Fatigue on Ultra-Long Range Flights. *The International Journal of Aerospace Psychology, 3-4*(3-4), 74–85. doi:10.1080/24721840.2019.1621177

Berry, L., Wall, E., & Carbone, L. (2006). Service Clues and Customer Assessment of the Service Experience: Lessons from Marketing. *The Academy of Management Perspectives, 20*(2), 43–57. doi:10.5465/amp.2006.20591004

Betts, T., & Tadisina, S. (2009). *Supply chain agility, collaboration and performance: how do they relate.* Academic Press.

Beuren, I. M., dos Santos, V., & Theiss, V. (2021). Organizational resilience, job satisfaction and business performance. *International Journal of Productivity and Performance Management.* doi:10.1108/IJPPM-03-2021-0158

Beveridge, D. (1991). *South African resumes flights to N.Y. Pittsburgh Post Gazette.*

Bielecki, M., Patel, D., Hinkelbein, J., Komorowski, M., Kester, J., Ebrahim, S., Rodriguez-Morales, A. J., Memish, Z. A., & Schlagenhauf, P. (2020). Reprint of: Air travel and COVID-19 prevention in the pandemic and peri-pandemic period: A narrative review. *Travel Medicine and Infectious Disease, 38*, 101939. Advance online publication. doi:10.1016/j.tmaid.2020.101939 PMID:33291000

Bielecki, M., Patel, D., Hinkelbein, J., Komorowski, M., Kester, J., Ebrahim, S., Rodriguez-Morales, A. J., Memish, Z. A., & Schlagenhauf, P. (2021). Air travel and COVID-19 prevention in the pandemic and peri-pandemic period: A narrative review. In *Travel Medicine and Infectious Disease* (Vol. 39). Elsevier Inc. doi:10.1016/j.tmaid.2020.101915

Billet, A. B. (1969). *Hydraulic System State-of-the-Art Advances on the 747 Airplane.* AE Technical Paper 690670, 1969, 1-11.

Bilotkach, V. (2019). Airline Partnerships, Antitrust Immunity, and Joint Ventures: What We Know and What I Think We Would Like to Know. *Review of Industrial Organization, 54*(1), 37–60. doi:10.100711151-018-9636-x

Bissessur, A., & Alamdari, F. (1998). Factors affecting the operational success of strategic airline alliances. *Transportation, 25*(4), 331–355. doi:10.1023/A:1005081621754

Bitner, M. J. (1995). Building service relationships: It's all about promises. *Journal of the Academy of Marketing Science, 23*(4), 246–251. doi:10.1177/009207039502300403

Bitner, M. J., Brown, S. W., & Meuter, M. L. (2000). Technology infusion in service encounters. *Journal of the Academy of Marketing Science, 28*(1), 138–149. doi:10.1177/0092070300281013

Blackhurst, J., Dunn, K., & Craighead, C. (2011). An empirically derived framework of global supply resiliency. *Journal of Business Logistics, 32*(4), 374–391. doi:10.1111/j.0000-0000.2011.01032.x

Blalock, G., Kadiyali, V., & Simon, D. (2007). The Impact of Post-9/11 Airport Security Measures on the Demand for Air Travel. *The Journal of Law & Economics*, *50*(4), 731–755. doi:10.1086/519816

Blickensderfer, E. C.-B. (1998). Assessing team shared knowledge: A field test and implications for team training. In *Proceedings of the 42nd Annual Meeting of the Human Factors* (p. 1630). Santa Monica, CA: HFES. 10.1177/154193129804202379

Bockelie, A., & Belobaba, P. (2017). Incorporating ancillary services in airline passenger choice models. *Journal of Revenue and Pricing Management*, *16*(6), 553–568. doi:10.105741272-017-0100-6

Boeing. (2013). *Made with Japan: A Partnership on the Frontiers of Aerospace*. Boeing.

Boeing. (2020). *World air cargo forecast 2020–2039*. https://www.boeing.com/commercial/market/cargo-forecast/

Boeing. (2021). *Boeing 787 Dreamliner*. Boeing. https://www.boeing.com/commercial/787/#/family

Boer, D., Deinert, A., Horman, A. C., & Voelpel, S. C. (2016). Revisiting the mediating role of leader-member exchange in transformational leadership: The differential impact model. *European Journal of Work and Organizational Psychology*, *25*(6), 883–899. doi:10.1080/1359432X.2016.1170007

Bolton, R. N., Grewal, D., & Levy, M. (2007). Six strategies for competing through service: An agenda for future research. *Journal of Retailing*, *83*(1), 1–4. doi:10.1016/j.jretai.2006.11.001

Bongiovanni, I., & Newton, C. (2019). Toward an epidemiology of safety and security risks: An organizational vulnerability assessment in international airports. *Risk Analysis*, *39*(6), 1281–1297. doi:10.1111/risa.13238 PMID:30452779

Bontis, N., Richards, D., & Serenko, A. (2011). Improving service delivery: Investigating the role of information sharing, job characteristics, and employee satisfaction. *The Learning Organization*, *18*(3), 239–250. doi:10.1108/09696471111123289

Borgardt, E. (2018). Conventional and extended versions of Means-End Chain theory. *Zeszyty Naukowe Uniwersytetu Ekonomicznego w Krakowie*, *3*(975), 191–204. doi:10.15678/ZNUEK.2018.0975.0312

Borgardt, E. (2019). Extending Means-End Chain theory by integrating a self-concept approach and behavioural perspective model. *Zeszyty Naukowe Uniwersytetu Ekonomicznego w Krakowie*, *979*(1), 47–61. doi:10.15678/ZNUEK.2019.0979.0103

Bose, R., & Sugumaran, V. (2003). Application of knowledge management technology in customer relationship management. *Knowledge and Process Management*, *10*(1), 3–17. doi:10.1002/kpm.163

Bouwer, J., Krishnan, V., & Saxon, S. (2020). *Will airline hubs recover from COVID-19?* McKinsey.

Brahmana, R., You, H., & Kontesa, M. (2021). Does CEO power matter for the performance of retrenchment strategy? *Journal of Strategy and Management*, *14*(1), 1–18. doi:10.1108/JSMA-10-2019-0186

Braun, V., & Clarke, V. (2012). Thematic analysis. In H. Cooper, P. M. Camic, D. L. Long, A. T. Panter, D. Rindskopf, & K. J. Sher (Eds.), APA handbook of research methods in psychology, Vol. 2. Research designs: Quantitative, qualitative, neuropsychological, and biological (pp. 57–71). American Psychological Association. doi:10.1037/13620-004

Braunscheidel, M. J., & Suresh, N. C. (2009). The organizational antecedents of a firm's supply Chain agility for risk mitigation and response. *Journal of Operations Management*, *27*(2), 119–140. doi:10.1016/j.jom.2008.09.006

Braun, V., & Clarke, V. (2006). Using thematic analysis in psychology. *Qualitative Research in Psychology*, *3*(2), 77–101. doi:10.1191/1478088706qp063oa

Brealey, A. R., Myers, C. S., & Marcus, J. A. (2007). *Fundamentals of Corporate Finance*. McGraw-Hill.

Brian K. Sperling, A. R. (2011). *Complementary information distribution to improve team performance in military helicopter operations: An experimental study*. Academic Press.

Compilation of References

British Broadcasting Corporation (BBC). (2007). *1952: Comet inaugurates the jet age.* British Broadcasting Corporation (BBC). http://news.bbc.co.uk/onthisday/hi/dates/stories/may/2/newsid_2480000/2480339.stm

British Broadcasting Corporation. (2020, August 9). *Coronavirus: The impact on Nigeria's airlines.* https://www.bbc.com/news/av/business-53715571

Broderick, S. (2022). *Corrosion From Inactivity Flagged On Pratt-powered 777 Engine Parts.* Academic Press.

Brueckner, J. K. (2001). The economics of international codesharing: an analysis of airline alliances. *International Journal of Industrial Organization, 19*(10), 1475-1498.

Brueckner, J. K., Lee, D. N., & Singer, E. S. (2011). Alliances, codesharing, antitrust immunity, and international airfares: Do previous patterns persist? *Journal of Competition Law & Economics, 7*(3), 573–602. doi:10.1093/joclec/nhr005

Brueckner, J., Lee, D., & Singer, E. (2013). Airline Competition and Domestic US Airfares: A Comprehensive Reappraisal. *Economics of Transportation, 2*(1), 1–17. doi:10.1016/j.ecotra.2012.06.001

Brueckner, J., & Whalen, W. (2000). The Price Effects of International Airline Alliances. *The Journal of Law & Economics, 43*(2), 503–546. doi:10.1086/467464

Brusset, X. (2016). Does supply chain visibility enhance agility? *International Journal of Production Economics, 171,* 46–59. doi:10.1016/j.ijpe.2015.10.005

Brusset, X., & Teller, C. (2017). Supply chain capabilities, risks, and resilience. *International Journal of Production Economics, 184,* 59–68. doi:10.1016/j.ijpe.2016.09.008

Budd, L., & Ison, S. (2020). *Air Transport Management: An International Perspective.* Routledge. doi:10.4324/9780429299445

Bueno, E. V., Weber, T. B. B., Bomfim, E. L., & Kato, H. T. (2019). Measuring customer experience in service: A systematic review. *Service Industries Journal, 39*(11-12), 779–798. doi:10.1080/02642069.2018.1561873

Bukar, A. B. U., & Garba, A. (2021). Effect of COVID-19 Pandemic on SME Performance in Nigeria. *Advanced International Journal of Business Entrepreneurship and SMES, 3*(7), 75–92. doi:10.35631/AIJBES.37007

Burke, K. (2013). How the DC-3 Revolutionized Air Travel. *Smithsonian.* https://www.smithsonianmag.com/history/how-the-dc-3-revolutionized-air-travel-5444300/

Butterfield, L., Borgen, W., Amundson, N., & Maglio, A. (2005). Fifty years of the critical incident technique: 1954-2004 and beyond. *Qualitative Research, 5*(4), 475–497. doi:10.1177/1468794105056924

Button, K. (2020). The economics of Africa's floriculture air-cargo supply chain. *Journal of Transport Geography, 86,* 102789. doi:10.1016/j.jtrangeo.2020.102789 PMID:32834672

Byington, M. R., & Miltiadous, M. (1990). Optimized Engine-Out Procedures to Extend the Range of Jet. *Journal of Aviation/Aerospace Education Research, 1*(1), 17–37. doi:10.15394/JAAER.1999.1007

Byrne, B. M. (2004). Testing for multigroup invariance using AMOS graphics: A road less traveled. *Structural Equation Modeling, 11*(2), 272–300. doi:10.120715328007sem1102_8

Byrnes, K. P., Rhoades, D. L., Williams, M. J., Arnaud, A. U., & Schneider, A. H. (2022). The effect of a safety crisis on safety culture and safety climate: The resilience of a flight training organization during COVID-19. *Transport Policy, 117,* 181–191. doi:10.1016/j.tranpol.2021.11.009 PMID:34803245

Byun, J., & Jang, S. (2018). Open kitchen vs. closed kitchen: Does kitchen design affect customers' causal attributions of the blame for service failures? *International Journal of Contemporary Hospitality Management*, *30*(5), 2214–2229. doi:10.1108/IJCHM-03-2016-0167

Byun, S. N., & Lee, D. H. (2001). *Preliminary Safety Review on the Design of Korea Next Generation Reactor: A Human Factors Evaluation of Advanced Control Facilities in Korea Next Generation Reactor* (404th ed.). Korea Institute of Nuclear Safety.

CAA. (2006). *Crew Resource Management Training: Guidance for Flight Crew, CRM Instructors and CRM Instructor-Examiners*. Safety Regulation Group.

Calisir, N., Basak, E., & Calisir, F. (2016). Key drivers of passenger loyalty: A case of Frankfurt–Istanbul flights. *Journal of Air Transport Management*, *53*, 211–217. doi:10.1016/j.jairtraman.2016.03.002

Camison, C., & Lopez, A. V. (2010). An examination of the relationship between manufacturing flexibility and firm performance: The mediating role of innovation. *International Journal of Operations & Production Management*, *30*(8), 853–878. doi:10.1108/01443571011068199

Campbell, M. C. (1999). Perceptions of price unfairness: Antecedents and consequences. *JMR, Journal of Marketing Research*, *36*(2), 187–199. doi:10.1177/002224379903600204

Caputo, F., Garcia-Perez, A., Cillo, V., & Giacosa, E. (2019). A knowledge-based view of people and technology: Directions for a value co-creation-based learning organisation. *Journal of Knowledge Management*, *23*(7), 1314–1334. doi:10.1108/JKM-10-2018-0645

Carpenter, M. A., & Sanders, W. G. (2014). *Strategic Management Concepts and Cases*. Pearson.

Cassell, C. (2005). Creating the interviewer: Identity work in the management research process. *Qualitative Research*, *5*(2), 167–179. doi:10.1177/1468794105050833

Center for Asia Pacific Aviation (CAPA). (2013). *Singapore Airlines upcoming termination of non-stops to US spells end to ultra long-range travel*. CAPA. https://centreforaviation.com/analysis/reports/singapore-airlines-upcoming-termination-of-non-

Center for Asia Pacific Aviation (CAPA). (2021). *Aviation Industry Glossary*. CAPA. https://centreforaviation.com/about/glossary

Cesare, A., & Gianluigi, G. (2011). Determinants of purchasing intention for fashion luxury goods in the Italian market: A laddering approach. *Journal of Fashion Marketing and Management*, *15*(1), 123–136. doi:10.1108/13612021111112386

Chamberlin, C. (2021). Did Qantas really 'invent' business class? *Executive Travelers*. https://www.executivetraveller.com/did-qantas-invent-business-class

Chan, A. T. L., Ngai, E. W. T., & Moon, K. K. L. (2017). The effects of strategic and manufacturing flexibilities and supply chain agility on firm performance in the fashion industry. *European Journal of Operational Research*, *259*(2), 486–499. doi:10.1016/j.ejor.2016.11.006

Chiambaretto, P. (2021). Air passengers' willingness to pay for ancillary services on long-haul flights. *Transportation Research Part E, Logistics and Transportation Review*, *147*, 102234.

Chidester, T. (1993). Role of dispatchers in CRM training. In *Proceedings of the Seventh International Symposium on Aviation Psychology* (pp. 182–185). Columbus, OH: The Ohio State University.

Compilation of References

Chinedu, E. (2017). *57 Years of Air Transport in Nigeria. Thisdaylive.* https://www.thisdaylive.com/index.php/2017/10/06/57-years-of-air-transport-in-nigeria/

Chinedu, E. (2021 December 3). As Omicron Raises Another Dilemma for Africa. *Thisdaylive.* https://www.thisdaylive.com/index.php/2021/12/03/as-omicron-raises-another-dilemma-for-africa/

Chinedu, E. (2021 July 30). Nigeria: Aviation Industry's Slow Recovery From Covid-19 Devastation. *Thisdaylive.* https://www.thisdaylive.com

Chin, W. W., & Dibbern, J. (2010). An introduction to a permutation based procedure for multi-group PLS analysis: Results of tests of differences on simulated data and a cross cultural analysis of the sourcing of information system services between Germany and the USA. In *Handbook of partial least squares* (pp. 171–193). Springer. doi:10.1007/978-3-540-32827-8_8

Cho, W., Windle, R., & Dresner, M. (2017). The impact of operational exposure and value-of-time on customer choice: Evidence from the airline industry. *Transportation Research Part A, Policy and Practice, 103,* 455–471.

Chow, C. K. W., & Tsui, W. H. K. (2017). Organizational learning, operating costs and airline consolidation policy in the Chinese airline industry. *Journal of Air Transport Management, 63,* 108–118. doi:10.1016/j.jairtraman.2017.06.018

Cho, Y., & McLean, G. (2009). Successful IT start-ups' HRD practices: Four cases in South Korea. *Journal of European Industrial Training, 33*(2), 125–141. doi:10.1108/03090590910939030

Chukwuma, M., & Wole, O. (2020 September 17). Fake COVID-19 Certificates bog air travel. *The Guardian.* https://guardian.ng/news/fake-covid-19-certifcates-bog-air-travel/

CIGEN. (2021, February 8). Retrieved from cigen.com: https://www.cigen.com.au/6-real-world-use-cases-robotic-process-automation-aviation/

Civil Aviation Authority Singapore (CAAS). (2017). *Air Operator Certificate Requirements.* Civil Aviation Authority Singapore. Retrieved from: https://www.caas.gov.sg

Clarke, V., & Braun, V. (2016). Thematic analysis. *The Journal of Positive Psychology, 12*(3), 297–298. doi:10.1080/17439760.2016.1262613

Clegg, C. (2010). The Aviation Industry and the Transmission of Communicable Disease: The Case of H1N1 Swine Influenza. *J. Air L. & Com., 75*(437). https://scholar.smu.edu/jalc/vol75/iss2/5

Cobena, M., Gallego, A., & Casanueva, C. (2019). Diversity in airline alliance portfolio configuartion. *Journal of Air Transport Management, 75,* 16–26. doi:10.1016/j.jairtraman.2018.11.004

Cogaltay, N., Yalcin, M., & Karadag, E. (2016). Educational Leadership and Job Satisfaction of Teachers: A Meta-Analysis Study on the Studies Published between 2000 and 2016 in Turkey. *Eurasian Journal of Educational Research, 26*(62), 255–282. doi:10.14689/ejer.2016.62.13

Cohen, M. Z., Kahn, D. L., & Steeves, R. H. (2000). *Hermeneutic phenomenological research: A practical guide for nurse researchers.* Sage Publications. doi:10.4135/9781452232768

Coldren, G., Koppelman, F. S., Kasturirangan, K., & Mukherjee, A. (2003). Modeling aggregate air-travel itinerary shares: Logit model development at a major US airline. *Journal of Air Transport Management, 6,* 361–369.

Cole, M. (2014). Towards proactive airport security management: Supporting decision making through systematic threat scenario assessment. *Journal of Air Transport Management, 35,* 12–18. doi:10.1016/j.jairtraman.2013.11.002

Cooper, G. E. (1980). Resource management the flightdeck. In *Proceedings of a NASNIndustry Workshop* (Rep. No. NASA CP-2120). Moffett Field, CA: NASA-Ames Research Center.

Cooper, M. D. (2000). Towards a model of safety culture. *Safety Science*, *36*(2), 111–136. doi:10.1016/S0925-7535(00)00035-7

Coulter, M. (2012). *Strategic Management in Action*. Pearson Education.

Crew Resource Management (CRM). (2021, December 8). *SKYbrary Aviation Safety*. Retrieved January 28, 2022, from https://skybrary.aero/articles/crew-resource-management-crm

Cui, Y., Duenyas, I., & Sahin, O. (2018). Unbundling of ancillary service: How does price discrimination of main service matter? *Manufacturing & Service Operations Management*, *20*(3), 455–466. doi:10.1287/msom.2017.0646

Curran, A. (2020). *The History of the Kangaroo Route*. Simple Flying. https://simpleflying.com/kangaroo-route-history/

Dagger, T. S., Danaher, P. J., Sweeney, J. C., & McColl-Kennedy, J. R. (2013). Selective halo effects arising from improving the interpersonal skills of frontline employees. *Journal of Service Research*, *16*(4), 488–502. doi:10.1177/1094670513481406

Dan Maurino, M. C. (2010). Human Factors in Aviation: An Overview. In E. Salas (Ed.), *Human Factors in Aviation* (p. 5). Elsevier.

Daniel, E., & Maurino, P. S. (2010). Crew Resource. In Human Factors in Transportation (pp. 10-4 to 10-5). Boca Raton, FL: CRC Press.

David Meister, V. G. (2010). Measurement in Aviation Systems. In *V. D. John A. Wise, Handbook of Aviation Human Factors* (pp. 9–11). CRC Press, Taylor & Francis Group.

David, B. (2019). Transportation Systems. Transportation Engineering and Planning. Encyclopedia of Life Support System, 1.

David, J. C. (2020). *Coronavirus Disease 2019 (COVID-19)*. Medscape. https://emedicine.medscape.com/article/2500114-overview

David, F. R. (2011). *Strategic Management Concepts And Cases*. Phi Learning.

David, F., & David, F. (2017). *Strategic Management: A Competitive Advantage Approach, Concepts and Cases*. Pearson Education Limited.

De Boer, E. (2018). The Different Types of Frequent Flyer Programs. In Strategy in Airline Loyalty. Frequent Flyer Programs. (pp. 29-57). Palgrave Macmillan. doi:10.1007/978-3-319-62600-0_2

de Groot, R. J., Baker, S. C., Baric, R. S., Brown, C. S., Drosten, C., Enjuanes, L., Fouchier, R. A., Galiano, M., Gorbalenya, A. E., Memish, Z. A., Perlman, S., Poon, L. L., Snijder, E. J., Stephens, G. M., Woo, P. C., Zaki, A. M., Zambon, M., & Ziebuhr, J. (2013). Middle East respiratory syndrome coronavirus (MERS-CoV): Announcement of the Coronavirus Study Group. *Journal of Virology*, *87*(14), 7790–7792. doi:10.1128/JVI.01244-13 PMID:23678167

De Man, A. P., & Luvison, D. (2019). Collaborative business models: Aligning and operationalizing alliances. *Business Horizons*, *62*(4), 473–482. doi:10.1016/j.bushor.2019.02.004

De Man, A. P., Roijakkers, N., & De Graauw, H. (2010). Managing dynamics through robust alliance governance structures: The case of KLM and Northwest Airlines. *European Management Journal*, *28*(3), 171–181. doi:10.1016/j.emj.2009.11.001

Compilation of References

Decision-Making (OGHFA BN). (2022, February 13). *SKYbrary Aviation Safety*. Retrieved February 14, 2022, from https://skybrary.aero/articles/decision-making-oghfa-bn#:%7E:text=The%20decision%2Dmaking%20process%20produces,the%20conduct%20of%20a%20flight

Decret nr. 195 din 16 martie 2020. Monitorul Oficial nr. 212 (2020) https://legislatie.just.ro/Public/DetaliiDocumentAfis/223831

Decreto do Presidente da República n.º 14-A/2020. Diário da República: Série I n.º 55 (2020) https://dre.pt/pesquisa/-/search/130399862/details/maximized

Dekker, S. W. (2009). The high reliability organization perspective. In Human factors in aviation (2nd ed., pp. 123–146). New York, NY: Wiley.

Delta Flight Museum. (2022). *Family Tree*. Delta Flight Museum. https://www.deltamuseum.org/exhibits/delta-history/family-tree/pan-am

Dempsey, C. A. (1985). *50 years of research on man in flight*. Wright-Patterson AFB.

Dennis, N. (2000). Scheduling issues and network strategies for international airline alliances. *Journal of Air Transport*, *11*(3), 175–183. doi:10.1016/j.jairtraman.2004.07.004

Dennis, N. (2005). Industry consolidation and future airline network structures in Europe. *Journal of Air Transport Management*, *6*(2), 75–85. doi:10.1016/S0969-6997(99)00027-7

Denton, N., & Dennis, N. (2000). Airline franchising in Europe: Benefits and disbenefits to airlines and consumers. *Journal of Air Transport Management*, *6*(4), 179–190. doi:10.1016/S0969-6997(00)00010-7

DeSantis, J. A. (2013). Engines Turn or Passengers Swim: A Case Study of How ETOPS Improved Safety and Economics in Aviation. *Journal of Air Law and Commerce*, *77*(4), 1–68.

DeSarbo, W. S., Di Benedetto, C. A., Song, M., & Sinha, I. (2005). Revisiting the Miles and Snow Strategic Framework: Uncovering Interrelationships Between Strategic Types, Capabilities, Environmental Uncertainty, and Firm Performance. *Strategic Management Journal*, *26*(1), 47–74. doi:10.1002mj.431

Dess, G. G., McNamara, G., Eisner, A. B., & Lee, S. (2019). *Strategic management: Text and cases*. McGraw-Hill Education.

Devine, P. J., Lee, N., Jones, R. M., & Tyson, W. J. (1993). *An Introduction to Industrial Economics* (4th ed.). Routledge.

Dick, A. S., & Basu, K. (1994). Customer loyalty: Toward an integrated conceptual framework. *Journal of the Academy of Marketing Science*, *22*(2), 99–113. doi:10.1177/0092070394222001

Dickinson, T. L., & McIntyre, R. M. (1997). *A conceptual framework for teamwork measurement. In Team performance assessment and measurement: Theory, methods, and applications*. Lawrence Erlbaum Associates Publishers.

Dinçer, Ö. (1998). *Stratejik Yönetim ve İşletme Politikası*. Beta Publishing.

Dirani, K., Abadi, M., Alizadeh, A., Barhate, B., Garza, R. C., Gunasekara, N., Ghassan, I., & Majzun, Z. (2020). Leadership competencies and the essential role of human resource development in times of crisis: A response to Covid-19 pandemic. *Human Resource Development International*, *23*(4), 380–294. doi:10.1080/13678868.2020.1780078

Dixon, J., Belnap, C., Albrecht, C., & Lee, K. (2010). The importance of soft skills. *Corporate Finance Review*, *14*(6), 35.

Doganis, R. (2002). *Flying Off Course: the Economics of International Airlines*. Routledge.

Doganis, R. (2005). *The Airline Business*. Routledge. doi:10.4324/9780203596807

Doganis, R. (2019). *Flying Off Course: airline economics and marketing* (5th ed.). Routledge. doi:10.4324/9781315402987

Doherty, B. (2020). *Thousands of Australians stranded overseas as countries close borders over Covid-19 fears*. https://www.theguardian.com/world/2020/mar/20/thousands-of-australians-

Dostaler, I., & Flouris, T. (2006). Stuck In the Middle Revisited: The Case of the Airline Industry. *Journal of Aviation/Aerospace Education Research*, *15*(2), 33–45. doi:10.15394/jaaer.2006.1502

Doyle, F., & Cosgrove, J. (2019). Steps towards digitization of manufacturing in an SME environment. *Proc. Manuf.*, *38*, 540–547. doi:10.1016/j.promfg.2020.01.068

Drescher, C. (2017). Why Airplanes Sometimes Fly Over the North Pole. *Condé Nast Traveler*. https://www.cntraveler.com/story/why-airplanes-sometimes-fly-over-the-north-pole

Dresner, M., & Windle, R. (1996). Alliances and Code-Sharing in the International Airline Industry. *Built Environment*, *22*(3), 201–211.

Drogoul, F., & Cabon, P. (2020). *Post COVID-19 fatigue management for ATCOs*. ResearchGate.

Duenyas, I. (2015). *Unbundling of Ancillary Service: How Does Price Discrimination of Main Service Matter?* Academic Press.

EASA. (2021a). *Review of Aviation Safety Issues Arising from the COVID-19 Pandemic-V2, April 2021 Review of Aviation Safety Issues Arising from the COVID-19 Pandemic Version 2-April, 2021*. https://www.easa.europa.eu/contact-us

EASA. (2021b). *Safety Information Bulletin Subject: Contamination of Air Data Systems During Aircraft Parking and / or Storage due to the COVID-19 Pandemic*. https://www.easa.europa.eu/sites/default/files/dfu/easa_sib_2020-14r1_1.pdf?msclkid=e2891536bbd511ec8be890d3d3d928f2

Economic Times. (2022). Bird Strike at Indian Airports. *Economic Times*. https://economictimes.indiatimes.com/industry/transportation/airlines/-aviation/limited-flights-but-bird-animal-strike-incidents-rose-significantly-at-indian-airports-in-2021/articleshow/90470596.cms?utm_source=contentofinterest&utm_medium=text&utm_campaign=cppst

Economics, O. (2012). *Nigeria Country Report: Economic Benefits from Air Transport in Nigeria*. Oxford Economics.

Eduardo Salas, M. L. (2010). Team Dynamics at 35,000 Feet. In D. M. Eduardo Salas (Ed.), Human Factors in Aviation (pp. 250-291). Elsevier.

Eduardo Salas, D. M. (2010). *Human Factors in Aviation*. Academic Press, Elsevier.

Egmond, R. v., & Westra, A. (2019). *Shell and aviation. The story of more than a century of collaboration*. Shell International B.V. HR.

Ellis, C. (2018). *PAL's non-stop Manila – New York JFK flight among world's longest*. Aerotime Hub. https://www.aerotime.aero/21979-pal-s-non-stop-manila-new-york-jfk-flight-among-world-s-longest

Elmelund-Præstekær, C., & Klitgaard, M. (2012). Policy or institution? The political choice of retrenchment strategy. *Journal of European Public Policy*, *19*(7), 1089–1107. doi:10.1080/13501763.2012.672112

Emirates. (2022). *About Us*. https://www.emirates.com/english/about-us/group-company/

Endsley, M. R. (1995b). Measurement of situation awareness in dynamic systems. *Human Factors*, *37*(1), 65–84. doi:10.1518/001872095779049499

Enoma, A., Allen, S., & Enoma, A. (2009). Airport redesign for safety and security: Case studies of three Scottish airports. *International Journal of Strategic Property Management*, *13*(2), 103–116.

Compilation of References

Erdoğan, B. (2019). Airline Alliances and Its Effects On Airlines: Turkish Airlines Case. *The Journal of Social Science*, *33*, 375–395.

Eurocontrol. (2021). *EUROCONTROL Data Snapshot #4 on CO_2 emissions by flight distance*. Eurocontrol. https://www.eurocontrol.int/publication/eurocontrol-data-snapshot-co2-emissions-flight-distance

European Commission. (2019). *Orientations towards the first Strategic Plan implementing the research and innovation framework programme Horizon Europe*. https://ec.europa.eu/research/pdf/horizon-europe/ec_rtd_orientations-towards-the-strategic-planning.pdf

European Council. (2020a). *Council Conclusions on COVID-19*. https://data.consilium.europa.eu/doc/document/ST-6038-2020-INIT/en/pdf

European Council. (2020b). *COVID-19 outbreak: the presidency steps up EU response by triggering full activation mode of IPCR*. https://www.consilium.europa.eu/en/press/press-releases/2020/03/02/covid-19-outbreak-the-presidency-steps-up-eu-response-by-triggering-full- activation-mode-of-ipcr

European Council. (2020c). *COVID-19: EU adopts slot waiver to help airlines*. https://www.consilium.europa.eu/en/press/press-releases/2020/03/30/covid-19-eu-adopts-slot-waiver-to-help-airlines

FAA. (2020). *Federal Aviation Administration National Part 139 Cert Alert*. FAA.

Fahimnia, B., & Jabbarzadeh, A. (2016). Marrying supply chain sustainability and resilience: A match made in heaven. *Transportation Research Part E, Logistics and Transportation Review*, *91*, 306–324. doi:10.1016/j.tre.2016.02.007

Fan, T., Vigeant-Langlois, L., Geissler, C., Bosler, B., & Wilmking, J. (2001). Evolution of global airline strategic alliance and consolidation in the twenty-first century. *Journal of Air Transport Management*, *7*(6), 349–360. doi:10.1016/S0969-6997(01)00027-8

Faraway, J., & Chatfield, C. (2008). Time series forecasting with neural networks: A comparative study using the airline data. *Journal of the Royal Statistical Society Applied Statistic Series C*, *47*(2), 231–250.

Farooq, M. S., Salam, M., Fayolle, A., Jaafar, N., & Ayupp, K. (2018). Impact of service quality on customer satisfaction in Malaysia airlines: A PLS-SEM approach. *Journal of Air Transport Management*, *67*, 169–180. doi:10.1016/j.jairtraman.2017.12.008

Fearn-Banks, K. (2011). *Crisis communications. A casebook approaches*. Routledge.

Featsystems. (n.d.). Retrieved from featsystems.com: https://www.featsystems.com/rpa-airline

Feiqi Huang, M. A. (2019). Applying robotic process automation (RPA) in auditing: A framework. *International Journal of Accounting Information Systems*, 11.

Feldscher, K. (2019). *The potentially unfriendly skies*. Harvard T.H Chan. https://www.hsph.harvard.edu/news/features/the-potentially-unfriendly-skies/

Felix, O. (2021, December 14). *Nigeria eyes diplomacy to resolve Omicron travel restrictions*. CNBCAFRICA. https://www.cnbcafrica.com/2021/nigeria-eyes-diplomatic-to-resovle-omicron-travel-restrictions/amp

Felix, R. (2021, February 12), Pandemic Results in Historic Decline in Air Passenger Traffic. *The Wire*. https://m.thewire.in/article/business/aviation-industry-covid-19/amp

Fereday, J., & Muir-Cochrane, E. (2006). Demonstrating rigor using thematic analysis: A hybrid approach of inductive and deductive coding and theme development. *International Journal of Qualitative Methods*, *5*(1), 80–92. doi:10.1177/160940690600500107

Fikayo, O. (2020, May 6). Nigerian govt. reveals worst hit sector from COVID-19. *Daily Post*. https://www.google.com/amp/s/dailypost.ng/2020/05/06/nigerian-govt-revealed-worst-hit-sector-from-covid-19/%3famp

Fitts, P. M. (1947). *Psychological aspects of instrument display. I. Analysis of 270 "pilot-error" experiences in reading and interpreting aircraft instruments* (Rep. No. TSEAA-694-12A). Dayton, OH: Aeromedical Laboratory, Air Materiel Command.

Flouris, T. G., & Oswald, S. L. (2016). *Designing and executing strategy in aviation management*. Routledge. doi:10.4324/9781315576718

Fontanet-Pérez, P., Vázquez, X. H., & Carou, D. (2022). The impact of the COVID-19 crisis on the US airline market: Are current business models equipped for upcoming changes in the air transport sector? *Case Studies on Transport Policy*, *10*(1), 647–656. doi:10.1016/j.cstp.2022.01.025

Fornell, C., & Larcker, D. F. (1981). Evaluating structural equation models with unobservable variables and measurement error. *JMR, Journal of Marketing Research*, *18*(1), 39–50.

Foroohar, R. (2018). *Corporate elites are overlooking deglobalization*. https://www.ft.com/content/df3ded82-ce32-11e8-b276-b9069bde0956

Forsyth, P., King, J., Rodoifo, C. L., & Trace, K. (2004). *Preparing ASEAN for open sky. AADCP Regional Economic Policy Support Facility Research Project 02/008*. Monash International Pty Ltd.

Forsyth, P., Niemeier, H.-M., & Wolf, H. (2011). Airport alliances and mergers – Structural change in the airport industry? *Journal of Air Transport Management*, *17*(1), 49–56. doi:10.1016/j.jairtraman.2010.10.011

Foster, H. D. (1993). Resilience Theory and System Evaluation. Verification and Validation of Complex Systems: Human Factors Issues. Academic Press.

Foushee, H. (1982). The role of communications, socio-psychological, and personality factors in the maintenance of crew coordination. *Aviation, Space, and Environmental Medicine*, *53*, 1062–1066. PMID:7150164

Foushee, H., & Helmreich, R. (1988). Group interaction and flight crew performance. In E. Wiener & D. Nagel (Eds.), *Human factors in aviation* (pp. 189–227). Academic Press.

Fraher, A. L. (2011). *Thinking through crisis: Improving teamwork and leadership in high-risk fields*. Academic Press.

Francis, G., Dennis, N., Ison, S., & Humphreys, I. (2007). The transferability of the low-cost model to long-haul airline operations. *Tourism Management*, *28*(2), 391–398. doi:10.1016/j.tourman.2006.04.014

Franzosi, R. (2008). Content analysis: Objective, systematic, and quantitative description of content. *Content Analysis*, *1*(1), 21-49.

Friedman, T. (2009, October 10). *Pigs in a Barrel*. Retrieved from https://taylorfriedman.wordpress.com/2009/10/10/fear-mongering-in-the-21st-century-newsroom/

Friesen, M. (2005, March). *Capital Market's Assessment of European Airline Mergers and Acquisitions–The Case of Air France and KLM* [Paper presentation]. In *5th Swiss Transport Research Conference*, Monte Verità/Ascona.

Gayle, P. G. (2008). An Empirical Analysis of the Competitive Effects of the Delta/Continental/Northwest Code-Share Alliance. *The Journal of Law & Economics*, *51*(4), 743–766. doi:10.1086/595865

Gentles, S. J., Charles, C., Ploeg, J., & McKibbon, K. A. (2015). Sampling in qualitative research: Insights from an overview of the methods literature. *Qualitative Report*, *20*(11), 1772–1789. doi:10.46743/2160-3715/2015.2373

Compilation of References

George, D., & Mallery, P. (2019). *IBM SPSS statistics 26 step by step: A simple guide and reference*. Routledge. doi:10.4324/9780429056765

Gherardi, S. (2006). *Organizational Knowledge: The Texture of Workplace Learning*. Wiley-Blackwell.

Giacomini, M. K., & Cook, D. J.Evidence-Based Medicine Working Group. (2000). Users' guides to the medical literature: XXIII. Qualitative research in health Care B. What are the results and how do they help me care for my patients? *Journal of the American Medical Association*, *284*(4), 478–482. doi:10.1001/jama.284.4.478 PMID:10904512

Gibcus, P., & Kemp, R. G. M. (2003). *Strategy and Small Firm Performance*. Research Report H200208, SCALES Scientific Analysis of Entrepreneurship and SMEs, Netherlands: Zoetermeer (EIM, Business & Policy Research).

Gilbert, D. (1996). *Airlines*. Paul Chapman Publishing.

Gilbert, D., & Wong, R. K. (2003). Passenger expectations and airline services: A Hong Kong based study. *Tourism Management*, *24*(5), 519–532.

Gillen, D. (2006). Airline business models and networks: Regulation, competition and evolution in aviation markets. *Review of Network Economics*, *5*(4), 366–385. doi:10.2202/1446-9022.1103

Gillen, D., & Morrison, W. G. (2005). Regulation, competition and network evolution in aviation. *Journal of Air Transport Management*, *11*(3), 161–174. doi:10.1016/j.jairtraman.2005.03.002 PMID:32572312

Gillen, D., & Morrison, W. G. (2015). Aviation security: Costing, pricing, finance and performance. *Journal of Air Transport Management*, *48*, 1–12. doi:10.1016/j.jairtraman.2014.12.005

Gilstrap, J. (2019, November 1). *Importance of Communication in Aviation. E2b Calibration Aerospace*. Retrieved February 14, 2022, from https://calibration.aero/importance-of-communication-in-aviation/

Gligor, D. M. (2016). The Role of Supply Chain Agility in Achieving Supply Chain Fit. *Decision Sciences*, *47*(3), 524–553. doi:10.1111/deci.12205

Gligor, D. M., Esmark, C. L., & Holcomb, M. C. (2015). Performance outcomes of supply chain agility: When should you be agile? *Journal of Operations Management*, *33-34*(1), 71–82. doi:10.1016/j.jom.2014.10.008

Global Aviation Industry High-Level Group. (2019). *Aviation Benefits Report 8*. Author.

Glueck, W. F., & Jauch, L. R. (1984). *Business Policy and Strategic Management*. McGraw-Hill.

Gogalniceanu, P., Calder, F., Callaghan, C., Sevdalis, N., & Mamode, N. (2021). Surgeons Are Not Pilots: Is the Aviation Safety Paradigm Relevant to Modern Surgical Practice? *Journal of Surgical Education*, *78*(5), 1393–1399. doi:10.1016/j.jsurg.2021.01.016 PMID:33579654

Goh, K., & Uncles, M. (2003). The benefits of airline global alliances: An empirical assessment of the perceptions of business travelers. *Transportation Research Part A, Policy and Practice*, *37*(6), 479–497. doi:10.1016/S0965-8564(02)00054-X

Gold, A. H., Malhotra, A., & Segars, A. H. (2001). Knowledge Management: An Organizational Capabilities Perspective. *Journal of Management Information Systems*, *18*(1), 185–214. doi:10.1080/07421222.2001.11045669

Goll, I., Johnson, N., & Rasheed, A. (2007). Knowledge Capability, Strategic Change, and Firm Performance: The Moderating Role of the Environment. *Management Decision*, *45*, 161-179. doi:10.1108/00251740710727223

Good, W., & Jebbin, M. F. (2015). Transportation and National Development. *Journal of Economics and Sustainable Development*, *6*(9).

Gostin, L. O., Bayer, R., & Fairchild, A. L. (2003). Ethical and Legal Challenges Posed by Severe Acute Respiratory Syndrome: Implications for the Control of Severe Infectious Disease Threats. *Journal of the American Medical Association*, *290*(24), 3229–3237.

Grace, G. (2020). *Assessing the Impact of COVID-19 on Africa's Economic Development*. United Nations Conference on Trade and Development. UNCTAD/ALDC/MISC/2020/3.

Graham, A. (2014). *Managing Airports: An International Perspective*. Routledge.

Grandinetti, R. (2016). Absorptive capacity and knowledge management in small and medium enterprises. *Knowledge Management Research and Practice*, *14*(2), 159–168. doi:10.1057/kmrp.2016.2

Grant, R. (2005). *Contemporary Strategy Analysis*. Backwell Publishing.

Grant, R. M. (2016). *Contemporary strategy analysis: Text and cases edition*. John Wiley & Sons.

Great Larousse. (1986). *Dictionary and Encyclopedia* (Vol. 16). Gelisim Publishing.

Green, P. (2021, March 8). *The Importance of Teamwork from a Cabin Crew Perspective*. CareerAddict. Retrieved February 14, 2022, from https://www.careeraddict.com/the-importance-of-teamwork-from-a-cabin-crew-perspective

Griffith, J. C., Roberts, D. L., & Ph.D., R. T. (2015). A Meta-Analysis of Crew Resource Management/Incident. *Journal of Aviation/Aerospace Education & Research (JAAER)*, *25*(1), 1-25.

Grimme, W., Bingemer, S., & Maerten, S. (2020). An analysis of the prospects of ultra-long-haul airline operations using passenger demand data. *Transportation Research Procedia*, *51*, 208–216.

Gronroos, C. (2008). Service logic revisited: Who creates value? And who co-creates? *European Business Review*, *20*(4), 298–314. doi:10.1108/09555340810886585

Gross, B., Rusin, L., Kiesewetter, J., Zottmann, J. M., Fischer, M. R., Prückner, S., & Zech, A. (2018). *Crew resource management training in healthcare: A systematic review of intervention design, training conditions and evaluation*. BMJ Open.

Group, D. H. (2011). *Investigation of the macondo well blowout disaster*. Retrieved from https://ccrm.berkeley.edu/pdfs_papers/bea_pdfs/dhsgfinalreportmarch2011-tag.pdf

Grundy, M., & Moxon, R. (2013). The Effectiveness of Airline Crisis Management on Brand Protection: A Case Study of British Airways. *Journal of Air Transport Management*, *28*, 55–61. doi:10.1016/j.jairtraman.2012.12.011

Grundy, T. (2006). Rethinking and Reinventing Michael Porter's Five Forces Model. *Strategic Change*, *15*(5), 213–229. doi:10.1002/jsc.764

Gruneberg, M. M. (1979). *Understand job satisfaction*. The Macmillan Press Ltd. doi:10.1007/978-1-349-03952-4

Grunert, K. G., & Grunert, S. C. (1995). Measuring Subjective Meaning Structures by the Laddering Method: Theoretical Considerations and Methodological Problems. *International Journal of Research in Marketing*, *12*(3), 209–225. doi:10.1016/0167-8116(95)00022-T

Gudmundsson, S. V., de Boer, E. R., & Lechner, C. (2002). Integrating frequent flyer programs in multilateral airline alliances. *Journal of Air Transport Management*, *8*(6), 409–417. doi:10.1016/S0969-6997(02)00043-1

Gudmundsson, S., & Rhoades, D. (2001). Airline alliance survival analysis: Typology, strategy and duration. *Transport Policy*, *8*(3), 209–218. doi:10.1016/S0967-070X(01)00016-6

Compilation of References

Gunasekaran, A., Lai, K., & Edwin Cheng, T. C. (2008). Responsive supply chain: A competitive strategy in a networked economy. *Omega*, *36*(4), 549–564. doi:10.1016/j.omega.2006.12.002

Gunessee, S., Subramanian, N., & Ning, K. (2018). Natural disasters, PC supply chain and corporate performance. *International Journal of Operations & Production Management*, *38*(9), 1796–1814. doi:10.1108/IJOPM-12-2016-0705

Guo, Q., Wang, J., Estill, J., Lan, H., Zhang, J., Wu, S., Yao, J., Yan, X., & Chen, Y. (2022). Risk of COVID-19 Transmission Aboard Aircraft: An Epidemiological Analysis Based on the National Health Information Platform. *International Journal of Infectious Diseases*, *118*, 270–276. doi:10.1016/j.ijid.2022.03.024 PMID:35331931

Gupta, D. (2008). Flexible carrier–forwarder contracts for air cargo business. *Journal of Revenue and Pricing Management*, *7*(4), 341–356. doi:10.1057/rpm.2008.29

Gutman, J. (1982). A Means-End Chain Model Based on Consumer Categorization Processes. *Journal of Marketing*, *46*(2), 60–72. doi:10.1177/002224298204600207

Habermann, M., Blackhurst, J., & Metcalf, A. Y. (2015). Keep Your Friends Close? Supply Chain Design and Disruption Risk. *Decision Sciences*, *46*(3), 491–526. doi:10.1111/deci.12138

Hackman, J. R., & Oldham, G. R. (1976). Motivation through the design of work: Test of a theory. *Organizational Behavior and Human Performance*, *16*(2), 250–279. doi:10.1016/0030-5073(76)90016-7

Hagemann, V., Kluge, A., & Greve, J. (2012). Measuring the effects of team resource management training for the fire service. *Human Factors and Ergonomics Society Annual Meeting*. 10.1037/e572172013-504

Hair, J. F., Black, W. C., Babin, B. J., & Anderson, R. E. (2010). *Multivariate Data Analysis: A Global Perspective* (7th ed.). Pearson Prentice Hall Publishing.

Ha, J., & Jang, S. (2013). Attributes, consequences, and consumer values: A means-end chain approach across restaurant segments. *International Journal of Contemporary Hospitality Management*, *25*(3), 383–409. doi:10.1108/09596111311311035

Hakeem, J. (2021 September 22). *Challenging COVID-19 Protocols air travellers must know about*. https://www.premiumtimesng.com/opinion/486310-challenging-covid-19-protocols-airtravellers-must-know-about-by-hakeem-jamiu.html

Haleem, O. (2020 December 10). NCAA: Increase in air fares caused by COVID-19 pandemic. *The Cable*. https://www.thecable.ng/ncaa-increase-in-fares-caused-by-covid-19-pandemic/amp

Hallstedt, S. I., Thompson, A. W., & Lindahl, P. (2013). Key elements for implementing a strategic sustainability perspective in the product innovation process. *Journal of Cleaner Production*, *51*, 277–288. doi:10.1016/j.jclepro.2013.01.043

Hamilton, I. W., Kazem, N. M. L., He, X., & Dumolo, D. (2013). Practical human factors integration in the nuclear industry. In *Cognition* (pp. 5–12). Technology & Work.

Hapsari, R., Clemes, M. D., & Dean, D. (2017). The impact of service quality, customer engagement and selected marketing constructs on airline passenger loyalty. *International Journal of Quality and Service Sciences*, *9*(1), 21–40. doi:10.1108/IJQSS-07-2016-0048

Hardie, J. A., & Brennan, P. A. (2020). Are You surgically current? Lessons from aviation for returning to non-urgent surgery following COVID-19. *Journal of Oral and Maxillofacial Surgery*.

Hassan, T. H., & Salem, A. E. (2021). Impact of Service Quality of Low-Cost Carriers on Airline Image and Consumers' Satisfaction and Loyalty during the COVID-19 Outbreak. *International Journal of Environmental Research and Public Health*, *19*(1), 83. doi:10.3390/ijerph19010083 PMID:35010341

Hazledine, T. (2011). Legacy Carriers Fight Back: Pricing and Product Differentiation in Modern Airline Marketing. *Journal of Air Transport Management, 17*(2), 130–135. doi:10.1016/j.jairtraman.2010.10.008

Heath, L., & Palenchar, M. (2009). Strategic issues management. *Sage (Atlanta, Ga.)*.

Hecht, H. (2004). Systems reliability and failure prevention. In H. Hecht (Ed.), *Systems reliability and failure prevention*. Artech House.

Heinonen, K., & Strandvik, T. (2009). Monitoring value-in-use of e-service. *Journal of Service Management, 20*(1), 33–51. doi:10.1108/09564230910936841

Heinonen, K., Strandvik, T., Mickelsson, K. J., Edvardsson, B., Sundström, E., & Andersson, P. (2010). A customer-dominant logic of service. *Journal of Service Management, 21*(4), 531–548. doi:10.1108/09564231011066088

Helfat, C. E., & Peteraf, M. A. (2003). The dynamic resource-based view: Capability lifecycles. *Strategic Management Journal, 24*(10), 997–1010. doi:10.1002mj.332

Helmreich, R. L. (1999). *The Line/LOS Checklist, Version 6.0: A checklist for human factors skills assessment, a log for external threats, and a worksheet for flightcrew error management.* Austin, TX: The University of Texas Team Research Project Technical Report 99-01.

Helmreich, R. L. (1992). Fifteen years of CRM wars: A report from the trenches. In *Towards 2000—future directions and new solutions* (pp. 73–88). The Australian Aviation Psychology Association.

Helmreich, R. L., & Foushee, H. C. (2010). Training, Why CRM? Empirical and Theoretical Bases of Human Factors. In B. G. Kanki, R. L. Helmreich, & J. Anca (Eds.), *Crew Resource Management*. Academic Press, Elsevier. doi:10.1016/B978-0-12-374946-8.10001-9

Helmreich, R. L., & Wilhelm, J. A. (1991). Outcomes of Crew Resource Management Training. *The International Journal of Aviation Psychology, 1*(4), 287–300. doi:10.120715327108ijap0104_3 PMID:11537899

Helms, M. M., Dibrell, C., & Wright, P. (1997). Competitive Strategies and Business Performance: Evidence from the Adhesives and Sealants Industry. *Management Decision, 35*(9), 689–703. doi:10.1108/00251749710186531

He, Q., Meadows, M., Angwin, D., Gomes, E., & Child, J. (2020). Strategic Alliance Research in the Era of Digital Transformation: Perspectives on Future Research. *British Journal of Management, 31*(3), 589–617. doi:10.1111/1467-8551.12406

Heracleous, L., & Wirtz, J. (2009). Strategy and Organization at Singapore Airlines: Achieving Sustainable Advantage Through Dual Strategy. *Journal of Air Transport Management, 15*(6), 274–279. doi:10.1016/j.jairtraman.2008.11.011

Higginbottom, G. (2004). Sampling issues in qualitative research. *Nurse Researcher, 12*(1), 7–19. doi:10.7748/nr2004.07.12.1.7.c5927 PMID:15493211

Hirche, C., & Kneser, U. (2021). What We Really can Learn From Aviation: Checklist-based Team Time-Out in Conjunction With Interpersonal Competence Training for the Daily Management of a Surgical Department. *Surgical Innovation, 28*(5), 642–646. doi:10.1177/15533506211018439 PMID:34319815

Hitt, M. A., Ireland, R. D., & Hoskisson, R. E. (2003). *Strategic Management: Competitiveness and Globalization* (5th ed.). Thomson South-Western.

Hitt, M. A., Ireland, R. D., & Hoskisson, R. E. (2020). *Strategic management: Concepts and Cases: Competitiveness and globalization*. Cengage Learning.

Compilation of References

Hoeller, S.-C. (2015). Here's the difference between a nonstop and direct flight. *Business Insider*. https://www.businessinsider.com/the-difference-between-a-nonstop-and-direct-flight-2015-9

Hofmann, K. (2012). ANA begins first 787 long-haul service. *Aviation Week*. Retreived from: https://aviationweek.com/air-transport/airports-routes/ana-begins-first-787-long-haul-service

Hollingham, R. (2017). *The British airliner that changed the world*. South African History Online. https://www.bbc.com/future/article/20170404-the-british-airliner-that-changed-the-world

Hollnagel, E., Woods, D., & Leveson, N. (2006). *Resilience Engineering: Concepts and Precepts*. Academic Press.

Holmström, J., & Partanen, J. (2014). Digital manufacturing-driven transformations of service supply chains for complex products. *Supply Chain Management, 19*(4), 421–430. doi:10.1108/SCM-10-2013-0387

Holtbrugge, D., Wilson, S., & Berg, N. (2006). Human resource management at Star Alliance: Pressures for standardization and differentiation. *Journal of Air Transport Management, 12*(6), 306–312. doi:10.1016/j.jairtraman.2006.07.006

Homburg, C., Jozić, D., & Kuehnl, C. (2017). Customer experience management: Toward implementing an evolving marketing concept. *Journal of the Academy of Marketing Science, 45*(3), 377–401. doi:10.100711747-015-0460-7

Hunt, J., & Truong, D. (2019). Low-fare flights across the Atlantic: Impact of low-cost, long- haul trans-Atlantic flights on passenger choice of Carrier. *Journal of Air Transport Management, 75*, 170–184.

Hussain, R., Al Nasser, A., & Hussain, Y. K. (2015). Service quality and customer satisfaction of a UAE-based airline: An empirical investigation. *Journal of Air Transport Management, 42*, 167–175. doi:10.1016/j.jairtraman.2014.10.001

Hwang, J., & Hyun, S. S. (2017). First-class airline travellers' perception of luxury goods and its effect on loyalty formation. *Current Issues in Tourism, 20*(5), 497–520. doi:10.1080/13683500.2014.918941

Hwang, J., & Lyu, S. O. (2018). Understanding first-class passengers' luxury value perceptions in the US airline industry. *Tourism Management Perspectives, 28*, 29–40. doi:10.1016/j.tmp.2018.07.001

Hwang, J., & Ok, C. (2013). The antecedents and consequence of consumer attitudes toward restaurant brands: A comparative study between casual and fine dining restaurants. *International Journal of Hospitality Management, 33*(1), 121–131. doi:10.1016/j.ijhm.2012.05.002

IAFC. (2005). Crew resource management manual. Fairfax, VA: IAFC.

IATA, ICAO, & IFALPA. (2015). Fatigue Risk Management Systems (FRMS) implementation Guide for Operators. IATA, ICAO, IFALPA.

IATA. (2012). *Introduction to the Airline Industry* (2nd ed.). IATA.

IATA. (2013). *Airline Customer Service* (3rd ed.). IATA.

IATA. (2020 May 6). *Calls on Nigerian Government to Support Aviation in the Face of COVID-19 Crisis*. https://www.iata.org/en.pressroom/pr/2020-05-07-01/

IATA. (2020, June 18). *The benefits of Robotic Process Automation*. Retrieved from airlines.iata.org: https://airlines.iata.org/white-papers/the-benefits-of-robotic-process-automation

IATA. (2020a). *Slower but Steady Growth in 2019*. https://www.iata.org/en/pressroom/pr/2020-02-06-01/

IATA. (2020b) *Economic Performance of the Airline Industry*. https://www.iata.org/en/iata-repository/publications/economic-reports/airline-industry-economic-performance---november-2020---report/

IATA. (2021). *Cargo chartbook Q4 2021*. https://www.iata.org/en/iata-repository/publications/economic-reports/cargo-chartbook---q4-2021/

IATA. (2022). *Airline Business Confidence Index Weighted Score (50 = No Change)*. www.iata.org/economics

Iatrou, K., & Alamdari, F. (2005). The empirical analysis of the impact of alliances on airline operations. *Journal of Air Transport Management*, *11*(3), 127–134. doi:10.1016/j.jairtraman.2004.07.005

IBM. (2021). *Automation and RPA in the enterprise*. IBM.

ICAO. (2014) *ICAO Crisis Management Framework*. https://www.icao.int/eurnat/eur%20and%20nat%20documents/forms/allitems.aspx?RootFolder=%2FEURNAT%2FEUR%20and%20NAT%20Documents%2FEUR%20Documents%2FEUR%20Documents%2F031%20ICAO%20Crisis%20Management%20Framework%20Document%202014&FolderCTID=0x012000DAF95319EADD9946B510C5D7B595637D00AA5EB47B299B9A4BAD1968B24E18655C&View=%7BE414A939-5FB4-4CB9-9139-466754ED0FA9%7D

ICAO. (2019) *Education and performance in aviation: Realising and sustaining benefits*. https://www.icao.int/Meetings/a40/Documents/WP/wp_408_en.pdf

ICAO. (2020). *Doc 10144 ICAO Handbook for CAAs on the Management of Aviation Safety Risks related to COVID-19*. ICAO.

ICAO. (2021a). *COVID Restart Risk Assessment Post-COVID Risk Assessment Checklist-V1.0*. https://www.icao.int/Security/COVID-19/Documents/COVID_Restart_Risk_Assessment_v1_1Nov2021.pdf?msclkid=7e03b659be1b11ecb2bce1954cd3c3f1

ICAO. (2021b). *Safety Report 2021 Edition*. https://www.icao.int/safety/Documents/ICAO%20Safety%20Report%202021%20Edition.pdf

INE PORDATA. (2018). *PORDATA - Base de Dados de Portugal Contemporâneo. Obtido em 6 de dezembro de 2020, de Tráfego de passageiros nos principais aeroportos: Lisboa, Porto e Faro*. https://www.pordata.pt/Portugal/Tr%C3%A1fego+de+passageiros+nos+principais+aeroportos+Lisboa++Porto+e+Faro-3248

INFOTECH. (2020). *Automation playbook airlines/aviation (AL)*. ITC Infotech.

International Air Transport Association (IATA). (1997). *Corporate Air Travel Survey*. IATA Aviation Information and Research.

International Civil Aviation Organization. (2021, January 15). *2020 Passenger totals drop 60 percent as COVID-19 assault on international mobility continues*. https://www.icao.int/Newsroom/Pages/2020-passenger-totals-drop-60-percent-as-covid-19assault-on-internationalmobility-continues.aspx

Investigation, A. C. (Director). (2006). *Crash of the Century* [Motion Picture].

Ireland, R., Hitt, M., & Vaidyanath, D. (2002). Alliance Management as a Source of Competitive Advantage. *Journal of Management*, *28*(3), 413–446. doi:10.1177/014920630202800308

Irma Becerra-Fernandez, R. S. (2001). Organizational Knowledge Management: A Contingency Perspective. *Journal of Management Information Systems*, *18*(1), 23–55. doi:10.1080/07421222.2001.11045676

Isermann, R. (2006). Fault-diagnosis systems: an introduction from fault detection to fault tolerance. In R. Isermann (Ed.), *Fault-diagnosis systems: an introduction from fault detection to fault tolerance*. Springer.

Ito, H., & Lee, D. (2005). Domestic codesharing practices in the US airline industry. *Journal of Air Transport Management*, *11*(2), 89–97. doi:10.1016/j.jairtraman.2004.09.003

Compilation of References

Ito, H., & Lee, D. (2007). Domestic code sharing, alliances, and airfares in the US airline industry. *The Journal of Law & Economics*, *50*(2), 355–380. doi:10.1086/511318

Jaakkola, E., Helkkula, A., & Aarikka-Stenroos, L. (2015). Service experience co-creation: Conceptualization, implications, and future research directions. *Journal of Service Management*, *26*(2), 182–205. doi:10.1108/JOSM-12-2014-0323

Jabbarzadeh, A., Fahimnia, B., & Sabouhi, F. (2018). Resilient and sustainable supply chain design: Sustainability analysis under disruption risks. *International Journal of Production Research*, *56*(17), 5945–5968. doi:10.1080/00207543.2018.1461950

Jaffe, S. D. (2015). *Airspace Closure and Civil Aviation: A Strategic Resource for Airline Managers*. Routledge.

Jalal Sarker, S., Crossman, A., & Chinmeteepituck, P. (2003). The relationships of age and length of service with job satisfaction: An examination of hotel employees in Thailand. *Journal of Managerial Psychology*, *18*(7), 745–758. doi:10.1108/02683940310502421

Janić, M. (2019). Modeling the resilience of an airline cargo transport network affected by a large scale disruptive event. *Transportation Research Part D, Transport and Environment*, *77*, 425–448. doi:10.1016/j.trd.2019.02.011

Jarry, G., Delahaye, D., & Feron, E. (2021). Flight safety during Covid-19: A study of Charles de Gaulle airport atypical energy approaches. *Transportation Research Interdisciplinary Perspectives*, *9*, 100327. Advance online publication. doi:10.1016/j.trip.2021.100327 PMID:33623897

Jenny, A., & Walker, G. M. (2016). *Human Factors of Leadership: What the Tenerife Plane Crash Taught the World About Cockpit Communication Dynamics. Human Factors and Applied Psychology*. Embry Riddle Aeronautical University.

Jiang, Y., Liao, F., Xu, Q., & Yang, Z. (2019). Identification of technology spillover among airport alliance from the perspective of efficiency evaluation: The case of China. *Transport Policy*, *80*(C), 49–58. doi:10.1016/j.tranpol.2019.05.004

Jimoh, A., Kafayat, A., & Maryam, C. D. (2020). Coronavirus outbreak in Nigeria: Burden and socio-medical response during the first 100 days. *International Journal of Infectious Diseases*, *98*, 218–224. doi:10.1016/j.ijid.2020.06.067 PMID:32585282

Joffe, H., & Yardley, L. (2003). Content and thematic analysis. In D. Marks & L. Yardley (Eds.), Research Methods for Clinical and Health Psychology (pp. 56-68). SAGE Publications, Ltd.

Johnston, A., & Ozment, J. (2011). Concentration in the Airline Industry: Evidence of Economies of Scale? *Journal of Transportation Management*, *22*(2), 59–74. doi:10.22237/jotm/1317427500

Johnston, R., & Clark, G. (2008). *Service operations management: improving service delivery* (3rd ed.). Prentice Hall.

Jorge Ribeiro, R. L. (2021). Robotic Process Automation and Artificial Intelligence in Industry 4.0 – A Literature review. Elsevier.

Jose, A. Y., Cecilla, P., Samuel, R., & Marco, A. R. D. (2020). Effectiveness of COVID-19 case definition in identifying SARS-CoV- 2 infection in northern Mexico. *Population Medicine*, *2*(October), 1–8. Advance online publication. doi:10.18332/popmed/127470

Joseph, O. (2020, February 1). Aviation operators fear travel ban as FG mulls lockdown. *Punch*. https://www.punchng.com/aviation-operators-fear-travel-ban-as-fg-mulls-lockdown/%3famp

Juliana, A. (2021, July 3). COVID-19: Concerns as Nigerian airlines, others face fresh setback. *Punch*. https://www.punchng.com/covid-19-concerns-as-nigerian-airlines-others-face-fresh-setback/%3famp

Junni, P., Sarala, R. M., Tarba, S. Y., & Weber, Y. (2015). The Role of Strategic Agility in Acquisitions. *British Journal of Management*, *26*(4), 596–616. doi:10.1111/1467-8551.12115

Juvan, J., Prezelj, I., & Kopač, E. (2020). Public dilemmas about security measures in the field of civil aviation. *Security Journal*, *34*(3), 410–428. doi:10.1057/s41284-020-00240-8

Kahneman, D., & Tversky, A. (1979). Prospect Theory: An Analysis of Decision Under Risk. *Econometrica*, *47*(2), 263–291. doi:10.2307/1914185

Kalogeraki, E.-M., Apostolou, D., Polemi, N., & Papastergiou, S. (2018). Knowledge management methodology for identifying threats in maritime/logistics supply chains. *Knowledge Management Research and Practice*, *16*(4), 508–524. doi:10.1080/14778238.2018.1486789

Kaminski-Morrow, D. (2021). Three airspeed incidents at Heathrow trigger alert over insect blockage. *Flight Global*. https://www.flightglobal.com/safety/three-airspeed-incidents-at-heathrow-trigger-alert-over-insect-blockage/144142.article?msclkid=17de37f4bbd911ecb32ecedbde9c1615

Kankaew, K. (2016). Thai Airways International: The World Economy Crisis Resolutions. *Actual Problems of Economics*, *2*(176), 261–265.

Kankaew, K., & Vadhanasindhu, C. (2020). Airline's human capital development: A case study of ground service officer in Thailand. *Journal of Critical Reviews*, *7*(11), 1780–1787.

Kantowitz, B. H. (2010). *Handbook of Aviation Human Factors*. Taylor & Francis Group.

Kantowitz, B. H. (2010). *Human Factors in Transportation*. Taylor & Francis Group.

Karia, N., & Hasmi Abu Hassan Asaari, M. (2006). The effects of total quality management practices on employees' work-related attitudes. *The TQM Magazine*, *18*(1), 30–43. doi:10.1108/09544780610637677

Kaynak, H., & Hartley, J. L. (2008). A replication and extension of quality management into the supply chain. *Journal of Operations Management*, *26*(4), 468–489. doi:10.1016/j.jom.2007.06.002

Kayode, O. (2020, June 4). Why flights after COVID-19 will be expensive-PTF. *Punch*. https://www.punchng.com/why-flights-after-covid-19-will-be-expensive-ptf/%3famp

Kennedy, R., & Kirwan, B. (1998). *Development of a Hazard and Operability-based method for identifying safety management vulnerabilities in high risk systems*. Academic Press.

Kiliç, D., Polat, G., & Sengur, F. (2021). Havayolu İşletmelerinin Covid-19 Pandemi Sürecindeki Yönetsel Tepkileri Üzerine Bir Araştırma. *Uluslararası Yönetim İktisat ve İşletme Dergisi*, *17*(2), 353–377.

Kılıç, D., Polat, G., & Şengür, F. (2021). Havayolu İşletmelerinin Covid-19 Pandemi *Sürecindeki Yönetsel Tepkileri Üzerine Bir Araştırma. Uluslararası Yönetim İktisat Ve İşletme Dergisi*, *17*(2), 353–377.

Kim, E. H., & Singal, V. (1993). Mergers and market power: Evidence from the airline industry. *The American Economic Review*, *83*(3), 549–569.

Kimes, S. E. (2010). *Strategic pricing through revenue management*. Academic Press.

Kim, M., & Sohn, J. (2022). Passenger, airline, and policy responses to the COVID-19 crisis: The case of South Korea. *Journal of Air Transport Management*, *98*, 102144. doi:10.1016/j.jairtraman.2021.102144 PMID:34539103

Compilation of References

Kim, S. K., & Byun, S. N. (2011). Effects of Crew Resource Management Training on the Team Performance of Operators in an Advanced Nuclear Power Plant. *Journal of Nuclear Science and Technology*, *48*(9), 1256–1264. doi:10.1080/18811248.2011.9711814

Kim, Y. K., & Lee, H. R. (2009). Passenger complaints under irregular airline conditions–cross-cultural study. *Journal of Air Transport Management*, *15*(6), 350–353. doi:10.1016/j.jairtraman.2008.11.007

Kim, Y. K., & Lee, H. R. (2011). Customer satisfaction using low cost carriers. *Tourism Management*, *32*(2), 235–243. doi:10.1016/j.tourman.2009.12.008

Kindström, D., & Kowalkowski, C. (2014). Service innovation in product-centric firms: A multidimensional business model perspective. *Journal of Business and Industrial Marketing*, *29*(2), 96–111. doi:10.1108/JBIM-08-2013-0165

Kitching, J., Blackburn, R., Smallbone, D., & Dixon, S. (2009). *Business Strategies and Performance during Difficult Economic Conditions*. Kingston University.

Kleymann, B., & Seristö, H. (2017). *Managing strategic airline alliances*. Routledge. doi:10.4324/9781315249858

Kling, J., & Smith, K. (1995). Identifying Strategic Groups in the US Airline Industry: An Application of the Porter Model. *Transportation Journal*, *35*(2), 26–34.

Klophaus, R., & Lordan, O. (2018). Codesharing network vulnerability of global airline alliances. *Transportation Research Part A, Policy and Practice*, *111*, 1–10. doi:10.1016/j.tra.2018.02.010

Knezevic, J. (2021). COVID-19 Pandemic as a Mechanism of the Motion of an Aircraft in MIRCE Mechanics. *American Journal of Engineering and Technology Management*, *6*(1), 1. doi:10.11648/j.ajetm.20210601.11

Koerber, A., & McMichael, L. (2008). Qualitative sampling methods: A primer for technical communicators. *Journal of Business and Technical Communication*, *22*(4), 454–473. doi:10.1177/1050651908320362

Kositchotethana, B. (2013). Economy passengers willing to pay more for comfort. *Bangkok Post*. https://www.bangkokpost.com/business/381103/economy-passengers-willing-to-pay-more-for-comfort

Kramer, L., Fowler, P., Hazel, R., Ureksoy, M., & Harig, G. (2010). *Marketing guidebook for small airports*. Transportation Research Board.

Krause, S. S. (2003). *Aircraft Safety: Accident Investigations, Analyses, & Applications* (2nd ed.). McGraw-Hill.

Krieger, N. (2005). *Embodiment: A conceptual glossary for epidemiology*. Academic Press.

Kumar, D. (2015). *Building Sustainable Competitive Advantage: Through Executive Enterprise Leadership*. Routledge.

Kumar, R., & Mishra, R. S. (2020). COVID-19 global pandemic: Impact on management of supply chain. *International Journal of Emerging Technology and Advanced Engineering*, *10*(04), 132–139. doi:10.46338/IJETAE0416

Kuo, C.-W., & Jou, R.-C. (2017). Willingness to pay for airlines' premium economy class: The perspective of passengers. *Journal of Air Transport Management*, *59*, 134–142.

La Guardia, J. G., Ryan, R. M., Couchman, C. E., & Deci, E. L. (2000). Within-person variation in security of attachment: A self-determination theory perspective on attachment, need fulfillment, and well-being. *Journal of Personality and Social Psychology*, *79*(3), 367–384. doi:10.1037/0022-3514.79.3.367 PMID:10981840

Ladan, S. I. (2012). An Analysis of Air Transportation in Nigeria. *Journal of Research in National Development*, *10*(2). https://www.ajol.info/index.php/jorind/article/view/92699

Lamb, L. T., Winter, R. S., Rice, S., Rustin, J. K., & Vaughn, A. (2020). Factors that Predict Passengers Willingness to Fly during and After the COVID-19 Pandemic. *Journal of Air Transport Management*, *89*, 101897. doi:10.1016/j.jairtraman.2020.101897 PMID:32837029

Langewiesche, W. (2010). *Fly by Wire: The Geese, the Glide, the Miracle on the Hudson* (2nd ed.). Picador.

Lapré, M. A. (2011). Reducing customer dissatisfaction: How important is learning to reduce service failure? *Production and Operations Management*, *20*(4), 491–507. doi:10.1111/j.1937-5956.2010.01149.x

Larson, P. D. (2001). Designing and Managing the Supply Chain: Concepts, Strategies, and Case Studies, David Simchi-Levi Philip Kaminsky Edith Simchi-Levi. *Journal of Business Logistics*, *22*(1), 259–261. doi:10.1002/j.2158-1592.2001.tb00165.x

Lawalni, M. (2021, March 25). Why flight delays, cancellations still persist after COVID-19 lockdown. *Vanguard*. https://www.vanguardngr.com/2021/03/why-flight-delay-cancellations-still-persist-after-covid-19-lockdown/amp

Lawani, M. (2020, June 28). Airfares may start from 100,000 as tough flying rules set to take effect. *Vanguard*. https://www.vanguardngr.com/2020/06/airfare-may-start-from-n10000-as-tough-flying-rules-set-effect/amp/

Law, C. (2017). The Study of Customer Relationship Management in Thai Airline Industry: A Case of Thai Travelers in Thailand. *Journal of Airline and Airport Management*, *7*(1), 13–42.

Law, C., & Doerflein, M. (2014). *Introduction to Airline Ground Service*. Cengage.

Lazare, L. (2017). EVA Air's long love affair with the iconic Boeing 747 is officially over. *Chicago Business Journal*. https://www.bizjournals.com/chicago/news/2017/08/22/eva-airs-longlove-affair-with-the-iconic-boeing.html

Lee, C. K., Ng, K. K. H., Chan, H. K., Choy, K. L., Tai, W. C., & Choi, L. S. (2018). A multi-group analysis of social media engagement and loyalty constructs between full-service and low-cost carriers in Hong Kong. *Journal of Air Transport Management*, *73*, 46–57. doi:10.1016/j.jairtraman.2018.08.009

Lee, K.-H., & Hyun, S. S. (2016). An extended model of employees' service innovation behavior in the airline industry. *International Journal of Contemporary Hospitality Management*, *28*(8), 1622–1648. doi:10.1108/IJCHM-03-2015-0109

Lee, M., Li, L. K., & Wong, W. (2019). Analysis of direct operating cost of wide-body passenger aircraft: A parametric study based on Hong Kong. *Chinese Journal of Aeronautics*, *32*(5), 1222–1243.

Lee, Y. (2016). Relationship Quality and Its Causal Link to Service Value, Satisfaction, and Word-of-Mouth. *Services Marketing Quarterly*, *37*(3), 171–184. doi:10.1080/15332969.2016.1184541

Lemon, K. N., & Verhoef, P. C. (2016). Understanding customer experience throughout the customer journey. *Journal of Marketing*, *80*(6), 69–96. doi:10.1509/jm.15.0420

Leschak, P. (2013, July 13). *Star Tribune*. Retrieved February 17, 2022, from https://www.startribune.com/opinion/commentaries/215309681.html

Li, E. Y., Chang, L. S., & Chang, L. F. (2016, June). Exploring Consumer Value of CrossBorder Online Shopping: an Application of means-End Chain Theory and Maslow's Hierarchy of Needs. In PACIS (p. 359). Academic Press.

Liamputtong, P. (2009). Qualitative data analysis: Conceptual and practical considerations. *Health Promotion Journal of Australia*, *20*(2), 133–139. doi:10.1071/HE09133 PMID:19642962

Li, J., & Herd, A. M. (2017). Shifting Practices in Digital Workplace Learning: An Integrated Approach to Learning, Knowledge Management, and Knowledge Sharing. *Human Resource Development International*, *20*(3), 185–193. doi:10.1080/13678868.2017.1308460

Compilation of References

Lijesen, M. G., Rietveld, P., & Nijkamp, P. (2002). How do carriers price connecting flights? Evidence from intercontinental flights from Europe. *Transportation Research Part E, Logistics and Transportation Review*, *28*(3-4), 239–252.

Likhacheva, A. (2006). SARS Revisited. *AMA Journal of Ethics*, *8*(4), 219–222. doi:10.1001/virtualmentor.2006.8.4.jdsc1-0604

Li, M. Z. (2000). Distinct features of lasting and non-lasting airline alliances. *Journal of Air Transport Management*, *6*(2), 65–73. doi:10.1016/S0969-6997(99)00024-1

Lin, C. (2010). The integrated secondary route network design model in the hierarchical hub- and-spoke network for dual express services. *International Journal of Production Economics*, *123*(1), 20–30.

Lin, C. F., & Fu, C. S. (2017a). Advancing the laddering and critical incident techniques by incorporating dramaturgical theory to reveal restaurant niches. *Service Industries Journal*, *37*(13–14), 801. doi:10.1080/02642069.2017.1351551

Lin, D., Lee, C. K. M., & Yang, J. (2017). Air cargo revenue management under buy-back policy. *Journal of Air Transport Management*, *61*, 53–63. doi:10.1016/j.jairtraman.2016.08.012

Lindenmeier, J., & Tscheulin, D. K. (2008). The effects of inventory control and denied boarding on customer satisfaction: The case of capacity-based airline revenue management. *Tourism Management*, *29*(1), 32–43. doi:10.1016/j.tourman.2007.04.004

Liou, J. J., & Tzeng, G. H. (2007). A non-additive model for evaluating airline service quality. *Journal of Air Transport Management*, *13*(3), 131–138. doi:10.1016/j.jairtraman.2006.12.002

Lipkin, M., & Heinonen, K. (2022). Customer ecosystems: Exploring how ecosystem actors shape customer experience. *Journal of Services Marketing*, *36*(9), 1–17. doi:10.1108/JSM-03-2021-0080

Li, T. (2020). A SWOT analysis of China's air cargo sector in the context of COVID-19 pandemic. *Journal of Air Transport Management*, *88*, 101875. doi:10.1016/j.jairtraman.2020.101875 PMID:32834695

Locke, E. (1976). The Nature and Causes of Job Satisfaction. The handbook of industrial and organizational psychology, 31.

Loh, C. (2021). *Record Smashing: What Is The Longest Airbus A380 Flight?* Simple Flying. https://simpleflying.com/longest-airbus-a380-flight/

Lohmann, G., Albers, S., Koch, B., & Pavlovich, K. (2009). From hub to tourist destination–An explorative study of Singapore and Dubai's aviation-based transformation. *Journal of Air Transport Management*, *15*(5), 205–211. doi:10.1016/j.jairtraman.2008.07.004

London Air Travel. (2018). *60 Years of the Transatlantic Jet Age*. London Air Travel. https://londonairtravel.com/2018/10/04/the-transatlantic-jet-age/

Longhurst, R. (2016). Semi-structured interviews and focus groups. In N. Clifford, M. Cope, T. Gillespie, & S. French (Eds.), *Key methods in geography* (3rd ed., pp. 143–156). SAGE Publication.

Lu, A. (2003). *International airline alliances: EC Competition Law, US Antitrust Law and International Air Transport*. Kluwer Law International.

Lubnau, I. I. T., & Okray, R. (2001, August 1). *Crew resource management for the fire service*. Retrieved February 17, 2022, from https://www.fireengineering.com/articles/print/volume154/issue-8/features/crew-resource-management-for-the-fire-service.html

Lucini, B. (2020). Soft skills for governing new threats: training methods for LEAs in preventing and countering violent extremism and radicalisation. *Sicurezza, Terrorismo e Società*, *45*.

Lufthansa. (2022). *Company*. https://www.lufthansagroup.com/en/company.html

Lusch, R. F., Vargo, S. L., & Tanniru, M. (2010). Service, value networks and learning. *Journal of the Academy of Marketing Science*, *38*(1), 19–31. doi:10.100711747-008-0131-z

Lusch, R. F., & Webster, F. E. Jr. (2011). A stakeholder-unifying, cocreation philosophy for marketing. *Journal of Macromarketing*, *31*(2), 129–134. doi:10.1177/0276146710397369

Lyon, J. (2018). First class is shrinking on airlines and it may disappear altogether. *Business Insider*. https://www.businessinsider.com/first-class-shrinking-airlines-may-disappear-altogether-2018-11

Macmillan, H., & Tampoe, M. (2001). Strategic management. Academic Press.

MacNealy, M. (1999). *Strategies for empirical research in writing*. Longman. doi:10.2307/358974

Maneenop, S., & Kotcharin, S. (2020). The impacts of COVID-19 on the global airline industry: An event study approach. *Journal of Air Transport Management*, *89*, 101920. doi:10.1016/j.jairtraman.2020.101920 PMID:32874021

Mantzana, V., Georgiou, E., Chasiotis, I., Gkotsis, I., Stelkens-Kobsch, T. H., Kazoukas, V., & Komninos, F. (2020). Airports' Crisis Management Processes and Stakeholders Involved. *Annals of Disaster Risk Sciences*, *3*(1).

Marcus, B., & Anderson, C. K. (2008). Revenue management for low-cost providers. *European Journal of Operational Research*, *188*(1), 258–272. doi:10.1016/j.ejor.2007.04.010

Mariya, A. I. (2009). *Analysis of the Interaction between Air Transportation and Economic Activity: A Worldwide Perspective* [Doctoral Dissertation]. Department of Aeronautics & Astronautics, Massachusetts Institute of Technology, Cambridge, MA.

Mark P. Alavosius, R. A. (2017). Leadership and Crew Resource Management in High-Reliability Organizations: A Competency Framework for Measuring Behaviors. *Journal of Organizational Behavior Management*, 142–170.

Martins, H., Rouco, C., Piedade, L., & Borba, F. (2020). Soft Skills for Hard Times: Developing a Framework of Preparedness for Overcoming Crises Events in Higher Education Students. *17th International Conference on Intellectual Capital, Knowledge Management & Organizational Learning*.

Martins, T. S., & Kato, H. T. (2010). *An Analytical Framework for Miles and Snow Typology and Dynamic Capabilities*. XXXIV Encontro da ANDAP.

Mason, K. J., & Alamdari, F. (2007). EU network carriers, low cost carriers and consumer behaviour: A Delphi study of future trends. *Journal of Air Transport Management*, *13*(5), 299–310. doi:10.1016/j.jairtraman.2007.04.011

Mathies, C., Gudergan, S. P., & Wang, P. Z. (2013). The effects of customer-centric marketing and revenue management on travelers' choices. *Journal of Travel Research*, *52*(4), 479–493. doi:10.1177/0047287513478499

Mathis, R., & Jackson, J. (2008). *Human resource management* (12th ed.). Thomson/South-western.

Mattila, A. S. (1999). The role of culture in the service evaluation process. *Journal of Service Research*, *1*(3), 250–261. doi:10.1177/109467059913006

Maureen, I. (2020, March 20). Coronavirus: Nigeria's aviation industry to lose N160 billion, 22,200 jobs. *Punch*. https://www.punchng.com/covid-19-aviation-industry-to-lose-n160bn-2220-jobs/%3famp

Maurino, D. E. (1992). Shall we add one more defense? In R. Heron (Ed.), *Third Seminar in Transportation*. Montreal, Canada: Transport Canada Development Centre.

Mazareanu, E. (2020). *Annual growth in global air traffic passenger demand from 2006 to 2021*. https://www.statista.com/statistics/193533/growth-of-global-air-traffic-passenger-demand/

McConaughey, E. (2008, April). Crew Resource Management in Healthcare: The Evolution of Teamwork Training and MedTeams. *The Journal of Perinatal & Neonatal Nursing*, 22(2), 96–104. doi:10.1097/01.JPN.0000319095.59673.6c PMID:18496068

McMahon-Beattie, U., McEntee, M., McKenna, R., Yeoman, I., & Hollywood, L. (2016). Revenue management, pricing and the consumer. *Journal of Revenue and Pricing Management*, 15(3), 299–305. doi:10.1057/rpm.2016.17

Midura, D. (2021, February 3). *CRM Risk Analysis & Management*. Technology Advisors. Retrieved January 28, 2022, from https://www.techadv.com/blog/crm-risk-analysis-management

Miles, R. E., Snow, C. C., Meyer, A. D., & Coleman, H. J. Jr. (1978). Organizational Strategy, Structure, and Process. *Academy of Management Review*, 3(3), 546–562. doi:10.2307/257544 PMID:10238389

Milioti, C., Karlaftis, M. G., & Akkogiounoglou, E. (2015). Traveler perceptions and airline choice: A multivariate probit approach. *Journal of Air Transport Management*, 49, 46–52.

Minichiello, A., Hood, J., & Harkness, D. (2018). Bringing User Experience Design to Bear on STEM Education: A Narrative Literature Review. *Journal For STEM Education Research*, 1(1-2), 7–33. doi:10.100741979-018-0005-3

Ministry of Tourism & Sports in Thailand. (2021). *Tourism Economic Review*. https://www.mots.go.th/more_news_new.php?cid=581

Mohammed, A., Harris, I., Soroka, A., & Nujoom, R. (2019). A hybrid MCDM-fuzzy multi-objective programming approach for a G-resilient supply chain network design. *Computers & Industrial Engineering*, 127, 297–312. doi:10.1016/j.cie.2018.09.052

Moller, K., & Rajala, A. (2007). Rise of strategic nets—New modes of value creation. *Industrial Marketing Management*, 36(7), 895–908. doi:10.1016/j.indmarman.2007.05.016

Montgomery, C. A., Thomas, A. R., & Kamath, R. (1984). Divestiture, market valuation, and strategy. *Academy of Management Journal*, 27(4), 830–840.

Morley, C. L. (2003). Impacts of international airline alliances on tourism. *Tourism Economics*, 9(1), 31–51. doi:10.5367/000000003101298259

Moroney, W. R. (1995). Evolution of human engineering: A selected review. In Research techniques in human factors. Englewood Cliffs, NJ: Prentice-Hall.

Morrish, S., & Hamilton, R. (2002). Airline alliances—Who benefits? *Journal of Air Transport Management*, 8(6), 401–407. doi:10.1016/S0969-6997(02)00041-8

Moses, E., & Kelvin, O. O. (2021 December 25). Omicron now spreading at Community level, says NCDC. *The Nation*. https://www.thenationonlineng.net/omicron-now-spread-at-community-levels-says-ncdc/amp

Mott, J. H., Hubbard, S. M., Lu, C. T., Sobieralski, J. B., Gao, Y., Nolan, M. S., & Kotla, B. (2019). Competency-based education: A framework for aviation management programs. *The Collegiate Aviation Review International*, 37(1).

Mutzabaugh, B. (2014). World's first Airbus A350 route will be Doha-Frankfurt. *USA Today*. https://www.usatoday.com/story/todayinthesky/2014/10/20/worlds-first-airbus-a350-route-will-be-doha-frankfurt/17644483/

Nag, R., Hambrick, D. C., & Chen, M.-J. (2007). What is strategic management, really? Inductive derivation of a consensus definition of the field. *Strategic Management Journal*, 28(9), 935–955. doi:10.1002mj.615

Nalisa. (2021, Feb 2). *Wīat čhet bin fā khōwit - sipkāo čhon mī kamrai* [Vietjet flies through COVID-19 until it's profitable]. Retrieved from: www.marketeeronline.co.th

National Bureau of Statistics. (2016). *2015 Summary Report Q3/Q4 in the Nigerian Aviation Sector.* http://nigerianstat.gov.ng

NDTV. (2022). *US Flight Passenger Who Was Duct-Taped To Her Seat Faces Record Fine.* https://www.ndtv.com/world-news/woman-on-us-flight-who-spit-at-headbutted-crew-faces-record-81-950-fine-2887078

Nishat Faisal, M., Banwet, D. K., & Shankar, R. (2006). Supply chain risk mitigation: Modeling the enablers. *Business Process Management Journal, 12*(4), 535–552. doi:10.1108/14637150610678113

NTSB. (1988). Aircraft Accident Report, Delta Airlines, Inc. National Transportation Safety Board, Bureau of Accident Investigation.

Nyadzayo, M. W., & Khajehzadeh, S. (2016). The antecedents of customer loyalty: A moderated mediation model of customer relationship management quality and brand image. *Journal of Business & Economic Research, 5*(2), 55-64.

O'Connell, J. F., & Warnock-Smith, D. (2013). An investigation into traveler preferences and acceptance levels of airline ancillary revenues. *Journal of Air Transport Management, 33*, 12–21. doi:10.1016/j.jairtraman.2013.06.006

O'Connell, J. F., & Williams, G. (2005). Passengers' perceptions of low cost airlines and full service carriers: A case study involving Ryanair, Aer Lingus, Air Asia and Malaysia Airlines. *Journal of Air Transport Management, 11*(4), 259–272. doi:10.1016/j.jairtraman.2005.01.007

O'Dwyer, M., & Gilmore, A. (2018). Value and alliance capability and the formation of strategic alliances in SMEs: The impact of customer orientation and resource optimization. *Journal of Business Research, 87*, 58–68. doi:10.1016/j.jbusres.2018.02.020

Obadiah, M. (2021). Aviation and national destiny. *Punch*, p. 1. https://www.google.come/amp/s/punch.com/aviation-and-national-destiny?%3famp

OECD. (1999). *Policy Roundtables Airline Mergers and Alliances.* https://www.oecd.org/daf/competition/mergers/2379233.pdf

Office of the Director-General Nigerian Civil Aviation Authority, All Operators Letter DG22/21 to All Airlines Operating International Flights into and out of Nigeria from Nigerian Civil Aviation Authority/ NCAA/DG/AIR/11/16/320, Revised Quarantine Protocol for Travellers Arriving Nigeria, 22nd October 2021.

Office of the Director-General Nigerian Civil Aviation Authority, All Operators Letter DG22/21 to All Airlines Operating International Flights into and out of Nigeria from Nigerian Civil Aviation Authority/NCAA/DG/AIR/11/16/319, Removal of Limitation of 200 Passengers Per Each International Flight Operating into Nigeria, 30 September 2021.

Okeleke, U. J., & Aponjolosun, M. O. (2020). A study on the effects of COVID–19 pandemic on Nigerian seafarers. *Journal of Sustainable Development of Transport and Logistics, 5*(2), 135–142. doi:10.14254/jsdtl.2020.5-2.12

Okray, R., & Lubnau, I. I. T. (2004). *Crew resource management for the fire service.* Penn Well Publishers.

Okumus, F., Altinay, L., & Chathoth, P. (2010). *Strategic Management in the International Hospitality and Tourism Industry.* Routledge. doi:10.4324/9780080940465

Olaganathan & Amihan. (2021). Impact of COVID -19 on Pilot Proficiency – A Risk Analysis. *Global Journal of Engineering and Technology Advances, 6*(3), 1–13. doi:10.30574/gjeta.2021.6.3.0023

Compilation of References

Olejniczak, D., & Nowacki, M. (2019). Assessment of the selected parameters of aerodynamics for Airbus A380 aircraft on the basis of CFD tests. *Transportation Research Procedia*, *40*, 839–846.

Oliver, R. L. (1999). Whence consumer loyalty. *Journal of Marketing*, *63*(4), 33–44. doi:10.1177/00222429990634s105

Oneworld. (2022). *14 Global Airlines. One Bright Alliance.* https://www.oneworld.com/members

Oniji, O. (2020). *Business Outlook: Impact of COVID-19 on the Aviation Sector in Nigeria.* Academic Press.

Orasanu, J. M. (1993). Shared problem models and flight crew performance. In N. M. A. N. Johnston (Ed.), *Aviation psychology in practice* (pp. 255–285). Averbury Technical.

Ordieres-meré, J. (2020). *Digitalization: An Opportunity for Contributing to Sustainability From Knowledge Creation.* Academic Press.

Organisation for Economic Cooperation and Development. (2020). *OECD Policy Response to Coronavirus (COVID-19), COVID-19 and the Aviation industry: Impact and Policy Response.* https://www.oecd.org/coronavirus/policy-response-/covid-19-and-the-aviation-industry-impact-and-policy-responses-26d521c1./

Oriol, M. (2006). Crew resource management: Applications in healthcare organizations. *JONA*, *36*(9), 402–406. doi:10.1097/00005110-200609000-00006 PMID:16969251

Otache, I. (2020). The Effects of the COVID-19 Pandemic on the Nigeria's Economy and Possible Coping Strategies. *Asian Journal of Social Sciences and Management Studies*, *7*(3), 173–179. doi:10.20448/journal.500.2020.73.173.179

Otto, J. E., & Ritchie, J. B. (1996). The service experience in tourism. *Tourism Management*, *17*(3), 165–174. doi:10.1016/0261-5177(96)00003-9

Oum, T., & Park, J.-H. (1997). Airline alliances: Current status, policy issues, and future directions. *Journal of Air Transport Management*, *3*(3), 133–144. doi:10.1016/S0969-6997(97)00021-5

Oum, T., Park, J.-H., & Zhang, A. (2000). *Globalization and Strategic Alliances: The Case of Airline Industry.* Elsevier Science Ltd.

Oum, T., Yu, C., & Zhang, A. (2001). Global airline alliances: International regulatory issues. *Journal of Air Transport Management*, *7*(1), 57–62. doi:10.1016/S0969-6997(00)00034-X

Oyebade, W. (2020, July 3). How new safety protocol changed air travel dynamics. *The Guardian.* https://guardian.ng/business-services/aviation-business/how-new-safety-protocol-changed-air-travel-dynamic/amp/

Oyebade, W. (2020, October 5). Test certificate rocks COVID-19 air travel protocol. *The Guardian.* https://theguardian.ng/news/test-certifcates-fraud-rocks-covid-19-air-travel-protocol-/

Oyebade, W. (2021 January 1). Local air travel in the year of pandemic. *The Guardian.* https://guardian.ng/business-services/aviation-business/local-air-travel-in-the-year-of-pandemic/

Oyebade, W. (2021 June 1). Travellers to face longer processing time over protocols, traffic. *The Guardian*, 1. https://guardian.ng/business-services/travellers-to-face-longer-processing-time-over-protocols-traffic/

Oyebade, W. (2021, January 22). Travel agencies to explore dynamics of new normal. *The Guardian.* https://guardian.ng/business-services/travel-agencies-to-explore-dynamics-of-new-normal/

Oyebade, W. (2021, October 8). Air Travellers express frustration over restrictions. *The Guardian.* https://guardian.ng/business-services-/aviation-business/air-travellers-express-frustration-over-resrrictions

Oyebade, W. (2021, September 17). Confusion in air travel over varying COVID-19 protocols. *The Guardian*. https://guardian.ng/business-services/confusion-in-air-travel-over-varying-covid-19-protocol/

Oyebade, W. (2022 February 10). Industry risks collapse as aviation fuel hits N400/litre. *The Guardian*. https://guardian.ng/news/industry-risks-collapse-as-aviation-fuel-hits-n400-litre/

Oyebade, W. (2022, January 14). Omicron restrictions, travel protocols stall air travel recovery. *The Guardian*. https://https:guardian.ng/business-services/omicron-restrictions-travel-protocols-stall-air-travel-recovery

Özdaşlı, K. (2012). Kurumsal (Şirket Düzeyi) Stratejiler. In F. Okumuş, M. Koyuncu, & E. Günlü (Eds.), *İşletmelerde Stratejik Yönetim*. Seçkin Publishing.

Özer, M. A. (2015). İşletmelerde Stratejinin Önemi Üzerine Değerlendirmeler. *International Journal of Economic and Administrative Studies*, 7(14), 69–84.

Pande, P. (2020). *How The Airbus A340-500 Opened The Door To The Longest Flight*. Simple Flying. https://simpleflying.com/airbus-a340-500-longest-flight/

Pandey, M., & Smith, B. (2014). *ETOPS: Expansion in the North Pacific Market*. Boeing. https://www.boeing.com/commercial/aeromagazine/aero_04/fo/fo01/index.html

Papatheodorou, A., & Lei, Z. (2006). Leisure travel in Europe and airline business models: A study of regional airports in Great Britain. *Journal of Air Transport Management*, 12(1), 47–52. doi:10.1016/j.jairtraman.2005.09.005

Parast, M. M., & Shekarian, M. (2019). The Impact of Supply Chain Disruptions on Organizational Performance: A Literature Review. In G. A. Zsidisin & M. Henke (Eds.), *Revisiting Supply Chain Risk* (pp. 367–389). Springer International Publishing. doi:10.1007/978-3-030-03813-7_21

Parasuraman, A., Zeithaml, V. A., & Berry, L. L. (1994). Alternative scales for measuring service quality: A comparative assessment based on psychometric and diagnostic criteria. *Journal of Retailing*, 70(3), 201–230. doi:10.1016/0022-4359(94)90033-7

Park, J. H., & Zhang, A. (1998). Airline alliances and partner firms' outputs. *Transportation Research Part E, Logistics and Transportation Review*, 34(4), 245–255. doi:10.1016/S1366-5545(98)00018-0

Pascual, M. E., & Cain, L. N. (2021). Loyalty programs: the vital safety feature for airlines to survive COVID-19. *International Hospitality Review*.

Patrick, K., & Xu, Y. (2018). Exploring generation y consumers' fitness clothing consumption: A means-end approach. *Journal of Textile & Apparel. Technology & Management*, 10(3), 1–15.

Patton, M. (2014). *Qualitative Evaluation and Research Methods: Integrating Theory and Practice* (4th ed.). Sage Publications.

Patton, M. Q. (1987). *How to Use Qualitative Methods in Evaluation* (4th ed.). SAGE.

Pels, E. (2001). A note on airline alliances. *Journal of Air Transport Management*, 7(1), 3–7. doi:10.1016/S0969-6997(00)00027-2

Pels, E. (2008). Airline network competition: Full-service airlines, low-cost airlines and long-haul markets. *Research in Transportation Economics*, 24(1), 68–74. doi:10.1016/j.retrec.2009.01.009

Pettit, T., Fiksel, J., & Croxton, K. (2010). Ensuring supply chain resilience: Development of a conceptual framework. *Journal of Business Logistics*, 31(1), 1–21. doi:10.1002/j.2158-1592.2010.tb00125.x

Compilation of References

Piers, Montijn, & Balk. (2009). *Safety Management System and Safety Culture Working Group Safety Management System and Safety Culture Working Group (SMS WG) Safety Culture Framework For The ECAST SMS-WG*. Academic Press.

Pine, B. J., & Gilmore, J. H. (1998). Welcome to the experience economy. *Harvard Business Review*, 76(4), 97–105. PMID:10181589

Pitfield, D. E. (2007). Ryanair's Impact on Airline Market Share from the London Area Airports: A Time Series Analysis. *Journal of Transport Economics and Policy*, 41(1), 75–92.

Podsakoff, P. M., MacKenzie, S. B., & Podsakoff, N. P. (2012). Sources of method bias in social science research and recommendations on how to control it. *Annual Review of Psychology*, 63(1), 539–569. doi:10.1146/annurev-psych-120710-100452 PMID:21838546

Porta, M. (2008). *A Dictionary of epidemiology*. American Journal of Epidemiology.

Porter, S. (2018). *The world's longest non-stop flight takes off from Singapore*. British Broadcasting Corporation. https://www.bbc.com/news/business-45795573

Porter, M. (1979). *How Competitive Forces Shape Strategy*. Harvard Business Review.

Porter, M. (1980). *Competitive Strategy: Techniques for Analyzing Industries and Competitors*. The Free Press.

Porter, M. (1985). *Competitive Advantage: Creating and Sustaining Superior Performance*. The Free Press.

Porter, M. (1996). What is Strategy? *Harvard Business Review*, 76(4), 61–78. PMID:10158474

Porter, M. (2008). The Five Competitive Forces that Shape Strategy. *Harvard Business Review*, 25–40. PMID:18271320

Porter, M. E. (1987). From competitive advantage to corporate strategy. *Harvard Business Review*, (59), 1–11. PMID:17183795

Pratt, S., Mann, S., Salisbury, M., Greenberg, P., Marcus, R., Stabile, B., McNamee, P., Nielsen, P., & Sachs, B. P. (2007). Impact of CRM based team training on obstetric outcomes and clinicians' patient safety attitudes. *Joint Commission Journal on Quality and Patient Safety*, 33(12), 720–725. doi:10.1016/S1553-7250(07)33086-9 PMID:18200896

Presidential Task Force on COVID-19. (2020, September 4). *COVID-19 Response: Provisional Quarantine Protocol for Travellers Arriving in Nigeria from any Country*. Academic Press.

Presidential Task Force on COVID-19. (2021, June 30). *COVID-19 Response: Provisional Quarantine Protocol for Travellers Arriving in Nigeria from any Country*. Academic Press.

Press, T. A. (2009, December 16). *CBS News*. Retrieved February 16, 2022, from https://www.nbcnews.com/id/wbna34447873

Price Water House Coopers Limited COVID-19 Resources. (2020). *Impact of COVID-19 on the Supply chain industry*. https://www.pwc.com/ng/covid-19

Professor Leslie Willcocks, P. M. (2015). The IT Function and Robotic Process Automation. *The Outsourcing Unit*, 15(5).

Prokesch, S. E. (1995). Competing on customer service: An interview with British Airways' Sir Colin Marshall. *Harvard Business Review*, 73(6), 100–112.

Qantas. (2019). *New Qantas Research Reveals What Customers Really Want on Ultra long Flights*. Qantas Airways. https://www.qantasnewsroom.com.au/media-releases/new-qantas-research-reveals-what-customers-really-want-on-ultra-long-haul-flights/

Qatar. (2022). https://www.qatarairways.com/tr-tr/about-qatar-airways/group-company.html

Qingbin, C., & Dangen, X. (2021). Research on Application of Blockchain Technology in Airport Aviation Security. *Proceedings of 2021 IEEE 3rd International Conference on Civil Aviation Safety and Information Technology, ICCASIT 2021*, 454–459. 10.1109/ICCASIT53235.2021.9633615

Qin, Y., Ng, K. K. H., Hu, H., Chan, F. T. S., & Xiao, S. (2021). Post disaster adaptation management in airport: A coordination of runway and hangar resources for relief cargo transports. *Advanced Engineering Informatics*, *50*, 101403. doi:10.1016/j.aei.2021.101403

Queirós, A., Faria, D., & Almeida, F. (2017). Strengths and limitations of qualitative and quantitative research methods. *European Journal of Education Studies*.

Rabionet, S. E. (2011). How I learned to design and conduct semi-structured interviews: An ongoing and continuous journey. *Qualitative Report*, *16*(2), 563–566.

Rahimi, R., Köseoglu, M. A., Ersoy, A. B., & Okumus, F. (2017). Customer relationship management research in tourism and hospitality: A state-of-the-art. *Tourism Review*, *72*(2), 209–220. doi:10.1108/TR-01-2017-0011

Ramirez, E., Jimenez, F. R., & Gau, R. (2015). Concrete and abstract goals associated with the consumption of environmentally sustainable products. *European Journal of Marketing*, *49*(9/10), 1645–1665. doi:10.1108/EJM-08-2012-0483

Ramp Resource Management. (2021, September 14). *SKYbrary Aviation Safety*. Retrieved January 29, 2022, from https://skybrary.aero/articles/ramp-resource-management

Ramyar Gilani, J. L. (2022). *Vascular Complications of Surgery and Intervention*. Springer. doi:10.1007/978-3-030-86713-3

Read, J. M., Diggle, J. P., Chirombo, J., Solomon, T., & Baylis, M. (2014). Effectiveness of screening for Ebola at airports. *Lancet*, *9962*(385), 23–24.

Redding, S. (1984). Cultural effects on cockpit communications in civilian aircraft. In *Flight Safety Foundation Conference*. Washington, DC: Flight Safety Foundation.

Redondi, R., Malighettu, P., & Paleari, S. (2011). Hub competition and travel times in the world-wide airport network. *Journal of Transport Geography*, *16*(6), 1260–1271. doi:10.1016/j.jtrangeo.2010.11.010

Redpath, N., O'Connell, J. F., & Warnock-Smith, D. (2017). The strategic impact of airline group diversification: The cases of Emirates and Lufthansa. *Journal of Air Transport Management*, *64*, 121–138. doi:10.1016/j.jairtraman.2016.08.009

Rehan Syeda, S. S. (2019). *Robotic Process Automation: Contemporary themes and challenges*. Elsevier.

Reinartz, W. J., & Kumar, V. (2003). The impact of customer relationship characteristics on profitable lifetime duration. *Journal of Marketing*, *67*(1), 77–99. doi:10.1509/jmkg.67.1.77.18589

Reporters, O. (2020). Coronavirus: Delta, Emirates, Air France, Lufthansa, KLM, others suspend flights to Nigeria. *Punch*. https://www.punchng.com/coronavirus-delta-emirates-air-france-lufthansa-klm-others-suspend-flights-to-nigeria/%3famp

Reynolds, T. J., & Olson, J. C. (Eds.). (2001). *Understanding consumer decision making: The means-end approach to marketing and advertising strategy*. Psychology Press. doi:10.4324/9781410600844

Rico, C. (2020). *Confirmado primeiro caso de coronavírus em Portugal. Segundo caso aguarda contra-análise*. https://www.tsf.pt/portugal/sociedade/confirmados-dois-primeiros-casos-de-contagio-pelo-novo-coronavirus-em-portugal-11876592.html

Compilation of References

Rivera, A. (2021). The impact of COVID-19 on transport and logistics connectivity in the landlocked countries of South America. Project Documents (LC/TS.2020/155), Santiago, Economic Commission for Latin America and the Caribbean (ECLAC).

Rivera-Santos, M., & Inkpen, A. (2009). Joint Ventures and Alliances. In M. Kotabe & K. Helsen (Eds.), *The SAGE Handbook of International Marketing* (pp. 198–217). SAGE Publications. doi:10.4135/9780857021007.n10

Robert L. Helmreich, A. C. (1999). The Evolution of Crew Resource Management Training in Commercial Aviation. *The International*, 19-32.

Robert, L., & Helmreich, J. A. (2001). Culture, Error, and Crew Resource Management. In Improving Teamwork in Organizations (p. 28). CRC Press.

Roberts, H. E., & Foti, R. J. (1998). Evaluating the Interaction Between Self-Leadership and Work Structure in Predicting Job Satisfaction. *Journal of Business and Psychology*, *12*(3), 257–267. doi:10.1023/A:1025067128193

Robertson, M. M. (1995). Maintenance CRM training: Assertiveness attitudes effect on maintenance performance in a matched sample. In N. J. R. Fuller (Ed.), *Human factors in aviation operations* (pp. 215–222). Averbury Technical.

Rubin, R. M., & Joy, J. N. (2005). Where Are the Airlines Headed? Implications of Airline Industry Structure and Change for Consumers. *The Journal of Consumer Affairs*, *39*(1), 215–228. doi:10.1111/j.1745-6606.2005.00010.x PMID:32336778

Rusi, S. (2013). *Singapore Airlines gives up the longest non-stop operating route (Newark – Singapore)*. Airlines Travel. https://en.airlinestravel.ro/singapore-airlines-has-discontinued-the-longest-non-stop-newark-singapore-route.html

Russon, M., & Vakil, F. (1995). Population, convenience and distance decay in a short-haul model of United States air transportation. *Journal of Transport Geography*, *3*(3), 179–195.

Salas, W., KA, B. C., & DC, W. (2006). Does crew resource management training work? An update, an extension, and some critical needs. *Human Factors*, 392–412.

Salas, E. B. (2019). *Airlines Alliances Dossier*. Statista.

Salas, E., Burke, C. S., Bowers, C. A., & Wilson, K. A. (2001). Team training in the skies: Does resource management training really work? *Human Factors*, *43*(4), 641–674. doi:10.1518/001872001775870386 PMID:12002012

Samanth, S. (2020 September 29). Inside airline industry's meltdown. *The Guardian*. https://www.theguardian.com/world/2020/sep/29/inside-the-airline-industry-meltdown-coronavirus-pandemic-/

Santos Bernardes, E., & Hanna, M. D. (2009). A theoretical review of flexibility, agility and responsiveness in the operations management literature. *International Journal of Operations & Production Management*, *29*(1), 30–53. doi:10.1108/01443570910925352

Sanyal, S. N., Datta, S. K., & Banerjee, A. K. (2014). Attitude of Indian consumers towards luxury brand purchase: An application of 'attitude scale to luxury items'. *International Journal of Indian Culture and Business Management*, *9*(3), 316–339. doi:10.1504/IJICBM.2014.064696

Sasu, D. D. (2022). *Coronavirus Cumulative cases in Nigeria 2020-2022*. Statista. https://www.statista.com/statistics/1110879/coronarius-cumulative-cases-in-nigeria/

Saunders, B., Kitzinger, J., & Kitzinger, C. (2015). Anonymising interview data: Challenges and compromise in practice. *Qualitative Research*, *15*(5), 616–632. doi:10.1177/1468794114550439 PMID:26457066

Saunders, M., Lewis, P., & Thornhill, A. (2007). *Research methods for business students*. Pearson Education.

Scarlett, G. H. (2021). Tourism Recovery and the Economic Impact: A Panel Assessment. *Research in Globalization*, *3*, 100044. doi:10.1016/j.resglo.2021.100044

Scheiwiller, S., & Zizka, L. (2021). Strategic Responses by European Airlines to the COVID-19 Pandemic: A Soft landing or a Turbulent Ride? *Journal of Air Transport Management*, *95*, 102103. doi:10.1016/j.jairtraman.2021.102103

Scurr, J. (2002). Travellers' thrombosis. *Perspectives in Public Health*, *122*(1), 11–13.

Sehl, K. (2020). *How the Airline Industry Survived SARS, 9/11, the Global Recession and More*. https://apex.aero/articles/aftershocks-coronavirus-impact/

Selivanovskikh, L., Latukha, M., Mitskevich, E., & Pitinov, S. (2020). Knowledge Management Practices as a Source of a Firm's Potential and Realized Absorptive Capacity. *Journal of East-West Business*, *26*(3), 293–325. doi:10.1080/10669868.2020.1716129

Sengur, Y., & Sengur, F. K. (2017). Airlines define their business models: A content analysis. *World Review of Intermodal Transportation Research*, *6*(2), 141–154. doi:10.1504/WRITR.2017.082732

Seuring, S. (2013). *A review of modeling approaches for sustainable supply chain management*. Academic Press.

Seuring, S. (2013, March). A review of modeling approaches for sustainable supply chain management. *Decision Support Systems*, *54*(4), 1513–1520. doi:10.1016/j.dss.2012.05.053

Seyi Samson, E., Surajudeen, A. J., Godwin, O. A., Kester, A. D., Adeolu, S. O., & Richard, Y. A. (2020, December 30). The Role of International Flights in Covid-19 Pandemic: Global, Africa and Nigeria's Narratives. *Iranian Journal of Health, Safety and Environment*, *6*(9), 696–710. www.academiascholarlyjournal.org/ijhse/index_ijhse.htm

Shaabani, E., Ahmadi, H., & Yazdani, H. (2012). Do interactions among elements of knowledge management lead to acquiring core competencies? *Business Strategy Series*, *13*(6), 307–322. doi:10.1108/17515631211286164

Shaban, I. A., Chan, F. T. S., & Chung, S. H. (2021). A novel model to manage air cargo disruptions caused by global catastrophes such as Covid-19. *Journal of Air Transport Management*, *95*, 102086. doi:10.1016/j.jairtraman.2021.102086 PMID:34548768

Shaikh, A. A., Glavee-Geo, R., Karjaluoto, H., & Ebo Hinson, R. (2019). *How is the use of mobile money services transforming lives in Ghana?* Marketing and Mobile Financial Services. doi:10.4324/9781351174466-12

Shaw, S. (2007). *Airline Marketing and Management*. Ashgate Publishing Limited.

Sheffi, Y. (2005). Building a resilient supply chain. *Harvard Business Review*, *1*(8), 1–4.

Sheffi, Y., & Rice, J. B. (2005). A supply chain view of the resilient enterprise. *MIT Sloan Management Review*, *47*(1), 41–48.

Shekarian, M., Reza Nooraie, S. V., & Parast, M. M. (2020). An examination of the impact of flexibility and agility on mitigating supply chain disruptions. *International Journal of Production Economics*, *220*, 107438. doi:10.1016/j.ijpe.2019.07.011

Sherman, A., & Hart, M. A. (2010). *Mergers and Acquisitions from A to Z* (2nd ed.). Amazon.

Siderska, J. (2021). *The Adoption of Robotic Process Automation Technology to Ensure Business Processes during the COVID-19 Pandemic*. MDPI.

Sieg, G. (2010). Grandfather Rights in the Market for Airport Slots. *Transportation Research Part B: Methodological*, *44*(1), 29–37. doi:10.1016/j.trb.2009.04.005

Simon, R. L. (2000). A successful transfer of lessons learned in aviation psychology and flight safety to health care. In *Patient Safety Initiative* (pp. 45–49). The MedTeams System.

Singh, J. (2003). Study on Pilot Alertness Highlights Feasibility for Ultra Long Range Flight Operations. *ICAO Journal*, *58*(1), 14–15.

Singh, R. K. (2015). Modelling of critical factors for responsiveness in supply chain. *Journal of Manufacturing Technology Management*, *26*(6), 868–888. doi:10.1108/JMTM-04-2014-0042

Singh, S. (2003). Simple random sampling. In *Advanced sampling theory with applications* (pp. 71–136). Springer. doi:10.1007/978-94-007-0789-4_2

Situational Awareness (OGHFA BN). (2022, February 12). *SKYbrary Aviation Safety*. Retrieved February 14, 2022, from https://skybrary.aero/articles/situational-awareness-oghfa-bn#:%7E:text=In%20other%20words%2C%20situational%20awareness,future%2C%20to%20feed%2Dforward

Siyan, P. A., & Adewale, E. A. O. (2020). Impact of COVID-19 on the Aviation Industry in Nigeria. *International Journal of Trend in Scientific Research and Development*, *4*(5), 234-239. www.ijtsrd.com/papers/ijtsrd31787.pdf

SkyTeam. (2022). *SkyTeam Airline Alliance*. https://www.skyteam.com/en/about

Skytrax. (2022). *World Airline Star Rating*. Skytrax. https://skytraxratings.com/about-airline-rating

Slutsken, H. (2020). *Five ways Boeing's 747 jumbo jet changed travel*. Cable News Network (CNN). https://edition.cnn.com/travel/article/boeing-747-jumbo-jet-travel/index.html

Smith, P. J., & Sadler-Smith, E. (2006). *Learning in Organizations: Complexities and Diversities*. New York: Routledge.

Smith, P. S. (2018). *'Kangaroo Route' Dynamics See New Market Entrants*. Aviation International News (AIN). https://www.ainonline.com/aviation-news/air-transport/2018-02-04/kangaroo-route-dynamics-see-new-market-entrants

Smith, K. G., Collins, C. J., & Clark, K. D. (2005). Existing Knowledge, Knowledge Creation Capability, and the Rate of New Product Introduction in High-Technology Firms. *Academy of Management Journal*, *48*(2), 346–357. doi:10.5465/amj.2005.16928421

Smith, M., & Graves, C. (2005). Corporate turnaround and financial distress. *Managerial Auditing Journal*, *20*(3), 304–320. doi:10.1108/02686900510585627

Snow, M., & Hrebiniak, D. C. (1980). Strategy, Distinctive Competence and Organizational Performance. *Administrative Science Quarterly*, *25*(2), 317–336. doi:10.2307/2392457

Sobieralski, J. B. (2020). COVID-19 and airline employment: Insights from historical uncertainty shocks to the industry. *Transportation Research Interdisciplinary Perspectives*, *5*, 100123. Advance online publication. doi:10.1016/j.trip.2020.100123 PMID:34173453

Socorro, M., & Viecens, M. (2013). The Effects of Airline and High Speed Train Integration. *Transportation Research Part A, Policy and Practice*, *49*, 160–177. doi:10.1016/j.tra.2013.01.014

Somayya Madakam, R. M. (2019). *Journal of Information Systems and Technology Management*, *16*.

Sorribes, J., Celma, D., & Martínez-Garcia, E. (2021). Sustainable human resources management in crisis contexts: Interaction of socially responsible labour practices for the wellbeing of employees. *Corporate Social Responsibility and Environmental Management*, *28*(2), 936–952.

Spulber, D. F. (2007). *Global Competitive Strategy*. Cambridge University Press. doi:10.1017/CBO9780511841651

Srihari, A., Mousumi, P., & Srivatsa, K. (2020). A Comparative Study and Analysis of Time Series Forecasting Techniques. *SN Computer Science, 1*, 175.

Stank, T. P., Paul Dittmann, J., & Autry, C. W. (2011). The new supply chain agenda: A synopsis and directions for future research. *International Journal of Physical Distribution & Logistics Management, 41*(10), 940–955. doi:10.1108/09600031111185220

Star Alliance. (2022). *About Star Alliance*. https://www.staralliance.com/en/about

Star Alliance. (2022). *Circle Pacific*. https://roundtheworld.staralliance.com/staralliance/EN/circle-pacific

Statista Research Department. (2022). *Coronavirus Cases in Nigeria March 2022 by state*. Statista. https://www.statista.com/statistics/1122620/coronavirus-cases-in-nigeria-by-state/

Statista. (2021). *The World's Longest Non-Stop Flights*. Statista. https://www.statista.com/chart/3761/the-worlds-longest-non-stop-flights/

Steven, M., & Merklein, T. (2013). The influence of strategic airline alliances in passenger transportation on carbon intensity. *Journal of Cleaner Production, 56*, 112–120. doi:10.1016/j.jclepro.2012.03.011

Story, V., Zolkiewski, J., Verleye, K., Nazifi, A., Hannibal, C., Grimes, A., & Abboud, L. (2020). Stepping out of the shadows: Supporting actors' strategies for managing end-user experiences in service ecosystems. *Journal of Business Research, 116*, 401–411. doi:10.1016/j.jbusres.2020.04.029

Stotz, T., Bearth, A., Ghelfi, S. M., & Siegrist, M. (2020). Evaluating the Perceived Efficacy of Randomized Security Measures at Airports. *Risk Analysis, 40*(7), 1469–1480. doi:10.1111/risa.13474 PMID:32356923

Strong, C. (2006). The influence of employee behavioural performance on customer focus strategies. *Service Industries Journal, 26*(2), 147–163. doi:10.1080/02642060500369180

Sullenberger, C. (2009). *Highest duty: My search for what really matters*. William Morrow & Company.

Sun, X., Wandelt, S., Zheng, C., & Zhang, A. (2021). COVID-19 Pandemic and Air Transportation: Successfully navigating the paper hurricane. *Journal of Air Transport Management, 94*, 102062. doi:10.1016/j.jairtraman.2021.102062 PMID:33875908

Swafford, P. M., Ghosh, S., & Murthy, N. (2008). Achieving supply chain agility through IT integration and flexibility. *International Journal of Production Economics, 116*(2), 288–297. doi:10.1016/j.ijpe.2008.09.002

Tang, C., & Tomlin, B. (2008). The power of flexibility for mitigating supply chain risks. *International Journal of Production Economics, 116*(1), 12–27. doi:10.1016/j.ijpe.2008.07.008

Taylor, H. L. (1993). Military psychology. In Encyclopedia of Human Behavior (pp. 503–542). San Diego, CA: Academic Press.

Teichert, T., Shehu, E., & von Wartburg, I. (2008). Customer segmentation revisited: The case of the airline industry. *Transportation Research Part A, Policy and Practice, 42*(1), 227–242. doi:10.1016/j.tra.2007.08.003

Tetiana Shmelova, A. S. (2020). Artificial Intelligence in Aviation Industries: Methodologies, Education, Applications, and Opportunities. IGI Global.

Thailandsha. (2022). *Amazing Thailand Safety and Health Administration*. Retrieved from: https://web.thailandsha.com/about/details

The Civil Aviation Authority of Thailand (CAAT). (2021). *Aviation Industry Review 2021*. https://www.caat.or.th

Compilation of References

Thomas, D. (2019). *Why did the Airbus A380 fail?* British Broadcast Corporation (BBC). https://www.bbc.com/news/business-47225789

Thomas, E. N. (2014). The Air Transportation System in the 21st Century. Sustainable Built Environment & Encyclopedia of Life Support Systems, 2.

Thompson, J., & Martin, F. (2005). *Strategic Management: Awareness and Change.* South Western a Division of Cengage Learning.

Thompson, J. L. (2001). *Strategic Management.* Thomson Learning.

THY. (2022). *Ortaklıklar.* https://www.turkishairlines.com/tr-tr/basin-odasi/hakkimizda/ortakliklar/

Tiernan, S., Rhoades, D., & Waguespack, B. (2008). Airline alliance service quality performance—An analysis of US and EU member airlines. *Journal of Air Transport Management, 14*(2), 99–102. doi:10.1016/j.jairtraman.2008.02.003

Topaloglu, H. (2012). A duality-based approach for network revenue management in airline alliances. *Journal of Revenue and Pricing Management, 11*(5), 500–517. doi:10.1057/rpm.2012.8

Tretheway, M. (2011). Comment on "legacy carriers fight back". *Journal of Air Transport Management, 17*(1), 40–43. doi:10.1016/j.jairtraman.2010.10.009

Trischler, J., & Westman Trischler, J. (2021). Design for experience–a public service design approach in the age of digitalization. *Public Management Review*, 1–20. doi:10.1080/14719037.2021.1899272

Trkman, P., & McCormack, K. (2009). Supply chain risk in turbulent environments—A conceptual model for managing supply chain network risk. *International Journal of Production Economics, 119*(2), 247–258. doi:10.1016/j.ijpe.2009.03.002

Truong, D., Pan, J. Y., & Buaphiban, T. (2020). Low cost carriers in Southeast Asia: How does ticket price change the way passengers make their airline selection? *Journal of Air Transport Management, 86*, 101836. doi:10.1016/j.jairtraman.2020.101836

Tsafarakis, S., Kokotas, T., & Pantouvakis, A. (2018). A multiple criteria approach for airline passenger satisfaction measurement and service quality improvement. *Journal of Air Transport Management, 68*, 61–75. doi:10.1016/j.jairtraman.2017.09.010

Tsai, T. H. (2016). Homogeneous service with heterogeneous products: Relationships among airline ticket fares and purchase fences. *Journal of Air Transport Management, 55*, 164–175. doi:10.1016/j.jairtraman.2016.05.008

Tsai, T. H., & Chen, C. M. (2019). Mixed logit analysis of trade-off effects between international airline fares and fences: A revenue management perspective. *Current Issues in Tourism, 22*(3), 265–275. doi:10.1080/13683500.2017.1402869

Tsantoulis, M., & Palmer, A. (2008). Quality convergence in airline co-brand alliances. *Managing Service Quality, 18*(1), 34–64. doi:10.1108/09604520810842830

Tunde, D. (2008). *A History of Aviation in Nigeria, 1925-2005.* Dele-Davis Publishers.

U.S-NRC. (n.d.). *Human-System Interface and Plant Modernization Process: Technical Basis and Human Factors Review Guidance. NUREG/CR-6637, BNL-NUREG-52567.* US Nuclear Regulatory Commission.

UIPATH. (n.d.). Retrieved from uipath.com: https://www.uipath.com/resources/covid-automations/process-opportunities-airlines

Ulas, D. (2019). Digital transformation process and SMEs. *Procedia Computer Science, 158*, 662–671. doi:10.1016/j.procs.2019.09.101

Ülgen, H., & Mirze, S. K. (2020). İşletmelerde Stratejik Yönetim. Beta Publishing.

Ülgen, H., & Mirze, S. K. (2013). *İşletmelerde Stratejik Yönetim* (6th ed.). Beta Basım A.Ş.

Um, J., Lyons, A., Lam, H. K. S., Cheng, T. C. E., & Dominguez-Pery, C. (2017). Product variety management and supply chain performance: A capability perspective on their relationships and competitiveness implications. *International Journal of Production Economics*, *187*, 15–26. doi:10.1016/j.ijpe.2017.02.005

UNDP. (2015). Work for human development. New York, NY: United Nations Development Programme.

UNDRR. (n.d.). *Disaster*. Retrieved December 01, 2020, from https://www.undrr.org/terminology/disaster

UNICEF Supply Division. (2020). *COVID-19 Impact Assessment and Outlook on Global Logistics*. https://www.unicef.org/

United Nations. (2015). *Sendai Framework for Disaster Risk Reduction 2015 – 2030*. Available at: https://www.preventionweb.net/files/43291_sendaiframeworkfordrren.pdf

United Nations. (2020). *Socio-Economic Impact Assessment of COVID- 19 in Thailand*. United Nations in Thailand.

Uzgör, M., & Sengur, F. (2021). Havayolu Sektöründe Devlet Destekleri: Türkiye'deki Teşvikli Uçuş Hatlarının İncelenmesi. *Anadolu Üniversitesi Sosyal Bilimler Dergisi*, 851-870.

Uzgör, M., & Sengur, F. (2022). Investigating an Underutilized Subsidized Routes Scheme: Underlying Reasons and Policy Recommendations. *Case Studies on Transport Policy*, *10*(1), 287–299. doi:10.1016/j.cstp.2021.12.010

Van Avermaete, J.A.G. (1998). *NOTECHS: Non-technical skill evaluation in JAR-FCL*. Academic Press.

Vancouver Airport Authority. (2015). *Philippine Airlines Flies Between Manila, Vancouver and New York*. Vancouver Airport Authority. https://www.yvr.ca/en/media/news-releases/2015/philippine-airlines-flies-between-manila-vancouver-and-new-york

Vargo, S. L., & Lusch, R. F. (2008). From goods to service (s): Divergences and convergences of logics. *Industrial Marketing Management*, *37*(3), 254–259. doi:10.1016/j.indmarman.2007.07.004

Vasconcellos, G. M., & Kish, R. J. (2013). Cross-border mergers and acquisitions. In C. F. Lee & A. C. Lee (Eds.), *Encyclopedia of Finance* (pp. 515–523). Springer. doi:10.1007/978-1-4614-5360-4_43

Verhoef, P. (2020). Customer experience creation in today's digital world. In B. Schlegelmilch & R. Wilner (Eds.), *The Routledge companion to strategic marketing* (pp. 107–122). Routledge. doi:10.4324/9781351038669-9

Verhoef, P. C., Lemon, K. N., Parasuraman, A., Roggeveen, A., Tsiros, M., & Schlesinger, L. A. (2009). Customer experience creation: Determinants, dynamics and management strategies. *Journal of Retailing*, *85*(1), 31–41. doi:10.1016/j.jretai.2008.11.001

Villamizar, H. (2021). Today in Aviation: First Commercial Jet Flies to South Africa. *Airways Magazine*. https://airwaysmag.com/today-in-aviation/first-commercial-jet-south-africa/

Virgin Atlantic. (2022). https://www.virgin.com/virgin-company

Wang, C.-N., Nguyen, X.-T., Le, T.-D., & Hsueh, M. (2018). A partner selection approach for strategic alliance in the global aerospace and defence industry. *Journal of Air Transport Management*, *69*, 190–204. doi:10.1016/j.jairtraman.2018.03.003

Wang, S. W., & Hsu, M. K. (2016). Airline co-branded credit cards—An application of the theory of planned behavior. *Journal of Air Transport Management*, *55*, 245–254. doi:10.1016/j.jairtraman.2016.06.007

Wansink, B. (2000). New techniques to generate key marketing insights. *Marketing Research*, (Summer), 28-36.

Compilation of References

Weatherford, L. R., Gentry, T. W., & Wilamowski, B. (2003). Neural network forecasting for airlines: A comparative analysis. *Journal of Revenue and Pricing Management, 1*, 319–331.

Weber, K. (2005). Travellers' Perceptions of Airline Alliance Benefits and Performance. *Journal of Travel Research, 43*(3), 257–265. doi:10.1177/0047287504272029

Weber, K., & Sparks, B. (2004). Consumer attributions and behavioral responses to service failures in strategic airline alliance settings. *Journal of Air Transport Management, 10*(5), 361–367. doi:10.1016/j.jairtraman.2004.06.004

Wen, C. H., & Lai, S. C. (2010). Latent class models of international air carrier choice. *Transportation Research Part E, Logistics and Transportation Review, 46*(2), 211–221. doi:10.1016/j.tre.2009.08.004

Wensveen, J. G., & Leick, R. (2009). The long-haul low-cost carrier: A unique business model. *Journal of Air Transport Management, 15*(3), 127–133. doi:10.1016/j.jairtraman.2008.11.012

Werfelman, L. (2015). *In It For the Ultra-Long-Haul.* Flight Safety Foundation. https://flightsafety.org/asw-article/in-it-for-the-ultra-long-haul/

Whiting, L. S. (2008). Semi-structured interviews: guidance for novice researchers. *Nursing Standard, 22*(23), 35-40.

Widtayakornbundit, S., & Phinaitrup, B.-A. (2021). A study of leadership in educational institution using dual systems and the effects on personal behavior: A case study of Thailand private vocational system. *Kasetsart Journal of Social Sciences, 42*(3), 527–534. doi:10.34044/j.kjss.2021.42.3.12

Wil, M. P., & van der Aalst, M. B. (2018). *Robotic Process Automation.* Springer Fachmedien Wiesbaden GmbH.

Wilkerson, J., Jacobson, M., Malwitz, A., Balasubramanian, S., Wayson, R., Fleming, G., Naiman, D., & Lele, S. (2010). Analysis of emission data from global commercial aviation: 2004 and 2006. *Atmospheric Chemistry and Physics, 2010*(10), 2945–2983.

Williams, B. D., Roh, J., Tokar, T., & Swink, M. (2013). Leveraging supply chain visibility for responsiveness: The moderating role of internal integration. *Journal of Operations Management, 31*(7), 543–554. doi:10.1016/j.jom.2013.09.003

Wilson, R. M., & Gilligan, C. (2005). *Strategic marketing management.* Routledge.

Windahl, C., & Lakemond, N. (2006). Developing integrated solutions: The importance of relationships within the network. *Industrial Marketing Management, 25*(7), 806–818. doi:10.1016/j.indmarman.2006.05.010

Wirtz, J., Kimes, S. E., Theng, J. H. P., & Patterson, P. (2003). Revenue management: Resolving potential customer conflicts. *Journal of Revenue and Pricing Management, 2*(3), 216–226. doi:10.1057/palgrave.rpm.5170068

Wole, O. (2020). Fresh concerns for operators as five airports reopen June 21. *The Guardian.* https://guardian.ng/business-services-fresh-concerns-for-operators-as-five-airports-reopen-june-21/

World Health Organization. (2020a). *Archived: WHO Timeline - COVID-19.* Retrieved January 08, 2021 from https://www.who.int/news/item/27-04-2020-who-timeline---covid-19

World Health Organization. (2020b). *Ebola virus disease.* https://www.who.int/health- topics/ebola/#tab=tab_1

Wozny, F. (2022). The Impact of COVID-19 on Airfares: A Machine Learning Counterfactual Analysis. *Econometrics, 10*(1), 8. doi:10.3390/econometrics10010008

Wright, C. P., Groenevelt, H., & Shumsky, R. A. (2010). Dynamic revenue management in airline alliances. *Transportation Science, 44*(1), 15–37. doi:10.1287/trsc.1090.0300

Xiao, L., Guo, Z., & D'Ambra, J. (2017). Analysing consumer goal structure in online group buying: A means–end chain approach. *Information & Management*, *54*(8), 1097–1119. doi:10.1016/j.im.2017.03.001

Xiaoqian, S., Sebastian, W., Changhong, Z., & Anming, Z. (2021), COVID-19 pandemic and air transportation: Successfully navigating the paper hurricane. *Journal of Air Transport Management*, *94*, 1-13. http://www.elsevier.com/locate/jairtraman

Xiong, G., & Helo, P. (2006). An application of cost-effective fuzzy inventory controller to counteract demand fluctuation caused by bullwhip effect. *International Journal of Production Research*, *44*(24), 5261–5277. doi:10.1080/00207540600600114

Xu, X., Liu, W., & Gursoy, D. (2019). The impacts of service failure and recovery efforts on airline customers' emotions and satisfaction. *Journal of Travel Research*, *58*(6), 1034–1051. doi:10.1177/0047287518789285

Xu, X., & Li, Y. (2016). Examining key drivers of traveler dissatisfaction with airline service failures: A text mining approach. *Journal of Supply Chain and Operations Management*, *14*(1), 30–50.

Yang, B., & Yang, Y. (2010). Postponement in supply chain risk management: A complexity perspective. *International Journal of Production Research*, *48*(7), 1901–1912. doi:10.1080/00207540902791850

Yang, W., Shao, J., Jiang, Y., Xu, Z., & Tsurdos, A. (2021). International Airline Alliance Network Design with Uncertainty. *Applied Sciences (Basel, Switzerland)*, *11*(7), 3065. doi:10.3390/app11073065

Yang, Z., & Peterson, R. (2004). Customer Perceived Value, Satisfaction, and Loyalty: The Role of Switching Costs. *Psychology and Marketing*, *21*(10), 799–822. doi:10.1002/mar.20030

Yao, X., & Vink, P. (2019). A Survey and a Co-creation Session to Evaluate Passenger Contentment on Long-haul Flight, with Suggestions for Possible Design Improvements to Future Aircraft Interiors. In *2nd International Comfort Congress August 29th and 30th, 2019* (pp. 1-9). Università degli Studi di Salerno.

Youn, B. D., Hu, C., & Wang, P. (2011). Resilience-Driven System Design of Complex Engineered Systems. *Journal of Mechanical Design*, *133*(10), 101011. doi:10.1115/1.4004981

Yusuf, Y. Y., Gunasekaran, A., Adeleye, E. O., & Sivayoganathan, K. (2004). Agile supply chain capabilities: Determinants of competitive objectives. *European Journal of Operational Research*, *159*(2), 379–392. doi:10.1016/j.ejor.2003.08.022

Zahra, S. A., & Pearce, J. A. II. (1990). Research Evidence on The Miles-Snow Typology. *Journal of Management*, *16*(4), 751–768. doi:10.1177/014920639001600407

Zhang, N. B. L. (2018). *ICCSE'18: Proceedings of the 3rd International Conference on Crowd Science and Engineering*. Academic Press.

Zhang, Z., Jia, M., & Gu, L. (2012). Transformational leadership in crisis situations: Evidence from the People's Republic of China. International Journal of Human Resource Management, 23(19), 4085–4109.

Zhang, C., & Jiang, X. (2019). Ultra Longhaul Flight and Its Impact on Air Travellers. *Journal of Transport & Health*, *14*, 100756.

Zhang, Q., Vonderembse, M. A., & Lim, J.-S. (2003). Manufacturing flexibility: Defining and analyzing relationships among competence, capability, and customer satisfaction. *Journal of Operations Management*, *21*(2), 173–191. doi:10.1016/S0272-6963(02)00067-0

Zhang, Y., Zheng, X., & Lu, W. (2018). Measuring the openness of Chinese International Air Transport Policy. *Transport Policy*, *72*, 208–217. doi:10.1016/j.tranpol.2018.03.014

Compilation of References

Zhun, L. (2021). Air Emergency Transport under COVID-19: Impact, Measures and the Future. *Hindawi Journal of Advanced Transportation*.

Zins, A. H. (2001). Relative attitudes and commitment in customer loyalty models: Some experiences in the commercial airline industry. *International Journal of Service Industry Management*, *12*(3), 269–294. doi:10.1108/EUM0000000005521

About the Contributors

Kannapat Kankaew is an Assistant Professor at College of Hospitality Industry Management; Suan Sunandha Rajabhat University. He received Doctor of Public Administration majoring in Human Resources Management. Prior his academic professional, he used to work in the aviation industry for more than 13 years. He has published and participated in International Conferences more than 20 papers in repute journals. And he has dedicated as an editorial board, associate editor, and reviewer for various journals both domestic and international. He is one of the working committee and examiner of Thailand Professional Qualification Institutes (Public Organization) for airport ground service professional.

* * *

Mert Akinet completed his master's degree at Hacettepe University, Department of Business Administration, Department of Marketing, and continues his doctoral studies at Eskişehir Technical University, Department of Aviation Management. AKINET has DGCA approved certificates such as Aviation Safety, Safety Management System (SMS) in the field of aviation, and field-specific certificates such as Quality Management System (ISO 9001:2015).

Hüseyin Önder ALDEMİR is an Assistant Professor at Özyeğin University, Faculty of Aviation and Aeronautical Sciences. He obtained his B.S. from Army School, Systems Engineering in 2000, M.S. in Mechanical Engineering from The Pennsylvania State University (PennState) in 2005, and Ph.D. in Civil Aviation Management from Anadolu University in 2018. During his Ph.D. education, he became a member of Air Transport and Regional Development (ATARD), which is a sub-organization of European Cooperation in Science and Technology (COST). By this scope, he participated two Ph.D. schools which were held at University of Bergamo, ITALY in 2017 and Poznan University of Economics and Business, POLAND in 2018. Dr. ALDEMİR accomplished Unmanned Aerial Vehicle (UAV) Systems pilot training in ISRAEL in 2008 and he has over 2500 hours of flight with different types of UAV systems as UAS pilot and UAS test/instructor pilot. His researches focus on strategic management, competition strategies, airline management, airport operations, safety management systems and Unmanned Aircraft Systems (UAS).

Abel Badillo-Portillo is a PhD student at the Instituto Politécnico Nacional, Mexico. His main research interests are related to safety, accidents in public transport systems.

About the Contributors

Vikrant Janawade is an associate professor at the University of Cote d'Azur. His research activities are mainly oriented to the field of marketing, services management, and international management.

Ibrahim Sarper Karakadilar is a scholar member of the Kahramanmaras Sutcu Imam University (KSU). In 2011, Ibrahim Sarper Karakadilar earned his PhD in Business Management from the Gebze Institute of Technology (GYTE). He was employed as a lecturer by KSU in 2017 and is currently teaching Transportation Systems, Freight Legislation, Customs Regulations, and Lean Management. He has co-authored manuscripts with his colleagues published in the 'Journal of Production Research', 'Expert Systems with Applications (ESWA)' and 'Total Quality Management Business Excellence'. His principal areas of research are logistics and supply chain management, marketing, lean management philosophy, and other current issues in business and operation management.

Sofia Khan is a research scholar in the Department of Business Administration, Manipal University Jaipur.

Doğan KILIÇ, won the Aviation Management Department of Ondokuz Mayıs University in 2011. Doğan KILIÇ, who successfully graduated from the Aviation Management Department of On Dokuz Mayıs University in his undergraduate education, was appointed as a lecturer in the Department of Civil Aviation Management at Bülent Ecevit University in Zonguldak in February 2020. KILIÇ also successfully completed the undergraduate program of Anadolu University, Faculty of Economics and Administrative Sciences, Department of Public Administration, within the scope of the second university program. Doğan KILIÇ completed his master's degree at Kocaeli University, Department of Aviation Management and continues his doctoral studies at Eskişehir Technical University, Department of Aviation Management. He is currently working as a lecturer in the Civil Air Transport management department at Zonguldak Bülent Ecevit University.

Ravi Lakshmanan is a postgraduate electrical engineer with a Master of Science in Quality Management and a PhD in Management. He has over 45 years of professional experience, 31 of which have been spent in the aviation industry. His areas of expertise include airport planning, design, development, and commissioning, as well as airport operations and management. His most recent full-time position was that of CEO of GMR Airport Developers Limited. After retirement, he continues to work as an advisor for GMR Infrastructure (Singapore) Pte Ltd. In addition, he is a visiting faculty member and guest lecturer at a few of India's top business schools. He has also authored a few research articles, two course books for a university, and guided two research scholars.

Colin C. H. Law is a Senior Lecturer at the Singapore Institute of Technology. He is specialised in airline business management, airlines operations, airlines economic and air deregulation. Colin is the author of numerous academic textbooks on airline and airport operations. He is the co-author of Introduction to Airline Ground Service and the author of A Practical Guide to Airline Customer Service: From Airline Operations to Passenger Services and A Flight Attendant's Essential Guide: From Passenger Relations to Challenging Situations.

Eliver Lin is an Associate Professor and the Programme Director of the Tourism, Hospitality and Event Management at Beijing Normal University-Hong Kong Baptist University United International

College. She has conducted a series of industry projects, in collaborations with industry partners, about tourism recovery post COVID-19 in the area of travel, air transport, and attractions. She is specialized in air transport management, deregulation, low-cost airlines, and airport and airlines relationship.

Chonnikarn Luanngpituksa is a lecturer at School of Integrated Science, Kasetsart University. A leading national institute in innovative integrated science to develop human resources capable of lifelong learning. Due to the study and research in Kobe, Japan for 7 years, the author has an ability to understand Japanese used in everyday situations, and in a variety of circumstances to a certain degree. Expert in marketing, consumer behaviour analysis, and retail internationalization. Moreover, with undergraduate degree of B.Sc. (product development), the author has skill on food processing, together with ability in sensory evaluation.

Hesham Magd has more than twenty-five years of combined experience in traditional and nontraditional higher education teaching, training, consultancy, community development, academic administration, curricula design, organizational change and development, distinguished research and scholarly writing, resulting in Honors, awards and recognition for academic excellence and outstanding achievement. Hesham is currently heavily involved in International accreditation and reshaping the aviation education in Oman and offer strategic direction on the direction of the sector In his previous appointments throughout the world in British, European, and American oriented Curriculum (Middle East, USA, and UK), he has been the driving force behind strategic institutional development during the time of profound change in the Higher Education in the Middle East. Hesham has broad knowledge of the UK, USA, Middle East University Systems, and Quality and accreditation systems (AACSB, AABI, OAAA, NCAAA…).

Bikal Jha is a professional educator in the field of Aviation. Mr. Jha holds a Commercial Pilot License, Master of Science in Aviation Management from London, and currently pursuing a Doctorate from UCAM, Spain. He has over ten years of experience in different areas of Aviation operations and he joined MCBS in 2015 as an Aviation lecturer in the faculty of Business. He has been involved in promoting Aviation Safety by presenting various Aviation safety-related topics on major platforms (World Aviation Safety Summit, Flight Safety Foundation, Singapore Aviation Academy, and IOSH) and by publishing Aviation articles in different magazines and newspapers. Some of his recent, Articles titled "Next Generation Equipment for Safer Skies" published in Himalayan Times (English Daily News Paper), Article titled "Enhancing Nepalese Air Traffic System" Published in Aviation Journal (Nepal Army Journal 7'th issue), Review of Investigation Report- Nepal Airlines crash: Published in AviationNepal.com (online News Portal), Presented New Airline Business Plan- Collective Investment by Non-Resident Nepali Association: (8'th Global NRNA Conference). His recent atrial titled "Inclusion of Human Factor Perspective towards Ensuring Quality in Accident Investigation Reports: A Case Study Approach in South Asia" was published in 'Global Business and Management Research: An International Journal' Vol. 13, No. 3 (2021). His expertise involves Aviation Safety and Security (Implementation of SMS and SSP), Investigation, Human Factors, Aviation Law and Policy, Air operations Management, Air Traffic Management, Aviation Meteorology, and other Aviation and Airport management topics.

Fahad ibne Masood, a seasoned aviator with 23 years of experience, has actively participated in the industry, training, and academics. Having gained experience of 1850 plus hours diversified flying to training as an instructor for 850 plus hours, Fahad is a proficient aircraft accident Investigation &

About the Contributors

Human Factors specialist with CRMI/T 'Train the trainer' credentials. Facilitated learning for 2000 plus aviation professionals internationally while generating value-added discussions on various global forums related to grey areas of human performance enhancement, NOTECHS/CRM, aircraft accident investigation, SMS, and HF to mention a few. Fahad holds a diverse set of competencies in aviation being a CPL holder & rated Flight Instructor on the commercial side, an academician, and an ex-military aviator. He has been there and done that on the grassroots tactical level, as well as, facilitated learning at the operational and not to mention, influenced strategic levels of policy. He has delivered talks in countries like Iceland, the UK, Singapore, Australia, Oman & Pakistan. His recent talk was on the TRT World International channel elaborating on the 5G challenge to aviation in the USA, one of his many appearances on international media. He continues to research and write for varying publishing houses as well. He is an active member of the RAeS -Royal Aeronautical Society, United Kingdom, and ISASI - International Society of Air Safety Investigators, USA. He is presently a doctoral student of Aviation Management from UCAM Universidad Católica San Antonio de Murcia, Spain.

Oluchukwu Ignatus Onianwa is a Nigerian Historian specializing in the Transnational Diplomatic and Military History and Social Media Studies. He obtained his PhD from the University of Ibadan in 2020. He has worked with the Swiss Military Academy ETH Zurich, Switzerland on a book project titled "Captivity in War"; "Visions of African Unity" with the International Studies Department University of Utrecht, Netherland and International Studies Group at the University of the Free State, Bloemfontein South Africa; A Tight-Embrace: Euro-Africa Relations" with the Department of Political and Social Science, the University of Bologna, Italy and "Human Rights Breakthrough of 1970" with the Department of International Studies University of Trento Italy. Onianwa is currently working with the Department of History and Political Science Alabama State University on "Africa: A Globalizing World, and the Challenges of Peace, Security, and Development". A Research Team Member with Department of History, Philosophy and Religious Studies Eastern Kentucky University, Richmond Kentucky USA on the book "African Experience. Onianwa is a Research Team Member on the Palgrave Handbook on Nigeria and Its History and Routledge Encyclopedia of African Studies (REAS) and Palgrave Handbook on Social Problems. He is currently conducting research on Social Media and EndSars Movement in Nigeria.

Jaime Santos-Reyes is a lecturer at the National Polytechnic Institute, Mexico, whose main research interests are seismic risk, safety management systems, critical infrastructures modelling, accident and risk analysis, reliability engineering. He obtained a PhD from Heriot-Watt University, UK, in 2001. He has spent 3 years working as a research associate at Heriot-Watt University, Edinburgh, Scotland, UK.

Ferhan K. Sengur currently is a member and the Head of the Department of Aviation Management, Faculty of Aeronautics and Astronautics, Eskisehir Technical University, Turkey. She earned her PhD in Aviation Management and completed her Master's and Bachelor's degrees in Aviation Management as well. She conducted her post-doctoral research at Embry Riddle Aeronautical University, Florida, the USA on a grant from the Turkish Higher Education Council in 2010. Currently, she also holds the position of the Director of the Women in Science and Technology Center at Eskisehir Technical University. As a Professor at the Department of Aviation Management, Faculty of Aeronautics and Astronautics, Eskisehir Technical University, she had gained valuable experience in teaching at both graduate and undergraduate levels. She had also conducted multiple international and national research projects, organized several conferences, delivered papers on national and international aviation and management symposiums, and published articles in national and international peer-reviewed journals. She also authored several chapters and books. Prof. Sengur had also consulted the Turkish State Planning Organization, Turkish Transportation Ministry and Turkish Directorate General of Civil Aviation for several National Aviation legislations and White Papers. Prof. Sengur is an expert in Airport and Airline Management and her research interests incorporate but are not limited to Strategic Management, Transportation Policies, and Corporate Social responsibility. Her current research interest focuses on Airport Governance Models, Airport Public-Private Partnerships, Airline Business models, and Responsible Management in Aviation.

Burak Erdogan received his bachelors degree in Civil Air Transportation Management from Kocaeli University in 2016. In September 2018, he started to work as a research assistant in the Aviation Management Department of Istanbul Aydın University. In March 2020, he transferred to Istanbul Bilgi University Aviation Management department and continues his research there. He received his master's degree in Aviation Management in 2019. He is in the thesis stage in his doctoral education in Aviation Management, which he started in 2020.

R K Tailor is an expert in Robotic Process automation and accounting in India. He is having research and teaching experience of more than 15 years. Dr. Tailor is an international author in the field of commerce and management. He is serving his services as the editorial board member in many international research associations and publication houses. He is also an international speaker of Robotic Process Automation in commerce and management and delivered his speeches in India, U.K. Turkey, Indonesia, Poland, Hungry, and many more.

Tanyeri Uslu is an Assistant Professor of Marketing at Altınbaş University, Department of Business Administration. She received her MSc. degree in Global Business and Transportation Management from State University of New York in 2009, and PhD degree in Business Administration from Gebze Technical University in 2018. Prior to her academic career she has worked at theTurkish General Consulate in New York, and as a manager in the private sector in the USA. She has an extensive experience in working with people who have diverse backgrounds, as well as from a variety of cultures. She has taught a variety of undergraduate and graduate level courses in universities including Boğaziçi University and Turkish- German University. She is currently teaching Global Marketing Dynamics, Contemporary Marketing Management, Consumer Behavior Theory, Service Marketing and Research Methods and Ethics courses. Besides her academic role, she has an administrative role for the graduate department of her current institution. Along with her colleagues, she has published books on supply chain management and airline industry dynamics, as well as academic articles in journals focusing on management, marketing, and interdisciplinary studies. Her latest publication is on the emerging specialty coffee sector in Turkey. Her research areas are; consumer behavior, industrial marketing, service marketing, branding, and sustainability.

Sarun Widtayakornbundit is a Lecturer at School of Integrated Science; Kasetsart University. He received Doctor of Public Administration majoring in Human Resources Management. His main research interests are related to human resource management, Organizational Behavior, Education Management, and Hotel and Tourism Management.

Index

A

agility 272, 274-275, 280-281, 283-288
air 1-39, 43, 45-46, 51-53, 56-57, 59-66, 74, 86, 88, 91, 94-96, 99, 102, 104, 106-107, 109, 114, 118-121, 124, 126-139, 142-147, 149, 152-154, 156-157, 159-162, 170, 175, 178, 180-183, 186-191, 194, 200, 204-206, 209, 211-213, 215, 224-227, 230, 232, 246-247, 249, 252, 262-263, 267, 272-278, 281, 284-287, 289, 293-294, 298
air cargo 30, 45, 143, 156, 160, 272-278, 284-287
Air Transport 1, 3, 6, 10, 12-14, 16-21, 23-24, 26, 29-34, 38-39, 53, 59-65, 86, 88, 91, 94-96, 118-120, 128, 135, 139, 142-146, 149, 157, 161-162, 186-191, 204-206, 224-227, 267, 272, 276, 284, 286-287
air travel 1-3, 5-16, 18-19, 26, 31, 33-34, 36-37, 95, 104, 119, 127, 142-143, 145, 209, 230, 232, 246-247, 263, 298
airline 14, 17, 20-24, 27-34, 37, 39-41, 43-56, 58-63, 66, 88, 92, 95-97, 101, 104, 113, 119-120, 122, 124, 126-127, 129, 133-134, 141-154, 156, 159-167, 170-172, 174-198, 200-215, 218-228, 230-231, 248-249, 252, 257, 263-265, 268, 270, 272-275, 281, 286, 289-298
airline alliance services 164-166, 174-175, 178
airline alliances 39, 53-55, 58-61, 141, 165-167, 172, 174, 177-178, 180-181, 184-191
Airline Competition 148, 154, 161
Airline Competitive Strategies 148
airline industry 31, 37, 39-41, 43, 45-47, 49-51, 53-55, 59-61, 95, 101, 144-145, 148-150, 152-154, 156, 159-162, 165-167, 170, 185, 188, 193, 205, 210, 223, 226-227, 248-249, 268, 270, 272, 286, 289, 295-296
Airline mergers and acquisitions 39, 50, 60
Airline strategies 39
airlines 1, 13, 27-33, 35-36, 43-44, 46-48, 51-56, 58-62, 65-66, 88, 92, 101-103, 107, 109, 116, 118-124, 126-143, 145-147, 149, 152-156, 159-163, 165-167, 170-171, 176-181, 183, 186, 190, 192-204, 206, 208-209, 211, 213-215, 220, 222-223, 226-227, 232-233, 235, 246, 248, 252, 262, 264, 272-275, 277, 284, 287, 290-291, 293-294, 296-299
airport management 45, 145, 229-234, 236-238, 240, 242, 244-246
and aviation 15, 144
Artificial Intelligence 112, 289-290, 293, 298-299
attribute 126, 175, 184, 192, 195, 197-204
aviation industry 16, 22, 24, 31, 33-37, 64, 66-67, 73-74, 83, 91, 99, 101, 106-107, 119, 143, 151-154, 160, 192-195, 211, 229-233, 246-247, 250-252, 262-264, 270, 291-292, 294, 296, 298

B

business 17, 20-21, 24, 26-27, 29, 31-34, 36, 40-41, 45, 48-53, 60-62, 65-66, 85, 91, 94, 96, 98, 109-110, 118, 123-127, 129-130, 133, 136, 141-145, 147-150, 152-158, 160-163, 166, 172, 176, 184, 186-190, 192-196, 204-210, 213-215, 219-224, 227, 232, 237, 241-243, 249, 255-258, 262, 264, 266-268, 270-275, 277-287, 289-296, 298-299

C

community of practice 251, 266, 271
Competency-Based Education Framework 229, 233, 236, 246, 250
connecting flights 51, 55, 118-119, 126-129, 132-133, 137-140, 142, 145, 147, 177-178, 214, 227
corporate strategies 39-41, 49, 58-59, 154
COVID-19 10, 12, 14-22, 24-38, 59, 61, 65, 86, 95-97, 142-143, 149, 152, 154, 159-162, 225, 229-232, 234-239, 241-242, 244-250, 252, 262, 272-278, 281, 283-284, 286-287, 292, 299
Crew Resource Management 98-101, 103, 107-109, 111-117
crisis 16-17, 29-31, 34, 48, 59, 95, 100, 114, 149, 153-

Index

154, 159-161, 229-237, 240-252, 262-267, 276, 279, 284, 286, 290
crisis management 161, 229, 233-234, 237, 244, 246, 248, 250, 252
critical incident technique 229, 246-247
culture 64, 72-75, 81, 84-86, 90-91, 93, 95-97, 101, 108, 110-111, 117, 156, 178-180, 192, 194-195, 205-206, 259-260, 268, 283
Customer Behavior 207
customer choice 118, 144
customer experience 164, 167-169, 186, 188-190, 193, 215, 223, 298
customer journey 164, 168-169, 188
customer loyalty 152, 160, 168, 205, 211, 223-225, 227
customer reactions 207-208

D

Delta 20, 23, 30, 37, 52, 57, 116, 121, 144, 159, 187
deregulation 49-50, 55, 148, 159, 194, 214, 227
direct flights 118-119, 128-129, 133, 135, 137-138, 147
disaster 32, 99, 101, 103, 110, 114, 231, 246, 248-250, 287
dual entitlement theory 207-208

E

emergency 22, 24, 30, 38, 93, 106, 111, 230-235, 237, 240, 243, 246, 250, 278, 284
employee behavior 251, 257, 262, 266-267, 271
epidemic 24-25, 149, 160, 231-232, 250, 252, 262, 264, 268, 274-275, 281, 290, 293
equity theory 207-208, 255
Extended-range Twin-engine Operational Performance Standards (ETOPS) 119, 122, 147

F

Fire-Services 98
flexibility 2, 47, 51, 118-119, 122, 142, 153, 155, 158-159, 176, 222, 224, 227, 236, 240-243, 262, 264, 266, 272-275, 280-281, 283, 287-288, 296
Full-Service Carrier 209, 214, 227

H

hazards 11-12, 64, 73-74, 76-77, 80-81, 85, 94, 100, 104, 106-107, 282-283
healthcare 107, 110-112, 114, 116
high reliability organization 98, 114
human capital 188, 232, 250, 255, 257, 267

Human Factor 64, 81, 93, 100, 108, 113

I

ICAO 35, 64-66, 73-76, 78-79, 81-82, 86-90, 94, 96-97, 102, 104, 120, 145-146, 232-235, 244, 248, 252
Image Value 192, 195, 197-199, 203

J

job satisfaction 251-255, 257-259, 262-263, 265-271, 292

K

knowledge management 248, 251-253, 255-260, 262, 265-271

L

leadership 32, 58, 81, 100-101, 105-106, 108, 111, 113-116, 145, 149, 155, 159-160, 229, 233, 235-237, 239, 244-247, 249-250, 268-269, 271, 282
Low-Cost Carrier 209, 214, 227
loyalty attitude 211-212, 214-216, 218, 223

M

Machine Learning 38, 289-290
management of change 64, 75, 80, 90-92
Mean-End approach 192, 196, 203
mergers and acquisitions 39, 41, 49-52, 58, 60, 62, 274
Mexico City 1-2, 4-5, 12-14, 18-19
models 20-21, 32, 34, 49, 51-52, 62, 64-65, 93-95, 99-100, 102, 116, 122, 127, 149-150, 163, 186, 189, 193, 205, 208-210, 214-215, 221-225, 227, 259, 264-265, 273, 279, 282, 284, 289, 291, 294
modes of transport 1-2, 5-7, 10, 20-21, 153

N

Needs Satisfaction 271
Nigeria 20-22, 24-37
nonstop flights 119, 121-122, 124-128, 140, 147
Nuclear 98-99, 103, 107, 110-113, 115, 117

O

Oaxaca 1-8, 10-12, 14, 18
Omicron 20, 30-31, 33-35, 37
Organizational Performance 163, 254, 265, 267, 271, 287

Index

P

pandemic 1, 10, 12, 14-17, 19-22, 25-34, 36-38, 59, 64-68, 73, 90, 92, 94-97, 142, 149, 152, 159-161, 199, 229-232, 234-242, 244-247, 250, 252, 262, 264, 266, 272-279, 282-284, 286, 299
perceived value 163, 209, 211-212, 215, 227, 254, 284
planning a trip 1-2, 5
premium cabins 130, 142, 147
premium class 118, 128, 130, 132-133, 135, 137, 139, 142
preventive measures 27, 77, 88-89
Prospect Theory 207-208, 225
public perception 1

R

reliability 7, 48, 74, 98, 102-103, 114-115, 120, 122, 216, 222, 272, 277, 281, 283, 289, 294, 298
resilience 29, 88, 95, 229, 233, 236, 240-246, 268, 272, 274-275, 280-281, 283-287
restoration 272, 281, 283
risk management 64, 75-76, 83, 100, 103, 110-111, 126, 145, 273, 281-283, 288
Robotic Process Automation 289-293, 295, 297-300

S

safety 1-2, 7, 12, 17, 26, 31-32, 36-37, 64-68, 72-81, 83-88, 90, 93-98, 100-104, 106-111, 113, 115-117, 144, 147, 170, 230, 232-233, 237, 240, 247, 252, 263, 281, 287
Security Program 64, 88
SeMS 64, 73, 90-91
service 5, 13, 21, 23, 29, 31, 39, 42-43, 48, 50-51, 53-55, 65-68, 72-74, 76-77, 83, 88-89, 93, 111, 114, 116, 119, 122, 124, 126, 129, 131-145, 151, 153-155, 159-160, 164-171, 174-182, 184-197, 201-206, 208-215, 220-228, 242, 251-253, 257, 262-264, 266-270, 281-282, 285-286, 289, 292-298
service experience 164-165, 167-169, 174, 185, 188-189
service quality 48, 55, 65-66, 175, 177, 179-180, 189-190, 195, 204-206, 209-212, 214-215, 221, 223-225, 228, 264, 296
SMS 64-65, 73-77, 80, 90, 97
soft skills 93, 103, 229, 232-234, 236, 244-248, 250
Southeast Asia airline 192-193, 196-198, 203-204
strategic alliances 39, 51-53, 61, 151, 166
supply chain 13, 37, 225, 227, 256, 272-277, 279-288, 292, 297

T

Transport 1-3, 5-8, 10, 12-21, 23-24, 26-27, 29-34, 36-39, 53, 59-65, 86, 88, 91, 94-96, 116, 118-120, 128, 135, 139, 142-147, 149, 153, 157, 161-163, 170, 186-191, 204-206, 221, 224-227, 230, 233, 262, 267, 272, 274, 276, 278, 281, 284-287
trust 73, 171, 201-202, 209-212, 215, 228, 230, 252-253, 257, 260, 268, 274, 280

U

Ultra Long Haul Flights 118, 129, 147

V

value creation 40, 165, 168-169, 185, 189, 251, 271, 281
value-added 54, 192-193, 195-196, 201-203
variant 20, 30-31

349

Recommended Reference Books

IGI Global's reference books are available in three unique pricing formats:
Print Only, E-Book Only, or Print + E-Book.

Shipping fees may apply.

www.igi-global.com

Data-Driven Optimization of Manufacturing Processes

ISBN: 9781799872061
EISBN: 9781799872085
© 2021; 298 pp.
List Price: US$ 225

Emerging Materials and Advanced Designs for Wearable Antennas

ISBN: 9781799876113
EISBN: 9781799876120
© 2021; 210 pp.
List Price: US$ 225

Emerging Applications and Implementations of Metal-Organic Frameworks

ISBN: 9781799847601
EISBN: 9781799847618
© 2021; 254 pp.
List Price: US$ 225

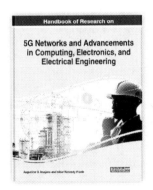

Handbook of Research on 5G Networks and Advancements in Computing, Electronics, and Electrical Engineering

ISBN: 9781799869924
EISBN: 9781799869948
© 2021; 522 pp.
List Price: US$ 295

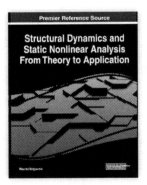

Structural Dynamics and Static Nonlinear Analysis From Theory to Application

ISBN: 9781799843993
EISBN: 9781799844006
© 2021; 347 pp.
List Price: US$ 195

Developing and Monitoring Smart Environments for Intelligent Cities

ISBN: 9781799850625
EISBN: 9781799850632
© 2021; 367 pp.
List Price: US$ 215

Do you want to stay current on the latest research trends, product announcements, news, and special offers?

Join IGI Global's mailing list to receive customized recommendations, exclusive discounts, and more.

Sign up at: **www.igi-global.com/newsletters**.

Publisher of Timely, Peer-Reviewed Inclusive Research Since 1988

www.igi-global.com   Sign up at www.igi-global.com/newsletters   facebook.com/igiglobal   twitter.com/igiglobal   linkedin.com/igiglobal

Ensure Quality Research is Introduced to the Academic Community

Become an Evaluator for IGI Global Authored Book Projects

 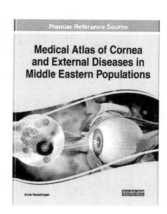  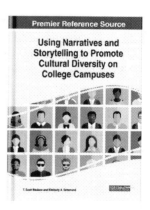

The overall success of an authored book project is dependent on quality and timely manuscript evaluations.

Applications and Inquiries may be sent to:
development@igi-global.com

Applicants must have a doctorate (or equivalent degree) as well as publishing, research, and reviewing experience. Authored Book Evaluators are appointed for one-year terms and are expected to complete at least three evaluations per term. Upon successful completion of this term, evaluators can be considered for an additional term.

If you have a colleague that may be interested in this opportunity, we encourage you to share this information with them.

Increase Your Manuscript's Chance of Acceptance
IGI Global Author Services

Copy Editing & Proofreading

Professional, native English language copy editors improve your manuscript's grammar, spelling, punctuation, terminology, semantics, consistency, flow, formatting, and more.

Scientific & Scholarly Editing

A Ph.D. level review for qualities such as originality and significance, interest to researchers, level of methodology and analysis, coverage of literature, organization, quality of writing, and strengths and weaknesses.

Figure, Table, Chart & Equation Conversions

Work with IGI Global's graphic designers before submission to enhance and design all figures and charts to IGI Global's specific standards for clarity.

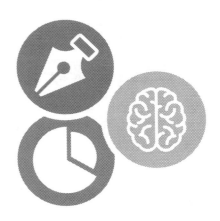

- Professional Service
- Quality Guarantee & Certificate
- Timeliness
- Affordable Pricing

What Makes IGI Global Author Services Stand Apart?

Services/Offerings	IGI Global Author Services	Editage	Enago
Turnaround Time of Projects	3-5 Business Days	6-7 Busines Days	6-7 Busines Days
Pricing	Fraction of our Competitors' Cost	Up to **2x** Higher	Up to **3x** Higher

Learn More or Get Started Here:

For Questions, Contact IGI Global's Customer Service Team at cust@igi-global.com or 717-533-8845

6,600+ E-BOOKS.
ADVANCED RESEARCH.
INCLUSIVE & ACCESSIBLE.
IGI Global e-Book Collection

- Flexible Purchasing Options (Perpetual, Subscription, EBA, etc.)
- Multi-Year Agreements with **No Price Increases** Guaranteed
- **No Additional Charge** for Multi-User Licensing
- No Maintenance, Hosting, or Archiving Fees
- Transformative **Open Access Options** Available

Request More Information, or Recommend the IGI Global e-Book Collection to Your Institution's Librarian

Among Titles Included in the IGI Global e-Book Collection

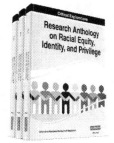

Research Anthology on Racial Equity, Identity, and Privilege (3 Vols.)
EISBN: 9781668445082
Price: US$ 895

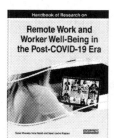

Handbook of Research on Remote Work and Worker Well-Being in the Post-COVID-19 Era
EISBN: 9781799867562
Price: US$ 265

Research Anthology on Big Data Analytics, Architectures, and Applications (4 Vols.)
EISBN: 9781668436639
Price: US$ 1,950

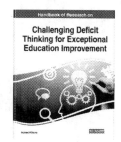

Handbook of Research on Challenging Deficit Thinking for Exceptional Education Improvement
EISBN: 9781799888628
Price: US$ 265

Acquire & Open

When your library acquires an IGI Global e-Book and/or e-Journal Collection, your faculty's published work will be considered for immediate conversion to Open Access *(CC BY License)*, at no additional cost to the library or its faculty *(cost only applies to the e-Collection content being acquired)*, through our popular **Transformative Open Access (Read & Publish) Initiative**.

For More Information or to Request a Free Trial, Contact IGI Global's e-Collections Team: eresources@igi-global.com | 1-866-342-6657 ext. 100 | 717-533-8845 ext. 100

Have Your Work Published and Freely Accessible
Open Access Publishing

With the industry shifting from the more traditional publication models to an open access (OA) publication model, publishers are finding that OA publishing has many benefits that are awarded to authors and editors of published work.

Freely Share Your Research | Higher Discoverability & Citation Impact | Rigorous & Expedited Publishing Process | Increased Advancement & Collaboration

Acquire & Open

 When your library acquires an IGI Global e-Book and/or e-Journal Collection, your faculty's published work will be considered for immediate conversion to Open Access *(CC BY License)*, at no additional cost to the library or its faculty *(cost only applies to the e-Collection content being acquired)*, through our popular **Transformative Open Access (Read & Publish) Initiative**.

Provide Up To 100% OA APC or CPC Funding

Funding to Convert or Start a Journal to Platinum OA

Support for Funding an OA Reference Book

IGI Global publications are found in a number of prestigious indices, including Web of Science™, Scopus®, Compendex, and PsycINFO®. The selection criteria is very strict and to ensure that journals and books are accepted into the major indexes, IGI Global closely monitors publications against the criteria that the indexes provide to publishers.

Learn More Here: For Questions, Contact IGI Global's Open Access Team at openaccessadmin@igi-global.com

Are You Ready to Publish Your Research

IGI Global offers book authorship and editorship opportunities across 11 subject areas, including business, computer science, education, science and engineering, social sciences, and more!

Benefits of Publishing with IGI Global:

- Free one-on-one editorial and promotional support.
- Expedited publishing timelines that can take your book from start to finish in less than one (1) year.
- Choose from a variety of formats, including Edited and Authored References, Handbooks of Research, Encyclopedias, and Research Insights.
- Utilize IGI Global's eEditorial Discovery® submission system in support of conducting the submission and double-blind peer review process.
- IGI Global maintains a strict adherence to ethical practices due in part to our full membership with the Committee on Publication Ethics (COPE).
- Indexing potential in prestigious indices such as Scopus®, Web of Science™, PsycINFO®, and ERIC – Education Resources Information Center.
- Ability to connect your ORCID iD to your IGI Global publications.
- Earn honorariums and royalties on your full book publications as well as complimentary copies and exclusive discounts.

Join Your Colleagues from Prestigious Institutions, Including:
Australian National University, MIT Massachusetts Institute of Technology, Johns Hopkins University, Harvard University, Tsinghua, Columbia University in the City of New York

Learn More at: www.igi-global.com/publish
or Contact IGI Global's Aquisitions Team at: acquisition@igi-global.com

Printed in the United States
by Baker & Taylor Publisher Services